Lecture Notes in Computer Science

Lecture Notes in Artificial Intelligence   14117

Founding Editor

Jörg Siekmann

Series Editors

Randy Goebel, *University of Alberta, Edmonton, Canada*
Wolfgang Wahlster, *DFKI, Berlin, Germany*
Zhi-Hua Zhou, *Nanjing University, Nanjing, China*

The series Lecture Notes in Artificial Intelligence (LNAI) was established in 1988 as a topical subseries of LNCS devoted to artificial intelligence.

The series publishes state-of-the-art research results at a high level. As with the LNCS mother series, the mission of the series is to serve the international R & D community by providing an invaluable service, mainly focused on the publication of conference and workshop proceedings and postproceedings.

Zhi Jin · Yuncheng Jiang ·
Robert Andrei Buchmann · Yaxin Bi ·
Ana-Maria Ghiran · Wenjun Ma
Editors

Knowledge Science, Engineering and Management

16th International Conference, KSEM 2023
Guangzhou, China, August 16–18, 2023
Proceedings, Part I

 Springer

Editors
Zhi Jin (iD)
Peking University
Beijing, China

Robert Andrei Buchmann (iD)
Babeş-Bolyai University
Cluj-Napoca, Romania

Ana-Maria Ghiran (iD)
Babeş-Bolyai University
Cluj-Napoca, Romania

Yuncheng Jiang (iD)
South China Normal University
Guangzhou, China

Yaxin Bi (iD)
Ulster University
Belfast, UK

Wenjun Ma (iD)
South China Normal University
Guangzhou, China

ISSN 0302-9743   ISSN 1611-3349 (electronic)
Lecture Notes in Artificial Intelligence
ISBN 978-3-031-40282-1   ISBN 978-3-031-40283-8 (eBook)
https://doi.org/10.1007/978-3-031-40283-8

LNCS Sublibrary: SL7 – Artificial Intelligence

This Springer imprint is published by the registered company Springer Nature Switzerland AG
The registered company address is: Gewerbestrasse 11, 6330 Cham, Switzerland

Preface

We are extremely pleased to introduce the Proceedings of the 16th International Conference on Knowledge Science, Engineering and Management (KSEM 2023), this is a four-volume set containing the papers accepted for this year's conference, which was organized by and hosted at the South China Normal University, Guangzhou, China during August 16–18, 2023.

Since its inaugural conference back in 2006, KSEM has accumulated great success under the immense efforts from each year's organizing committee and beyond. Previous years' events were held in Guilin, China (KSEM 2006); Melbourne, Australia (KSEM 2007); Vienna, Austria (KSEM 2009); Belfast, UK (KSEM 2010); Irvine, USA (KSEM 2011), Dalian, China (KSEM 2013); Sibiu, Romania (KSEM 2014); Chongqing, China (KSEM 2015); Passau, Germany (KSEM 2016); Melbourne, Australia (KSEM 2017); Changchun, China (KSEM 2018); Athens, Greece (KSEM 2019). Even during the COVID pandemic, KSEM was continued and held in Hangzhou, China (KSEM 2020); Tokyo, Japan (KSEM 2021) and Singapore (KSEM 2022), respectively.

The objective of KSEM is to create a forum that gathers researchers and practitioners from academia, industry, and government around the globe to present advancements in theories and state-of-the-art technologies in the field of knowledge science, engineering, and management. Attendees were encouraged to present prototypes and deploy knowledge-based systems, discuss and debate practical challenges as well as opportunities for the research community. With its interdisciplinary nature, KSEM 2023 focused on four broad areas: Knowledge Science with Learning and AI (KSLA), Knowledge Engineering Research and Applications (KERA), Knowledge Management Systems (KMS), and Emerging Technologies for Knowledge Science, Engineering and Management (ETKS).

In this year's conference, we received 395 submissions. Single-blind review was adopted for the conference review process. Each submission was peer reviewed by 2 to 4 reviewers from the program committee members and external reviewers. Among them, 114 regular papers (28.8% acceptance rate) and 30 short papers were selected, giving a total of 144 papers. We have separated the proceedings into four volumes: LNCS 14117, 14118, 14119, and 14120. The collection of papers represents a wide range of research activities, covering knowledge representation and reasoning, knowledge extraction, knowledge integration, data mining and knowledge discovery, and beyond.

In addition to the regular sessions, this year's event featured the following keynote speakers:

- Witold Pedrycz, University of Alberta, Canada, with the presentation titled *Credibility of Machine Learning Through Information Granularity*;
- Zhi-Hua Zhou, Nanjing University, China, with the presentation titled *A New Paradigm to Leverage Formalized Knowledge and Machine Learning*;

- Geoff Webb, Monash University, Australia, with the presentation titled *Recent Advances in Assessing Time Series Similarity Through Dynamic Time Warping*;
- Jie Tang, Tsinghua University, China, with the presentation titled *ChatGLM: Run Your Own "ChatGPT" on a Laptop*.

We would like to express our sincere gratitude to the many contributors who were steadfast supporters and made KSEM 2023 a great success. First of all, we would like to thank the KSEM 2023 Organizing Committee, the School of Computer Science at South China Normal University, Sun Yat-sen University, and our publisher Springer, without their crucial support the conference would not have been possible. Secondly, we would like to thank the members of our Steering Committee (Honorary General Chairs), Ruqian Lu from the Chinese Academy of Sciences, and Dimitris Karagiannis from the University of Vienna, Austria, for their invaluable guidance throughout the event; the General Co-chairs, Zhi Jin from Peking University, Christos Douligeris from the University of Piraeus, Daniel Neagu from the University of Bradford, and Weihua Ma from South China Normal University. They were involved in the whole process of the organization efforts, and provided various critical resources, including but not limited to connections to external reviewers and professional advice. Last but not least, we would like to thank the authors who submitted their papers to this year's conference, the Program Committee and the external reviewers, without whom the daunting tasks of paper reviews would not have been accomplished in time.

We hope that the reader finds the results of the conference program valuable and thought-provoking, and we hope attendees had a valuable opportunity to share ideas with other researchers and practitioners from institutions around the world.

August 2023

Zhi Jin
Yuncheng Jiang
Robert Andrei Buchmann
Yaxin Bi
Ana-Maria Ghiran
Wenjun Ma

Organization

Honorary General Chairs

Ruqian Lu   Chinese Academy of Sciences, China
Dimitris Karagiannis   University of Vienna, Austria

General Chairs

Zhi Jin   Peking University, China
Christos Douligeris   University of Piraeus, Greece
Daniel Neagu   University of Bradford, UK
Weihua Ma   South China Normal University, China

Program Chairs

Yuncheng Jiang   South China Normal University, China
Robert Buchmann   Babeş-Bolyai University, Romania
Yaxin Bi   Ulster University, UK

Publication Chairs

Ana-Maria Ghiran   Babeş-Bolyai University, Romania
Wenjun Ma   South China Normal University, China

Publicity Chairs

Ye Zhu   Deakin University, Australia
Jieyu Zhan   South China Normal University, China

Steering Committee

Ruqian Lu (Honorary Chair)   Chinese Academy of Sciences, China
Dimitris Karagiannis (Chair)   University of Vienna, Austria

Bo Yang	Jilin University, China
Chengqi Zhang	University of Technology, Sydney, Australia
Christos Douligeris	University of Piraeus, Greece
Claudiu Kifor	Lucian Blaga University of Sibiu, Romania
Gang Li	Deakin University, Australia
Hui Xiong	State University of New Jersey, USA
Jörg Siekmann	German Research Centre of Artificial Intelligence, Germany
Martin Wirsing	Ludwig-Maximilians-Universität München, Germany
Meikang Qiu	Texas A&M University-Commerce, USA
Xiaoyang Wang	Zhejiang Gongshang University, China
Yaxin Bi	Ulster University, UK
Yoshiteru Nakamori	Japan Advanced Institute of Science and Technology, Japan
Zhi Jin	Peking University, China
Zili Zhang	Southwest University, China

Technical Program Committee

Achim D. Brucker	University of Exeter, UK
Achim Hoffmann	University of New South Wales, Australia
Agostino Cortesi	Universita' Ca' Foscari di Venezia, Italy
Andrea Polini	University of Camerino, Italy
Ben Roelens	Open Universiteit, Netherlands
Bo Luo	University of Kansas, USA
Bowen Zhao	Singapore Management University, Singapore
Chaobo He	South China Normal University, China
Chenyou Fan	South China Normal University, China
Cheng Huang	Sichuan University, China
Chunxia Zhang	Beijing Institute of Technology, China
Claudiu Kifor	Lucian Blaga University of Sibiu, Romania
Cungen Cao	Chinese Academy of Sciences, Beijing, China
Dan Oleary	University of Southern California, USA
Daniel Volovici	Lucian Blaga University of Sibiu, Romania
Dantong Ouyang	Jilin University, China
Dimitris Apostolou	University of Piraeus, Greece
Dongning Liu	Guangdong University of Technology, China
Florin Leon	Gheorghe Asachi Technical University of Iasi, Romania
Haibo Zhang	University of Otago, New Zealand

Hans Friedrich Witschel	Fachhochschule Nordwestschweiz, Switzerland
Hansi Jiang	SAS Institute, USA
Hao Tang	City University of New York, USA
Hechang Chen	Jilin University, China
Jiahao Cao	Tsinghua University, China
Jan Vanthienen	KU Leuven, Belgium
Jia-Huai You	University of Alberta, Canada
Jianfei Sun	University of Science and Technology of China, China
Jiangning Wu	Dalian University of Technology, China
Jianquan Ouyang	Xiangtan University, China
Jianting Ning	Singapore Management University, Singapore
Jiaqi Zhu	Chinese Academy of Sciences, China
Juan Manuel Vara	University Rey Juan Carlos, Spain
Jue Wang	Chinese Academy of Sciences, China
Jun Zheng	New Mexico Institute of Mining and Technology, USA
Junwei Zhang	Xidian University, China
Krzysztof Kluza	AGH University of Science and Technology, Poland
Leilei Sun	Beihang University, China
Lihua Cai	South China Normal University, China
Liang Chang	Guilin University of Electronic Science and Technology, China
Luca Cernuzzi	Universidad Católica, Chile
Man Zhou	Huazhong University of Science and Technology, China
Marite Kirikova	Riga Technical University, Latvia
Md Ali	Rider University, USA
Meiyong Liu	Sun Yat-sen University, China
Meng Li	Hefei University of Technology, China
Mengchi Liu	South China Normal University, China
Naveed Khan	Ulster University, UK
Nick Bassiliades	Aristotle University of Thessaloniki, Greece
Norbert Pataki	Eötvös Loránd University, Hungary
Pengfei Wu	National University of Singapore, Singapore
Pietro Ferrara	Ca' Foscari University of Venice, Italy
Priscila Cedillo	Universidad de Cuenca, Ecuador
Qiang Gao	Southwestern University of Finance and Economics, China
Qianli Ma	South China University of Technology, China
Qingtian Zeng	Shandong University of Science and Technology, China

Qingzhen Xu	South China Normal University, China
Radu Tudor Ionescu	University of Bucharest, Romania
Remus Brad	Lucian Blaga University of Sibiu, Romania
Ruisheng Shi	Beijing University of Posts & Telecommunications, China
Shaojing Fu	National University of Defense Technology, China
Songmao Zhang	Chinese Academy of Sciences, China
Suqin Tang	Guangxi Normal University, China
Takeshi Morita	Aoyama Gakuin University, Japan
Wei Luo	Deakin University, Australia
Weina Niu	UESTC, China
Weipeng Cao	Guangdong Laboratory of Artificial Intelligence and Digital Economy (Shenzhen), China
Xiang Zhao	National University of Defense Technology, China
Xiangyu Wang	Xidian University, China
Xiangru Li	South China Normal University, China
Xingfu Wu	Argonne National Laboratory, USA
Ye Zhu	Deakin University, Australia
Yiming Li	Tsinghua University, China
Yong Tang	South China Normal University, China
Yongmei Liu	Sun Yat-sen University, China
Yuxin Ye	Jilin University, China
Zehua Guo	Beijing Institute of Technology, China
Zengpeng Li	Lancaster University, UK
Zheng Wang	Northwestern Polytechnical University, China
Zhiping Shi	Capital Normal University, China
Zhiwen Yu	South China University of Technology, China
Zili Zhang	Deakin University, Australia
Zongming Fei	University of Kentucky, USA

Keynotes Abstracts

Credibility of Machine Learning Through Information Granularity

Witold Pedrycz[iD]

Department of Electrical and Computer Engineering, University of Alberta, Edmonton, Canada
wpedrycz@ualberta.ca

Abstract. Over the recent years, we have been witnessing numerous and far-reaching developments and applications of Machine Learning (ML). Efficient and systematic design of their architectures is important. Equally important are comprehensive evaluation mechanisms aimed at the assessment of the quality of the obtained results. The credibility of ML models is also of concern to any application, especially the one exhibiting a high level of criticality commonly encountered in autonomous systems and critical processes of decision-making. With this regard, there are a number of burning questions: how to quantify the quality of a result produced by the ML model? What is its credibility? How to equip the models with some self-awareness mechanism so careful guidance for additional supportive experimental evidence could be triggered?

Proceeding with a conceptual and algorithmic pursuits, we advocate that these problems could be formalized in the settings of Granular Computing (GrC). We show that any numeric result be augmented by the associated information granules being viewed as an essential vehicle to quantify credibility. A number of key formalisms explored in GrC are explored, namely those involving probabilistic, interval, and fuzzy information granules. Depending on the formal settings, confidence levels and confidence intervals or coverage and specificity criteria are discussed in depth and we show their role as descriptors of credibility measures.

The general proposals of granular embedding and granular Gaussian Process models are discussed along with their ensemble architectures. In the sequel, several representative and direct applications arising in the realm of transfer learning, knowledge distillation, and federated learning are discussed.

A New Paradigm to Leverage Formalized Knowledge and Machine Learning

Zhi-Hua Zhou

Department of Computer Science and Technology, School of Artificial Intelligence,
Nanjing University, China
zhouzh@nju.edu.cn

Abstract. To develop a unified framework which accommodates and enables machine learning and logical knowledge reasoning to work together effectively is a well-known holy grail problem in artificial intelligence. It is often claimed that advanced intelligent technologies can emerge when machine learning and logical knowledge reasoning can be seamlessly integrated as human beings generally perform problem-solving based on the leverage of perception and reasoning, where perception corresponds to a data-driven process that can be realized by machine learning whereas reasoning corresponds to a knowledge-driven process that can be realized by formalized reasoning. This talk ill present a recent study in this line.

Recent Advances in Assessing Time Series Similarity Through Dynamic Time Warping

Geoff Webb

Department of Data Science and Artificial Intelligence, Monash Data Futures Institute,
Monash University, Australia
Geoff.Webb@monash.edu

Abstract. Time series are a ubiquitous data type that capture information as it evolves over time. Dynamic Time Warping is the classic technique for quantifying similarity between time series. This talk outlines our impactful program of research that has transformed the state of the art in practical application of Dynamic Time Warping to big data tasks. These include fast and effective lower bounds, fast dynamic programming methods for calculating Dynamic Time Warping, and intuitive and effective variants of Dynamic Time Warping that moderate its sometimes-excessive flexibility.

ChatGLM: Run Your Own "ChatGPT" on a Laptop

Jie Tang

Department of Computer Science, Tsinghua University, China
jietang@tsinghua.edu.cn

Abstract. Large language models have substantially advanced the state of the art in various AI tasks, such as natural language understanding and text generation, and image processing, multimodal modeling. In this talk, I am going to talk about how we build GLM-130B, a bilingual (English and Chinese) pre-trained language model with 130 billion parameters. It is an attempt to open-source a 100B-scale model at least as good as GPT-3 and unveil how models of such a scale can be successfully pre-trained. Based on GLM-130B, we have developed ChatGLM, an alternative to ChatGPT. A small version, ChatGLM-6B, is opened with weights and codes. It can be deployed with one RTX 2080 Ti (11G) GPU, which makes it possible for everyone to deploy a ChatGPT! It has attracted over 2,000,000 downloads on Hugging Face in one month, and won the trending #1 model for two weeks.

GLM-130B: https://github.com/THUDM/GLM-130B.
ChatGLM: https://github.com/THUDM/ChatGLM-6B.

Contents – Part I

Knowledge Science with Learning and AI

Joint Feature Selection and Classifier Parameter Optimization: A Bio-Inspired Approach

Zeqian Wei, Hui Kang, Hongjuan Li, Geng Sun$^{(\boxtimes)}$, Jiahui Li$^{(\boxtimes)}$, Xinyu Bao, and Bo Zhu

College of Computer Science and Technology and College of Software, Jilin University, Changchun 130012, China
{kanghui,sungeng}@jlu.edu.cn, lijiahui0803@foxmail.com

Abstract. Feature selection has been proven to be an effective method for handling large amounts of data, which together with the parameter settings of the classifier determines the performance of the classifier. However, many studies have considered the two separately, ignoring the intrinsic connection between them. Thus, in this work, we formulate a joint feature selection and parameters optimization problem, which is NP-hard and mixed-variable structured. Then we propose an improved binary honey badger algorithm (IBHBA) to solve the formulated problem. First, a novel initialization strategy based on the fast correlation-based filter (FCBF) method is proposed to generate promising initial solutions. Second, IBHBA introduces a local search factor based on simulated annealing (SA), a crossover operator based on tournament selection, and a mutation mechanism to improve the performance of conventional HBA. Finally, a binary mechanism is adopted to make it suitable for the feature selection problem. Experiments conducted in 27 public datasets have demonstrated that the proposed approach can outperform some well-known swarm-based algorithms.

Keywords: Feature selection · Support vector machines · Honey badger algorithm

1 Introduction

As a popular research area in computer science, machine learning is widely used in pattern recognition [11], data mining, machine vision, text processing and other fields [6], accompanied by increasingly diverse and large datasets. However, high-dimensional datasets in machine learning contain a number of irrelevant and redundant features, which then degrade classification accuracy and consume a significant amount of computing resources [7]. Feature selection is an effective approach to overcome this issue which receives growth attention.

Through the exclusion of redundant and irrelevant features, feature selection strives to find an optimal subset of features and extract the most pertinent information from high-dimensional data. Feature selection methods mainly include

© The Author(s), under exclusive license to Springer Nature Switzerland AG 2023
Z. Jin et al. (Eds.): KSEM 2023, LNAI 14117, pp. 3–14, 2023.
https://doi.org/10.1007/978-3-031-40283-8_1

three categories that are the filters, wrapper, and embedded approaches [7]. The filter-based approaches calculate the scores of all features and then filter out the features with lower scores through a predefined threshold. The wrapper-based methods use a subset of features as the input vector to the classifier, and the classification results guide the selection of features in turn. Thus, the wrapper-based methods acquire higher classification accuracy while using more computing resources. Moreover, the embedded methods perform feature selection during classifier training which are seen as particular wrapper-based methods.

Aside from feature selection, the setting of classification parameters has a significant impact on classification outcomes [4]. For example, if a radial basis function (RBF) kernel is selected for the support vector machine (SVM), then the penalty parameter C and the kernel function parameter γ must be set appropriately. The value of C that is too large or too small, and will result in a poor model generalization effectiveness and failure to achieve the learning effect. In addition, parameter γ has a much greater influence on classification outcomes than parameter C, since its value affects the partitioning outcome in the feature space [10]. However, most of the methods can only individually optimize either feature subset selection or SVM parameters [3], greatly limiting the classification potential of SVM. Zhou et al. [24] used the genetic algorithm (GA) to optimize feature subset selection and SVM parameters at the same time, and the experimental result demonstrated that the approach can reduce the time complexity of the operation and improve the classification accuracy simultaneously. Therefore, we propose to optimize joint feature subset selection and SVM parameters in this work.

However, it is not straightforward to find the better feature subset and SVM parameters since the problem is NP-hard and involves mixed decision variables. The swarm intelligence algorithm has excellent search capabilities for high-dimensional spaces, which makes it well-suitable for wrapper-based feature selection problems. Some researchers have adopted several swarm intelligence algorithms such as particle swarm optimization (PSO) [19], salp swarm algorithm (SSA) [21], whale optimization algorithm 5 (WOA) [1], cuckoo search (CS) [16], harris hawk optimization (HHO) [23], as well as variants of these algorithms for solving the feature selection problems.

Honey badger algorithm (HBA) [12] is a novel swarm intelligence algorithm proposed in 2022, which has an easier mechanism and better performance compared to some other algorithms. However, according to the no free lunch (NFL) theory, no algorithm can solve all optimization problems suitably. Moreover, HBA is proposed for solving continuous optimization problems, and it cannot be used directly for solving our considered mixed-variable optimization problem. In addition, HBA may have several certain downsides, e.g., it is prone to stagnate to a local optimum solution due to insufficient exploration capabilities and population diversity. Therefore, the above conditions motivate us to improve conventional HBA and employ it to optimize the classifier parameters and feature subset selection simultaneously.

The main contributions of this paper are summarized as follows:

1. We formulate a joint feature selection problem to simultaneously optimize feature subset selection and SVM parameters. The formulated problem is NP-hard and difficult to be solved since it involves mixed decision variables.
2. Due to the difficulty of the formulated problem, we propose an improved binary HBA (IBHBA) to solve the formulated feature selection problem. IBHBA introduces a novel initial strategy, a local search operator, a population diversity improvement factor, and a binary mechanism to improve the performance of HBA and make it suitable for feature selection problems.
3. Experiments are conducted on 27 UC Irvine Machine Learning Repository, and the performance of the proposed IBHBA is verified by comparing it with several other algorithms.

The rest of this paper is organized as follows. Section 2 reviews the related work. Section 3 describes the proposed IBHBA. Section 4 shows the experiment results and Sect. 5 provides a synopsis of the findings and conclusions.

2   Related Work

Swarm intelligence algorithms have the traits of self-learning, self-adaptive and self-organizing. Given that the majority of them have simple structures and fast convergence rates, they and their variants are widely used for solving feature selection problems, e.g., PSO, SSA, CS, HHO, and WOA.

Too et al. [20] introduced opposition-based learning and conditional strategy to enhance the performance of the PSO. Tubishat et al. [21] presented a dynamic SSA for the feature selection. Mehedi et al. [16] used the modified CS to minimize the power quality disturbances within the network. Moreover, in [25], an improved greedy HHO was proposed to achieve classification purposes.

Recently, some studies using swarm intelligence algorithms for parameter setting have also been applied to the feature selection problem. Dai and Zhao [5] used an improved PSO for parameters optimization of SVM. In [9], multi-layer perceptron was trained based on the newly upgraded bat algorithm for cyber intrusion detection. However, the above studies do not consider the relation between parameters and features, which may miss the optimal solution. Karthikeyan and Alli [14] fused SVM with a hybrid glowworm swarm optimization and GA to generate joint chromosomes that were used to classify diabetic retinopathy. Karn et al. [13] used PSO to select a suitable feature subset and set an apposite value for each parameter simultaneously. Ren et al. [18] realized joint feature subset selection and parameter optimization of an echo state network by a modified binary SSA.

The above-mentioned approaches can solve feature selection problems in various applications. However, as a newly proposed swarm intelligence algorithm, there is no study of joint feature selection and parameter tuning based on HBA. Moreover, HBA has some weaknesses that need to be optimized to fit the feature selection. Thus, in this paper, a novel IBHBA is proposed to address the aforementioned shortcomings.

3   Algorithm Description

The solution space of the formulated problem is discrete and vast, especially when the parameters are also encoded, making it difficult to be solved. Thus, we propose an IBHBA to make it more suitable for the formulated problems.

3.1   Honey Badger Algorithm

The HBA is a bio-inspired evolutionary algorithm, which is inspired by the food-searching behaviors of honey badgers in nature. HBA has two candidate solution update phases, i.e., the digging phase and the honey phase. In the digging phase, the solutions are updated by using Eq. (1), and in the honey phase via Eq. (2):

$$x_{\text{new}} = x_{\text{prey}} + F \times \beta \times I \times x_{\text{prey}} + F \times r_1 \times \alpha \times d_i$$
$$\times |\cos(2\pi r_2) \times [1 - \cos(2\pi r_3)]| , \tag{1}$$
$$x_{\text{new}} = x_{\text{prey}} + F \times r_4 \times \alpha \times d_i, \tag{2}$$

where x_{prey} is the position of the prey, namely, the best position found so far. Moreover, β is set as a constant greater than or equal to 1, which is used to adjust the hunting ability. In addition, d_i is the distance between prey and the ith honey badger. Additionally, r_1, r_2, r_3 and r_4 are four random numbers between 0 and 1. Furthermore, F is 1 or -1 with the same odds which prevents the search process from trapping in the local optimum. Also, α is a self-adaptive factor and I_i is the smell intensity of the ith prey. Specifically, the definitions are as follows:

$$\alpha = C \times \exp\left(\frac{-t}{t_{\max}}\right),$$
$$I_i = r_5 \times \frac{(x_i - x_{i+1})^2}{4\pi d_i^2}, \tag{3}$$

where C is a constant ≥ 1, t_{max} is the maximum number of iteration and r_5 is a random number between 0 and 1.

3.2   IBHBA

HBA has several inherent defects. Moreover, HBA is originally designed to solve continuous space optimization problems, so it is not suitable directly for feature selection. Thus, we propose an IBHBA for solving the above questions and the details of the introduced improved factors are as follows.

Initialization Strategy Based on the FCBF Method. Population initialization is a significant step for bio-inspired algorithms. In general, random initialization is always used for generating a well-distributed population, which may not omit some potential solutions. However, if we can get the initial population close enough to the optimal solution, the algorithm could find a better solution promisingly and quickly. Thus, we proposed an initialization method based on the fast correlation-based filter (FCBF) approach [22]. The FCBF method assigns each feature a weight, ranks all features, and gets rid of redundant features by computing symmetrical uncertainty (SU) between features or features and categorical variables. The dimension corresponding to the filtered features will be initialized to 1. Furthermore, 70% of the individuals in the population, the rest of the features are initialized randomly to preserve the diversity of the population and the rest are initialized with the probability defined in Eq. (4).

$$P_i = \frac{SU_i}{max(SU_j)}, j \neq i. \tag{4}$$

Simulated Annealing Operator. The simulated annealing (SA) algorithm avoids the local optima stagnation problem by introducing a distinct mechanism, that is, the worst solution will be taken with a well-defined probability [8]. In this study, SA is applied to avoid trapping into the local optimum.

Genetic Operators. G_{best} is the leader of all solutions in HBA, as a result, the optimization performance of the algorithm relies too much on it without taking advantage of the other solutions with the experience they collect, and this experience may be more valuable for directing the optimizer to the global solution. Thus, to further enhance the exploitation ability of HBA, a crossover operator based on tournament selection is proposed and described as follows:

$$
\begin{aligned}
X_{new} &= X_{best} \times X_{tour}, \\
X_{new}^d &= \begin{cases} X_{best}^d, & rand < 0.5, \\ X_{tour}^d, & otherwise, \end{cases}
\end{aligned} \tag{5}
$$

where X_{best} is the best solution, X_{tour} is generated using binary tournament selection for each dimension. The two individuals mentioned above are crossed with a crossover probability of 0.5 to create X_{new}, as shown in Eq. (5). Furthermore, the subset size-oriented mutation (SSOM) operator [15] is employed to increase population diversity.

Binary Mechanism. In this work, a kind of V-shaped function [17] is adopted for the solution mappings, and the details of this function are as follows:

$$x_v = \left| \frac{x}{\sqrt{1+x^2}} \right|, \tag{6}$$

$$x_{binary} = \begin{cases} 1, & N_{random} \leqslant x_v, \\ 0, & N_{random} > x_v, \end{cases} \tag{7}$$

where x_{binary} is the converted binary solution of the feature selection problem and N_{random} is a random number which is used as the threshold.

Table 1. Solution representation

the ith solution	feature mask	C		γ	
representation	$x_{i,1}$ $\cdots$ $x_{i,D}$	$x_{i,D+1}$ $\cdots$ $x_{i,D+9}$		$x_{i,D+10}$ $\cdots$ $x_{i,D+19}$	

Table 2. Benchmark datasets

Number	Dataset	Number of feature	Number of instance
1	Arrhythmia	278	452
2	Breastcancer	10	699
3	BreastEW	30	569
4	Congress	16	435
5	Exactly	13	1000
6	German	24	1000
7	Glass	9	214
8	Lung-Cancer	56	32
9	Heart-StatLog	13	270
10	HeartEW	13	294
11	Hepatitis	19	142
12	Hillvalley	100	106
13	Ionosphere	34	351
14	Lymphography	18	148
15	sonar	60	208
16	Spect	22	267
17	Vehicle	18	846
18	Vote	16	300
19	Vowel	10	901
20	WDBC	30	569
21	Wine	13	178
22	Krvskp	36	3196
23	tic-tac-toe	9	958
24	Zoo	16	101
25	Dermatology	33	366
26	divorce	54	170
27	Movementlibras	90	360

Table 3. Parameters setting

No	Algorithm	Values of key parameters
1	BCS	Discovery rate $= 0.25$, $\alpha = 1$
2	BWOA	$b = 1$
3	BPSO	$c_1 = c_2 = 2, w = 0.9$
4	BHBA	$C = 2, \beta = 6$
5	IBHBA	$C = 2, \beta = 6, T_{init} = 1000, T_{min} = 1, \alpha_t = 0.95, k = 1$

3.3   Complexity Analysis of IBHBA

The most time-consuming step in feature selection is the calculation of fitness function value, compared to which the other computational steps are negligible. Therefore, the computational complexity of the proposed IBHBA is $\mathcal{O}(t_{max} \cdot N)$, where t_{max} shows the maximum number of iterations and N is the population size, which is the same as that of HBA. However, IBHBA may take more time in practical application, and the reason may be that the introduced improved factors or larger search space require additional computing time, which is difficult to predict. Thus, to assess the computational complexity of IBHBA more comprehensively, the experiment time is recorded in Sect. 4.

Table 4. Fitness function values obtained by different algorithms

	BHHO	BSSA	BWOA	BCS	BPSO	BHBA	IBHBA
Arrhythmia	0.3300	0.3382	0.3224	0.3215	0.3134	0.2994	**0.2370**
Breastcancer	0.0302	0.0281	0.0286	0.0278	0.0276	0.0284	**0.0267**
BreastEW	0.0516	0.0549	0.0467	0.0509	0.0509	0.0440	**0.0267**
Congress	0.0294	0.0281	0.0275	0.0231	0.0265	0.0233	**0.0127**
Exactly	0.2242	0.1637	0.1483	0.1455	0.2055	0.1948	**0.0046**
German	0.2663	0.2614	0.2621	0.2560	0.2594	0.2550	**0.2153**
Glass	0.4396	0.4294	0.4279	0.4263	0.4263	0.4276	**0.2564**
Lung-Cancer	0.0409	0.0929	0.0304	0.0266	0.0268	**0.0249**	0.0250
Heart-StatLog	0.1629	0.1620	0.1810	0.1479	0.1555	0.1515	**0.1245**
HeartEW	0.1908	0.1836	0.1885	0.1840	0.1850	0.1817	**0.1279**
Hepatitis	0.2841	0.2991	0.2776	0.2642	03089	0.2856	**0.2382**
Hillvalley	0.5206	0.5232	0.5151	0.5207	0.5206	0.5087	**0.3256**
Ionosphere	0.0499	0.0442	0.0501	0.0380	0.0406	0.0390	**0.0285**
Lymphography	0.5846	0.5819	0.5936	0.5566	0.5789	0.5694	**0.5347**
sonar	0.1119	0.1183	0.1115	0.0854	0.0922	0.0689	**0.0280**
Spect	0.2858	0.2752	0.2752	0.2535	0.2677	0.2590	**0.2288**
Vehicule	0.3561	0.3386	0.3735	0.3140	0.3267	0.3131	**0.1618**
Vote	0.0621	0.0590	0.0625	0.0510	0.0531	0.0468	**0.0432**
Vowel	0.1876	0.1894	0.1863	0.1776	0.1852	0.1872	**0.0112**
WDBC	0.0579	0.0544	0.0532	0.0502	0.0541	**0.0440**	0.0294
Wine	0.0777	0.0751	0.0756	0.0703	0.0684	0.0699	**0.0225**
Krvskp	0.0536	0.0435	0.0435	0.0343	0.0406	0.0364	**0.0130**
tic-tac-toe	0.1157	0.1295	0.1155	0.1151	0.1173	0.1151	**0.0100**
Zoo	0.0856	0.0724	0.0770	0.0456	0.0472	0.0558	**0.0031**
Dermatology	0.0244	0.0230	0.0218	0.0162	0.0173	0.0168	**0.0154**
divorce	0.0306	0.0419	0.0334	0.0312	0.0330	0.0249	**0.0004**
Movementlibras	0.1849	0.1820	0.1820	0.1728	0.1685	0.1658	**0.0869**

3.4   Feature Selection Based on IBHBA

We design the fitness function based on the linear weighting method as follows:

$$f_{FS} = a \cdot Acc + b \cdot \frac{S}{D}, \tag{8}$$

where Acc is the classification accuracy, S and D represent the number of selected features and the total number of features, respectively. Moreover, a and b are the corresponding weights, and they are set to 0.99 and 0.01, respectively.

Table 5. CPU time occupied by different algorithms

	BHHO	BSSA	BWOA	BCS	BPSO	BHBA	IBHBA
Arrhythmia	6503.9	3660.2	3297.1	7546.6	**3029.1**	3861.6	4433.2
Breastcancer	369.1	238.8	**169.1**	501.1	315.2	194.6	375.7
BreastEW	315.3	**193.1**	211.3	400.3	273.3	225.0	346.1
Congress	218.3	128.7	**127.0**	268.0	165.1	139.2	198.3
Exactly	1409.8	921.7	**834.3**	1884.9	1305.7	1013.6	2497.0
German	1549.5	917.0	**905.0**	2045.1	1286.1	1103.8	1564.1
Glass	967.6	786.4	514.4	1047.5	**490.8**	854.6	634.8
Lung-Cancer	87.9	53.6	**53.4**	122.2	81.2	73.1	69.9
Heart-StatLog	204.1	124.0	**114.7**	276.8	173.6	135.8	164.6
HeartEW	159.5	118.5	**93.6**	264.3	165.4	120.5	181.6
Hepatitis	121.0	**76.3**	87.1	165.2	111.1	93.3	116.4
Hillvalley	1026.5	646.5	**564.6**	1285.3	1026.5	1001.3	2336.6
Ionosphere	236.1	**132.5**	162.2	285.1	190.3	154.4	178.2
Lymphography	1206.1	**735.3**	737.0	1571.0	1094.2	933.2	901.2
sonar	220.9	164.1	123.3	226.8	**104.9**	233.0	140.3
Spect	217.8	**128.2**	158.7	273.1	181.6	168.3	184.8
Vehicule	2839.5	**1503.4**	1555.3	3185.7	2192.9	1696.7	1724.3
Vote	168.7	**94.6**	101.5	206.0	95.2	118.6	137.1
Vowel	7480.7	**3295.4**	3716.0	6616.7	3360.9	5117.8	3546.7
WDBC	330.8	**218.7**	221.1	475.7	283.5	226.5	347.7
Wine	236.2	**133.6**	135.1	286.7	208.4	162.5	169.5
Krvskp	8996.7	**4666.5**	4916.1	11475.4	5078.9	8266.5	11632.5
tic-tac-toe	1535.1	881.7	**869.4**	1839.5	1272.4	1011.1	2060.9
Zoo	1563.1	**520.5**	666.4	1172.0	807.4	763.1	816.1
Dermatology	1301.5	**564.7**	645.1	1222.0	580.5	1290.9	718.8
divorce	127.3	**63.4**	65.5	136.2	93.6	84.1	110.4
Movementlibras	5553.3	**3119.7**	3139.7	6639.1	5062.6	4450.9	3917.2

In addition, the representation of solutions needs to be designed. This research uses the RBF kernel for SVM because the RBF kernel can analyze higher dimensional data and require that only two parameters, C and γ be defined [10]. Moreover, each feature corresponds to one of the solution's dimensions. Thus, one solution is comprised of three parts, the features mask, C, and γ.

Table 1 shows the representation of the ith solution with a dimension of $D+9+10$, where D is the number of features. The feature mask is Boolean that 1 represents the feature selected, and 0 indicates the feature is not selected. Moreover, to fit into the discrete space, C and γ are encoded, taking up 9 and 10 dimensions, respectively. With a precision of two decimal places, the adjustment ranges for these two parameters are [0.1, 500] and [0.00001, 0.6].

4   Experiment and Analysis

In this section, we conduct tests to evaluate the performance of IBHBA. First, the experimental setups are displayed. Furthermore, the test results obtained by IBHBA and several comparison algorithms are presented and analyzed.

4.1   Experiment Setup

The experiment uses 27 benchmark datasets that were acquired from the famed UCI Machine Learning Repository [2]. Table 2 lists the number of features, and instances used in each dataset.

Binary honey badger algorithm (BHBA), binary harris hawk optimization (BHHO), binary salp swarm algorithm (BSSA), binary whale optimization algorithm (BWOA), cuckoo search (BCS), and binary particle swarm optimization (BPSO) are introduced as comparison algorithms. Furthermore, the key parameters setting of these algorithms are listed in Table 3. In addition, for a fair comparison, the maximum number of iterations and the swarm size are the same for each algorithm. In this work, they are set as 100 and 20.

The algorithm is implemented in python 3.6 on an Intel dual core with 12 GB RAM. To avoid the random bias of the experiment, each algorithm is run 5 times independently. Moreover, in each classification evaluation, we use 90 % of the instances for training, and the rest is used for testing.

4.2   Results and Analysis

In this section, the feature selection results in terms of the fitness function value, convergence rate, and CPU time are presented. Moreover, the best results obtained by a particular algorithm are displayed in bold font for a clear overview.

Tables 4 and 5 show the numerical statistical results of the mean fitness function values and CPU time of different algorithms for each dataset, respectively. It is easy to see that IBHBA outperforms the competitors on 26 selected datasets in terms of the mean fitness function value. However, IBHBA consumes more CPU time to solve feature selection issues. On the one hand, the newly incorporated improved factors necessitate additional solution processes, which lengthens experiment times. On the other hand, the involvement of classifier parameters expands the search space, which also increases the time consumption.

In addition, Fig. 1 shows the convergence rates of different algorithms during the 3rd iteration. As can be seen, IBHBA exposes the best curves on 26

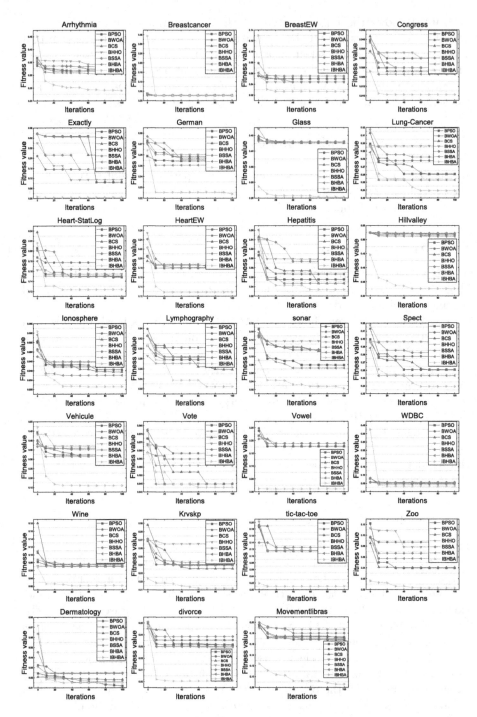

Fig. 1. Convergence rates obtained by different algorithms.

datasets, which performs the best convergence ability among all the comparison algorithms. Thus, We may conclude that the proposed IBHBA has the best overall performance on the chosen datasets after combining the above analysis for the tables and figures.

5   Conclusions

In this paper, IBHBA was proposed to simultaneously adjust the parameter values of SVM and find the optimal subset of features to obtain optimal classification results for the constructed classifiers. In IBHBA, we first proposed a novel initial strategy to improve initialization population quality. Second, a simulated annealing operator was introduced to enhance the local search performance of the algorithm. Moreover, we used the crossover and mutation mechanism to improve the population diversity. Finally, a binary method was adopted to make the continuous algorithm suitable for the feature selection problem. Experiments were conducted on several classical datasets, and the results showed that the overall performance of IBHBA outperforms BHHO, BSSA, BCS, BPSO, and BHBA in solving feature selection problems. In our future work, more datasets will be considered to further evaluate the proposed algorithm.

Acknowledgements. This work is supported in part by the National Key Research and Development Program of China (2022YFB4500600), in part by the National Natural Science Foundation of China (61872158, 62002133, 62172186, 62272194), in part by the Science and Technology Development Plan Project of Jilin Province (20200201166JC, 20190701019GH, 20190701002GH), in part by Graduate Innovation Fund of Jilin University (2022028, 2022155, 2023CX013), and in part by the Excellent Young Talents Program for Department of Science and Technology of Jilin Province (Grant 20190103051JH).

References

1. Agrawal, R.K., Kaur, B., Sharma, S.: Quantum based whale optimization algorithm for wrapper feature selection. Appl. Soft Comput. **89**, 106092 (2020)
2. Blake, C.: UCI repository of machine learning databases. http://www.ics.uci.edu/~mlearn/MLRepository.html (1998)
3. Cervantes, J., García-Lamont, F., Rodríguez-Mazahua, L., López Chau, A.: A comprehensive survey on support vector machine classification: applications, challenges and trends. Neurocomputing **408**, 189–215 (2020)
4. Chen, H., Zhang, Z., Yin, W., Zhao, C., Wang, F., Li, Y.: A study on depth classification of defects by machine learning based on hyper-parameter search. Measurement **189**, 110660 (2022)
5. Dai, Y., Zhao, P.: A hybrid load forecasting model based on support vector machine with intelligent methods for feature selection and parameter optimization. Appl. Energy **279**, 115332 (2020)
6. Deng, Y., Guan, D., Chen, Y., Yuan, W., Ji, J., Wei, M.: SAR-ShipNet: SAR-Ship detection neural network via bidirectional coordinate attention and multi-resolution feature fusion. In: Proceedings IEEE ICASSP, pp. 3973–3977 (2022)

7. Dhal, P., Azad, C.: A comprehensive survey on feature selection in the various fields of machine learning. Appl. Intell. **52**(4), 4543–4581 (2022)
8. Elgamal, Z.M., Sabri, A.Q.M., Tubishat, M., Tbaishat, D., Makhadmeh, S.N., Alomari, O.A.: Improved reptile search optimization algorithm using chaotic map and simulated annealing for feature selection in medical field. IEEE Access **10**, 51428–51446 (2022)
9. Ghanem, W.A.H.M., et al.: Cyber intrusion detection system based on a multiobjective binary bat algorithm for feature selection and enhanced bat algorithm for parameter optimization in neural networks. IEEE Access **10**, 76318–76339 (2022)
10. Ghosh, S., Dasgupta, A., Swetapadma, A.: A study on support vector machine based linear and non-linear pattern classification. In: Proceedings IEEE ICISS, pp. 24–28 (2019)
11. Guan, D., et al.: A novel class noise detection method for high-dimensional data in industrial informatics. IEEE Trans. Ind. Informatics **17**(3), 2181–2190 (2021)
12. Hashim, F.A., Houssein, E.H., Hussain, K., Mabrouk, M.S., Al-Atabany, W.: Honey badger algorithm: new metaheuristic algorithm for solving optimization problems. Math. Comput. Simul. **192**, 84–110 (2022)
13. Karn, R.R.P., et al.: A feature and parameter selection approach for visual domain adaptation using particle swarm optimization. In: Proceedings IEEE CEC, pp. 1–7. IEEE (2022)
14. Karthikeyan, R., Alli, P.: Feature selection and parameters optimization of support vector machines based on hybrid glowworm swarm optimization for classification of diabetic retinopathy. J. Med. Syst. **42**(10), 1–11 (2018)
15. Li, A., Xue, B., Zhang, M.: Multi-objective feature selection using hybridization of a genetic algorithm and direct multisearch for key quality characteristic selection. Inf. Sci. **523**, 245–265 (2020)
16. Mehedi, I.M., et al.: Optimal feature selection using modified cuckoo search for classification of power quality disturbances. Appl. Soft Comput. **113**(Part), 107897 (2021)
17. Mirjalili, S., Lewis, A.: S-shaped versus v-shaped transfer functions for binary particle swarm optimization. Swarm Evol. Comput. **9**, 1–14 (2013)
18. Ren, W., Ma, D., Han, M.: Multivariate time series predictor with parameter optimization and feature selection based on modified binary salp swarm algorithm. IEEE Trans. Indust. Inf. **19**, 6150–6159 (2022)
19. Sakri, S.B., Rashid, N.B.A., Zain, Z.M.: Particle swarm optimization feature selection for breast cancer recurrence prediction. IEEE Access **6**, 29637–29647 (2018)
20. Too, J., Sadiq, A.S., Mirjalili, S.M.: A conditional opposition-based particle swarm optimisation for feature selection. Connect. Sci. **34**(1), 339–361 (2022)
21. Tubishat, M., et al.: Dynamic salp swarm algorithm for feature selection. Expert Syst. Appl. **164**, 113873 (2021)
22. Yu, L., Liu, H.: Feature selection for high-dimensional data: a fast correlation-based filter solution. In: Fawcett, T., Mishra, N. (eds.) Proceedings ICML, pp. 856–863. AAAI Press (2003)
23. Zhang, Y., Liu, R., Wang, X., Chen, H., Li, C.: Boosted binary Harris Hawks optimizer and feature selection. Eng. Comput. **37**(4), 3741–3770 (2021)
24. Zhou, T., Lu, H., Wenwen, W., Xia, Y.: GA-SVM based feature selection and parameter optimization in hospitalization expense modeling. Appl. Soft Comput. **75**, 323–332 (2019)
25. Zou, L., Zhou, S., Li, X.: An efficient improved greedy Harris Hawks optimizer and its application to feature selection. Entropy **24**(8), 1065 (2022)

Automatic Gaussian Bandwidth Selection for Kernel Principal Component Analysis

Kai Shen, Haoyu Wang$^{(\boxtimes)}$, Arin Chaudhuri, and Zohreh Asgharzadeh

SAS Institute Inc, Cary, NC 27513, USA
haoyu.wang@sas.com

Abstract. Kernel principal component analysis (KPCA) has been proved to be useful in many applications as a dimension reduction technique. Compared with PCA, KPCA better exploits the complicated spatial structure of high-dimensional features. Because of the high computational cost of exact KPCA, however, research has focused on the fast computation of KPCA, through techniques such as matrix sketching, the Nyström method, and random Fourier features. There has been little discussion of the selection of kernel bandwidth, which is critical in practice. In this paper, we propose a new data-driven bandwidth selection method, called the criterion of the maximum sum of eigenvalues (CMSE) method and a scalable variation (SCMSE) to handle big data. Both feature high time efficiency and achieve performance better than or comparable to that of the existing methods. We conduct both simulation study and real-world data analyses to support our conclusions.

Keywords: Kernel PCA · Gramian matrix · Pre-image problem · Reconstruction error · Gaussian kernel bandwidth selection

1 Introduction

Kernel principal component analysis (KPCA) [16] is a well-known technique for dimension reduction. It shares the same underlying idea as PCA: it projects data into a lower-dimensional space that captures the highest possible amount of variance in the data. Instead of performing a linear transformation of the data, KPCA expands the features by nonlinear transformations and then applies PCA in this transformed feature space, called reproducing kernel Hilbert space (RKHS). KPCA has been proved to be useful in many application areas, such as visualization, pattern recognition, data compression, image denoising, and novelty detection.

Exact KPCA requires the full construction of the centered kernel matrix and expensive eigendecomposition, with computational complexity $\mathcal{O}(n^3)$, making it difficult to apply to massive data sets. Fast computation of KPCA has been achieved by either using a sample of data points to construct a much smaller Gramian matrix or using feature maps to provide an approximate embedding of the RKHS in Euclidean space [4,7–9,11–13]. Kernel PCA has been made more scalable by the aforementioned approximation methods. However, there has been

Z. Jin et al. (Eds.): KSEM 2023, LNAI 14117, pp. 15–26, 2023.
https://doi.org/10.1007/978-3-031-40283-8_2

little research on another important issue of KPCA: selection of the kernel bandwidth. Because different bandwidth values correspond to different RKHS, it is almost impossible to incorporate bandwidth selection into any RKHS theory framework. However, in practice, the choice of the kernel bandwidth is extremely important for almost all kernel-based methods. Bandwidth values that are either too large or too small for kernel PCA fail to serve the purpose of data visualization, dimension reduction, or anomaly detection. For instance, Fig. 1 shows the results of data visualization using KPCA for the Statistical Control Chart Time Series data set available in the UCI Machine Learning Repository [5]. An appropriate bandwidth value (Fig. 1a) can effectively separate the data into different clusters, and thus visualization is meaningful. On the other hand, if the bandwidth is inappropriate (too small in this case, as shown in Fig. 1b), all the data points are clustered together. Therefore, kernel bandwidth selection becomes essential for solving real-world problems. In [10], the Gaussian kernel bandwidth is set to default value, $\sigma_{kt} = \sqrt{\frac{1}{2n(n-1)} \sum_{i,j=1}^{n} ||\boldsymbol{x}_i - \boldsymbol{x}_j||^2}$, which turns out to be a good practical choice. The method proposed in [1] chooses hyperparameters in KPCA based on cross-validation for the comparable reconstruction errors of pre-images in the original space. In [19], a new data-driven bandwidth selection criterion for KPCA is proposed that is related to least squares cross-validation for kernel density estimation. These two methods either are completely heuristic or require cross-validation, which is very time-consuming. In this paper, we propose a new data-driven bandwidth selection method, which is based on the sum of the first k largest eigenvalues when the value of k is given, as well as a variation of this method to handle big data. These methods do not require cross-validation and thus are much more time-efficient. Note that in this paper we focus only on the Gaussian kernel, which is the most commonly used kernel.

The rest of the paper is organized as follows. In Sect. 2, we first give some background information about KPCA and the pre-image issue, and then we introduce the problem setup and propose our bandwidth selection methods. In Sect. 3, we conduct a real-world data analysis to support the proposed methods. In Sect. 4, both simulation study and real-world data analysis are conducted to illustrate the efficiency of our proposed methods. Further discussion is presented in the final section.

2   Methodology

In this section, we introduce the methodology of our proposed bandwidth selection method. We call it the criterion of the maximum sum of eigenvalues (CMSE) method. We also introduce a variation of this method, called scalable CMSE (SCMSE), which handles large amounts of data in an efficient way.

2.1   Preliminaries

We start with some preliminaries for the proposed bandwidth selection method. The KPCA problem is well defined in [16,17]. We introduce the concept of the

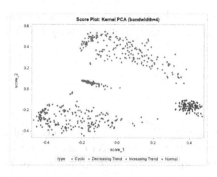 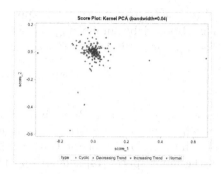

(a) KPCA using appropriate bandwidth   (b) KPCA using inappropriate bandwidth

Fig. 1. Data visualization using KPCA for Statistical Control Chart Time Series data set available in the UCI Machine Learning Repository. The first two KPCA score values are plotted against each other. An appropriate bandwidth gives much better clustering results (clusters are completely separated) than an inappropriate bandwidth (clusters are heavily overlapped).

KPCA pre-image [18], which is the mapping of a projection in the RKHS to the original input space. The KPCA reconstruction error [17] can be calculated as the distance between the pre-image and the original input point. Throughout this paper, we use reconstruction error as a performance measure of the different bandwidth selection methods.

KPCA Pre-image. The pre-image technique proves to be useful in denoising applications. The rationale behind this is our assumption that the directions of eigenvectors corresponding to small eigenvalues contain only information about noise, because small eigenvalues suggest small variances. In contrast, leading eigenvectors that correspond to large eigenvalues are assumed to contain relevant pattern information. Linear PCA can also be applied to the denoising problem, but the linear limitation makes it impossible for linear PCA to identify noise that has a nonlinear pattern. KPCA denoises the data by first applying linear PCA to the $\phi(\boldsymbol{x})$ in the feature space and then projecting the data onto the subspace spanned by the leading eigenvectors. However, these projections still lie in the feature space, and we have to map them back to the input space to recover the denoised patterns. Note that the eigenvectors for KPCA, and hence the projections in the feature space, are expressed in terms of the mapped input data $\sum_{i=1}^{n} \alpha_i \phi(\boldsymbol{x}_i)$. The mapping $\phi(\cdot)$ is usually nonlinear and thus not necessarily invertible. Therefore, it cannot generally be guaranteed that the exact pre-image exists, and in most cases we must settle for only an approximate solution [14].

Since we are focusing on Gaussian kernel bandwidth selection, here we restrict our discussion of the pre-image problem to the Gaussian kernel,

$$K(\boldsymbol{x}_i, \boldsymbol{x}_j) = \exp(-\frac{\|\boldsymbol{x}_i - \boldsymbol{x}_j\|^2}{2\sigma^2}) \qquad (1)$$

With the Gaussian kernel, one approximate solution for the pre-image problem is obtained by minimizing the Euclidean distance between $\phi(z)$ and the projection $P_J\phi(x)$ in feature space, which is denoted by

$$\arg\min_{z}\|\phi(z) - P_J\phi(x)\|^2 \tag{2}$$

The projection operator P_J is given as $P_J\phi(x) = \sum_{j=1}^{J} \beta_j v_j$, where v_j is the jth leading eigenvector of the covariance matrix and β_j is the projection of a data point x onto v_j. For the Gaussian kernel that satisfies $K(x, x) = 1$ for all x in the input space, [14] showed that the minimization of formula (2) can be achieved by fixed-point iterations.

KPCA Reconstruction Error. In this paper, we use the reconstruction error of KPCA projection as an objective loss function to evaluate the performance of the proposed kernel bandwidth selection method. However, in contrast with PCA, the reconstruction error of projection is not straightforwardly applicable to KPCA because the Euclidean norm in RKHS is not comparable for different kernel bandwidths. To tackle this problem, we need to find the pre-image of the KPCA projection in RKHS, which lies in the original input space. Here the pre-image is defined as the approximate inverse image of the feature map. After obtaining the pre-image, we can calculate its squared reconstruction error [1] in the input space—namely,

$$E_r = \|z - x\|^2, \tag{3}$$

where x is a test point and z is the corresponding pre-image of x's KPCA projection in RKHS. Because the reconstruction error is now calculated with respect to input space, these errors are comparable for different kernel bandwidths.

2.2   Criterion of the Maximum Sum of Eigenvalues (CMSE) Method

A lot of research has been done in the setting where the RKHS is fixed—in other words, where the kernel and the bandwidth associated with that kernel remain unchanged. Both the theoretical framework and the computational improvement are implemented in that setting. However, in practice, an appropriate kernel bandwidth is always needed in order to ensure a satisfactory performance of KPCA. Little work has been done with regard to bandwidth selection for KPCA (see, for instance, [19]).

The bandwidth selection method that we propose is called the criterion of the maximum sum of eigenvalues (CMSE) method. As we discussed earlier, KPCA expands the features by nonlinear transformations and then applies PCA in the RKHS. It is commonly acknowledged that when PCA is applied to a covariance matrix, the first k eigenvalues (k should be large enough to identify a major variance pattern) explain the majority of variance underlying the data. For KPCA, each kernel bandwidth corresponds to a unique RKHS, and the first k eigenvalues explain a certain amount of variance of features in a certain RKHS. The proposed criterion is thus that for a given value of k, the bandwidth that has the maximum sum of the first k largest eigenvalues is the ideal bandwidth, because it tends to explain the largest amount of variance in the data set.

Our method is similar in spirit to the principle of maximum likelihood for parameter selection. In the problem of maximum likelihood, we are given a family of probability distributions indexed by a set of parameters θ, and different values of θ correspond to different probability distributions. If $p_\theta(x)$ denotes the probability density of the data under the distribution corresponding to θ, we choose the θ that maximizes $p_\theta(x)$. In KPCA, where different values of bandwidth σ correspond to different embedding spaces, we choose a value of σ that maximizes the variation due to the principal subspace of dimension k. In Sect. 3, we show that our proposed CMSE method performs well in a real-world data analysis.

2.3 Scalable CMSE (SCMSE) Method

Although the CMSE method provides a systematic way to perform Gaussian kernel bandwidth selection, the time that it takes to apply CMSE to an even moderately large data set is still too long, given that the time complexity of CMSE is $\mathcal{O}(n^3)$, where n is the size of the data set. The $\mathcal{O}(n^3)$ complexity of CMSE comes from the fact that we use the finite-difference method to approximate the derivative. Therefore, evaluating the objective function—namely, the sum of eigenvalues—is the dominant cost, and it involves an eigendecomposition that takes $\mathcal{O}(n^3)$ time [15]. For practical applications involving moderate to large amounts of data, we propose a variation: the scalable CMSE (SCMSE) method for large data sets. The SCMSE method uses a new Gaussian-based kernel function inspired by the Nyström method [4]. Specifically, we choose q landmark points, $\mathcal{Z} = \{z_j\}_{j=1}^q$, by using k-means clustering, and then we construct the new kernel function $K_{new}(\boldsymbol{x}_i, \boldsymbol{x}_j)$ as

$$K_{new}(\boldsymbol{x}_i, \boldsymbol{x}_j) = K(\boldsymbol{x}_i, \mathcal{Z})K(\mathcal{Z}, \mathcal{Z})^{-1}K(\mathcal{Z}, \boldsymbol{x}_j), \tag{4}$$

where K denotes the standard Gaussian kernel function. Now let us denote G as $K(\boldsymbol{X}, \mathcal{Z})K(\mathcal{Z}, \mathcal{Z})^{-1/2} = G$, and then the new kernel matrix can be expressed as $K_{new} = GG^T$.

Kernel PCA is performed on the centered kernel matrix as

$$\tilde{K}_{n \times n} = K_{n \times n} - \mathbf{1}_{1/n}K_{n \times n} - K_{n \times n}\mathbf{1}_{1/n} + \mathbf{1}_{1/n}K_{n \times n}\mathbf{1}_{1/n}, \tag{5}$$

where $\mathbf{1}_{1/n}$ is an $n \times n$ matrix with all elements equal to $1/n$. More details can be found in [16]. For the new kernel matrix defined in equation (4), the centering can be done by subtracting the column means of G matrix from each element in G, as follows:

$$\tilde{K}_{new} = (G - \bar{G})(G - \bar{G})^T = \tilde{G}\tilde{G}^T, \tag{6}$$

where $\bar{G}$ is the matrix of column mean of G and $\tilde{G}$ is the centered version of G.

Since $\tilde{G}\tilde{G}^T$ and $\tilde{G}^T\tilde{G}$ share the same nonzero eigenvalues, the SCMSE method obtains its scalability from applying the CMSE method to the eigensystem of

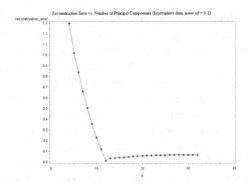

Fig. 2. Hypersphere data. The number of selected PCs is 12.

$\tilde{G}^T \tilde{G}$, which is a matrix of size $q \times q$. When we choose a much smaller set of q landmark points from the original data points, SCMSE offers a huge improvement in time complexity (from $\mathcal{O}(n^3)$ to $\mathcal{O}(nq^2)$) over the CMSE method. In Sect. 4, we will give a simulation study and a real data example to show the efficiency of SCMSE method.

2.4   Choosing the Number of Principal Components

The number of principal components k plays an important role in the proposed methods. It determines how many principal variance directions we want to consider. Here we select the k value for the CMSE and SCMSE methods by using the following heuristic:

1. Find a range of k values (e.g., 1% to 10% of the number of the observations) and a desired step size.
2. For each k value in the preceding range, calculate the Gaussian kernel bandwidth by using the CMSE method and plot the reconstruction error.
3. Create the plot of the reconstruction error (y-coordinate) versus the k values (x-coordinate). Then choose the inflection point or some point near the inflection point in the plot and use its x-coordinate as the k value.

The concept of an inflection point is similar to that discussed in [2], which provides a detailed explanation. We find that this heuristic method works well in practice. See Figs. 2 for plots of reconstruction error versus the number of principal components for the simulated hypersphere data set (which is introduced in Sect. 4.1).

3   Experiment

In this section, we compare the performance of four bandwidth selection methods: the default bandwidth of [10] (KT), $\sigma_{kt} = \sqrt{\frac{1}{2n(n-1)} \sum_{i,j=1}^{n} ||\boldsymbol{x}_i - \boldsymbol{x}_j||^2}$;

the modified default bandwidth (MKT), $\sigma_{mkt} = \sqrt{\frac{1}{4n(n-1)} \sum_{i,j=1}^{n} \|\boldsymbol{x}_i - \boldsymbol{x}_j\|^2}$ (this is a slight modification by a different scaling factor from the σ_{kt}, yet we find that it leads to considerable performance improvement); the criterion of the maximum sum of eigenvalues (CMSE); and the five-fold cross-validation method of [1]. The comparison is done by applying KPCA denoising to a real-world data example. The reconstruction error is used as an objective loss function to compare the performance of different bandwidths. The experiments in this paper are conducted using the SAS/IML® programming language.

In all the results tables, we provide the reconstruction error for five kernel bandwidths: σ_{kt}, σ_{mkt}, σ_{gs}, σ_{opt}, and σ_{5cv}. Here σ_{5cv} denotes the kernel bandwidth obtained by five-fold cross-validation; this method uses a candidate bandwidth set for grid search. Both σ_{gs} and σ_{opt} denote the bandwidth that is obtained by the CMSE method. The difference is that σ_{gs} is found by a plain grid search over the candidate bandwidth set, and σ_{opt} is found by the Newton method, which optimizes the bandwidth to maximize the sum of the first k eigenvalues. The method of [19] is not included in the experiment because it is computationally too expensive, involving a multidimensional integration in a leave-one-out cross-validation (LOOCV) setting. Because of space limitations, we have put supplementary simulation results as well as code online.

To test our bandwidth selection methods on real-world data, here we consider the MNIST data set [3]. It contains 28×28-pixel labeled images of handwritten digits. The pixel values are scaled to range from 0 to 1. There are a total of 60,000 digits, and each digit is represented by a 784-dimensional real value vector and the corresponding integer label. For each of the 10 digits, we randomly selected 300 examples for training and 50 examples for testing. The test data were rendered noisy by Gaussian noise, which is characterized by zero mean and standard deviation $\sigma = 0.4$.

Figures 3a and 3b illustrate the first appearance of each digit in the test data set, without and with Gaussian noise, respectively.

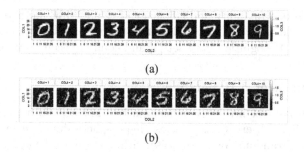

(a)

(b)

Fig. 3. Digits (a) with and (b) without Gaussian Noise

Since we have 300 samples for each digit, the total training data set size is $3,000 \times 784$. The grid search implementation of CMSE is done over the bandwidth set [0.1, 10] with a step size of 0.1. Because this is a relatively large data set, LOOCV is too expensive to run. Therefore we use five-fold cross-validation instead. The grid search of cross-validation is done over the same bandwidth set as that of CMSE. A variable number of principal components (NPC=60, 70, 80, 90) is applied in KPCA implementation. From the results in Table 1, we see that CMSE and five-fold cross-validation achieves comparable performance. The MKT method performs somewhat worse, and the KT method's performance is the worst. In Figs. 4a, 4b, 4c, 4d, and 4e, we provide the denoised digits that correspond to NPC = 90 and five bandwidths, σ_{gs}, σ_{opt}, σ_{mkt}, σ_{loocv}, and σ_{kt}, respectively. From the plots, we see that σ_{gs}, σ_{opt}, σ_{mkt}, and σ_{loocv} generate almost equally good denoising results, whereas σ_{kt} gives results that are less clear and sharp, especially for the digits "2", "4", and "5" (as highlighted in Fig. 4e). These plots are consistent with the reconstruction errors we observed in Table 1. With respect to the time taken, the two heuristic methods (KT and MKT) take the least time (0.01 secs), followed by the CMSE method (the grid search method takes 400 secs per bandwidth, and the optimization method takes 53 secs), and five-fold cross-validation takes the most time (34 mins).

Table 1. Mean Reconstruction Errors over Different σ's for MNIST Data

NPC	ME_{kt}	ME_{mkt}	ME_{gs}	ME_{opt}	ME_{5cv}
60	35.30	21.25	19.08	18.57	17.27
70	33.96	20.16	18.31	17.78	16.49
80	32.59	19.28	17.61	17.02	16.04
90	31.49	18.69	17.07	16.50	15.60

4   Efficiency of SCMSE

To demonstrate the capability and efficiency of the SCMSE method in handling large data sets, we apply SCMSE and CMSE to the simulated data sets and the real-world Letter Recognition data set [5] and compare their performance.

4.1   Ten-Dimensional Hyperspheres

The simulated data set involves denoising a ten-dimensional hypersphere with a radius of 1. The observations in these hypersphere data are uniformly distributed. We add random Gaussian noise with a standard deviation of δ to the radius when generating each training and test observation. Here we investigate four δ value settings: 0.05, 0.1, 0.2, and 0.4. The training set consists of 5,000 observations, and the test set consists of 100 observations. The denoising performance is measured by the reconstruction error between the denoised test set and the clean test set without noise. The purpose is to compare the bandwidth selection quality and time consumed between the CMSE and SCMSE methods.

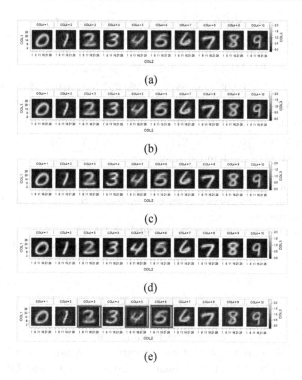

Fig. 4. Denoised Digits with 90 PCs and (a) σ_{gs}, (b) σ_{opt}, (c) σ_{mkt}, (d) σ_{loocv}, (e) σ_{kt}

The comparison results are summarized in Table 2. Here we choose 100 land-mark points for all the comparison settings and use mean reconstruction error and mean time consumed (in seconds) as evaluation metrics. From the results presented in the table, we see that the bandwidth selected by SCMSE achieves almost the same reconstruction error as CMSE, but the time consumed is much less. Therefore, by employing the new kernel function (4), the SCMSE method demonstrates great efficiency in handling large data sets, and we suggest that whenever the data set is of moderate or large size, SCMSE should be used in place of CMSE.

4.2   A Real Large-Scale Data Example: Letter Recognition Data Set

To further explore the performance of the proposed SCMSE method on a large data set, here we use the Letter Recognition data set from the UCI Machine Learning Repository [5]. The data set includes a large number of black-and-white pixel images of rectangular shape, each of them corresponding to one of the 26 capital letters in the English alphabet. These letter pictures use 20 different fonts, and each picture was randomly altered to generate a total of 20,000 unique instances. Each instance was then transformed into 16 statistical attributes (edge counts and statistical moments). All these attributes were further scaled to a

Table 2. CMSE and SCMSE Performance Comparison over Different σ's for Hypersphere Data with Number of PCs = 12 and Number of Iterations = 100

δ	ME_{opt_cmse} (SE)	ME_{opt_scmse} (SE)	MT_{opt_cmse} (SE)	MT_{opt_scmse} (SE)
0.05	0.005 (0.0006)	0.005 (0.0008)	500.337 (30.3420)	3.701 (0.3101)
0.1	0.007 (0.0006)	0.007 (0.0007)	533.404 (31.2712)	15.989 (1.3334)
0.2	0.029 (0.0037)	0.030 (0.0042)	165.332 (19.5674)	0.959 (0.0322)
0.4	0.252 (0.0371)	0.264 (0.0421)	157.460 (15.2115)	0.941 (0.0378)

σ: standard deviation of random Gaussian noise.

SE: standard error.

ME_{opt_cmse}: mean reconstruction error corresponding to CMSE.

ME_{opt_scmse}: mean reconstruction error corresponding to approximate CMSE using low-rank approximation.

MT_{opt_cmse}: mean time consumed (in seconds) for CMSE.

MT_{opt_scmse}: mean time consumed (in seconds) for approximate CMSE using low-rank approximation.

range of integer values from 0 to 15 [6]. In this example, a training set of size 16,000 instances is randomly selected, and the remaining 4,000 instances are used as a test set. To test the denoising performance of different kernel bandwidths, here we add iid Gaussian noise of zero mean and standard deviation of 2 to the test data set. The KPCA pre-image of the test set is calculated using 320 principal components. The mean reconstruction error is calculated between the denoised test set and the clean test set without noise. SCMSE (with 400 k-means clustering centroids) and CMSE are applied to find the optimal bandwidth. The results are summarized in Table 3. As a benchmark, in the table 3 we also provide the mean reconstruction error obtained from the bandwidth selected by five-fold cross-validation over the bandwidth set $\{0.001, 0.01, 0.1, 0.5, 0.75, 1, 5, 10, 20, 50\}$.

Table 3. Mean Reconstruction Error over Different σ's for Letter Recognition Data Set

NPC	ME_{opt_cmse}	ME_{opt_scmse}	ME_{5cv}	MT_{opt_cmse}	MT_{opt_scmse}	MT_{5cv}
320	26.84	27.91	26.87	4773.11	14.25	15355.450

From the results in Table 3, we see that the SCMSE method achieves reconstruction error comparable to that of the CMSE method and five-fold cross-validation, but the time taken is much less.

5   Discussion

In this paper, we have discussed the problem of Gaussian kernel bandwidth selection for KPCA. We have proposed a quick and easy way to choose the bandwidth for the Gaussian kernel by calculating the sum of eigenvalues of the centered kernel matrix and selecting the bandwidth associated with the maximum sum of the first k eigenvalues. We call this method the criterion of the maximum sum of eigenvalues (CMSE). For a fixed number of principal components, a larger sum of eigenvalues suggests that eigenvectors of the mapped pattern in RKHS potentially explain more variance, thus leading to a better candidate for the kernel bandwidth.

In practice, the CMSE method can be implemented by either grid search or the Newton optimization method. We conducted empirical studies by using real-world data sets to evaluate the proposed method. Because KPCA uses an unsupervised algorithm, the reconstruction error between the pre-image and the original test image in the input space is used as an objective loss function in evaluating the performance of our proposed method. We observed that, in general, the CMSE method leads to a smaller reconstruction error than the heuristic methods and a reconstruction error similar to that of the cross-validation method. When it comes to run-time cost, CMSE takes longer than the heuristic methods, but much less time than cross-validation, which is known to be computationally expensive. Overall, the CMSE method achieves the best balance between performance and computational efficiency.

When it is applied to data sets of moderate or large size, the CMSE method, which involves multiple eigendecompositions of the kernel matrix, becomes very slow to run. To handle this issue, we propose the SCMSE method, which is inspired by a new kernel function derived from the Gaussian kernel between the original input data points and k-means clustering centroids. From our experiments, we observed that SCMSE achieves performance comparable to that of CMSE, while also greatly reducing the time and space complexity.

References

1. Alam, M.A., Fukumizu, K.: Hyperparameter selection in kernel principal component analysis. J. Comput. Sci. **10**(7), 1139–1150 (2014). https://doi.org/10.3844/jcssp.2014.1139.1150
2. Chaudhuri, A., et al.: The trace kernel bandwidth criterion for support vector data description. Pattern Recogn. **111**, 107662 (2021)
3. Deng, L.: The MNIST database of handwritten digit images for machine learning research. IEEE Signal Process. Mag. **29**(6), 141–142 (2012)
4. Drineas, P., Mahoney, M.W., Cristianini, N.: On the nyström method for approximating a gram matrix for improved kernel-based learning. J. Mach. Learn. Res. **6**(12) (2005)
5. Dua, D., Graff, C.: UCI Machine Learning Repository. University of California, Irvine, USA, School of Information and Computer Sciences (2019)
6. Frey, P.W., Slate, D.J.: Letter recognition using Holland-style adaptive classifiers. Mach. Learn. **6**(2), 161–182 (1991)
7. Gittens, A., Mahoney, M.W.: Revisiting the Nyström method for improved large-scale machine learning. J. Mach. Learn. Res. **17**(1), 3977–4041 (2016)

8. Kimura, S., Ozawa, S., Abe, S.: Incremental kernel PCA for online learning of feature space. In: International Conference on Computational Intelligence for Modelling, Control and Automation and International Conference on Intelligent Agents, Web Technologies and Internet Commerce (CIMCA-IAWTIC'06), vol. 1, pp. 595–600. IEEE (2005)

9. Kumar, S., Mohri, M., Talwalkar, A.: Sampling methods for the Nyström method. J. Mach. Learn. Res. **13**(Apr), 981–1006 (2012)

10. Kwok, J.T., Tsang, I.W.: The pre-image problem in kernel methods. IEEE Trans. Neural Netw. **15**(6), 1517–1525 (2004)

11. Liberty, E.: Simple and deterministic matrix sketching. In: Proceedings of the 19th ACM SIGKDD International Conference on Knowledge Discovery and Data Mining, pp. 581–588 (2013)

12. Lopez-Paz, D., Sra, S., Smola, A., Ghahramani, Z., Schölkopf, B.: Randomized nonlinear component analysis. In: International Conference on Machine Learning, pp. 1359–1367 (2014)

13. Mahoney, M.W., et al.: Randomized algorithms for matrices and data. Found. Trends Mach. Learn. **3**(2), 123–224 (2011)

14. Mika, S., Schölkopf, B., Smola, A., Müller, K.R., Scholz, M., Rätsch, G.: Kernel pca and de-noising in feature spaces. In: Advances in Neural Information Processing Systems, vol. 11 (1998)

15. Pan, V.Y., Chen, Z.Q.: The complexity of the matrix eigenproblem. In: Proceedings of the Thirty-first Annual ACM Symposium on Theory of Computing, pp. 507–516 (1999)

16. Schölkopf, B., Smola, A., Müller, K.-R.: Kernel principal component analysis. In: Gerstner, W., Germond, A., Hasler, M., Nicoud, J.-D. (eds.) ICANN 1997. LNCS, vol. 1327, pp. 583–588. Springer, Heidelberg (1997). https://doi.org/10.1007/BFb0020217

17. Shen, K., Asgharzadeh, Z.: Kernel principal component analysis using SAS. SAS Technical Paper (2019)

18. Teixeira, A.R., Tomé, A.M., Stadlthanner, K., Lang, E.W.: KPCA denoising and the pre-image problem revisited. Digital Signal Process. **18**(4), 568–580 (2008)

19. Thomas, M., Brabanter, K.D., Moor, B.D.: New bandwidth selection criterion for kernel PCA: approach to dimensionality reduction and classification problems. BMC Bioinform. **15**, 1–12 (2014)

Boosting LightWeight Depth Estimation
via Knowledge Distillation

Junjie Hu[1] , Chenyou Fan[2], Hualie Jiang[3], Xiyue Guo[4], Yuan Gao[1],
Xiangyong Lu[5], and Tin Lun Lam[1,3(✉)]

[1] Shenzhen Institute of Artificial Intelligence and Robotics for Society, Shenzhen,
China
[2] South China Normal University, Guangzhou, China
[3] The Chinese University of Hong Kong, Shenzhen, China
tllam@cuhk.edu.cn
[4] Zhejiang University, Hangzhou, China
[5] Tohoku University, Sendai, Japan

Abstract. Monocular depth estimation (MDE) methods are often
either too computationally expensive or not accurate enough due to
the trade-off between model complexity and inference performance. In
this paper, we propose a lightweight network that can accurately estimate depth maps using minimal computing resources. We achieve this by
designing a compact model that maximally reduces model complexity. To
improve the performance of our lightweight network, we adopt knowledge
distillation (KD) techniques. We consider a large network as an expert
teacher that accurately estimates depth maps on the target domain. The
student, which is the lightweight network, is then trained to mimic the
teacher's predictions. However, this KD process can be challenging and
insufficient due to the large model capacity gap between the teacher and
the student. To address this, we propose to use auxiliary unlabeled data
to guide KD, enabling the student to better learn from the teacher's predictions. This approach helps fill the gap between the teacher and the
student, resulting in improved data-driven learning. The experiments
show that our method achieves comparable performance to state-of-the-
art methods while using only 1% of their parameters. Furthermore, our
method outperforms previous lightweight methods regarding inference
accuracy, computational efficiency, and generalizability.

Keywords: Depth estimation · lightweight network · Knowledge
distillation · Auxiliary data

1 Introduction

Monocular depth estimation has gained widespread attention as an economical
and convenient alternative to depth sensors, providing applications in obstacle
avoidance [16], simultaneous localization and mapping (SLAM) [10,25], robot
navigation [18]. With the rapid development of deep learning in recent years,
significant progress has been made in this field.

ⓒ The Author(s), under exclusive license to Springer Nature Switzerland AG 2023
Z. Jin et al. (Eds.): KSEM 2023, LNAI 14117, pp. 27–39, 2023.
https://doi.org/10.1007/978-3-031-40283-8_3

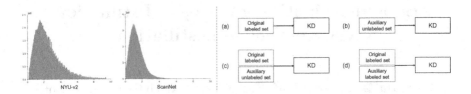

Fig. 1. The left side shows the depth histogram of NYU-v2 training set and ScanNet validation set, respectively. Both of the two histograms exhibit a long-tailed distribution and they are highly similar. The right side shows the configuration of knowledge distillation (KD) considered in this paper. (a) is the standard method that applies KD with the original labeled set. (b) applies KD with only the auxiliary unlabeled set. (c) applies KD with the original labeled set and the auxiliary unlabeled set. (d) applies KD with both the original and auxiliary labeled set.

Most of the previous works mainly focused on the improvement of estimation accuracy [13,14]. However, the depth estimation has to be both computationally efficient and accurate. It is essential for real-world applications with limited computation resources. Although several prior works have attempted to improve the computational efficiency with lightweight networks [19,26], they often come at the cost of significantly decreased inference accuracy. There is an urgent need for MDE to achieve satisfactory performance while maintaining good efficiency.

In this paper, we propose a novel approach to monocular depth estimation that aims to achieve high inference accuracy with minimal hardware resources. To achieve this goal, we introduce a lightweight network with a compact architecture design that reduces the model complexity while maximizing the accuracy of the depth estimation. Our network, built on MobileNet-v2, has only 1.7M parameters, making it one of the most lightweight networks in the literature. By minimizing the model complexity, we aim to strike a balance between accuracy and computational efficiency, making our approach well-suited for real-world applications with limited hardware resources.

We next describe our approach to training the lightweight network using knowledge distillation (KD) [21]. Specifically, we leverage a large network trained on the target domain $\mathcal{X}$ to serve as an expert teacher. Given any input image from $\mathcal{X}$, the teacher network outputs the corresponding depth map. Our approach is motivated by two considerations. First, since depth estimation is a nonlinear mapping from RGB space to depth space, KD can be seen as an approximation of this mapping in a data-driven way. Therefore, the more high-quality data we have, the more accurately we can approximate the mapping. Second, in depth estimation, we find that auxiliary data can be more easily collected since many real-world scenarios share similar scene scales and demonstrate similar depth histograms. For example, two popular indoor benchmarks, NYU-v2 and ScanNet, exhibit similar long-tailed depth distributions and depth ranges, as shown in Fig. 1. This observation motivates our proposal to use auxiliary data to guide KD, which enables the lightweight network to leverage additional training signals and improve its accuracy.

Our study focuses on two scenarios: labeled and unlabeled data. In the labeled case, ground truths can be obtained using depth sensors such as Kinect. In the unlabeled case, auxiliary data can be collected using a visual camera in scenarios with similar scene scales. Therefore, leveraging auxiliary data is practical for improving the performance of depth estimation in real-world applications. In this paper, we propose to take the following learning strategies for these two specific cases.

- When auxiliary data is unlabeled, we first train the teacher on the original labeled set and then apply KD with both the original labeled set and the auxiliary unlabeled set to improve the student.
- When auxiliary data is labeled, we first train the teacher on the combined original and auxiliary sets, which provides a more discriminative teacher. We then apply KD to further enhance the student with the mixed dataset.

As a result, our proposed method achieves comparable results to state-of-the-art methods, while utilizing only 1% of the parameters, and outperforms other lightweight approaches by a large margin. To evaluate the effectiveness of our approach, we conduct a series of experiments and confirm that:

- Even without access to the original training set, our approach can still be effective if enough auxiliary unlabeled samples are available and they have similar scene scales to the original training samples.
- Combining the original trained set and auxiliary unlabeled set in KD can significantly improve performance by better bridging the gap between the teacher and student.
- Directly training the lightweight network with a mixed dataset of both original and auxiliary labeled data has limited improvement due to its low capacity. However, the two-stage learning strategy of first training a larger teacher and then applying KD is more effective in this case.

2   Related Work

In previous studies, monocular depth estimation has been addressed in a supervised learning approach by minimizing the pixel-wise loss between the predicted and ground truth depth [8,13]. Various network architectures have been proposed, including the basic encoder-decoder network [14], networks with skip connections [13], dilated convolution [9], and pyramid pooling [17], all of which have shown improved performance. Additionally, the problem can be formulated as an unsupervised learning task, where the geometry consistency of multi-view images is taken into account [28]. However, the performance of unsupervised approaches still lags behind supervised methods.

Real-time depth estimation has also been investigated in several studies. For example, lightweight networks based on MobileNet and MobileNet-v2 were introduced for fast depth estimation in [19,26], using traditional supervised learning methods. Additionally, an unsupervised approach for depth estimation was proposed in [15] using a lightweight network with recurrent modules. While these small networks demonstrate superior computation speed, their accuracy tends to be significantly lower compared to larger networks. A few works also have applied knowledge distillation to depth estimation [1, 20].

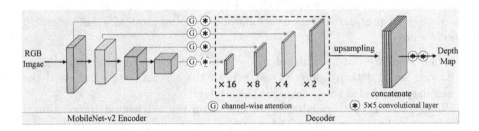

Fig. 2. Diagram of the proposed lightweight network.

3   Lightweight Network

Most previous works for pixel to pixel regression tasks use a symmetric encoder-decoder network [12,14]. However, these networks can be computationally inefficient, requiring significant GPU memory during computation. Furthermore, research on CNNs has shown that there is a high degree of redundancy within them, with multiple filters capturing similar feature representations [2]. To improve the efficiency of depth estimation networks, we propose an extremely compact network architecture in this paper.

The network architecture we propose is depicted in Fig. 2 and is based on a lightweight design that achieves high inference efficiency. Specifically, given a set of feature maps extracted by encoder blocks, we first apply channel-wise attention [11] to attribute weights to each feature map. We then fuse them using the convolutional layer and compress them to a fixed number of channels (16 channels) to reduce the model's complexity. For features extracted with an encoder at multiple scales, we apply the above operation at each scale, and the outputted feature maps are upsampled by factors of ×2, ×4, ×8, and ×16, respectively. Finally, we concatenate them and feed them into two 5 × 5 convolutional layers to obtain the final depth map.

We adopt ResNet-34 and MobileNet-v2 as backbone networks for the teacher and student, respectively, resulting in 21.9 M and 1.7 M parameters, respectively.

4   Promoting KD with Auxiliary Data

Standard KD. We adopt the classical knowledge distillation framework, which involves a well pre-trained teacher network on a labeled set $\mathcal{X}$. The student network is trained using the ground truth depths and estimations from the teacher network as supervision. We denote the teacher and student networks as N_t and

N_s, respectively. The loss function used to train the student network is defined as follows:

$$\mathcal{L} = \frac{1}{|\mathcal{X}|} \sum_{x_i, g_i \in \mathcal{X}} (\lambda L(N_s(x_i), N_t(x_i)) + (1 - \lambda)L(N_s(x_i), g_i)) \tag{1}$$

Here, g_i represents the ground truth depth for input x_i, L is an error measure between two depth maps, and λ is a hyperparameter that balances the two loss terms. To compute L, we use the error measure proposed in [13], which takes into account depth, gradient, and normal losses.

Learning with Auxiliary Data. We hypothesize that auxiliary data can be effective for knowledge distillation (KD) in depth estimation, as long as it shares similar scene scales. To verify this assumption, we conducted a preliminary experiment using a teacher network trained on the NYU-v2 dataset and performing KD with cross-domain datasets. The loss function used for training the student is defined as:

$$\mathcal{L} = \frac{1}{\mathcal{U}} \sum_{u_j \in \mathcal{U}} \lambda L(N_s(u_j), N_t(u_j)) \tag{2}$$

where $\mathcal{U}$ denotes the unlabeled set, N_s and N_t are the student and teacher networks, respectively, and L is the error measure between two depth maps.

To evaluate the effectiveness of using auxiliary data, we selected two datasets with different characteristics: ImageNet, an out-of-distribution dataset, and ScanNet, another indoor dataset with similar scene scales. Note that only RGB images from these datasets were used. We found that using ScanNet as auxiliary data resulted in slightly better performance than the original training data alone, while using ImageNet led to a 15.5% accuracy drop. These findings confirm our hypothesis that KD with unlabeled data is effective for depth estimation, provided that the data has similar scene scales to the original data. Moreover, we found that incorporating both the original training data and auxiliary data further improves the performance of the lightweight network. We considered two scenarios for using auxiliary data, which are discussed in detail in Sec. 5.1.

The use of auxiliary unlabeled data: The teacher network, denoted as N_t, is trained on the original labeled set $\mathcal{X}$. During the knowledge distillation process, we have access to both $\mathcal{X}$ and an auxiliary unlabeled set $\mathcal{U}$. The loss function used to train the student network is formulated as follows:

$$\mathcal{L} = \frac{1}{\mathcal{X}} \sum_{x_i, g_i \in \mathcal{X}} (\lambda L(N_s(x_i), N_t(x_i)) + (1 - \lambda)L(N_s(x_i), g_i)) + \frac{1}{\mathcal{U}} \sum_{u_j \in \mathcal{U}} (L(N_s(u_j), N_t(u_j)) \tag{3}$$

The use of auxiliary labeled data: In this case, the auxiliary data $\mathcal{U}'$ is fully labeled, which means that we have access to both the input images and their ground truth depth maps. We use this data to train a teacher network, denoted as N_t', on a mixed dataset, i.e., $\mathcal{X} \cup \mathcal{U}'$. Since the teacher network is trained on a larger and more diverse dataset, it is expected to be more discriminative than the one trained on $\mathcal{X}$ only. Next, we use the teacher network N_t' to perform KD on a student network N_s, which is learned using both the labeled set $\mathcal{X}$ and the auxiliary labeled set $\mathcal{U}'$. The loss for the student is formulated as:

$$
\mathcal{L} = \frac{1}{\mathcal{X}} \sum_{x_i, g_i \in \mathcal{X}} (\lambda L(N_s(x_i), N_t'(x_i)) + (1 - \lambda)L(N_s(x_i), g_i)) +
$$
$$
\frac{1}{\mathcal{U}'} \sum_{u_j, g_j \in \mathcal{U}'} (\lambda L(N_s(u_j), N_t'(u_j)) + (1 - \lambda)L(N_s(u_j), g_j'))
$$

(4)

where g_j' denotes ground truth of u_j.

5   Experiments

5.1   Implementation Details

We conducted all experiments on the NYU-v2 dataset [22], which is widely used in previous studies and contains various indoor scenes. We followed the standard preprocessing procedure [14]. Specifically, we used the official splits of 464 scenes, with 249 scenes for training and 215 scenes for testing. This resulted in approximately 50,000 unique pairs of images and depth maps with a size of 640×480 pixels. To reduce the computational complexity, we resized the images down to 320×240 pixels using bilinear interpolation and then cropped their central parts to 304×228 pixels, which served as inputs to the networks. The depth maps were resized to 152 × 114 pixels. For testing, we used the same small subset of 654 samples as in previous studies. To obtain auxiliary data, we randomly selected 204,000 images from 1,513 scenarios of the ScanNet dataset [6].

We adopt ResNet-34 as the teacher network and MobileNet-v2 as the student network. Both networks are trained for 20 epochs, and the loss weight λ is set to 0.1. We initialize the encoder module in the network with a model pre-trained on the ImageNet dataset [7], while the other layers are initialized randomly. We employ the Adam optimizer with an initial learning rate of 0.0001, a weight decay of 0.0001, and $\beta_1 = 0.9$ and $\beta_2 = 0.999$. We reduce the learning rate to 10% for every 5 epochs.

5.2   Quantitative Evaluation

To simplify our notation, we use the following conventions throughout the paper. Specifically, we use $\mathcal{X}$, $\mathcal{U}$, and $\mathcal{U}'$ to refer to the NYU-v2 dataset, the unlabeled ScanNet dataset, and the labeled ScanNet dataset, respectively. The teacher models trained on $\mathcal{X}$ and $\mathcal{X} \cup \mathcal{U}'$ are denoted as $N_t(\mathcal{X})$ and $N_t(\mathcal{X} \cup \mathcal{U}')$, respectively. Similarly, the student models trained on $\mathcal{X}$, $\mathcal{X} \cup \mathcal{U}$, and $\mathcal{X} \cup \mathcal{U}'$ are denoted as $N_s(\mathcal{X})$, $N_s(\mathcal{X} \cup \mathcal{U})$, and $N_s(\mathcal{X} \cup \mathcal{U}')$, respectively.

Performance Without KD. We first evaluate the teacher and student network with supervised learning. We perform experiments on $\mathcal{X}$ and the mixed dataset $\mathcal{X} \cup \mathcal{U}'$, respectively. The results are shown in Fig. 3 (a). It can be observed that increasing the amount of labeled data leads to performance improvements for both the teacher and student networks, with the teacher improving from 0.845 to 0.874 and the student improving from 0.802 to 0.825. However, a significant performance gap still exists between the teacher and student networks, with the teacher outperforming the student, e.g., 0.845 vs 0.802 and 0.874 vs 0.825.

Performance with KD. We conducted a series of experiments to validate our proposed method. We began by training the teacher networks $N_t(\mathcal{X})$ and $N_t(\mathcal{X} \cup \mathcal{U}')$ on the datasets $\mathcal{X}$ and $\mathcal{X} \cup \mathcal{U}'$, respectively. Subsequently, we trained the student network in four different settings:

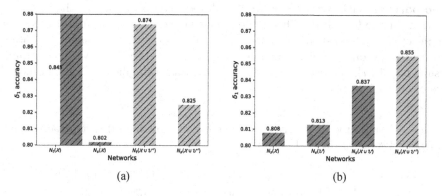

(a)   (b)

Fig. 3. (a) Results of the teacher and student network trained with supervised learning. The blue color denotes results trained on $\mathcal{X}$ and the green color denotes results with $\mathcal{X} \cup \mathcal{U}'$. (b) Results of the student network learned with KD. The blue color denotes results of $N_s(\mathcal{X})$, $N_s(\mathcal{U})$ and $N_s(\mathcal{X} \cup \mathcal{U})$, respectively, and the green color denotes results of $N_s(\mathcal{X} \cup \mathcal{U}')$. (Color figure online)

1. Using a trained teacher network on the original dataset, we applied knowledge distillation with the original training set, i.e., $N_t(\mathcal{X}) \rightarrow N_s(\mathcal{X})$.
2. Using a trained teacher network on the original dataset, we applied knowledge distillation with the auxiliary unlabeled set, i.e., $N_t(\mathcal{X}) \rightarrow N_s(\mathcal{U})$.
3. Using a trained teacher network on the original dataset, we applied knowledge distillation with both the original training set and the auxiliary unlabeled set, i.e., $N_t(\mathcal{X}) \rightarrow N_s(\mathcal{X} \cup \mathcal{U})$.
4. Using a trained teacher network on both the original training set and auxiliary labeled set, we applied knowledge distillation with the mixed labeled set, i.e., $N_t(\mathcal{X} \cup \mathcal{U}') \rightarrow N_s(\mathcal{X} \cup \mathcal{U}')$.

The results in Fig. 3 (b) demonstrate a notable performance gap between the teacher and student networks when standard KD is applied in setting 1), with a drop in performance from 0.845 to 0.808. Interestingly, using only auxiliary unlabeled data in setting 2) leads to even better performance compared to standard KD. Combining the original training set and auxiliary unlabeled data in setting 3) results in a significant performance boost.

As shown in Fig. 3 (a) for $N_s(\mathcal{X} \cup \mathcal{U}')$, when auxiliary data is labeled, the lightweight network's performance can be improved through supervised learning. However, due to the small network's limited capacity, the improvement is modest, and the network's performance is still inferior to that trained with KD and auxiliary unlabeled data, as seen in the result of $N_s(\mathcal{X} \cup \mathcal{U})$ in Fig. 3 (b). Moreover, a more accurate teacher can be learned to further improve the lightweight network's performance through KD, as seen in $N_s(\mathcal{X} \cup \mathcal{U}')$ of Fig. 3 (b).

5.3 Comparison with Previous Methods

Comparison with Large Networks: Table 1 compares our method against previous methods built on different backbone networks, ranging from ResNet-50 to SeNet-154, demonstrating a clear trend of accuracy improvement. Notably, when utilizing only auxiliary unlabeled data, our method achieves comparable results to [13,27], and even outperforms [9,14] with a significantly smaller model size of only 1.7 M parameters.

Table 1. Quantitative comparisons between our method and other approaches built on large networks on the NYU-v2 dataset.

Method	Backbone	Params (M) ↓	RMSE ↓	REL ↓	δ_1 ↑
Laina et al. [14]	ResNet-50	60.6	0.573	0.127	0.811
Hu et al. [13]	ResNet-50	63.6	0.555	0.126	0.843
Zhang et al. [27]	ResNet-50	95.4	0.497	0.121	0.846
Fu et al. [9]	ResNet-101	110.0	0.509	0.115	0.828
Hu et al. [13]	SeNet-154	149.8	0.530	0.115	0.866
Chen et al. [4]	SeNet-154	210.3	0.514	0.111	0.878
Chen et al. [3]	ResNet-101	163.4	**0.376**	**0.098**	**0.899**
Ours $N_s(\mathcal{X} \cup \mathcal{U})$	MobileNet-V2	1.7	0.482	0.131	0.837
Ours $N_s(\mathcal{X} \cup \mathcal{U}')$	MobileNet-V2	1.7	**0.461**	**0.121**	**0.855**

Table 2. Quantitative comparison of lightweight approaches on the NYU-v2 dataset. The best and the second best results are highlighted in red and blue, respectively.

Method	Backbone	Params (M)	GPU [ms]	δ_1
Fast-depth [26]	MobileNet	3.9	7	0.775
Joint-depth [19]	MobileNet-V2	3.1	21	0.790
Ours $N_s(\mathcal{X} \cup \mathcal{U})$	MobileNet-V2	1.7	11	**0.837**
Ours $N_s(\mathcal{X} \cup \mathcal{U}')$	MobileNet-V2	1.7	11	0.855

In terms of methods utilizing extra labeled data, the best performance in Table 1 is achieved by [3], where six auxiliary datasets with a total of 120K extra training data are carefully selected to handle hard cases for depth estimation, such as spurious edges and reflecting surfaces. While our method uses randomly selected auxiliary data from the ScanNet dataset, we believe that utilizing similar carefully selected data could further improve our method's performance.

Comparison with lightweight Networks: We conducted a comparison between our proposed method and two previous approaches for lightweight depth estimation: Fast-depth [26], a traditional encoder-decoder net, and Joint-depth [19], which jointly learns semantic and depth information. Table 2 presents the quantitative results of this comparison, which show that our method outperforms the other two methods by a significant margin, even with only about half of the parameters. Specifically, the δ_1 accuracy of our method, $N_s(\mathcal{X} \cup \mathcal{U})$, is 83.7%, which outperforms Joint-depth and Fast-depth by 4.7% and 6.2%, respectively. Furthermore, when the auxiliary data is labeled, the improvement is more significant, as the accuracy of $N_s(\mathcal{X} \cup \mathcal{U}')$ is 85.5%, representing 6.5% and 8% improvement over Joint-depth and Fast-depth, respectively. In addition, the qualitative comparisons in Fig. 4 show that the estimated depth maps of our method are more accurate and have finer details.

We also compared the GPU time required to infer a depth map from an input image. To conduct this comparison, we used a computer with an Intel(R) Xeon(R) CPU E5-2690 v3 and a GT1080Ti GPU card. We calculated the computation time for the other two methods using their official implementations. The results show that our method infers a depth map using only 11 ms of GPU time, which is much faster than Joint-depth. However, it is worth noting that Fast-depth achieves the smallest inference speed at the expense of degradation of accuracy and demonstrates the worst accuracy among the three methods.

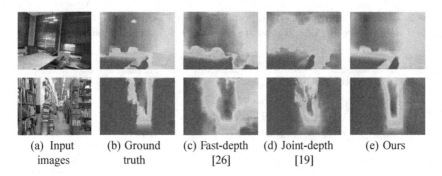

| (a) Input images | (b) Ground truth | (c) Fast-depth [26] | (d) Joint-depth [19] | (e) Ours |

Fig. 4. Qualitative comparison of different methods for lightweight depth estimation on the NYU-v2 dataset.

5.4 Effect of Varying the Number of Auxiliary Data

We conducted an ablation study to investigate the impact of varying the number of auxiliary data on the performance of our lightweight network. Specifically, we used the teacher model trained on the original labeled set and applied knowledge distillation with different numbers of unlabeled samples taken from $\mathcal{U}$. In our experiments, we evaluated our approach using 11.6K, 22.0K, 40.2K, 67.6K, 153.0K, and 204.2K auxiliary samples.

As shown in Fig. 5, our results indicate that increasing the number of auxiliary data samples generally leads to better knowledge distillation performance. However, we observed diminishing returns after a certain number of samples, beyond which adding more samples did not yield any additional improvement.

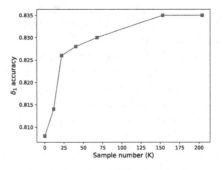

Fig. 5. Results of KD that applies $N_t(\mathcal{X}) \rightarrow N_s(\mathcal{X} \cup \mathcal{U})$ with different number of training samples from $\mathcal{U}$.

5.5 Cross-Dataset Evaluation

To assess the generalization performance of our lightweight model, we conduct a cross-dataset evaluation on two widely used datasets: SUNRGBD [23] and TUM

Table 3. The results of different methods on the SUNRGBD dataset. The best and the second best results are highlighted in red and blue, respectively.

Method	RMSE	REL	δ_1
Fast-depth [26]	0.662	0.376	0.404
Joint-depth [19]	0.634	**0.338**	0.454
Ours $N_s(\mathcal{X} \cup \mathcal{U})$	**0.577**	**0.338**	0.430
Ours $N_s(\mathcal{X} \cup \mathcal{U}')$	0.531	0.306	**0.446**

Table 4. The δ_1 accuracy of different methods on the five sequences from TUM dataset. The best and the second best results are highlighted in red and blue, respectively.

Method	360	desk	desk2	rpy	xyz
Fast-depth [26]	0.548	0.308	0.358	0.333	0.287
Joint-depth [19]	0.512	0.410	0.441	0.552	**0.583**
Ours $N_s(\mathcal{X} \cup \mathcal{U})$	**0.615**	**0.442**	**0.498**	**0.611**	0.486
Ours $N_s(\mathcal{X} \cup \mathcal{U}')$	0.854	0.695	0.772	0.679	0.905

[24]. We directly apply our method, $N_s(\mathcal{X} \cup \mathcal{U})$ and $N_s(\mathcal{X} \cup \mathcal{U}')$, to evaluate on these datasets without any fine-tuning. Note that the comparison between $N_s(\mathcal{X} \cup \mathcal{U}')$ and other methods may not be entirely fair as our method employs auxiliary labeled data. However, we include these results to demonstrate the effectiveness and reliability of utilizing auxiliary data to improve KD in a data-driven manner. The results for each dataset are presented below.

Results on SUNRGBD. Table 3 presents the results, where the best and second best results are highlighted in red and blue, respectively. Our method achieves the lowest RMSE and REL error, while Joint-depth outperforms others in δ_1 accuracy and ranks second in REL.

Results on TUM. We select five sequences from the TUM dataset, including fr1/360, fr1/desk, fr1/desk2, fr1/rpy, and fr1/xyz, as in [5]. Depth accuracy was measured by δ_1. As shown in Table 4, our method significantly outperforms the other methods, demonstrating a better generalization performance.

6   Conclusion

In this paper, we revisit the problem of monocular depth estimation by focusing on the balance between inference accuracy and computational efficiency. We identify the inherent challenge of striking a balance between accuracy and model size. To address this challenge, our method proposes a lightweight network architecture that significantly reduces the number of parameters. We then demonstrate that incorporating auxiliary training data with similar scene scales is an effective strategy for enhancing the performance of the lightweight network. We conduct two experiments, one with auxiliary unlabeled data and one with auxiliary labeled data, both utilizing knowledge distillation. Our method achieves comparable performance with state-of-the-art methods built on much larger networks, with only about 1% of the parameters, and outperforms other lightweight methods by a significant margin.

Acknowledgements. This work is supported by the Shenzhen Science and Technology Program (JSGG20220606142803007) and the funding AC01202101103 from the Shenzhen Institute of Artificial Intelligence and Robotics for Society.

References

1. Aleotti, F., Zaccaroni, G., Bartolomei, L., Poggi, M., Tosi, F., Mattoccia, S.: Real-time single image depth perception in the wild with handheld devices. Sensors (Basel, Switzerland) **21**(1), 15 (2021)

2. Bau, D., Zhou, B., Khosla, A., Oliva, A., Torralba, A.: Network dissection: quantifying interpretability of deep visual representations. In: Proceedings of the IEEE Conference on Computer Vision and Pattern Recognition (CVPR), pp. 3319–3327 (2017)

3. Chen, T., et al.: Improving monocular depth estimation by leveraging structural awareness and complementary datasets. In: Vedaldi, A., Bischof, H., Brox, T., Frahm, J.-M. (eds.) ECCV 2020. LNCS, vol. 12359, pp. 90–108. Springer, Cham (2020). https://doi.org/10.1007/978-3-030-58568-6_6

4. Chen, X., Zha, Z.: Structure-aware residual pyramid network for monocular depth estimation. In: Proceedings of the Twenty-Eighth International Joint Conference on Artificial Intelligence (IJCAI), pp. 694–700 (2019)

5. Czarnowski, J., Laidlow, T., Clark, R., Davison, A.: Deepfactors: real-time probabilistic dense monocular SLAM. IEEE Robot. Autom. Lett. **5**, 721–728 (2020)

6. Dai, A., Chang, A.X., Savva, M., Halber, M., Funkhouser, T., Nießner, M.: Scannet: richly-annotated 3D reconstructions of indoor scenes. In: Proceedings of the IEEE Conference on Computer Vision and Pattern Recognition (CVPR), pp. 2432–2443 (2017)

7. Deng, J., Dong, W., Socher, R., Li, L.J., Li, K., Fei-Fei, L.: ImageNet: a large-scale hierarchical image database. In: Proceedings of the IEEE Conference on Computer Vision and Pattern Recognition (CVPR), pp. 248–255 (2009)

8. Eigen, D., Puhrsch, C., Fergus, R.: Depth map prediction from a single image using a multi-scale deep network. In: Advances in Neural Information Processing Systems (NIPS), pp. 2366–2374 (2014)

9. Fu, H., Gong, M., Wang, C., Batmanghelich, K., Tao, D.: Deep ordinal regression network for monocular depth estimation. In: Proceedings of the IEEE Conference on Computer Vision and Pattern Recognition (CVPR), pp. 2002–2011 (2018)

10. Guo, X., Hu, J., Chen, J., Deng, F., Lam, T.L.: Semantic histogram based graph matching for real-time multi-robot global localization in large scale environment. IEEE Robot. Autom. Lett. **6**(4), 8349–8356 (2021)

11. Hu, J., Shen, L., Sun, G.: Squeeze-and-excitation networks. In: Proceedings of the IEEE Conference on Computer Vision and Pattern Recognition (CVPR), pp. 7132–7141 (2018)

12. Hu, J., Guo, X., Chen, J., Liang, G., Deng, F., Lam, T.L.: A two-stage unsupervised approach for low light image enhancement. IEEE Robot. Autom. Lett. **6**(4), 8363–8370 (2021)

13. Hu, J., Ozay, M., Zhang, Y., Okatani, T.: Revisiting single image depth estimation: Toward higher resolution maps with accurate object boundaries. In: IEEE Winter Conference on Applications of Computer Vision (WACV), pp. 1043–1051 (2019)

14. Iro, L., Christian, R., Vasileios, B., Federico, T., Nassir, N.: Deeper depth prediction with fully convolutional residual networks. In: International Conference on 3D Vision (3DV), pp. 239–248 (2016)
15. Liu, J., Li, Q., Cao, R., Tang, W., Qiu, G.: MiniNet: an extremely lightweight convolutional neural network for real-time unsupervised monocular depth estimation. ArXiv abs/2006.15350 (2020)
16. Mancini, M., Costante, G., Valigi, P., Ciarfuglia, T.A.: Fast robust monocular depth estimation for obstacle detection with fully convolutional networks. In: IEEE International Conference on Intelligent Robots and Systems (IROS), pp. 4296–4303 (2016)
17. Mendes, R.Q., Ribeiro, E.G., Rosa, N.S., Grassi, V.: On deep learning techniques to boost monocular depth estimation for autonomous navigation. Robot. Auton. Syst. **136**, 103701 (2021)
18. Mendes, R.D.Q., Ribeiro, E.G., Rosa, N.D.S., Grassi Jr, V.: On deep learning techniques to boost monocular depth estimation for autonomous navigation. arXiv preprint arXiv:2010.06626 (2020)
19. Nekrasov, V., Dharmasiri, T., Spek, A., Drummond, T., Shen, C., Reid, I.: Real-time joint semantic segmentation and depth estimation using asymmetric annotations. In: IEEE International Conference on Robotics and Automation (ICRA), pp. 7101–7107 (2019)
20. Pilzer, A., Lathuilière, S., Sebe, N., Ricci, E.: Refine and distill: dxploiting cycle-inconsistency and knowledge distillation for unsupervised monocular depth estimation. In: Proceedings of the IEEE Conference on Computer Vision and Pattern Recognition (CVPR), pp. 9760–9769 (2019)
21. Romero, A., Ballas, N., Kahou, S., Chassang, A., Gatta, C., Bengio, Y.: FitNets: hints for thin deep nets. In: International Conference on Representation Learning (ICLR) (2015)
22. Silberman, N., Hoiem, D., Kohli, P., Fergus, R.: Indoor segmentation and support inference from RGBD images. In: European Conference on Computer Vision (ECCV), vol. 7576, pp. 746–760 (2012)
23. Song, S., Lichtenberg, S.P., Xiao, J.: Sun RGB-D: A RGB-D scene understanding benchmark suite. In: Proceedings of the IEEE Conference on Computer Vision and Pattern Recognition (CVPR), pp. 567–576 (2015)
24. Sturm, J., Engelhard, N., Endres, F., Burgard, W., Cremers, D.: A benchmark for the evaluation of RGB-D slam systems. In: IEEE International Conference on Intelligent Robots and Systems (IROS), pp. 573–580 (2012)
25. Tateno, K., Tombari, F., Laina, I., Navab, N.: CNN-SLAM: real-time dense monocular slam with learned depth prediction. In: Proceedings of the IEEE Conference on Computer Vision and Pattern Recognition (CVPR), pp. 6565–6574 (2017)
26. Wofk, D., Ma, F., Yang, T.J., Karaman, S., Sze, V.: FastDepth: fast monocular depth estimation on embedded systems. In: IEEE International Conference on Robotics and Automation (ICRA), pp. 6101–6108 (2019)
27. Zhang, Z., Cui, Z., Xu, C., Yan, Y., Sebe, N., Yang, J.: Pattern-affinitive propagation across depth, surface normal and semantic segmentation. In: Proceedings of the IEEE Conference on Computer Vision and Pattern Recognition (CVPR), pp. 4106–4115 (2019)
28. Zhou, T., Brown, M.R., Snavely, N., Lowe, D.G.: Unsupervised learning of depth and ego-motion from video. In: Proceedings of the IEEE Conference on Computer Vision and Pattern Recognition (CVPR), pp. 6612–6619 (2017)

Graph Neural Network
with Neighborhood Reconnection

Mengying Guo[1,2], Zhenyu Sun[1,2], Yuyi Wang[3], and Xingwu Liu[4(✉)]

[1] Institute of Computing Technology, Chinese Academy of Sciences, Beijing, China
{guomengying,sunzhenyu}@ict.ac.cn
[2] University of Chinese Academy of Sciences, Beijing, China
[3] CRRC Zhuzhou Institute, Zhuzhou, China
[4] School of Mathematical Sciences, Dalian University of Technology, Dalian, China
liuxingwu@dlut.edu.cn

Abstract. Graph Neural Network (GNN) models have become increasingly popular for network analysis, especially in node classification tasks. However, the effectiveness of GNNs is compromised by two limitations. First, they implicitly assume that networks are homophilous, leading to decreased performance on heterophilous or random networks commonly found in the real world. Second, they tend to ignore the known node labels, inferring node labels merely from the node features and network structure. This is mainly rooted in the non-uniformity of node degrees, which makes it hard to directly aggregate label information. Hence, we propose a novel framework NRGNN, short for Graph Neural Network with Neighborhood Reconnection. NRGNN adjusts the network structure to increase homophily and uniformize node degrees. Then it applies message-passing-based or PageRank-based GNNs to the reconstructed networks, addressing the two limitations of GNNs. We evaluate NRGNN against 14 state-of-the-art baselines for node classification tasks. The empirical results demonstrate that NRGNN outperforms almost all the baselines, regardless of whether the datasets are homophilous, heterophilous, or random. The techniques might be adapted to more network analysis tasks.

Keywords: Graph Neural Network · Heterophilous Graph · Network Reconnection · Label Propagation Algorithm · Node Classification

1 Introduction

Node classification is a crucial task in network analysis, and Graph Neural Network (GNN) models have gained widespread attention due to their state-of-the-art performance [3–6,17]. However, typical GNN models are faced with two common drawbacks: the homophily assumption [21] and label ignorance [25].

First, the homophily assumption assumes that links tend to exist between nodes with similar features or labels, which limits the practical applicability of GNNs since many real-world networks are strongly heterophilous or randomly

Z. Jin et al. (Eds.): KSEM 2023, LNAI 14117, pp. 40–50, 2023.
https://doi.org/10.1007/978-3-031-40283-8_4

linked. Although GNNs perform satisfactorily for some tasks on heterophilous networks [8], this only occurs in rare cases where the label distribution of neighbors is a strong predictor and sufficiently distinguishable [8]. **Second**, GNNs tend to ignore the known node labels since they predict node labels based merely on node representations that are learned from the node features and network structure [12]. One simple solution named *label trick* [19] is to enrich the feature of a node by concatenating it and the node's label. However, this approach works unsatisfactorily in general [26]. Another natural idea is to concatenate the labels of all neighbors, not just of the node itself, to the node feature. However, this would only be feasible if node degrees were nearly uniform. Otherwise, different nodes would have different feature dimensions, breaking a strict prerequisite of GNNs: since GNNs use matrix multiplication to aggregate neighbors' information, dimensional consistency is required.

Several approaches have been proposed to address the limitations of GNNs. To address the issue of label ignorance, GMNN [12] uses two GNNs to model node label dependencies through conditional random fields. GCN-LPA [18] combines label propagation and GCN [6] to aggregate neighbor features based on label similarity, but it is only suitable for homophilous datasets. To address the homophily assumption, H2GCN [26], JKNet [20], Mixhop [1], Geom-GCN [11], and FSGNN [9] enrich the amount of aggregated information to improve the performance of GNNs on heterophilous datasets. However, they still suffer from label ignorance, and aggregating too much information may cause feature over-smoothing. APPNP [4] and GPRGNN [3] use the PageRank-based GNN to alleviate over-smoothing. However, APPNP is also unsuitable for heterophilous datasets, and learned weights in GPRGNN may yield oversimplified or ill-posed filters [9]. As far as we know, it remains open to simultaneously address both label ignorance and homophily assumption in GNNs.

We propose NRGNN (Neighborhood Reconnection Graph Neural Network), a novel graph neural network framework that simultaneously tackles the label ignorance and homophily assumption. Our contribution lies in three aspects.

- We propose a novel network reconnection model that adjusts the network's topology by reconnecting each node's neighborhood using the hard attention mechanism. The resulting network has uniform node degrees and high homophily, which enables GNNs to process it effectively, even if the original network is heterophilous.
- We design the NRGNN framework to combine the proposed network reconnection model with a separated PageRank-based GNN model to classify nodes. The framework is designed to be loosely coupled, making it easily adaptable to other GNN models.
- We evaluate the performance of NRGNN against 14 state-of-the-art baselines on nine datasets with extreme homophily or heterophily, as well as six newly proposed random datasets. Results demonstrate that NRGNN outperforms all baselines on the six new datasets and achieves the best performance on six of the nine datasets, showcasing the effectiveness of our proposed approach.

2   Notation and Preliminary

Problem Statement. We model a network as an undirected graph $G = (V, E)$ with node set V and edge set E. Let $A \in \mathbb{R}^{|V| \times |V|}$ represent the adjacency matrix of G, with entry $a_{ij} > 0$ being the weight of the edge between nodes v_i and v_j while $a_{ij} = 0$ for non-adjacency. Every node has a f-dimensional feature vector, and all the feature vectors form the feature matrix $X \in \mathbb{R}^{|V| \times f}$. Each node has a label l_i from a finite set L, but only the labels on a subset $V' \subset V$ are known. The node classification problem is to infer the unknown labels on $V \setminus V'$.

Graph Neural Network (GNNs) extend the idea of convolutional neural networks to graph-structured data, enabling end-to-end training. GNNs classify nodes by iteratively aggregating their neighbor features. The Graph Convolutional Network (GCN) [6] is a typical example of GNNs. In GCN, $H^{(t)}$ represents the result aggregated by the t-th layer, with $H^{(0)} = X$ being the node feature matrix. The aggregation function can be defined as follows:

$$H^{(t+1)} = \sigma(\tilde{A} H^{(t)} W^{(t)}) \tag{1}$$

Here, $\tilde{A}$ is the symmetric normalized adjacency matrix, $\sigma(\cdot)$ denotes the ReLU activation function, and $W^{(t)}$ and $H^{(t)}$ are the weight matrix and the hidden node representation in the t-th layer.

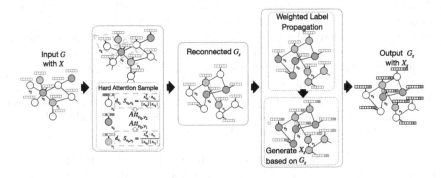

Fig. 1. Network Reconnection process of NRGNN.

3   Network Reconnection

Our proposed approach aims to fully utilize known label information and overcome the homophily assumption by reconnecting the network. As illustrated in Fig. 1, this involves two steps: structure reconnection and feature regeneration.

Structure Reconnection. In order to improve homophily and fully utilize known node labels in the network, we propose a reconnection method that removes all the edges and reconnects each node to a fixed number of its original k-neighbors that might have the same label. This ensures uniform node degrees while prioritizing nodes sharing similar labels. However, since many node labels are initially unknown, and it is expected that similar nodes tend to have the same label, we define attention values that capture the similarity of two nodes and use stochastic hard attention to select the k-neighbors for reconnection.

Specifically, the attention values are defined in terms of both the *node features* and *local structure* to capture node similarity comprehensively. For *node features*, we adopt the approach in [24] of calculating attention values using cosine similarity, which assigns smaller attention values to edges connecting dissimilar nodes. Thus, we define the similarity between nodes v_i and v_j as $s_{ij} = \frac{\mathbf{x_i}^T \cdot \mathbf{x_j}}{|\mathbf{x_i}||\mathbf{x_j}|}$, where $\mathbf{x_i}, \mathbf{x_j}$ are the feature vectors of v_i, v_j, respectively.

To capture *local structural information*, we consider the degree of nodes as a critical indicator of their importance and preferentially connect nodes with higher degrees [15]. For any $v_j \in \mathcal{N}_k(v_i)$ ($\mathcal{N}_k(v_i)$ is the set of nodes **within** k-hops of v_i) with degree d_j, we define attention value Att_{ij} that represents the likelihood of establishing an arc from node v_i to v_j. As in [15], establishing an arc from v_i to v_j is modeled by d_j independent Bernoulli trials, each with a success probability of s_{ij}. No arc exists if and only if no trials succeed, so we have:

$$Att_{ij} \triangleq 1 - (1 - s_{ij})^{d_j} \approx 1 - e^{-d_j s_{ij}} \qquad (2)$$

We employ min-max normalization, due to its high performance and low time complexity [2]. By rescaling both measures to $[0, 1]$, denoted as d'_j and s'_{ij} respectively, we ensure they have a balanced influence on the attention calculation.

Then, the attention value is redefined to be $Att'_{ij} \triangleq 1 - e^{-d'_j s'_{ij}}$. To obtain a fixed number of p neighbors, we first normalize the attention values $Att'_{ij} : v_j \in \mathcal{N}_k(v_i)$ for any v_i to form a probability vector denoted by $\hat{Att}_{ij}$, and sample with replacement p neighbors using stochastic hard attention. For each sampled neighbor $v_j \in \mathcal{N}_k(v_i)$, the arc weight from v_i to v_j is defined as $a'_{ij} = n_j \cdot \hat{Att}_{ij}$.

Finally, due to the permutation invariance required, the final edge weight between any nodes v_i and v_j is obtained by accumulating the two arc weights, namely $a_{ij} = a_{ji} \triangleq a'_{ij} + a'_{ji}$.

Feature Regeneration. To incorporate node labels into the GNNs, we need pre-processed labels to concatenate with the node features. Since many nodes have unknown labels, we use a weighted label propagation algorithm to obtain these labels. The algorithm utilizes the reconnection network G_s and its adjacency matrix A_s. The formula for weighted label propagation is as $L^{(t+1)} = D_s^{-1/2} A_s D_s^{-1/2} L^{(t)}$. Here, D_s denotes the node degree matrix of A_s, where the i-th diagonal entry is the sum of edge weights incident to node i, represented as $\sum_{j=0}^{|V|} a_{ij}$ [22]. $L^{(t+1)}$ contains the node labels obtained through weighted label propagation, where $L^{(0)}$ is the initial known node label matrix. We use the obtained node labels to create a new feature matrix X_s for the reconnected network G_s. Specifically, we concatenate the labels of each node's neighbors in descending order of edge weight with its original feature vector X.

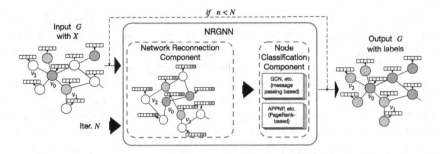

Fig. 2. The framework of NRGNN. The model runs for user-specific N epochs on the input network G.

4 The Framework of NRGNN

This section presents NRGNN, a loosely coupled end-to-end framework for node classification (see Fig. 2). The framework operates on a given network G for N epochs, and at each epoch, NRGNN applies network reconnection to generate a new network G_s with a feature matrix X_s. Next, it applies any off-the-shelf node classification model to classify nodes, such as message passing-based, PageRank-based, or MLP. If further epochs are required, NRGNN updates X_s by concatenating X with the new labels of neighbors in G_s, which are classified by the classification model, before passing G and X_s to the next epoch. The iteration continues until convergence or the user-specified N epochs are reached.

Separated Personalized PageRank. As observed in the node classification task, node features play a more critical role than the network's structure [26]. Additionally, [23] shows that even simple MLPs can distill rich information from node features, indicating the importance of node features. In order to further utilize X_s and alleviate over-smoothing, we propose a simple and effective optimization approach called *Separated Personalized PageRank* for personalized PageRank used in APPNP. This approach mimics the separation of propagation and classification in GPRGNN [3], while avoiding the use of learned weights to combine results from different layers, thus reducing the number of parameters to be trained in comparison with GPRGNN.

We add an MLP layer to pre-classify nodes using hidden features $Z^{(0)}$ learned from personalized PageRank used in APPNP [4]:

$$Z^{(0)} = H = f_{\theta_0}(X_s)$$
$$Z^{(t+1)} = (1 - \alpha)\hat{A}_s Z^{(t)} + \alpha H \tag{3}$$
$$Z = \text{softmax}((1 - \alpha)\hat{A}_s Z^{(T)} + \alpha H)$$

Then, propagate the intermediate classification results calculated by $Z^{(1)} = H = f_{\theta_1}(Z^{(0)})$, where f_{θ_1} represent another neural network with parameter set $\{\theta_1\}$. The rest training process is similar to Eq. (3), except that the matrix $\hat{A}_s$ is not symmetrically normalized, but *row normalized*. The model is also trained end-to-end, with gradients flowing through backpropagation.

Convergence and Over-Smoothing. We present proof of convergence for the Separated Personalized PageRank model. After the t-th propagation step, the result is:

$$Z^{(t)} = ((1-\alpha)^t \hat{A}_s^{\ t} + \alpha \sum_{i=0}^{t-1}(1-\alpha)^i \hat{A}_s^{\ i})H \qquad (4)$$

Here, $\hat{A}_s$ is the row-normalized adjacency matrix, and H is the pre-classified node labels obtained from the MLP layer. Convergence of $Z^{(t)}$ is known when $\hat{A}_s$ is symmetrically normalized [4]. It can be proved that Eq. (4) converges when $\hat{A}_s$ is row normalized. Moreover, the proposed model mitigates feature over-smoothing, similar to Personalized PageRank. In both models, the node's self-information is incorporated during propagation. However, Personalized PageRank uses the node's hidden features, whereas Separated Personalized PageRank uses pre-classified node labels.

5 Experiments

5.1 Experimental Setting

Datasets and Baselines. To evaluate the performance of NRGNN, we used 15 public datasets, each serving a unique purpose. For standard homophilous benchmark datasets, we selected Cora, Citeseer, and Pubmed [10,14]. For widely used small-size heterophilous datasets, we chose Tex. (Texas), Wisc. (Wisconsin), and Corn. (Cornell) [11]. In addition, we incorporated Actor [16], Squi. (Squirrel), and Cham. (Chameleon) [13], which have relatively larger sizes. We also incorporated Twitch-explicit datasets (six networks) [7], new high-quality datasets with moderate homophily. All datasets are summarized in Table 1, where the edge homophily ratio h is calculated by $h = \frac{|\{(v_i,v_j)\in E : l_i = l_j\}|}{|E|}$ [26].

Table 1. Statistics of datasets

Datasets	# Nodes	# Edges	# Labels	# Node feat	Edge hom.(h)	Node. hom.($\bar{h}$)
Cora	2,708	5,429	7	1,433	.81	.83
Citeseer	3,327	4,732	6	3,703	.74	.71
Pubmed	19,717	44,338	3	500	.80	.79
Actor	7,600	33,544	5	932	.22	.22
Squirrel	5,201	217,073	5	2,089	.22	.22
Chameleon	2,277	36,101	5	2,325	.23	.25
Texas	183	309	5	1,703	.11	.06
Wisconsin	251	499	5	1,703	.21	.16
Cornell	183	295	5	1,703	.30	.30
Twitch-DE	9,498	76,569	2	2,514	.63	.54
Twitch-ENGB	7,126	17,662	2	2,545	.56	.42
Twitch-ES	4,648	29,691	2	2,148	.58	.53
Twitch-FR	6,549	56,333	2	2,275	.56	.51
Twitch-PTBR	1,912	15,650	2	1,449	.57	.52
Twitch-RU	4,385	18,652	2	2,224	.62	.52

We evaluated NRGNN against 14 state-of-the-art baselines, including models that perform well on homophilous datasets (GCN, GCN-Cheby, GAT, and GraphSAGE), heterophilous datasets (Geom-GCN, H2GCN, DEGNN, Mixhop, FSGNN, CS-GNN, and JKNet), a baseline that considers label dependencies when classifying nodes (GMNN), and two PageRank-based GNN models (APPNP and GPRGNN). In addition to the standard NRGNN model, we also evaluated four variants where different widely-used node classification models were used in place of the Separated Personalized PageRank component. These models include GCN, APPNP, GraphSAGE, and MLP.

Performance Measurement. We evaluated each model on the node classification task, using the commonly used metric of accuracy to measure performance. Following [26], we randomly split each dataset into 60% training, 20% validation, and 20% testing nodes per class. To ensure the reliability of our results, we repeated each baseline five times and reported the average accuracy and standard deviation. We selected hyperparameters using grid search.

5.2   Performance on Classical Datasets

See Table 2 for the performance of NRGNN and its variants on classical datasets. The results indicate that, in most cases, NRGNN achieves performance superior to other methods, even on heterophilous datasets. The excellent performance on small or feature-dominant datasets can be attributed to the method's ability to adjust local structure and filter features during network reconnection.

However, it is worth noting that on the Pubmed, Chameleon, and particularly on Squirrel datasets, NRGNN exhibits lower accuracy than the baseline FSGNN. This disparity may be attributed to the fact that node features in Pubmed and first-hop features without self-loop in Squirrel and Chameleon play a more critical role than in other datasets [9]. It is possible that reconnected networks with fixed neighborhood sizes may lose some key information in these datasets.

Table 2. The node classification task performance on classical datasets (Percent).

	Cora	Pubmed	Citeseer	Actor	Squi	Cham.	Texa	Wisc	Corn
GCN	88.51 ±0.54	87.29 ±0.30	76.97 ±1.72	29.37 ±1.50	24.82 ±1.32	34.82 ±2.23	58.95±4.88	50.59 ±4.87	60.53±2.35
GCN-Cheby	87.85 ±0.84	87.93±0.53	77.06 ±2.01	34.08±1.25	30.64 ±0.90	47.98±2.53	81.05 ±4.21	80.39±2.48	75.79 ±1.05
GAT	84.16 ±1.42	84.66±0.25	75.17 ±0.88	27.26±1.15	23.46 ±2.19	35.39±0.77	57.89 ±6.86	50.59±6.61	59.47 ±6.98
GraphSAGE(Mean)	88.08±1.93	88.82 ±0.58	75.38 ±1.82	35.55 ±1.19	42.25 ±1.05	58.99 ±2.64	86.49 ±3.31	84.71 ±6.71	77.84 ±4.44
Geom-GCN	86.67 ±0.78	88.31 ±0.27	76.28 ±1.95	32.67 ±0.77	37.94 ±2.35	61.84 ±1.65	70.00 ±9.05	67.84 ±4.74	57.37 ±9.62
H2GCN	88.10 ±0.56	88.58 ±0.44	77.78 ±2.16	37.72 ±0.82	39.35 ±1.50	60.48 ±3.05	85.26 ±3.00	86.67 ±1.64	82.63 ±4.40
DEGNN	84.24 ±0.91	85.02 ±0.51	75.25 ±1.04	35.85 ±1.58	36.10 ±1.58	60.35 ±2.86	80.54 ±2.02	74.00 ±6.69	72.97 ±7.05
Mixhop	86.41 ±2.47	83.37 ±0.51	75.71 ±0.72	26.51 ±1.50	25.49 ±2.52	43.33 ±3.98	64.74 ±3.94	67.45 ±6.63	65.26 ±6.94
CS-GNN	85.16 ±6.95	85.00 ±6.89	70.77 ±10.49	30.83 ±5.65	35.29 ±6.44	45.00 ±16.96	81.05 ±6.32	74.51 ±4.29	70.00 ±6.78
FSGNN	87.85 ±1.28	**89.82 ±0.36**	76.70 ±1.28	34.86 ±0.75	**73.87 ±1.38**	**77.85 ±0.34**	87.57 ±5.57	87.45 ±2.93	87.03 ±5.51
GMNN	88.80 ±0.38	86.15 ±0.06	76.01 ±0.64	31.21 ±0.50	22.13 ±2.34	57.54 ±0.84	70.53 ±1.05	60.78 ±4.80	58.42 ±3.49
JKNet	86.37 ±2.50	87.36 ±0.43	75.61 ±1.41	29.49 ±1.12	41.02 ±6.19	63.37 ±1.26	77.05 ±3.74	61.75 ±5.68	66.56 ±8.14
APPNP	87.98 ±0.86	87.07 ±0.51	80.19 ±1.13	38.80 ±0.37	28.76 ±1.48	46.35 ±3.00	92.46 ±3.04	94.00 ±3.10	91.15 ±2.45
GPRGNN	88.44 ±0.59	89.47 ±0.32	79.84 ±0.80	38.67 ±0.56	52.39 ±2.66	68.10 ±1.49	92.13 ±2.62	90.75 ±3.84	90.82 ±3.38
NRGNN	93.30 ±0.64	84.76 ±0.22	84.26 ±2.32	47.92 ±2.51	51.83 ±1.54	70.18 ±2.07	**95.26 ±1.97**	**97.25 ±2.93**	**93.16 ±2.11**
NRGNN-MLP	78.27 ±1.17	85.68 ±0.30	77.23 ±1.54	37.30 ±0.51	36.57 ±0.50	51.24 ±0.37	89.47 ±2.15	89.54 ±0.92	86.84 ±2.15
NRGNN-GCN	84.59 ±0.53	86.94 ±0.26	77.38 ±0.07	38.03 ±0.25	38.23 ±1.02	54.97 ±0.45	92.11 ±2.15	88.89 ±1.85	86.84 ±2.15
NRGNN-APPNP	**93.37 ±0.97**	84.22 ±0.45	**84.35 ±1.81**	49.21 ±2.44	52.24 ±0.79	71.10 ±0.80	93.16 ±3.94	96.47 ±2.29	93.16 ±3.94
NRGNN-GraphSAGE	86.56 ±0.91	88.31 ±0.35	76.97 ±1.49	35.54 ±1.26	34.91 ±7.96	53.51 ±0.77	84.74 ±4.82	86.67 ±2.29	81.05 ±3.87

5.3   Performance on Twitch Datasets

Due to the classical datasets being either extremely homophilous or heterophilous, to ensure the robustness of our experiments, we also perform experiments on the Twitch datasets, which are featured by the middle homophily ratio. The results of our experiments are presented in Table 3, indicating that NRGNN achieves the highest accuracy on almost all datasets, with the exception of Twitch-RU, where GPRGNN outperforms NRGNN marginally.

The lower accuracy of NRGNN on Twitch-RU could be attributed to the regenerated features containing noisy information, particularly on middle homophily ratio datasets with smaller sizes. The separated personalized PageRank-based model involves classifying nodes first and propagating intermediate classification results, which may not fully leverage the regenerated feature information of neighboring nodes. Nonetheless, the NRGNN-GCN variant still outperforms all other methods on this dataset, highlighting the effectiveness of our proposed network reconnection component.

Table 3. The node classification task performance on Twitch datasets (Percent).

	DE	ENGB	ES	FR	PTBR	RU
GCN	65.29 ±1.28	58.69 ±1.43	70.34 ±1.36	63.15 ±1.14	63.56 ±2.64	73.80 ±0.97
GCN-Cheby	66.51 ±0.96	57.92 ±0.56	71.51 ±0.61	64.92 ±1.12	65.65 ±1.57	74.32 ±1.60
GAT	61.09 ±1.70	55.68 ±0.18	72.02 ±1.65	63.48 ±1.05	63.56 ±0.51	75.26 ±0.83
GraphSAGE(Mean)	60.14 ±0.81	55.08 ±0.81	70.62 ±1.07	62.31 ±0.91	65.17 ±1.77	75.46 ±0.79
H2GCN	67.07 ±0.66	59.89 ±1.63	71.29 ±0.85	65.30 ±1.43	65.34 ±3.13	73.89 ±1.12
DEGNN	*N.A.*	56.59 ±2.53	70.82 ±0.19	63.11 ±0.03	67.43 ±1.27	75.48 ±0.00
Mixhop	63.07 ±2.40	59.49 ±2.15	70.95 ±3.09	64.83 ±0.93	62.71 ±9.93	75.53 ±1.52
CS-GNN	66.82 ±3.96	42.35 ±4.40	68.82 ±3.53	60.67 ±2.49	63.23 ±2.77	64.89 ±1.67
FSGNN	66.86 ±0.96	58.76 ±4.16	71.55 ±2.26	64.22 ±2.40	68.33 ±4.40	74.79 ±1.48
GMNN	68.17 ±0.42	59.55 ±0.31	69.68 ±0.00	64.12 ±0.05	66.96 ±0.42	75.03 ±0.10
JKNet	64.84 ±0.58	57.63 ±0.99	72.84 ±0.72	66.02 ±1.45	67.96 ±0.71	75.60 ±0.62
APPNP	65.29 ±0.29	58.36 ±0.90	70.02 ±1.17	64.63 ±0.47	66.34 ±1.48	75.03 ±1.68
GPRGNN	64.25 ±2.35	58.01 ±2.03	71.33 ±1.30	66.40 ±2.04	68.32 ±2.68	75.64 ±1.66
NRGNN	70.72 ±0.50	**70.95 ±1.96**	**76.28 ±2.33**	**68.96 ±4.42**	**79.90 ±3.10**	74.32 ±1.41
NRGNN-MLP	67.30 ±0.36	61.36 ±0.20	71.22 ±0.70	64.02 ±0.16	67.54 ±0.37	75.03 ±1.45
NRGNN-GCN	67.61 ±0.40	62.25 ±0.83	73.37 ±1.14	66.01 ±0.97	68.32 ±0.93	**76.55 ±0.39**
NRGNN-APPNP	**71.62 ±1.49**	68.55 ±3.21	73.38 ±3.70	65.22 ±2.88	79.48 ±2.40	74.32 ±1.41
NRGNN-GraphSAGE	65.72 ±1.03	55.66 ±5.16	69.85 ±1.21	62.70 ±0.86	66.70 ±1.14	74.32 ±1.41

5.4   Ablation Study

The network reconnection model comprises two crucial components that significantly impact its performance: the structure reconnection and the feature regeneration via the weighted label propagation. To gain a more in-depth understanding of the contributions of each component, we conducted comparative experiments on NRGNN and its variants. We refer to the variants as NRGNN-PR and NRGNN-G, where NRGNN-PR employs random initialization instead of weighted label propagation to predict the unknown node labels. NRGNN-G uses the original network G instead of the reconnected network G_s when classifying nodes, namely, the newly generated features (X_s) are propagated over the original network G instead of the reconnected network G_s. We conducted one run of NRGNN and its variants on classical datasets, and the results are presented in Table 4. The results reveal that NRGNN-PR and NRGNN-G outperform NRGNN on homophilous datasets and Cham., respectively. This finding indicates that while node label information and network reconnection are crucial in heterophilous datasets, they may be less critical in homophilous networks.

Table 4. The node classification task accuracy(%) of NRGNN and its variants.

	Cora	Pubm.	Cite.	Actor	Squi	Cham.	Texa	Wisc	Corn
NRGNN-PR	92.08	85.27	**85.14**	47.43	48.80	**71.05**	94.74	97.98	94.60
NRGNN-G	**93.37**	**86.61**	83.33	45.66	30.64	70.27	94.37	97.76	93.37
NRGNN	92.63	85.22	84.08	**49.76**	**53.89**	70.63	**95.37**	**98.04**	**94.74**

6   Conclusion

GNNs are popular tools for network analysis, but their applicability and performance are often limited by the homophily assumption and label ignorance. To address these issues, we propose NRGNN, a novel framework that leverages a stochastic hard attention mechanism to reconnect the network, which connects each node to a fixed number of its k-neighbors based on feature similarity and neighbors degree. NRGNN's loosely coupled framework also incorporates a separated personalized PageRank method to further enhance node classification accuracy. Our experiments show that NRGNN consistently outperforms state-of-the-art baselines, especially on random datasets.

Acknowledgement. Thanks to Sa Wang and Yungang Bao for their help. This work is supported in part by the Strategic Priority Research Program of the Chinese Academy of Sciences under grant numbers XDA0320000 and XDA0320300, the National Natural Science Foundation of China (Grant No. 62072433 and 62090022), the Fundamental Research Funds for the Central Universities (DUT21RC(3)102).

References

1. Abu-El-Haija, S., et al.: MixHop: higher-order graph convolutional architectures via sparsified neighborhood mixing. In: Proceedings of the 36th International Conference on Machine Learning, pp. 21–29 (2019)
2. Al Shalabi, L., Shaaban, Z.: Normalization as a preprocessing engine for data mining and the approach of preference matrix. In: 2006 International Conference on Dependability of Computer Systems, pp. 207–214 (2006)
3. Chien, E., Peng, J., Li, P., Milenkovic, O.: Adaptive Universal Generalized PageRank Graph Neural Network (2021)

4. Gasteiger, J., Bojchevski, A., Günnemann, S.: Predict then Propagate: Graph Neural Networks meet Personalized PageRank (2022)
5. Hamilton, W., Ying, Z., Leskovec, J.: Inductive Representation Learning on Large Graphs. In: Advances in Neural Information Processing Systems. vol. 30 (2017)
6. Kipf, T.N., Welling, M.: Semi-Supervised Classification with Graph Convolutional Networks (2017)
7. Lim, D., Li, X., Hohne, F., Lim, S.N.: New Benchmarks for Learning on Non-Homophilous Graphs (2021)
8. Ma, Y., Liu, X., Shah, N., Tang, J.: Is homophily a necessity for graph neural networks? In: International Conference on Learning Representations (2022)
9. Maurya, S.K., Liu, X., Murata, T.: Improving Graph Neural Networks with Simple Architecture Design (2021)
10. Namata, G., London, B., Getoor, L., Huang, B.: Query-driven active surveying for collective classification. In: 10th International Workshop on Mining and Learning with Graphs. vol. 8, p. 1 (2012)
11. Pei, H., Wei, B., Chang, K.C.C., Lei, Y., Yang, B.: Geom-GCN: geometric graph convolutional networks. In: International Conference on Learning Representations (2019)
12. Qu, M., Bengio, Y., Tang, J.: GMNN: graph markov neural networks. In: Proceedings of the 36th International Conference on Machine Learning, pp. 5241–5250 (2019)
13. Rozemberczki, B., Allen, C., Sarkar, R.: Multi-scale attributed node embedding. J. Complex Netw. 9(2), cnab014 (2021)
14. Sen, P., Namata, G., Bilgic, M., Getoor, L., Galligher, B., Eliassi-Rad, T.: Collective classification in network data. AI Mag. 29(3), 93–93 (2008)
15. Şimşek, Ö., Jensen, D.: Navigating networks by using homophily and degree. Proc. Natl. Acad. Sci. 105(35), 12758–12762 (2008)
16. Tang, J., Sun, J., Wang, C., Yang, Z.: Social influence analysis in large-scale networks. In: Proceedings of the 15th ACM SIGKDD International Conference on Knowledge Discovery and Data Mining, pp. 807–816. Paris France (2009)
17. Veličković, P., Cucurull, G., Casanova, A., Romero, A., Liò, P., Bengio, Y.: Graph attention networks. In: International Conference on Learning Representations. arXiv:1710.10903 (2018)
18. Wang, H., Leskovec, J.: Unifying Graph Convolutional Neural Networks and Label Propagation (2020)
19. Wang, Y., Jin, J., Zhang, W., Yu, Y., Zhang, Z., Wipf, D.: Bag of Tricks for Node Classification with Graph Neural Networks (2021)
20. Xu, K., Li, C., Tian, Y., Sonobe, T., Kawarabayashi, K.I., Jegelka, S.: Representation learning on graphs with jumping knowledge networks. In: Proceedings of the 35th International Conference on Machine Learning, pp. 5453–5462 (2018)
21. Yan, Y., Hashemi, M., Swersky, K., Yang, Y., Koutra, D.: Two sides of the same coin: heterophily and oversmoothing in graph convolutional neural networks. In: 2022 IEEE International Conference on Data Mining (ICDM), pp. 1287–1292 (2022)
22. Yoshua, B., Olivier, D., Nicolas Le, R.: Label propagation and quadratic criterion. In: Chapelle, O., Scholkopf, B., Zien, A. (eds.) Semi-Supervised Learning, pp. 192–216. The MIT Press (2006)
23. Zhang, S., Liu, Y., Sun, Y., Shah, N.: Graph-less neural networks: teaching old MLPs new tricks via distillation. In: International Conference on Learning Representations (2022)

24. Zhang, X., Zitnik, M.: GNNGuard: defending graph neural networks against adversarial attacks. In: Advances in Neural Information Processing Systems, vol. 33, pp. 9263–9275 (2020)
25. Zhu, J., et al.: Graph neural networks with heterophily. Proc. AAAI Conf. Art. Intell. **35**(12), 11168–11176 (2021)
26. Zhu, J., Yan, Y., Zhao, L., Heimann, M., Akoglu, L., Koutra, D.: Beyond homophily in graph neural networks: current limitations and effective designs. In: Advances in Neural Information Processing Systems. vol. 33, pp. 7793–7804 (2020)

Critical Node Privacy Protection Based on Random Pruning of Critical Trees

Lianwei Qu[⬛], Yong Wang[✉][⬛], and Jing Yang

College of Computer Science and Technology, Harbin Engineering University,
Heilongjiang 150001, China
{qlw95,yangjing}@hrbeu.edu.cn, paperworkhrbeu@163.com

Abstract. With the popularity of social networks, the conflict between the heterogeneous social network data publishing and user privacy leakage is becoming very obvious. Especially for critical node users, if the critical node users suffer from background knowledge attacks during data publishing, it can not only lead to the privacy information leakage of the critical user but also lead to the privacy leakage of their friends. To address this issue, we propose a critical node privacy protection method based on random pruning of critical trees. First, we obtain the critical node candidate set by the degree centrality. Then, we calculate the candidate node's global and local criticality to get the critical node set. Next, we extract the critical tree with the critical node as the root node. Finally, we design a critical tree privacy protection strategy based on random pruning. The experimental results show that the proposed method can balance the privacy and availability of critical nodes in the network data publishing.

Keywords: Heterogeneous social networks · Node criticality · Critical node · Critical tree · Random pruning

1 Introduction

In heterogeneous social networks, which contain some critical node users [1]. When critical nodes suffer from background knowledge attacks, it leads to privacy leakage of critical users. In addition, its neighboring users can also be attacked by using the existing background knowledge [2]. Therefore, the critical node is important, but the structure composed of the critical node and its neighbors is more important. So, we use the network structure privacy protection method to solve the privacy protection problem of critical nodes.

In the current study, the structural privacy-preserving approaches based on anonymity are not resistant to background knowledge-based attacks [3–5]. The random perturbation-based graph structure privacy protection [6] can resist the attack of strong background knowledge, but the availability of the graph structure is sacrificed. However, the differential privacy-based privacy protection [7–10] can be resistant to attacks with strong background knowledge, there is still an imbalance between privacy

Z. Jin et al. (Eds.): KSEM 2023, LNAI 14117, pp. 51–58, 2023.
https://doi.org/10.1007/978-3-031-40283-8_5

and availability. In addition, the current study lacks a comprehensive consideration of the local and global importance of the nodes [11].

To solve these issues, we propose the CNPP model. First, the measure node criticality method considers both local and global node criticality. Then, the proposed method extracts critical trees based on node criticality. Finally, the critical trees' privacy is protected using random pruning. The CNPP model can effectively protect the privacy of critical nodes in network publishing while maintaining data availability.

The main contributions of this paper are as follows.

(1) A fine-grained node criticality calculation method is proposed, which effectively fine-grained calculates node criticality. This method can calculate node criticality more comprehensively.
(2) The proposed method combines critical nodes and structural features to extract critical trees, which are then used for graph structure privacy protection. This method effectively ensures the privacy of the critical structure.
(3) Personalized privacy protection strategies are proposed based on random pruning, effectively protecting critical structures in the published network. This method improves the privacy protection of critical structures.

The rest of the paper is organized as follows. Section 2 introduces the CNPP model. Section 3 introduces the specific scheme. Section 4 analyzes the experimental results and performance metrics of the method. Section 5 gives our conclusions.

2   CNPP Model

CNPP model aims at randomly perturbing the critical structures in the network structure. The model contains node criticality calculation, critical structure extraction and critical structure privacy protection methods. In the critical structure privacy protection, we design the critical tree privacy protection strategy based on random pruning. The specific process is shown in Fig. 1.

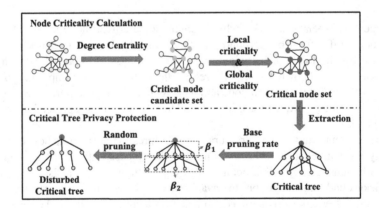

Fig. 1. Flow chart of CNPP implementation.

3   Scheme

3.1   Node Criticality Calculation

Critical Node Candidate Set. In the network, the higher node degree means the higher degree centrality, which means the node is more important in the network. Therefore, we select the critical node candidate set by calculating the node degree centrality in the network.

$$DC(v_i) = D(v_i)/N - 1 \tag{1}$$

where N denotes the number of nodes in the network. $D(v_i)$ denotes the degree of node v_i. Specifically, if the node degree centrality is higher than the average node degree centrality, the node is selected into the critical node candidate set.

Node Criticality Calculation. We extract the first-order neighbor node structure and second-order neighbor node structure for node local criticality calculation. The node local criticality is calculated by the structural entropy [12], as shown in the following equation.

$$S(v_i) = -\sum_{i=1}^{n} \frac{D(v_i)}{\sum_{i=1}^{n} D(v_i)} log \frac{D(v_i)}{\sum_{i=1}^{n} D(v_i)} \tag{2}$$

where $S(v_i)$ denotes the local structural entropy of the node. $D(v_i)$ denotes the degree of node v_i. $\sum_{i=1}^{n} D(v_i)$ denotes the sum of the node degree in the network.

In the node global critical calculation, we introduce the node betweenness to measure the node global critical in the network. The specific equation is as follows.

$$B_i = \sum_{i \neq j \neq k \in N} \frac{P_{jk}^i}{P_{jk}} \tag{3}$$

where, B_i denotes the betweenness of node i. P_{jk} denotes the number of shortest paths from node j to node k. P_{jk}^i represents the number of nodes i that pass through in the shortest path between node j and node k.

Therefore, based on the node local criticality and node global criticality, we propose a node criticality calculation method based on structural entropy and betweenness. The specific equation is shown below.

$$NC_i = \alpha S(v_i) + (1 - \alpha)B_i \tag{4}$$

where, NC_i indicates the node criticality. $\alpha \in (0,1)$ is a modified coefficient. When the NC value is larger, it indicates that the node is more critical and central in the network.

Finally, we sort the nodes in the candidate set in descending order. On this basis, we propose a protection parameter $\rho \in (0, 1]$, which is determined by the users. The final critical nodes are determined based on the protection parameters.

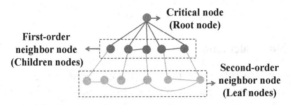

Fig. 2. Critical Tree Structure NC-T$_i$.

3.2 Critical Structure Extraction

Based on the final critical node set, we extract the structure with the critical node as the root node, called the critical tree NC-T$_i$. The specific structure is shown in Fig. 2.

We design a preprocessing method to avoid excessive privacy protection leading to poor availability of the published network structure. First, we delete critical nodes exist among the critical tree's first and second-order neighbor nodes. Then, the similarity between critical trees is calculated based on the Jaccard index. The specific formula is as follows.

$$NS_{i,j} = |E_i \cap E_j|/|E_i| + |E_j| - |E_i \cap E_j| \tag{5}$$

where $NS_{i,j}$ denotes the similarity between root nodes. $|E_i|$, $|E_j|$ denote the number of edges of root nodes i and j in the critical tree, respectively. $|E_i \cap E_j|$ indicates the number of the same edges between root node i and root node j in the critical tree.

3.3 Random Pruning Based on Critical Tree Privacy Protection (RPCT)

First, we must determine the base pruning rate β_{base}. Then, we calculate critical tree final pruning rate β_{v_i}.

$$\beta_{v_i} = [S(v_i)/S(G)]\beta_{base} \tag{6}$$

where, β_{v_i} denotes the final pruning rate of the critical tree with root node vi. $S(v_i)$ represents the structural entropy of the critical tree. S(G) indicates the structural entropy of the whole network. β_{base} is the base pruning rate.

Then, we determine the pruning rate of each order structure.

$$\beta_j = [S(o_j)/S(v_i)]\beta_{v_i} \tag{7}$$

where, β_j denotes every order structural pruning rate. $S(o_j)$ represents every order structural entropy. $S(v_i)$ is the structural entropy of the critical tree. β_{v_i} indicates the total pruning rate of the critical tree.

Next, we add to each edge in the critical tree the Laplace uncertainty value that satisfies the differential privacy. The aim is to satisfy the randomness in pruning. Finally, random pruning of critical trees is achieved based on uncertainty and pruning rate.

4 Experiment

4.1 Experiment Preparation

In this paper, we choose to compare and analyze with the PBCN [2] in the real dataset Yelp. This model combines differential privacy and random perturbation to achieve structure and node protection. Where, there also exists a privacy protection parameter k in the PBCN model similar to this paper, and the larger k the greater the privacy protection strength. Therefore, we perform the comparative analysis of privacy and availability in terms of both structural features and clustering. The dataset specific information is shown in Table 1.

Table 1. The information of the three size datasets.

Name	Node	Edge	Average node Degree
D1	522	18618	71.333
D2	1127	46498	82.516

The experiment uses RE to analyze the privacy and availability of the published network. The formula for RE is as follows:

$$RE = |Q_i - \tilde{Q}_i|/Q_i \tag{8}$$

where Q_i is the original data and $\tilde{Q}_i$ represents the network after privacy protection.

4.2 Global Network Analysis

Edge. Figure 3 shows the RE values of the original edges in the network after PBCN and CNPP privacy protection with different protection parameters. In different size datasets, the RE values of the CNPP method are consistently lower than those of the PBCN method and gradually decrease as the protection parameters increase. This indicates that the CNPP method can better balance privacy and availability and provide personalized privacy protection. In addition, we dynamically adjust the NS values in the CNPP method in our experiments. The experimental results prove that the privacy and availability of the publishing network can also be effectively balanced by adjusting the NS value in any protection parameter and the base pruning rate.

Figure 4 shows the distribution of RE values of the original edges at different pruning rates in the same protection level and NS value. The experimental results show that in the same protection level and NS value, the RE value decreases with the decrease of the pruning rate. In addition, the RE values under different protection parameters are closer in the same base pruning rate and NS value. We need to remove other critical nodes during critical tree construction, which leads to a decrease in the similarity between critical trees and the number of edges.

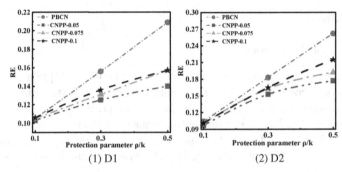

Fig. 3. RE values of the original edges after privacy protection with different protection parameters.

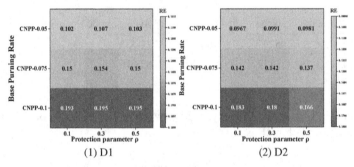

Fig. 4. RE values of the original edges at different pruning rates in the same protection level and NS value.

Critical Node Analysis. Based on the critical node criticality ranking positions, we propose a privacy measurement formula for the critical nodes obtained after CNPP privacy protection.

$$\Pr(\tilde{CN}) = [B(CN) - A\left(\tilde{CN}\right) + F\left(\tilde{CN}\right)]/B(CN) \tag{9}$$

where $B(CN)$ represents the number of original critical node sets. $A(\tilde{CN})$ indicates the number of original critical nodes after CNPP privacy protection. $F(\tilde{CN})$ indicates the number of critical nodes with the wrong criticality ranking position in the critical node set after CNPP privacy protection.

Figure 5 shows the privacy of the critical node set after the CNPP privacy protection. According to the analysis of the experimental results, as the protection parameter increases, the Pr value is closer in the same pruning rate and NS value. Conversely, the Pr value increases with the base pruning rate increases at the same protection parameter, indicating enhanced privacy.

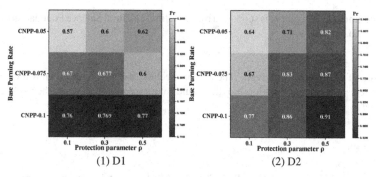

Fig. 5. The Pr value of critical node set after CNPP privacy protection.

4.3 Clustering Analysis

F-score. Figure 6 shows the F1 scores of the network clustering results after privacy protection. In this experiment, we set $\beta = 1$ and consider that precision and recall have the same effect. When the base pruning rate or protection level is small, the F-score of the CNPP method is slightly higher than that of the PBCN method, and it can be concluded that the network after privacy protection by the CNPP method has better availability. However, when the base pruning rate or protection level is high, the F-value of the CNPP method is slightly lower than that of the PBCN method.

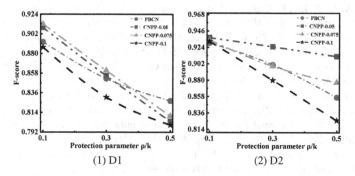

Fig. 6. The F1-score of the network clustering results after privacy protection.

5   Conclusions

The CNPP method proposed in this paper addresses the limitations of current privacy protection methods for graph structures, such as the lack of simultaneous consideration of critical nodes and critical structure privacy, and the lack of research on the comprehensive measurement of node criticality in the network structure. The experimental results demonstrate the effectiveness of the CNPP method in balancing the privacy and availability of network structures, especially for critical nodes, and providing personalized privacy protection for different privacy needs.

Acknowledgments. This paper is supported by the National Natural Science Foundation of China under Grant no.61672179.

Declaration of Competing Interest. The authors declare that they have no known competing financial interests or personal relationships that could have appeared to influence the work reported in this paper.

References

1. Weihua, G., Song, S., Xiaobing, P., Xuhua, Y.: Clustering and associating method of dual heterogeneous communities in location based social networks. Chin. J. Comput. **43**(10), 1910–1922 (2020)
2. Huang, H., Zhang, D., Wang, K., Gu, J., Wang, R.: Privacy-preserving approach PBCN in social network with differential privacy. IEEE Trans. Netw. Serv. Manage. **17**, 931–945 (2020)
3. Samarati, P., Sweeney, L.: Generalizing data to provide anonymity when disclosing information. In: Proceedings of the 17th ACMSIGMODSIGACT - SIGART Symposium on the Principles of Database Systems, Seattle, WA, USA, vol. 188, pp. 10–1145 (1998)
4. Zhang, J., Xu, L., Tsai, P.-W.: Community structure-based trilateral stackelberg game model for privacy protection. Appl. Math. Model. **86**, 20–35 (2020)
5. Jiang, H., Jiguo, Yu., Cheng, X., Zhang, C., Gong, B., Haotian, Yu.: Structure-attribute-based social network deanonymization with spectral graph partitioning. IEEE Trans. Comput. Soc. Syst. **9**(3), 902–913 (2022)
6. Zhang, X., Li, J., Liu, J., Zhang, H., Liu, L.: Social network sensitive area perturbance method based on firefly algorithm. IEEE Access **7**, 137759–137769 (2019)
7. Wei, J., Lin, Y., Yao, X., Zhang, J.: Differential privacy-based location protection in spatial crowdsourcing. IEEE Trans. Serv. Comput. **15**(1), 45–58 (2022)
8. Xiao, X., Xiong, L., Yuan, C.: Differential privacy via wavelet transforms. IEEE Trans. Knowl. Data Eng. **23**(8), 1200–1214 (2011)
9. Lei, H., Li, S., Wang, H.: A weighted social network publishing method based on diffusion wavelets transform and differential privacy. Multimedia Tools Appl. **81**, 20311–20328 (2022)
10. Gao, T., Li, F.: Differential private social network publication and persistent homology preservation. IEEE Trans. Netw. Sci. Eng. **8**(4), 3152–3166 (2021)
11. Han, Y., Sun, B., Wang, J., Du, Y.: Object person analysis based on critical node recognition algorithm. J. Beijing Univ. Aeronaut. Astronaut. **48**, (2022)
12. Wu, Z., Hu, J., Tian, Y., Shi, W., Yan, J.: Privacy preserving algorithms of uncertain graphs in social networks. J. Softw. **30**(4), 1106–1120 (2019)

DSEAformer: Forecasting by De-stationary Autocorrelation with Edgebound

Peihao Ding[ID], Yan Tang[(✉)][ID], Yingpei Chen[ID], and Xiaobing Li[ID]

School of Computer and Information Science, Southwest University, Chongqing,
China
{dph365475889,chenyingpei1,1597438586}@email.swu.edu.cn,
tangyan1800@163.com

Abstract. Time series analysis is vital for various real-world scenarios. Enhancing multivariate long-sequence time-series forecasting (MLTF) accuracy is crucial due to the increasing data volume and dimensionality. Current MLTF methods face challenges such as over-stationarization and distribution shift, affecting prediction accuracy. This paper proposes DSEAformer, a unique MLTF method that addresses distribution shift by normalizing and de-normalizing time series data. To avoid over-stationarization, a de-stationary autocorrelation method is suggested. Additionally, a time series optimization regularization based on weighted moving average helps prevent overfitting. Tests on three datasets confirm that DSEAformer outperforms existing MLTF techniques. In conclusion, DSEAformer introduces innovative ideas and methods to enhance time series prediction and offers improved practical applications.

Keywords: Multivariate long-sequence time-series forecasting ·
Encoder-decoder · Autocorrelation mechanism · Temporal optimization
regularization · Sequence decomposition

1 Introduction

Long sequence time-series forecasting, which refers to predicting future data in weeks, months, or even years through learning from existing data, is a significant subfield of data mining [3]. There are several real-world uses for long sequence time-series forecasting, including anticipating traffic flow [12], weather [12], and electrical load [12]. Because the interplay of numerous factors can result in complex dynamic interactions, multivariate long-sequence time-series forecasting (MLTF) is the most challenging of these applications to apply. The primary focus of this article will be on multivariate long-sequence time-series forecasting.

© The Author(s), under exclusive license to Springer Nature Switzerland AG 2023
Z. Jin et al. (Eds.): KSEM 2023, LNAI 14117, pp. 59–65, 2023.
https://doi.org/10.1007/978-3-031-40283-8_6

Traditional time series prediction is inadequate for multivariate long-sequence time-series, high-dimensional data, or long-term trends. In the informer [12] and autoformer [10] models by Zhou et al. and Wu et al., self-attention and auto-correlation tackle these issues. Yet, normalization-induced distribution shift [5] and over-stationarization [8] can lower prediction accuracy and erase intricate sub-sequence relationships. Moreover, noise terms [2] pose challenges for current approaches, leading to potential overfitting.

Inspired by the aforementioned problems, we propose DSEAformer, an encoder-decoder model for MLTF. The main contributions of this paper can be summarized as follows:

- We proposed a sequence preprocessing module that solves distribution shift and designed a de-stationary mechanism based on autocorrelation, which effectively prevents over-stationarization.
- We proposed a regularization optimization method for multivariate long time series, which prevents overfitting during the training process.
- We extensively experimented on three benchmark datasets and found that DSEAfomer outperforms current baseline models significantly.

2   Model

2.1   Encoder

The encoder extracts seasonal information from a multivariate long-sequence time-series $(l * m)$ through preprocessing and mapping to the de-stationary auto-correlation module. It outputs preserved seasonal items for the decoder via two sequence decompositions [10]. With M layers, the encoder's gradient is updated through edgebound after each layer's iteration in training. The decoder also has N layers.

2.2   Decoder

The decoder extracts seasonal and trend information by integrating the encoder's assistance [3]. It decomposes the input sequence into seasonal and trend com-ponents, combining seasonal information from the encoder through recursive decomposition and DSA to obtain the final seasonal component. The decomposed trend component is integrated and concatenated with the seasonal component, and a prediction result is obtained via de-normalization.

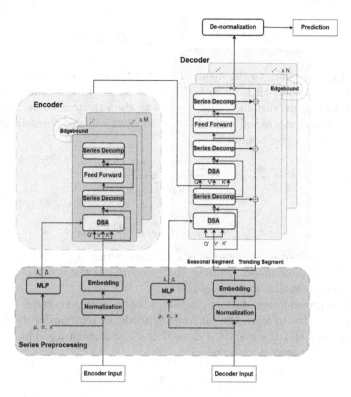

Fig. 1. The architecture of DSEAformer.

2.3   Sequence Preprocessing

Using sequence decomposition [13], we split time series into trend and seasonal components. Wavelet packet decomposition [11] is employed for sub-sequence separation, and the roughness $L(X)$ serves as the weight for the trend component. Weight distribution is derived using the softmax function. Average pooling filters [13] are selected based on different weights, yielding the trend component. The rest of the sequence shows the seasonal component.

$$T_x = AvgPool(X)^* Softmax(L(X)) \tag{1}$$

$$S_x = X - T_x \tag{2}$$

By normalizing the range of sequence values to a relatively small range [5], it effectively prevents distribution shift and makes the model more capable of learning the data patterns [5] of time series. In the output end of the model, the original distribution information of the sequence is restored through de-normalization.

$$E_t[x_{mt}^i] = \frac{1}{L_x} \sum_{j=1}^{L_x} x_{mj}^i \tag{3}$$

$$Var[x_{mt}^i] = \frac{1}{L_x} \sum_{j=1}^{L_x} (x_{mj}^i - E_t[x_{mj}^i])^2 \tag{4}$$

Where $E_t[x_{mt}^i]$ refers to the mean of the $t - th$ time step, $Var[x_{mt}^i]$ refers to the variance of the t-th time step, L_x is the length of the time series, m is the number of feature variables, and i refers to the i-th item in the minibatch. Based on the above statistical variables, the output results of normalization and de-normalization can be obtained:

$$\hat{x}_{mt}^i = \frac{x_{mt}^i - E_t\left[x_{mt}^i\right]}{\sqrt{Var\left[x_{mt}^i\right]}} \tag{5}$$

$$\hat{y}_{mt}^i = \sqrt{Var\left[x_{mt}^i\right]} \cdot (\widetilde{y}_{mt}^i) + E_t\left[x_{mt}^i\right] \tag{6}$$

$\hat{x}_{mt}^i$ is the result of normalizing the input time series, $\hat{y}_{mt}^i$ is the result of de-normalization [8] after model training ends, and $\widetilde{y}_{mt}^i$ is the result of prediction after input normalization and model learning.

In order to prevent over-stationarization, a multi-layer perceptron [8] is introduced as a projector to learn the inherent dependence relationship between the original sequence and the standard deviation σ_x and mean μ_x. This results in the de-stationary parameters λ and Δ:

$$\log \lambda, \Delta = MLP(\sigma_x, \mu_x, x) \tag{7}$$

2.4   De-stationary Autocorrelation(DSA)

Subsequences contain similar periodic dependencies as the original sequence, and mining potential development patterns through autocorrelation mechanisms [10] is of great help for time series prediction. According to the discrete autocorrelation coefficient A_{xx} the correlation between a subsequence of length L and a time delay of η of the original sequence can be calculated.

$$A_{xx(\eta)} = \lim_{L\to\infty} \frac{1}{L} \sum_{t=0}^{L-1} X_t X_{t-\eta} \tag{8}$$

After normalization, the sequence X_t' is projected to obtain the query Q', key K', and value V' through a projector. K' is split into n segments with different time delays and autocorrelated with Q'. The resulting sequence is $A_{Q'K'(\eta_1)}, A_{Q'K'(\eta_2)} \cdots A_{Q'K'(\eta_n)}$. At this point, the autocorrelation between the sequences is the result of the stationary, having a similar distribution at different time delays. By establishing the relationship between the stationary and original sequence autocorrelations, it can be concluded that:

$$A_{Q'K'(\eta)} = \lim_{L\to\infty} \frac{1}{L} \sum_{t=1}^{L} \frac{QK(\eta) - K(\eta)\mu_Q}{\sigma_x^2} \tag{9}$$

To correct for the de-stationarity of the original sequence, the detrending coefficients λ and Δ are introduced.

$$A'_{Q'K'(\eta)} = \lim_{L \to \infty} \frac{1}{L} \sum_{t=1}^{L} (\lambda Q'K'(\eta) + \Delta) \tag{10}$$

From the n time delays of K', the top k correlation coefficients are selected, and the subsequence correlation aggregation is performed on them through softmax. As a result, the distribution estimate of the de-stationary autocorrelation of Q' and K' is obtained as $\hat{A}_{Q'K'(\eta)}$:

$$\hat{A}_{Q'K'(\eta_1)}, ..., \hat{A}_{Q'K'(\eta_k)} = Softmax(A'_{Q'K'(\eta_1)}, ..., A'_{Q'K'(\eta_k)}) \tag{11}$$

Concatenating the obtained distribution with the corresponding values of V' at k time delays, the complete de-stationary autocorrelation mechanism (DSA) is obtained:

$$DSA(Q', K', V', \lambda, \Delta) = \sum_{i=1}^{k} \hat{A}'_{Q'K'(\eta_i)} TimeDelay(V', \eta_i) \tag{12}$$

2.5 Edgebound

Deep learning time series models can overfit by learning noise. Edgebound dynamically sets a lower bound on the loss to capture the unpredictability of current observations. N_1 and N_2 [2], with identical network structures, use a weighted moving average to compute N2's parameters from N_1's weights.

$$W_{N_2}^t = \frac{nW_{N_1}^t + (n-1)W_{N_1}^{t-1} + ... + 2W_{N_1}^{t-n+2} + W^{t-n+1}}{n + (n-1) + ... + 2 + 1} \tag{13}$$

The prediction estimate of the target network sets a lower bound on the source network's loss, with $W_{N_1}^t$ and $W_{N_2}^t$ as parameter weights for the source and target networks at time t, and n as the weight coefficient across different time points. The training loss is expressed as:

$$R_{LM}(f(W_{N_1})) = \frac{1}{LM} \sum_{l=1}^{L} \sum_{m=1}^{M} |f(W_{N_1}) - y_{lm}| \tag{14}$$

$$\hat{R}_{LM}(f(W_{N_1})) = \frac{1}{NLM} \sum_{i=1}^{N} \sum_{l=1}^{L} \sum_{m=1}^{M} |f(W_{N_1}) - y_{lm}| \tag{15}$$

$$\hat{R}_{LM}^{edgebound}(f(W_{N_1})) = |\hat{R}_{LM}(f(W_{N_1})) - \hat{R}_{LM}(f(W_{N_2}))| + \hat{R}_{LM}(f(W_{N_2})) \tag{16}$$

When $R_{LM}(f(W_{N_1}))$ represents the risk of a time series (length L, M features) in source network $N1$, $\hat{R}_{LM}(f(W_{N_1}))$ is the empirical risk version [4], and

$\hat{R}_{LM}^{edgebound}(f(W_{N_1}))$ is the regularized empirical risk optimized by edgebound. Update gradient descent when source network's empirical risk exceeds target network's, and update gradient ascent when source network's empirical risk is below target network's.

3 Experiments

3.1 Datasets and Evaluation Metrics

We applied DSEAformer to three real-world datasets, which are ETTm1 [12] (transformer oil temperature), ECL [12] (electric power consumption), and Weather [12] (weather data). We used MSE (mean square error) and MAE (mean absolute error) as evaluation metrics.

3.2 Baselines

We compared DSEAformer with the state-of-the-art methods in the MLTF field in the past five years, including FEDformer [13], Autoformer [10], Inform-er [12], ETSformer [9], Logtrans [7], LSTnet [6], and TCN [1] as baseline algorithms. The forecast step lengths were selected as 96, 192, and 720.

Table 1. Multivariate long-sequence time-series forecast comparison

Method		DSEAformer		FEDformer		Autoformer		Informer		ETSformer		LogTrans		LSTnet		TCN	
Metric		MSE	MAE	MSE	MAE	MSE	MAE	MSE	MAE	MSE	MAE	MSE	MAE	MSE	MAE	MSE	MAE
ETTm1	96	**0.041**	**0.156**	0.103	0.245	0.171	0.242	0.395	0.362	0.128	0.268	0.953	0.742	1.218	1.760	1.243	1.828
	192	**0.105**	**0.214**	0.132	0.279	0.301	0.370	0.521	0.589	0.261	0.372	0.818	0.771	1.244	1.467	1.261	1.757
	720	**0.345**	**0.373**	0.478	0.501	0.546	0.619	3.749	1.639	0.478	0.453	3.184	1.772	2.331	1.612	2.435	1.719
ECL	96	**0.185**	**0.297**	0.194	0.299	0.201	0.317	0.327	0.367	0.187	0.307	0.258	0.359	0.703	0.755	0.988	0.882
	192	**0.197**	**0.305**	0.204	0.308	0.225	0.334	0.314	0.408	0.199	0.315	0.266	0.368	0.725	0.676	0.997	0.821
	720	**0.229**	**0.340**	0.231	0.343	0.254	0.361	0.373	0.439	0.233	0.345	0.283	0.376	0.958	0.815	1.441	0.792
Weather	96	**0.217**	**0.295**	0.218	0.297	0.266	0.337	0.300	0.384	0.197	0.281	0.458	0.490	0.594	0.587	0.616	0.590
	192	**0.232**	**0.305**	0.276	0.307	0.307	0.364	0.598	0.574	0.237	0.312	0.659	0.589	0.561	0.565	0.630	0.602
	720	**0.343**	**0.378**	0.405	0.429	0.419	0.428	1.059	1.747	0.352	0.388	0.870	0.676	0.618	0.601	0.640	0.611

3.3 Results

The comparison results between DSEAformer and other baseline methods are shown in Table 1, from which we obtained the following results:

- Our DSEAformer excels over recent baselines in MLTF tasks of various lengths, displaying superior MSE and MAE. It sustains robust prediction even for longer time series, avoiding overfitting with edgebound.
- Compared to self-attention methods like Informer and LogTrans, our DSEAformer utilizes autocorrelation mechanisms to aggregate time series information, improving efficiency and information utilization.

- Compared to Fedformer, Autoformer, and ETSformer, DSEAformer improves the predictability of time series and uncovers potential dependencies among time series by introducing sequence preprocessing.
- Compared with CNN-based LSTnet and TCN, DSEAformer can better capture the periodic patterns and long-term dependencies of time series.

4   Conclusion

In our paper, we introduce the DSEAformer approach to address distribution shift and over-stationarization concerns in MLTF. With regard to the MLTF problem, we adopt an optimization regularization strategy to mitigate overfitting brought on by noise interference. Numerous tests show that our suggested approach works well in raising the MLTF task's prediction accuracy. Future research will focus on sequence decomposition and a deeper examination of the periodic information in terms of trends.

References

1. Bai, et al.: An empirical evaluation of generic convolutional and recurrent networks for sequence modeling. arXiv preprint arXiv:1803.01271 (2018)
2. Cho, Y., Kim, D., Kim, D., Khan, M.A., Choo, J.: WaveBound: dynamic error bounds for stable time series forecasting. arXiv preprint arXiv:2210.14303 (2022)
3. Hyndman, R.J., Athanasopoulos, G.: Forecasting: principles and practice. OTexts (2018)
4. Ishida, T., Yamane, I., Sakai, T., Niu, G., Sugiyama, M.: Do we need zero training loss after achieving zero training error? arXiv preprint arXiv:2002.08709 (2020)
5. Kim, T., Kim, J., Tae, Y., Park, C., Choi, J.H., Choo, J.: Reversible instance normalization for accurate time-series forecasting against distribution shift. In: International Conference on Learning Representations (2021)
6. Lai, G., Chang, W.C., Yang, Y., Liu, H.: Modeling long-and short-term temporal patterns with deep neural networks. In: The 41st international ACM SIGIR Conference on Research & Development in Information Retrieval, pp. 95–104 (2018)
7. Li, S., et al.: Enhancing the locality and breaking the memory bottleneck of transformer on time series forecasting. In: Advances in Neural Information Processing Systems 32 (2019)
8. Liu, Y., et al.: Non-stationary transformers: exploring the stationarity in time series forecasting. In: Advances in Neural Information Processing Systems (2022)
9. Woo, G., Liu, C., Sahoo, D., Kumar, A., Hoi, S.: ETSformer: exponential smoothing transformers for time-series forecasting. arXiv preprint arXiv:2202.01381 (2022)
10. Wu, H., Xu, J., Wang, J., Long, M.: Autoformer: decomposition transformers with auto-correlation for long-term series forecasting. Adv. Neural. Inf. Process. Syst. **34**, 22419–22430 (2021)
11. Zhang, Y., et al.: Classification of EEG signals based on autoregressive model and wavelet packet decomposition. Neural Process. Lett. **45**, 365–378 (2017)
12. Zhou, H., et al.: Informer: Beyond efficient transformer for long sequence time-series forecasting. In: Proceedings of the AAAI Conference on Artificial Intelligence, vol. 35, pp. 11106–11115 (2021)
13. Zhou, T., Ma, Z., Wen, Q., Wang, X., Sun, L., Jin, R.: FEDformer: frequency enhanced decomposed transformer for long-term series forecasting. In: International Conference on Machine Learning, pp. 27268–27286. PMLR (2022)

Multitask-Based Cluster Transmission for Few-Shot Text Classification

Kaifang Dong⬤, Fuyong Xu, Baoxing Jiang, Hongye Li, and Peiyu Liu(✉)

Shandong Normal University, Jinan, Shandong, China
liupy@sdnu.edu.cn

Abstract. Few-shot text classification aims to perform class prediction by learning from a few examples on labels. Prototypical Network (ProtoNet) is often used to solve the few-shot problem, devoted to constructing a metric space between classes and samples. However, the ProtoNet-based works of building meta-learners have inadequately developed the potential of metric space for the discriminative representation of text, which lead to the deficiency of classification tasks. To improve the above problem, we propose a smoothing strategy combining averaging and prototyping based on ProtoNet. Specifically, we generate a new cluster by cluster transmission algorithm and combine it with a label vector of the pooling function to enrich the distinguishability representation. The proposed algorithm makes the features of the samples more compact and improves the learning efficiency. Then, we use the representation of basic classification features as an auxiliary task to further enhance the diversity of spatial vectors and alleviate the over-fitting problem. Experiments show that our approach further improves the performance of the few-shot text classification task.

Keywords: Few-shot learning · Cluster transmission · Text classification · Prototypical network · Multi-task learning

1 Introduction

Few-shot text classification (FSTC) [17, 21, 27] is a fundamental and urgent task in natural language processing. Traditional classification methods rely heavily on a large amount of labeled training data. Therefore, using general text classification strategies is not feasible when the number of available samples in the real world is tiny. FSTC aims to allow the model to master the ability to distinguish different classes by learning from a few samples to predict the unseen classes in training. In recent years, two approaches based on meta-learning strategies have emerged to address the problem of few-shot classification urgently: metric-based meta-learning [4, 11, 29] and optimization-based meta-learning [7, 9, 18].

Optimization-based meta-learning continuously learns the implicit features of the support set through multiple gradient updates [1, 14, 20, 28]. To improve the performance of optimization algorithm-based tasks, Bansal et al. [2] added

BERT [6] to few-shot text classification. On this basis, Bao et al. [3] proposed a way to enhance the effectiveness of meta-learning by using the distributional signatures of words. In recent work, Lei et al. [13] proposed an adaptive meta-learner based on gradient similarity to improve the generalization of the model to new tasks.

The metric-based algorithm is more concise and effective than the optimization-based algorithm approach. The prototype network is a concrete implementation based on this algorithm. The metric-based approach uses certain distance metric criteria to build a metric space. Some of the work [8,12] revolves around metric learning and graphs, focusing on constructing graphs and edge features. There are also many models based on the improvement of the prototypical network based on the euclidean distance algorithm. For example, Chen et al. [4] proposed ContrastNet by incorporating contrast learning. Sun et al. [22] added hierarchical attention to ProtoNet. However, the traditional prototypical network and its improved models [4,22,25,26], both fail to fully exploit the value of the metric space. The presence of some population sample points whose coordinates are too dispersed makes models an obstacle to the class determination of the query points.

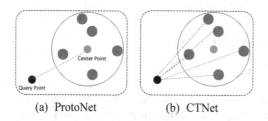

(a) ProtoNet   (b) CTNet

Fig. 1. Comparative diagram of different label representation methods. Picture (a) shows the traditional prototypical network using the population center point as the feature representation of the labels. Picture (b) shows the proposed method to calculate the distance from the query point to each point in the cluster.

Single-task supervised learning acquires the knowledge to determine the sample labels by fitting the mapping relationship between the sample features and the labels. In some cases, however, we collect or construct multiple labels for a sample, each label corresponding to a learning task. In these multiple tasks, we want the model to improve the performance effectively in one of the tasks, then this task is the main task, and the rest are auxiliary tasks. The auxiliary task improves the learning efficiency [24] of the main task and further enhance the generalization ability of the model [16].

To alleviate the troubles caused by the above problems, we have adapted the prototypical network and proposed the Cluster Transmission Network (CTNet). This network uses cluster transmission to further tap metric space's potential in the differentiated text representation. We make full use of the location points in the metric space beyond the sample points by algorithmic mapping, which makes the sample representation more delicate. The cluster transmission algorithm generates more independent new clusters based on the original ones, thus further enhancing the compactness of the space vector in terms of distribution. The difference between the focus of CTNet and the traditional prototypical network is shown in Fig. 1. In the process of continuously updating the parameters, the traditional method makes the query point close to the center point, while our method makes the query point the center point. In addition, to alleviate the distress caused by over-fitting, CTNet incorporates auxiliary tasks [15,16,24] to help the model learn to have more diverse feature representations and to improve the model's generalization ability. Our contributions are summarized as follows:

1) We proposed a cluster transmission network (CTNet) that can be applied to few-shot text classification, and elaborate a cluster transmission algorithm to effectively improve the utilization value of the metric space.

2) CTNet uses auxiliary task to alleviate the over-fitting problem of few-shot text classification. The auxiliary task enables the main task to learn more distinctive text representations and enhance the ability of the model to adapt to new tasks.

3) We designed the corresponding experiments. Experimental results show that the proposed CTNet is effective and outperforms the baseline model. Available codes at https://github.com/LZXYF/CTNet.

2   Environment Setting

2.1   Task Definition

Before tackling the few-shot text classification task, the dataset is first divided into a training set Set_{train}, a validation set Set_{val}, and a test set Set_{test}, where the classes in the three do not intersect each other. When training, validating, and testing the meta-learner, a task consisting of a support set S and a query set Q is extracted from the corresponding dataset. In an episode of a n-way k-shot text classification problem, n classes are intercepted in the dataset, and then $k + m$ sample examples are intercepted in each class. The support set S comprises these $n \times k$ samples and the corresponding labels. We will only talk about the cases of $k = 1$ and $k = 5$ later. The query set Q consists of $n \times m$ samples and does not contain true labels.

The task of the model is to try to obtain the ability to accurately classify each sample in the query set Q by training and learning from a small amount of labeled text in the support set S.

2.2   Encoder

The text is vector transformed using the BERT encoder [6] in the proposed method. BERT is both a pre-trained model and a transformer-based bidirectional feature extraction tool. Multiple sub-encoders form the coding layer of BERT. Moreover, each sub-encoder contains a multi-headed attention mechanism [5] and a feed-forward neural network [23] layer. This construction enables

BERT to use the contextual information of words for feature extraction. BERT is used as an encoder for converting text to feature vectors in many tasks [4,17,21], which facilitates the construction of a uniform metric space.

3 Algorithm and Architecture

3.1 Text Encoding

Figure 2 shows the architecture of our proposed cluster transmission network (CTNet). CTNet requires an encoder to convert text into a form of word vectors. Here we choose the most suitable BERT as the encoder based on the previous study [3,19,21].

For an episode, we define the support set S with n classes as follows: $S = \{(x_j, y_j) | j \in \{0, 1, ..., n \times k - 1\}\}$. The query set Q that has the same class is defined as: $Q = \{q_i | i \in \{0, 1, ..., n \times m - 1\}\}$. The BERT encoder is defined as $B(\cdot)$. x_j and q_i are input to $B(\cdot)$ in for encoding.

Then the encoded vectors $\tilde{x}_j \in \mathbb{R}^d$, $\tilde{q}_i \in \mathbb{R}^d$ are obtained, where d denotes the dimensionality of the word vector. The above operation can be defined as follows:

$$\tilde{x}_j, \tilde{q}_i = B(x_j, q_i). \tag{1}$$

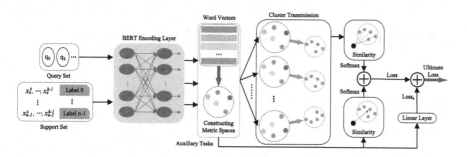

Fig. 2. CTNet model architecture diagram. We first convert the text into vectors and build up the metric space. The cluster transmission algorithm is then applied to construct new clusters. We combine the prototype approach and the smoothing of the cluster transmission as cluster representation. The final loss of the classification task must be connected to the loss of the auxiliary task.

3.2 Cluster Transmission

Here, we refer to the sample points the cluster transmission algorithm generated in the metric space as the target points $t_\ell^\nu \in \mathbb{R}^d$, where ℓ denotes the cluster's label and ν represents the index of different elements in the same class. Similarly, we can represent the different classes of $\tilde{x}_j$ in this way. In $\tilde{x}_\ell^\nu$, $\ell = \{0, 1, ..., n - 1\}$

and $\nu = \{0, 1, ..., k-1\}$. The number of target points in a cluster must be greater than or equal to 1. The general form of prototype $s_\ell \in \mathbb{R}^d$ can be obtained by the operation of average pooling function $P(\cdot)$ on $\tilde{x}_\ell^\nu$. Many previous approaches have used this format [17,19,21]. The prototype s_ℓ can represent the features of the class, and ℓ represents the class label. The process by which we obtain the prototype is shown below:

$$s_\ell = P\left(\tilde{x}_\ell^0, ..., \tilde{x}_\ell^{k-1}\right). \tag{2}$$

The cluster transmission algorithm can be used when $k = 5$. In particular, we first consider the k same-labeled elements in the support set S as a cluster C, and denote the region of this cluster by O_C. Secondly, the elements in the cluster are connected to each other by lines. Finally, we obtain an arbitrary point from the line as a target point. To avoid the number of target points explosion, we choose only the first k middle position points as target points. Our newly acquired points must be in the original cluster region. A new cluster G is formed with these target points, and O_G denotes its region. Figure 3(a) can represent the relationship between O_G and O_C: $O_G \subseteq O_C$. This variation in cluster regions enables the model to learn features with compactness and diversity. The points in the middle position provide fair and stable features, equivalent to giving equal weight to each element in the cluster. The process of extracting the target points can be expressed as follows:

$$t_\ell^\nu = \frac{\tilde{x}_\ell^j + \tilde{x}_\ell^r}{2}, \tag{3}$$

where $\nu = \{0, 1, ..., k-1\}$, $\ell = \{0, 1, ..., n-1\}$, $r \neq j$, $0 \leq j, r \leq k-1$.

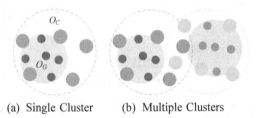

(a) Single Cluster   (b) Multiple Clusters

Fig. 3. Picture (a) compares cluster area size before and after cluster transmission. Larger points represent the original samples, while smaller points represent the feature points generated by the algorithm. Previous models did not easily distinguish confusable sample points. Yet, as represented in Picture (b), this feature transfer increases the distance between clusters, thus enhancing the model's ability to represent diverse types.

However, when performing one-shot tasks, the number of target points can only be one. Cluster transmission can no longer generate new sample points in this case. To be consistent with the purpose of cluster transmission, we need a special treatment for $k = 1$. Cluster transmission makes clusters more independent from each other, enhancing the compactness of data distribution and expanding diversity. For an element representing a cluster, we only need to expand the distance between each element to achieve the same purpose. As a result, we calculate the distance between the prototypes in different clusters and use this distance as a loss value $\mathcal{L}_s$, which is calculated as shown:

$$\mathcal{L}_s = \frac{1}{N+1} \sum_{j=0}^{N} E(s_\alpha, s_\beta). \tag{4}$$

Here, $N = n(n-1)/2 - 1$, $E(\cdot)$ is a function that evaluates the similarity based on the euclidean distance. s_α and s_β are in Eq. (2). $\beta \neq \alpha, 0 \leq \alpha, \beta \leq n-1$. Finally we need to maximize the value of $\mathcal{L}_s$.

3.3 Loss Calculation

The model first calculates the prototype similarity between $\tilde{q}_i$ and s_ℓ in Eq. (2). The procedure for calculating the probability distribution is shown below:

$$p_1(j|s_0, ..., s_{n-1}, \tilde{q}_i) = \frac{e^{E(s_j, \tilde{q}_i)}}{\sum_j e^{E(s_j, \tilde{q}_i)}}. \tag{5}$$

When $k = 5$, it is also necessary to calculate the similarity between $\tilde{q}_i$ and t_ℓ^ν in Eq. (3). We match the similarity between $\tilde{q}_i$ and all t_ℓ^ν in the same cluster and take its average $\mathcal{A}_\ell$ as the similarity between $\tilde{q}_i$ and this cluster. The process of calculating the target similarity is shown below:

$$\mathcal{A}_\ell = \frac{1}{n} \sum_{v=0}^{n-1} \|t_\ell^v - \tilde{q}_i\|_2, \tag{6}$$

$$p_2(j|\mathcal{A}_0, ..., \mathcal{A}_{n-1}) = \frac{e^{\mathcal{A}_j}}{\sum_j e^{\mathcal{A}_j}}. \tag{7}$$

Then the target similarity and prototype similarity are combined to get the final similarity result. Fusing the two similarity representations allows the model to learn more detailed and tighter features. When $k = 1$, $p = p_1$, and when $k > 1$, by the following calculation:

$$p = \eta p_1 + (1 - \eta)p_2, \tag{8}$$

where $\eta \in (0, 1)$ is a tunable weight parameter.

Finally, we calculate the negative log-likelihood loss values based on similarity.

$$\mathcal{L} = \begin{cases} -\frac{1}{nm} \sum_{j=0}^{nm-1} \log p(y_i) & k > 1 \\ \left[-\frac{1}{m} \sum_{j=0}^{m-1} \log p(y_i)\right] / \mathcal{L}_s & k = 1 \end{cases} \tag{9}$$

Here, y_i is the gold-standard label of $\tilde{q}_i$. We use $\mathcal{L}_s$ as the denominator of the final loss so that $\mathcal{L}_s$ can be maximized when minimizing the final loss.

3.4   Auxiliary Learning

In order to generate representations with diversity, we use learning the basic class feature representation as a auxiliary task. Specifically, we use a feedforward neural network layer f_ω to regulate the dimensionality of $\tilde{x}_j$, where ω denotes a parameter in the feedforward neural network. $\mathcal{C}(\cdot)$ denotes the cross-entropy loss function. The calculation is shown below:

$$X_j = f_\omega(\tilde{x}_j), \tag{10}$$

$$\mathcal{L}_a = \frac{1}{n \times k} \sum_{j=0}^{n \times k - 1} \mathcal{C}(X_j, y_j), \tag{11}$$

where y_j is the true label of X_j.

Finally, we give a weight ρ to the loss value of the auxiliary task:

$$\tilde{\mathcal{L}} = \mathcal{L} + \rho \mathcal{L}_a. \tag{12}$$

We have compiled algorithms for model learning, which are presented in Algorithm 1.

Algorithm 1: CTNet learning algorithm

Data: Support for task datasets $S = \{(x_j, y_j) | j \in \{0, 1, ..., n \times k - 1\}\}$.
   Query for task datasets $Q = \{q_i | i \in \{0, 1, ..., n \times m - 1\}\}$.

1 **while** not done **do**
2 | Text encoder is used $\tilde{x}_j, \tilde{q}_i \leftarrow B(x_j, q_i)$
3 | Find the prototype s_ℓ according to Eq. 2
4 | **if** $k = 1$ **then**
5 | | Calculate the loss value $\mathcal{L}_s$ by Eq. 4
6 | | Calculate the prototype similarity of $\tilde{q}_i$ to s_ℓ
7 | **else**
8 | | t_ℓ^ν is obtained through cluster transmission
9 | | Calculate the target similarity by Eq. 7
10 | | Combining target similarity and prototype similarity
11 | **end**
12 | The final loss value $\mathcal{L}$ is calculated according to Eq. 9
13 | Calculate $\tilde{\mathcal{L}}$ by adding the auxiliary task loss value $\mathcal{L}_a$
14 | Update learning parameters
15 **end**

---

4   Experiment

4.1   Experimental Conditions and Dataset

For the fairness of the experiment, we use Huffpost[1] and FewRel [10] as benchmarks and keep the same experimental conditions as the previous research

---

[1] https://www.huffpost.com/.

[3,19,22]. We use 1000 episodes to evaluate the performance of each model. In addition, five different random number seeds are used for training, and the macro average accuracy is calculated as the final result.

Huffpost: The task is to predict the class of the article based on its title. The training, validation, and test set in this data set contain 20, 5, and 16 types of labels, respectively. Each label contains 900 samples.

FewRel: The task is to predict the relationships between entities. The training, validation, and test set in this data set contain 65, 5, and 10 types of labels, respectively. Each label contains 700 samples.

4.2   Results Analysis

We compare the proposed cluster transmission network (CTNet) with the methods proposed by Bao et al. [3] and Ohashi et al. [19], respectively. In addition, four models [7,17,21,28] have been added for reference. The scores are compared in Table 1, and the table's rightmost column indicates the average results. We provide three types of averaging: *5-way*, *10-way*, and *All*, which represent the average score in the 5-way environment only, the average score in the 10-way environment only, and the average score for all results, respectively.

Table 1. Table for model score comparison

	Huffpost				FewRel				Average
	5-Way		10-Way		5-Way		10-Way		
	1-Shot	5-Shot	1-Shot	5-Shot	1-Shot	5-Shot	1-Shot	5-Shot	*5-Way / 10-Way / All*
Bao et al. [3]	42.12	62.97	-	-	70.08	88.07	-	-	65.81 / - / 65.81
MLMAN [28]	47.07	57.80	33.86	43.79	73.61	82.75	60.28	71.48	65.30 /52.35 /58.83
MAML [7]	51.10	65.23	37.37	51.74	68.94	76.49	58.07	65.01	65.44 /53.05 /59.24
ProtoNet [21]	51.03	68.36	37.42	55.81	78.61	88.92	65.97	80.38	71.73 /59.89 /65.81
Meta-FCS [17]	51.07	68.49	38.98	57.06	75.24	88.36	66.19	81.93	70.79 /61.04 /65.92
Ohashi et al. [19]	52.34	69.66	38.83	57.26	79.52	89.28	**68.08***	82.51	72.70 /61.67 /67.19
Ours CTNet	**53.58**	**69.90**	**39.74**	57.16	78.58	**91.08***	66.51	**83.03**	73.29 /61.61 /67.45
CTNet+ρ	**54.36***	**70.64***	**40.54***	**57.96***	**80.26***	91.00	67.21	**83.57***	74.07 /62.32 /68.19

Bold in the table indicates that the score has been improved, and bold with "*" indicate that it is the most advanced score. "CTNet" means that only the mainline task is used, while "CTNet+ρ" means that the auxiliary task is added.

Table 1 shows that some of the results have been improved with the use of CTNet only. This indicates that combining prototype and average similarity is better than using only prototypes in predicting the accuracy of unknown classes. When the auxiliary task with CTNet is involved in training, the fit state of the model can be further improved to achieve the highest scores.

On the Huffpost dataset, our CTNet outperforms the ProtoNet by 2.15%-3.33% and the baseline [19] by 0.7%-2.02%. Compared with optimization-based meta-learning like MAML [7], the advantages of CTNet are more obvious. The

10-way 1-shot experiment on the FewRel dataset did not beat the baseline, although it scored higher than ProtoNet.

In terms of average scores, CTNet improved by 2.34% (*5-Way*), 2.43% (*10-Way*), and 2.38% (*All*) compared to ProtoNet. CTNet improved by 1.37% (*5-Way*) and 0.65% (*10-Way*) and 1.0% (*All*) compared to baseline. Overall, the advantages of CTNet are most prominent in the *5-Way* environment.

Relying only on our proposed algorithm has a small gain in a *10-way* environment. This is because, as the number of categories increases, the diversity of features needs to be enhanced even more. We add the auxiliary task to optimize the representation of the basic classes generated by the encoder and further improve the diversity of features.

There are two main reasons for the excellent performance of our proposed model: (i) We apply the proposed cluster transmission algorithm to the model to help it build a richer text representation. Cluster transmission builds a more compact new cluster on top of the old one, and the model can get more distinguishing features in the metric space. (ii) CTNet utilizes the optimized representation of the basic classes. The auxiliary task enhances the diversity of spatial vector representations, which improves the model's ability to adapt quickly to new tasks.

4.3 Visualization Analysis

We collect a random sample of 100 query sets for each label, and visualize their feature vectors after dimensionality reduction. The purpose of this experiment was to explore the ability of the model to represent distinguishing features. The results are shown in Fig. 4, where each point represents a sample, and different colors indicate different classes.

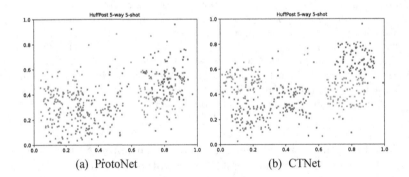

Fig. 4. Text-representation of ProtoNet and CTNet on Huffpost.

Figure 4(a) shows a visualization of the ProtoNet, where many points do not belong to the same class but cross over. There are also some points that cannot be accurately classified. Figure 4(b) shows the visualization of CTNet, which distances the samples of different classes and uses the cluster transmission algorithm to make the samples of the same class more concentrated. In addition, it also reduces the number of samples that cannot be accurately classified. Similar elements after cluster transmission are significantly better in terms of compactness performance. These phenomena reflect the effectiveness of the proposed approach in enhancing discriminatory.

4.4 Fitting Verification

To verify the effectiveness of CTNet in mitigating over-fitting using auxiliary tasks. We set the weight ρ of the auxiliary task to 1e-2 and adjust the number of times the model is trained. Figure 5 plots the accuracy change curves of ProtoNet and CTNet during the training process.

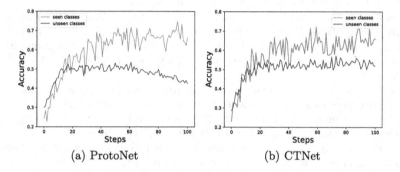

(a) ProtoNet   (b) CTNet

Fig. 5. Learning curve of ProtoNet (left) v.s. Our (right) on 5-way 1-shot task of the Huffpost dataset. We plot average accuracy from seen classes (red) and unseen classes (blue). (Color figure online)

As can be seen in Fig. 5(a) and 5(b), there is little difference between the two models in the early stage, and CTNet shows its advantages in the middle stage, performing a better fit than ProtoNet. ProtoNet is gradually overfitted as the number of training increases. In contrast, CTNet is relatively more stable and easier to generalize to unseen classes. These show that our proposed method generalizes better and is easily adaptable to the few-shot task.

5 Conclusion

In this paper, we propose a few-shot text classification method using cluster transmission and auxiliary tasks to alleviate the over-fitting problem in the model. Cluster transmission is smoothing by averaging all members of the cluster instead of just using the center as the prototype. This strategy generates more compact clusters based on the original clusters, making the clusters behave more independently from each other. Previous works have always focused on making the prototype carry more information. Unlike these works, we focus on developing the application value of metric space. Experiments show that our method can further improve the performance of few-shot classification. In the future, we will further explore new coding methods based on this foundation.

Acknowledgements. This work is supported by part Key R & D project of Shandong Province 2019JZZY010129.

References

1. Andrychowicz, M., et al.: Learning to learn by gradient descent by gradient descent. In: NIPS, pp. 3981–3989. Barcelona, Spain (2016)
2. Bansal, T., Jha, R., Munkhdalai, T., McCallum, A.: Self-supervised meta-learning for few-shot natural language classification tasks. In: EMNLP, pp. 522–534. ACL (2020). https://doi.org/10.18653/v1/2020.emnlp-main.38
3. Bao, Y., Wu, M., Chang, S., Barzilay, R.: Few-shot text classification with distributional signatures. In: ICLR, OpenReview.net, Addis Ababa, Ethiopia (2020)
4. Chen, J., Zhang, R., Mao, Y., Xu, J.: ContrastNet: a contrastive learning framework for few-shot text classification. In: AAAI, pp. 10492–10500. AAAI Press (2022)
5. Dar, R.A., Dileep, A.D.: Multi-headed self-attention-based hierarchical model for extractive summarization. In: Nagar, A.K., Deep, K., Bansal, J.C., Das, K.N. (eds.) Soft Computing for Problem Solving 2019. AISC, vol. 1138, pp. 87–96. Springer, Singapore (2020). https://doi.org/10.1007/978-981-15-3290-0_7
6. Devlin, J., Chang, M., Lee, K., Toutanova, K.: BERT: pre-training of deep bidirectional transformers for language understanding. In: NAACL-HLT, vol. 1, pp. 4171–4186. ACL, Minneapolis, MN, USA (2019). https://doi.org/10.18653/v1/n19-1423
7. Finn, C., Abbeel, P., Levine, S.: Model-agnostic meta-learning for fast adaptation of deep networks. In: ICML, vol. 70, pp. 1126–1135. PMLR, Sydney, NSW, Australia (2017)
8. Fu, W., Zhou, L., Chen, J.: Bidirectional matching prototypical network for few-shot image classification. IEEE Signal Process. Lett. **29**, 982–986 (2022). https://doi.org/10.1109/LSP.2022.3152686
9. Han, C., Fan, Z., Zhang, D., Qiu, M., Gao, M., Zhou, A.: Meta-learning adversarial domain adaptation network for few-shot text classification. In: ACL/IJCNLP, pp. 1664–1673. ACL (2021). https://doi.org/10.18653/v1/2021.findings-acl.145
10. Han, X., et al.: FewRel: a large-scale supervised few-shot relation classification dataset with state-of-the-art evaluation. In: EMNLP, pp. 4803–4809. ACL, Brussels, Belgium (2018). https://doi.org/10.18653/v1/d18-1514
11. Jia, X., Su, Y., Zhao, H.: Few-shot learning via relation network based on coarse-grained granulation. Appl. Intell. **53**(1), 996–1008 (2023). https://doi.org/10.1007/s10489-022-03332-7
12. Jiang, B., Zhao, K., Tang, J.: RGTransformer: region-graph transformer for image representation and few-shot classification. IEEE Signal Process. Lett. **29**, 792–796 (2022). https://doi.org/10.1109/LSP.2022.3155991
13. Lei, T., Hu, H., Luo, Q., Peng, D., Wang, X.: Adaptive meta-learner via gradient similarity for few-shot text classification. In: COLING, pp. 4873–4882. ICCL, Gyeongju, Republic of Korea (2022)

14. Li, Z., Zhou, F., Chen, F., Li, H.: Meta-SGD: learning to learn quickly for few shot learning. arXiv:1707.09835 (2017)

15. Liu, H., Chi, Z., Yu, Y., Wang, Y., Chen, J., Tang, J.: Meta-auxiliary learning for future depth prediction in videos. In: WACV, pp. 5745–5754. IEEE, Waikoloa, HI, USA (2023). https://doi.org/10.1109/WACV56688.2023.00571

16. Liu, S., Davison, A.J., Johns, E.: Self-supervised generalisation with meta auxiliary learning. In: NIPS, pp. 1677–1687. Vancouver, BC, Canada (2019)

17. Liu, W., Pang, J., Li, N., Yue, F., Liu, G.: Few-shot short-text classification with language representations and centroid similarity. Appl. Intell. **53**(7), 8061–8072 (2023). https://doi.org/10.1007/s10489-022-03880-y

18. Mishchenko, K., Hanzely, S., Richtárik, P.: Convergence of first-order algorithms for meta-learning with Moreau envelopes. arXiv:2301.06806 (2023)

19. Ohashi, S., Takayama, J., Kajiwara, T., Arase, Y.: Distinct label representations for few-shot text classification. In: ACL/IJCNLP, vol. 2, pp. 831–836. ACL (2021). https://doi.org/10.18653/v1/2021.acl-short.105

20. Ravi, S., Larochelle, H.: Optimization as a model for few-shot learning. In: ICLR, pp. 1–11. OpenReview.net, Toulon, France (2017)

21. Snell, J., Swersky, K., Zemel, R.S.: Prototypical networks for few-shot learning. In: NIPS, pp. 4077–4087. MIT Press, Long Beach, CA, USA (2017)

22. Sun, S., Sun, Q., Zhou, K., Lv, T.: Hierarchical attention prototypical networks for few-shot text classification. In: EMNLP-IJCNLP, pp. 476–485. ACL, Hong Kong, China (2019). https://doi.org/10.18653/v1/D19-1045

23. Xian-Lun, T., Yin-Guo, L., Ling, Z.: A hybrid particle swarm algorithm for the structure and parameters optimization of feed-forward neural network. In: Liu, D., Fei, S., Hou, Z., Zhang, H., Sun, C. (eds.) ISNN 2007. LNCS, vol. 4493, pp. 213–218. Springer, Heidelberg (2007). https://doi.org/10.1007/978-3-540-72395-0_27

24. Wang, X., Hu, P., Liu, P., Peng, D.: Deep semisupervised class- and correlation-collapsed cross-view learning. IEEE Trans. Cybern. **52**(3), 1588–1601 (2022). https://doi.org/10.1109/TCYB.2020.2984489

25. Wu, Z., Zhao, H.: Hierarchical few-shot learning based on coarse- and fine-grained relation network. Artif. Intell. Rev. **56**(3), 2011–2030 (2023). https://doi.org/10.1007/s10462-022-10223-3

26. Xiao, Y., Jin, Y., Hao, K.: Adaptive prototypical networks with label words and joint representation learning for few-shot relation classification. IEEE Trans. Neural Networks Learn. Syst. **34**(3), 1406–1417 (2023). https://doi.org/10.1109/TNNLS.2021.3105377

27. Xu, J., Du, Q.: Learning transferable features in meta-learning for few-shot text classification. Pattern Recognit. Lett. **135**, 271–278 (2020). https://doi.org/10.1016/j.patrec.2020.05.007

28. Ye, Z., Ling, Z.: Multi-level matching and aggregation network for few-shot relation classification. In: ACL, vol. 1, pp. 2872–2881. ACL, Florence, Italy (2019). https://doi.org/10.18653/v1/p19-1277

29. Zhou, J., Lv, Q., Chen, C.Y.: Dynamic concept-aware network for few-shot learning. Knowl. Based Syst. **258**, 110045 (2022). https://doi.org/10.1016/j.knosys.2022.110045

Hyperplane Knowledge Graph Embedding with Path Neighborhoods and Mapping Properties

Yadan Han[1,2], Guangquan Lu[1,2(✉)], Jiecheng Li[1,2], Fuqing Ling[1,2], Wanxi Chen[1,2], and Liang Zhang[1,2]

[1] Key Lab of Education Blockchain and Intelligent Technology, Ministry of Education, Guangxi Normal University, Guilin 541004, China
[2] Guangxi Key Lab of Multi-Source Information Mining and Security, Guangxi Normal University, Guilin 541004, China
{hanyadan,memorydobby}@stu.gxnu.edu.cn, lugq@mailbox.gxnu.edu.cn,
ljc120801@gmail.com, LingFQ123@163.com, zhangliangcsuer@gmail.com

Abstract. Knowledge representation learning(KRL) is significant for the knowledge graph completion(or link prediction) task, it aims to project entities and relations to a low-dimensional vector space. There are two topics have been widely studied in KRL: one is the ability of the model to handle complex relations(i.e., N-to-1, 1-to-N and N-to-N), and the other is whether the model integrates multi-source information. However, the existing methods rarely consider both topics. To mitigate this problem, this paper proposes TransPMH, a hyperplane knowledge graph embedding model with path neighborhoods and mapping properties, which models the relation as a hyperplane. Besides, this paper introduces path neighborhoods as the multi-source information to improve the model's knowledge representation ability, and also introduces the relational mapping properties to enhance the model's ability to handle complex relations. We conducted extensive experiments for link prediction and triplet classification on benchmark datasets like WordNet and Freebase. Experimental results show that the proposed method achieves significant improvements in multiple evaluation metrics.

Keywords: Knowledge representation learning · Knowledge graph completion · Path neighborhoods · Mapping properties · Link prediction · Triplet classification

1 Introduction

knowledge Graphs (KGs) store a large number of facts in the real world, and it is a multi-relational graph composed of entities (nodes) and relations (different types of edges), which is usually represented in the form of a triplet (head-entity, relationship, tail-entity) or (h, r, t) for short. Nowadays, Knowledge graphs such as WordNet [2], Freebase [2] and WikiData [3] are widely applied to various fields, e.g., sentiment analysis [4,5], question answering [6], and node clustering [7]. However, since KGs are constantly expanding and difficult to construct,

© The Author(s), under exclusive license to Springer Nature Switzerland AG 2023
Z. Jin et al. (Eds.): KSEM 2023, LNAI 14117, pp. 78–91, 2023.
https://doi.org/10.1007/978-3-031-40283-8_8

KGs are usually incomplete. Thus, knowledge graph completion(KGC) (or link prediction) becomes a very important task.

For this task, knowledge representation learning has been proposed, which projects entities and relations into a low-dimensional vector space. Distance-based knowledge representation learning models from TransE [8] to the state-of-the-art TranSHER [9], have greatly improved on knowledge graph completion tasks. There are two major topics have been widely studied. The first one refers to handling complex relations, such as 1-to-N, N-to-1 and N-to-N relations. TransE has attracted many researchers' attention because of its leading performances and fewer parameters. However, TransE only performs well for 1-to-1 relations and is weak in dealing with 1-to-N, N-to-1, and N-to-N relations. The latter is whether to integrate multi-source information. Traditional knowledge representation learning methods only utilize triplet facts and ignore rich additional information of entities, such as entity descriptions, hierarchical types, images, relation paths and neighborhood information, etc. Among them, neighborhood information can provide much useful information for predicting the missing relations. For example, considering the KB fragment given in Fig. 1, if we know that *Taylor_Swift* sang *Fearless*, which can help us predict *Taylor_Swift* is a *Singer* rather than an *Actor*. Thus, the rich information contained neighborhood can assist the model to better model entities and relations.

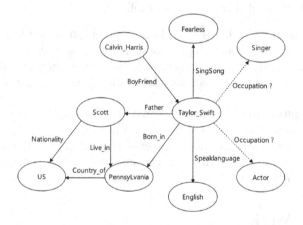

Fig. 1. An example fragment of a KB

Previous methods solve these two problems separately. Since TransE has flaws when dealing with complex relations, many variant models of TransE have been proposed, such as TransH [10], TransR [11] and TransD [12], etc. These models are all dedicated to dealing with complex relations. DKRL [13], TKRL [14] and IKRL [15] utilize entity descriptions, hierarchical types and images respectively to improve the knowledge representation ability of the model. These models consider different multi-source information to learn triplet representations. However, few models consider these two topics together.

In this paper, we present TransPMH, a knowledge graph embedding method that is capable of incorporating multi-source information and encoding complex relations. It introduces relational mapping properties to improve the model's ability to handle complex relations. Besides, we consider multi-source information, i.e., relation path neighborhoods to learn representations of entities and relations. As shown in Fig. 1, we want to infer the relation between $Taylor\_Swift$ and US, there are three relation paths that are helpful in predicting the relations between them: $Taylor\_Swift$ $\xrightarrow{Born\_in} PennsyLvania \xrightarrow{Country\_of} US$, $Taylor\_Swift \xrightarrow{Father} Scott$ $\xrightarrow{Live\_in} PennsyLvania \xrightarrow{Country\_of} US$, and $Taylor\_Swift \xrightarrow{Father} Scott$ $\xrightarrow{Nationality} US$. Then we can denote $Taylor\_Swift$ as a relation path-specific mixture of its neighbors as follows:

$$Taylar\_Swift = \alpha_{p,1}[(PennsyLvania, Born\_in^{-1}) + (US, Country\_of^{-1})]$$
$$+ \alpha_{p,2}[(Scott, Father^{-1}) + (US, Nationality^{-1})]$$
$$+ \alpha_{p,3}[(Scott, Father^{-1}) + (PennsyLvania, Live\_in^{-1})$$
$$+ (US, Country\_of^{-1})]$$

where $\alpha_{p,i}$ is the weight, denoting the importance of each path for predicting relation r. The knowledge of different paths may have different information, thus different paths have different weights.

The contributions of this paper are as follows:

- This paper proposed a hyperplane knowledge graph embedding model with path neighborhoods and mapping properties—TransPMH, which projects entities to a relation-specific hyperplane. In order to improve ability of the model to handle complex relations, the relational mapping property is introduced;
- It utilizes multi-source information—relation path neighborhoods to enhance the knowledge representation ability of the model;
- The extensive experiments are conducted on benchmark datasets, and the experimental results show that our method outperforms baseline models on link prediction and triplets classification tasks.

2   Related Work

2.1   Translation-Based Embedding Methods

TransE [8] is the earliest proposed translation-based model and the triplet (h, r, t) is called the translation from h to t using the relation r, it defines $h + r \approx t$. However, TransE only performs well when dealing with 1-to-1 relations, and it has flaws when modeling 1-to-N, N-to-1, and N-to-N relations. For this problem, TransH [10] and TransR [11] were proposed. For a triplet (h, r, t), TransH projects h and t into a relation-specific hyperplane using the following formula: $h_{\perp} = h - w_r^T h w_r$, $t_{\perp} = t - w_r^T t w_r$, where w_r is the normal vector of the hyperplane.

TransR is slightly different from TransH. TransR projects h/t to the relation-specific subspace: $h_r = hM_r$, $t_r = hM_r$, where w_r is the mapping matrix from entity space to relation subspace. TransE, TransH and TransR all consider that each relation only corresponds to one semantic representation, but in actual situations, relation r may represent different meanings. TransD [12] proposes a dynamic matrix-based model to solve this problem. However, these traditional methods only learn knowledge representation from structured triplets and ignore the multi-source information related to triplets.

2.2   Muti-source Information Learning

Multi-source information like textual, images and attribute information, considered as auxiliary information to the structured information in triplets, is significant for representation learning in KGs. DKRL [13] learns representations about textual descriptions of entities using Continuous Bag-Of-Words (CBOW) encoder and Convolutional Neural Network (CNN) encoder. TKRL [14] proposes Recursive Hierarchical Encoder (RHE) and Weighted Hierarchical Encoder (WHE) to construct type-specific projection matrices, mapping entities into different semantic spaces respectively. IKRL [15] designs an image encoder consisting of a neural representation module and a projection module to generate image-based representations for different images of each entity. The above multi-source information is auxiliary information outside of triplets. In addition, there is another kind of auxiliary information derived from triplets, such as relation paths, which contain a large amount of semantic information and can improve the effectiveness of knowledge graph completion. PTransE [16] integrates relation paths into the knowledge representation learning model, and describes the reasoning information at the relation level through a multi-step path. The relation path model utilizes the longer paths existing in KBs to utilize extra information, which improves the knowledge representation ability of the model. In this paper, we introduce the neighborhood information of entities and combine it with relation paths to improve the knowledge representation ability of the model.

3   Methodology

In this section, we will introduce the proposed knowledge representation learning model— TransPMH in detail. The overall architecture of our model is shown in Fig. 2. TransPMH is also a translation-based model, which uses relational mapping properties and relation path neighborhoods to overcome the shortcomings of the existing methods, i.e., they cannot simultaneously consider the problem of complex relations and multi-source information.

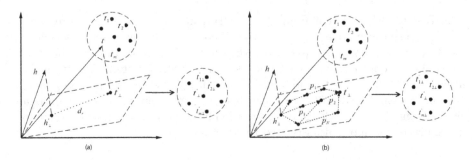

Fig. 2. TransPMH model. The 1-N relation is taken as an example to illustrate our proposed model. (a): h and t are connected by a direct path. (b): h and t are connected by indirect paths, where p_i represents the relation path between h and t. $h'_\perp$ and $t'_\perp$ are the representations of h and t in the hyperplane with the wight specific to the relation type (ω_r): $h'_\perp = \omega_r\, h_\perp$, $t'_\perp = \omega_r\, t_\perp$.

3.1   TransPMH

Aiming at the problem that the existing knowledge representation learning models cannot simultaneously deal with complex relations and integrate multi-source information, we propose TransPMH, this is a hyperplane knowledge graph embedding model with relational mapping properties and relation path neighborhoods. We first project entities into a relation-specific hyperplane, and then join relational mapping properties to define different weights for different relation types, so that the model can better handle complex relations. Besides, in order to enhance the knowledge representation ability of the model, relation path neighborhood as the multi-source information is introduced, making TransPMH more suitable for knowledge graph completion.

Joining Relational Mapping Properties. For a given triplet (h, r, t), we first project entities into a relation-specific hyperplane, which utilizes the idea of TransH's hyperplane projection. Specifically, h and t are first projected into a hyperplane via a relation-specific normal vector w_r, denoted as $h_\perp$ and $t_\perp$, respectively, then connect $h_\perp$ and $t_\perp$ through the relation vector d_r on the hyperplane:

$$h_\perp = h - w_r^T h w_r, t_\perp = t - w_r^T t w_r \tag{1}$$

where $h_\perp + d_r = t_\perp$.

TransH alleviates the problem of dealing with complex relations in the TransE to a certain extent. However, existing work divides the relations into 1-to-1, 1-to-N, N-to-1, and N-to-N, TransH does not consider the relation types of h and t when projecting entities. To overcome this problem, we introduce a weight ω_r related to the relation types. The weight of each triplet denotes the degree of mapping, and the mapping property of each triplet depends on its relation. For example, the relation between *husband* and *wife* is one-to-one, and the relation between *teacher* and *student* is one-to-many. Therefore, the weight is relation-specific. Specifically, we give a higher weight to 1-to-1 relations because the weight is fully expressed by this one triplet, and a lower weight is given to 1-to-N relations because the weight is expressed by multiple triplets together, so each triplet's own weight should be reduced. Similarly, we define weights for N-to-1 and N-to-N relations. Different relations have different weights, thus the model can handle complex relations. In addition, the weight w_r is related to $h_r q t_r$ and $t_r q h_r$, the calculation formula of the weight is shown in Eq.(2):

$$w_r = \frac{1}{\log(t_r q h_r + h_r q t_r)} \tag{2}$$

where $t_r q h_r$ is the average number of tail entities per distinct head entity, and $h_r q t_r$ is the average number of head entities per distinct tail entity. Then the representations of h and t projected from the two-dimensional plane to the hyperplane through the relational mapping properties become $h'_\perp = w_r \, h_\perp$, $t'_\perp = w_r \, t_\perp$. Combined Eq.(2), the score function is defined as Eq.(3):

$$f_r(h,t) = w_r \|h_\perp + d_r - t_\perp\|_{L_1/L_2} \tag{3}$$

Incorporating Relation Path Neighborhoods. Traditional knowledge representation learning models only consider the direct relations between h and t, but there are often relation paths between entities in large-scale knowledge graphs. These relation paths usually contain rich semantic information, and considering the characteristics of the relation paths is of great significance to better knowledge representation. For example, there is a relation path in Fig. 1: $Taylor\_Swift \xrightarrow{Born\_in} PennsyLvania \xrightarrow{Country\_of} US$, then it can be inferred that the triplet $(Taylor\_Swift, Nationality, US)$ holds.

In order to enhance the knowledge representation ability of the model, we consider incorporating multi-source information—relation path neighborhoods, so that the model can learn more useful information when embedding entities. For the triplet (h, r, t), there are two ways to connect h and t. In the first case, h and t are directly connected to form a direct path, as shown in Fig. 2(a), we denote it as (h, r, t); the second case is that h and t are indirectly connected to form indirect paths, as shown in Fig. 2(b), we denote it (h, P, t), P is the set of multiple relation paths between entity pairs (h, t), $P(h, t) = (p_1, ...p_N)$, where $p = (r_1, ...r_l)$, the calculation formula of p is shown in Eq.(4), and the distance of the relation path between h and t is shown in Eq.(5).

$$p = r_1 + r_2 + ... + r_l \tag{4}$$

$$|p| = |r_1| + |r_2| + ... + |r_l| \tag{5}$$

Since h and t have two connection ways, there should be two cases when embedding entities and relations. Specifically, for the triplet (h, r, t) that forms a direct path, we directly use Eq.(3) to learn the embeddings of h and t. However, in real-world factual KBs, there may be multiple different relation paths for the entity pair (h, t). For such paths, computing the vectors for all relation paths can be computationally expensive and time-consuming. To overcome this problem, we introduce a threshold τ in our implementation and consider in the vector representation construction only those relation paths sets for $|\mathcal{N}| \leq \tau$, where $\mathcal{N}$ represents the number of nodes connecting relation paths. In the experimental part of the fourth section, it can be known that the experimental result is the best when $\tau=5$. Therefore, we choose the set of relation paths with $|\mathcal{N}| \leq 5$, then we calculate the distance of each multi-step relation paths between the entity pair (h, t) according to Eq.(5), and get a set of the relation paths distance $|P| = (|p_1|, |p_2|, ... |p_N|)$ of the entity pair (h, t). For the entity pair (h, t) with relation paths, each relation path has different importance for predicting relation r, that is, different relation paths have different weights. For example, in Fig. 2, for predicting the relation between $Taylor\_Swift$ and US, the knowledge of relation path $Taylor\_Swift \xrightarrow{Father} Scott \xrightarrow{Live\_in} PennsyLvania \xrightarrow{Country\_of} US$ may not be so informative, so the corresponding weight may be small. Therefore, in this paper, we choose the smallest distance of relation paths $|p_{min}|$ and take its reciprocal as the weight:

$$\alpha = \frac{1}{|p_{min}|} \tag{6}$$

The relation path with greater weight contains more information, which is more conducive to inferring the missing relations between entities.

In summary, combined with Eq.(3), the score function of the TransPMH model is shown in Eq. (7):

$$f_r(h, t) = w_r \left\| h_\perp + d_r - t_\perp + \alpha \left(h_\perp + d_r - t_\perp \right) \right\|_{L_1/L_2} \tag{7}$$

3.2 Objective Formalization

In the model training process, to encourage discrimination between golden triplets and incorrect triplets, we use the following margin-based ranking loss:

$$L = \sum_{(h,r,t)\in S} \sum_{(h',r,r')\in S'} \max \left(f_r(h, t) + \gamma - f_r(h', t'), 0 \right) \tag{8}$$

In Eq.(8), S is the set of positive triplets, S' is the set of negative triplets, $max(x, y)$ denotes to return the larger value between x and y, and γ is the margin. The optimization goal of this objective function is to separate the positive triplets from the negative triplets to the greatest extent possible.

In the process of minimizing the objective function L, we consider the following constraints, mainly including:

$$\forall h, t \in E, \|h\|_2 \leq 1, \|t\|_2 \leq 1 \tag{9}$$

$$\forall r \in R, |w_r^\top r|/\|r\|_2 \leq \varepsilon \tag{10}$$

$$\forall r \in R, \|r\|_2 = 1 \tag{11}$$

Constraint (9) ensures that the entity vector's length is less than or equal to 1, constraint (10) guarantees the translation vector d_r is in the hyperplane, and constraint (11) makes sure that the hyperplane is the normal unit vector.

Table 1. Dataset Statistics

Dataset	Entities	Relations	Train	Valid	Test
WN18	40,943	18	141,442	5,000	5,000
FB15K	14,951	1,345	483,142	50,000	59,071
WN11	38,696	11	112,581	2,609	10,544
FB13	75,043	13	316,232	5,908	23,733
WN18RR	40,943	11	86,835	3,034	3,134
FB15K-237	14,541	237	272,115	17,535	20,466

4 Experiments

4.1 Dataset

We evaluate our proposed model on several benchmark datasets. WN18 and WN11 are two subsets of WordNet, a dataset that describes the characteristics of associations between words. FB15K and FB13 are two subsets of Freebase, a large dataset containing real-world facts. To further demonstrate the effectiveness of our model, we also conduct experiments on WN18RR and FB15K-237, which are subsets of WN18 and FB15K, respectively, where the inverse relation is deleted. The statistics of these knowledge graphs are summarized in Table 1.

4.2 Link Prediction

Evaluation Metrics. Link prediction task is to complete the missing h or t in the triplet (h, r, t), it aims to obtain the correct entity ranking, rather than finding a best one, so we consider the following evaluation metrics. Consistent with the baseline models, we report two metrics in our experiments: one is the average ranking of the correct entities($MeanRank/MR$), and the other is the proportion of the correct entities ranking in the top 10($Hits@10$). A lower $MeanRank$ and a higher $Hit@10$ indicate a better model. Besides, for comparison with classical models, we also use $Mean\ Reciprocal\ Rank(MRR)$ and $Hit@3$ as metrics. MRR is the reciprocal of the average ranking, and $Hit@3$ is the proportion of the correct entities ranking in the top 3. The higher MRR and $Hit@3$ indicate a better model.

Table 2. Link prediction experiment on WN18 and FB15K

Method	WN18				FB15K			
	MR		Hit@10		MR		Hit@10	
	Raw	Filt	Raw	Filt	Raw	Filt	Raw	Filt
SE [20]	1011	985	68.5	80.5	273	162	28.8	39.8
SME [21]	545	533	65.1	74.1	274	154	30.7	40.8
TransE [8]	263	251	75.4	89.2	243	125	34.9	47.1
TransM [23]	292	280	75.7	85.4	196	93	44.6	55.2
TransH [10]	401	388	73.0	82.3	212	87	45.7	64.4
TransR [11]	238	255	79.8	92.0	198	77	48.2	68.7
STransH [24]	347	330	77.1	90.6	196	68	46,6	69.5
OPTransE [25]	211	199	79.2	91.7	141	53	51.0	69.9
RPJE [26]	205	183	79.1	91.1	186	50	51.5	70.3
ERDERP [27]	258	246	79.9	93.2	189	54	49.1	71.1
TransP [28]	171	155	77.4	91.9	168	32	51.3	75.6
TransPMH (unif)	**162**	**147**	79.4	**93.9**	160	**25**	52.9	**78.9**
TransPMH (bern)	164	150	**80.5**	93.2	**138**	38	**54.0**	78.6

Table 3. Link prediction experiment on WN18RR and FB15K-237

Method	FB15K-237				WN18RR			
	MR	MRR	Hit@3	Hit@10	MR	MRR	Hit@3	Hit@10
DistMult [17]	254	.241	.263	.419	5110	.43	.44	.49
ComplEx [18]	339	.247	.275	.428	5261	.44	.46	.51
ConvE [19]	244	.325	.356	.501	4187	.43	.44	.52
CAKE [20]	170	.321	.355	**.515**	-	-	-	-
TransPMH	120	**.327**	**.361**	.513	1695	**.237**	**.391**	**.503**

Implementation. We perform link prediction experiments on WN18 and FB15K. In addition, we also conduct experiments on WN18RR and FB15K-237 to prove the effectiveness of our proposed model. In the experiment, we use "$unif$" to denote the traditional method of replacing the head entity or tail entity with equal probability, and "$bern$" to denote the method of adopting the Bernoulli sampling strategy, i.e. according to different relations types to replace h and t with different probabilities respectively. Under the "$unif$" setting, the optional hyperparameters are: learning rate α =0.0001, margin $\gamma = 4.5$, embedding dimension $k = 100$, batch size $B = 1200$ on WN18; learning rate $\alpha = 0.0001$, margin $\gamma = 1.5$, embedding dimension $k = 100$, batch size $B = 9600$ on FB15K. Under the "$bern$" setting, the optional hyperparameters are: learning rate α =0.0001, margin $\gamma = 4.5$, embedding dimension $k = 100$, batch size $B = 1200$ on WN18; learning rate $\alpha = 0.0001$, margin $\gamma = 1.5$, embedding dimension

$k = 100$, batch size $B = 1200$ on FB15K. For both datasets, we iterate all the training triplets for 500 epochs.

Experimental Results and Analysis. Link prediction experiments result on FB15K and WN18 are shown in Table 2; results on WN18RR and FB15K-237 with inverse relations removed are shown in Table 3. Table 2 shows that our proposed model, TransPMH, achieves state-of-the-art performance on WN18 and FB15K. From Table 3, we can know that our model has better performance than baselines in general. In addition, we noticed that the $Hit@10$ of CAKE on FB15K-237 is the best. This may be related to the common sense negative sampling mechanism introduced by CAKE, we will also consider applying this method to negative sampling in future work.

Performance of Complex Relation Types. In order to verify the ability of TransPMH for complex relations, we also perform complex relation experiment on FB15K. As seen from Table 4, compared with the baseline models, TransPMH achieves state-of-the-art performance on 1-1, 1-n, and n-1. Among them, the $Hit@10$ value of 1-n reaches 96.0% on Predicting Left and the $Hit@10$ value of n-1 reaches 94.9% on Predicting Right. Additionally, we find that our model does not perform as well as ERDERP in predicting n-n relations, which may be due to the fact that it considers the embedding of relations separately, so the model is more suitable for n-n relations. In future work, we plan to improve relation embeddings.

Table 4. Hit@10 of each type of relations on FB15K

Method	Predicting Left(Hits@10)				Predicting Right(Hits@10)			
	1-1	1-n	n-1	n-n	1-1	1-n	n-1	n-n
SE [20]	35.6	62.6	17.2	37.5	34.9	14.6	68.3	41.3
SME [21]	35.1	53.7	19.0	40.3	32.7	14.9	61.6	43.3
TransE [8]	43.7	65.7	18.2	47.2	43.7	19.7	66.7	50.0
TransM [23]	76.8	86.3	23.1	52.3	76.3	29.0	85.9	56.7
TransH [10]	66.8	87.6	28.7	28.7	65.5	39.8	83.3	67.2
TransR [11]	78.8	89.2	34.1	69.2	79.2	37.4	90.4	72.1
TransRD [29]	79.9	92.7	33.9	66.7	79.3	37.2	92.7	71.1
STransH [24]	76.7	88.2	35.8	68.1	73.6	42.4	85.2	70.6
ERDERP [27]	78.1	86.3	49.5	**70.3**	79.1	51.7	85.6	**73.7**
TransP [28]	85.9	92.7	53.5	46.2	87.4	45.1	94.7	51.1
TransPMH (unif)	88.2	94.8	**58.3**	69.8	87.1	**60.2**	93.8	72.2
TransPMH (bern)	**92.1**	**96.0**	51.9	69.3	**91.8**	51.8	**94.9**	72.5

4.3 Triplet Classification

Evaluation Metrics. The triplet classification task is to judge whether a given triplet(h, r, t) is correct or not. It mainly uses $accuracy(ACC)$ as the evaluation metric. The higher the ACC represents the better performance of the model on the triplet classification task. The calculation formula of the ACC is as follows:

$$ACC = \frac{T_p + T_n}{N_{pos} + N_{neg}} \tag{12}$$

In Eq.(12), T_p is the number of correctly predicted positive triplets; T_n is the number of correctly predicted negative triplets; N_{pos} and N_{neg} denote the number of positive triplets and negative triplets in the training set, respectively.

Implementation. We perform triplets classification experiment on WN11, FB13 and FB15K. The optional hyperparameters are: learning rate $\alpha = 0.1$, margin $\gamma = 4.5$, embedding dimension $k = 20$, batch size $B = 4800$, and L_1 as dissimilarity on WN11; learning rate $\alpha = 0.001$, margin $\gamma = 5$, embedding dimension $k = 50$, batch size $B = 4800$, and L_1 as the dissimilarity on FB13; learning rate $\alpha = 0.0001$, margin $\gamma = 2$, embedding dimension $k = 100$, batch size $B = 4800$, and L_1 as the dissimilarity on FB15K.

Experimental Results and Analysis. Table 5 shows the experimental result for triplet classification. It shows that the triplet classification result of TransPMH on WN11, FB13, and FB15k reached 90.7%, 90.1%, and 93.2%, respectively, which achieves state-of-the-art performance compared to baseline models. The result of triplet classification experiment shows that our model can easily extract new information from existing knowledge graphs, which demonstrates the effectiveness of our proposed model.

Table 5. Triplet classification accuracy of different models

Method	WN11	FB13	FB15K
SE [20]	53.0	75.2	72.2
SME [21]	70.0	63.7	71.6
TransE [8]	75.8	81.5	79.7
TransM [23]	77.8	72.1	89.9
TransH [10]	78.8	83.3	87.7
TransR [11]	85.9	82.5	83.9
STransH [24]	79.6	85.2	89.6
OPTransE [25]	82.3	87.2	90.5
RPJE [26]	84.7	-	91.3
ERDERP [27]	-	-	91.2
TransP [28]	89.8	87.0	93.1
TransPMH(unif)	88.2	88.7	91.3
TransPMH(bern)	**90.7**	**90.1**	**93.2**

4.4   Auxiliary Experiment

Influence of Adjacent Nodes' Numbers. In order to choose the optimal adjacent nodes' numbers between relation paths, we perform the experiment for the influence of adjacent nodes' numbers on ACC on FB15K. The specific result is shown in Fig. 3. It can be seen from Fig. 3 that when adjacent nodes' numbers are in the range of [0,5], the value of ACC increases gradually with the increase of the nodes' numbers; when adjacent nodes' numbers are in the range of [5,8], the value of ACC decreases gradually with the increase of the nodes' numbers. Experimental result shows that adjacent nodes' number between relation paths has an impact on ACC, and the value of ACC is the best when the number of adjacent nodes is 5. Therefore, in this paper, we choose relation paths with 5 adjacent nodes.

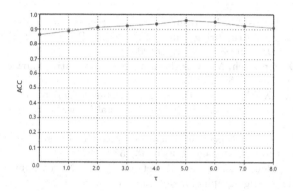

Fig. 3. Influence of adjacent nodes' numbers on ACC

5   Conclusion

In this paper, we proposed TransPMH, a hyperplane knowledge embedding model with path neighborhoods and mapping properties. This model mainly aims at knowledge graph completion, and solves the problem that the existing models can't simultaneously deal with complex relations and integrate multi-source information. Specifically, drawing on ideas from TransH, the proposed method first projects entities to a relation-specific hyperplane. Besides, we introduce relational mapping properties to improve the model's ability to handle complex relations. Finally, to enhance the model's knowledge representation learning ability, we consider multi-source information, i.e., relation path neighborhoods to learn representations of triplet facts. We perform extensive experiments on benchmark datasets for link prediction and triplets classification tasks. The results show that the proposed method outperforms most of the baselines and can be applied to the completion and reasoning of large-scale KGs.

Acknowledgements. The work is supported partly by National Natural Science Foundation of China (No. 62166003), the Project of Guangxi Science and Technology (GuiKeAB23026040), the Project of Guangxi Science and Technology

(GuiKeAD20159041, 2022AB07002), Key Lab of Education Blockchain and Intelligent Technology, Ministry of Education, Guangxi Normal University, Guilin, 541004, China, Intelligent Processing and the Research Fund of Guangxi Key Lab of Multi-source Information Mining & Security (No. 20-A-01-01, MIMS21-M-01, MIMS20-M-01), the Guangxi Collaborative Innovation Center of Multi-Source Information Integration and the Guangxi "Bagui" Teams for Innovation and Research, China.

References

1. Miller, G.A.: WordNet: a lexical database for English. Commun. ACM **38**(11), 39–41 (1995)
2. Bollacker, K., Evans, C., Paritosh, P., et al.: Freebase: a collaboratively created graph database for structuring human knowledge. Proceed. ACM SIGMOD Int. Conf. Manage. Data **2008**, 1247–1250 (2008)
3. Vrandečić, D., Krötzsch, M.: Wikidata: a free collaborative knowledgebase. Commun. ACM **57**(10), 78–85 (2014)
4. Huang, F., Li, X., Yuan, C., et al.: Attention-emotion-enhanced convolutional LSTM for sentiment analysis. IEEE Trans. Neural Netw. Learn. Syst. **33**(9), 4332–4345 (2021)
5. Lu, G., Li, J., Wei, J.: Aspect sentiment analysis with heterogeneous graph neural networks. Inf. Process. Manage. **59**(4), 102953 (2022)
6. Yasunaga, M., Ren, H., Bosselut, A., et al.: QA-GNN: reasoning with language models and knowledge graphs for question answering. Proceed. Conf. North Am. Chapt. Assoc. Comput. Linguist. Human Lang. Technol. **2021**, 535–546 (2021)
7. Li, J., Lu, G., Wu, Z., et al.: Multi-view representation model based on graph autoencoder. Inf. Sci. **632**, 439–453 (2023)
8. Bordes, A., Usunier, N., Garcia-Duran, A., et al.: Translating embeddings for modeling multi-relational data. In: Advances in Neural Information Processing Systems 26 (2013)
9. Li, Y., Fan, W., Liu, C., et al.: TransHER: translating knowledge graph embedding with hyper-ellipsoidal restriction. arXiv preprint arXiv:2204.13221 (2022)
10. Wang, Z., Zhang, J., Feng, J., et al.: Knowledge graph embedding by translating on hyperplanes. In: Proceedings of the AAAI Conference on Artificial Intelligence, vol. 28, no. 1 (2014)
11. Lin, Y., Liu, Z., Sun, M., et al.: Learning entity and relation embeddings for knowledge graph completion. In: Proceedings of the AAAI Conference on Artificial Intelligence, vol. 29, no. 1 (2015)
12. Ji, G., He, S., Xu, L., et al.: Knowledge graph embedding via dynamic mapping matrix. In: Proceedings of the 53rd Annual Meeting of the Association for Computational Linguistics and the 7th International Joint Conference on Natural Language Processing (volume 1: Long papers), pp. 687–696 (2015)
13. Xie, R., Liu, Z., Jia, J., et al.: Representation learning of knowledge graphs with entity descriptions. In: Proceedings of the AAAI Conference on Artificial Intelligence, vol. 30, no. 1 (2016)
14. Xie, R., Liu, Z., Sun, M.: Representation learning of knowledge graphs with hierarchical types. In: IJCAI, vol. 2016, pp. 2965–2971 (2016)
15. Xie, R., Liu, Z., Luan, H., et al.: Image-embodied knowledge representation learning. In: Proceedings of the 26th International Joint Conference on Artificial Intelligence, vol. 2017, pp. 3140–3146 (2017)

16. Lin, Y., Liu, Z., Luan, H., et al.: Modeling relation paths for representation learning of knowledge bases. Proceed. Conf. Emp. Meth. Nat. Lang. Process. **2015**, 705–714 (2015)

17. Yang, B., Yih, S.W., He, X., et al.: Embedding entities and relations for learning and inference in knowledge bases. In: Proceedings of the International Conference on Learning Representations (ICLR) 2015 (2015)

18. Trouillon, T., Welbl, J., Riedel, S., et al.: Complex embeddings for simple link prediction. In: International Conference on Machine Learning. PMLR, vol. 2016, pp. 2071–2080 (2016)

19. Dettmers, T., Minervini, P., Stenetorp, P., et al.: Convolutional 2D knowledge graph embeddings. In: Proceedings of the AAAI Conference on Artificial Intelligence, vol. 32, no. 1 (2018)

20. Niu, G., Li, B., Zhang, Y., et al.: CAKE: a scalable commonsense-aware framework for multi-view knowledge graph completion. In: Proceedings of the 60th Annual Meeting of the Association for Computational Linguistics (Volume 1: Long Papers), pp. 2867–2877 (2022)

21. Bordes, A., Weston, J., Collobert, R., et al.: Learning structured embeddings of knowledge bases. Proceed. AAAI Conf. Artif. Intell. **25**(1), 301–306 (2011)

22. Bordes, A., Glorot, X., Weston, J., et al.: A semantic matching energy function for learning with multi-relational data: application to word-sense disambiguation. Mach. Learn. **94**, 233–259 (2014)

23. Fan, M., Zhou, Q., Chang, E., et al.: Transition-based knowledge graph embedding with relational mapping properties. In: Proceedings of the 28th Pacific Asia Conference on Language, Information and Computing, pp. 328–337 (2014)

24. Xiaojun, C., Yang, X.: STransH: a revised translation-based model for knowledge representation. Comput. Sci. **46**(09), 184–189 (2019)

25. Zhu, Y., Liu, H., Wu, Z., et al.: Representation learning with ordered relation paths for knowledge graph completion. In: Proceedings of the 2019 Conference on Empirical Methods in Natural Language Processing and the 9th International Joint Conference on Natural Language Processing (EMNLP-IJCNLP), pp. 2662–2671 (2019)

26. Niu, G., Zhang, Y., Li, B., et al.: Rule-guided compositional representation learning on knowledge graphs. Proceed. AAAI Conf. Artif. Intell. **34**(03), 2950–2958 (2020)

27. Lin, L., Liu, J., Guo, F., et al.: ERDERP: entity and relation double embedding on relation hyperplanes and relation projection hyperplanes. Mathematics **10**(22), 4182 (2022)

28. Ma, Y., Altenbek, G., Wu, X.: Knowledge graph embedding via entity and relationship attributes. Multimed. Tools Appl. 1–16 (2023). https://doi.org/10.1007/s11042-023-15070-0

29. Yanli, Z., Xiaoping, Y., Liang, W., et al.: TransRD: a knowledge graph embedding representation model with asymmetric features. Chin. J. Inf. **33**(11), 73–82 (2019)

RTAD-TP: Real-Time Anomaly Detection Algorithm for Univariate Time Series Data Based on Two-Parameter Estimation

Qiyun Fan, Yan Tang$^{(\boxtimes)}$, Xiaoming Ding, Qianglong Huangfu, and Peihao Ding

School of Computer and Information Science, Southwest University, Chongqing, China
tangyan1800@163.com, {xmding,soyoung,dph365475889}@email.swu.edu.cn

Abstract. The anomaly detection of univariate time series data is becoming increasingly important, as early detection of anomalies is valuable in practical applications. However, due to the continuous influx of data streams and the dynamic changes in data patterns, real-time anomaly detection still poses challenges. Algorithms such as SPOT, DSPOT, and FluxEV are efficient unsupervised anomaly detection algorithms for data streams, but their detection performance still needs to be improved when processing large-scale data streams. To address this, we propose the Real-Time Anomaly Detection Algorithm for Univariate Time Series Data Based on Two-Parameter Estimation (RTAD-TP), a fast and effective unsupervised real-time anomaly detection algorithm. We calculate the residual between the current value and the predicted value using Exponential Moving Average (EMA), and apply extreme value distribution to determine the threshold for the residual. In addition, we use two-parameter estimation to improve the speed and accuracy of parameter estimation in automatic thresholding, addressing the limitations of SPOT, DSPOT, and FluxEV. Experimental results show that the RTAD-TP algorithm has better detection performance than the baseline algorithm.

Keywords: Univariate time series data · real-time anomaly detection · unsupervised learning

1 Introduction

Single variable time series data refers to a series of data points of a single variable recorded over a specific period of time [10], which is a very common data type in practical applications. In monitoring important systems and processes, such as industrial equipment [5], transportation [4], and energy consumption [6], detecting anomalies in single variable time series data is particularly critical. Timely detection of anomalies and taking appropriate measures can prevent or mitigate the potential impact of problems. In practical applications such as IoT

Z. Jin et al. (Eds.): KSEM 2023, LNAI 14117, pp. 92–101, 2023.
https://doi.org/10.1007/978-3-031-40283-8_9

systems, stationary mode and periodic mode univariate time series data are common data types. Despite the simplicity of the data patterns, there are still two major challenges in detecting anomalies in such data: large data volumes and rapid response. In recent years, various algorithms have been proposed, but their performance in large data volume and rapidly responsive systems is limited, and there are issues such as the need for a large number of labels, retraining, and low detection efficiency. Therefore, designing an adaptive, unsupervised, and efficient anomaly detection algorithm is very challenging.

In existing methods, SPOT [11], DSPOT [11], and FluxEV [6] algorithms based on extreme value theory do not require training and only need a small amount of data for initialization. They use incremental learning to automatically update thresholds and can detect extreme outliers in real-time from single-variable time series data. Inspired by them, we found that if we use a more efficient method to smooth the data and extract residual values, we can effectively address the influence of data fluctuations. At the same time, we also found that if we can replace maximum likelihood estimation (MLE) [7,13] and method of moments (MOM) [7,13] with faster and more accurate parameter estimation methods, we can solve the complexity and inaccuracy of automatic threshold parameter estimation. To address these issues, we propose RTAD-TP, which uses an exponentially weighted moving average (EMA) method that focuses more on recent data points to remove periodic changes in the data while retaining the trend of the data stream and extracting residuals. We introduce a faster and more accurate probability weighted moment (PWM) method [7,13] for parameter estimation and use MOM to further refine parameter values. By using a two-parameter estimation approach, we can accelerate parameter estimation while ensuring accuracy.

Our contributions in this work can be summarized as follows:

- We propose a very fast and efficient real-time anomaly detection method for single-variable time series data. It is an unsupervised learning anomaly detection approach that can quickly detect extreme value anomalies in stationary and periodic patterns.
- We start with the contextuality of time-series data, using EMA to perform weighted averaging on historical data, so that the EMA prediction value contains the recent data trend. Then we extract the residual values and apply extreme value distribution analysis to quickly identify anomalies.
- With the assistance of the two-parameter estimation method and the EMA method, the RTAD-TP algorithm achieves a 5-20 times improvement in detection efficiency compared to the baseline algorithm.

2   Related Work

Real-time anomaly detection algorithms for univariate time series data can be classified into three categories: machine learning-based methods, neural network-based methods, and statistical methods [2,3]. Research findings [3] show that in the field of single variable time series data anomaly detection, the comprehensive performance of machine learning and neural network-based methods is inferior to statistical methods. In the field of statistical methods, some new methods have been proposed in recent years, among which the SPOT [11] algorithm that uses extreme value theory for detecting anomalies in data streams for the first time has performed well on unlabeled data streams. The SPOT algorithm is a streaming version of the second theorem of extreme value theory Peaks-Over-Threshold (POT). According to the extreme value theory , the tail distribution is fitted using the Generalized Pareto Distribution (GPD):

$$\overline{F}_t(x) = \mathbb{P}(X - t > x | X > t) \underset{t \to \tau}{\sim} (1 + \frac{\gamma x}{\sigma(t)})^{-\frac{1}{\gamma}} \tag{1}$$

The POT method fits the excesses over a threshold t $(X_i > t)$ of a peak with a generalized Pareto distribution (GPD) having α and γ parameters. After estimating the parameters, the threshold can be calculated using the following formula:

$$z_q \simeq t + \frac{\widehat{\sigma}}{\widehat{\gamma}} \left(\left(\frac{qn}{N_t} \right)^{-\widehat{\gamma}} - 1 \right) \tag{2}$$

3   Methodology

Figure 1 illustrates the overall framework of the proposed RTAD-TP algorithm, which consists of five parts: the initial sequence modeling module, the GPD parameter estimation module, the threshold updating module, the anomaly detection module, and the data smoothing module.

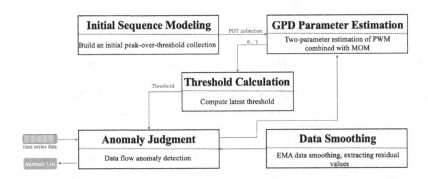

Fig. 1. Framework of the RTAD-TP algorithm.

3.1   Initial Sequence Modeling Module

As shown in Fig. 2, to construct the initial POT set and the initial threshold t, the initial sequence is first read, and a sliding window is moved to calculate the mean of the window, generating a sequence of window means M. Next, the difference between the sample value X_i and the nearest window M_{i-1} is calculated. After traversal, a sequence S of differences between sample values and window means is obtained. Then, the S sequence is sorted, and the initial threshold t is determined based on the empirical percentile 98

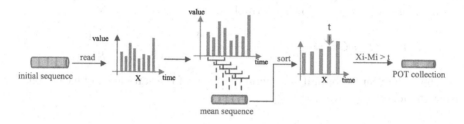

Fig. 2. The process of the initial sequence modeling.

3.2   GPD Parameter Estimation Module

The estimation values of σ and γ parameters are crucial for calculating the final threshold. MLE is a high-precision parameter estimation method, but it involves complex calculations. The MOM estimates parameters based on sample moments, but its estimated parameter values have lower accuracy. PWM is an extension of the method of moments that uses probability-weighted sample moments to estimate the parameter values of the distribution. It has better accuracy properties than MOM and is easier to compute than MLE. We adopt a two-parameter estimation method, which involves first estimating parameter values using the PWM method, and then using the extremely fast computational speed of MOM to further correct the PWM parameter estimates, thereby improving accuracy and detection rate.

The principle of MOM is to replace the population moments with sample moments. For GPD, the variance can be expressed as $E(Y) = \frac{\sigma}{1-\gamma}$ [13], The mean can be expressed as $var(Y) = \frac{\sigma^2}{(1-\gamma)^2(1-2\gamma)}$ [13]. For sample data, the variance is calculated by the formula s $S^2 = \sum_{i=1}^{N_t} \frac{(Y_i-\mu)^2}{N_t-1}$, The mean is calculated by the formula $\mu = \sum_{i=1}^{N_t} \frac{Y_i}{N_t}$, Where Nt is the length of the POT set, Y_i is the element of the POT set $(Xi - t \mid Xi > t)$, and the parameter estimation values can be calculated using the following formula [13]:

$$\hat{\sigma} = \frac{\mu}{2}\left(1 + \frac{\mu^2}{s^2}\right) \tag{3}$$

$$\hat{\gamma} = \frac{1}{2}\left(1 - \frac{\mu^2}{S^2}\right) \tag{4}$$

The PWM formula is as follows [7,13]:

$$w_k(\theta) = E[YF^k(Y;\theta)] \tag{5}$$

where w_k is the k-th order probability-weighted moment, θ is the parameter of GPD, E is the expectation value, and by substituting the GPD distribution function into formula (5), the k-th order probability-weighted moment of GPD can be expressed as the following formula [7,13]:

$$w_k = E(YG^k) = \frac{\sigma}{\gamma} \times [\frac{r!}{(k+1-\gamma)(k-\gamma)...(1-\gamma)} - \frac{1}{k+1}] \tag{6}$$

The k-th order probability-weighted moment of the sample can be calculated using the following formula [7,13]:

$$W_k = \frac{1}{N_t} \sum_{i=1}^{N_t} \frac{(i-1)(i-2)...(i-k)}{(N_t-1)(N_t-2)...(N_t-k)} Y_{(i)} \tag{7}$$

where Y_i represents the i-th data after sorting the sample data, by combining formula (6) and formula (7) to solve the equations, w_0 and w_1 can be expressed using the following formula [7,13].:

$$w_0 = \frac{1}{N_t} \sum_{i=1}^{N_t} \frac{i}{N_t} Y_{(i)} = \frac{1}{N_t^2} \sum_{i=1}^{N_t} Y_{(i)} i \tag{8}$$

$$w_1 = \frac{1}{N_t} \sum_{i=1}^{N_t} \frac{i-1}{N_t-1} Y_{(i)} = \frac{N_t}{N_t-1} w_0 - \frac{1}{N_t(N_t-1)} E(Y) \tag{9}$$

By replacing population moments with sample moments, the estimated parameter values can be expressed using the following formula [7,13]:

$$\begin{matrix} w_0 = \frac{\sigma}{1-\gamma} \\ w_1 = \sigma \frac{3-\gamma}{2(1-\gamma)(2-\gamma)} \end{matrix} \rightarrow \begin{matrix} \widehat{\sigma} = \frac{2w_0(w_1-w_0)}{w_0-2w_1} \\ \widehat{\gamma} = 2 + \frac{w_0}{w_0-2w_1} \end{matrix} \tag{10}$$

Finally, the average of the σ and γ estimates from both the PWM and MOM methods are computed, and the final parameter estimate is represented using the following formula:

$$\widehat{\sigma} = \frac{1}{2}(\widehat{\sigma}_{MOM} + \widehat{\sigma}_{PWM}) \tag{11}$$

$$\widehat{\gamma} = \frac{1}{2}(\widehat{\gamma}_{MOM} + \widehat{\gamma}_{PWM}) \tag{12}$$

3.3   Threshold Calculation Module

The threshold calculation module serves as the center for dynamically updating the threshold, which calculates the threshold according to Eq. 2. Here, t is the initial threshold used to retrieve peaks based on empirical quantiles, $\widehat{\sigma}$ and $\widehat{\gamma}$ are the parameter values calculated by calling the GPD parameter estimation module, q is an empirical risk parameter used to determine anomalies (recommended initial values are in the range of 1e–3 to 1e–5 based on data patterns [11]), n is the length of the current observed time series, and N_t is the number of values in the peak set that exceed the threshold ($X_i > t$). The latest obtained threshold is used by the anomaly detection module for anomaly detection.

3.4 Anomaly Detection Module

When a new data point X_i arrives, simply comparing it with a certain threshold and regarding X_i exceeding the threshold as abnormal data is too simplistic and cannot achieve satisfactory detection performance. Therefore, the anomaly detection module automatically sets the threshold using the extreme value distribution model provided by SPOT. Specifically, the module first calculates the latest EMA value using the data smoothing module, and then calculates the residual value X_i' of X_i in the local sequence trend. Next, the extreme value distribution model is used to determine whether X_i' is abnormal data. The criterion for anomaly detection is the latest threshold z_q calculated based on the extreme distribution of residual values since the last anomaly detection. For data between the threshold z_q and the initial threshold t, they are added to the POT set and trigger threshold updating. After the threshold updating is completed, the module continues to perform anomaly detection on the next data point.

3.5 Data Smoothing Module

The data smoothing operation is intended to preserve the normal trend of the time-series data stream and overcome the impact of data fluctuations. EMA is a weighted average of observed values over a period of time, with exponentially decreasing weights. Compared to a simple moving average, the more recent observations have greater weights. Anomalies in time-series data are strongly correlated with the local context, and data points closer to the current point have a greater influence. Therefore, RTAD-TP uses EMA for data smoothing, and the formula for calculating EMA is:

$$EMA_t = \alpha \times y_t + (1 - \alpha) \times EMA_{t-1} \tag{13}$$

where y_t is the observation value at time t, EMA_{t-1} is the previous EMA value, and α is the smoothing factor, which represents the weight of the current observation value in the weighted average, with a range of 0 to 1. To improve the speed of the algorithm, the EMA is calculated recursively to avoid reweighting all historical data each time. Specifically, the first EMA value is equal to the first observed value, and then each subsequent EMA value is calculated by taking the weighted average of the current observation value and the previous EMA value, providing a fast EMA value calculation for the anomaly detection module to calculate the residual value.

4   Experiments

4.1   Datasets

Experimental evaluation on two popular public datasets.

- Yahoo S5-A1A2 dataset [8]: Real traffic data from Yahoo's production environ-ment, containing 167 univariate time series with manually labeled anoma-lies, averaging 1420 timestamps per time series.
- Twitter-volume-AAPL dataset [1]: Consisting of the number of tweets about Apple Inc. on Twitter, with approximately 16000 timestamps and labeled anomalies.

4.2   Metrics

We use popular metrics such as precision, recall, F1-score, and the number of data processed per unit time to evaluate the detection performance of RTAD-TP.

4.3   Baselines

We compare RTAD-TP with the following baseline algorithms, including machine learning-based method SR [9], neural network-based method DONUT [12], and statistical methods such as SPOT [11], DSPOT [11], and FluxEV [8].

- SPOT [11]: A univariate time series anomaly detection algorithm based on extreme value theory, which performs well on unlabeled datasets.
- DSPOT [11]: An algorithm that introduces a moving average window method to solve the problem of SPOT algorithm being affected by data stream fluc-tuations.
- FluxEV [8]: An algorithm that uses two-step smoothing operations to enlarge the difference between anomalous and normal values, and uses moment esti-mation to improve the efficiency of the SPOT algorithm.
- SR [9]: An industrial anomaly detection service proposed by Microsoft, which is a time series anomaly detection algorithm based on spectrum reconstruc-tion.
- DONUT [12]: An unsupervised anomaly detection algorithm based on vari-ational auto-encoder (VAE), which has excellent performance in terms of accuracy.

4.4   Experiment 1

The experimental results of the processing speed of RTAD-TP and the baseline algorithms are shown in Fig 3:

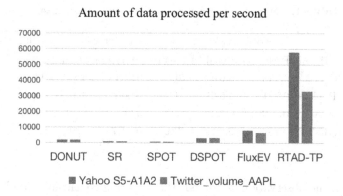

Fig. 3. Experimental results of efficiency comparison test.

The following conclusions can be drawn by observing the experimental results:

- RTAD-TP outperforms the baseline algorithms with an absolute advantage, indicating that the RTAD-TP algorithm, using a double-parameter estimation method combining probability-weighted moment and moment estimation, greatly improves the computational efficiency while ensuring superior anomaly detection accuracy. Additionally, the use of a recursive EMA calculation method avoids the need for reweighting and calculation of all historical data each time, further improving the computational efficiency.
- The FluxEV algorithm replaces the maximum likelihood estimation method with moment estimation, greatly improving the detection efficiency in terms of parameter estimation. This further shows that the limitations that affect the detection efficiency of the SPOT and DSPOT algorithms are related to parameter estimation. The FluxEV algorithm introduces complex data smoothing processing, which brings unnecessary computational overhead in stationary mode and periodic mode data streams, while RTAD-TP uses a fast and efficient EMA for data smoothing, greatly improving computational efficiency.

4.5 Experiment 2

The experimental results of the accuracy of RTAD-TP and the baseline algorithms are shown in Table 1:

Table 1. Detection accuracy comparison experiment results.

	Yahoo S5-A1A2			Twitter-volume-AAPL		
Algorithm	Precision	Recall	F1-score	Precision	Recall	F1-score
SPOT	0.548	0.610	0.514	0.384	**1.000**	0.556
DSPOT	0.521	0.646	0.511	0.500	**1.000**	0.667
FluxEV	**0.763**	0.712	0.737	0.364	0.286	0.500
RTAD-TP	0.757	**0.787**	**0.739**	**0.667**	0.800	**0.727**

Based on the observation of Table 1, the following conclusions can be drawn:

- On the Yahoo S5-A1A2 dataset, RTAD-TP performs equally well as FluxEV in terms of accuracy, indicating that the use of two-parameter estimation in RTAD-TP algorithm can improve its accuracy. Although FluxEV uses a two-step smoothing operation to enlarge the difference between normal and anomalous values, its use of lower-accuracy moment estimation partially offsets the detection accuracy. Comparison with SPOT and DSPOT algorithms further indicates that the two-parameter correction estimation in RTAD-TP algorithm can improve the accuracy of anomaly detection.
- The results of the Twitter-volume-AAPL dataset also demonstrate that RTAD-TP algorithm outperforms other baseline algorithms. FluxEV performs poorly on this dataset because Twitter-volume-AAPL is a stationary dataset with few anomalous points, and the additional two-step smoothing operation in FluxEV may remove some anomalous features, leading to a failure to detect most of the anomalies. SPOT and DSPOT are not adaptive to data fluctuations, resulting in overfitting, which also indicates that RTAD-TP can cope well with the impact of data fluctuations.

5   Conclusion

In this paper, We proposed the RTAD-TP algorithm for real-time anomaly detection in univariate time series data. By modeling the extreme value distribution of the residual values after EMA smoothing, the two-parameter estimation was introduced to ensure the accuracy of anomaly detection and improve detection efficiency. It effectively meets the real-time anomaly detection requirements for stationary mode and periodic mode univariate time series data. For future work, we plan to use a correlation mechanism to automatically determine the algorithm's anomaly risk parameters based on the characteristics of the data stream, instead of manual configuration.

References

1. Ahmad, S., Lavin, A., Purdy, S., Agha, Z.: Unsupervised real-time anomaly detection for streaming data. Neurocomputing **262**, 134–147 (2017)
2. Blázquez-García, A., Conde, A., Mori, U., Lozano, J.A.: A review on outlier/anomaly detection in time series data. ACM Comput. Surv. (CSUR) **54**(3), 1–33 (2021)
3. Braei, M., Wagner, S.: Anomaly detection in univariate time-series: a survey on the state-of-the-art. arXiv preprint arXiv:2004.00433 (2020)
4. Chakraborty, N., et al.: Structural attention-based recurrent variational autoencoder for highway vehicle anomaly detection. arXiv preprint arXiv:2301.03634 (2023)
5. Chatterjee, A., Ahmed, B.S.: IoT anomaly detection methods and applications: a survey. Internet Things **19**, 100568 (2022)
6. Himeur, Y., Ghanem, K., Alsalemi, A., Bensaali, F., Amira, A.: Artificial intelligence based anomaly detection of energy consumption in buildings: a review, current trends and new perspectives. Appl. Energy **287**, 116601 (2021)
7. Hosking, J.R., Wallis, J.R.: Parameter and quantile estimation for the generalized pareto distribution. Technometrics **29**(3), 339–349 (1987)
8. Li, J., Di, S., Shen, Y., Chen, L.: FluxEV: a fast and effective unsupervised framework for time-series anomaly detection. In: Proceedings of the 14th ACM International Conference on Web Search and Data Mining, pp. 824–832 (2021)
9. Ren, H., et al.: Time-series anomaly detection service at Microsoft. In: Proceedings of the 25th ACM SIGKDD International Conference on Knowledge Discovery & Data Mining, pp. 3009–3017 (2019)
10. Seymour, L.: Introduction to time series and forecasting. J. Am. Stat. Assoc. **92**(440), 1647 (1997)
11. Siffer, A., Fouque, P.A., Termier, A., Largouet, C.: Anomaly detection in streams with extreme value theory. In: Proceedings of the 23rd ACM SIGKDD International Conference on Knowledge Discovery and Data Mining, pp. 1067–1075 (2017)
12. Xu, H., et al.: Unsupervised anomaly detection via variational auto-encoder for seasonal KPIs in web applications. In: Proceedings of the 2018 World Wide Web Conference, pp. 187–196 (2018)
13. de Zea Bermudez, P., Kotz, S.: Parameter estimation of the generalized pareto distribution–part I. J. Statist. Plann. Inference **140**(6), 1353–1373 (2010)

Multi-Sampling Item Response Ranking Neural Cognitive Diagnosis with Bilinear Feature Interaction

Jiamei Feng, Mengchi Liu[✉], Tingkun Nie, and Caixia Zhou

School of Computer Science, South China Normal University,
Guangzhou 510631, China
{jiamei,2020022990,zcxcs}@m.scnu.edu.cn, liumengchi@scnu.edu.cn

Abstract. Cognitive diagnosis is a fundamental task in educational data mining that aims to discover students' proficiency in knowledge concepts. Neural cognitive diagnosis combines deep learning with cognitive diagnosis, breaking away from artificially defined interaction functions. However, existing cognitive diagnosis models mostly start from the interaction of students' answers, ignoring the feature interaction between test items and knowledge concepts. Meanwhile, few of the previous models consider the monotonicity of knowledge concept proficiency. To address these issues, we present a novel cognitive diagnosis method, called multi-sampling item response ranking neural cognitive diagnosis with bilinear feature interaction. We first allow the ratio in loss function to adjust the impact between pointwise sampling and pairwise sampling to strengthen the monotonicity. At the same time, we replace element product feature interaction with bilinear feature interaction in the multi-sampling item response ranking neural cognitive diagnosis to enhance interaction in the deep learning process. Specifically, our model is stable and can be easily applied to cognitive diagnosis. We observed improvements over the previous state-of-the-art baselines on real-world datasets.

Keywords: Cognitive diagnosis · Sampling · Feature interaction · Neural network

1 Introduction

During the pandemic, online education [15] is widely used, and the magnitude of educational information continues to increase. Faced with these complex and diverse educational information, students may experience information disorientation. Therefore, educational data mining [4,8] has become particularly important. Cognitive diagnosis is an important component of educational information mining, and it plays an important role in intelligent education area [2,20]. It ensures that test recommendations are interpretable and that students and teachers can intuitively obtain student cognitive diagnosis results. It also provides information about students' proficiency in knowledge concepts.

Z. Jin et al. (Eds.): KSEM 2023, LNAI 14117, pp. 102–114, 2023.
https://doi.org/10.1007/978-3-031-40283-8_10

Cognitive diagnosis model originated in the 1990 s s and evolved from the item response theory (IRT) [10–12,14] to the dichotomous cognitive diagnosis (DINA) [3]. The core innovation of DINA is taking Q-matrix into consideration, which also marks the maturity of cognitive diagnosis. FuzzyCDM [9] is an improved version of DINA that introduces guess parameters to determine whether an item is a guess based on a student's performance on other test items in the same knowledge concept. However, they all have the problem of requiring manual setting of interaction functions. Neural cognitive diagnosis(NCD) [17] combines deep learning neural networks with cognitive diagnosis for the first time, breaking away from artificially defined interaction functions in IRT and DINA models. DeepCDM [5] and ECDM [19] are two deep cognitive diagnosis models based on NCD. However, previous works [5,17,19] mainly focus on the representation learning of trait features. IRR-NCD [16] proposes an Item Response Ranking framework (IRR), aiming to introduce pairwise learning into cognitive diagnosis to well model monotonicity between item responses. However, IRR lacks the interactive expression ability of feature vectors.

In order to process the above problem, we propose a novel cognitive diagnosis method, called multi-sampling item response ranking neural cognitive diagnosis with bilinear feature interaction or RNCD for short. As the naming suggest, this model considers multi-sampling item response ranking to improve monotonicity and bilinear feature interaction to strengthen feature interaction. The main contributions of this work are as follows:

1. A novel multi-sampling item response ranking neural cognitive diagnosis model is proposed, which allows the ratio in loss function to adjust the impact between pointwise sampling and pairwise sampling, and strengthens the monotonicity of proficiency knowledge concepts.
2. Bilinear feature interaction replaces element product feature interaction in multi-sampling item response ranking neural cognitive diagnosis to enhance interactions during the deep learning process. The model realizes the common advantages of deep learning and feature representation.
3. Our model RNCD is comprehensively evaluated on numerical experiments and shows that it consistently outperforms the existing six baselines across all metrics. The cognitive states are continuous, achieving proficiency levels suitable for large sample datasets. Especially, we demonstrate the good monotonicity of RNCD and the automatic training of feature interaction.

2   Preliminaries

The definition of cognitive diagnosis is that the response log R and Q-matrix are given and the goal is to mine students' proficiency on on knowledge concepts. The premise of cognitive diagnosis is monotonicity. According to the monotonicity theory, a student's proficiency is monotonic. Specifically, a student who responds correctly to a test item is assumed to be more skilled than one who responds incorrectly [13,17]. Under massive education data, NCD modeling has been investigated for cognitive diagnosis to achieve good performance. We use $S = \{s_1, s_2, \ldots s_N\}$ to indicate all students, the number of students are N. $E = \{e_1, e_2, \ldots e_M\}$ be the set of all test items (or test questions) in the number of M. $L = \{k_1, k_2, \ldots k_L\}$ be the set of knowledge concepts, and the number is L. The inclusion relationship between test items and concepts is expressed as a matrix $Q = \{q_{ij}\}_{M \times L}$ and labeled by experts, where $q_{ij} \in \{0, 1\}$ indicates whether test item e_i contains concept k_j. A set of triplet (s, e, r) are setted as response log R, where $s \in S$, $e \in E$. Here, r is a real score between 0 and 1. $r_{se} = 0$ indicates the normalized score of a student s wrong answer a test item e, and $r_{se} = 1$ otherwise. The prediction of the normalized predicted score of student s_i answering test item e_j.

2.1   Item Response Ranking (IRR)

Pairwise learning is a method of exploring pairwise relationships and has been studied in many fields, such as natural language processing [6] and computer vision [18]. As the importance of learning has grown in these areas, IRR has also introduced it into the field of cognitive diagnosis. IRR includes pairwise learning and pairwise construction.

$$(r_{ie}) \leftarrow P(y_{ie}) \tag{1}$$

P is the prediction probability of the correct response in cognitive diagnosis, and r is the true response. The overall meaning of pointwise learning Eq. (1) is to minimize the difference between P and r. The objective function of pairwise learning is shown in Eq. (2):

$$(r_{ie} - r_{je}) \leftarrow P(y_{ie} - y_{je}) \tag{2}$$

Traditional pointwise learning cannot optimize the monotonicity between responses, but pairwise learning objective functions can directly optimize the monotonicity in the objective function. The group that has completed the test is called the observation group S^O, while the group that has not completed the test is called the unobserved group S^U. The pairwise construction is shown in Eq. (3):

$$S = S^O(e) + S^U(e); S^O(e) = S^+(e) + S^-(e)$$
$$S^+(e) = \{u \mid u \in S^O(e), r = 1\}; S^-(e) = \{u \mid u \in S^O(e), r = 0\} \tag{3}$$

where S^+ is the positive sampling group, S^- is the negative sampling group, and both of them belong to the observation group S^O.

Unobserved samples should not be directly classified as answer errors, so these samples need to be divided twice. The classification equation is shown in Eq. (4):

$$P(r_{ue}) \geq P(r_{S^-(e)}) \geq 0; P(r_{ue}) \leq P(r_{S^+(e)}) \leq 1 \tag{4}$$

The meaning of Eq. (4) is that the probability that student u correctly answer e is $0 \leq P(r_{S^-(e)}) \leq P(r_{ue}) \leq P(r_{S^+(e)}) \leq 1$, where $S^-(e)$ is the negative set that has been observed, $S^+(e)$ is the positive set that has been observed, and $S^-(e)$ means that e is a sample of the negative set that has been observed.

2.2 Bilinear Feature Interaction

FiBiNET [7] greatly promotes the development of bilinear feature interaction. There are three combinations of bilinear structures. All: all features share a W matrix. Each: each feature field uses a W matrix. Interaction: each feature interaction uses a W matrix. Interaction combination method is selected in this paper. The calculation of output P in Eq. (5)is represented by the symbol $\bullet$.

$$\bullet \leftarrow P_{ij} = v_i \cdot W_{ij} \odot v_j \tag{5}$$

W_{ij} is generated by the interaction of two feature vectors, which needs to be derived from the parameter matrix, v_i and v_j refers to two characteristic fields, with the index i and j ranging from $1 \leq i \leq f$, $1 \leq j \leq f$, f refers to the total number of characteristic fields, and the number of parameter matrices W is N_W. $N_W = \frac{f(f-1)}{2}$. The calculation for the parameter quantity $W_x = k \times k$ required for training a W parameter matrix is obtained through neural network training. k is the length of the embedded vector.

3 Proposed Model

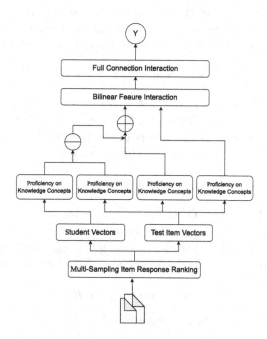

Fig. 1. The Overall Framework of RNCD.

RNCD mainly consists of two parts. The first part is multi-sampling item response ranking (MIRR), which is mainly used to process sampling before entering the cognitive diagnosis to ensure monotonicity. The second part is the improved NCD model, which is responsible for the interaction between feature vectors and obtaining the final cognitive diagnosis results. Next, we will introduce two structural parts. The overall framework is shown in Fig. 1.

3.1   The Design of Farmework

NCD introduces neural networks into the field of cognitive diagnosis, solving the problem of manually setting interaction functions. The framework of the NCD consists of three factors: student factors, test item factors, and the interaction between students and test items.

Student factors refer to the characteristics of students, which affect their scores in answering questions. The goal of NCD and IRR is to explore students' proficiency of knowledge concepts, which is the basis for the integration of the two structures. In order to enhance interpretability and improve students' self-assessment ability, NCD did not use discontinuous potential feature vectors in IRT and MIRT, but instead chose a method similar to DINA, continuous element features. For example, if a student has done multiple test items, and these items examine a total of three knowledge concepts, the student's proficiency of knowledge concepts is represented by a vector, $h^s = [0.8, 0.4, 0.5]$, which means that the student's mastery of the first knowledge concept is 0.8, and the proficiency is good, while the mastery of the second knowledge concept is 0.4, and the proficiency is poor. The h^s can be obtained through model training.

$$h^s = sigmoid\left(x^s \times A\right) \tag{6}$$

Here $h^s \in (0,1)^{1 \times K}$, $x^s \in (0,1)^{1 \times N}$, $A \in R^{N \times K}$. x^s is the student's one-hot code. h^s is obtained by multiplying x^s with a trainable matrix A.

Test item factors refer to the factors of the item itself, mainly reflected in the Q-matrix Q. The treatment of Q is shown in Eq. (7).

$$Q^e = x^e \times Q \tag{7}$$

Q^e is the processed Q matrix, $Q^e \in (0,1)^{1 \times K}$. x^e is the test items's one-hot code, $x^e \in (0,1)^{1 \times M}$. Test item factors also include difficulty of knowledge concepts h_{diff} and discrimination of knowledge concepts h_{disc}. Test items are shown in Eq. (8) and Eq. (9). $B \in R^{M \times K}$ and $D \in R^{M \times 1}$ are trainable parameter matrices.

$$h_{diff} = sigmoid\left(x^e \times B\right) \tag{8}$$

$$h_{disc} = sigmoid\left(x^e \times D\right) \tag{9}$$

The interaction between students and test items is implemented through interaction functions. Interaction functions are divided into two parts, namely, the feature interaction layer and the full connection layer. Compared to the interaction function of NCD, RNCD changes the interaction mode of vectors in the interaction function from an element product to a bilinear feature interaction that better represents the characteristics of vectors themselves. Bilinear feature interaction enables interaction between student factors (h^s) and test item factors (h_{diff}, h_{disc} and Q^e).

$$x = Q_e \bullet (h^s - h_{diff}) \times h_{disc} \qquad (10)$$

x is the vector obtained after bilinear feature interaction($\bullet$) is shown in Eq. (10). $\bullet$ represents the bilinear feature interaction. Refer to Sect. 2.2 for bilinear interaction method. $-$ represents the subtraction between vectors, subtracts elements within vectors, and $\times$ represents the multiplication operation between vectors. To achieve bilinear interaction, we need to add a neural network structure for training. Here, RNCD uses a three-layer fully connected neural network.

3.2   Multi-Sampling Item Response Ranking

A novel model that we extend an IRR method by adding multi-sampling, which is denoted as MIRR. The traditional IRR method only result in pairwise sampling which is a single selection form.

The sampling method is to first divide all samples into positive samples, negative samples, and unobserved samples, and then randomly select samples from the observed samples (positive samples, negative samples). If a positive sample is selected, a negative sample is supplemented, and vice versa. Unobserved samples also require random sampling, with the total number of observed samples being N^O and the total number of unobserved samples being N^U. Together, the two constitute the training sample T(R), as shown in Eq. (11):

$$\text{T(R)} = \begin{cases} \{(s, s^l) \mid S^l \in \Lambda_{N^O} (s^-(e)) \oplus \Lambda_{N^U} (S^U(e))\} & r_{se} = 1 \\ \{(s, s^l) \mid S^l \in \Lambda_{N^O} (s^+(e)) \oplus \Lambda_{N^U} (S^U(e))\} & r_{se} = 0 \end{cases} \qquad (11)$$

where $\Lambda_x (S)$ means randomly selecting up to x elements from the set S form a subset, while $\oplus$ is a set addition. r_{se} is the correct answer to the first sample selected.

The likelihood function of IRR is different from traditional cognitive diagnostic models. The likelihood model of IRR consists of two parts: IRR^+ and IRR^-, IRR^+ representing the likelihood function of positive samples, and IRR^- representing the likelihood function of negative samples. The overall likelihood function in Eq. (12), Eq. (13) and Eq. (14) for IRR is as follows:

$$\ln IRR = \ln IRR^+ + \ln IRR^- \qquad (12)$$

$$\ln IRR^+ = \prod_{e \in E} \prod_{i \in S^+(e)} \prod_{j \in S - S^+(e)} P(r_{ie} \geq r_{je}) \times (1 - P(r_{je} \geq r_{ie})) \qquad (13)$$

$$\ln IRR^- = \prod_{e \in E} \prod_{i \in S^-(e)} \prod_{j \in S - S^-(e)} P(r_{ie} \leq r_{je}) \times (1 - P(r_{je} \leq r_{ie})) \qquad (14)$$

The pairwise training loss function is $\text{LOSS}_{\text{pair}}$

$$\text{LOSS}_{\text{pair}} = - \sum_{(i,j) \in T(R)} \log \frac{\exp\left(P\left(r_{ie} \mid \theta\right)\right)}{\exp\left(P\left(r_{ie} \mid \theta\right)\right) + \exp\left(P\left(r_{je} \mid \theta\right)\right)} + \lambda(\theta) \quad (15)$$

The pointwise training loss function is $\text{LOSS}_{\text{point}}$

$$\text{LOSS}_{\text{point}} = - \sum_i \left(r_i \log y_i + (1 - r_i) \log\left(1 - y_i\right)\right) \quad (16)$$

Due to the extensive use of unobserved data by IRR, but without distinguishing between student identities, and the randomness of the sampling method may lead to poor results. Taking university learning as an example, assuming that the number of samples and the type of students are increased, it may become meaningless to predict the performance of students in different learning directions on test items. For example, a sample of liberal arts students and science and engineering students was selected for pairwise learning, so in order to optimize for this possible situation, we set a hyperparameter *ratio* to adjust the proportion of pointwise training and pairwise training. Finally, we use multi-sampling' $\text{LOSS}_{\text{final}}$ to update the neural network.

$$\text{LOSS}_{\text{final}} = \text{mean}\left((1 - \text{ratio}) * \text{LOSS}_{\text{point}} + \text{ratio} * \text{LOSS}_{\text{pair}}\right) \quad (17)$$

4   Experiments

4.1   Experiment Platform and Datasets

The experimental environment uses the 64-bit operating system of the flagship version of Windows 10. The CPU is AMD Raptor 7, the graphics card is NVIDIA RTX1650TI, the programming language is python 3.6, the deep learning language is pytorchCUDA10.2, and the tensorflow 1.14-gpu version of the tensorflow package is used. The main software used in the experiment is pycharm.

We conducted our empirical evaluations on two real world social media and publicly available datasets: ASSISTments[1] and MATH[2]. Both of which are open datasets provided by iFLYTEK. For these two datasets, we first filtered out students with ASSISTments and MATH response logs smaller than 15 and 30, respectively. That is, students with fewer answer records are filtered to ensure that the remaining students have sufficient data to support cognitive diagnosis. For the division of data sets, both data sets are divided using a training set and testing set ratio of $8 : 2$. The statistics of datasets after the preprocessing steps are depicted in Table 1.

---

[1] https://sites.google.com/site/ assistmentsdata/home/assistment-2009–2010data.
[2] https://edudata.readthedocs.io/en/latest/build/blitz/math2015.

Table 1. Statistics of all datasets.

Dataset	ASSISTments	MATH
Number of students	4,163	10,268
Number of test items	17,746	917,495
Number of knowledge concepts	123	1,488
Number of response logs	324,572	864,722

4.2 Evaluation Indicators and Baselines

Three standard metrics are utilized for evaluating the quality of cognitive diagnosis, including AUE, Accuracy and F1.

AUE is the surface level, which randomly selects a positive sample and a negative sample from the positive and negative sample sets. The predictive value of the positive sample is greater than the probability of the negative sample. The value range of AUE is [0,1].

Accuracy is the accuracy rate. In the confusion matrix, TP is the positive and actual positive case of model prediction, and TN is the actual positive case of prediction negative case. Accuracy is defined as:

$$\text{Accuracy} = \frac{TP + TN}{total} \tag{18}$$

Precision and Recall in Eq. (19) can also be used as evaluation indicators, while F1 in Eq. (20) focuses on both factors and is more comprehensive.

$$\text{Precision} = \frac{TP}{TP + FP}; \ \text{Recall} = \frac{TP}{TP + FN} \tag{19}$$

$$F1 = \frac{2 * \text{Precision} * \text{Recall}}{\text{Precision} + \text{Recall}} \tag{20}$$

We compare the results with the standard state-of-the-art models that have been introduced in the Sect. 1 as baselines: IRT [12], MIRT [1], DINA [3], Fuzzy-CDM [9], NCD [17], IRR-NCD [16]

4.3 Experimental Results and Analysis

In order to ensure the authenticity of the results during the experiment, each model uses the parameters recommended in its original text, such as the value of the constant D in IRT, which is 1.702. For example, the common structure used is that the neural network layer number of IRT and NCD are set to 3 layers, with the number of nodes per layer being (512, 256, 1), and the batchsize being uniformly set to 256.

Table 2. RNCD compare with six kinds of models on two datasets. Bold indictes the overall best.

Datasets	ASSISTments			MATH		
	AUC	Accuracy	F1	AUC	Accuracy	F1
RNCD	**0.752443**	**0.727827**	**0.806025**	**0.865704**	**0.774100**	**0.757903**
IRR-NCD	0.749447	0.721003	0.797927	0.861245	0.773321	0.757514
NCD	0.748809	0.721718	0.795541	0.858742	0.771041	0.755132
FuzzyCDM	0.729862	0.705470	0.782520	0.831404	0.750734	0.747655
MIRT	0.698982	0.679872	0.749667	0.830429	0.751288	0.745278
DINA	0.718423	0.683786	0.760365	0.824463	0.746687	0.742479
IRT	0.742494	0.712255	0.794281	0.799718	0.730697	0.733847

Overall Performance of RNCD. For competing models in the comparison, we have used metrics reported in prior results. The results in Table 2 clearly show that the performance of RNCD on each dataset surpasses other baselines.

The experimental results on the ASSISTments show that RNCD performs better than other models, with the second-best model, IRR-NCD, improving by 0.4%, 1%, and 1.1% respectively. Compared to the poorly performing MIRT, RNCD improves by 7.7%, 6.9%, and 7.6% respectively. The experimental results of various models show that models with machine learning or deep learning perform better than models that do not use both. For example, IRT uses a machine learning algorithm. Compared to DINA that is not used, IRT is 3.3% higher in AUC than DINA. MIRT performs poorly in all models, and we analyze the reason is that there are fewer sample features, and the extended features of MIRT are not fully utilized. On the MATH dataset, RNCD also performed better than other models, increasing second best IRR-NCD by 0.04%, 0.01%, and 0.001% respectively. Compared to the poorly performing IRT, RNCD increased by 8.3%, 6.0%, and 3.2% on the three evaluation indicators. It can be noted that RNCD still performs better than other models on a larger dataset.

Diagnostic Results Analysis. The content in Table 3 is a prior knowledge of student cognitive diagnosis, which includes the answers of three students during their actual problem-solving process. It can be seen that student A has achieved good results on test items: Test 1, Test 2, and Test 3. While student B only answered Test 3 correctly. And student C only answered Test 2 incorrectly. With the support of this prior knowledge and other data, the accuracy rate of the three students' answers predicted by the model is shown in Fig. 2.

We set the threshold for the prediction value at 0.5, the student can be judged to be able to answer correctly. Based on this criterion, it can be seen that the model's prediction is consistent with the actual situation. For student A, both prediction values are greater than 0.9, and the other prediction value is 0.75, so it can be judged that the student is excellent and can achieve good results on all

Table 3. Response logs (student-knowledge concepts).

ID	Knowledge Concepts	Student A	Student B	Student C
Test 1	addition, subtraction, division	√	×	√
Test 2	addition, subtraction, multiplication, power	√	×	×
Test 3	power	√	√	√

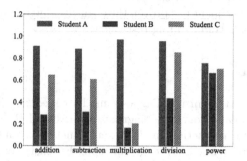

Fig. 2. Student-Item prediction results

three test items. Student B's predicted value on Test 1 and Test 2 is lower than 0.5, so it is judged that he cannot correctly answer Test 1 and Test 2, while the predicted value on Test 3 is greater than 0.5, so it is judged that the student can correctly answer Test 3. Student C's judgment is similar to Student A and Student B.

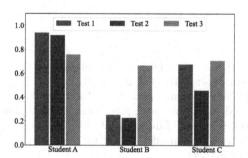

Fig. 3. Students' proficiency on knowledge concepts

Figure 3 shows the proficiency of knowledge concepts, which is the goal of a cognitive diagnostic and the most important predictive data for the model. Student A has a high level of proficiency of each knowledge concept and overall performance is excellent, but with a low proficiency of the power operation. Therefore, it is possible to recommend this knowledge concept to student A. Student B has a low proficiency of each knowledge concept, so it is reasonable to recommend the more basic test items in each knowledge concept to student B, that is, recommend the test items with a lower degree of distinction or difficulty. For student C, the overall proficiency is qualified, but there is an obvious weakness, multiplication. Therefore, it is necessary to recommend test items about multiplication from basic to advanced. So far, we have completed a cognitive diagnosis of the proficiency of several students' knowledge concepts, and this cognitive diagnosis information can provide more help to professional teachers. In summary, this experiment has proven the cognitive diagnostic ability of RNCD and its potential for recommending test items.

5   Conclusion

This paper presents a cognitive diagnosis model called RNCD based on deep learning model NCD and cognitive diagnosis algorithm IRR. The RNCD model can increase feature interaction in deep neural network, and strengthens the monotonicity of proficiency knowledge concepts. Extensive experiments on two open education datasets under AUE, Accuracy and F1 evaluation metric settings demonstrate that RNCD outperforms other baselines. Ultimately, optimize student cognitive diagnosis modeling in personalized learning, improve student learning efficiency, reduce the burden on students and teachers, and optimize the allocation of educational resources.

Acknowledgement. This work was partly supported by the Guangzhou Key Laboratory of Big Data and Intelligent Education [grant numbers 201905010009, Mengchi Liu]; and National Natural Science Foundation of China [grant numbers 61672389, Mengchi Liu].

References

1. Chalmers, R.P.: MIRT: a multidimensional item response theory package for the r environment. J. Stat. Softw. **48**(1), 1–29 (2012)
2. Cheng, Y., et al.: Neural cognitive modeling based on the importance of knowledge point for student performance prediction. In: 16th International Conference on Computer Science & Education, ICCSE 2021, Lancaster, United Kingdom, August 17–21, 2021, pp. 495–499. IEEE (2021). https://doi.org/10.1109/ICCSE51940.2021.9569724
3. De, L., Torre, J.: Dina model and parameter estimation: a didactic. J. Educ. Behav. Stat. **34**(1), 115–130 (2009)
4. Fischer, C., Pardos, Z., Baker, R., Warschauer, M.: Mining big data in education: Affordances and challenges. SAGE PublicationsSage CA: Los Angeles, CA **44**, 130–160 (2020). https://doi.org/10.3102/0091732X20903304
5. Gao, L., Zhao, Z., Li, C., Zhao, J., Zeng, Q.: Deep cognitive diagnosis model for predicting students' performance. Future Gener. Comput. Syst. **126**, 252–262 (2022). https://doi.org/10.1016/j.future.2021.08.019

6. Huang, J., Wei, Z., Zhao, S., Ding, S., Wang, H.: Learning to explain entity relationships by pairwise ranking with convolutional neural networks. In: Proceedings of the Twenty-Sixth International Joint Conference on Artificial Intelligence, IJCAI 2017, Melbourne, Australia, August 19–25, 2017, pp. 4018–4025 (2017). https://doi.org/10.24963/ijcai.2017/561

7. Huang, T., Zhang, Z., Zhang, J.: Fibinet: combining feature importance and bilinear feature interaction for click-through rate prediction. In: Proceedings of the 13th ACM Conference on Recommender Systems, RecSys 2019, Copenhagen, Denmark, September 16–20, 2019, pp. 169–177 (2019). https://doi.org/10.1145/3298689.3347043

8. Kaur, H., Kaur, T.: A prediction model for student academic performance using machine learning-based analytics. In: Proceedings of the Future Technologies Conference, FTC 2022, Virtual Event, 20–21 October 2022, Volume 1. vol. 559, pp. 770–775. Springer (2022). https://doi.org/10.1007/978-3-031-18461-1_50

9. Liu, Q., et al.: Fuzzy cognitive diagnosis for modelling examinee performance. ACM Trans. Intell. Syst. Technol. **9**(4), 48:1-48:26 (2018). https://doi.org/10.1145/3168361

10. Lord, F.M.: Applications of item response theory to practical testing problems. Lawrence Erlbaum Asscciaates (1980)

11. Muraki, E.: A generalized partial credit model. Handbook of Modern Item Response Theory, pp. 153–164 (1997)

12. Rasch, G.: Probabilistic models for some intelligence and attainment tests. Achievement Tests, p. 199 (1993)

13. Rosenbaum, P.R.: Testing the conditional independence and monotonicity assumptions of item response theory **49**(3), 425–435 (1984)

14. Samejima, F.: Graded response model. Handbook of Modern Item Response Theory, pp. 85–100 (1997)

15. Sanz-Martínez, L., Er, E., Martínez-Monés, A., Dimitriadis, Y., Bote-Lorenzo, M.L.: Creating collaborative groups in a MOOC: a homogeneous engagement grouping approach. Behav. Inf. Technol. **38**(11), 1107–1121 (2019). https://doi.org/10.1080/0144929X.2019.1571109

16. Tong, S., et al.: Item response ranking for cognitive diagnosis. In: Proceedings of the Thirtieth International Joint Conference on Artificial Intelligence, IJCAI-21, pp. 1750–1756 (8 2021). https://doi.org/10.24963/ijcai.2021/241

17. Wang, F., Liu, Q., Chen, E., Huang, Z., Wang, S.: Neural cognitive diagnosis for intelligent education systems. Proc. AAAI Conf. Artif. Intell. **34**(4), 6153–6161 (2020)

18. Wang, T., Sun, Q., Ge, Q., Ji, Z., Chen, Q., Xia, G.: Interactive image segmentation via pairwise likelihood learning. In: Proceedings of the Twenty-Sixth International Joint Conference on Artificial Intelligence, IJCAI 2017, Melbourne, Australia, August 19–25, 2017, pp. 2957–2963 (2017). https://doi.org/10.24963/ijcai.2017/412

19. Yang, H., et al.: A novel quantitative relationship neural network for explainable cognitive diagnosis model. Knowl. Based Syst. **250**, 109156 (2022). https://doi.org/10.1016/j.knosys.2022.109156

20. Zheng, Y., Li, C., Liu, S., Lu, W.: An improved genetic approach for composing optimal collaborative learning groups. Knowl. Based Syst. **139**, 214–225 (2018). https://doi.org/10.1016/j.knosys.2017.10.022

A Sparse Matrix Optimization Method for Graph Neural Networks Training

Tiechui Yao[1,2], Jue Wang[1,2(✉)], Junyu Gu[1,2], Yumeng Shi[1,2], Fang Liu[1,2], Xiaoguang Wang[2], Yangang Wang[1,2], and Xuebin Chi[1,2]

[1] Computer Network Information Center, Chinese Academy of Sciences, Beijing, China
wangjue@sccas.cn
[2] University of Chinese Academy of Sciences, Beijing, China

Abstract. Graph neural networks (GNN) have shown great application potential in scientific research applications, biomedicine, and other fields, which exhibit superior feature representation capabilities for graph data with non-Euclidean structures. These capabilities are enabled efficiently by sparse matrix-matrix multiplication (SPMM) and sparse matrix-vector multiplication (SPMV) that operate on sparse matrix representations of graph structures. However, SpMM has the characteristics of high memory occupation and irregular memory access, which leads to low storage and computational efficiency. To address the above issues, this paper proposes a sparse matrix optimization method, including a sparse matrix format and a performance model. The format, namely BMCOO, divides the sparse matrix into multiple blocks and adopts the bitmap to compress the position information of non-zero elements in each block. This paper further designs an SpMV algorithm in BMCOO format on GPU. In addition, a multi-channel SpMV performance model is constructed to predict the execution time of SpMV by combining the sparse matrix scale and system architecture parameters. Then the performance model fine-tunes the graph partitioning of the GNN training process. Experiments on the SuiteSparse and the Open Graph Benchmark datasets verify the effectiveness and superiority of the proposed method.

Keywords: Sparse matrix format · Sparse matrix-vector multiplication · Performance model · Graph neural networks

1 Introduction

Graph neural networks (GNN) have shown potential in new energy prediction [13], traffic flow prediction [11], text classification [14], etc. The underlying core of GNN is the operations between sparse matrices and dense matrices, including sparse matrix-matrix multiplication (SpMM) and sparse matrix-vector multiplication (SpMV). Sparse matrices represent the topological structure of the graph. Dense matrices represent the graph's node features and the model's weights.

Z. Jin et al. (Eds.): KSEM 2023, LNAI 14117, pp. 114–123, 2023.
https://doi.org/10.1007/978-3-031-40283-8_11

SpMM can be simply defined as a parallel version of multiple SpMV operations. SpMM is one of the top three important modes in parallel computing [1]. With the rapid growth of graph data volume, both storage compression and computing load balancing have become more prominent. On the one hand, large-scale sparse graph data cannot be stored and computed in dense matrices because that would waste a lot of memory usage and computing power. On the other hand, processing graph data requires a careful consideration of node and edge features as well as the topological structure of the graph. These data are essentially different from Euclidean data, and we can hardly apply Euclidean space data processing methods. The performance, storage overhead and indirect access operations of sparse matrix operation kernels directly reduce the computational efficiency of overall GNN training. Therefore, efficient SpMM for GNN training is of great significance. Specifically, optimizing the SpMV of GNN is necessary by combining sparse matrix formats and hardware features.

For general graphs, existing large-scale zero elements in their adjacency matrices are obvious. Using sparse matrix compression format storage can avoid the problems of large memory footprints and long calculation time caused by indirect access. However, there are still some challenges in SpMM operations: 1) low access efficiency caused by the uneven distribution of non-zero elements in memory, discontinuous access, complex indexing, etc.; 2) load imbalance caused by the uneven distribution of non-zero elements on each compute unit [4]. The sparse matrices storage format plays a critical role in the performance of SpMM [6]. To improve cache utilization and avoid cache space waste, a common method is to store sparse matrices in blocks. The BCOO and BCSR [5] formats store non-zero elements in sub-blocks in COO and CSR format. The BCCOO [12] format extends the COO format using bit methods, which significantly reduces the memory usage of row and column index arrays. Many well-known sparse matrix formats have been developed, including DIA, ELL, CSR5 [8], Merge-SpMV [9], etc., but the current GNN framework only supports COO and CSR formats. Thus, storage optimization of sparse matrices for GNN is still challenging.

On the other hand, for distributed full-batch training of GNN on GPUs, graph partitioning techniques are required to distribute the training process across multiple computing nodes. However, the computational load of each computing node is imbalanced [10]. The search space for automatically tuning the SpMV operations of each computing node is enormous. Early performance models focus on hardware characteristics and are partially used for automatically selecting sparse matrix formats [4,12]. Performance models based on convolutional neural networks (CNN) consider the computational characteristics of applications [15]. The performance of SpMV can reflect the execution performance of SpMM. However, early performance models based on hardware characteristics or CNN rarely consider the fine-grained representation method of sparse matrices, which results in significant prediction errors. Therefore, it is necessary to establish a CNN-based SpMV performance model to reduce the tuning cost of full-batch training of GNN.

To address the above challenges, this paper proposes a new sparse matrix storage format and constructs an SpMV performance model based on deep learning. The main contributions of this paper are summarized as follows:

1. We propose a sparse matrix storage format based on blocks and bit compression (BitMap-based COOrdinate, BMCOO). BMCOO first divides the sparse matrix into blocks and then compresses the coordinate information of non-zero elements with bit markers to achieve compressed storage of sparse matrix rows and columns. Based on this format, the SpMV algorithm is further implemented on GPU.
2. We propose an SpMV performance model based on deep learning. This model uses a similarity matrix representation method, SimPooling, to enhance the position information of non-zero elements in the thumbnail of the sparse matrix. Then, combined with the matrix parameters and system architecture parameters, this model uses multi-channel CNN to extract matrix spatial features and predicts SpMV execution time. Specifically, this model guides fine-tuning of graph partitioning before full-batch training of GNN, instead of actually executing the forward and backward propagation processes.
3. We verified the method's effectiveness in experiments on the public dataset SuiteSparse matrix library and the Open Graph Benchmark (OGB). The BMCOO format has an average compression ratio of 45.16% and 65.3% compared with the COO and CSR formats, respectively. Besides, the average compression ratio of the BMCOO format can reach 45.04% while the execution efficiency is close to BCCOO. On the OGB dataset, compared with the COO and CSR formats that are commonly used in GNN frameworks, BMCOO saves an average of 30.73% and 9.75% memory usage. The performance model has an accuracy rate of 82% in time prediction for SpMV.

2 Sparse Matrix Format and Performance Model

2.1 Overview

The workflow of full-batch training of GNN based on sparse matrix storage format and SpMV performance model is shown in Fig. 1. We use the multi-level graph partition algorithm in Metis [7] to partition the original graph, then predict the training time of the sub-graph via the SpMV performance model. We fine-tune the partition results based on the predicted time to achieve computing load balance. Then we use the sparse matrix format to store the obtained subgraphs and send the matrix to the graph convolution layer in the GNN. The sparse matrix calculation operation of GCN calls the SpMM algorithm. Similarly, the SpMM algorithm is also invoked during the back-propagation process, which obtains the gradient of loss to update the weights of the GNN. Finally, the above forward propagation and back-propagation processes are repeated until a preset number of training iterations is reached, or the model converges.

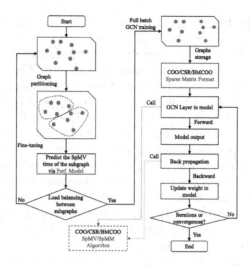

Fig. 1. Flowchart of Sparse Matrix Optimization Method for GNN Training

2.2   BMCOO Storage Format for Graphs

The core idea of the BMCOO storage format is to use block partitioning of sparse matrices based on the classic COO format, combined with bit marking of the coordinate information of non-zero elements in the submatrix, to compress row indexes (indices). In addition, the row index of the submatrix is subtracted from adjacent positions in a way similar to BCCOO and then negated. The row index is recorded using bit positions to compress further the space occupied by row indices.

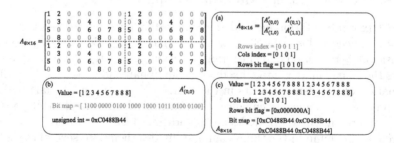

Fig. 2. Schematic Diagram of Block Method in BMCOO Format

We first define the block row size of the partitioned submatrix as *block row* and the column size of the partitioned submatrix as *block column*. We partition the matrix $A_{8 \times 16}$ according to the block size of *block row* $\times$ *block column*. In the example shown in Fig. 2(a), block_row is 4 and block_col is 8. The sparse matrix $A_{8 \times 16}$ is divided into four submatrices, marked as $A'(0,0)$, $A'(0,1)$, $A'(1,0)$, and $A'(1,1)$ in order from left to right and top to bottom. We only store the submatrices existing non-zero elements.

At the block level of a large sparse matrix, the row index *Rows index* and column index *Cols index* of each submatrix are marked. These indices facilitate the confirmation of the relative position of the submatrix during SpMV operation. Specifically, the *Rows index* array will be replaced by the *Rows bit flag* array when the BMCOO actually stored. In the *Rows bit flag* array, a bit value of 0 indicates that the submatrix is at the end of a row in the original sparse matrix. The transfer process is divided into two steps: (1) We subtract adjacent positions from *Rows index* [0 0 1 1], i.e., subtract the value of the $n + 1^{th}$ bit from that of the nth bit. When the last bit is the same as the previous bit, a *1* is added to the end of the *temporary* array; otherwise, a 0 is added. Then we get an *temporary* array [0 1 0 1]. (2) For the convenience of calculation, we negate the *temporary* array to store the *Rows bit flag* [1 0 1 0] as an unsigned integer.

At the submatrix level after partitioning, as shown in Fig. 2(b), we store the value array *Value* of non-zero elements according to the submatrix block. In this way, all non-zero elements in a submatrix block can share the row and column indices of the partition level, which greatly reduces memory overhead.

For partitioned submatrices, we use a mask to mark the relative position within the block. Specifically, as shown in Eq. 1, when the element in row i and column j in the submatrix is non-zero, its corresponding $bitmap[i * block\_col + j]$ is set to 1; otherwise it is set to 0.

$$bitmap[i * block\_col + j] = \begin{cases} 0 & A'_{(m,n)}[i, j] = 0, \\ 1 & \text{otherwise.} \end{cases} \quad (1)$$

m and n are the row and column indices of the submatrix.

2.3   SpMV Performance Model for Graph Partitioning

The matrix representation method, named SimPooling2D, combines image processing and vector clustering. The algorithm mainly includes two steps: pooling dimensionality reduction and clustering partitioning. Firstly, the reduction compresses the sparse matrix into a fixed-sized thumbnail and preserves the position information of non-zero elements in the sparse matrix. Then, the image sharpening processing technology enhances the contrast of non-zero element positions in the thumbnail. Next, the K-Means algorithm clusters non-zero elements of each row and column in the thumbnail and divides them into several categories. In this way, the sparse matrix can be divided into several sub-blocks, and each non-zero element in each sub-block belongs to the same category. The SimPooling2D algorithm can extract memory access mode features of non-zero elements in sparse matrices, i.e., storage location and access order of non-zero elements in each sub-block.

As shown in Fig. 3, we use multi-channel CNNs to extract features of enhanced thumbnail, compressed thumbnail, row similarity vector, column similarity vector, and other compressed information, respectively. The features are

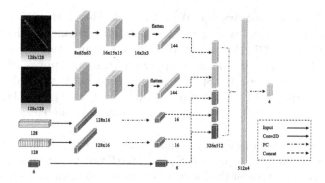

Fig. 3. Architecture of Multi-channel Performance Model

concatenated together and input into the fully connected layer to generate the output. The first and second convolutional channels extract the primary and secondary non-zero element distribution information, whose inputs are the Laplacian differential operator enhanced thumbnail and compressed thumbnail generated via SimPooling2D. To cover the information of the sparse matrix and access rules, the third and fourth channels extract row and column similarity vectors obtained by SimPooling2D. These two vectors represent the memory access mode between each row/column and other rows/columns, which reflect the structural information in the sparse matrix. To consider more structural and feature information, this model selects some parameters related to compression in the fifth channel. These parameters include the number of rows, columns, and non-zero elements in a sparse matrix, kernel row size, kernel column size, and compression ratio used by SimPooling2D. These parameters can reflect the scale, density, distribution, and compression effect of a sparse matrix, which are important for the model to perceive the SpMV execution time scale.

3 Experiments

3.1 Datasets

We first use the dataset SuiteSparse [2], which is a sparse matrix benchmark set used in circuit simulation, materials science, and other fields. We select 1872 sparse matrices with rows and columns greater than or equal to 1024. Each matrix is executed 1000 times for SpMV operation in different formats, respectively. Then, the basic dataset is divided into the training, validation, and test set according to the ratio of 8:1:1. In addition, this experiment also selects the authoritative Open Graph Benchmark (OGB) [3] for testing compression ratio and training GNN.

3.2 Experiment Setting

The numerical calculations in this study were carried out on the ORISE Supercomputer. The supercomputer system has thousands of computing nodes with the CentOS 7.6 operating system. We set k in K-Means clustering to 32 and the iterations are 50. The training epochs for the performance model are 50 and the learning rate is 0.001. Besides, we determine four intervals according to the lower bound, lower quartile, median, upper quartile, and upper bound of the box plot as category labels for SpMV runtime. The full-batch training experiments using multiple GPUs share the same hyperparameters: the learning rate is 0.0001, epochs are 1000, the optimizer is Adam, and the size of the hidden layer is 256.

The calculation methods for the memory usage of storage formats are listed as follows. $S_{\mathrm{idx}} = sizeof(\mathrm{idx\_type})$ and $S_{\mathrm{val}} = sizeof(\mathrm{val\_type})$ represent the space occupied by the data type of the index and non-zero element value, respectively. ptr_len is the length of the row index in CSR format, b_num is the number of blocks in BCCOO and BMCOO formats, and $block\_row$ and $block\_col$ are the row size and column size of blocks in BCCOO and BMCOO formats, respectively.

$$\begin{cases} S_{\mathrm{COO}} = 2 \times nnz \times S_{\mathrm{idx}} + nnz \times S_{\mathrm{val}} \\ S_{\mathrm{CSR}} = (ptr\_len + 2 \times nnz) \times S_{\mathrm{idx}} + nnz \times S_{\mathrm{val}} \\ S_{\mathrm{BCCOO}} = 2 \times b\_num \times S_{\mathrm{idx}} \\ \qquad + b\_num \times block\_row \times block\_col \times S_{\mathrm{val}} \\ S_{\mathrm{BMCOO}} = (2 \times b\_num + b\_num/32) \times S_{\mathrm{idx}} + nnz \times S_{\mathrm{val}} \end{cases} \quad (2)$$

Let TP_i be the number of samples of i class correctly predicted to i class, and FP_i be the number of incorrectly predicted samples, then accuracy is the proportion of the total number of samples with the correct predicted, which can be expressed as the Eq. 3.

$$accuracy = \sum_{i=1}^{n} TP_i / (\sum_{i=1}^{n} (TP_i + FP_i)) \quad (3)$$

3.3 Results and Analysis

The memory usage of different storage formats for each matrix is shown in Table 1. The BMCOO format greatly reduces the storage size of various sparse matrices. Compared with COO, CSR, and BCCOO, the average compression ratio is 49.57%, 70.36%, and 35.45%, respectively.

We evaluate the SpMV operation efficiency of BMCOO. Table 2 shows the running time of the SpMV algorithm in BMCOO and BCCOO, as well as four benchmark testing algorithms. The specific row and column numbers and non-zero element numbers of the matrices are detailed in Table 1. Compared with CPU single-threaded, the average speedup ratio of our proposed algorithm is 34.44X. Compared with multi-threaded parallel algorithms based on OpenMP, the average speedup ratio is 11.08X. Compared with the SpMV algorithms based on CSR provided in cuSPARSE and CUSP library, the average speedup ratios are 1.82X and 1.78X. Although for some sparse matrices, the SpMV performance of BMCOO is slightly worse than that of CSR, BMCOO has a better compression rate within the same range of execution time. Compared with the SpMV based on BCCOO, our algorithm achieves an average speedup ratio of 1.54X.

Table 1. Memory usage of different storage formats (MB)

Matrix Name	Row	Col	Nnz	COO	CSR	BCCOO	BMCOO
af_shell7	504,855	504,855	17,588,875	211.07	142.73	140.66	**82.89**
af_5_k101	503,625	503,625	17,550,675	210.61	142.42	139.96	**82.68**
gyro_k	17,361	17,361	1,021,159	12.25	8.24	15.04	**5.42**
Pres_Poisson	14,822	14,822	715,804	8.59	5.79	7.94	**3.57**
Zhao2	33,861	33,861	166,453	2.00	1.47	6.82	**1.26**
Goodwin_030	10,142	10,142	312,814	3.75	2.54	4.73	**1.67**
tuma1	22,967	22,967	87,760	1.05	0.79	3.62	**0.67**
t2d_q4_A_09	9,801	9,801	87,025	1.04	0.74	1.67	**0.50**
ex26	2,163	2,163	94,033	1.13	0.76	1.11	**0.47**

Table 2. Execution time of different SpMV algorithms (ms)

Name	CPU	OpenMP	CuSparse	CUSP	BCCOO	BMCOO
af_shell7	24.064	5.969	**0.285**	0.560	0.296	0.316
af_5_k101	22.362	5.946	**0.288**	0.559	0.297	0.314
gyro_k	1.362	0.353	0.032	0.034	0.031	**0.031**
Pres_Poisson	0.845	0.194	0.027	0.028	0.020	**0.019**
Zhao2	0.241	0.093	0.017	0.013	0.018	**0.013**
Goodwin_030	0.362	0.100	0.019	0.018	0.012	**0.011**
tuma1	0.136	0.081	0.016	0.013	0.012	**0.008**
t2d_q4_A_09	0.092	0.071	0.014	0.013	0.012	**0.006**
ex26	0.108	0.061	0.014	0.012	0.012	**0.005**

Table 3. Compression ratio of OGB datasets

Format	ogbn-arxiv	ogbn-proteins	ogbn-products	ogbn-papers100m
COO	18.6599 MB	632.9800 MB	989.7462 MB	51.7019 GB
CSR	14.6723 MB	475.26516 MB	752.1058 MB	39.6649 GB
BCCOO	157.0370 MB	2556.2471 MB	8401.9644 MB	439.4552 GB
BMCOO	**14.0468 MB**	**316.9362 MB**	**749.3922 MB**	**39.1797 GB**

From the OGB datasets in Table 3, it can be analyzed that BMCOO utilizes the locality and sparsity of graph structure and stores non-zero elements according to blocks. This can reduce memory usage and improve access efficiency, such as BMCOO saving 4.1%, 33.3%,0.4%, and 1.2% memory usage, respectively, compared with the CSR format.

We evaluate the accuracy of the performance model predictions presented in this paper. First, we train three types of performance models based on deep

Table 4. Prediction accuracy of multi-channel performance model

Model	Acc. (COO)	Acc. (CSR)	Acc. (BMCOO)
2-channel Perf. Model	72.68%	74.14%	67.32%
4-channel Perf. Model	71.46%	75.61%	68.29%
Ours	**84.39%**	**87.32%**	**75.37%**

learning in five channels. Table 4 shows the SpMV runtime prediction accuracy of the performance model under different formats. The accuracy under COO, CSR, and BMCOO formats are 84.39%, 87.32%, and 75.37%, respectively. These results show that the proposed performance model has high prediction accuracy and can effectively capture the impact of matrix and vector features on SpMV runtime. It should be noted that COO and CSR are commonly used formats for adjacency matrices in GNN training, whereas BCCOO has poor compression performance in the OGB datasets due to its compress mode. Hence this experiment skips the performance model for BCCOO.

Subsequently, we keep only two SimPooling convolution channels (2-channel perf. model) and the four channels of SimPooling (4-channel perf. model) to retrain the performance models. The accuracy of the COO and CSR model declines by about 12%, while the BMCOO model declines by about 7%. This result implies that the proposed parameters can reflect the scale, density, distribution, and compression effect of sparse matrices.

Finally, we train a three-layer graph convolutional neural network on the ogbn-products dataset using 2 to 64 GPUs, respectively. After the ogbn-products dataset is divided into multiple subgraphs, the accuracy of the training, validation, and test set is still stable. Meanwhile, we can almost achieve a linear speedup on 8 GPUs, which demonstrates the strong scalability of the proposed sparse matrix optimization method in full-batch training of GNN.

4   Conclusion

This paper first proposed a BMCOO format to partition the matrix and compressed the coordinate information of non-zero elements with bit marking. We then implemented the SpMV algorithm on GPU. Secondly, for the performance model, this paper extracted the distribution characteristics of non-zero elements in sparse operations and conducted a multi-channel CNN combined with architectural parameters to support SpMV performance prediction of various storage formats. Finally, in the experiments, compared with common formats such as COO, BMCOO saved an average of 51.83% memory usage on the SuiteSparse dataset and achieved a 1.82X speedup ratio compared with cuSPARSE library in SpMV. Compared with the CSR storage format, it saved 4.1%, 33.3%, 0.4%, and 1.2% memory usage, respectively on OGB datasets. Under multiple storage formats, the average accuracy of the multi-channel SpMV performance model reached 82%. The performance model was used to guide the graph partitioning process in full-batch training of GNN.

Acknowledgement. This work was supported by National Key R&D Program of China (No. 2021ZD0110403). We would like to thank the MindSpore team for their support.

References

1. Asanovic, K., et al.: The landscape of parallel computing research: a view from Berkeley. EECS Department, University of California, Berkeley, Tech. rep. (2006)
2. Davis, T.A., Hu, Y.: The university of Florida sparse matrix collection. ACM Trans. Math. Softw. (TOMS) **38**(1), 1–25 (2011)
3. Hu, W., et al.: Open graph benchmark: datasets for machine learning on graphs. Adv. Neural. Inf. Process. Syst. **33**, 22118–22133 (2020)
4. Huang, G., Dai, G., Wang, Y., Yang, H.: GE-SPMM: general-purpose sparse matrix-matrix multiplication on GPUs for graph neural networks. In: SC20: International Conference for High Performance Computing, Networking, Storage and Analysis, pp. 1–12. IEEE (2020)
5. Im, E.J., Yelick, K., Vuduc, R.: Sparsity: optimization framework for sparse matrix kernels. Int. J. High Perform. Comput. Appl. **18**(1), 135–158 (2004)
6. Karakasis, V., Gkountouvas, T., Kourtis, K., Goumas, G., Koziris, N.: An extended compression format for the optimization of sparse matrix-vector multiplication. IEEE Trans. Parall. Distrib. Syst. **24**(10), 1930–1940 (2012)
7. Karypis, G., Kumar, V.: A fast and high quality multilevel scheme for partitioning irregular graphs. SIAM J. Sci. Comput. **20**(1), 359–392 (1998)
8. Liu, W., Vinter, B.: CSR5: an efficient storage format for cross-platform sparse matrix-vector multiplication. In: Proceedings of the 29th ACM on International Conference on Supercomputing, pp. 339–350 (2015)
9. Merrill, D., Garland, M.: Merge-based parallel sparse matrix-vector multiplication. In: SC'16: Proceedings of the International Conference for High Performance Computing, Networking, Storage and Analysis, pp. 678–689. IEEE (2016)
10. Mu, Z., Tang, S., Zong, C., Yu, D., Zhuang, Y.: Graph neural networks meet with distributed graph partitioners and reconciliations. Neurocomputing **518**, 408–417 (2023)
11. Wu, Z., Pan, S., Chen, F., Long, G., Zhang, C., Philip, S.Y.: A comprehensive survey on graph neural networks. IEEE Trans. Neural Netw. Learn. Syst. **32**(1), 4–24 (2020)
12. Yan, S., Li, C., Zhang, Y., Zhou, H.: YASPMV: yet another SPMV framework on GPUs. Acm Sigplan Notices **49**(8), 107–118 (2014)
13. Yao, T., et al.: Very short-term forecasting of distributed PV power using GSTANN. CSEE J. Power Energy Syst. (2022)
14. Zhao, Q., Yang, J., Wang, Z., Chu, Y., Shan, W., Tuhin, I.A.K.: Clustering massive-categories and complex documents via graph convolutional network. In: Qiu, H., Zhang, C., Fei, Z., Qiu, M., Kung, S.-Y. (eds.) KSEM 2021. LNCS (LNAI), vol. 12815, pp. 27–39. Springer, Cham (2021). https://doi.org/10.1007/978-3-030-82136-4_3
15. Zhao, Y., Li, J., Liao, C., Shen, X.: Bridging the gap between deep learning and sparse matrix format selection. In: Proceedings of the 23rd ACM SIGPLAN Symposium on Principles and Practice of Parallel Programming, pp. 94–108 (2018)

Dual-Dimensional Refinement of Knowledge Graph Embedding Representation

Jie Cui, Fei Pu, and Bailin Yang[✉]

School of Computer Science and Technology, Zhejiang Gongshang University,
Hangzhou, China
ybl@zjgsu.edu.cn

Abstract. Knowledge graph representation learning aims to embed knowledge facts into a continuous vector space, enabling models to capture semantic connections within and between triples. However, existing methods primarily focus on a single dimension of entities or relations, limiting their ability to learn knowledge facts. To address this issue, this paper proposes a dual-dimension refined representation model. At the entity level, we perform residual semantic stratification of entities based on modulus and phase information. At the relation level, we introduce an adaptive direction mapping property, allowing entities to have different mapping directions in different relations, and employ negative sampling to further enhance the model's ability to refine relations. Experimental results show that our model exhibits outstanding link prediction performance on datasets such as WN18RR, FB15k-237, and UMLS. Through validation experiments, we substantiate our assumptions and analyses regarding datasets and model capabilities, thereby addressing the interpretability shortcomings of existing embedding models on underperforming datasets.

Keywords: Knowledge graph · Representation learning ·
Dual-dimensional · Link prediction · Validation experiment

1 Introduction

Knowledge graphs typically represent facts as triples (h, r, t), where h stands for head entities, r for relations and t for tail entities. Entities correspond to real-world objects or abstract concepts, while relations represent semantic links between entities. Knowledge graphs have been extensively used in recommender systems [25], question-answering systems [8], intelligent search [22], and other domains, promoting the advancement of artificial intelligence information services [10]. Structured knowledge representation in knowledge graphs enhances their manageability, scalability, and understandability.

Early representation learning models like UM [4] assessed the probability of facts by measuring the distance between head and tail entities. Subsequent researchers developed improved knowledge embedding methods from multiple perspectives. However, current knowledge graph representation learning [3]

J. Cui and F. Pu—These authors contributed equally to this work.

Z. Jin et al. (Eds.): KSEM 2023, LNAI 14117, pp. 124–137, 2023.
https://doi.org/10.1007/978-3-031-40283-8_12

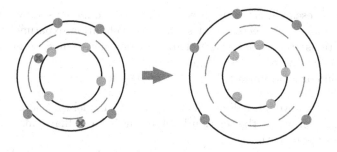

Fig. 1. DRKE(right) addresses the flaws of HAKE(left).

mainly focuses on a single level of either relations or entities. The HAKE [25] model can effectively improve the capture of semantic features in triples after achieving semantic stratification of entities. However, due to the lack of research on relational refinement, it has two shortcomings under the interference of relational noise: 1) insufficient classification ability at the semantic level; 2) inability to effectively identify semantic features in entities at the same level.

To address these issues, we propose a dual-dimensional refinement model, DRKE (**D**ual-dimensional **R**efinement of **K**nowledge graph **E**mbedding). At the relation level, an adaptive directional mapping attribute is introduced, which allows entities to have different directions under different relations, thereby overcoming noise interference caused by other relations. At the same time, at the entity level, the residual information of entities is exploited based on their modulus and phasor representation to achieve more effective semantic layering. Figure 1 shows that during the entity feature embedding process in HAKE, due to the fact that the distribution of some entities is not close enough to the semantic level to which they belong, entities may be misclassified to adjacent levels, thereby reducing the classification accuracy. By introducing the directional mapping attribute of the relationship and the residual semantics of the entities, DRKE can effectively expand the differences between levels and make the misclassified entities return to the correct semantic level.

In knowledge representation models, negative example sampling is typically used to learn the semantic connections of correct triples more effectively. Since most current models mainly focus on the entity level, they generally only negatively sample head and tail entities. The DRKE model aims to explore the dual-dimensional modeling of entities and relations. Therefore, we also introduce a negative sampling strategy for relations, allowing the model to more accurately capture the directionality of relations and reduce the ambiguity caused by other relations. To ensure the effectiveness of the dual-dimensional refinement, we conduct not only link prediction experiments on entities but also relation prediction experiments. Most knowledge graph representation models currently do not enumerate experimental results on datasets with relatively poor performance or provide insufficient explanations for these datasets. Therefore, we divide the link prediction experiment into two parts: the first part, consistent with previous research, is mainly used to evaluate the model's knowledge graph completion ability; the second part serves as a validation experiment to verify our assumptions about the dataset characteristics and to analyse in detail how DRKE improves the prediction ability.

The main contributions of the DRKE model include:

1) We propose a novel dual-dimensional refinement model that adds a direction-mapping attribute at the relation level and uses a residual semantic layering of entities at the entity level.
2) We employ a new negative sampling strategy that increases the negative samples of relations, thereby enhancing the model's ability to learn at the relational level.
3) Our DRKE achieves state-of-the-art results on prediction tasks and provides more comprehensive performance analysis.

2   Related Work

In the development of knowledge graph representation learning research, the concept of knowledge graphs was first proposed by Google, which subsequently attracted a large number of researchers to conduct studies on existing knowledge base datasets such as WordNet, Freebase and Probase. A large number of methods and models have contributed to achieving more complete knowledge graphs, and we classify these models mainly into three categories: geometric translation models, neural network models, and semantic matching models.

Geometric translation models describe the relations among triples in geometric forms, clearly demonstrating the model construction ideas. In the series of models based on TransE [5], such as TransH [21], TransD [9] and TransA [11], their core idea is to consider the relation as the difference between head and tail entities, i.e. $t=h+r$. In RotatE [17], the relation is considered as the rotation angle between head and tail entities in the complex vector space, i.e. $t=hr$. Inspired by the rotation operation in the RotatE model, DensE [13] and ConE [2] embed triples into 3D Euclidean space and double-cone hyperbolic space, respectively, utilizing different geometric features for modeling. The HAKE model introduces modulus and phase attributes for both entities and relations, using modulus information to distinguish entities of different categories and phase information to differentiate entities within the same category. Since entities of the same category have similar modulus sizes, HAKE has semantic stratification capabilities.

Neural network models mainly leverage the powerful feature capturing ability of neural networks, but they lack interpretability. ConvE [6] uses a convolutional neural network to apply a two-dimensional convolution to the input triples, enhancing the interaction between entities and relations. ConvKB [14] addresses the problem that ConvE does not embed entities and relations in the same dimension and only concatenates head entities and relations, thereby enhancing the semantic properties of triples. InteractE [19] uses different concatenation arrangements for relation and entity embedding vectors, while using circular convolution to further improve interaction within triples. With the significant impact of Transformer [20] in the field of artificial intelligence, the Transformer-based SAttLE [1] emerged, which uses self-attention mechanisms for low-dimensional embedding of knowledge facts. SAttLE captures the dependencies and interactions among triples, solving the overfitting and instability issues caused by high-dimensional embeddings.And KG-BERT [24] uses BERT [7] to construct a richer knowledge graph context semantics.

Semantic matching models compute the relevance of entities and relations through multiplication operators, with the relation representation reflecting the latent semantics of the entities during the matching process. RESCAL [15] models asymmetric relations and employs collective learning to perform collective classification inference on knowledge facts, extracting deeper dependencies from instances. DistMult [23] suggests that bilinear target learning is good at capturing relational semantics while reducing the number of parameters in bilinear models through diagonal matrices. ComplEx [18] introduces complex vectors, embedding triples into the complex space, and calculates the triple scores through the Hermitian product of complex numbers.

3   Method

In this section, we propose a novel model called DRKE that refines the study of entities and relations in two dimensions. This is achieved by implementing residual semantic stratification for entities and introducing directional mapping attributes for relations.

3.1   Entity Level

In the entity set of a knowledge graph, different entities possess their unique semantic properties. Due to the similarity of semantics for some entities, they are categorized into different semantic classes. To classify entities more effectively, we assign different moduli to entities of different categories. This means that entities of the same category are distributed in the same hierarchy, so that different hierarchical knowledge graphs are embedded in the geometric form of concentric circles. The modulus of the tail entity can be defined as the Hermitian product of the head entity modulus and the relation modulus, given by the following formula:

$$(1 + \beta_1)\boldsymbol{t}_m = (1 + \beta_1)\boldsymbol{h}_m \circ \boldsymbol{r}_m \tag{1}$$

where $\boldsymbol{h}_m, \boldsymbol{t}_m \in \mathbb{R}^d$, $\boldsymbol{r}_m \in \mathbb{R}^d_+$, and the parameter β_1 to preserve the residual semantics of the entity after the calculation of relations.

To ensure the identification of different entities in the same semantic hierarchy, entities also have phase attributes. Different phase information implies different positions within the same hierarchy. The phase of the tail entity is equal to the sum of the phase of the head entity and the phase of the relation, modulo 2π. The formula is defined as:

$$(1 + \beta_2)t_p = ((1 + \beta_2)h_p + r_p) \bmod 2\pi \tag{2}$$

where $h_p, t_p, r_p \in [0, 2\pi)^d$, and the parameter β_2 controls the residual semantics of the entity phase information.

3.2   Relation Level

The classification of semantic hierarchies of entities is a coarse-grained classification. Under different relation conditions, entities in the same hierarchy still have completely different semantic information. For example, the semantics of the entities "Obama" and "Biden" are more similar under the "position" relation and exhibit greater differences under the "ethnicity" relation. To effectively segment or integrate entities under various relations, we divide relations into three semantic features: relational directional mapping information, relation modulus information, and relation phase information. The relational directionality represents the mapping tendency of an entity's modulus and phase information under different relations, defined by the formula:

$$\begin{aligned} E_m &= O_{(\eta,\mu)} \circ E_m \\ E_p &= O_{(\eta,\mu)} \circ E_p \end{aligned} \tag{3}$$

where O is the directional mapping matrix of the relation, (η, μ) represents the value range of the average distribution of the directional matrix, i.e., $|O_{ij}| \in [\eta, \mu]$, and it must satisfy $\eta < \mu$.

The values of η and μ determine the distribution of the entities after the directional mapping, which in turn affects the learning performance of the model on the dataset, as shown in Fig. 2. When μ is too small, the Hermitian product of the entity will weaken or even eliminate its semantic features. As shown in Fig. 2a, after the entity undergoes directional mapping, the effect of semantic stratification is no longer obvious, and the differences between entities of the same hierarchy are weakened. In the extreme case of $\mu = 0$, there are no semantic differences between all entities. When μ is too large, the mapping distance of each entity under different relations is different, and the excessively large μ causes some entities in the same hierarchy to have a large variance in mapping

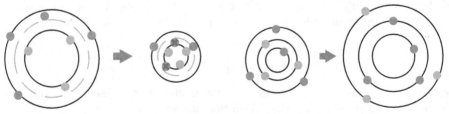

(a) The semantic hierarchy is weakened and entities are more homogeneous if μ is too small.

(b) The semantic hierarchy will be weakened or even confused if μ is too large.

Fig. 2. Influence of relational projection distribution.

distances, so the entities may be too dispersed after mapping, which is not conducive to the semantic hierarchy modeling of the model. Figure 2b shows a special case when μ is too large: three layers of semantic entities undergo relation directional mapping, but the order of the first and second outer layers changes under this mapping, causing the semantic hierarchy of the whole knowledge graph to become confused. Therefore, in subsequent experiments, the value distribution of (η, μ) is different under different datasets.

3.3   Model Computing and Training

Combining the dual-dimensional modeling of entities and relations, the scoring function of DRKE for modulus information is:

$$f_m(\boldsymbol{h}, \boldsymbol{r}, \boldsymbol{t}) = \left\|(\boldsymbol{O}_{(\eta,\mu)} \circ \boldsymbol{h}_m + \beta_1 \boldsymbol{h}_m) \circ \boldsymbol{r}_m - (\boldsymbol{O}_{(\eta,\mu)} \circ \boldsymbol{t}_m + \beta_1 \boldsymbol{t}_m)\right\|_2 \quad (4)$$

where $\boldsymbol{h}_m$, $\boldsymbol{t}_m$ represents the modulus information of the head and tail entities, $\boldsymbol{r}_m$ represents the modulus information of the relation, and the L_2 norm is used to calculate the triplet modulus information. Similarly, the scoring function of DRKE for the phase information is:

$$f_p(\boldsymbol{h}, \boldsymbol{r}, \boldsymbol{t}) = \left\|\sin\left((\boldsymbol{O}_{(\eta,\mu)} \circ \boldsymbol{h}_p + \beta_2 \boldsymbol{h}_p) + \boldsymbol{r}_p - (\boldsymbol{O}_{(\eta,\mu)} \circ \boldsymbol{t}_p + \beta_2 \boldsymbol{t}_p)\right)/2\right\|_1 \quad (5)$$

where $\boldsymbol{h}_p$, $\boldsymbol{t}_p$ and $\boldsymbol{r}_p$ represent the phase information of the triplet, and the L_1 norm is used to calculate the phase information. The final scoring function of DRKE is:

$$f_s(\boldsymbol{h}, \boldsymbol{r}, \boldsymbol{t}) = -\lambda_m f_m(\boldsymbol{h}, \boldsymbol{r}, \boldsymbol{t}) - \lambda_p f_p(\boldsymbol{h}, \boldsymbol{r}, \boldsymbol{t}) \quad (6)$$

where λ_m, λ_p represents the weights of modulus and phase features.

In order to enhance the adaptability of the relation direction attribute, a relation negative sampling strategy is implemented in DRKE. At the same time, the self-adversarial negative example training method [17] is adopted to better train the model. The negative sampling strategy is as follows:

$$p\left(h'_j, r'_j, t'_j \mid \{(h_i, r_i, t_i)\}\right) = \frac{\exp \alpha f_s\left(\boldsymbol{h}'_j, \boldsymbol{r}'_j, \boldsymbol{t}'_j\right)}{\sum_i \exp \alpha f_s\left(\boldsymbol{h}'_i, \boldsymbol{r}'_i, \boldsymbol{t}'_i\right)} \quad (7)$$

Therefore, the loss function is defined as:

$$L = -\log \sigma\left(\gamma - f_s(\boldsymbol{h}, \boldsymbol{r}, \boldsymbol{t})\right) - \sum_{i=1}^n p\left(h'_i, r'_i, t'_i\right) \log \sigma\left(f_s\left(\boldsymbol{h}', \boldsymbol{r}', \boldsymbol{t}'\right) - \gamma\right) \quad (8)$$

where σ denotes the sigmoid activation function, and γ represents the margin parameter.

Table 1. Dataset statistics.

Datasets	#E	#R	#Train	#Valid	#Test
WN18RR	40,943	11	86,835	3,034	3,134
FB15k-237	14,541	237	272,115	17,535	20,466
UMLS	135	46	5,216	652	661
Nations	14	55	1,592	199	201
FB15k	14,951	1345	48,3142	50,000	59,071

4 Experiments

4.1 Experimental Setup

Evaluation Task and Metrics. We evaluated the model's ability to complete knowledge graph entities using link prediction task, divided into performance tests and validation experiments. We also conducted relation prediction experiments and ablation studies to demonstrate the effectiveness of the model's improvements in dual dimensions. Evaluation metrics include Mean Rank (MR), Mean Reciprocal Rank (MRR), and Hits@k.

Datasets. Experiments were performed on five knowledge graph datasets: WN18 RR and FB15K-237 for link prediction performance testing, UMLS and Nations for link prediction validation, and relation prediction experiments on the FB15k dataset. Dataset statistics are in Table 1.

Hyperparameters. During the training process, we used the Adam optimizer [32]. To select the best hyperparameters, we performed a grid search on the validation set, and the specific hyperparameter settings are shown in Table 2.

4.2 Link Prediction

Performance Test Experiment. Table 3 compares DRKE's performance with other models on the WN18RR and FB15k-237 datasets. DRKE outperforms

Table 2. Hyperparameter settings.

Datasets	batch	dim	lr	epoch	adv	γ	λ_m	λ_p	η	μ
WN18RR	256	500	0.00005	80,000	1.0	5.0	2.0	0.5	1.5	2.0
FB15k-237	256	1,000	0.00005	100,000	1.0	9.0	4.0	0.5	0.5	1.5
Nations	128	500	0.001	10,000	0.5	6.0	0.5	4.0	1.0	2.0
UMLS	256	500	0.0005	10,000	0.5	36.0	2.0	0.5	1.0	2.0
FB15k	512	1,000	0.00005	100,000	1.0	32.0	4.0	0.5	0.5	1.5

other models in all evaluation metrics. Compared to HAKE, the improvement of DRKE in Hits@1 and Hits@3 on the WN18RR dataset is limited, but Hits@10 shows more significant improvement. On FB15k-237, although the improvement in Hits@10 is smaller, performance increased by 6.0% and 4.2% in Hits@1 and Hits@3, respectively.

Table 3. Results of the performance tests of the link prediction.

Methods	WN18RR				FB15k-237			
	MRR	Hits@1	Hits@3	Hits@10	MRR	Hits@1	Hits@3	Hits@10
TransE	0.226	–	–	0.501	0.294	–	–	0.465
DistMult	0.430	0.390	0.440	0.490	0.241	0.155	0.263	0.419
ComplEx	0.440	0.410	0.460	0.510	0.247	0.158	0.275	0.428
ConvE	0.430	0.400	0.440	0.520	0.325	0.237	0.356	0.501
RotatE	0.476	0.428	0.492	0.571	0.338	0.241	0.375	0.533
HAKE	0.497	0.452	0.516	0.582	0.346	0.250	0.381	0.542
ConE	0.496	0.453	0.515	0.579	0.345	0.247	0.381	0.540
KG-BERT	0.216	0.041	0.302	0.524	–	–	–	0.420
DensE	0.492	0.443	0.509	0.516	0.351	0.256	0.386	0.544
SAttLE	0.491	0.454	0.508	0.558	**0.360**	**0.268**	0.396	0.545
DRKE	**0.502**	**0.456**	**0.523**	**0.596**	**0.360**	0.265	**0.397**	**0.549**

The improvements of DRKE on the two datasets can be observed in different evaluation metrics. Therefore, we further analyzed the dataset and the model itself. The Hits@10 metric reflects the coarse-grained semantic learning capability of the model, mainly reflecting the classification performance of different semantic levels. In contrast, the Hits@1 and Hits@3 metrics focus more on the fine-grained semantic discriminative ability, mainly reflecting the model's recognition of different entities within the same semantic level.

In the WN18RR dataset, describing lexical relationships, the differences between different semantic levels are relatively small, leading to ambiguities in the boundary entities between levels. This ambiguity limits the performance of the HAKE model, while the relational directional mapping of the DRKE model expands the differences between levels, resulting in a significant improvement in the Hits@10 metric. The FB15k-237 dataset includes facts from multiple domains, making the entity levels more diverse and prominent. Therefore, HAKE can identify different semantic levels, resulting in a relatively smaller improvement in the Hits@10 metric for DRKE. However, the significant improvements in Hits@1 and Hits@3 metrics show that DRKE compensates for HAKE's entity recognition ability at the same level.

Figure 3a visualizes triplets on the WN18RR dataset, showing the embedding results of entities in the polar coordinate system. HAKE classifies 'psychological_feature', 'hoops', 'husbandry', and 'cards' at the same semantic level,

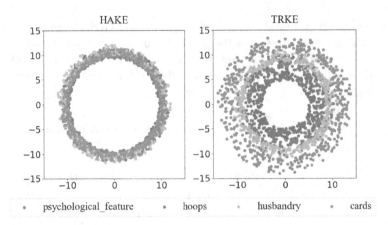

(a) Visualization of entity semantic hierarchy in HAKE and DRKE.

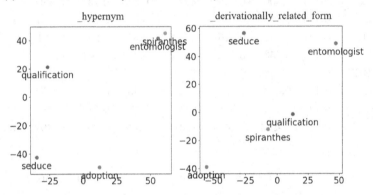

(b) DRKE entity embedding visualization under different relations.

Fig. 3. Embedding visualization.

while DRKE captures the hierarchical differences accurately. Figure 3b reduces all triplet features in the WN18RR dataset to 2D Euclidean space and randomly selects some entities and relations for visualization. The entities "spiranthes" and "entomologist" are both related to the natural world, so under the "_hypernym" relation their semantic differences are smaller. However, in the context of the "_derivationally_related_form" relation, their semantic differences are more significant due to the dissimilarities in their etymological origins. The relation mapping visualization demonstrates that DRKE can present different semantic information for entities under different relations.

Validation Experiment. To validate the dataset and model analysis, we selected the UMLS and Nations datasets for the experiments. The Nations dataset contains only 14 country entities and 55 relations, meaning all entities in this dataset will be at the same semantic level during the DRKE modeling

Table 4. Results of the validation experiments of the link prediction.

Methods	Nations				UMLS			
	MRR	Hits@1	Hits@3	Hits@10	MRR	Hits@1	Hits@3	Hits@10
TransE	0.481	0.219	0.667	0.980	0.797	0.645	0.942	0.984
DistMult	0.713	0.597	0.776	0.978	0.868	0.821	–	0.869
ComplEx	0.668	0.527	0.741	0.995	0.934	0.890	–	0.992
ConvE	**0.817**	**0.718**	**0.883**	**1.000**	0.940	0.916	0.972	0.991
RotatE	0.716	0.580	0.799	**1.000**	0.927	0.874	**0.979**	0.995
HAKE	0.732	0.595	0.853	0.988	0.932	0.893	0.966	0.995
DRKE	0.766	0.657	0.868	0.990	**0.952**	**0.926**	0.976	**0.996**

process, rendering the model's semantic layering capability ineffective. In contrast, the semantic features of the UMLS dataset are richer. We predict that DRKE's performance on this dataset may not be optimal.

Table 4 shows the link prediction experiment results of DRKE and other models on the UMLS and Nations datasets. The experimental results validate our assumptions and analysis. On the Nations dataset, DRKE was not the best-performing model. ConvE performed best on this dataset, with DRKE closely following but still having a gap in accuracy. On the UMLS dataset, DRKE outperformed other models on several evaluation metrics. Although slightly inferior to RotatE on Hits@3, it led RotatE by a more significant margin on the finer-grained Hits@1 metric.

The experiments on the Nations and UMLS datasets confirmed the inductive properties of the datasets. Simultaneously, it also proves that the DRKE model, when dealing with complex knowledge graphs, uses specific ways to improve its ability to learn knowledge facts.

4.3 Relation Prediction

Link prediction experiments are primarily designed to evaluate entity prediction capabilities. However, in real-world knowledge graphs, predicting relations between entities is also crucial. To verify DRKE's effectiveness at the relation level, we selected the FB15k dataset for relation prediction experiments, with results shown in Table 5.

The experimental results show that DRKE performs well. Although PTransE [12], ProjE [16], and KG-BERT lead in MR, they still lag behind DRKE in the more critical prediction accuracy metric, Hits@1. Although the average comprehensive performance of the KG-BERT model is close to DRKE, KG-BERT not only uses pre-training with text information outside the dataset, but its time complexity is also 52.5 times that of DRKE. Compared to the HAKE model, DRKE has an improved performance of 27.8% and 7.6% in the MR and Hits@1 evaluation metrics, respectively. This also proves that by introducing relational mapping matrices and negative sampling strategies for relations, the entity prediction and relation prediction capabilities of the model have been improved.

Table 5. Results of the relation prediction.

Methods	MR	Hits@1
TransE	2.5	0.843
PTransE (ADD, len-2 path)	**1.2**	0.936
PTransE (RNN, len-2 path)	1.4	0.932
PTransE (ADD, len-3 path)	1.4	0.940
ProjE (pointwise)	1.3	0.956
ProjE (listwise)	**1.2**	0.957
ProjE (wlistwise)	**1.2**	0.956
HAKE	1.8	0.909
KG-BERT	**1.2**	0.960
DRKE	1.3	**0.978**

4.4 Ablation Studies

We performed ablation studies on the FB15k-237 dataset, with results shown in Table 6. w/o RDM represents the DRKE model without relation directional mapping, w/o ERS represents the model without entity residual semantics, w/o RNS represents the model without negative sampling of relations, and $\Delta(\eta, \mu)$-small and $\Delta(\eta, \mu)$-big represent the model directional mapping value range of [0, 0.2] and [1.0, 5.0], respectively. The original DRKE model performs best in all evaluation metrics.

The comparison of the original DRKE model with w/o RDM and w/o RNS confirms that without refined approaches on directional mapping and negative sampling of relations, the ability of the model to complete knowledge graphs will

Table 6. Results of Ablation Studies.

Methods	MRR	Hits@1	Hits@3	Hits@10
DRKE	**0.360**	**0.265**	**0.397**	**0.549**
$\Delta(\eta, \mu)$-smill	0.353	0.260	0.389	0.539
$\Delta(\eta, \mu)$-big	0.320	0.221	0.359	0.516
w/o RDM	0.346	0.253	0.379	0.534
w/o ERS	0.357	0.262	0.393	0.544
w/o RNS	0.343	0.246	0.382	0.540

be limited. The method of RNS in the promotion of RDM is very important, because there is no negative sampling of relations, the model can not accurately represent the relationship, resulting in a great impact on the learning of entities under the wrong relationship feature mapping. Compared to w/o ERS, the lack of residual semantics of the entities also affects its predictive performance. Overall, the ablation experiments confirm the effectiveness of two-dimensional refinement. At the same time, $\Delta(\eta, \mu)$-small and $\Delta(\eta, \mu)$-big also show that the range of directional mapping values has a significant impact on DRKE performance.

5   Conclusion

In this work, we propose the DRKE model that refines the modeling of entities and relations in a dual-dimensional manner by employing residual semantic stratification of entities and directional mapping attributes of relations. In addition, based on entity negative sampling, we introduce a relation negative sampling method to improve the model's ability to capture semantic information at the relation level. In the link prediction experiments on WN18RR and FB15k-237, DRKE shows excellent performance. In addition, we verify our analysis of the datasets and the model performance through validation experiments, showing that DRKE indeed has strong performance interpretability. The DRKE model can flexibly adapt to the characteristics of different types of knowledge graphs, achieving excellent results on various evaluation metrics.

In future work, we will conduct more in-depth research on the dual-dimension of entities and relations. For instance, under different relations, the semantic hierarchies of entities might be entirely different, and thus they will be embedded into different semantic levels.

Acknowledgement. This research is supported by the Key R&D Program Project of Zhejiang Province (No. 2021C02004, 2019C01004), and Zhejiang Gongshang University "Digital+" Disciplinary Construction Management Project (No. SZJ2022A009).

References

1. Baghershahi, P., Hosseini, R., Moradi, H.: Self-attention presents low-dimensional knowledge graph embeddings for link prediction. Knowl.-Based Syst. **260**, 110124 (2023)
2. Bai, Y., Ying, Z., Ren, H., Leskovec, J.: Modeling heterogeneous hierarchies with relation-specific hyperbolic cones. Adv. Neural. Inf. Process. Syst. **34**, 12316–12327 (2021)
3. Bengio, Y., Courville, A., Vincent, P.: Representation learning: a review and new perspectives. IEEE Trans. Pattern Anal. Mach. Intell. **35**(8), 1798–1828 (2013)
4. Bordes, A., Glorot, X., Weston, J., Bengio, Y.: Joint learning of words and meaning representations for open-text semantic parsing. In: Artificial Intelligence and Statistics, pp. 127–135. PMLR (2012)
5. Bordes, A., Usunier, N., Garcia-Duran, A., Weston, J., Yakhnenko, O.: Translating embeddings for modeling multi-relational data. In: Advances in Neural Information Processing Systems, vol. 26 (2013)

6. Dettmers, T., Minervini, P., Stenetorp, P., Riedel, S.: Convolutional 2D knowledge graph embeddings. In: Proceedings of the AAAI Conference on Artificial Intelligence. vol. 32 (2018)

7. Devlin, J., Chang, M.W., Lee, K., Toutanova, K.: BERT: Pre-training of deep bidirectional transformers for language understanding. arXiv preprint arXiv:1810.04805 (2018)

8. Hao, Y., et al.: An end-to-end model for question answering over knowledge base with cross-attention combining global knowledge. In: Proceedings of the 55th Annual Meeting of the Association for Computational Linguistics (Volume 1: Long Papers), pp. 221–231 (2017)

9. Ji, G., He, S., Xu, L., Liu, K., Zhao, J.: Knowledge graph embedding via dynamic mapping matrix. In: Proceedings of the 53rd Annual Meeting of the Association for Computational Linguistics and the 7th International Joint Conference on Natural Language Processing (volume 1: Long papers), pp. 687–696 (2015)

10. Ji, S., Pan, S., Cambria, E., Marttinen, P., Philip, S.Y.: A survey on knowledge graphs: representation, acquisition, and applications. IEEE Trans. Neural Netw. Learn. Syst. **33**(2), 494–514 (2021)

11. Jia, Y., Wang, Y., Lin, H., Jin, X., Cheng, X.: Locally adaptive translation for knowledge graph embedding. In: Proceedings of the AAAI Conference on Artificial Intelligence, vol. 30 (2016)

12. Lin, Y., Liu, Z., Luan, H., Sun, M., Rao, S., Liu, S.: Modeling relation paths for representation learning of knowledge bases. arXiv preprint arXiv:1506.00379 (2015)

13. Lu, H., Hu, H., Lin, X.: Dense: an enhanced non-commutative representation for knowledge graph embedding with adaptive semantic hierarchy. Neurocomputing **476**, 115–125 (2022)

14. Nguyen, T.D., Nguyen, D.Q., Phung, D., et al.: A novel embedding model for knowledge base completion based on convolutional neural network. In: Proceedings of the 2018 Conference of the North American Chapter of the Association for Computational Linguistics: Human Language Technologies, Volume 2 (Short Papers), pp. 327–333 (2018)

15. Nickel, M., Tresp, V., Kriegel, H.P., et al.: A three-way model for collective learning on multi-relational data. In: ICML, vol. 11, pp. 3104482–3104584 (2011)

16. Shi, B., Weninger, T.: Proje: embedding projection for knowledge graph completion. In: Proceedings of the AAAI Conference on Artificial Intelligence, vol. 31 (2017)

17. Sun, Z., Deng, Z.H., Nie, J.Y., Tang, J.: Rotate: knowledge graph embedding by relational rotation in complex space. arXiv preprint arXiv:1902.10197 (2019)

18. Trouillon, T., Welbl, J., Riedel, S., Gaussier, É., Bouchard, G.: Complex embeddings for simple link prediction. In: International Conference on Machine Learning, pp. 2071–2080. PMLR (2016)

19. Vashishth, S., Sanyal, S., Nitin, V., Agrawal, N., Talukdar, P.: Interacte: improving convolution-based knowledge graph embeddings by increasing feature interactions. In: Proceedings of the AAAI Conference on Artificial Intelligence, vol. 34, pp. 3009–3016 (2020)

20. Vaswani, A., et al.: Attention is all you need. In: Advances in Neural Information Processing Systems, vol. 30 (2017)

21. Wang, Z., Zhang, J., Feng, J., Chen, Z.: Knowledge graph embedding by translating on hyperplanes. In: Proceedings of the AAAI Conference on Artificial Intelligence, vol. 28 (2014)

22. Xiong, C., Power, R., Callan, J.: Explicit semantic ranking for academic search via knowledge graph embedding. In: Proceedings of the 26th International Conference on World Wide web, pp. 1271–1279 (2017)
23. Yang, B., Yih, W.t., He, X., Gao, J., Deng, L.: Embedding entities and relations for learning and inference in knowledge bases. arXiv preprint arXiv:1412.6575 (2014)
24. Yao, L., Mao, C., Luo, Y.: KG-BERT: bert for knowledge graph completion. arXiv preprint arXiv:1909.03193 (2019)
25. Zhang, F., Yuan, N.J., Lian, D., Xie, X., Ma, W.Y.: Collaborative knowledge base embedding for recommender systems. In: Proceedings of the 22nd ACM SIGKDD International Conference on Knowledge Discovery and Data Mining, pp. 353–362 (2016)

Contextual Information Augmented Few-Shot Relation Extraction

Tian Wang[1,2] , Zhiguang Wang[1,2](✉), Rongliang Wang[1,2] , Dawei Li[3], and Qiang Lu[1,2]

[1] Beijing Key Laboratory of Petroleum Data Mining,
China University of Petroleum, Beijing, China
`cwangzg@cup.edu.cn`
[2] Department of Computer Science and Technology,
China University of Petroleum, Beijing, China
[3] Research Institute of Petroleum Exploration and Development,
Beijing, China

Abstract. Few-Shot Relation Extraction is a challenging task that involves extracting relations from a limited number of annotated data. While some researchers have proposed using sentence-level information to improve performance on this task with Prototype Network, most of these methods do not adequately leverage this valuable source of sentence-level information. To address this issue, we propose a novel sentence augmentation method that utilizes abundant relation information to generate additional training data for few-shot relation extraction. In addition, we add a new "None of Above" class for each task, thereby enhancing the model's classification ability for similar relations and improving its overall performance. Experimental results on the FewRel demonstrate that our method outperforms existing methods on three different few-shot relation extraction tasks. Moreover, our method also provides a new idea for both few-shot learning and data augmentation research.

Keywords: Few-Shot · Relation Extraction · Contextual Sentence · Relation Information · Data Augmentation

1 Introduction

Relation Extraction (RE) [1] is a crucial task in natural language processing that aims to extract the relations between entities in a given sentence. However, RE faces a significant challenge due to the lack of high-quality annotated data, which results in time-consuming manual annotation and poor generalization of relation extraction models. To address this issue, Few-Shot Relation Extraction

This work is supported by National Natural Science Foundation of China (No. 61972414), National Key R&D Program of China (No. 2019YFC0312003) and Beijing Natural Science Foundation (No. 4202066).

(FSRE) has emerged as a popular research topic in recent years intending to enable effective relation extraction with limited annotated data.

Researchers have applied N-way-K-shot meta-learning to the task division criteria for precise FSRE's definition, shown in Fig. 1. In this framework, FSRE is viewed as a series of relation extraction meta-tasks, with each meta-task randomly selecting N types of relations from the Support Set (S), where each relation type consists of K annotated samples. The model then learns relation extraction abilities by studying these samples and performs relation extraction on sentence samples of the unknown relations in the Query Set (Q). Besides, the Prototype Network [15]-based method is the most common method used in N-way-K-shot FSRE. Specifically, this method computes the centroid of the prototype representation of all samples of the same relation as the relation prototypes and then compares the distances between the prototype of the relation-unknown sample and the centroids for determining the unknown relation. This method is effective for RE with limited annotated data and has demonstrated promising results in recent studies.

Fig. 1. 3-Way-1-Shot FSRE. There are 3 relations, which have 1 sentence sample, and a relation-unknown sentence q. The goal of FSRE is extracting relation from q.

Peng et al. [13] have demonstrated through extensive experiments that contextual information in the text is a crucial factor that affects the accuracy of RE. However, in recent years, some researchers [4,5,17,19] have overlooked the information in contextual sentences, treating them merely as a means of obtaining entity information or as a part of the final prototype representation. These methods ignore the fact that some words that are not directly related to the entities themselves in contextual sentences may contain valid relation information. For instance, the sentence "*However, in 1992, then-owner Aamulehti sold Pohjalainen to Ilkka.*" contains the "*sold $\cdots$ to $\cdots$*" that represents the ownership of the item. But some words in this sentence, such as "*However*" and "*in 1992*", are meaningless for RE. Overall, In FSRE, the information contained in contextual sentences is crucial and can have a significant impact on the results of relation extraction. At the same time, it is also essential to filter out useless words in contextual sentences. By doing so, the model can more accurately identify and extract the relation between entities and improve the overall performance of FSRE.

Based on the issues mentioned above in FSRE, we propose a novel relation-based sentence augmentation method. This method leverages relation information to augment the limited annotated dataset. It employs pre-defined sentence structures and information elimination to mitigate the impact of diverse sentence structures and irrelevant information. We also integrate entity information with contextual sentence information using the Prototype Network to obtain the final prototype representation. Moreover, we add the "None of Above" as the $(N+1)$th relation to improve the model's ability to distinguish similar relations. At the same time, we modify the commonly used cross-entropy loss function accordingly to adapt to practical situations. The experimental results on FewRel [9] demonstrate that our proposed method outperforms existing methods on three FSRE tasks: 5-way-1-shot, 5-way-5-shot, and 10-way-1-shot.

2   Related Work

In the traditional relation extraction datasets, there are fewer types of relation but more sentence samples in a single relation, which is not suitable for FSRE. To address this issue, Han et al. [9] created the FewRel dataset, which was specifically designed for FSRE and was extracted and screened from Wikipedia and Wikidata using computer software and human judgment. Along with the FewRel, they also released a basic FSRE framework. Since then, various FSRE methods have emerged, including exploring internal data, introducing external data, and prompt-based fine-tuning.

The goal of exploring the internal information in data is to improve model performance by extracting additional information from the data itself. This information may originate from entities, relations, or sentences, and it is extracted and integrated using a variety of methods. For instance, Qu et al. [14] utilized a Bayesian meta-learning technique to construct a global relationship graph, thereby improving the model's ability to handle novel and unknown relations. Liu et al. [12] directly incorporated entity and relationship prototypes to construct a more comprehensive prototype representation. Brody et al. [2], on the other hand, focused on making FSRE more applicable in real-world settings and devised a data augmentation approach to adapt to more practical scenarios.

The characteristic of introducing external data information is the use of external data to enrich the information of known data thereby enhancing the accuracy of FSRE. Yang et al. [19] improved the Prototype Network-based TD-proto by integrating text descriptions of entities and relations. Concept-FERE [20] augmented the relation prototype by adding entity description information on the textual entities. Wang et al. [17] separately encoded entity types and sentence structures and fused them to obtain an enhanced prototype representation for relation extraction.

The prompt-based fine-tuning method has gained popularity in the FSRE field due to the availability of pre-trained language models such as BERT [11]. Researchers are now exploring how prompt-based fine-tuning methods can improve the performance of RE. He et al. [10] proposed a virtual prompt pre-training method that allows the model to explore the potential space of relations and improve its performance. Chen et al. [3] transformed FSRE into a masked text prediction problem by inserting text fragments.

3 Proposed Method

In this section, we present our proposed method for augmenting sentences using relation information, which is detailed in Sect. 3.1. We first extract relation information to expand the dataset and apply predefined sentence structures and information elimination to reduce irrelevant words. Then we fuse both the sentences and entities to obtain the final relation prototype representation. Additionally, we modify the N-way-K-shot setting by adding a "None of Above" as the $(N + 1)$th relation and adjust the loss function to improve practicality. Finally, we discuss the principles of relation extraction.

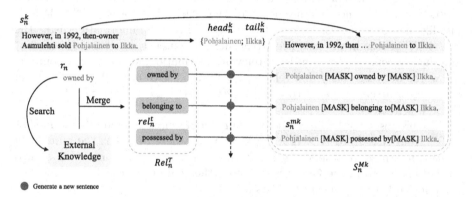

Fig. 2. The Sentence Augmentation Method by Relation Information. In this figure, s represents a sentence, and S represents a set of sentences. rel represents a piece of relation information, and Rel represents a set of relation information. N is the number of relations, K is the number of samples of a single relation, T is the number of relation information, and M is the number of sentences in S_n^{Mk}, while $T + 1 = M$.

3.1 Sentence Augmentation Method by Relation Information

We use relation information to augment samples on contextual sentences in the FSRE, which is shown in Fig. 2, thereby changing N-way-K-shot to N-way-$M \times K$-shot.

First, we obtain the information of the head entity $head_n^k$ and the tail entity $tail_n^k$ of the given sentence s_n^k in the Support Set S_N^K (s_n^k represents the kth sentence of the nth relation). Then we query the relevant information of the relation r_n between entity pairs in the external knowledge, such as synonyms, explanation information, etc., which are very easy to obtain, and integrate it with r_n itself to obtain the relation information set Rel_n^T. After that, we concatenate entities information and relation information by relying on a format like $\{head_n^k, rel_n^t, tail_n^k\}$, where rel_n^t is the tth relation information in Rel_n^T, and obtain a sentence set S_n^{Mk} composed of new sentence samples s_n^{mk} based on the relation information. Finally, we combine all sentence sets $S_n^{Mk}(n \in \{1, 2, \cdots, N\}, k \in \{1, 2, \cdots, K\})$ to get the final Support Set S_N^{MK} which is used for FSRE.

The new sentence s_n^{mk} obtained by the method described in Sect. 3.1 is not a grammatically correct sentence in the strict sense. For example, for the original sentence "*However, in 1992, then-owner Aamulehti sold Pohjalainen to Ilkka*" with the head entity "*Pohjalainen*", tail entity "*Ilkka*", and the relation "owned by", the new sentence "*Pohjalainen owned by Ilkka*" is grammatically incorrect because of lack of the verb "*is*". However, humans can still understand the meaning of the new sentence after reading it. To avoid serious grammatical errors, the word connecting the entity and the relation is replaced by "$[MASK]$", just like masking the word except the entity and relation information using the "$[MASK]$" token in the sentence. To ensure the sentence structure is consistent and the new sentence contains less irrelevant information, we replace the connecting words between entity and relation information with one "$[MASK]$" token, resulting in a sentence structure of $\{head_n^k, [MASK], rel_n, [MASK], tail_n^k\}$ for the new sentences.

The proposed method increases the number of sentences in an N-way-K-shot FSRE from $N \times K$ to $N \times K \times M(M \in N^+)$, where $M - 1$ is the number of relation information as shown in Fig. 2. However, this method cannot be applied to the sentence q in the Query Set Q since the goal of the FSRE is to identify the relation between the entity pairs in q.

3.2   Relation Prototype Representation

The generation of relation prototype representation and the process of a relation-unknown sentence relation extraction are shown in Fig. 3. This section will explain how we generate the relation prototype representation shown in the light gray boxes on the left side of Fig. 3.

Sentence Prototype. First, we use the sentence augmentation method of Sect. 3.1 on the original sentence set S_n^K of the relation r_n to obtain the sentence set S_n^{MK}. In detail, the sentence s_n^{mk} is obtained by expanding the kth sentence in the original sentence set S_n^K through relation information. We use BERT [11] as the sentence encoder to obtain the text embedding representation $SenSP_n^{mk}$ of s_n^{mk}:

$$SenSP_n^{mk} = BERT(s_n^{mk}) \tag{1}$$

where $BERT(\cdot)$ represents using BERT to obtain text embedding representation of the sentence. For the $K \times M$ sentences of r_n, we also use Formula 1 to obtain those text embedding representations.

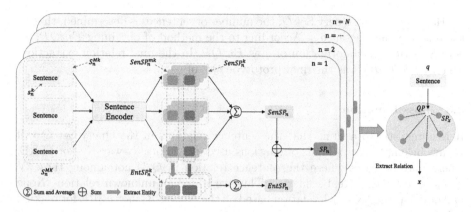

Fig. 3. Relation Prototype Representation Generation and Sentence Relation Extraction. The prototype generation of the nth relation is shown in the gray box on the left side of this figure. And the relation extraction of a relation-unknown sentence is shown on the right side of this figure. (Color figure online)

The prototype representations of all sentences in S_N^{MK} are summed and averaged to obtain the final sentence prototype $SenSP_n$:

$$SenSP_n = \frac{\sum_{m=1}^{M} \sum_{k=1}^{K} SenSP_n^{mk}}{M \times K} \tag{2}$$

where $SenSP_n^{mk}$ represents the sentence prototype representation of s_n^{mk}, and $M - 1$ represents the amount of relation information of relation r_n.

Entity Prototype. The intermediate state $\{head_n^{mk}, tail_n^{mk}\}$ is obtained by concatenating the hidden states corresponding to the start tokens of the head entity and the tail entity in $SenSP_n^{mk}$ following Baldini Soares et al. [16]. At the same time, we can get the entity prototype $EntSP_n^{mk}(EntSP_n^{mk} \in R^{2d})$ of the intermediate state, where d represents the text input size of the sentence encoder. For $S_n^{mk}(m \in \{1, 2, \cdots, M\})$, all entity pair information is exactly the same, so $EntSP_n^{mk}$ can be simplified as $EntSP_n^k$. At last, the final entity prototype representation $EntSP_n$ is obtained using a method similar to Formula 1:

$$EntSP_n = \frac{\sum_{k=1}^{K} EntSP_n^k}{K} \tag{3}$$

Relation Prototype. We obtain the final prototype representation SP_n of the relation r_n on the Support Set according to the direct addition method by Liu et al. [12], where $SenSP_n$ and $EntSP_n$ represent the sentence prototype and entity prototype of relation r_n, respectively:

$$SP_n = SenSP_n + EntSP_n \tag{4}$$

However, for the Query Set Q, the number of sentences is determined, that is, there is only one sentence q. According to the method of obtaining $EntQP$, we get the entity pair information of q as $EntQP$. In the final relation extraction, we only use $EntQP$ as the final prototype QP of q.

3.3   Loss Function

It is unrealistic to assume that the sentence relations in the Query Set Q will always belong to the N kinds of relations used in practical N-way-K-shot FSRE. There may be cases where the sentence relation in Q is not among these N kinds of relations in real scenarios. Thus we added an unknown relation "None of Above" as the $(N+1)$th relation based on the N-way-K-shot FSRE for making it have a strong generalization. And at the same time, we derive the $(N+1)$th relation from the existing N relations to enhance the ability of the model to distinguish similar relations and then obtain its prototype representation SP_{n+1}:

$$SP_{n+1} = \frac{\sum_{n=1}^{N} SP_n}{N} \tag{5}$$

where SP_n represents the prototype representation of the r_n. Besides, SP_{n+1} is added to the prototype representation set SP of the Support Set.

After that, we make a small adjustment to the cross-entropy loss function L_{ce} for the newly added $(N+1)$th relation:

$$L_{ce}(p, q) = -log(q_n) \quad n = p \tag{6}$$

$$L_{N+1}(p, q, x) = \begin{cases} L_{ce}(p, q) & res(q) = x \\ 0 & res(q) \neq x \end{cases} \tag{7}$$

In L_{ce}, p represents the actual result, q represents the array of predicted results, q_n represents the predicted probability of the nth relation, and $n = p$ represents that q is consistent with the actual result. In L_{N+1}, p, q is the same as L_{ce}'s, x represents the $(N+1)$th relation, and $res(\cdot)$ means obtaining the final predicted result. The Formula 7 indicates that when the predicted result is the $(N+1)$th relation, the loss function will perform the cross-entropy calculation on the results of all $(N+1)$ relations.

$$L_{total} = L_{ce}(p, q_{[0:N]}) + \lambda L_{N+1}(p, q, x) \tag{8}$$

The final loss function L_{total} is shown in Formula 8, where p, $q \in R^{b \times (N+1)}$, x have the same meanings as in Formula 6 and 7, λ represents the coefficient of L_{N+1}, b represents the batch size, and $q_{[0:N]}$ represents that we intercept the first N prediction results. L_{total} means that if the prediction result $res(q)$ is not the $(N+1)$th relation, it calculates the cross entropy of the first N prediction results, and if not, performs cross entropy calculation on the results of all $(N+1)$ relations.

3.4   Relation Extraction

The process of relation extraction is shown on the right side of Fig. 3. We obtain all relation prototype representations $SP_n(n \in \{1, 2, \ldots, N\})$ through Sect. 3.2, and then obtain the prototype representation QP of relation-unknown sentence q, and add SP_{n+1} to SP according to Sect. 3.3. The model uses the vector dot product way to calculate the distance between QP and $SP_n(n \in \{1, 2, \ldots, N, N + 1\})$, and select the relation with the closest distance to QP as the final prediction result. During the entire experiment, we use L_{total} as the final loss function.

4   Experiments

Table 1. The Situation of FewRel's Relations and Sentences.

Dataset	Relation	Sentence
Train Set	64	44800
Valid Set	16	11200
Test Set	20	14000
Sum	100	70000

4.1   Dataset

We conduct experiments on the publicly available FSRE dataset FewRel [9]. FewRel, shown in Table 1, contains 100 relations, each with 700 sentences, all extracted from Wikipedia and Wikidata by computer software and human judgment. Our experiment follows the official standard and divides the dataset into the train set, valid set, and test set. The relation types of the three datasets are 64, 16, and 20 respectively, and the three datasets are disjoint with each other. In FewRel, each relation has a corresponding relationship name and a description which can be used as the relation information.

4.2   Training and Validation

We use bert-base-uncased [11] as the sentence encoder. We set the number of training epochs to 30000, the number of validation epochs to 1000, the learning rate to 1e-5, and the λ in the loss function L_{total} to 1. We use the common N-way-K-shot (N-w-K-s) on the FewRel as the definition to distinguish different tasks and use the accuracy rate to measure the effect of the model.

4.3   Comparable Models

The models compared with our model include two CNN-based models Proto-HATT [6] and MLMAN [21], as well as eight BERT-based models BERT-PAIR [7], REGRAB [14], TD-proto [19], CTEG [18], ConceptFERE [20], DRK [17], HCRP [8], SimpleFSRE [12]. The relevant results are all from their papers or CodeLab[1].

4.4   Results

Table 2. The Results on the FewRel Valid Set and Test Set. We use "N-w-K-s" as "N-way-K-shot". The experimental results are displayed in the form of "Valid Set/ Test Set", respectively in the accuracy rate on Valid Set and Test Set, and the unit is the percentage. "— —" indicates that the result is unknown. Bold indicates the best results in our experiment.

Encoder	Model	5-w-1-s	5-w-5-s	10-w-1-s	10-w-5-s
CNN	Proto-HATT	72.65/74.52	86.15/88.40	60.13/62.38	76.20/80.45
	MLMAN	75.01 /— —	87.09/90.12	62.48 /— —	77.50/83.05
BERT	BERT-PAIR	85.66/88.32	89.48/93.22	76.84/80.63	81.76/87.02
	REGRAB	87.95/90.30	92.54/94.25	80.26/84.09	86.72/89.93
	TD-proto	— —/ 84.76	— —/ 92.38	— —/ 74.32	— —/ 85.92
	CTEG	84.72/88.11	92.52/95.25	76.01/81.29	84.89/91.33
	ConceptFERE	— —/ 89.21	— —/ 90.34	— —/ 75.72	— —/ 81.82
	DRK	— —/ 89.94	— —/ 92.42	— —/ 81.94	— —/ 85.23
	HCRP (BERT)	90.90/93.76	93.22/95.66	84.11/89.95	87.79/92.10
	SimpleFSRE (BERT)	91.29/94.42	94.05/96.37	86.09/90.73	89.68 /**93.47**
	Ours (BERT)	**93.30/94.69**	**94.79/96.67**	**88.09/91.64**	**90.68**/ 93.10

All experimental results are shown in Table 2, and the CNN-based and BERT-based models are both in the table. We can obtain three observations: (i) In this experiment, our model achieves the best results on the valid set and test set of 5-way-1-shot, 5-way-5-shot, and 10-way-1-shot respectively. While in the 10-way-5-shot task, our model is only the best result on the valid set, and slightly worse than SimpleFSRE on the test set. (ii) Our model improves results on the valid set more than on the test set. (iii) Our model performs best on the 10-way-1-shot task.

4.5   Result Analysis

Under the premise that the number of relation types (N) is determined, increasing the number of sentences (K) in the type can improve the accuracy of FSRE

---

[1] https://competitions.codalab.org/competitions/27980#results.

results obviously. Our relation-based sentence augmentation method has better results in the four few-shot tasks in the experiment, especially for 10-way-1-shot where the effect is the most significant because the 10-way-1-shot task is changed to 10-way-3-shot through the sentence augmentation method, which greatly increases the sample size in a single relation. This phenomenon is in good agreement with the above rule. However, the number of samples for each relation is already 5, and the improvement effect of adding 3 sentences is insignificant for the other three tasks, especially in the N-way-5-shot task.

4.6   Ablation Study

Because FewRel does not have a public test set, we conduct an ablation study on the valid set, and the validation iteration number is set to 1000. The ablation study results are shown in Table 3, and we can obtain two observations: (i) The original sentence information is helpful to improve the accuracy of the FSRE model. (ii) After using the sentence augmentation method mentioned in Sect. 3.1, the accuracy of relation extraction is greatly improved. These show that our proposed sentence augmentation method based on relation information is of great help to improve the accuracy of FSRE.

Table 3. Ablation Experimental Results. L_{total}, "Sen-Info", and "Data-Argue" represent that the ablation model uses the total loss function, uses sentence prototype as a part of relation prototype, and uses the method mentioned in Sect. 3.1, respectively. "✓" represents the corresponding method or data used in the ablation experiment. The unit is the percentage.

L_{total}	Sen-Info	Data-Argue	5-w-1-s	10-w-1-s
✓			87.43	79.32
✓	✓		87.72	79.36
✓	✓	✓	93.30	88.09

4.7   Limitation

The method proposed in this paper is simple and efficient, but it has two limitations: (i) It generates $M - 1$ times sentences in one FSRE which can lead to increased computer resource consumption. This may result in slower training and inference speeds, particularly on low-specification computers. (ii) The quality of the obtained relation information determines the quality of the generated sentences and ultimately affects the accuracy of FSRE. Research on the above two limitations will be the focus of our future research.

5 Conclusion

In this paper, we propose a sentence augmentation method based on relation information, that can generate a series of high-quality sentence samples with the same sentence structure and fewer irrelevant words. At the same time, we obtain the relation prototype representation for the Prototype Network by directly adding the entity prototype and the sentence prototype. Finally, considering that the existing N-way-K-shot task setting is unrealistic, we add the "None of Above" as the $(N + 1)$th relation based on N-way-K-shot, and modify the loss function to accommodate this modification. Experiments show that our method achieves the best results on three few-shot relation extraction tasks.

Our sentence augmentation method offers a simple and efficient approach that generates a substantial number of high-quality sentence samples for FSRE research. It provides valuable insights for data augmentation in future related studies. However, it is important to address the challenges of computer resource consumption and the quality of obtained relation information, as these factors can impact the speed and accuracy of FSRE. Hence reducing computer resource consumption and getting high-quality relation information will be the content of future research.

References

1. Bach, N., Badaskar, S.: A survey on relation extraction. Lang. Technol. Inst. Carnegie Mellon Univ. **178**, 15 (2007)
2. Brody, S., Wu, S., Benton, A.: Towards realistic few-shot relation extraction. In: Proceedings of the 2021 Conference on Empirical Methods in Natural Language Processing, pp. 5338–5345 (2021)
3. Chen, X., et al.: Knowprompt: knowledge-aware prompt-tuning with synergistic optimization for relation extraction. In: Proceedings of the ACM Web Conference 2022, pp. 2778–2788 (2022)
4. Dong, M., Pan, C., Luo, Z.: Mapre: an effective semantic mapping approach for low-resource relation extraction. In: Proceedings of the 2021 Conference on Empirical Methods in Natural Language Processing, pp. 2694–2704 (2021)
5. Fan, S., Zhang, B., Zhou, S., Wang, M., Li, K.: Few-shot relation extraction towards special interests. Big Data Res. **26**, 100273 (2021)
6. Gao, T., Han, X., Liu, Z., Sun, M.: Hybrid attention-based prototypical networks for noisy few-shot relation classification. In: Proceedings of the AAAI Conference on Artificial Intelligence, vol. 33, pp. 6407–6414 (2019)
7. Gao, T., et al.: Fewrel 2.0: towards more challenging few-shot relation classification. In: Proceedings of the 2019 Conference on Empirical Methods in Natural Language Processing and the 9th International Joint Conference on Natural Language Processing (EMNLP-IJCNLP), pp. 6250–6255 (2019)
8. Han, J., Cheng, B., Lu, W.: Exploring task difficulty for few-shot relation extraction. In: Proceedings of the 2021 Conference on Empirical Methods in Natural Language Processing, pp. 2605–2616 (2021)
9. Han, X., et al.: Fewrel: a large-scale supervised few-shot relation classification dataset with state-of-the-art evaluation. In: Proceedings of the 2018 Conference on Empirical Methods in Natural Language Processing, pp. 4803–4809 (2018)

10. He, K., Huang, Y., Mao, R., Gong, T., Li, C., Cambria, E.: Virtual prompt pre-training for prototype-based few-shot relation extraction. Expert Syst. Appl. **213**, 118927 (2023)
11. Kenton, J.D.M.W.C., Toutanova, L.K.: BERT: pre-training of deep bidirectional transformers for language understanding. In: Proceedings of NAACL-HLT, pp. 4171–4186 (2019)
12. Liu, Y., Hu, J., Wan, X., Chang, T.H.: A simple yet effective relation information guided approach for few-shot relation extraction. In: Findings of the Association for Computational Linguistics: ACL 2022, pp. 757–763 (2022)
13. Peng, H., et al.: Learning from context or names? An empirical study on neural relation extraction. In: Proceedings of the 2020 Conference on Empirical Methods in Natural Language Processing (EMNLP), pp. 3661–3672 (2020)
14. Qu, M., Gao, T., Xhonneux, L.P., Tang, J.: Few-shot relation extraction via Bayesian meta-learning on relation graphs. In: International Conference on Machine Learning, pp. 7867–7876. PMLR (2020)
15. Snell, J., Swersky, K., Zemel, R.: Prototypical networks for few-shot learning. In: Proceedings of the 31st International Conference on Neural Information Processing Systems, pp. 4080–4090 (2017)
16. Soares, L.B., Fitzgerald, N., Ling, J., Kwiatkowski, T.: Matching the blanks: distributional similarity for relation learning. In: Proceedings of the 57th Annual Meeting of the Association for Computational Linguistics, pp. 2895–2905 (2019)
17. Wang, M., Zheng, J., Cai, F., Shao, T., Chen, H.: DRK: discriminative rule-based knowledge for relieving prediction confusions in few-shot relation extraction. In: Proceedings of the 29th International Conference on Computational Linguistics, pp. 2129–2140 (2022)
18. Wang, Y., Verspoor, K., Baldwin, T.: Learning from unlabelled data for clinical semantic textual similarity. In: Proceedings of the 3rd Clinical Natural Language Processing Workshop, pp. 227–233 (2020)
19. Yang, K., Zheng, N., Dai, X., He, L., Huang, S., Chen, J.: Enhance prototypical network with text descriptions for few-shot relation classification. In: Proceedings of the 29th ACM International Conference on Information and Knowledge Management, pp. 2273–2276 (2020)
20. Yang, S., Zhang, Y., Niu, G., Zhao, Q., Pu, S.: Entity concept-enhanced few-shot relation extraction. In: Proceedings of the 59th Annual Meeting of the Association for Computational Linguistics and the 11th International Joint Conference on Natural Language Processing (Volume 2: Short Papers), pp. 987–991 (2021)
21. Ye, Z.X., Ling, Z.H.: Multi-level matching and aggregation network for few-shot relation classification. In: Proceedings of the 57th Annual Meeting of the Association for Computational Linguistics, pp. 2872–2881 (2019)

Dynamic and Static Feature-Aware Microservices Decomposition via Graph Neural Networks

Long Chen, Mingjian Guang, Junli Wang, and Chungang Yan[✉]

Key Laboratory of Embedded System and Service Computing,
Ministry of Education, and the National (ProvinceMinistry Joint)
Collaborative Innovation Center for Financial Network Security,
Tongji University, Shanghai 201804, China
{2133030,mjguang,junliwang,yanchungang}@tongji.edu.cn

Abstract. Microservices architecture has gained significant success in software development due to its flexibility and scalability. Decomposing a monolithic system into microservices can increase code reusability and reduce reconstruction costs. However, existing microservices decomposition approaches only utilize dynamic or static feature to represent the monolithic system, leading to low coverage of classes and inadequate information. To address these issues, we propose a novel Microservices Decomposition approach with the Dynamic and Static feature-aware called MDDS, which combines dynamic and static feature to construct a graph that represents the monolithic system. We also propose an approach based on variational graph auto-encoders to learn the nodes' representations in the graph, providing similar encodings to functionally similar classes to enhance microservices clustering. Extensive experiments on four traditional monolithic systems demonstrate that MDDS outperforms other baselines in several significant metrics.

Keywords: Dynamic feature · monolithic system · microservices decomposition · graph neural network · static feature

1 Introduction

With the increasing popularity of cloud-native development, microservices are becoming an essential part of modern software architecture [1]. The design philosophy behind microservices is to adopt multiple small-scale and independently deployable microservices instead of a monolithic system with complex functions [2]. Despite this, many software systems are still constructed utilizing a monolithic architecture, making system expansion and maintenance difficult. Microservices decomposition has been proposed to solve this problem, whereby a monolithic application is decomposed into microservices. Leading organizations such as Netflix, Amazon, and eBay have recognized the significance of microservices decomposition and have invested heavily in its development [1,3].

This work was supported in part by the Shanghai Science and Technology Innovation Action Plan Project under Grant 22511100700.

In microservices decomposition, most approaches construct a graph to represent the monolithic system and then utilize graph clustering algorithms to cluster the nodes in the graph to obtain the microservices candidates [2]. Graph construction approaches can be categorized into two types. The first category consists of dynamic analysis approaches [4–7], which rely on the calling relationship and frequency between classes to construct a graph that represents the monolithic system. These dynamic analysis approaches have received considerable attention recently as they can improve the cohesiveness of microservices and reduce communication between services [8]. The second category is static analysis approaches [9–12], which construct a graph based on the structural dependencies or semantic relationships between classes. These static analysis approaches are relatively simple to implement and are frequently used in existing approaches. In the clustering step, existing approaches generally rely on community discovery algorithms based on heuristics, such as the GN algorithm [13], AP clustering, and hierarchical clustering for microservices decomposition.

However, the aforementioned approaches have several limitations. Firstly, dynamic analysis approaches suffer from the class coverage problem and static analysis approaches face the problem of inadequate information. Specifically, dynamic analysis heavily relies on test cases, and designing test cases to cover a large number of classes in large monolithic systems can be a challenge. For example, [4,7] can only cover 70%-80% of the classes in large systems, while classes without covered require manual delineation, which is inefficient and laborious. For the static analysis, related approaches merely analyze the system structure while ignoring the system's runtime state, which results in increased communication costs and reduced cohesiveness within services. Secondly, for graph clustering, the above clustering approaches are difficult to utilize both node features and topology information, resulting in information loss. Recently, graph neural networks [14,15] have shown significant performance in various domains. For example, variational graph autoencoder (VGAE) [16] has been particularly effective in improving the performance of graph clustering tasks [17]. VGAE is extensively used in graph clustering tasks as it relies on unsupervised learning and plays a crucial role in graph representation learning. However, few studies have applied VGAE to microservices decomposition.

To solve the above limitations, we propose a dynamic and static feature-aware microservices decomposition via graph neural network. Our approach combines static and dynamic features to construct a more holistic representation graph, which effectively addresses the class coverage problem and enriches the information in the graph. To cluster the graph, we propose a VGAE based approach to learn the graph structure and the node features. With this model, classes with similar functions are assigned similar encodings, which can improve the effectiveness of clustering to obtain microservices candidates. To evaluate the effectiveness of our approach, we conduct experiments on four standard monolithic systems and compare our approach with several state-of-the-art approaches. We also perform ablation experiments to illustrate the performance of the dynamic and static analysis. The main contributions of this work are as follows:

– For graph construction, we propose an approach that combines dynamic and static features of monolithic systems to solve the problem of class coverage and inadequate information.
– We propose a VGAE-based graph representation learning approach to enhance clustering to obtain microservices candidates.
– The experiments conducted on several monolithic systems validate that MDDS outperforms other baselines in cohesion and coupling metrics.

2   Related Work

Researchers have proposed many approaches to help identify or decompose microservices. These approaches can be categorized by how they analyze monolithic systems and how they perform microservices clustering.

Several studies have analyzed the static structure and semantic relations of monolithic systems to decompose microservices. Kamimura et al. [9] propose an approach that utilizes the results of a static analysis tool to extract potential microservices candidates. Martinek et al. [10] utilize a distributed representation of the source code to decompose microservices, while Mazlami et al. [18] analyze the version control repository of a monolithic application. Li et al. [19] present a novel approach for identifying microservices by considering quality expectations and deployment constraints. However, the limitation of these approaches is that they only rely on the static structure or semantic relationships of the monolithic system, which can lead to incomplete or suboptimal microservices.

Other approaches rely on dynamic analysis to uncover more information about the system operation. Jin et al. [4] propose a function-oriented microservices extraction approach based on execution trace clustering. Abdullah et al. [5] propose an unsupervised learning approach for web application auto-decomposition into microservices. Taibi et al. [6] develop a decomposition framework based on process mining to help identify candidates for microservices. Kalia et al. [7] propose the Mono2micro model, which utilizes marked execution traces and specific hierarchical clustering algorithms to obtain microservices. However, these approaches suffer from the problem of insufficient coverage since the paths for test case execution may only cover a part of the classes.

Some research focuses on improving microservices decomposition in terms of clustering algorithms. Most approaches utilize clustering approaches based on heuristic algorithms. For example, Nunes et al. [11] utilize hierarchical clustering to decompose the call graph to obtain microservices candidates. However, these clustering algorithms heavily rely on graph construction and need to work better for clustering graphs with complex information. Kinoshita et al. [20] propose an approach to decompose microservices using multi-objective optimization and transform monolithic system information into constraints to avoid information loss. Sellami et al. [12] introduce an evolutionary search-based technique to improve the extraction of microservices from monolithic applications. These approaches rely on the design of the optimization objective and finding the optimal solution from the results set is also tricky.

3 Proposed Approach

This section describes the overview of our proposed approach and the design of the various parts.

3.1 Approach Overview

The approach overview is illustrated in Fig. 1, which comprises four main stages. 1) The monolithic system performs static and dynamic analyses to obtain the system's static structure, *class-level* and *method-level* call relations, and semantic vectors of methods. 2) The relations between classes are identified by combining the system's static structure and class-level call relations, which are exploited to construct a class call graph, with classes serving as vertices and relations as edges. Additionally, MDDS calculates method weights based on the *method-level* call relations and aggregates the method vectors into class vectors according to the weights. 3) The class call graph and class vectors are utilized to create the dynamic and static features graph. VGAE is utilized to learn the graph structure and node features. After training the model, MDDS obtains the node embedding matrix Z. 4) Finally, the matrix Z contains the embedding representation of each vertex in the graph and we utilize k-means to cluster these vertices to obtain the microservices candidates.

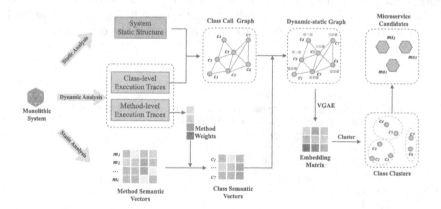

Fig. 1. Approach Overview

3.2 Problem Formulation

A monolithic system is defined by a set $C = \{c_1, c_2, \ldots, c_n\}$, where n denotes the number of classes in the monolithic system. Let $MS = \{ms_1, ms_2, \ldots, ms_k\}$ be the set of microservices ms, where k denotes the number of microservices.

Microservices decomposition is to cluster these n classes into k small sets, where each set forms a microservice ms.

MDDS constructs a system graph to represent the monolithic system and then transforms the microservices decomposition problem into a graph clustering problem. A system graph G is defined by a tuple (V, E, W_e, X) where $V = \{v_i\}_{i=1}^{|V|}$ is the set of vertices. $E \subseteq V \times V$ is the set of edges where each edge between vertex v_i and vertex v_j can be denoted as (v_i, v_j), $v_i, v_j \in V$. W_e is the weight on the edge and X is the node feature matrix. In the following steps, MDDS utilizes dynamic and static analysis to obtain the information that exploits to construct the system graph.

3.3 Dynamic Analysis

The dynamic analysis process can be divided into three steps. Firstly, we utilize the Kieker [21] to obtain the execution trace logs. Then we extract the *Method-level* call relations from the logs. Thirdly, we extract the *Class-level* call relations based on the *Method-level* call relations.

1) Execution trace. The execution of the monolithic system is monitored and recorded in Kieker's log file. Figure 2 shows a record in the log file. The record consists of ten items, including *Type, SeqID, Method, SessionID, TraceID, Tin, Tout, HostName, Eoi* and *Ess*. Among them, *Method, Eoi* and *Ess* are information related to method call relationships and are selected to generate the *Method-level* call relations, where *Method* denotes the full signature of a method, *Eoi* is the order of method calls and *Ess* is the depth of the call stack.

```
Type : $1;
SeqID : 1668923437043728958;
Method : private void org.mybatis.jpetstore.domain.CartItem.calculateTotal();
SessionID : 6EAF07C5595B9A73BAEAF1D8991F142A;
TraceID : 684828618337026411;
Tin : 1668923437043724292;
Tout : 1668923437043728708;
HostName : MacBook-Air.local;
Eoi : 12;
Ess : 3
```

Fig. 2. One record in the Log

2) *Method-level* call relations. Let $r_i = (m_i, \lambda_i, \mu_i)$ be the call relation corresponding to the ith log record, where m_i denotes the *Method*, λ_i denotes the *Eoi* and μ_i denotes the *Ess* in the record. We define $S_{log} = \{r_1, r_2, \ldots, r_m\}$ as the set of call relations. We can extract the method call relations from S_{log}. According to [8,21], if two records r_i and r_j satisfy the rule: $\mu_i = \mu_j - 1$, $\lambda_i < \lambda_j$, then m_i is the caller of m_j. Considering there may be multiple calls between two methods, we merge these same call relations and record the number of calls between them using k_{ij} for ease of handling. We can represent each call relation by a triple $M_{ij} = (m_i, m_j, k_{ij})$ that indicates the call relation between m_i and m_j and the number of calls is k_{ij}.

3) *Class-level* **call relations.** A class contains multiple methods, so the call relations between classes can be accessed by *Method-level* call relations. With S_M, we can extract *Class-level* call relations. We similarly utilize a triple $D_{pq} = (c_p, c_q, Calls_D(c_p, c_q))$ to represent the call relationship between two classes c_p and c_q, where $Calls_D(c_p, c_q)$ denotes the number of calls between the two classes. $Calls_D(c_p, c_q)$ can be calculated by the following formula:

$$Calls_D(c_p, c_q) = \sum_{\forall m_i \in c_p} \sum_{\forall m_j \in c_q} k_{ij} \tag{1}$$

where k_{ij} denotes the number of calls between m_i and m_j. If there is no call relation between the two methods, then let $k_{ij} = 0$.

3.4 Static Analysis

Source code dependencies are widely used in software engineering to measure how strongly the classes of a software system are related to each other [12]. MDDS detects dependencies between classes in terms of structural dependencies and semantic similarity.

1) **Structural dependencies.** The more structural dependencies between two classes, the more closely they are connected [22]. Clustering such classes into the same microservices can effectively reduce the cost of communication between services. According to this principle, we define the structural dependencies between two classes in terms of their method dependencies. Let $d_{ij} = (m_i, m_j)$ be the structural dependency between two methods m_i and m_j. We define the set $S_S = \{d_1, d_2, \ldots, d_t\}$ to contain these structural dependencies. The following formula can calculate the dependencies between classes:

$$Calls_S(c_p, c_q) = \sum_{\forall m_i \in c_p} \sum_{\forall m_j \in c_q} g_{ij} \tag{2}$$

where g_{ij} denotes whether a structural dependency exists between m_i and m_j. If $d_{ij} \in S_S$, $g_{ij} = 1$, otherwise $g_{ij} = 0$.

We utilize dynamic call relations and static structural dependencies to jointly reflect the relations between classes. Let $\sigma(c_p, c_q)$ be the degree of association between two classes c_p and c_q. $\sigma(c_p, c_q)$ is defined as follows:

$$\sigma(c_p, c_q) = \alpha \times Calls_D(c_p, c_q) + \beta \times Calls_S(c_p, c_q) \tag{3}$$

where α and β are weights, and $\alpha + \beta = 1$.

2) **Semantic similarity.** The concept of bounded context, derived from domain-driven design, is used as a fundamental design principle to define microservices

boundaries [23]. Based on this design principle, we analyze the semantics of the source code to enhance the microservices decomposition.

During the semantic analysis of this work, we utilize the Code2Vec [24] to generate vector representations of the entity class instead of the traditional approach (*tf-idf*). Code2Vec is a deep learning-based code vector generation model designed to generate vector representations of code fragments by analyzing the semantic structure of the code. The vectors obtained by Code2Vec are more representative of the code's functionality than *tf-idf*. Let y_i be the semantic vector of method m_i. A class contains multiple methods, and we can represent these method vectors with a matrix $Y = [y_1, y_2, \ldots, y_l]^\mathsf{T}$, where l denotes the number of methods in the class.

In this work, we utilize classes as nodes for clustering. However, the vectors generated by Code2Vec are method vectors of codes, and an entity class may contain one or more methods. We propose a weight-based approach to aggregate method vectors to obtain class vectors instead of the aggregation approaches (e.g., mean) utilized by existing microservices decomposition approaches [10].

Methods utilized frequently in an entity class are more representative of the functionality of that class and should therefore receive more weight. We record *Method-level* call relations in our dynamic analysis, and we can calculate the percentage weights based on this. We can employ the following formula to calculate the method weights:

$$w_i = \tau_i \Big/ \sum_{\forall m_j \in c} \tau_j \qquad (4)$$

where c represents a class containing methods m_j, τ_i denotes the number of calls and invocations of method m_i.

The weights of all methods in a class can be obtained according to Eq. 4, and let $W = [w_1, w_2, \ldots, w_l]$ be the vector of these weights. MDDS calculates the class vector (x) by $x = WY$.

3.5   Construction of Dynamic and Static Features Graph

Based on the information obtained from the dynamic and static analysis, we construct graph $G = (V, E, W_e, X)$ to represent the monolithic system. Each vertex in set V corresponds to a class in the monolithic system. We utilize the degree of association between two classes $\sigma(c_i, c_j)$ to determine whether an edge exists between two vertices. For $\forall v_i, v_j \in V$, if $i \neq j$ and $\sigma(c_i, c_j) \neq 0$, then we form an edge (v_i, v_j) between v_i and v_j. We add the edge (v_i, v_j) to the edge set E and add $\sigma(c_i, c_j)$ to the weight set W_e. In addition, we define the node features matrix $X = [x_1^\mathsf{T}, x_2^\mathsf{T}, \ldots, x_n^\mathsf{T}]$, where x_i denotes the class vector of the ith class and n denotes the number of classes.

3.6   Training and Clustering

To facilitate VGAE in learning the graph structure and node features, we utilize the matrix A to represent the graph's adjacency matrix where A_{ij} is the weight of edge (v_i, v_j) if it exists, otherwise $A_{ij} = 0$. According to [16], a two layer-graph convolution encoder is utilized to obtain the representation of nodes. The formula is as follows:

$$Z = f(X, A) = \text{ReLU}\left(\hat{A}\,\text{ReLU}\left(\hat{A}XW^{(0)}\right)W^{(1)}\right) \tag{5}$$

where Z denotes the node representation matrix, $W^{(0)}$ and $W^{(1)}$ are the training parameters of the encoder. We normalize the adjacency matrix A by $\hat{A} = \tilde{D}^{-\frac{1}{2}}(A + I)\tilde{D}^{-\frac{1}{2}}$, where I is the identity matrix and $\tilde{D}$ is the degree diagonal matrix. VGAE determines the loss by utilizing the gap before and after the graph reconstruction and we can utilize the matrices Z and A to calculate the structural loss of the graph. In addition, to represent the impact of node attributes on training, we should also calculate the attribute loss after decoding. The loss function is calculated as follows:

$$Loss = \left\|X - \hat{X}\right\|_2^2 + \left\|A - ZZ^{\mathsf{T}}\right\|_2^2 + KL(Z, p(Z)) \tag{6}$$

where $\hat{X}$ is the node attribute matrix obtained by decoding. $KL(Z, p(Z))$ denotes the KL divergence to ensure that the embedding matrix is a normal distribution, where $p(Z)$ is the prior distribution of Z.

Following obtaining the matrix Z, we cluster nodes utilizing the k-means algorithm. In microservices decomposition, existing approaches rely on relevant experts or experience to determine the number of microservices to be split. In this work, we utilize the Elbow approach to determine the k. After k-means clustering, we obtain clusters of classes and each cluster forms a microservice.

4   Evaluation

4.1   Evaluation Applications

In order to evaluate our approach, we conduct experiments on four traditional monolithic systems: JPetstore[1] SpringBlog[2], JForum[3], and Roller[4]. JPetstore is a small pet store system, SpringBlog is a blogging website, JForum is a forum system, and Roller is a multi-user, group blogging service system. Table 1 shows the details of these four systems.

We chose these four open-source monolithic systems because they represent a common scenario for large-scale legacy Web applications. Due to degraded designs and growing complexity, such legacy applications typically suffer from modularity, maintainability, and scalability issues. In addition, these four systems vary in size from 24 to 534 classes, so they have been utilized as benchmarks in recent microservices decomposition studies.

---

[1] https://github.com/mybatis/jpetstore-6.
[2] https://github.com/Raysmond/SpringBlog.
[3] https://github.com/rafaelsteil/jforum2.
[4] https://github.com/apache/roller.

Table 1. Monolithic systems metadata

System	Version	Domain	SLOC	# of classes
JPetstore	6.0.2	e-store	1438	24
SpringBlog	2.8.0	blogging	3583	85
JForum	2.1.9	forum	29550	340
Roller	5.2.0	blogging	47602	534

4.2 Baselines

To assess the efficacy of our approach, we select four approaches as comparative standards: LIMBO [25], MEM [10], FoME [8] and MSExtractor [18]. LIMBO is a classical software decomposition approach that utilizes information loss to represent the distance between entity classes. For MEM, it proposes three logical, semantic, and contributor coupling strategies to measure the correlation between classes. FoME, as an approach for tracking test case execution, is considered the originator of dynamic analysis. MSExtractor transforms the clustering problem of microservices splitting into a multi-objective optimization problem by continuously optimizing the cohesiveness and coupling to obtain better microservices partitioning results. Above approaches have been widely utilized as baseline approaches for comparison in recent studies.

4.3 Metrics

Recently, studies on the quality of microservices decomposition have primarily utilized cohesiveness and coupling to evaluate the decomposing effect. Therefore, this work evaluates the quality of extracted microservices utilizing four coupling and cohesion-based evaluation metrics, widely utilized in recent studies to evaluate the quality of microservices candidates.

CHM and CHD. CHM (CoHesion at Message level) [26] is a widely utilized metric to measure the cohesiveness of services at the message level and CHD (CoHesion at Domain level) [26]is used to measure the average cohesion of service interfaces at the domain level. The higher the CHM (or CHD), the better the cohesiveness of microservices.

OPN (OPeration Number). OPN [12] computes the number of public operations exposed by an extracted microservice to other candidate microservices. It can be defined by the following equation:

$$OPN = \frac{1}{|MS|} \times \sum_{\forall ms_i \in MS} \left| \bigcup_{\forall op_i \in ms_i} op_j \right| \tag{7}$$

where op_j is an operation provided by the extracted microservices. OPN is less, the better.

IRN (InteRaction Number). IRN [12] represents the number of method calls across two services. It can be defined by the following equation:

$$IRN = \sum_{\substack{\forall(ms_i,ms_j)\in MS \\ ms_i \neq ms_j}} \sum_{\substack{\forall p_k \in ms_i \\ \forall op_q \in ms_j}} \text{calls}\,(op_k, op_q) \tag{8}$$

where $calls(Op_k, Op_q)$ is the calling frequency from Op_k to Op_q. Op_k and Op_q are involved in inter-service interactions between the extracted microservices. The smaller the IRN, the looser coupling of candidate microservices.

4.4   Results and Discussion

The results and discussion section present the evaluation results of our approach and four baseline approaches. In Table 2, to follow Jin et al.'s [4] recommendation, we report the cohesion results in interval form rather than specific values, as slight differences between CHM (or CHD) scores are not significant. "Total" shows the number of metrics, in which an approach outperforms others.

Table 2. Comparison of evaluation results

System	Metric	MSExtractor	FoME	MEM	LIMBO	MDDS
Jpetstore	CHM	0.4–0.5	**0.7–0.8**	0.5–0.6	0.5–0.6	**0.7–0.8**
	CHD	**0.6–0.7**	**0.6–0.7**	**0.6–0.7**	**0.6–0.7**	**0.6–0.7**
	OPN	26	**22**	39	68	28
	IRN	**32**	35	48	329	**32**
	Total	2	**3**	1	1	**3**
SpringBlog	CHM	0.5–0.6	0.7–0.8	0.6–0.7	0.6–0.7	**0.8–0.9**
	CHD	0.6–0.7	**0.8–0.9**	**0.8–0.9**	0.7–0.8	**0.8–0.9**
	OPN	10	**7**	21	147	**7**
	IRN	**21**	26	30	238	24
	Total	1	2	1	0	**3**
Jforum	CHM	0.6–0.7	0.7–0.8	0.6–0.7	0.6–0.7	**0.8–0.9**
	CHD	0.4–0.5	**0.7–0.8**	0.6–0.7	0.6–0.7	**0.7–0.8**
	OPN	36	70	**11**	94	29
	IRN	**71**	97	145	993	86
	Total	1	1	1	0	**2**
Roller	CHM	0.5–0.6	**0.6–0.7**	**0.6–0.7**	**0.6–0.7**	**0.6–0.7**
	CHD	0.6–0.7	**0.8–0.9**	**0.8–0.9**	0.7–0.8	**0.8–0.9**
	OPN	63	56	66	1062	**52**
	IRN	**946**	1441	2786	46964	1654
	Total	1	2	1	1	**3**

The results show that our proposed approach outperforms the four baseline approaches in terms of cohesiveness and coupling. For Jpetstore, which has a small number of classes, the differences in results among different approaches are slight. However, for the other three systems, MDDS shows a more significant advantage in terms of cohesiveness.

Figure 3 indicates the number of the superiority of each metric on the four systems. From this, we find that MDDS maintains the best performance among the four experiments in CHM and CHD, which evaluate cohesiveness. Our approach exploits more information about the monolithic system and makes the classes with similar functions have similar encoding through the graph embedding representation of VGAE. This increases the effect of clustering and the final results show better cohesiveness. In addition, our approach also has the best results on OPN, a metric for evaluating coupling, which means that microservices obtained by MDDS have fewer interfaces. For IRN, MSExtractor maintains better results because MSExtractor is a static analysis-based approach, and the number of communications between its services is relatively low compared to dynamic analysis approaches. Overall, the evaluation results demonstrate the effectiveness of our proposed approach in microservices decomposition.

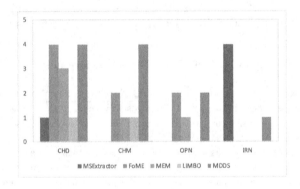

Fig. 3. Overall winners among all the approaches

To verify the effectiveness of dynamic and static feature, we conduct ablation experiments on SpringBlog. Experiment I represents our approach, while Experiment II utilizes only data from dynamic analysis and Experiment III utilizes only static feature. In each case, semantic information serves as the attribute vector of the nodes. The results of these experiments are shown in Table 3, where the metric "Coverage" denotes the coverage of classes in the system.

Table 3. Results of ablation experiments

Metric	Experiment I	Experiment II	Experiment III
CHM	**0.8–0.9**	0.7–0.8	0.5–0.6
CHD	**0.8–0.9**	**0.8–0.9**	0.6-0.7
OPN	7	7	10
IRN	24	26	**21**
Coverage	**91.76**%	72.94%	88.24%

The results show that dynamic analysis-based approaches outperform static analysis in terms of cohesiveness, while static analysis is better at decoupling and improving class coverage. MDDS combines the two and significantly improves the cohesiveness and class coverage. Low class coverage is a common problem in dynamic analysis, causing significant challenges in designing test cases and requiring extensive manual work to produce splitting results. Our proposed approach successfully addresses this issue and offers significant reference value to help engineers in related fields overcome the problem.

5   Conclusions

We propose a novel approach called MDDS to tackle the challenge of microservices decomposition. Our approach combines dynamic and static features to construct a monolithic system representation graph. We apply VGAE to the decomposing process to reduce information loss when dealing with graphs with complex information. Our experimental results demonstrate that our approach achieves lower coupling and higher cohesion compared to other approaches.

In future work, we plan to refine our approach by addressing the issue of coupling between microservices caused by certain classes in the monolithic system that contain many methods. We aim to split these classes into smaller, more granular methods and assign them to different microservices to reduce coupling and improve system performance.

References

1. Fritzsch, J., Bogner, J., Wagner, S., Zimmermann, A.: Microservices migration in industry: intentions, strategies, and challenges. In: 2019 IEEE International Conference on Software Maintenance and Evolution (ICSME), pp. 481–490. IEEE (2019)
2. Gonzalez, D., Ravesh, R., Sharma, S.: Microservices: Building Scalable Software. Packt Publishing (2017)
3. Taibi, D., Kehoe, B., Poccia, D.: Serverless: from bad practices to good solutions. In: 2022 IEEE International Conference on Service-Oriented System Engineering (SOSE), pp. 85–92. IEEE (2022)

4. Jin, W., Liu, T., Zheng, Q., Cui, D., Cai, Y.: Functionality-oriented microservice extraction based on execution trace clustering. In: 2018 IEEE International Conference on Web Services (ICWS), pp. 211–218. IEEE (2018)

5. Abdullah, M., Iqbal, W., Erradi, A.: Unsupervised learning approach for web application auto-decomposition into microservices. J. Syst. Softw. **151**, 243–257 (2019)

6. Taibi, D., Systä, K.: From monolithic systems to microservices: a decomposition framework based on process mining (2019)

7. Kalia, A.K., Xiao, J., Krishna, R., Sinha, S., Vukovic, M., Banerjee, D.: Mono2micro: a practical and effective tool for decomposing monolithic java applications to microservices. In: Proceedings of the 29th ACM Joint Meeting on European Software Engineering Conference and Symposium on the Foundations of Software Engineering, pp. 1214–1224 (2021)

8. Al Maruf, A., Bakhtin, A., Cerny, T., Taibi, D.: Using microservice telemetry data for system dynamic analysis. In: 2022 IEEE International Conference on Service-Oriented System Engineering (SOSE), pp. 29–38. IEEE (2022)

9. Kamimura, M., Yano, K., Hatano, T., Matsuo, A.: Extracting candidates of microservices from monolithic application code. In: 2018 25th Asia-Pacific Software Engineering Conference (APSEC), pp. 571–580. IEEE (2018)

10. Al-Debagy, O., Martinek, P.: A microservice decomposition method through using distributed representation of source code. Scal. Comput. Pract. Exp. **22**(1), 39–52 (2021)

11. Nunes, L., Santos, N., Rito Silva, A.: From a monolith to a microservices architecture: an approach based on transactional contexts. In: Bures, T., Duchien, L., Inverardi, P. (eds.) ECSA 2019. LNCS, vol. 11681, pp. 37–52. Springer, Cham (2019). https://doi.org/10.1007/978-3-030-29983-5_3

12. Sellami, K., Ouni, A., Saied, M.A., Bouktif, S., Mkaouer, M.W.: Improving microservices extraction using evolutionary search. Inf. Softw. Technol. **151**, 106996 (2022)

13. Newman, M.E., Girvan, M.: Finding and evaluating community structure in networks. Phys. Rev. E **69**(2), 026113 (2004)

14. Guang, M., Yan, C., Xu, Y., Wang, J., Jiang, C.: A multichannel convolutional decoding network for graph classification. IEEE Trans. Neural Netw. Learn. Syst. (2023)

15. Guang, M., Yan, C., Wang, J., Qi, H., Jiang, C.: Benchmark datasets for stochastic petri net learning. In: 2021 International Joint Conference on Neural Networks (IJCNN), pp. 1–8. IEEE (2021)

16. Kipf, T.N., Welling, M.: Variational graph auto-encoders. arXiv preprint arXiv:1611.07308 (2016)

17. Guang, M., Yan, C., Liu, G., Wang, J., Jiang, C.: A novel neighborhood-weighted sampling method for imbalanced datasets. Chin. J. Electron. **31**(5), 969–979 (2022)

18. Mazlami, G., Cito, J., Leitner, P.: Extraction of microservices from monolithic software architectures. In: 2017 IEEE International Conference on Web Services (ICWS), pp. 524–531. IEEE (2017)

19. Li, J., Xu, H., Xu, X., Wang, Z.: A novel method for identifying microservices by considering quality expectations and deployment constraints. Int. J. Softw. Eng. Knowl. Eng. **32**(03), 417–437 (2022)

20. Kinoshita, T., Kanuka, H.: Automated microservice decomposition method as multi-objective optimization. In: 2022 IEEE 19th International Conference on Software Architecture Companion (ICSA-C), pp. 112–115. IEEE (2022)

21. Van Hoorn, A., Waller, J., Hasselbring, W.: Kieker: a framework for application performance monitoring and dynamic software analysis. In: Proceedings of the 3rd ACM/SPEC International Conference on Performance Engineering, pp. 247–248 (2012)
22. Cerny, T., Taibi, D.: Static analysis tools in the era of cloud-native systems. arXiv preprint arXiv:2205.08527 (2022)
23. Evans, E.: Domain-Driven Design: Tackling Complexity in the Heart of Software. Addison-Wesley Professional, Boston (2004)
24. Alon, U., Zilberstein, M., Levy, O., Yahav, E.: Code2vec: learning distributed representations of code. Proc. ACM Program. Lang. 3(POPL), 1–29 (2019)
25. Andritsos, P., Tzerpos, V.: Information-theoretic software clustering. IEEE Trans. Softw. Eng. 31(2), 150–165 (2005)
26. Athanasopoulos, D., Zarras, A.V., Miskos, G., Issarny, V., Vassiliadis, P.: Cohesion-driven decomposition of service interfaces without access to source code. IEEE Trans. Serv. Comput. 8(4), 550–562 (2014)

An Enhanced Fitness-Distance Balance Slime Mould Algorithm and Its Application in Feature Selection

Haijia Bao, Yu Du, and Ya Li[✉]

College of Computer and Information Science, Southwest University,
Chongqing 400715, China
swu_yali@163.com

Abstract. Recently, the slime mould algorithm (SMA) has become popular in function optimization due to its simple structure and excellent optimization capability. However, it suffers from the shortcomings of easily falling into local optimum and unbalance exploration and exploitation. To address above limitations, an enhanced fitness-distance balance SMA (EFDB-SMA) is proposed in this paper. Firstly, fitness-distance balance (FDB) is an effective method to identify candidate solutions from the population with the highest potential to guide the search process. The FDB score is calculated from the fitness value of the candidate solution and the distance to the current optimal solution. In order to trade off exploration and exploitation, a candidate solution with high potential, which is selected based on FDB score through the roulette wheel method, is used to replace random choosing individual in position update mechanism. Secondly, an elite opposition-based learning strategy is adopted in the population initialization for increasing population diversity. Then chaotic tent sequence, with traversal property, is integrated into the position updating of SMA to perturb the position and jump out of local optima. Finally, EFDB-SMA greedily selects the position with superior fitness values during search process instead of indiscriminately accepting position updates to improve search performance. The experimental results on CEC2020 functions indicate that the proposed algorithm outperforms other optimizers in terms of accuracy, convergence speed and stability. Furthermore, classic datasets were tested to demonstrate practical engineering value of EFDB-SMA in spatial search and feature selection.

Keywords: Slime mould algorithm · Fitness-distance balance · Function optimization · Feature selection · Metaheuristic algorithm

1 Introduction

In scientific research and daily production life, optimization problems are commonly appear in practical areas, such as scheduling [19,27], prediction problem

Z. Jin et al. (Eds.): KSEM 2023, LNAI 14117, pp. 164–178, 2023.
https://doi.org/10.1007/978-3-031-40283-8_15

[12, 26]. However, traditional optimization methods have many limitations, such as the precocity of algorithms, the difficulty of solving combinatorial optimization problems. In recent decades, researchers have gained inspiration from the evolution of natural and biological life activities, the metaheuristic algorithms (MAs) have been developed and considered as an effective method to solve the global optimization problem.

The slime mould algorithm (SMA) [11] is a novel metaheuristic algorithm proposed by Li et al. in 2020, which simulates the behavior and morphological changes of multi-headed slime mould during foraging. To simulate positive and negative feedback during foraging, weights are used in SMA and three different position update mechanisms are generated. It has been shown that the foraging pattern of slime mould is based on the optimization theory [18].

SMA has been widely used in optimization problems with efficient performance due to simple structure and powerful local search capability. Many researchers make improvements on SMA with satisfactory results. Jia et al. [9] proposed an ensemble mutation slime mould algorithm with a restart mechanism. The composite mutation strategy was introduced to increase population diversity, the restart strategy was used to improve individuals and avoid getting into local optimum. Abdel-Basset et al. [1] developed an efficient binary SMA algorithm integrated with an attacking-feeding strategy, first a binary version was developed by using a transfer function, then a two-phase mutation was combined with it to further exploit the best solution so far and improve exploitation, finally, a novel attacking-feeding strategy was used to balance exploration and exploitation based on the previous state of each individual. Altay et al. [2] presented a global optimized chaotic SMA algorithm, which added chaotic mappings to improve the global convergence speed of SMA and prevent it from plunging into local solutions. Houssein et al. [7] proposed an efficient maximum power point tracking SMA algorithm based on orthogonal opposition-based learning, which contained Lévy flights and an orthogonal learning strategy that can find the best combinations between factor levels with a small number of experiments and provide new combinations of solutions in the best search direction. An equilibrium SMA algorithm was presented by Naik et al. [17], which integrated the equilibrium pool concept from the equilibrium optimizer into the search pattern of SMA to update position, then used it for color image threshold processing. Multi-objective slime mould algorithm (MOSMA) has also been developed recently. Houssein et al. [8] incorporated non-dominated sorting and crowding distance operator with SMA for solving multi-objective optimization problems, and the Pareto optimal solutions were stored in an external archive. Yacoubi et al. [23] combined MOSMA with orthogonal learning to solve the association rule mining problem, and got satisfactory results in the aspects of average support and average confidence.

The metaheuristic search (MHS) process is a population-based search method, which usually includes two steps. In the first step, candidate solutions are selected from the population according to the selection method adopted, called reference positions. In the second step, the search process is led by the selected reference positions. The direction and success of search process are directly affected by the candidate solutions from the population in the search process. In most MHS algorithms, the search process suffers from premature convergence, similarity of candidate solutions to each other, and the trend of falling into local optimum. Based on the above defects, Kahraman et al. [10] proposed a new selection method based on the fitness-distance balance (FDB) of the candidate solutions. In this idea, the reference positions are selected based on the score obtained from the fitness value of the candidate solution and the distance from the current optimal candidate solution. This selection method effectively identifies candidate solutions from the population with the highest potential to improve the search process, and has shown excellent performance in other metaheuristic algorithms (MAs) [3,4,21].

SMA is a novel optimizer with few improvements and applications. It is interesting to discover strategies that might improve efficiency and performance of SMA, further exploration is needed to enrich its vitality in the field of optimization technology. The drawbacks such as unbalanced exploration-exploitation and easy to plunge into local optimum need to be handled. For this purpose, an enhanced fitness-distance balance slime mould algorithm (EFDB-SMA) is proposed and applied in feature selection problem. The contributions of this paper are as follows:

1. The fitness-distance balance (FDB) method is introduced to the position update mechanism, with the aim of trading off exploration and exploitation.
2. To increase population diversity and enhance the global exploration ability and convergence speed of SMA, the elite opposition-based learning (EOBL) strategy is added to population initialization.
3. Chaotic tent sequences are used to the position of slime moulds for perturbation, which helps to jump out of local optimal capture. Moreover, the individuals with superior fitness values are remained by using a greedy selection strategy in each iteration.
4. The experiments are conducted on CEC2020 benchmark functions for the performance comparison of EFDB-SMA with other algorithms. The binary EFDB-SMA is developed to solve the feature selection problem.

2   Slime Mould Algorithm

Slime mould algorithm (SMA) is a novel metaheuristic algorithm proposed by Li et al. [11] to simulate the diffusion and foraging behavior of the slime mould. Adaptive weights are used to simulate the process of positive and negative feedback generated by propagating waves form biological oscillators. There are three behaviors: finding food, approaching food and wrapping food.

Supposing that there are N slime moulds, in the iteration $t+1$ the position of the i-th slime individual $Xi\,(i=1,2,...,N)$ is updated as Eq. (1) shown:

$$\overrightarrow{X_i(t+1)} = \begin{cases} \text{rand} \cdot (\text{UB} - \text{LB}) + \text{LB} & r_1 < z \\ \overrightarrow{X_b(t)} + \overrightarrow{v_b}\left(\overrightarrow{W} \cdot \overrightarrow{X_A(t)} - \overrightarrow{X_B(t)}\right) & r_1 \geq z\ \&\ r_2 < p_i(t) \\ \overrightarrow{v_c} \cdot \overrightarrow{X_i(t)} & r_1 \geq z\ \&\ r_2 \geq p_i(t) \end{cases} \quad (1)$$

where UB and LB are the upper and lower boundary of the search space. r_1 and r_2 are random values in $[0, 1]$. $\overrightarrow{v_b}$ represents the position of the best individual up to the current iteration t. $\overrightarrow{X_A(t)}$ and $\overrightarrow{X_B(t)}$ represent randomly selected individual from the current population, respectively. $\overrightarrow{W}$ is the weight factor. z is the probability of initializing individual to a random position, which is set to 0.03 in the original paper.

The p_i is calculated as Eq. (2):

$$p_i = \tanh |f(X_i) - f_{gb}| \tag{2}$$

where $f(X_i)$ denotes the fitness value of the i-th slime individual, f_{gb} represents the global best fitness value obtained so far.

The weight of N slime moulds in the iteration t is as shown in Eq. (3):

$$\overrightarrow{W(f\,\text{Index}(i))} = \begin{cases} 1 + r_3 \cdot \log\left(\frac{f_{lb} - f(X_i)}{f_{lb} - f_{lw}} + 1\right) & 1 \le i \le \frac{N}{2} \\ 1 - r_3 \cdot \log\left(\frac{f_{lb} - f(X_i)}{f_{lb} - f_{lw}} + 1\right) & \frac{N}{2} < i \le N \end{cases} \tag{3}$$

where r_3 is a random number in $[0, 1]$. f_{lb} and f_{lw} represent the local best and local worst fitness value in the current iteration, respectively. For a minimization problem, the fitness values are sorted in ascending order as Eq. (4) shown:

$$f\,\text{Index} = \text{sort}(f) \tag{4}$$

The $\overrightarrow{v_b}$ is a parameter with the range of $[-a, a]$ and $\overrightarrow{v_c}$ is between $[-b, b]$, T shows the maximum number of iterations.

$$a = arctanh\left(-\left(\frac{t}{T}\right) + 1\right) \tag{5}$$

$$b = 1 - \left(\frac{t}{T}\right) \tag{6}$$

3   The Proposed EFDB-SMA Algorithm

In this section, the improved factors adopted by the proposed EFDB-SMA algorithm are described in detail.

3.1   Elite Opposition-Based Learning

The population is initialized randomly in original SMA algorithm. In this way, the population has no prior knowledge with low quality, which limits the exploration ability of SMA. Effective information carried by elite individual is utilized through the elite opposition-based learning (EOBL) mechanism and an opposite population is generated. In this section, the EOBL [28] is adopted to improve the population initialization.

The original population based on random initialization $P_1 = \{X_1, X_2, \ldots, X_n\}$ and the population based on EOBL $P_2 = \{X_1^{op}, X_2^{op}, \ldots, X_n^{op}\}$ are merged into one population $\{P_1 \cup P_2\}$, then N optimal individuals are selected to form a new initial population P.

Firstly, the original population based on random initialization way is generated, the j-th dimensional position of i-th individual $\overrightarrow{X_{ij}}$ is calculated as follows:

$$\overrightarrow{X_{ij}} = \text{rand} \cdot (\text{ub} - \text{lb}) + \text{lb} \tag{7}$$

where $i = 1, 2, \ldots, n; j = 1, 2, \ldots, m$, n is the number of individuals in the population, and m is the number of variables. ub and lb represent the upper and lower value of the search space, respectively. The individual with the best fitness value is described as X_e, and its j-th dimensional position is denoted as $\overrightarrow{X_{ej}}$. The j-th dimensional position of the individual based on EBOL $\overrightarrow{X_{ij}^{op}}$ is calculated as shown in Eq. (8):

$$\overrightarrow{X_{ij}^{op}} = \text{r} \cdot (da_j + db_j) - \overrightarrow{X_{ej}} \tag{8}$$

where r is a dynamic parameter in $[0, 1]$. $da_j = \min(\overrightarrow{X_j}), db_j = \max(\overrightarrow{X_j})$, da_j and db_j denote the dynamic bounds of the j-th decision variable, which solve the problem that it is difficult to preserve the search experience with fixed bounds and help to reduce the search time of algorithm.

The j-th dimensional position of the elite opposition-based solution $\overrightarrow{X_{ij}^{op}}$ is reset by using random generation if it exceeds the boundary, the equation is shown in Eq. (9):

$$\overrightarrow{X_{ij}^{op}} = \text{rand}(da_j, db_j) \tag{9}$$

3.2 Roulette-Wheel Fitness-Distance Balance

Fitness-distance balance (FDB) is a selection method proposed by Kahrama et al. [10] to solve the problems of premature convergence, similarity among candidate solutions and easily falling into local optimum. The FDB score consists of the fitness value of the candidate solution and the distance from the current optimal solution. The steps to calculate the FDB scores of candidate solutions in population are as follows: (1) Calculating the fitness value of each candidate solution in the population. (2) Calculating the distance between the candidate solution and the optimal solution. The distance metric used is Euclidean. (3) Calculating the FDB score of candidate solution, which is obtained from the weighted summation of the normalized fitness value of each candidate solution and the normalized distance value between the candidate solution and the optimal solution, with the weight of 0.5 in the original paper.

The position update of slime mould as Eq. (1) shown is determined by the convergence factor and its position in the first condition. In the second condition, it is related to the current optimal individual position and two random individual positions. It is the most important update operator in the search process, which determines the performance of the algorithm. In the last condition, the position update of slime mould is expressed as a random search close to the current optimal individual position. However, the aimless random search may reduce the convergence speed in the early stage, with the iteration increases, it is easy to plunge into local optimal capture while solving functions with multiple local optimum, which limits its exploration and exploitation. In this section, in an attempt to overcome above shortcomings, the position update mechanism in second situation is improved based on FDB.

The selection method considered FDB and roulette-wheel FDB (RFDB), and the replaced individuals considered the best individual X_b, a random individual X_A, another random individual X_b, both X_A and X_B. Eight cases are obtained by combining the selection method and the replaced individual. After conducting 30, 50, 100 dimensional experiments on 23 benchmark test functions (including unimodal, multimodal and fixed dimensional functions) in 30 times, the experimental results are shown in Table 1, the minimum value of each different dimensional function is expressed in bold. As the non-parametric Friedman test results suggested, the selection method-RFDB and the replaced individual-X_A are finally selected.

Table 1. Friedman test results of the SMA and eight cases (selection method and replaced individual) according to different dimensional function types.

Function Type	Dimension	SMA	FDB X_b	FDB X_A	FDB X_B	FDB X_A, X_B	RFDB X_b	RFDB X_A	RFDB X_B	RFDB X_A, X_B
Unimodal	$D = 30$	4.4286	4.7143	4.1429	7.0000	4.5714	5.1429	**4.0000**	4.2857	6.7143
	$D = 50$	5.4286	**3.1429**	5.4286	4.5714	5.7143	6.4286	3.7143	4.4286	6.1429
	$D = 100$	3.7857	5.4286	6.6429	4.0000	5.2857	5.2857	4.5714	**3.1429**	6.8571
Multimodal	$D = 30$	4.5000	5.3333	**4.1667**	5.3333	6.5000	5.5000	4.5000	4.5000	4.6667
	$D = 50$	5.0000	5.3333	5.3333	3.8333	6.3333	5.3333	**3.1667**	4.8333	5.8333
	$D = 100$	5.5000	5.1667	5.0000	4.3333	5.6667	4.3333	5.1667	**4.1667**	5.6667
Fixed	$D =$ fixed	5.0000	5.3000	5.7500	5.3000	5.4500	6.4000	**3.6000**	4.5000	3.7000
Friedman's mean rank		4.8061	4.9170	5.2092	4.9102	5.6459	5.4891	**4.1027**	4.2653	5.6544
Rank		3	5	6	4	8	7	1	2	9

3.3   Chaotic Perturbation

According to the position update mechanism of SMA, there is a trend that leads the population to converge in the direction of the origin. The SMA has limitations in solution accuracy without providing an effective convergence mechanism. To overcome these deficiencies, increase the traversal search capability and avoid guiding slime moulds close to the origin, tent mapping is introduced.

Chaotic sequences have been widely used in various optimization search problems on account of pseudo-randomness, ergodicity, and sensitivity to initial values. Zhang et al. [25] developed a tent mapping expression as Eq. (10) shown:

$$z_{j+1} = \begin{cases} 2z_j + \text{rand}(0,1) \times \frac{1}{NT}, 0 \leq z \leq \frac{1}{2} \\ 2(1 - z_j) + \text{rand}(0,1) \times \frac{1}{NT}, \frac{1}{2} < z \leq 1 \end{cases} \tag{10}$$

Equation (10) is transformed by Bernoulli shift [25]:

$$z_{j+1} = (2z_j) + \text{rand}(0,1) \times \frac{1}{NT} \tag{11}$$

where NT denotes the number of particles in the chaotic sequence, which is product of the number of slime mould individuals in the population and the dimension of decision variables in EFDB-SMA, j represents the current dimension.

The tent mapping, with traversal property, is added to the original position update mechanism as a perturbation factor in proposed EFDB-SMA. The position update of slime mould is shown in Eq. (12):

$$\overrightarrow{X_i(t+1)} = \overrightarrow{v_c} \cdot z_i \cdot \overrightarrow{X_i(t)} \tag{12}$$

Combining the RFDB selection method and tent mapping, the position update mechanism in the proposed EFDB-SMA is as Eq. (13) shown:

$$\overrightarrow{X_i(t+1)} = \begin{cases} \text{rand} \cdot (\text{UB} - \text{LB}) + \text{LB} & r_1 < z \\ \overrightarrow{X_b(t)} + \overrightarrow{v_b} \left(\overrightarrow{W} \cdot \overrightarrow{X_A(t)} - \overrightarrow{X_B(t)} \right) & r_1 \geq z \ \& \ r_2 < p_i(t) \ \& \ r_3 \geq 0.5 \\ \overrightarrow{X_b(t)} + \overrightarrow{v_b} \left(\overrightarrow{W} \cdot \overrightarrow{X_{RFDB}(t)} - \overrightarrow{X_B(t)} \right) & r_1 \geq z \ \& \ r_2 < p_i(t) \ \& \ r_3 < 0.5 \\ \overrightarrow{v_c} \cdot \overrightarrow{X_i(t)} & r_1 \geq z \ \& \ r_2 \geq p_i(t) \end{cases} \tag{13}$$

3.4   Greedy Selection Strategy

Different from the general MHS algorithms [24], the elite selection strategy or hierarchy mechanism are not used in the standard SMA. All individuals are simply and equally selected close to or away from the best current food source. The greedy selection strategy is proposed to improve search performance. At the end of each iteration, if the current fitness value is not as good as that of the previous iteration for each slime mould, the updated position is not considered and the position of the previous iteration is maintained. In the iteration $t + 1$, the position of i-th slime mould is described as $\overrightarrow{Xa_i(t)}$, then the greedy selection strategy is executed as shown in Eq. (14):

$$\overrightarrow{X_i(t+1)} = \begin{cases} \overrightarrow{Xa_i(t)} & if \ f(Xa_i(t)) < f(X_i(t)) \\ \overrightarrow{X_i(t)} & if \ f(Xa_i(t)) \geq f(X_i(t)) \end{cases} \tag{14}$$

Based on the above improvements, the pseudocode of the proposed EFDB-SMA algorithm is presented in Algorithm 1.

4   Experimental Results and Analysis

In this section, the proposed EFDB-SMA algorithm is compared with two classic optimizers (grey wolf optimization (GWO) [14], particle swarm optimization (PSO) [6]) and three advanced optimizers (adaptive opposition slime mould algorithm (AOSMA) [16], enhanced whale optimization algorithm (EWOA) [15], FDB teaching-learning-based artificial bee colony (FDB-TLABC) [5]).

Algorithm 1. Pseudo-code of EFDB-SMA

Input: *Popsize, Dim, Max_iteration*;
Output: *Bestfitness*;
1: Initialize the position of slime mould
   $X_i(i = 1, 2, 3 \ldots n)$ base on EOBL strategy by Eq. (7) to Eq. (8);
2: **while** $t <= Max\_iteration$ **do**
3:    Calculate the fitness of all slime moulds;
4:    Update *Bestfitness*, X_b;
5:    Calculate the W by Eq. (3);
6:    Calculate the FDB scores of all individuals
7:    **for** each slime mould i **do**
8:       Update p, v_b, v_c;
9:       Select a slime mould r based on FDB score by roulette-wheel method;
10:      Update position by Eq. (13) as X_a;
11:      Calculate the fitness $f(X_a)$ of the slime mould;
12:      **if** $f(X_a) < f(X_i)$ **then**
13:         $X_i = X_a$;
14:      **else**
15:         $X_i = X_i$;
16:      **end if**
17:   **end for**
18:   $t = t + 1$;
19: **end while**
20: **return** *Bestfitness*.

4.1   Parameter Settings

All algorithms are conducted under the same conditions for fairness. The dimension is 30, and the number of search individuals and iterations are 30 and 1000, respectively. The experimental results of all algorithms are obtained after 30 independent runs, and the average fitness value (Avg), the standard deviation (Std) and the running time (Time) are used to evaluate the performance.

The parameter settings of other algorithms are detailed in Table 2, which are used in the original paper or widely adopted by various researchers. Friedman test is conducted to verify the average performance of all optimizers for further statistical judgment, mean rank and final rank are assumed. The experiments were executed on Windows 10 OS with Intel(R) Core(TM) i7-10700 CPU @ 2.90 GHz and 16 GB RAM. The algorithms for comparison were coded by MATLAB R2020b.

Table 2. Parameter settings of optimization algorithms.

Algorithm	Parameters	Algorithm	Parameters
EFDB-SMA	$z = 0.03$	GWO	$a = [2, 0]$
PSO	$c_1 = 2, c_2 = 2, w = 0.9$	AOSMA	$del = 0.03$
EWOA	$P = 20\%, k = 1.5 \times N, x_0 = 0.5, \gamma = 0.1$	FDB-TLABC	$Limit = 200, CR = 0.5$

4.2   Comparison with Other Algorithms

The experimental results are shown in Table 3 and EFDB-SMA ranks first. The obtained fitness values are smaller than other MAs except on F8 and F10, which indicates that it has strong exploitation capability. EFDB-SMA has smaller Std values. All the above results show that the introduction of FDB selection method and the replacement of a random individual can find potential candidate solutions, so that the proposed algorithm can achieve an excellent balance between exploration and exploitation, as well as effectively avoid plunging into local optimum.

Table 3. The comparison results of the EFDB-SMA against other algorithms.

Function	Metric	EFDB-SMA	GWO	PSO	AOSMA	EWOA	FDB-TLABC
F1	Avg	**4.820E+03**	2.240E+09	1.272E+11	1.145E+04	3.109E+04	8.173E+04
	Std	**5.719E+03**	1.315E+09	1.878E+10	1.642E+04	4.821E+04	2.204E+05
	Time	21.974	6.336	**5.907**	10.57	15.477	22.617
F2	Avg	**4.285E+03**	5.247E+03	1.087E+04	5.156E+03	5.023E+03	8.562E+03
	Std	6.875E+02	1.398E+03	5.018E+02	6.550E+02	7.316E+02	**2.973E+02**
	Time	25.230	8.033	**7.586**	13.053	16.959	26.267
F3	Avg	**8.554E+02**	8.934E+02	3.565E+03	1.082E+03	9.729E+02	9.627E+02
	Std	3.863E+01	3.863E+01	3.275E+02	9.640E+01	6.813E+01	**1.391E+01**
	Time	24.672	7.504	**7.055**	12.420	16.389	24.835
F4	Avg	**1.900E+03**	1.900E+03	1.768E+06	1.900E+03	1.911E+03	1.915E+03
	Std	**0.000E+00**	2.103E-01	8.929E+05	0.000E+00	3.328E+00	2.705E+00
	Time	22.050	6.754	**6.382**	9.403	16.043	23.561
F5	Avg	**8.431E+05**	2.418E+06	5.355E+08	2.107E+06	1.140E+06	4.112E+06
	Std	**4.569E+05**	2.369E+06	2.667E+08	1.598E+06	7.960E+05	2.202E+06
	Time	24.771	7.891	**7.423**	12.448	16.795	25.580
F6	Avg	**2.142E+03**	2.167E+03	1.044E+04	2.675E+03	2.366E+03	3.338E+03
	Std	**1.481E+02**	2.642E+02	3.326E+03	3.416E+02	2.674E+02	2.510E+02
	Time	24.188	7.415	**6.873**	11.955	16.182	24.794
F7	Avg	**2.632E+05**	1.627E+06	3.073E+08	5.615E+05	4.992E+05	7.983E+05
	Std	**2.129E+05**	2.956E+06	2.147E+08	3.901E+05	4.755E+05	4.386E+05
	Time	24.782	7.243	**7.036**	11.829	16.520	25.081
F8	Avg	2.620E+03	5.499E+03	1.235E+04	5.650E+03	2.303E+03	**2.302E+03**
	Std	1.121E+03	2.115E+03	5.639E+02	1.822E+03	**2.755E+00**	3.756E+00
	Time	32.698	11.683	**11.271**	18.252	21.103	33.687
F9	Avg	**2.913E+03**	2.956E+03	4.504E+03	3.004E+03	2.975E+03	3.029E+03
	Std	2.255E+01	6.462E+01	4.421E+02	6.650E+01	5.537E+01	**1.057E+01**
	Time	35.993	13.507	**12.900**	22.616	22.616	37.166
F10	Avg	2.914E+03	3.015E+03	1.969E+04	2.916E+03	2.902E+03	**2.889E+03**
	Std	1.465E+01	5.826E+01	4.191E+03	2.444E+01	1.709E+01	**7.265E+00**
	Time	31.944	11.512	**11.102**	18.048	20.969	33.735
Friedman's mean rank		**1.500**	3.500	6.000	3.500	2.700	3.800
Rank		**1**	3	6	3	2	5

The SMA algorithm itself takes a relatively long time because of the calculation of oscillation factors. The proposed EFDB-SMA takes a amount of time to generate the elite opposition-based learning population in the initialization

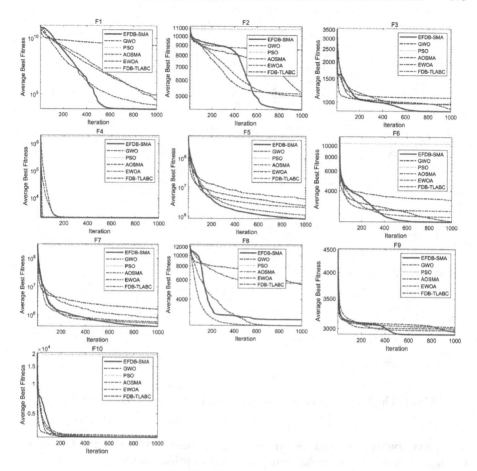

Fig. 1. The convergence curves of the EFDB-SMA against other algorithms.

stage. The FDB score, which is composed of fitness value and distance value also increases the calculation time. Finally, chaotic perturbation and greedy selection strategy for each position update also contribute to the increase of running time. Even if it is relatively time-consuming, EFDB-SMA still possesses effective advantages over other algorithms, so the time results are expected.

The convergence diagram is shown in Fig. 1. It can be seen that on F1-F7 and F9, EFDB-SMA finally obtained the minimum average fitness value with fast convergence speed, which may be attributed to the EOBL strategy in the population initialization stage, it makes slime moulds approach the optimal value as soon as possible and accelerates the convergence rate, thus having excellent exploration capability. While on F8 and F10, the EFDB-SMA is slightly inferior to EWOA and FDB-TLABC, respectively. With the number of iterations increasing, most algorithms converge to plateaus, but EFDB-SMA can continue

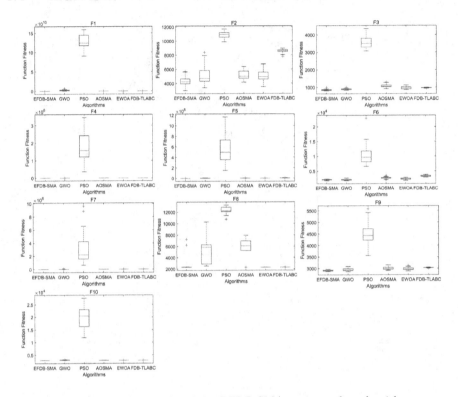

Fig. 2. The boxplot graphs of the EFDB-SMA against other algorithms.

to explore, because chaotic perturbation and roulette wheel method improve population diversity and help jump out of local optimal value.

As boxplot graph illustrates data distribution, it is appropriate to depict an agreement between the experimental results. Figure 2 shows the best fitness obtained for 6 algorithms run 30 times independently. From the figure, it can be seen that EFDB-SMA has smaller median, quartile and narrow distribution frame than other algorithms, which reveals that the EFDB-SMA is stably consistent in various comparison algorithms.

5   Application in Feature Selection

In this section, the proposed EFDB-SMA is applied in feature selection problem.

5.1   Feature Selection

Feature selection (FS) is an effective data preprocessing method [22]. In recent years, metaheuristic algorithms (MAs) with global search capability have been applied to feature selection problem with excellent performance. The objectives of FS are usually maximizing the classification accuracy rate and minimizing the number of selected features. Therefore, the fitness function is designed as shown in Eq. (15):

$$\text{Fitness} = w_1 \cdot (1 - Acc) + w_2 \cdot \frac{|\text{sNF}|}{|\text{NF}|} \tag{15}$$

where w_1 is the weight of the classification error rate and w_2 is the weight of the number of selected features, $w_1 + w_2 = 1$. Acc represents the accuracy obtained by the classifier using the selected subset of features. $|\text{sNF}|$ denotes the number of selected features, and $|\text{NF}|$ denotes the total number of features.

5.2   Binary EFDB-SMA

Feature selection is a discrete combinatorial optimization problem, so the original continuous EFDB-SMA needs to be modified to binary version (BEFDB-SMA). The transfer function, the Sigmoid function [13], is adopted to map continuous values to 1 or 0, where 1 means the feature is selected and 0 means not. In the iteration t, the binary j-th position of i-th slime mould $X_{ij}^b(t)$ is shown in Eq. (17), $X_{ij}(t)$ is a continuous value in $[0, 1]$:

$$S(X_{ij}(t)) = \frac{1}{1 + e^{-X_{ij}(t)}} \tag{16}$$

$$X_{ij}^b(t) = \begin{cases} 1 \; if \; rand \geq S(X_{ij}(t)) \\ 0 \; if \; rand < S(X_{ij}(t)) \end{cases} \tag{17}$$

5.3   Datasets and Parameters

Six classic datasets from the UCI repository are employed to validate the performance of BEFDB-SMA in feature selection.

The k-nearest neighbor (KNN) [20], one of the common classification algorithms in machine learning, is adopted to measure the classification accuracy of the selected features. According to most researchers' suggestions $K = 5$. For feature selection, the classification accuracy is more important than the number of selected features, so refer to most researchers' experience, w_1 is 0.99 and w_2 is 0.01. The values of parameters of other MAs for comparison are taken from the original papers. Other parameters are consistent with the previous experimental settings except that the number of search agents is 10. The evaluation indicators include the average fitness value (Fitness), the average classification error rate (Error) and the average number of selected features (Size).

5.4   Experimental Results and Analysis

The experimental results are given in Table 4. The BEFDB-SMA algorithm ranks first and obtains the smallest average fitness value on 83% datasets. It performs well in terms of classification accuracy, but moderately in terms of the number of selected features, as the two objectives are conflicting. The search space is

Table 4. Comparison of fitness, error and size of each algorithm on six datasets.

Dataset	Metric	BEFDB-SMA	BHHO	BWOA	BMFO	BGWO	BPSO
Zoo	Fitness	**1.475E−02**	2.349E−02	1.899E−02	2.540E−02	2.318E−02	2.536E−02
	Error	**0.010**	0.019	0.014	0.021	0.019	0.021
	Size	7.8	7.7	7.5	7.2	7.2	**7.1**
Ionosphere	Fitness	8.113E−02	8.173E−02	**7.536E−02**	8.018E−02	7.848E−02	7.737E−02
	Error	0.078	0.080	**0.074**	0.078	0.077	0.076
	Size	11.9	9.7	8.3	9.7	**8.2**	8.7
Promoters	Fitness	**9.427E−02**	1.131E−01	1.146E−01	1.207E−01	1.124E−01	1.124E−01
	Error	**0.090**	0.110	0.112	0.118	0.110	0.110
	Size	27.6	25.6	22.2	**20.8**	21.6	21.8
Urban land cover	Fitness	**1.596E−01**	1.681E−01	1.597E−01	1.625E−01	1.629E−01	1.613E−01
	Error	**0.157**	0.165	0.157	0.161	0.161	0.159
	Size	60.3	64.1	56.6	**52.4**	55.6	53.6
MUSK	Fitness	**1.078E−01**	1.184E−01	1.160E−01	1.139E−01	1.165E−01	1.151E−01
	Error	**0.104**	0.115	0.113	0.111	0.114	0.113
	Size	72.6	79.3	62.2	61.9	62.7	**59.4**
LSVT	Fitness	**7.470E−02**	8.072E−02	8.713E−02	8.569E−02	8.754E−02	8.480E−02
	Error	**0.071**	0.077	0.085	0.083	0.085	0.082
	Size	131.4	124.6	**102.0**	112.6	114.9	112.7
Friedman's mean rank		**1.67**	4.54	3.13	4.38	4.08	3.21
Rank		1	6	2	5	4	3

expanded and the population is more uniformly distributed through the initialization strategy based on EOBL. Individuals are selected with probability based on their FDB scores to guide the evolution of the population, hence individuals learn from the excellent, then the features with useful information are more likely to be selected to improve the classification accuracy. Combined with chaotic perturbation and greedy selection strategy, the BEFDB-SMA algorithm can avoid getting stuck in local solutions and get smaller fitness value. Therefore, the proposed algorithm has excellent performance in solving feature selection problem.

6   Conclusion

Aiming at the shortcomings of SMA algorithm, such as easily falling into local optimum and insufficient balance between exploration and exploitation, EFDB-SMA is proposed in this paper. The FDB selection method is introduced to balance the exploitation and exploration capabilities, the population quality and diversity are improved by the EOBL strategy, EFDB-SMA also designs the chaotic perturbation for avoiding the local optimal capture, and the greedy selection strategy in each iteration contributes to find the global optimal value. The experimental results on CEC2020 benchmark functions and Friedman test show that the proposed EFDB-SMA performs outstanding competitiveness compared to classic and advanced optimizers. Moreover, the binary version of EFDB-SMA is developed by a transfer function and applied to feature selection. Experimental results demonstrate that the proposed algorithm may be useful for feature selection and become an ideal data preprocessing tool. Future work is to investigate an improved multi-objective SMA for solving feature selection problem.

References

1. Abdel-Basset, M., Mohamed, R., Chakrabortty, R.K., Ryan, M.J., Mirjalili, S.: An efficient binary slime mould algorithm integrated with a novel attacking-feeding strategy for feature selection. Comput. Ind. Eng. **153**, 107078 (2021)
2. Altay, O.: Chaotic slime mould optimization algorithm for global optimization. Artif. Intell. Rev. **55**(5), 3979–4040 (2022)
3. Aras, S., Gedikli, E., Kahraman, H.T.: A novel stochastic fractal search algorithm with fitness-distance balance for global numerical optimization. Swarm Evol. Comput. **61**, 100821 (2021)
4. Duman, S., Kahraman, H.T., Guvenc, U., Aras, S.: Development of a Lévy flight and FDB-based coyote optimization algorithm for global optimization and real-world ACOPF problems. Soft. Comput. **25**, 6577–6617 (2021)
5. Duman, S., Kahraman, H.T., Sonmez, Y., Guvenc, U., Kati, M., Aras, S.: A powerful meta-heuristic search algorithm for solving global optimization and real-world solar photovoltaic parameter estimation problems. Eng. Appl. Artif. Intell. **111**, 104763 (2022)
6. Eberhart, R., Kennedy, J.: Particle swarm optimization. In: Proceedings of the IEEE International Conference on Neural Networks, vol. 4, pp. 1942–1948. Citeseer (1995)
7. Houssein, E.H., Helmy, B.E.d., Rezk, H., Nassef, A.M.: An efficient orthogonal opposition-based learning slime mould algorithm for maximum power point tracking. Neural Comput. Appl. 1–25 (2022)
8. Houssein, E.H., Mahdy, M.A., Shebl, D., Manzoor, A., Sarkar, R., Mohamed, W.M.: An efficient slime mould algorithm for solving multi-objective optimization problems. Expert Syst. Appl. **187**, 115870 (2022)
9. Jia, H., Zhang, W., Zheng, R., Wang, S., Leng, X., Cao, N.: Ensemble mutation slime mould algorithm with restart mechanism for feature selection. Int. J. Intell. Syst. **37**(3), 2335–2370 (2022)
10. Kahraman, H.T., Aras, S., Gedikli, E.: Fitness-distance balance (FDB): a new selection method for meta-heuristic search algorithms. Knowl.-Based Syst. **190**, 105169 (2020)
11. Li, S., Chen, H., Wang, M., Heidari, A.A., Mirjalili, S.: Slime mould algorithm: a new method for stochastic optimization. Futur. Gener. Comput. Syst. **111**, 300–323 (2020)
12. Luo, J., Chen, H., Xu, Y., Huang, H., Zhao, X., et al.: An improved grasshopper optimization algorithm with application to financial stress prediction. Appl. Math. Model. **64**, 654–668 (2018)
13. Mirjalili, S., Lewis, A.: S-shaped versus v-shaped transfer functions for binary particle swarm optimization. Swarm Evol. Comput. **9**, 1–14 (2013)
14. Mirjalili, S., Mirjalili, S.M., Lewis, A.: Grey wolf optimizer. Adv. Eng. Softw. **69**, 46–61 (2014)
15. Nadimi-Shahraki, M.H., Zamani, H., Mirjalili, S.: Enhanced whale optimization algorithm for medical feature selection: a COVID-19 case study. Comput. Biol. Med. **148**, 105858 (2022)
16. Naik, M.K., Panda, R., Abraham, A.: Adaptive opposition slime mould algorithm. Soft. Comput. **25**(22), 14297–14313 (2021). https://doi.org/10.1007/s00500-021-06140-2
17. Naik, M.K., Panda, R., Abraham, A.: An entropy minimization based multilevel colour thresholding technique for analysis of breast thermograms using equilibrium slime mould algorithm. Appl. Soft Comput. **113**, 107955 (2021)

18. Nakagaki, T., Yamada, H., Ueda, T.: Interaction between cell shape and contraction pattern in the physarum plasmodium. Biophys. Chem. **84**(3), 195–204 (2000)
19. Pang, J., Zhou, H., Tsai, Y.C., Chou, F.D.: A scatter simulated annealing algorithm for the bi-objective scheduling problem for the wet station of semiconductor manufacturing. Comput. Ind. Eng. **123**, 54–66 (2018)
20. Peterson, L.E.: K-nearest neighbor. Scholarpedia **4**(2), 1883 (2009)
21. Xu, Y., Peng, Y., Su, X., Yang, Z., Ding, C., Yang, X.: Improving teaching-learning-based-optimization algorithm by a distance-fitness learning strategy. Knowl.-Based Syst. **257**, 108271 (2022)
22. Xue, Y., Xue, B., Zhang, M.: Self-adaptive particle swarm optimization for large-scale feature selection in classification. ACM Trans. Knowl. Discov. Data (TKDD) **13**(5), 1–27 (2019)
23. Yacoubi, S., Manita, G., Amdouni, H., Mirjalili, S., Korbaa, O.: A modified multi-objective slime mould algorithm with orthogonal learning for numerical association rules mining. Neural Comput. Appl. 1–27 (2022)
24. Yu, W.J., Zhan, Z.H., Zhang, J.: Artificial bee colony algorithm with an adaptive greedy position update strategy. Soft. Comput. **22**, 437–451 (2018)
25. Zhang, N., Zhao, Z., Bao, X., Qian, J., Wu, B.: Gravitational search algorithm based on improved tent chaos. Control Decis. **35**(4), 893–900 (2020)
26. Zhang, Y., et al.: Towards augmented kernel extreme learning models for bankruptcy prediction: algorithmic behavior and comprehensive analysis. Neurocomputing **430**, 185–212 (2021)
27. Zhou, H., Pang, J., Chen, P.K., Chou, F.D.: A modified particle swarm optimization algorithm for a batch-processing machine scheduling problem with arbitrary release times and non-identical job sizes. Comput. Ind. Eng. **123**, 67–81 (2018)
28. Zhou, Y., Wang, R., Luo, Q.: Elite opposition-based flower pollination algorithm. Neurocomputing **188**, 294–310 (2016)

Low Redundancy Learning for Unsupervised Multi-view Feature Selection

Hong Jia[(✉)] and Jian Huang

Guangdong Key Laboratory of Intelligent Information Processing,
College of Electronics and Information Engineering, Shenzhen University,
Shenzhen, China
hongjia1102@szu.edu.cn, 2060432042@email.szu.edu.cn

Abstract. Multi-view feature selection is an important research direction in multi-view learning. Most of the existing multi-view feature selection methods focus on the correlation between features and data category structure, while ignoring the redundancy between features. In this paper, we propose a multi-view feature selection method based on low redundancy learning, which introduces and automatically assigns the weight of feature redundancy in each view to the projection space matrix. Subsequently, by applying $l_{2,1}$ norm to the projection space matrix to constrain row sparsity, the feature subsets with high correlation and low redundancy can be selected. In order to make full use of the consistency of multiple views, we also utilize spectral analysis to learn the potential category structure of each view, and minimize the difference between single-view category structure and consensus clustering indication matrix. Finally, an alternating iterative updating method is presented to solve the optimization problem. Experiments on different public multi-view data sets verify the effectiveness of the proposed method.

Keywords: Unsupervised learning · Multi-view data · Feature selection · Feature redundancy · Spectral analysis

1 Introduction

In recent years, with the continuous development of data collection technology, high-dimensional multi-view data is common in practice and can provide more comprehensive information. However, they also contain a lot of noise, which may damage the performance of learning algorithms and consume expensive computational cost. Multi-view feature selection can effectively alleviate such problem and has received widespread attention in multi-view learning. Since true class labels are always difficult to obtain in reality, we are committed to the research of multi-view unsupervised feature selection in this paper.

This work was supported by the National Natural Science Foundation of China under Grant 61806131 and the Natural Science Foundation of Guangdong Province under Grant 2018A030310510.

There are mainly two different kinds of ways for multi-view unsupervised feature selection. The first kind of methods connect the features from different views together and then apply traditional single-view feature selection approaches to the concatenated data. Typically, unsupervised feature selection methods for single view data include Laplacian Score (LS) [6], Spectral Feature Selection(SPEC) [18], Multi-Cluster Feature Selection (MCFS) [3], Nonnegative Discriminative Feature Selection (NDFS) [9], and so on. These methods can achieve satisfying performance on single view data in most cases. However, they are usually not suitable for multi-view data as the potential correlations between different views are ignored. The other way for multi-view feature selection is to use methods specifically designed for multi-view data. This kind of methods often mine the diversity and complementary information between different views. Representative approaches include Multi-view Feature Selection(MVFS) [14], Adaptive Unsupervised Multi-view Feature Selection (AUMFS) [5], and Adaptive Multi-view Feature Selection (AMFS) [15]. These methods build a similarity graph for each view based on the spectral graph theory, and then use these pre-calculated local geometric structures to select relevant features. However, as the similarity graphs are constructed directly from the original features, they often contain noise. Therefore, some other methods proposed to learn better clustering structure and feature subset alternately, such as Multi-view Unsupervised Feature Selection with Adaptive Similarity and View Weight (ASVW) [7], Adaptive Collaborative Similarity Learning (ACSL) [4], Multilevel Adaptive neighbor graph for Multi-view Feature Selection (MAMFS) [17], and Cross-view Locality Preserved Diversity and Consensus Learning model (CvLP-DCL) [13].

As most existing multi-view feature selection methods only focus on the importance of features for the learning tasks while ignore the correlations between different features, the selected feature subsets may retain features that are relevant to the learning task but highly redundant with each other. Therefore, this paper proposes a low redundancy learning method for multi-view unsupervised feature selection. Specifically, a unified framework, which simultaneously learns the consensus clustering structure and performs multi-view feature selection is presented. To conduct low redundancy learning, feature redundancy matrix is further introduced, which collaborates with the feature weighting matrix to select feature subsets with high relevance and low redundancy. Finally, we present an effective alternate optimization method to solve the proposed learning model. Experimental results on real multi-view data sets demonstrate the superiority of the proposed method.

2   Multi-view Feature Selection with Low Redundancy Learning

2.1   Notations

Throughout this paper, vectors and matrices are denoted as boldface lowercase letters and boldface capital letters, respectively. For a matrix $\mathbf{A} \in \mathbb{R}^{m \times n}$, $A_{i,j}$

represents the element in the i_{th} row and j_{th} column, $\mathbf{A}^i$ denote its i_{th} row and $\mathbf{A}_j$ denote its j_{th} column. The trace of square matrix $\mathbf{A}$ is denoted as $Tr(\mathbf{A})$. The transpose of matrix $\mathbf{A}$ is denoted as $\mathbf{A}^T$. The inverse of matrix $\mathbf{A}$ is denoted as $\mathbf{A}^{-1}$. $\mathbf{I}_m$ is the identity matrix with size $m \times m$. The $l_{2,1}$ norm of the matrix $\mathbf{A}$ is denoted as $\|\mathbf{A}\|_{2,1}$, which is calculated by $\sum_{i=1}^m \sqrt{\sum_{j=1}^n A_{i,j}^2}$. The Frobenius norm of the matrix $\mathbf{A}$ is denoted as $\|\mathbf{A}\|_F$, which is calculated by $\sqrt{\sum_{i=1}^m \sum_{j=1}^n A_{i,j}^2}$. The hadamard product of matrix is denoted as $\mathbf{A} \odot \mathbf{B}$, which means the matrix obtained by multiplying the corresponding elements of matrix $\mathbf{A}$ and matrix $\mathbf{B}$. $diag(\mathbf{A})$ represents a vector composed of diagonal elements of matrix $\mathbf{A}$.

Suppose we have a multi-view data set with V views. We denote it as $\mathbf{X} = [\mathbf{X}^{(1)}, \mathbf{X}^{(2)}, \ldots, \mathbf{X}^{(v)}] \in \mathbb{R}^{n \times d}$, where n is the number of data samples and d is the number of features. The feature matrix of data in the v_{th} view is denoted as $\mathbf{X}^{(v)} = [\mathbf{x}_1^{(v)^T}; \mathbf{x}_2^{(v)^T}; \ldots; \mathbf{x}_{d_v}^{(v)^T}] \in \mathbb{R}^{n \times d_v}$, where d_v is the number of features in the v_{th} view and $d = \sum_{v=1}^V d_v$. The goal of multi-view feature selection is to select s most valuable features from d features without label information.

2.2 Formulation

Although most data has multiple view information with different feature distributions, they still have common information because they represent different aspects of the sample. To take full advantage of this common information, we project feature information from different views into a shared semantic space that reflects the categorical structure of the original data. The projection space learning can be expressed as follows:

$$\min_{\mathbf{W}^{(v)}, \mathbf{Y}} \sum_{v=1}^V \|\mathbf{X}^{(v)} \mathbf{W}^{(v)} - \mathbf{Y}\|_F^2, \text{s.t. } \mathbf{Y} \in \{0,1\}^{n \times c}, \tag{1}$$

where $\mathbf{W}^{(v)} \in \mathbb{R}^{d_v \times c}$ is the projection matrix for the v_{th} view, $\mathbf{Y} \in \mathbb{R}^{n \times c}$ is the common cluster indicator matrix which can represent the common semantic information, and c is the number of clusters. In order to perform feature selection, we want the projection space $\mathbf{W}^{(v)}$ of Eq. (1) to be as sparse as possible in rows. Therefore, we add an $l_{2,1}$ norm regularization term. Additionally, as it is difficult to solve Eq. (1) with the constrain $\mathbf{Y} \in \{0,1\}^{n \times c}$, we use the orthogonality constraint instead, which can be written as follow:

$$\min_{\mathbf{W}^{(v)}, \mathbf{Y}} \sum_{v=1}^V \|\mathbf{X}^{(v)} \mathbf{W}^{(v)} - \mathbf{Y}\|_F^2 + \|\mathbf{W}^{(v)}\|_{2,1}, \text{s.t. } \mathbf{Y}^T \mathbf{Y} = \mathbf{I}, \mathbf{Y} \geq 0. \tag{2}$$

Most of the multi-view feature selection methods are based on the above regression model. However, this model has not considered the redundancy of features. Therefore, we further use a diagonal matrix $\mathbf{\Theta}^{(v)} \in \mathbb{R}^{d_v \times d_v}$ to weight the components of the projection space in the v_{th} view. Then, the learning model can be rewritten as

$$\min_{\mathbf{W}^{(v)}, \mathbf{Y}} \sum_{v=1}^{V} \|\mathbf{X}^{(v)}\mathbf{\Theta}^{(v)}\mathbf{W}^{(v)} - \mathbf{Y}\|_F^2 + \|\mathbf{W}^{(v)}\|_{2,1} \tag{3}$$
$$\text{s.t. } \mathbf{Y}^T\mathbf{Y} = \mathbf{I}, \mathbf{Y} \geq 0, Tr(\mathbf{\Theta}^{(v)}) = d_v, \Theta_{i,i}^{(v)} \geq 0.$$

The diagonal matrix $\mathbf{\Theta}^{(v)}$ assigns different weights to variant feature pairs based on the redundancy between them. In our work, we use cosine similarity to calculate the redundancy between different features:

$$R_{i,j}^{(v)} = \frac{\mathbf{f}_i^{(v)^T} \mathbf{f}_j^{(v)}}{\|\mathbf{f}_i^{(v)}\|\|\mathbf{f}_j^{(v)}\|}. \tag{4}$$

Here, $\mathbf{f}_i^{(v)} \in \mathbb{R}^{n \times 1}$ and $\mathbf{f}_j^{(v)} \in \mathbb{R}^{n \times 1}$ are the i_{th} and j_{th} feature of the v_{th} view, respectively. The feature redundancy represented by Eq. (4) is utilized to allocate the value of the diagonal elements of the weight matrix. The model can be mathematically formulated as

$$\min_{\theta^{(v)} \in \mathbb{R}^{d_v \times 1}} \sum_{i=1}^{d_v} \sum_{j=1}^{d_v} \theta_i^{(v)} R_{i,j}^{(v)} \theta_j^{(v)} = \theta^{(v)^T} \mathbf{R}^{(v)} \theta^{(v)}, \tag{5}$$

where $\theta^{(v)}$ is a vector consisting of diagonal elements of $\mathbf{\Theta}^{(v)}$. Equation (5) will give priority to features with low-redundancy and assign larger weights to them. However, this may also lead to a situation that irrelevant features with low redundancy are assigned larger weights. Therefore, considering the feature relevance, a new diagonal matrix $\mathbf{C}^{(v)} \in \mathbb{R}^{d_v \times d_v}$ is introduced, whose diagonal elements are calculated by

$$C_{i,i}^{(v)} = 1 - \frac{\|\mathbf{W}^{i^{(v)}}\|_2^2}{\sum_{i=1}^{d_v} \|\mathbf{W}^{i^{(v)}}\|_2^2}. \tag{6}$$

Generally, the smaller the value of $\mathbf{C}_{i,i}^{(v)}$, the more relevant the feature is. In addition, the feature redundancy matrix $\mathbf{R}^{(v)} \in \mathbb{R}^{d_v \times d_v}$ can prevent two highly similar features from being allocated with large weights simultaneously. However, the cosine similarity calculated by Eq. (4) may have a negative element. This will result in two highly negatively related features to allocate large weight simultaneously if we use Eq. (5) exactly. To solve this problem, we square the elements on $\mathbf{R}^{(v)}$. Combining Eq. (4) and Eq. (6), we get a new feature redundancy matrix and its elements are

$$\mathbf{S_f}_{i,j}^{(v)} = R_{i,j}^{(v)^2} + tC_{i,j}^{(v)^2}, \tag{7}$$

where t is a parameter to adjust the balance between redundancy and correlation. According to Eq. (3)–(7), the learning model can be further written as

$$\min_{\mathbf{W}^{(v)}, \mathbf{Y}} \sum_{v=1}^{V} \|\mathbf{X}^{(v)}\mathbf{\Theta}^{(v)}\mathbf{W}^{(v)} - \mathbf{Y}\|_F^2 + \|\mathbf{W}^{(v)}\|_{2,1} + \theta^{(v)^T} \mathbf{S_f}^{(v)} \theta^{(v)} \tag{8}$$
$$\text{s.t. } \mathbf{Y}^T\mathbf{Y} = \mathbf{I}, \mathbf{Y} \geq 0, Tr(\mathbf{\Theta}^{(v)}) = d_v, \Theta_{i,i}^{(v)} \geq 0.$$

Moreover, high-dimensional data often contain important local geometric information, which is conducive to unsupervised feature selection. According to [2], we can obtain the category structure information of each view through spectral analysis. The mathematical expression is

$$\min_{\mathbf{Y}^{(v)}} \frac{1}{2} \sum_{i=1}^{n} \sum_{j=1}^{n} \|\mathbf{y}_i - \mathbf{y}_j\|_2^2 \mathbf{S}_{ij}^{(v)} = Tr(\mathbf{Y}^{(v)^T} \mathbf{L}^{(v)} \mathbf{Y}^{(v)}), \tag{9}$$

where $\mathbf{L}^{(v)} = \mathbf{D}^{(v)} - \mathbf{S}^{(v)}$ is the Laplacian matrix for the v_{th} view. $\mathbf{D}^{(v)}$ is a diagonal matrix, whose diagonal elements are defined as $D_{i,i}^{(v)} = \sum_{i=1}^{n} S_{ij}^{(v)}$. $\mathbf{S}^{(v)}$ is the similarity matrix of the samples from the v-th view, which can be obtained through

$$S_{ij}^{(v)} = \begin{cases} e^{-\frac{\|\mathbf{x}_i^{(v)} - \mathbf{x}_j^{(v)}\|^2}{\sigma^2}}, & if\ \mathbf{x}_i^{(v)} \in N(\mathbf{x}_j^{(v)})\ or\ \mathbf{x}_j^{(v)} \in N(\mathbf{x}_i^{(v)}), \\ 0, & otherwise. \end{cases} \tag{10}$$

Here $\mathbf{x}_i^{(v)}$ and $\mathbf{x}_j^{(v)}$ are the i-th and j-th sample of the v-th view, respectively. $N(\mathbf{x}_j^{(v)})$ is the k-nearest neighbor set of $\mathbf{x}_j^{(v)}$. Although the feature distribution in different views may be different, the category structure should be similar. Therefore, we integrate the category structures of different views to learn a consensus clustering indicator matrix:

$$\min_{\mathbf{Y},\mathbf{Y}^{(v)}} \alpha_v^r \|\mathbf{Y} - \mathbf{Y}^{(v)}\|_F^2, \text{s.t. } \mathbf{Y}^{(v)^T} \mathbf{Y}^{(v)} = \mathbf{I}, \mathbf{Y}^{(v)^T} \geq 0, \sum_{v=1}^{V} \alpha_v = 1, \alpha \geq 0, \tag{11}$$

where α_v is a balance parameter to balance the effectiveness of different views. By combining Eq. (8)–(11), we obtain the mathematical model for Multi-view Feature Selection with Low Redundancy Learning (LR-MVFS) as follows:

$$\min_{\mathbf{W}^{(v)},\mathbf{Y},\mathbf{Y}^{(v)},\Theta^{(v)}} \sum_{v=1}^{V} [\|\mathbf{X}^{(v)}\Theta^{(v)}\mathbf{W}^{(v)} - \mathbf{Y}\|_F^2 + \|\mathbf{W}^{(v)}\|_{2,1}$$

$$+ \lambda_1 (Tr(\mathbf{Y}^{(v)^T}\mathbf{L}^{(v)}\mathbf{Y}^{(v)}) + \alpha_v^r \|\mathbf{Y} - \mathbf{Y}^{(v)}\|_F^2) + \lambda_2 \theta^{(v)^T} \mathbf{S_f}^{(v)} \theta^{(v)}],$$

$$\text{s.t. } \mathbf{Y}^T\mathbf{Y} = \mathbf{I}, \mathbf{Y} \geq 0, Tr(\Theta^{(v)}) = d_v, \Theta_{i,i}^{(v)} \geq 0, \mathbf{Y}^{(v)^T}\mathbf{Y}^{(v)} = \mathbf{I}, \tag{12}$$

$$\mathbf{Y}^{(v)^T} \geq 0, \sum_{v=1}^{V} \alpha_v = 1, \alpha \geq 0.$$

2.3   Optimization

The objective function in Eq. (12) is not convex to all variables simultaneously. Therefore, we provide an effective alternate optimization method to solve it.

Update $\mathbf{W}^{(v)}$ and Fix the Other Variables. When other variables are fixed, we treat the last three terms of Eq. (12) as a constant as the change of W has little effect on their values. Then, Eq. (12) can be reformulated as

$$\min_{\mathbf{W}^{(v)}} \|\mathbf{X}^{(v)}\mathbf{\Theta}^{(v)}\mathbf{W}^{(v)} - \mathbf{Y}\|_F^2 + \|\mathbf{W}^{(v)}\|_{2,1}. \tag{13}$$

According to [10], Eq. (13) can be transformed into following equation:

$$\min_{\mathbf{W}^{(v)}} \|\mathbf{X}^{(v)}\mathbf{\Theta}^{(v)}\mathbf{W}^{(v)} - \mathbf{Y}\|_F^2 + Tr(\mathbf{W}^{(v)^T}\mathbf{U}^{(v)}\mathbf{W}^{(v)}), \tag{14}$$

where $\mathbf{U}^{(v)}$ is a diagonal matrix and the i-th diagonal element is calculated by $\frac{1}{2\|\mathbf{W}^{i(v)}\|_2+\varepsilon}$. ε is a small constant to avoid overflow. Subsequently, taking the derivative of Eq. (14) with $\mathbf{W}^{(v)}$ and set it to zero, we obtain the updating rule for $\mathbf{W}^{(v)}$ as follows:

$$\mathbf{W}^{(v)} = (\mathbf{\Theta}^{(v)}\mathbf{X}^{(v)^T}\mathbf{X}^{(v)}\mathbf{\Theta}^{(v)} + \mathbf{U}^{(v)})^{-1}\mathbf{\Theta}^{(v)}\mathbf{X}^{(v)^T}\mathbf{Y}. \tag{15}$$

Then, $\mathbf{W}^{(v)}$ and $\mathbf{U}^{(v)}$ can be updated in an alternative manner until convergence.

Update $\mathbf{\Theta}^{(v)}$ and Fix the Other Variables When other variables are fixed, Eq. (12) can be reformulated as

$$\min_{\mathbf{\Theta}^{(v)}} \|\mathbf{X}^{(v)}\mathbf{\Theta}^{(v)}\mathbf{W}^{(v)} - \mathbf{Y}\|_F^2 + \lambda_2\boldsymbol{\theta}^{(v)^T}\mathbf{S_f}^{(v)}\boldsymbol{\theta}^{(v)}, \text{s.t. } Tr(\mathbf{\Theta}^{(v)}) = d_v, \Theta_{i,i}^{(v)} \geq 0. \tag{16}$$

Further ignoring the irrelevant items, we obtain:

$$\min_{\mathbf{\Theta}^{(v)}} Tr(\mathbf{X}^{(v)}\mathbf{\Theta}^{(v)}\mathbf{W}^{(v)}\mathbf{W}^{(v)^T}\mathbf{\Theta}^{(v)}\mathbf{X}^{(v)^T} - 2\mathbf{\Theta}^{(v)}\mathbf{W}^{(v)}\mathbf{Y}^T\mathbf{X}^{(v)}) + \lambda_2\boldsymbol{\theta}^{(v)^T}\mathbf{S_f}^{(v)}\boldsymbol{\theta}^{(v)},$$

$$\text{s.t. } Tr(\mathbf{\Theta}^{(v)}) = d_v, \Theta_{i,i}^{(v)} \geq 0. \tag{17}$$

Lemma 1. If $\mathbf{\Theta}$ is a diagonal matrix, then $Tr(\mathbf{\Theta}\mathbf{A}\mathbf{\Theta}\mathbf{B}) = \boldsymbol{\theta}^T(\mathbf{A}^T \odot \mathbf{B})\boldsymbol{\theta}$.

The proof of Lemma 1 can be found in the literature [16]. Then we apply Lemma 1 to Eq. (17), the equation can be rewritten as

$$\min_{\mathbf{\Theta}^{(v)}} \boldsymbol{\theta}^{(v)^T}[(\mathbf{W}^{(v)}\mathbf{W}^{(v)^T}) \odot (\mathbf{X}^{(v)^T}\mathbf{X}^{(v)}) + \lambda_2\mathbf{S_f}^{(v)}]\boldsymbol{\theta}^{(v)} - 2\boldsymbol{\theta}^{(v)^T} diag(\mathbf{W}^{(v)}\mathbf{Y}^T\mathbf{X}^{(v)}),$$

$$\text{s.t. } Tr(\mathbf{\Theta}^{(v)}) = d_v, \Theta_{i,i}^{(v)} \geq 0. \tag{18}$$

Equation (18) is a quadratic programming problem as follow:

$$\min_{\boldsymbol{\theta}} \boldsymbol{\theta}^T\mathbf{A}\boldsymbol{\theta} - 2\boldsymbol{\theta}^T\mathbf{b}, \text{s.t. } \boldsymbol{\theta} \geq 0, \sum_{i=1}^{d_v}\theta_i = d_v, \tag{19}$$

where

$$\begin{cases} \mathbf{A} = (\mathbf{W}^{(v)}\mathbf{W}^{(v)^T}) \odot (\mathbf{X}^{(v)^T}\mathbf{X}^{(v)}) + \lambda_2\mathbf{S_f}^{(v)}, \\ \mathbf{b} = diag(\mathbf{W}^{(v)}\mathbf{Y}^T\mathbf{X}^{(v)}). \end{cases}$$

Equation (19) can be easily solved by using quadratic programming solving toolbox.

Update $\mathbf{Y}^{(v)}$ and fix the Other Variables. When other variables are fixed, Eq. (12) can be reformulated as

$$\min_{\mathbf{Y}^{(v)}} \lambda_1 (Tr(\mathbf{Y}^{(v)^T}\mathbf{L}^{(v)}\mathbf{Y}^{(v)}) + \alpha_v^r \|\mathbf{Y} - \mathbf{Y}^{(v)}\|_F^2), \text{s.t. } \mathbf{Y}^{(v)^T}\mathbf{Y}^{(v)} = \mathbf{I}, \mathbf{Y}^{(v)^T} \geq 0. \tag{20}$$

Then we construct the Lagrange function as follows:

$$\begin{aligned} L(\mathbf{Y}^{(v)}, \mathbf{\Phi}) =& \lambda_1 (Tr(\mathbf{Y}^{(v)^T}\mathbf{L}^{(v)}\mathbf{Y}^{(v)}) + \alpha_v^r \|\mathbf{Y} - \mathbf{Y}^{(v)}\|_F^2) \\ &+ \rho\|\mathbf{Y}^{(v)^T}\mathbf{Y}^{(v)} - \mathbf{I}\|_F^2 + Tr(\mathbf{\Phi}^T\mathbf{Y}^{(v)}). \end{aligned} \tag{21}$$

By taking the derivative of Eq.(21) with $\mathbf{Y}^{(v)}$ and setting it to zero, we obtain:

$$\begin{aligned} \frac{\partial L(\mathbf{Y}^{(v)}, \mathbf{\Phi})}{\partial \mathbf{Y}^{(v)}} =& 2\lambda_1 \mathbf{L}^{(v)}\mathbf{Y}^{(v)} + 2\lambda_1 \alpha_v^r (\mathbf{Y}^{(v)} - \mathbf{Y}) \\ &+ 4\rho(\mathbf{Y}^{(v)}\mathbf{Y}^{(v)^T}\mathbf{Y}^{(v)} - \mathbf{Y}^{(v)}) + \mathbf{\Phi} = 0. \end{aligned} \tag{22}$$

According to the Karush-Kuhn-Tuckre(KKT) condition $\Phi_{i,j}Y_{i,j}^{(v)} = 0$, $\mathbf{Y}^{(v)}$ can be updated via following strategy:

$$Y_{i,j}^{(v)} \leftarrow Y_{i,j}^{(v)} \frac{[\lambda_1 \alpha_v^r \mathbf{Y} + 2\rho \mathbf{Y}^{(v)}]_{i,j}}{[\lambda_1 (\mathbf{L}^{(v)}\mathbf{Y}^{(v)} + \alpha_v^r \mathbf{Y}^{(v)}) + 2\rho \mathbf{Y}^{(v)}\mathbf{Y}^{(v)^T}\mathbf{Y}^{(v)}]_{i,j}}, \tag{23}$$

where ρ is a relatively large value to constrain $\mathbf{Y}^{(v)}$ satisfying the orthogonal condition. In this work, we set $\rho = 10^8$. Subsequently, we should normalize $\mathbf{Y}^{(v)}$ such that $[\mathbf{Y}^{(v)^T}\mathbf{Y}^{(v)}]_{i,i} = 1$.

Update Y and Fix the Other Variables. When other variables are fixed, Eq. (12) can be reformulated as

$$\min_{\mathbf{Y}} \sum_{v=1}^{V} \|\mathbf{X}^{(v)}\mathbf{\Theta}^{(v)}\mathbf{W}^{(v)} - \mathbf{Y}\|_F^2 + \lambda_1 \alpha_v^r \|\mathbf{Y} - \mathbf{Y}^{(v)}\|_F^2, \text{s.t. } \mathbf{Y}^T\mathbf{Y} = \mathbf{I}, \mathbf{Y} \geq 0. \tag{24}$$

Then, we construct the Lagrange function and take the derivative with $\mathbf{Y}$:

$$\begin{aligned} \frac{\partial L(\mathbf{Y}, \mathbf{\Psi})}{\partial \mathbf{Y}} =& \sum_{v=1}^{V} [-2\mathbf{X}^{(v)}\mathbf{\Theta}^{(v)}\mathbf{W}^{(v)} + 2\lambda_1 \alpha_v^r (\mathbf{Y} - \mathbf{Y}^{(v)}) \\ &+ 2\mathbf{Y}] + 4\gamma(\mathbf{Y}\mathbf{Y}^T\mathbf{Y} - \mathbf{Y}) + \mathbf{\Psi} = 0. \end{aligned} \tag{25}$$

Based on the Karush-Kuhn-Tuckre(KKT) condition $\Psi_{i,j}Y_{i,j} = 0$, we can obtain the updating formula of $\mathbf{Y}$ as follows:

$$Y_{i,j} \leftarrow Y_{i,j} \frac{[\sum_{v=1}^{V}(\mathbf{X}^{(v)}\mathbf{\Theta}^{(v)}\mathbf{W}^{(v)} + \lambda_1 \alpha_v^r \mathbf{Y}^{(v)}) + 2\gamma \mathbf{Y}]_{i,j}}{[\sum_{v=1}^{V}(1 + \lambda_1 \alpha_v^r)\mathbf{Y} + 2\gamma \mathbf{Y}\mathbf{Y}^T\mathbf{Y}]_{i,j}}. \tag{26}$$

We also set $\gamma = 10^8$ and normalize $\mathbf{Y}$ such that $[\mathbf{Y}^T\mathbf{Y}]_{i,i} = 1$.

Update α and fix the Other Variables. When other variables are fixed, Eq. (12) can be reformulated as

$$\min_{\alpha} \sum_{v=1}^{V} \alpha_v^r \|\mathbf{Y} - \mathbf{Y}^{(v)}\|_F^2, \quad \text{s.t.} \sum_{v=1}^{V} \alpha_v = 1, \alpha \geq 0. \tag{27}$$

The Lagrange function can be constructed as

$$L(\alpha, \tau) = \sum_{v=1}^{V} \alpha_v^r f(v) - \tau(\sum_{v=1}^{V} \alpha_v - 1), \tag{28}$$

where $f(v) = \|\mathbf{Y} - \mathbf{Y}^{(v)}\|_F^2$. Taking the derivative with α_v and setting it to zero, we can derive its solution with closed form:

$$\alpha_v = \frac{f(v)^{\frac{1}{1-r}}}{\sum_{v=1}^{V} f(v)^{\frac{1}{1-r}}}. \tag{29}$$

Finally, based on the previous analysis, the main procedure for solving LR-MVFS can be summarized as Algorithm 1.

Algorithm 1. LR-MVFS algorithm

Input: multi-view data $\{\mathbf{X}^{(v)}\}_{v=1}^{V}$, the number of clusters c, the parameters r, λ_1, λ_2.
Output: the selected feature subset.
1: Initialize $\{\Theta^{(v)}\}_{v=1}^{V} = \mathbf{I}, \alpha_v = \frac{1}{v}$. Construct feature redundancy matrix $\mathbf{S_f}$ and Laplacian matrix $\mathbf{L}$ for each view.
2: Repeat
3:     Update $\mathbf{W}^{(v)}$ with Eq.(15)
4:     Update $\Theta^{(v)}$ by solving Eq.(19)
5:     Update $\mathbf{Y}^{(v)}$ with Eq.(23)
6:     Update $\mathbf{Y}$ with Eq.(26)
7:     Update α_v with Eq.(29)
8: until Convergence
9: Calculate the l_2 norm of the rows of $\{\mathbf{W}^{(v)}\}_{v=1}^{V}$ and then sort them in descending order. Select the top features as the feature subset.

2.4   Convergence Analysis

In this part, we make a simple analysis of the convergence for each step in Algorithm 1. According to the Theorem 1 in [10], the iterative optimization process of $\mathbf{W}^{(v)}$ and $\mathbf{U}^{(v)}$ will monotonically decrease the objective function value until convergence. In step 4, $\Theta^{(v)}$ is updated by solving the quadratic programming problem. It is easy to prove that $\mathbf{A}$ is a positive semi-definite matrix, so Eq. (19) has a global optimal solution. For the steps of updating $\mathbf{Y}^{(v)}$ and $\mathbf{Y}$, the Karush-Kuhn-Tuckre (KKT) condition can ensure that the value of the objective function decreases with each iteration [8]. For updating α_v in step 7, Lagrange multiplier method can also ensure the convergence.

3   Experiments

This section investigates the performance of proposed LR-MVFS algorithm. The main information of utilized data sets has been summarized in Table 1. In experiments, the k-means clustering algorithm has been employed to verify the effectiveness of the feature subsets and the clustering results were evaluated by the clustering accuracy index (ACC) [1].

Table 1. Details of the multi-view data sets used in the experiments

Dataset	View dimension	Data points	Classes	View redundancy
Handwritten	47/240/6/64/76/216	2000	10	0.6184/0.3290/0.5200/0.0195/0.6605/0.8082
MSRC-V1	24/576/512/256/254	210	7	0.8759/0.7802/0.6760/0.8858/0.8644
Caltech101-7	48/40/254/1984/512/928	1474	7	0.8468/0.6752/0.6728/0.4117/0.6180/0.7862
ORL	4096/3304/6750	400	40	0.8894/0.0784/0.6038
NUSWIDE	65/226/145/74/129	30000	31	0.0340/0.0504/0.0417/0.1055/0.3958
BBCSport	3183/3203	544	5	0.0025/0.0025

The performance of LR-MVFS has be compared with three single view feature selection methods, i.e., Laplacian Score(LS) [6], Spectral Feature Selection(SPEC) [18], and SLSDR [11], and three multi-view feature selection methods, i.e., CGMV-UFS [12], ACSL [4], and NSGL [1]. For LS, SPEC, SLSDR, CGMV-UFS, ACSL and LR-MVFS, the neighborhood size for constructing the similarity graph was set as 5 and the HeatKernel parameter was set as 10. For CGMV-UFS, the values of r_1, r_2, and r_3 were set as 2. For the hyperparameters in SLSDR, ACSL, NSGL and LR-MVFS, we all tuned their values by a grid-search strategy from 10^{-4} to 10^4 at 10 times intervals. For LR-MVFS, the value of r was set as 2 and the setting of parameter t was variant to different data sets according to the average redundancy of each single-view feature set. To formulate the setting rule of t, we define an indirect variable t_v, whose value is 25 percent of the average total redundancy between a feature and all the other features in the v-th view and can be calculated by

$$t_v = \frac{Avr_v * d_v}{4}, \quad v = 1, \dots, V, \tag{30}$$

where Avr_v records the average redundancy of the v-th view. Subsequently, for a data set, if the average redundancy of most views is greater than 0.5, we set $t = \min\{t_1, t_2, \dots, t_V\}$. Otherwise, if the average redundancy of most views is less than 0.5, we set $t = \max\{t_1, t_2, \dots, t_V\}$ to make the correlation playing a greater role. For a data set with similar number of views having average redundancy greater than 0.5 or lower than 0.5, we take the average value of t_v for t.

Since k-means algorithm is sensitive to initializations, it has been executed 20 times with different random initializations under each situation and the average clustering accuracy and standard deviation have been recorded. Table 2 summarizes the best results of different methods on variant data sets. It can be

Table 2. Clustering accuracy of seven algorithms on six data sets (ACC±STD%).

	Handwritten	MSRC-V1	Caltech101-7	ORL	NUSWIDE	BBCSport
Baseline	58.69 ± 4.11	48.14 ± 3.13	40.38 ± 4.22	48.11 ± 3.13	13.82 ± 0.36	**62.97 ± 11.67**
LS	60.87 ± 4.94	49.71 ± 4.7	41.12 ± 3.9	36.08 ± 2.03	13.34 ± 0.33	45.48 ± 7.38
SPEC	60.79 ± 4.67	50.05 ± 3.8	41.53 ± 3.13	38.66 ± 1.96	13.37 ± 0.22	42.52 ± 6.54
SLSDR	71.55 ± 4.11	65.62 ± 5.17	60.24 ± 6.18	45.85 ± 2.2	14.35 ± 0.24	55.42 ± 10.97
CGMV-UFS	75.43 ± 6.7	68.07 ± 6.55	62.13 ± 6.07	47.44 ± 3.07	14.32 ± 0.38	55.55 ± 9.44
ACSL	76.11 ± 7.97	62.57 ±5.23	58.22 ± 6.07	48.46 ± 3.01	13.78 ± 0.32	55.52 ± 8.73
NSGL	78.45 ± 6.85	72.19 ± 6.39	61.11 ± 3.74	56.69 ± 2.47	14.15 ± 0.37	53.69 ± 11.24
LR-MVFS	**80.67 ± 6.28**	**74.9 ± 5.28**	**63.18 ± 4.04**	**57.88 ± 3.77**	**15.15 ± 0.6**	59.41 ± 9.83

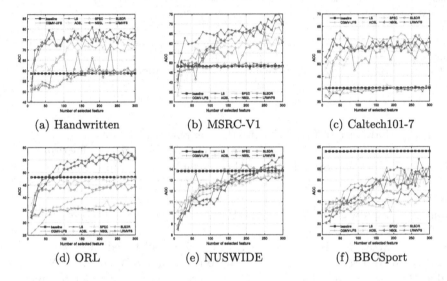

(a) Handwritten   (b) MSRC-V1   (c) Caltech101-7

(d) ORL   (e) NUSWIDE   (f) BBCSport

Fig. 1. The clustering accuracy (ACC) of different methods on different feature subsets.

observed that most feature selection algorithms perform better than the baseline, which indicates that feature selection can not only reduce data dimensions, but also improve the performance of learning algorithms. Moreover, we can find that multi-view feature selection methods overall perform better than single-view approaches. The main reason is that simply combining the features from different views together may ignore the connection between different views. More importantly, our proposed LR-MVFS method shows superior performance than other multi-view feature selection approaches. Especially, in comparison with the CGMV-UFS method, which is also characterized by improving the effectiveness of feature selection by considering feature redundancy and projection space weight, the presented LR-MVFS approach can still reach higher clustering accuracy.

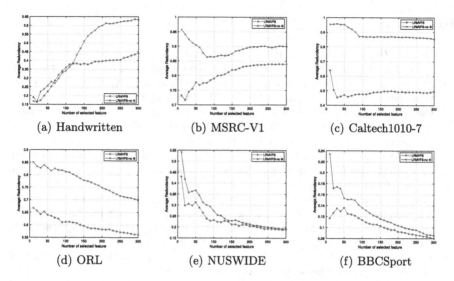

Fig. 2. Comparison of average redundancy before and after removing Θ on different data sets.

In order to further illustrate the detailed performance, we show the clustering accuracy curves of different methods obtained on variant size of feature subsets. The results are shown in Figs. 1. It can be observed from the figure that the curve of LR-MVFS is basically higher than that of other methods. Especially, for the Handwritten, MSRC-V1 and ORL data sets, due to the high redundancy between features, the proposed method performs much better than the others. Additionally, to further validate the effectiveness of proposed redundancy learning mechanism, we removed Θ and the last term of Eq. (12), and updated the new objective function iteratively according to the updating rules similar to Algorithm 1. Subsequently, the average redundancy of the selected feature subsets before and after removing Θ were compared in Fig. 2. It can be observed from the figures that the average redundancy of the feature subsets selected by LRMVFS is significantly lower, which shows the effectiveness of feature redundancy matrix Θ in low redundancy learning.

4   Conclusion

In this paper, we have proposed a multi-view unsupervised feature selection method with low redundancy learning, which adaptively weights the projection space according to the redundancy between features. This method also combines the local geometric structure of each single view to learn the consensus clustering indicator matrix. Subsequently, sparse constraints are applied to the projection space to complete the feature selection. An alternative iterative solution has been developed for the proposed model and experimental results on real-world multi-view data sets have demonstrated the superiority of this method.

References

1. Bai, X., Zhu, L., Liang, C., Li, J., Nie, X., Chang, X.: Multi-view feature selection via nonnegative structured graph learning. Neurocomputing **387**, 110–122 (2020)
2. Belkin, M., Niyogi, P.: Laplacian eigenmaps for dimensionality reduction and data representation. Neural Comput. **15**(6), 1373–1396 (2003)
3. Cai, D., Zhang, C., He, X.: Unsupervised feature selection for multi-cluster data. In: Proceedings of the 16th ACM SIGKDD International Conference on Knowledge Discovery and Data Mining, pp. 333–342 (2010)
4. Dong, X., Zhu, L., Song, X., Li, J., Cheng, Z.: Adaptive collaborative similarity learning for unsupervised multi-view feature selection. arXiv preprint arXiv:1904.11228 (2019)
5. Feng, Y., Xiao, J., Zhuang, Y., Liu, X.: Adaptive unsupervised multi-view feature selection for visual concept recognition. In: Lee, K.M., Matsushita, Y., Rehg, J.M., Hu, Z. (eds.) ACCV 2012. LNCS, vol. 7724, pp. 343–357. Springer, Heidelberg (2013). https://doi.org/10.1007/978-3-642-37331-2_26
6. He, X., Cai, D., Niyogi, P.: Laplacian score for feature selection. In: Advances in Neural Information Processing Systems, vol. 18 (2005)
7. Hou, C., Nie, F., Tao, H., Yi, D.: Multi-view unsupervised feature selection with adaptive similarity and view weight. IEEE Trans. Knowl. Data Eng. **29**(9), 1998–2011 (2017)
8. Lee, D.: Algorithms for non-negative matrix factorization. In: NIPS 2000 (2000)
9. Li, Z., Yang, Y., Liu, J., Zhou, X., Lu, H.: Unsupervised feature selection using nonnegative spectral analysis. In: Proceedings of the AAAI conference on artificial intelligence. vol. 26 (2012)
10. Nie, F., Huang, H., Cai, X., Ding, C.: Efficient and robust feature selection via joint l2, 1-norms minimization. In: Advances in Neural Information Processing Systems, vol. 23 (2010)
11. Shang, R., Xu, K., Shang, F., Jiao, L.: Sparse and low-redundant subspace learning-based dual-graph regularized robust feature selection. Knowl.-Based Syst. **187**, 104830 (2020)
12. Tang, C., et al.: Consensus learning guided multi-view unsupervised feature selection. Knowl.-Based Syst. **160**, 49–60 (2018)
13. Tang, C., et al.: Cross-view locality preserved diversity and consensus learning for multi-view unsupervised feature selection. IEEE Trans. Knowl. Data Eng. **34**(10), 4705–4716 (2022)
14. Tang, J., Hu, X., Gao, H., Liu, H.: Unsupervised feature selection for multi-view data in social media. In: Proceedings of the 2013 SIAM International Conference on Data Mining, pp. 270–278. SIAM (2013)
15. Wang, Z., Feng, Y., Qi, T., Yang, X., Zhang, J.J.: Adaptive multi-view feature selection for human motion retrieval. Signal Process. **120**, 691–701 (2016)
16. Xu, X., Wu, X., Wei, F., Zhong, W., Nie, F.: A general framework for feature selection under orthogonal regression with global redundancy minimization. IEEE Trans. Knowl. Data Eng. (2021)
17. Zhang, H., Wu, D., Nie, F., Wang, R., Li, X.: Multilevel projections with adaptive neighbor graph for unsupervised multi-view feature selection. Inf. Fusion **70**, 129–140 (2021)
18. Zhao, Z., Liu, H.: Spectral feature selection for supervised and unsupervised learning. In: Proceedings of the 24th International Conference on Machine Learning, pp. 1151–1157 (2007)

Dynamic Feed-Forward LSTM

Chengkai Piao[iD], Yuchen Wang, and Jinmao Wei[✉]

Nankai University, 38 Tongyan Road, Tianjin 300350, Tianjin, China
{apark,wyc}@mail.nankai.edu.cn, weijm@nankai.edu.cn

Abstract. We address the insufficient hidden states capabilities and single-direction feeding flaws of existing LSTM caused by its horizontal recurrent steps. To this end, we propose the Dynamic Feed-Forward LSTM (D-LSTM). Specifically, our D-LSTM first expands the capabilities of hidden states by assigning an exclusive state vector to each word. Then, the Dynamic Additive Attention (DAA) method is utilized to adaptively compress local context words into a fixed size vector. Last, a vertical feed-forward process is proposed to search context relations by filtering informative features in the compressed context vector and updating hidden states. With the help of exclusive hidden states, each word can preserve its most correlated context features and hidden states do not interfere with each other. By setting an appropriate context window size for DAA and stacking multiple such layers, the context scope can be gradually expanded from a central word to both sides and achieve the whole sentence at the top layer. Furthermore, the D-LSTM module is compatible with parallel computing and amenable to training via back-propagation for its vertical prorogation. Experimental results on both classification and sequence tagging datasets insist that our models achieve competitive performance compared to existing LSTMs.

Keywords: Dynamic Process · Feed Forward · LSTM · Full Context

1 Introduction

Albeit the rapid development of Neural Network (NN) model, context patterns, the relations between a word and its neighbors, still play an important role. Long-Short Term Memory (LSTM), as well as its variants [13] are powerful models for modeling context patterns. Thanks to the horizontal recurrent property that searches relations between a word and the shared historical context vector, LSTMs could iteratively update and enrich the hidden state, and to generate satisfying representations.

Despite the success, horizontal LSTMs are suffering from the limitations of insufficient hidden states capabilities and single-direction feeding [5]. On the one hand, all words share a single hidden state vector, which may not have enough capability to store adequate context information for all words, and new words may dilute previous hidden state values and disturb context patterns [6]. On the other hand, LSTMs can take only single-direction information into account since the horizontal recurrent structures are designed to search relations between a word and its historical contexts. Although Bi-directional LSTM (BiLSTM) can alleviate this limitation, it merely provides an additional reverse order sequence, which still faces the same issue. Furthermore, attributed to their sequential nature, LSTMs do not support parallel computing, which may constrain the industrial deployment.

To increase the capabilities of hidden states, Dense Connections [6] were inserted between two LSTM layers. To take multi-direction context information into consideration, different sequence orders were learned by the Self-Attention mechanism and Multi-channel Features (SAMF) [13] method. To conquer the limitation of single-direction feeding, researchers used fixed context window [23] and Convolution Neural Network (CNN) [2] to dismiss the local context dependencies. However, the above limitations were not completely solved. Although dense connections can expand the capabilities of hidden states, it is still suffering from the limitation of shared hidden states. Meanwhile, since an Attention method can only provide a fixed order of sequence, it is essentially equal to an enhanced Bi-LSTM model that has multiple input sequences. For different sentences, stacking insufficient layers is not expected to expand their fixed size context scope to cover all words of long sequences, while redundant layers are unnecessary for short sentences and lead to high computational complexities.

In this paper, we propose Dynamic Feed Forward LSTM (D-LSTM) to alleviate, even eliminate, the aforementioned limitations. Firstly, each word is assigned an exclusive hidden state vector to store specific context information. Then, a Dynamic Additive Attention (DAA) method is proposed to adaptively compress local words, covered by its context window, into a single context vector. Last, a feed-forward process is adopted to search context relations by filtering informative features in the compressed context vector and updating hidden states.

With the help of specific hidden states, each word has adequate storage to preserve the most correlated context relations and all hidden states do not interfere with each other. Meanwhile, since the number of hidden states is determined by the sentence length, the capability of hidden states can be adaptively allocated, long sentences will be assigned more state vectors than the shorts. Consequently, the problem of insufficient context information caused by the shared hidden state can be solved.

By stacking multiple layers, the context scope of DAA is expanded layer by layer. This method is coherence with the theory that context words closer to the target word should be more important, and the importance decreases with the distance gets larger. Meanwhile, the dynamic context window of DAA ensures the context scope of the model can be expanded to the whole sentence at the top layer, independent with the sentence length. Consequently, D-LSTM can take reasonable context weights and appropriate context orders into account, and to address the limitation of single direction feeding. Furthermore, our model is capable of taking full advantage of parallel computing since the vertical feed-forward process has few recurrent steps. Experimental results on both classification and sequence labeling show that our model achieves or exceeds existing LSTMs using the same number of parameters while being faster. The main contributions of this paper are listed as follows.

- Specific hidden states used to solve the limitation of insufficient capabilities of hidden states.
- A Dynamic Local Context method used to address the problem of single-direction feeding.
- A parallel structure that can convert the updating process of hidden states from horizontal recurrent steps into a vertical feed-forward process.

2   Related Work

LSTM and its variants have achieved satisfying results in NLP tasks, such as Sentiment Analysis(SA) [11], Sequence Labeling (SL) [10], Fake News Detection (FND) [19] and Topic Modeling (TM) [1], etc. However, the limitations of insufficient hidden states capabilities and single-direction feeding may impede the model from searching context relations. The former shortcoming may cause gradient vanishing [8] and lacking long-range relations [15] since new words will disturb previous hidden state values. The latter problem may lead to high computational cost [9] for its horizontal recurrent steps.

To expand the capabilities of hidden states, researchers have proposed two kinds of methods, additional structures and extra semantic spaces. In the former aspect, Dense [6] connections were inserted between layers to provide additional hidden state storage. Similarly, [21] proposed to construct Residual Connections between layers and achieved similar performance with fewer parameters. In the latter domain, [12] proposed to use more channels to expand the capability of its hidden state vector. Extra word embeddings can also provide local context combinations [16]. [22] proposed to use Latent Dirichlet Allocation (LDA) to search context patterns in an extra semantic space, and thus to decrease the demand of context information. Besides, several existing methods [24] adopted the same idea to alleviate this limitation.

Another line of research aimed at multi-direction context information, there are two kinds of mainstream methods, additional sequence information, context window and global states. Specifically, Bi-LSTM [14] adopted an additional reverse order sequence to build more context relations and achieved satisfying performances. Following this idea, Multi-Head Attention (MHA) [20] was equipped to explore more sequence orders by its row transformations. Context window based models [23] collected local information and iteratively expanded the context scope layer by layer to learn context relations. Researchers also used global states to search interactions between local- and global-scale context features [17]. [3] split a sentence into segments and used a two-layer RNN to independently extract segment and global features. Similarly, local and global attention were integrated into LSTM to generate informative features [7].

3   Model

Existing LSTMs store all historical information in a single hidden state vector, which may be insufficient to represent specific context relations for each word. Meanwhile, horizontal recurrent steps can only take single-direction context information into account, although Bi-LSTM adopts an additional reverse order of sequence, the single-direction problem still unsolved. Figure 1a illustrates the structure of Existing LSTMs.

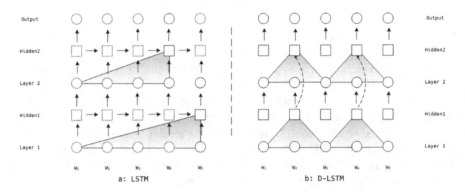

Fig. 1. The comparison between LSTM and D-LSTM.

The proposed D-LSTM assigns a specific hidden state and a recurrent cell to each word and gradually enriches the representations of hidden states as the model goes deeper. Since the specific hidden states cuts off the dependencies of context words, the updating process of hidden states can be converted from horizontal recurrent steps into a feed forward process. Equation (1) illustrates the computing process of D-LSTM.

$$
\begin{aligned}
F &= \sigma\left(E \times W_f + H^{l-1} \times U_f + b_f\right), \\
D &= \sigma\left(E \times W_d + H^{l-1} \times U_d + b_d\right), \\
I &= tanh\left(E \times W_i + H^{l-1} \times U_i + b_i\right), \\
O &= \sigma\left(E \times W_o + H^{l-1} \times U_o + b_o\right), \\
C^l &= C^{l-1} \odot F + D \odot I, \\
H^l &= O \odot tanh(H^{l-1}).
\end{aligned}
\tag{1}
$$

where F, D, I, O represent the values of D-LSTM gates respectively used to control the information flow for a layer cell C and hidden state vectors H, W_*, U_* and b_* are trainable parameters. σ is the sigmoid function, $E = DAA(S)$ are compressed local context vectors. Since there are few recurrent steps, the gates and hidden states can be written in matrix forms.

To compute the context matrix E, a Dynamic Additive Attention (DAA) is used to compress context words into a single vector. Equation (2) illustrates the computing process.

$$DAA(S) = \{\sigma(Q_i) \odot \sum_{i=i-ctx/2}^{i+ctx/2} [\sigma(K_i) \odot V_i]\}|_{i=1}^{m}. \tag{2}$$

where $Q = S \times W_q + b_q$, $K = S \times W_k + b_k$ and $V = S \times W_v + b_v$ are linear transformations of S, W_q, W_k and W_v are trainable matrices, b_q, b_k and b_v are corresponding biases, E are compressed contexts, ctx denotes the context window size.

Since sentences have different lengths, it is hard to determine the value of ctx. Although stacking multiple layers can gradually expand the context scope as the model goes deeper, a fixed number of layers and context window size can not precisely cover all words of different sentences. Suppose the model depth is l and context window size is ctx, the context scope of the top layer is fixed as $(ctx - 1) \cdot l + 1$. Insufficient layers and a small context window may not be able to cover a long sentence, while redundant layers and a large context window will exceed the boundary of a short sentence. To address this limitation, we compute a specific context window for each sentence to ensure the top layer can access the full-scale context words. Equation (3) illustrates the computing process.

$$ctx = \lceil \frac{m + l - 1}{l} \rceil. \tag{3}$$

For a fixed model depth l, a long sentence will be assigned a large ctx while a short sentence will have a small ctx, to expand of compress its context scope. Consequently, the context scope can be adaptively adjusted to cover the whole sentence and provide precisely context information.

Since D-LSTM breaks the horizontal recurrent property, it is compatible with parallel computing and we use matrix operations in this section to emphasis this feature. It is worth noting that Eq. (2) has two loop steps, and we propose a matrix multiplication based parallel solution.

First, shown in Eq. (4), we compute the second part of Eq. (2). Since this step only contains matrix multiplications, it could be implemented in parallel.

$$KV = \sigma(K) \odot V. \tag{4}$$

Then, a row-transformation matrix $T \in \mathbb{R}^{m \times m}$ is constructed to perform left multiply with KV. T is a square matrix in which each row represents a word's context window, and the values are set with 1 if the corresponding positions are covered by the context window. T is shown in Equation (5).

$$T_{ij} = \begin{cases} 1 & i - ctx \leq j \leq i + ctx, \\ 0 & otherwise. \end{cases} \tag{5}$$

At last, the transformed matrix is performed an item-wise product with Q. Particularly, for boundary conditions, context window should be moved to central direction accordingly. Consequently, the parallel DAA could be rewritten as Eq. (6).

$$DAA(S) = \sigma(Q) \odot [T \times (K \cdot V)]. \tag{6}$$

4 Experiments

4.1 Datasets

We choose 5 datasets for classification evaluation, which contains Cook[1], Flip-kart[2], IMDB[3], SMS [4] and Tweet[5]. For Sequence Labeling tasks, we choose POS-GMB-e and POS-GMB-p datasets[6]. We randomly split the movie review dataset into training (70%), development (10%) and test (20%) sections.

4.2 Competitor Models

Previous works have proposed various methods to solve the aforementioned limitations, but not all of them can be applied to our tasks. We chose the 6 most related neural models and implemented them as competitor methods.

We used classical LSTM and Bi-LSTM as the baseline models. We used Dense-LSTM [6] to validate the influences of exclusive hidden states. It used full connections between neighbor layers to expand the capabilities of hidden states. We used Res-LSTM [21] to compare the parameter number of different hidden states. Used residual connections, instead of full connections, between layers. We used SAMF [13] as the baseline of extra sequence order. It imposed an Attention module to generate an additional order of the sequence on a Bi-LSTM to take multiple directions of context information into account. We used S-LSTM [23] to compare the differences between fixed-size and dynamic context window. It used stacked structures to iteratively expand the context scope. We used CNN-LSTM [2] as the baseline of context module. It used a CNN model to learn local context information. We used LDA-LSTM [22] as the additional comparison, it used LDA to provide semantic distribution and to decrease the demand for context information.

4.3 Ablation Study

The Influence of Layers and Dimensions. Figure 2 draws the accuracies of D-LSTM with various embedding dimensions and layer numbers on the Tweet dataset. From the viewpoint of the x-axis, when the number of embedding dimensions varied from 100 to 600, the accuracies insistently increases before reaching a peak value, and then decreases slightly. It can be explained by the intuition that insufficient dimensions can not provide enough semantic spaces but abundant dimensions can not indefinitely improve the performance. On the y-axis, the

---

[1] http://archive.ics.uci.edu/ml/datasets/Youtube+cookery+channels+viewers+comments+in+Hinglish.

[2] https://www.kaggle.com/kabirnagpal/flipkart-customer-review-and-rating.

[3] https://www.cs.cornell.edu/people/pabo/movie-review-data/.

[4] https://www.kaggle.com/lishaoshao/tweet-sentiment-extraction-wpf?select=test.csv.

[5] https://www.kaggle.com/ishantjuyal/emotions-in-text.

[6] https://www.kaggle.com/shoumikgoswami/annotated-gmb-corpus.

accuracies achieved the best results at 4 layers. Using more layers can achieve similar performances, indicating that our model can collect full-scale context information within any number of layers. This shows the smoothness of our model in various embedding dimensions.

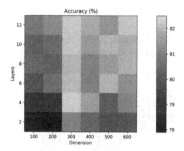

Fig. 2. The accuracies of D-LSTM on different dimensions and layers.

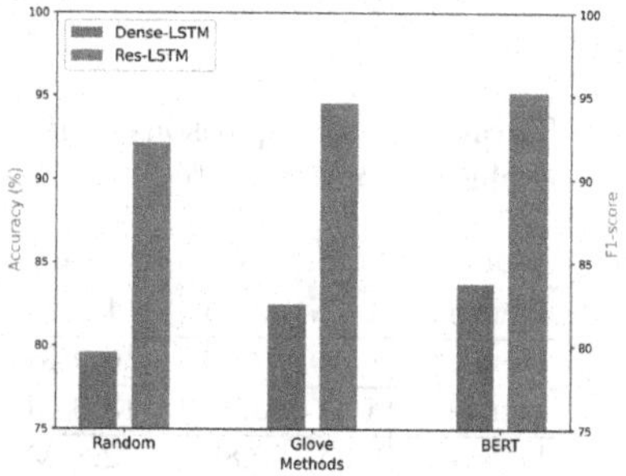

Fig. 3. The performance of D-LSTM on different word embeddings.

The Influence of Word Embeddings. To test if the D-LSTM is compatible with different word embeddings, we used three kinds of methods, random, Global vectors for word representation (Glove) [18] and Bidirectional Encoder Representations from Transformers (BERT) [4], to initialize the word vectors. Figure 3 illustrates the corresponding results on Tweet and POS-EMB-e datasets. It can be easily find that the random method reported inferior performance than the others while BERT reports the highest accuracies. Due to the limited dataset, simply using random values to initialize word vectors may lead to over-fitting. Since Glove has many pre-training samples, its word embeddings naturally contain abundant semantic knowledge, which will benefit the downstream tasks. Similar with the Glove, BERT uses Transformer based models to pre-train word embeddings in a dataset that contains more than 3300M words. Since the main purpose of this paper is not to present a pre-train method, while the competitor models were used Glove. Consequently, we used Glove in the remaining experiments for the fair comparisons.

The Influence of Exclusive Hidden States. To validate if the exclusive hidden states can improve the performances, we compared our model with Dense-LSTM and Res-LSTM. Table 1 illustrates the corresponding results, where the column of **States** indicates whether each word has specific hidden states. With the help of exclusive hidden states, all models reported higher accuracies than their original versions. D-LSTM reports 1.35% ∼ 1.47% accuracy gain with the specific hidden states equipped, Dense-LSTM and Res-LSTM have similar trends. This phenomena can be explained by the theory of specific hidden states can preserve the most correlated features for each word while shared hidden states are prone to be affected by different words.

Since Dense-LSTM adopts trainable dense connections to store hidden state information, it should use larger linear models to store the expanded hidden states and its parameters will be significantly increased. Res-LSTM has few trainable parameters between two layers, adopting specific hidden states will not make the model complicated. D-LSTM has fewer parameters than the competitors, and whether using specific hidden states or not has no apparent effect on the parameter number. This is becaus the hidden states are not trainable parameters.

Table 1. Comparisons against exclusive context states.

Model	L.	S.	Acc (%)	Param
Dense	4	N	80.85	11.4 M
Dense	8	N	79.20	16.9 M
Dense	4	Y	80.91	13.0 M
Dense	8	Y	80.87	22.8 M
Res	4	N	79.13	9.6 M
Res	8	N	78.55	17.5 M
Res	4	Y	80.49	9.6 M
Res	8	Y	81.06	17.5 M
D-LSTM	4	N	80.10	10.9 M
D-LSTM	8	N	80.67	14.3 M
D-LSTM	4	Y	82.45	10.9 M
D-LSTM	8	Y	82.14	14.3 M

Table 2. Comparisons against dynamic context window.

Model	L.	Ctx	Acc (%)	Param
S-LSTM	4	2	77.36	13.9 M
S-LSTM	8	2	79.72	23.6 M
S-LSTM	4	5	79.85	13.9 M
S-LSTM	8	5	81.01	23.6 M
S-LSTM	4	D	80.98	13.9 M
S-LSTM	8	D	81.68	23.6 M
D-LSTM	4	2	80.16	10.9 M
D-LSTM	8	2	81.42	14.3 M
D-LSTM	4	5	81.58	10.9 M
D-LSTM	8	5	82.03	14.3 M
D-LSTM	4	D	82.45	10.9 M
D-LSTM	8	D	82.14	14.3 M

The Influence of Dynamic Context Window. We compared the experimental results of our model and S-LSTM to investigate the effectiveness of dynamic context window. Specifically, we set the number of layers and context window as the variables, and other hyper-parameters were frozen. According to Table 2, both D-LSTM and S-LSTM showed increasing trends with layers and context window size, which indicate the necessity of context information. Meanwhile, both of the models achieved better performances with a larger context window, which implies that expanding the context window will help the model to extract semantic features. Particularly, with the dynamic context window equipped, S-LSTM exceeds fixed-size context window D-LSTM. Intuitively a fixed-size context window can not perfectly cover all words when handling different sentences, therefore S-LSTM reports relatively inferior accuracy. To make sure that the context window indeed affects the model performance, we equipped a fixed-size context window on D-LSTM, and it reported 1.03% ∼ 2.29% accuracy inferior, demonstrating the necessity of dynamic context window.

Both S-LSTM and D-LSTM reported few differences in parameter number, which insists that our DAA is capable of handling various context words without changing its structure. Meanwhile, our model has half as many parameters as S-LSTM, which indicates D-LSTM is more light-weighted and easier for deployment.

The Influence of Sentence Length. Figure 4 shows the accuracies of different sentence lengths on the Tweet dataset, where "+" on the x-axis represents the sentence length is greater than 25. It can be seen that the performances of all models decrease as the sentence lengths increase, indicating that the long sentences are harder to understand by a model. D-LSTM reports an relative horizontal curve, showing that our model can access the full-scale context of different length sentences. This confirms our intuition that using a specific dynamic context window and the feed-forward structure to collect context information is a feasible way.

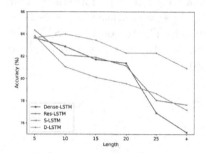

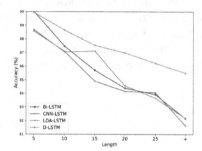

Fig. 4. The accuracies with different sentence lengths on the Tweet dataset.

Fig. 5. The accuracies with different sentence lengths on the IMDB dataset.

To further test the affections of sentence lengths, we compared the D-LSTM with its competitors on the IMDB dataset, which has the average length of 269. The corresponding results are illustrated in Fig. 5 The overall accuracy trends are consistent with the previous experiment, in which the performances decreases as the lengths increasing. Since the length of sentences varies significantly, the accuracy curves are steeper then Fig. 4. In comparison, D-LSTM still reported relatively flat accuracy curves, indicating that the robustness of D-LSTM.

Table 3. Statistics of 5 classification datasets.

Dataset	Cook	Flipkart	IMDB	SMS	Tweet	Average (%)
LSTM	71.35	72.84	85.93	70.85	79.75	75.51
Bi-LSTM	72.04	74.74	86.41	72.13	81.84	76.77
Dense-LSTM	73.77	74.40	85.66	**74.33**	80.25	77.08
Res-LSTM	74.59	73.96	84.67	71.73	79.13	76.28
SAMF	73.25	73.98	86.67	69.09	80.78	75.99
S-LSTM	68.06	74.66	85.33	68.94	81.01	75.03
CNN-LSTM	72.76	73.61	86.49	70.08	80.49	75.94
LDA-LSTM	72.56	74.81	86.33	71.61	79.32	76.29
D-LSTM	**75.23**	**75.57**	**87.54**	73.86	**82.45**	**78.47**

4.4   The Statistic of Classification Task

The result statistics of 5 classification datasets are illustrated in Table 3. The experimental results on Tweet are consistent with the previous results, where D-LSTM outperforms all competitors significantly. Meanwhile, BiLSTM gives an average accuracy of 76.77%, which achieved 1.26% average accuracy improvement compared with LSTM. Dense-LSTM and Res-LSTM expands the hidden state capability, Bi-LSTM, LDA-LSTM and SAMF adopted additional input sequences, S-LSTM and CNN-LSTM utilized local context window to alleviate the limitations of LSTM, and they achieved relatively better performances. Our model gives the best results on other datasets, and its average accuracy is 78.47%, significantly higher compared with existing models. The reason is D-LSTM can access full-scale context information of different length sentences, and preserve the most related context features for each word.

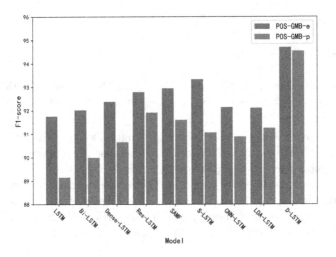

Fig. 6. Statistic of sequence labeling tasks.

4.5   The Statistic of Sequence Labeling Task

Figure 6 illustrates the F1-score on sequence labeling tasks. Firstly, coherence with previous classification experimental results, Bi-LSTM exceeds LSTM, which insists Bi-directional information will benefit sequence labeling task. Meanwhile, Dense-LSTM achieved relatively high performance compared with competitors, which implies the capabilities of hidden states is a more important factor. For our D-LSTM, it achieved the best results among the competitors, since our model is capable of addressing both context direction and hidden states capability limitations. Consequently, D-LSTM has stronger adaptability. Furthermore, D-LSTM can access the full-scale context window of different sentences without changing their structure, which makes it easier to deploy.

5   Conclusion

We have investigated D-LSTM, a dynamic feed-forward network for sentence representation, which offers full-scale context information of arbitrary length sentences to the model. In a D-LSTM layer, each word is assigned a group of hidden states to preserve exclusive context vectors. Meanwhile, a vertical feed-forward propagation is incorporated to generate a representation vector for each word independently. Results on a range of classification and sequence labeling tasks show that D-LSTM outperforms existing LSTMs with a notable gap and maintains stable results, demonstrating that D-LSTM can be a useful addition to the neural toolbox for encoding sentences. The structural nature of our model supports parallel computing, making it easier to deploy commercially.

Acknowledgments. This work was partially supported by the National Key R&D Programs of China (2018YFC1603800, 2018YFC1603802, 2020YFA0908700, 2020YFA0908702), the National Natural Science Foundation of China (61772288, 61872115) and the Natural Science Foundation of Tianjin City (18JCZDJC30900).

References

1. Asghari, M., Sierra-Sosa, D., Elmaghraby, A.S.: A topic modeling framework for spatio-temporal information management. Inf. Process. Manage. **57**(6), 102340 (2020)
2. Behera, R.K., Jena, M., Rath, S.K., Misra, S.: Co-LSTM: Convolutional LSTM model for sentiment analysis in social big data. Inf. Process. Manage. **58**(1), 102435 (2021)
3. Dennis, D., et al.: Shallow RNN: accurate time-series classification on resource constrained devices. In: Advances in Neural Information Processing Systems, pp. 12896–12906 (2019)
4. Devlin, J., Chang, M.W., Lee, K., Toutanova, K.: Bert: Pre-training of deep bidirectional transformers for language understanding. In: Proceedings of the 2019 Conference of the North American Chapter of the Association for Computational Linguistics: Human Language Technologies, Volume 1 (Long and Short Papers), pp. 4171–4186 (2019)
5. Ding, Y., Zhu, Y., Feng, J., Zhang, P., Cheng, Z.: Interpretable Spatio-temporal attention LSTM model for flood forecasting. Neurocomputing **403**, 348–359 (2020)
6. Ding, Z., Xia, R., Yu, J., Li, X., Yang, J.: Densely connected bidirectional LSTM with applications to sentence classification. In: Zhang, M., Ng, V., Zhao, D., Li, S., Zan, H. (eds.) NLPCC 2018. LNCS (LNAI), vol. 11109, pp. 278–287. Springer, Cham (2018). https://doi.org/10.1007/978-3-319-99501-4_24
7. Hanunggul, P.M., Suyanto, S.: The impact of local attention in LSTM for abstractive text summarization. In: 2019 International Seminar on Research of Information Technology and Intelligent Systems (ISRITI), pp. 54–57. IEEE (2019)
8. Hochreiter, S.: Gradient flow in recurrent nets: the difficulty of learning long-term dependencies. A Field Guide to Dynamical Recurrent Neural Networks, pp. 237–244 (2001)
9. Hosseini, M., Maida, A.S., Hosseini, M., Raju, G.: Inception LSTM for next-frame video prediction (student abstract). In: Proceedings of the AAAI Conference on Artificial Intelligence, vol. 34, pp. 13809–13810 (2020)

10. Jörke, M., Gillick, J., Sims, M., Bamman, D.: Attending to long-distance document context for sequence labeling. In: Proceedings of the 2020 Conference on Empirical Methods in Natural Language Processing: Findings, pp. 3692–3704 (2020)

11. Ke, P., Ji, H., Liu, S., Zhu, X., Huang, M.: Sentilare: linguistic knowledge enhanced language representation for sentiment analysis. In: Proceedings of the 2020 Conference on Empirical Methods in Natural Language Processing (EMNLP), pp. 6975–6988 (2020)

12. Le, H.T., Cerisara, C., Denis, A.: Do convolutional networks need to be deep for text classification? In: Workshops at the Thirty-Second AAAI Conference on Artificial Intelligence, pp. 29–36 (2018)

13. Li, W., Qi, F., Tang, M., Yu, Z.: Bidirectional LSTM with self-attention mechanism and multi-channel features for sentiment classification. Neurocomputing **387**, 63–77 (2020)

14. Lin, B.Y., Xu, F.F., Luo, Z., Zhu, K.: Multi-channel BILSTM-CRF model for emerging named entity recognition in social media. In: Proceedings of the 3rd Workshop on Noisy User-generated Text, pp. 160–165 (2017)

15. Liu, G., Guo, J.: Bidirectional LSTM with attention mechanism and convolutional layer for text classification. Neurocomputing **337**, 325–338 (2019)

16. Lu, C., Huang, H., Jian, P., Wang, D., Guo, Y.-D.: A P-LSTM neural network for sentiment classification. In: Kim, J., Shim, K., Cao, L., Lee, J.-G., Lin, X., Moon, Y.-S. (eds.) PAKDD 2017. LNCS (LNAI), vol. 10234, pp. 524–533. Springer, Cham (2017). https://doi.org/10.1007/978-3-319-57454-7_41

17. Niu, G., Xu, H., He, B., Xiao, X., Wu, H., Gao, S.: Enhancing local feature extraction with global representation for neural text classification. In: Proceedings of the 2019 Conference on Empirical Methods in Natural Language Processing and the 9th International Joint Conference on Natural Language Processing (EMNLP-IJCNLP), Hong Kong, China, pp. 496–506. Association for Computational Linguistics, November 2019. https://doi.org/10.18653/v1/D19-1047, https://www.aclweb.org/anthology/D19-1047

18. Pennington, J., Socher, R., Manning, C.D.: Glove: global vectors for word representation. In: Proceedings of the 2014 Conference on Empirical Methods in Natural Language Processing (EMNLP), pp. 1532–1543 (2014)

19. Song, C., Ning, N., Zhang, Y., Wu, B.: A multimodal fake news detection model based on crossmodal attention residual and multichannel convolutional neural networks. Inf. Process. Manage. **58**(1), 102437 (2021)

20. Vaswani, A., et al.: Attention is all you need. In: Advances in Neural Information Processing Systems, pp. 5998–6008 (2017)

21. Wang, J., Peng, B., Zhang, X.: Using a stacked residual LSTM model for sentiment intensity prediction. Neurocomputing **322**, 93–101 (2018)

22. Wang, Y., Wang, X., Chang, X.: Sentiment analysis of consumer-generated online reviews of physical bookstores using hybrid LSTM-CNN and LDA topic model. In: 2020 International Conference on Culture-oriented Science & Technology (ICCST), pp. 457–462. IEEE (2020)

23. Zhang, Y., Liu, Q., Song, L.: Sentence-state LSTM for text representation. In: Proceedings of the 56th Annual Meeting of the Association for Computational Linguistics (Volume 1: Long Papers), pp. 317–327 (2018)

24. Zulqarnain, M., Ishak, S., Ghazali, R., Nawi, N.M., Aamir, M., Hassim, Y.M.M.: An improved deep learning approach based on variant two-state gated recurrent unit and word embeddings for sentiment classification. Int. J. Adv. Comput. Sci. Appl. **11**, 594–603 (2020)

Black-Box Adversarial Attack on Graph Neural Networks Based on Node Domain Knowledge

Qin Sun, Zheng Yang, Zhiming Liu, and Quan Zou[✉]

College of Computer and Information Science, Southwest University,
Chongqing 400715, China
swu116840@email.swu.edu.cn

Abstract. The sensitivity of Graph Neural Networks (GNNs) to their input graph data has drawn increasing attention to adversarial graphs. Given the widespread application of GNNs in various graph tasks, it is particularly important to study the principles and implementation of graph adversarial attacks for understanding the robustness of GNNs. Previous studies have attempted to reduce the prediction accuracy of GNNs by adding small perturbations to the graph structure or node features. However, these methods typically limit the perturbation strength within a small budget and fix the perturbation budget to a constant value when perturbing the graph structure or node features. In downstream node classification tasks, the required perturbation strengths to misclassify different nodes vary. Therefore, it is important to take domain knowledge of nodes or edges into account when setting the perturbation vector. To address this issue, we propose a special adversarial graph called DK-AdvGraph, where we meticulously tailor the perturbation vector of adversarial graphs in a highly limited black-box setting. Additionally, to better confuse GNNs, we ensure a higher similarity between nodes after perturbation while setting the perturbation vector. Our extensive experimental results demonstrate that the proposed DK-AdvGraph has practical significance in promoting the progress of GNNs in considering graph domain knowledge.

Keywords: Graph neural networks · Adversarial graphs · Domain knowledge

1 Introduction

Deep neural networks have demonstrated outstanding performance in processing Euclidean data and have attracted increasing attention in various fields, such as image retrieval [30], natural language processing [19], and recommendation systems [8]. However, graph data in the non-Euclidean space often present challenges for efficient processing using deep learning techniques. Graph data provide a general representation method that can clearly describe the relationships

Supported by Southwest University.

between entities and have a wide range of applications in real-world scenarios such as communication networks [21], social networks [26], and molecular structure networks [27] in biology or chemistry. Therefore, in recent years, there has been a surge of research interest in representation learning for graph networks and processing of graph data.

Graph neural networks (GNNs) [6,16,20] have pioneered the application of deep learning to graph data, and have found rapid development in graph embedding, node classification, link prediction and other graph tasks. Despite demonstrating excellent performance on various graph tasks, recent studies have shown that GNNs exhibit significant performance degradation when facing meticulously designed adversarial graphs. Adversarial attacks on existing GNNs [7,10] can be classified into white-box attacks [1,4] and black-box attacks [3,22]. White-box attackers can efficiently launch attacks by obtaining the gradient of the loss function when they have knowledge of GNN parameters and node labels. However, obtaining the parameters of a GNN model and a large number of node labels in real-world scenarios is impractical. In contrast, black-box attackers can launch attacks on GNNs without any knowledge of the internal structure or training parameters, based only on knowledge of the inputs and outputs of the GNNs.

Although black-box attacks are more applicable to real-world scenarios, they are less efficient than white-box attacks in terms of attack performance. Therefore, achieving high-performance and low-perturbation attacks in extremely limited black-box settings presents a significant challenge. Despite the proposal of state-of-the-art attacks [15,22], most existing attackers have not taken into account node domain knowledge when setting the perturbation strength, especially in feature attacks, where a constant perturbation value is used for different nodes to generate adversarial graphs. We argue that different nodes in the network pose varying levels of difficulty in being misclassified by GNNs, and thus the perturbation strength should be set based on domain knowledge of the nodes. Additionally, in topology attacks, defenders based on preprocessing techniques [9,25] mitigate the attacks by removing edges between nodes with low similarity. However, this measure only considers the addition of edges by attackers and neglects the removal of edges. Therefore, topology attacks need to conceal similarities between nodes.

To simulate real-world attack scenarios, we designed a high-performance iterative selection black-box attack that does not require accessing the GNN parameters and node labels. We refer to the adversarial graph generated by our attack method as DK-AdvGraph. To our knowledge, our work is the first to attempt to set the perturbation vector based on domain knowledge of different nodes to generate an adversarial graph. By perturbing specific nodes, we aim to increase the similarity between nodes, making it more challenging for GNNs to distinguish between them. Our attack strategy is limited to accessing node features and graph topology. We conduct experiments on three classic graph network public datasets: Cora, Citeseer, and Pubmed. The experimental results show that our proposed DK-AdvGraph has significantly better attack performance than other baselines, thus prompting GNNs to fully consider the domain knowledge of nodes or edges when performing node representation and prediction. In the field of network security research, adversarial attacks and defenses are interdependent. The purpose of designing effective attack algorithms is to promote the progress of models in robustness, and better attack algorithms can be designed by fully researching defense methods.

In summary, our contributions are as follows:

- We propose a node domain knowledge adversarial graph and have demonstrated through experiments that our proposed DK-AdvGraph has higher attack performance.
- Building on domain knowledge adversarial graphs, we also utilize the intrinsic principles of GNNs to increase the similarity between nodes, thus achieving the goal of high probability model confusion.
- We incorporate both feature attacks using node domain knowledge and topology attacks with node similarity masking in our proposed approach.
- We conduct extensive comparative experiments to demonstrate the practical significance of our proposed DK-AdvGraph in promoting the performance of GNNs.

2 Related Work

Currently, researchers have made many attempts in very limited black-box attacks. For instance, Metattck [18] optimizes the input graph data as hyperparameters based on meta-learning for poisoning attacks under black-box settings, which makes small perturbations significantly degrade the model's performance. Additionally, GNNStealing [17] uses a query graph as input and constructs a surrogate model with similar performance to the target model based on the different responses of the target model, achieving model stealing attacks. In addition to optimization-based attacks [23] and model stealing [29], the topology attack proposed in [2] modifies edges by attacking the model's graph filter and leverages feature matrix to obtain adversarial samples to achieve better attack performance than RL-S2V [4]. However, RL-S2V strictly limits attacker's access to the target model by only allowing modifications to the graph structure based on the model's output, while GF-Attack requires accessing to the model's graph filters.

Regarding the perturbation of graph structures and node features, the differences in degree distribution before and after the perturbation and the magnitude of the perturbation in node features represent the level of ease for the defender to distinguish the adversarial graph, which we refer to as the concealment of the attack. Nettack [31] ensures the concealment of its attacks by controlling the sampling of degree distributions belonging to the same distribution for the original and adversarial graphs and avoiding the emergence of new co-occurring relationships between node features after perturbation. In feature attacks, the concealment of the attack is an important evaluation criterion for adversarial attacks. Researchers typically control the magnitude of the perturbation to ensure the concealment of the attack. For example, PEEGA [11] generates an adversarial graph while ensuring that $\|\hat{A} - A\| + \|\hat{X} - X\| < \delta$, and then assesses their impact on node representations. In addition, Infmax [12] significantly reduces the performance of several popular GNNs by perturbing the features of a very small number of specific nodes. However, most existing graph adversarial attacks sacrifice attack performance for higher attack concealment.

3   Preliminary

In this section, we introduce the commonly used notations in graph adversarial attacks. We then present the target model for the attack, and finally describe the attack setting of our proposed method.

3.1   Notations

Our attack method mainly targets non-targeted attacks on node classification tasks, which means that the goal is to cause GNNs to misclassify the nodes without misclassifying them into specific classes. Generally, we represent an undirected attributed graph as $G = (\mathcal{V}, E, X, C)$, where $\mathcal{V}$ represents a set of N nodes in the graph, E represents the set of edges, $X \in R^{N \times D}$ represents the $N \times D$ dimensional feature vector of the graph, and C represents the one-dimensional vector of node labels. Additionally, we use $A \in \{0,1\}^{N \times N}$ to represent the adjacency matrix of the graph, where $A[u][v] = 1$ and $A[u][v] = 0$ respectively indicate the presence and absence of an edge between nodes u and v. We denote the perturbed feature vector as $\hat{X}$ and the perturbed adjacency matrix as $\hat{A}$.

3.2   Graph Neural Network

Graph neural networks take A and X as input and iteratively aggregate information from neighboring nodes to represent nodes $\mathcal{V}$ as a vector space H. With an increasing number of iterations, a node can aggregate information from higher-order neighbors. Graph convolutional network (GCN) is the most representative example of graph neural networks. The representation of the $(l + 1)$-th layer nodes, denoted as H^{l+1}, can be expressed as follows:

$$H^{l+1} = \sigma(\tilde{D}^{-\frac{1}{2}} \tilde{A} \tilde{D}^{-\frac{1}{2}} H^l W^l) \tag{1}$$

where σ represents a non-linear activation function (e.g., ReLU), $\tilde{A} = A + I$ represents the adjacency matrix with self-loop edges added to each node, where I is the identity matrix. $\tilde{D}$ is the degree matrix of $\tilde{A}$, and $\tilde{D}^{-\frac{1}{2}} \tilde{A} \tilde{D}^{-\frac{1}{2}}$ is the symmetric normalization of A. Initially, $H^0 = X$, and H^l represents the node representation vector after l iterations. W^l is the weight matrix used for linear transformation. Finally, an L-layer GCN can be expressed as:

$$Z = f_\theta(A, X) = softmax(\tilde{D}^{-\frac{1}{2}} \tilde{A} \tilde{D}^{-\frac{1}{2}} \sigma(\tilde{D}^{-\frac{1}{2}} \tilde{A} \tilde{D}^{-\frac{1}{2}} \sigma(...) W^{L-1}) W^L) \tag{2}$$

where $Z \in R^{N \times C}$ is the final output matrix of the GCN, representing the predicted probabilities of each node belonging to different classes.

In addition to the symmetrically normalized aggregation of neighbor node information used in GCN, researchers have proposed various practical GNNs by adopting different ways of aggregating node embeddings. For example, Graph Isomorphism Network [24] employs summation to aggregate all node information, while Graph Sampling and Aggregation [7] uses averaging operations to aggregate neighbor node information.

3.3 The Graph Adversarial Attack Settings

Our attack aims to select a subset of nodes in the graph, add perturbations to their features, and add or delete edges between them to significantly reduce the classification accuracy of GNNs on the generated adversarial graph. In realistic scenarios, it is difficult to manipulate a large amount of data and obtain key nodes in the graph. Therefore, we assume that our attack can only manipulate a limited number of ordinary nodes.

In addition to limiting the number of nodes that can be perturbed, we aim to preserve the fundamental properties of the graph while modifying its topology to ensure the concealment of the topology attack. Specifically, after the topology modification, the total number of edges in the graph and the degree sequence of the nodes should not exhibit significant differences.

4 Methodology

In this section, we introduce the DK-AdvGraph generated using our black-box attack method. Our work primarily focuses on selecting the target nodes and features to attack, as well as setting the perturbation vectors. In the attacks of features and topology, feature attack is the main focus of our work.

4.1 Attack Model

Our attack aims to achieve a high-performance, low-perturbation iterative attack. High-performance can be achieved by maximizing the difference in node representation before and after being perturbed, which can be expressed as:

$$\max \sum_{v \in \mathcal{V}} \|\hat{H}_v - H_v\| \tag{3}$$

where H_v is unknown due to the black-box assumption that does not access GNN parameters and internal structure. In general, $A_n^l X$ can simulate the process of aggregating neighbor node information in a GNN with l layers. Therefore, $A_n^l X$ can be used as a surrogate model in a black-box scenario. Low-perturbation requires that $\sum_{v \in \mathcal{V}} \|X_v - \hat{X}_v\| + \|A - \hat{A}\|$ is as small as possible. In order to achieve both high-performance and low-perturbation, we need to find the adversarial node features $\hat{X}_v$ and an adversarial adjacency matrix $\hat{A}$ to minimize the ratio of perturbation strength and node difference before and after perturbation. Therefore, our optimization problem can be expressed as:

$$\min \mathcal{F}(\hat{X}_v, \hat{A}) = \frac{\sum\limits_{v \in \mathcal{V}} \|X_v - \hat{X}_v\| + \|A - \hat{A}\|}{\sum\limits_{v \in \mathcal{V}} \|A_n^l X_v - \hat{A}_n^l \hat{X}_v\|} \tag{4}$$

where A_n represents the normalized adjacency matrix, and l represents the alternative representation parameter of the l-layer GNN.

When the attacker can only access a limited number of nodes, Eq. 4 can only obtain a locally optimal solution, and the number of parameters depends on the number of nodes that the attacker can access. This significantly reduces the generalization ability of the attack algorithm. In order to enhance the transferability of the attack model, we propose an iterative selection attack model, where topology modifications and feature perturbations are treated as discrete actions. The proposed attack model is illustrated in Fig. 1.

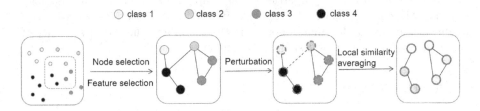

Fig. 1. Framework.

4.2   Node Selection

The selection of target attack nodes is the first step in our feature attack under the assumption that the attacker can only access a small number of nodes. In recent years, researchers have proposed various methods for selecting nodes for perturbation based on the node centrality scores, such as Degree, Betweenness, and PageRank. Inspired by the PGD algorithm [14], nodes that are close to the classification boundary are more likely to produce different classification results with lower perturbations. Therefore, to set a lower perturbation strength for each node without sacrificing attack performance, we need to select nodes closer to the classification boundary for perturbation. As shown in Fig. 2, we calculate the maximum feature distance between nodes of the same predicted class (same-max) and the minimum feature distance between nodes of different predicted classes (dif-min) by analyzing the characteristic of the nodes close to the classification boundary. The larger the difference between same-max and dif-min, the closer the node is to the classification boundary. We iteratively select the target attack nodes based on this characteristic of nodes close to the classification boundary until the total number of target attack nodes $\left| \bigcup\limits_{i=0}^{i=k} S_i \right|$ reaches a certain budget η, where S_i refers to the set of target attack nodes selected in the i-th iteration, and k is the number of iterations.

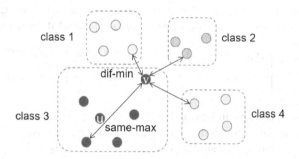

Fig. 2. Selection of target attack nodes.

4.3 Feature Selection

The nodes $\bigcup_{i=0}^{i=k} S_i$ that we have selected will serve as our target attack nodes. Next, we need to select the attack feature targets for the selected nodes. A node's feature vector represents multiple characteristics of an entity. We aim to perturb some of the crucial features to interfere with the classification performance of GNNs. We calculate the gradient of the classification loss with respect to node features for the surrogate model $A_n^l X$, and perturb the features that have higher average gradients, considering them as important features.

4.4 The Setting of the Feature Perturbation Vector

In citation networks, when classifying papers based on their word vector features, cross-disciplinary papers are more likely to be misclassified than papers from a single discipline. Inspired by the BP attack [28] in adversarial image samples, we perturb nodes based on the feature distances between different classes of nodes. In Fig. 2, if same-max is greater than dif-min, the current node is closer to the classification boundary (e.g., node v), whereas if same-max is less than dif-min, the current node is closer to the class center (e.g., node u). We take the smaller value between same-max and dif-min as the perturbation strength. For nodes in S_i, we set a specific perturbation feature vector $P_{i,v}$ for each node as follows:

$$P_{i,v} = min\left(min_{C_u}\|X_{S_{i,v}} - X_{S_{i,C_u}}\|, max_{C_v}\|X_{S_{i,v}} - X_{S_{i,C_v}}\|\right) \quad (5)$$

where C_u represents the nodes that are classified differently from node v by GNNs and C_v represents the nodes that are classified the same as node v by GNNs. Our idea is to explore the boundary problem between nodes of different classes by considering the feature distances between different node subsets selected at multiple iterations.

According to the intrinsic characteristics of GNNs, increasing the similarity between nodes can better confuse the model. Therefore, we aim to ensure that the perturbed nodes exhibit higher feature similarity, so that the overall feature of each selected node set in each iteration is at a relatively average level. Our proposed approach for adversarial node feature representation is as follows:

$$\hat{X}_v = \begin{cases} X_v\,[i] + P_{i,v}, \; if I\,(X_v\,[i] \neq 0) < \underset{v \in S_i}{avg}\, I\,(X_v \neq 0) \\ X_v\,[i] - P_{i,v}, \; if I\,(X_v\,[i] \neq 0) > \underset{v \in S_i}{avg}\, I\,(X_v \neq 0) \end{cases} \tag{6}$$

where $I(\cdot)$ represents the indicator function. Our basic idea involves iterative local averaging of the input node features, which makes it challenging for GNNs to handle locally sparse and similar nodes, thus effectively influencing the classification results of GNNs.

4.5   Topology Attack

In the link prediction scenario, Fang et al. [5] proposed the use of Neural Networks with Elementary Subgraphs Features to encode the one-hop neighborhood of the target link as topology features. These features are then utilized to predict the likelihood of the edge between two nodes. Generally, the feature distance between nodes increases with their dissimilarity, resulting in a lower probability of the existence of an edge between them. Our topology attack aims to modify the topology features by adding edges between nodes with high similarity and removing edges between nodes with low similarity. This attack is carried out on the iteratively selected node set S_i, and its adversarial adjacency matrix is represented as $\hat{A}_{u,v} = A_{u,v} + \Delta A_{u,v}$. The perturbation vector of the adjacency matrix $\Delta A_{u,v}$ is represented as follows:

$$\Delta A_{u,v} = \begin{cases} 1, \text{ for } A^{\iota}\,[u]\,[v] \neq 0, A^{\iota-i}\,[u]\,[v] = 0 \\ -1, \text{ for } u = argmax \| X_v - X_u \| \\ 0, \text{ for } else \end{cases} \tag{7}$$

where $\Delta A_{u,v} = 1$ indicates adding an edge between nodes u and v, while $\Delta A_{u,v} = -1$ represents deleting an edge between nodes u and v. $A^{\iota}\,[u]\,[v] \neq 0, A^{\iota-i}\,[u]\,[v] = 0$ indicate that node u can reach node v with at least ι edges. Our topology attack takes into account both the feature distance and spatial distance of nodes, and we restrict the removal or addition of a limited number of edges in each iteration to ensure the concealment of the topology attack. Our experiments demonstrate that our topology attack can resist preprocessing-based defenders.

5   Experiments

In this section, we will introduce our experimental setup, the evaluation of experimental effectiveness, and the experimental results. We conduct comparative experiments between our proposed DK-AdvGraph and several advanced baseline attack strategies. Additionally, we conduct separate experiments for feature attacks and topology attacks to better analyze the differential impact of these attacks on the performance of GNNs.

5.1 Experimental Setting

Our experimental code is implemented in PyTorch and the model training and attack testing are conducted on a computer with an AMD threadripper 3975wx CPU and an NVIDIA RTX 3090 graphics card with 24GB of memory.

We test three currently popular GNNs, GCN, GAT, and JK-Net, as target attack models. We use citation network datasets, Cora, Citeseer, and Pubmed, for node classification tasks in graph network learning. In these citation network datasets, nodes represent publications, edges represent citation relationships between publications, and the node features are word vectors of publications, where each element is a binary variable indicating the presence of each word in the publication.

To evaluate the effectiveness of our proposed DK-AdvGraph, we compare our attack with four state-of-the-art black-box attack algorithms: GF-Attack [2], PEEGA [11], RWCS [13], and InfMax [12], by generating adversarial graphs against three GNNs. Next, we will briefly introduce our baseline strategies.

GF-Attack uses graph signal processing to describe graph embeddings and modifies edges by manipulating the graph filters of the target model. PEEGA iteratively perturbs the adjacency matrix and node features by maximizing the difference in node representations before and after the perturbation and the difference in node representations within the same class. RWCS algorithm perturbs the nodes with the highest importance scores by utilizing a random walk transition matrix selection method. InfMax transforms the problem of maximizing the misclassification rate into a problem of selecting the set of nodes that can propagate the largest number of influences in the network. Nettack [31] requires accessing to the training dataset to build a surrogate model, so we exclude it from our comparison. To ensure fairness in the comparison, we select the same number of nodes to be perturbed for each attack method. To ensure the efficiency of the attacks, we set the maximum number of iterations for selecting the node set to $k = 10$. For topology attack, we set $\iota = 3$ in the condition for adding edges $A^{\iota}[u][v] \neq 0$ in Eq. 7. To consider the scenario where the attacker may not have access to the most important nodes in the network, we exclude the top 10% of nodes based on the importance metrics of Degree, Betweenness, and PageRank when iteratively selecting the nodes.

5.2 Effectiveness Evaluation

We present the performance comparison of our proposed attack and the baselines on different GNNs across different datasets in Table 1. The row corresponding to the clean graph shows the original classification accuracy of the GNNs trained on the unperturbed graph. The other rows show the classification accuracy of the

GNNs on the adversarial graph. The purpose of the attack research is to reduce the accuracy of the GNNs, so a lower classification accuracy indicates stronger attack performance. Bold numbers indicate the lowest classification accuracy.

Table 1. Attack performance summary of different attack methods when the same number of nodes is selected.

	GCN			GAT			JK-Net		
	Citeseer	Cora	Pubmed	Citeseer	Cora	Pubmed	Citeseer	Cora	Pubmed
Clean Graph	0.7520	0.8550	0.8570	0.7500	0.8770	0.8520	0.7320	0.8590	0.8570
GF-Attack($\downarrow$)	0.6472	0.7314	0.7421	0.6435	0.7512	0.7395	0.6162	0.7283	0.7388
PEEGA($\downarrow$)	0.6620	0.7430	0.7510	0.6937	0.7779	0.7833	0.5110	0.6980	0.7061
RWCS($\downarrow$)	0.6050	0.7000	0.7040	0.6240	0.5750	0.5760	0.4500	0.5760	0.5870
InfMax($\downarrow$)	0.6070	0.6880	0.6950	0.6240	0.5590	0.5600	0.4440	0.5650	0.5760
Ours($\downarrow$)	**0.4526**	**0.5080**	**0.5775**	**0.4490**	**0.4030**	**0.4722**	**0.3308**	**0.3179**	**0.4840**

It is worth noting that the black-box attacks of GF-Attack and PEEGA have lower attack performance than RWCS and Infmax. This is because GF-Attack attacks the graph by compromising the quality of node output embeddings. Similarly, the output embedding of the graph embedding model used by PEEGA exhibits very low node characteristics. Therefore, both GF-Attack and PEEGA do not directly impact the attack performance of GNNs significantly. RWCS and Infmax focus on selecting nodes with high importance scores for attack. However, the attack strategies for the selected target nodes are not meticulously designed, resulting in suboptimal impact on the classification accuracy of GNNs.

Furthermore, it should be noted that RWCS and Infmax require accessing to both GNN parameters and node labels to evaluate the importance of node features, whereas GF-Attack, PEEGA, and our proposed attack only need to access node feature vectors and adjacency matrix. However, GF-Attack and PEEGA ensure attack concealment by limiting the number of modified edges and the perturbation budget, respectively, while ignoring attack performance. Meanwhile, RWCS and Infmax neglect perturbation budget when attacking the target node set. To address these limitations, we propose a DK-AdvGraph, which aims to strike a balance between perturbation strength and attack performance.

In addition to the attack performance, the attack algorithm also needs to ensure that the generated adversarial examples can effectively evade detection models. Generally, it is believed that a smaller perturbation strength leads to stronger attack concealment. We iteratively select node subsets for perturbation on three datasets and record the averages of same-max and dif-min in each iteration of the first five iterations, as shown in Table 2. In each iteration, same-max should be significantly larger than dif-min in the selected subset. To evaluate the impact of different perturbation strengths on the classification performance of GNNs, we use same-max and dif-min as node feature perturbation strengths and test the classification performance of GNNs. As shown in Fig. 3, although same-max is considerably larger than dif-min in the selected target attack nodes, both have comparable effects on the classification performance of GCN. As the number of iterations increases, the classification accuracy of GCN on adversarial examples generated using same-max and dif-min as the perturbation strength tends to coincide.

Table 2. The average of same-max and dif-min in each iteration of the first five iterations.

iterations	Cora		Citeseer		Pubmed	
	same-max	dif-min	same-max	dif-min	same-max	dif-min
1	0.6075	0.2907	0.3080	0.2158	0.4668	0.1968
2	0.6823	0.3001	0.2869	0.2183	0.4683	0.1997
3	0.6345	0.2907	0.3059	0.2181	0.4700	0.1976
4	0.6258	0.2908	0.3161	0.1803	0.4597	0.1964
5	0.6759	0.3074	0.3201	0.1895	0.4231	0.1999

In the black-box setting, GF-Attack is restricted to adding or deleting only one edge for a node, which involves only topology modifications and not feature perturbation. RWCS and Infmax set their feature perturbation strength to 10, which is much larger than that we set. PEEGA sets the perturbation budget to $\delta = r \cdot \|A\|$, which yields a perturbation strength only slightly smaller than ours, but its attack performance is inferior to ours.

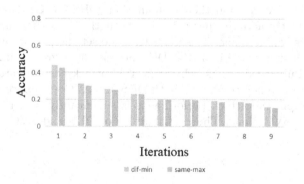

Fig. 3. The impact of adversarial graphs generated with different perturbation strengths on the classification accuracy of GCN.

We also evaluate the impact of the number of attacked nodes on the performance of GNNs. During the stage of selecting nodes for the targeted attack, we initially choose 10% of the total number of nodes to be attacked, and subsequently record the classification accuracy of GNNs after the attack. Table 3 shows that as the proportion of the target attack nodes increases in the three datasets, the classification accuracy of the three models decreases significantly. The experimental results indicate that our attack algorithm still has a significant impact on the classification performance of GNNs even when only a small number of nodes are selected for perturbation. Moreover, when our attacker can access a large number of nodes, the impact on the classification performance of GNNs is devastating.

Table 3. The influence of different attack node thresholds on the classification accuracy of the model.

η	GCN			GAT			JK-Net		
	Citeseer	Cora	Pubmed	Citeseer	Cora	Pubmed	Citeseer	Cora	Pubmed
0(Clean graph)	0.7609	0.8817	0.8575	0.7534	0.8799	0.8443	0.7398	0.8503	0.8521
0.3	0.2406	0.2440	0.3862	0.2722	0.2107	0.3436	0.2286	0.1701	0.3546
0.4	0.1880	0.2089	0.3416	0.2015	0.1867	0.3246	0.1910	0.1738	0.3365
0.5	0.1308	0.1423	0.3208	0.1594	0.1368	0.3131	0.1714	0.1627	0.3241

5.3   Ablation Studies

To separately evaluate the effects of perturbation strength and local similarity averaging in DK-AdvGraph on GNNs' classification performance, we conduct ablation experiments using GCN on three datasets. We test the performance of the GCN under three different scenarios: perturbation strength (DKS), local similarity averaging (AVG), and their combination (DKS+AVG). Under the DKS attack, we directly add the perturbation strength $P_{i,v}$ to the feature of the attacked nodes, while under the AVG attack, we set the perturbation strength to $\epsilon = 0.1$. As shown in Fig. 4, the DKS attack has a greater impact on the Citeseer and Pubmed datasets, while the AVG attack has a greater impact on the Cora dataset. When combining both DKS and AVG attacks to generate the adversarial graph, the attack performance is significantly better than that of either DKS or AVG alone. The contributions of DKS and AVG in producing

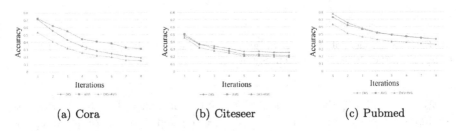

| (a) Cora | (b) Citeseer | (c) Pubmed |

Fig. 4. The impact of different attack behaviors on the GCN classification accuracy on three datasets: Cora, Citeseer, and Pubmed.

effective attacks differ depending on the feature distance between the nodes of different classes and the global characteristics close to the classification boundary nodes, which also confirms that our attack algorithm is based on specific node domain knowledge. We further evaluate the differential impact of feature perturbations and topology modifications on GNNs' performance using GCN. We test the performance of the GCN under three scenarios: feature perturbation (FP), topology modification (TM), and the combination of both (FP+TM). As shown in Fig. 5, in our proposed attack algorithm, FP has a much greater impact than TM. However, when combining the attack impact of both, it is significantly greater than that of either FP or TM alone.

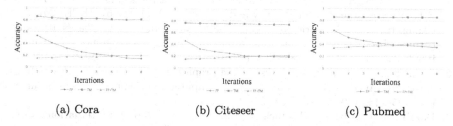

(a) Cora   (b) Citeseer   (c) Pubmed

Fig. 5. The impact of different attack types on the GCN classification accuracy on three datasets: Cora, Citeseer, and Pubmed.

6 Conclusion and Future Works

We conduct a security risk assessment of GNNs in a highly limited black-box setting, particularly for node classification tasks. We propose an attack algorithm based on node domain knowledge to perform feature perturbations and topology modifications, which significantly reduces the classification performance of GNNs on our proposed DK-AdvGraph. We focus on attack concealment and performance, ensuring that the attack algorithm has sufficient concealment without sacrificing attack performance. Specifically, we iteratively search for target attack nodes close to the classification boundary by analyzing the relationship between the same-max and the dif-min and then adding perturbations to them. To better fit real-world attacks, we strictly limit the attacker's access to GNN parameters and internal structure, as well as the number of nodes the attacker can obtain. We conduct extensive experiments on three benchmark datasets for graph representation learning, targeting three mainstream GNNs, and demonstrate that our proposed DK-AdvGraph can effectively impact different node classification models while maintaining sufficient concealment.

As for future work, there is still room for improvement in the time efficiency of our attack algorithm, which requires iterative selection of the target attack node set and calculation of feature distances between nodes. Furthermore, existing defender models focus more on the information transmission process between nodes and our work provides a new perspective for studying the robustness of GNNs. Detection and defense methods for low-perturbation adversarial samples will be an important part of our future research.

Acknowledgements. This paper is funded in part by the National Natural Science Foundation of China (62032019) and the Capacity Development Grant of Southwest University (SWU116007).

References

1. Carlini, N., Wagner, D.: Towards evaluating the robustness of neural networks. In: 2017 IEEE Symposium on Security and Privacy (SP), pp. 39–57. IEEE (2017)
2. Chang, H., et al.: A restricted black-box adversarial framework towards attacking graph embedding models. In: Proceedings of the AAAI Conference on Artificial Intelligence, vol. 34, pp. 3389–3396 (2020)
3. Chen, Y., et al.: Practical attacks against graph-based clustering. In: Proceedings of the 2017 ACM SIGSAC Conference on Computer and Communications Security, pp. 1125–1142 (2017)
4. Dai, H., et al.: Adversarial attack on graph structured data. In: International Conference on Machine Learning, pp. 1115–1124. PMLR (2018)
5. Fang, Z., Tan, S., Wang, Y., Lu, J.: Elementary subgraph features for link prediction with neural networks. IEEE Trans. Knowl. Data Eng. (2021)
6. Gao, H., Ji, S.: Graph U-Nets. In: International Conference on Machine Learning, pp. 2083–2092. PMLR (2019)
7. Hamilton, W., Ying, Z., Leskovec, J.: Inductive representation learning on large graphs. In: Advances in Neural Information Processing Systems, vol. 30 (2017)
8. Hao, Y., Meng, G., Wang, J., Zong, C.: A detection method for hybrid attacks in recommender systems. Inf. Syst. **114**, 102154 (2023)
9. Hsieh, I.C., Li, C.T.: Netfense: adversarial defenses against privacy attacks on neural networks for graph data. IEEE Trans. Knowl. Data Eng. (2021)
10. Kipf, T.N., Welling, M.: Semi-supervised classification with graph convolutional networks. arXiv preprint arXiv:1609.02907 (2016)
11. Li, H., Di, S., Li, Z., Chen, L., Cao, J.: Black-box adversarial attack and defense on graph neural networks. In: 2022 IEEE 38th International Conference on Data Engineering (ICDE), pp. 1017–1030. IEEE (2022)
12. Ma, J., Deng, J., Mei, Q.: Adversarial attack on graph neural networks as an influence maximization problem. In: Proceedings of the Fifteenth ACM International Conference on Web Search and Data Mining, pp. 675–685 (2022)
13. Ma, J., Ding, S., Mei, Q.: Towards more practical adversarial attacks on graph neural networks. In: Advances in Neural Information Processing Systems, vol. 33, pp. 4756–4766 (2020)
14. Madry, A., Makelov, A., Schmidt, L., Tsipras, D., Vladu, A.: Towards deep learning models resistant to adversarial attacks. arXiv preprint arXiv:1706.06083 (2017)
15. Mu, J., Wang, B., Li, Q., Sun, K., Xu, M., Liu, Z.: A hard label black-box adversarial attack against graph neural networks. In: Proceedings of the 2021 ACM SIGSAC Conference on Computer and Communications Security, pp. 108–125 (2021)
16. Scarselli, F., Gori, M., Tsoi, A.C., Hagenbuchner, M., Monfardini, G.: The graph neural network model. IEEE Trans. Neural Networks **20**, 61–80 (2008)

17. Shen, Y., He, X., Han, Y., Zhang, Y.: Model stealing attacks against inductive graph neural networks. In: 2022 IEEE Symposium on Security and Privacy (SP), pp. 1175–1192. IEEE (2022)
18. Sun, Y., Wang, S., Tang, X., Hsieh, T.Y., Honavar, V.: Adversarial attacks on graph neural networks via node injections: A hierarchical reinforcement learning approach. In: Proceedings of the Web Conference 2020, pp. 673–683 (2020)
19. Suyeon, H., et al.: A fast and flexible FPGA-based accelerator for natural language processing neural networks. ACM Trans. Archit. Code Opt. **20**, 1–24 (2023)
20. Veličković, P., Cucurull, G., Casanova, A., Romero, A., Lio, P., Bengio, Y.: Graph attention networks. arXiv preprint arXiv:1710.10903 (2017)
21. Xiao, Y., Sun, Z., Shi, G., Niyato, D.: Imitation learning-based implicit semantic-aware communication networks: Multi-layer representation and collaborative reasoning. IEEE J. Sel. Areas Commun. (2022)
22. Xu, J., et al.: Blindfolded attackers still threatening: strict black-box adversarial attacks on graphs. In: Proceedings of the AAAI Conference on Artificial Intelligence, vol. 36, pp. 4299–4307 (2022)
23. Xu, K., et al.: Topology attack and defense for graph neural networks: an optimization perspective. arXiv preprint arXiv:1906.04214 (2019)
24. Xu, K., Hu, W., Leskovec, J., Jegelka, S.: How powerful are graph neural networks? arXiv preprint arXiv:1810.00826 (2018)
25. Xu, X., Yu, Y., Li, B., Song, L., Liu, C., Gunter, C.: Characterizing malicious edges targeting on graph neural networks. https://openreview.net/forum?id=HJxdAoCcYX (2019)
26. Yin, X., Lin, W., Sun, K., Wei, C., Chen, Y.: A 2 s 2-GNN: rigging GNN-based social status by adversarial attacks in signed social networks. IEEE Trans. Inf. Forensics Secur. **18**, 206–220 (2022)
27. Yu, Z., Gao, H.: Molecular representation learning via heterogeneous motif graph neural networks. In: International Conference on Machine Learning, pp. 25581–25594. PMLR (2022)
28. Zhang, H., Avrithis, Y., Furon, T., Amsaleg, L.: Walking on the edge: fast, low-distortion adversarial examples. IEEE Trans. Inf. Forensics Secur. **16**, 701–713 (2020)
29. Zhang, J., Peng, S., Gao, Y., Zhang, Z., Hong, Q.: APMSA: adversarial perturbation against model stealing attacks. IEEE Trans. Inf. Forensics Secur. **18**, 1667–1679 (2023)
30. Zhang, Z., Wang, L., Wang, Y., Zhou, L., Zhang, J., Chen, F.: Dataset-driven unsupervised object discovery for region-based instance image retrieval. IEEE Trans. Pattern Anal. Mach. Intell. **45**, 247–263 (2022)
31. Zügner, D., Akbarnejad, A., Günnemann, S.: Adversarial attacks on neural networks for graph data. In: Proceedings of the 24th ACM SIGKDD International Conference on Knowledge Discovery & Data Mining, pp. 2847–2856 (2018)

Role and Relationship-Aware Representation Learning for Complex Coupled Dynamic Heterogeneous Networks

Jieya Peng, Jiale Xu, and Ya Li[✉]

College of Computer and Information Science, Southwest University,
Chongqing 400715, China
swu_yali@163.com

Abstract. Representation learning for dynamic heterogeneous networks with complex coupling relationships in the real world can play an important role in the research of downstream tasks such as node classification, link prediction and recommendation systems. However, the existing network representation learning methods are difficult to retain the dynamic and heterogeneous nature of the network at the same time, and it is difficult to capture information with complex coupling and dynamic changes. At the same time, some potential but equally valuable information in the real network has not been fully mined and utilized. This work proposes a complex coupling dynamic heterogeneous role and relationship awareness model, which is a method that can effectively preserve network structure information and relationship information. In the model, a historical memory map is constructed at a given time step to preserve historical and current network information. On the historical memory map, through the guidance of the meta-path, a random walk process based on the role-aware strategy is performed to obtain the node sequence and effective semantic information. Finally, the node sequence is input into the proposed improved skip-gram model based on relationship awareness for training, so as to learn node embedding more effectively. Experiments on two real-world datasets confirm that the proposed model consistently outperforms the state-of-the-art representation learning methods on downstream tasks including node classification and link prediction.

Keywords: Network embedding · Dynamic networks · Random walk · Heterogeneous networks · Network representation learning

1 Introduction

Network representation learning can represent the nodes in the network into a low-dimensional, real-valued and dense vector form while retaining the rich information of the original real network, which plays an extremely important role

Z. Jin et al. (Eds.): KSEM 2023, LNAI 14117, pp. 218–233, 2023.
https://doi.org/10.1007/978-3-031-40283-8_19

in solving some practical application problems. As the scale of network structure data gradually increases, the coupling and interaction become more and more complex. Traditional network representation learning methods can no longer meet the increasingly complex network analysis needs of users. The entities in the real network are modeled as different types of nodes, and the relationships between entities are modeled as edges to construct a heterogeneous information network. Mining the rich information contained in the heterogeneous network is of great significance for us to complete network application tasks such as node classification [1, 11, 22, 24, 27], network visualization [2, 6, 9, 15, 21], and link prediction [5, 10, 31–33].

At present, the existing network representation methods can be divided into three categories: methods based on matrix factorization such as GraRep [3], hyperbolic SVD [19] and M-NMF [30]. The method based on matrix factorization is lack of scalability, and its representation performance is often very dependent on the construction of the relation matrix, and the results under different construction criteria often have great differences in performance. Random walk based methods generate node sequences by walking through the network, and generate relevant network representations by word embedding models. Deep-Walk [20], Node2vec [10], and LINE [26] are classic algorithms. Methods based on graph neural network models have also been extensively studied. GAE [14] algorithm, through Graph Convolutional Network (GCN) [13] encoder and inner product encoder for unsupervised learning and network representation of graph structure. GraphGAN [29] applies the idea of generative adversarial networks to graph representation learning.

Compared with homogeneous network embedding, heterogeneous network embedding has greater complexity and heterogeneity [23]. Methods based on natural language model embedding usually use techniques commonly used in natural language processing to capture the relationship between nodes. Classical algorithms include PTE [25] algorithm, LSHM [12] algorithm, Metapath2vec [7] and similar HIN2Vec [8] et al. Neural network-based embedding methods are also used in heterogeneous network representation learning, and HNE [4] and DHNE [28] are the representative methods.

DANE [16] uses matrix factorization theory to obtain the eigenvectors, and then further updates the two matrices to obtain the output of the embedding. DepthLGP [18] is a network representation learning method based on deep transformation of high-order Laplacian Gaussian processes. However, the representation learning methods for dynamic networks are difficult to adapt to the characteristics of heterogeneous networks.

Traditional network representation learning methods do not fully consider the dynamics and heterogeneity of the network when modeling. In response to the above challenges, this work proposes an embedding model of complex coupled dynamic heterogeneous networks based on role and relationship-aware representation, named RRDNE, which learns more effective heterogeneous network representation by deeply mining structural relationships and interaction relationships. Firstly, in order to obtain all the domain information of the target node in a given time step, the historical memory graph of the dynamic heterogeneous network is constructed by the snapshot graph. On this basis, a meta-path is used to guide a role-aware random walk strategy to generate node sequences. Finally, in order to effectively obtain the interaction between nodes in the network and further retain the node feature information, we construct an improved skip-gram model based on relation-aware strategy to learn the node embedding vector. We also conduct extensive experiments on real datasets to demonstrate the effectiveness of our proposed method. In summary, the main contributions of this work include: 1) A structural role aware random walk strategy guided by meta-path is designed, which can not only reflect the heterogeneous characteristics and complex coupling relationships of dynamic heterogeneous networks, but also reveal the global structural information of nodes in the network. 2) Structural criteria for relationships in heterogeneous networks are explored and summarized. An improved skip-gram model based on the relationship awareness strategy is proposed, which can effectively integrate the topology and interaction information of heterogeneous networks to improve the representation learning performance.

The remainder of this paper is organized as follows: Sect. 2 presents related work. Section 3 presents the relevant concepts used in the work. The specific structure of the RRDNE model is presented in detail in Sect. 4. Section 5 presents a discussion of the experimental results. In the last section, the present work is summarized.

2   Preliminaries

In this section, some basic concepts concerning dynamic heterogeneous network embedding are elaborated and some concepts appearing in this paper are further explained.

Theorem 1. *A dynamic heterogeneous network within T can be defined as a collection of networks $G = \{G_1, G_2, ..., G_T\}$ containing a sequence of time snapshots. Where at $T = t$, the current snapshot can be represented as a heterogeneous network G_t, which is defined as $G_t = (V_t, E_t, T, \phi, \gamma)$, where V_t and E_t denote the set of all nodes and edges in the heterogeneous network graph at time t, respectively. Each node v in Gt corresponds to A specific node type, and v is associated with the node type mapping function $\phi : V_t \rightarrow A$. Each edge e in Gt corresponds to a specific edge type, and e is associated with the edge type mapping function $\gamma : E_t \rightarrow R.A$ and R represents the collection of node and edge types, their limitation is $|A| + |R| > 2$.*

Theorem 2. *Given a network $G = (V, E)$, the goal of network representation learning is to map the nodes in the network into a latent low-dimensional representation space through vector representation. Embedded in the network, each node $v \in V$ needs to be projected into the low-dimensional vector space R_d by the mapping function $f : v \rightarrow R_d$, so as to maintain the network structure and semantic relationship, where $d \ll |V|$.*

Theorem 3. *In heterogeneous networks, meta-paths describe the composite rela-tionships between different types of objects. Figure 1 consists of multiple types of objects, including author (A), paper (P), conference (C). In heterogeneous net-works, two objects can be connected by different semantic paths, which are called meta-paths. Specifically, it can be expressed as $\rho : K_1 \overset{R_1}{\to} K_2 \overset{R_2}{\to} ... \overset{R_{c-1}}{\to} K_c \overset{R_c}{\to} K_{c+1}$. This is the node sequence of different types of nodes connecting different types of edges. Where K_c is a node of type C, and R_c is the connection relation-ship between nodes. Specifically, the node sequence $A \overset{R_1}{\to} P \overset{R_2}{\to} C$ indicates that the author's paper is published in a certain conference. Sequence $A \overset{R_1}{\to} P \overset{R_2}{\to} A$ repre-sents the co-author relationship of a paper. Sequence $A \overset{R_1}{\to} P \overset{R_2}{\to} C \overset{R_3}{\to} P \overset{R_4}{\to} A$ rep-resents two papers published at the same conference with their different authors.*

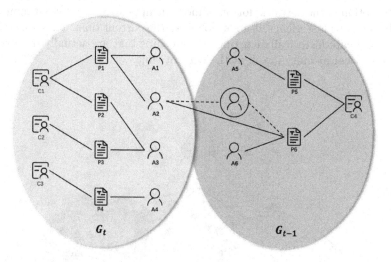

Fig. 1. Examples of node interactions guided by different meta-paths.

3   The Proposed Model: RRDNE

In order to solve the problem that network heterogeneity and dynamics cannot be used simultaneously, the proposed RRDNE method consists of three main components. Firstly, a historical memory graph containing all neighborhoods of time step τ is constructed to retain as much historical information as possible. Next, considering the structural role proximity of network nodes, under the guid-ance of meta-paths, a role-aware random walk strategy is used to capture the complex interactions and potentially important information between nodes in the historical network graph. Finally, since the various heterogeneous relations in the dynamic heterogeneous network have significantly different structural character-istics, the skip-gram model is improved based on the relation-aware strategy to complete the embedding task.

3.1   Construct a Historical Memory Graph

To maintain the temporal smoothness of the network, we plot nodes at different times and their corresponding neighborhoods in adjacent locations. Generally, for a target node, the closer the interaction time between the historical neighbor nodes and the target node is, the more influence the historical neighbor node has on the target node. The influence weight can be quantified in functional form as follows.

$$W\left(v_{t_j} \mid v_{T_i}\right) = \frac{exp\left[-\left(T_i - t_j\right)\right]}{\sum_{T_i - \tau < t_m < T_i} exp\left[-\left(T_i - t_m\right)\right]} \qquad (1)$$

where $W\left(v_{t_j} \mid v_{T_i}\right)$ is the edge weight between nodes v_{t_j} and v_{T_i}, where T_i is the current time and t_j is historical time in time step τ.

As shown in Fig. 2, in time step τ, in order to succinctly represent the semantic information of the network, for the same node appearing at different moments, we only keep one historical self-node closest to the current time. The dashed lines in Fig. 2 indicate historically existing relationships that are actually not present in the historical memory graph at the current time.

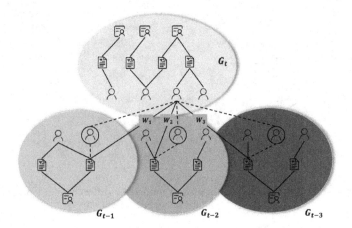

Fig. 2. An example of a historical memory graph. The node vt represents the node in the current graph G_t, and v_{t-1}, v_{t-2}, v_{t-3} represent the historical self-nodes of v_t at historical moments. In order to preserve the semantic information contained in the node path, this work directly constructs weighted edges between the current node and its historical neighbors in snapshots G_{t-1}, G_{t-2}, G_{t-3}.

3.2   Random Walk Strategy Based on Role Perception

Many complex coupling and interaction features contained in the network often play an important role. Mining these features abstractly and deeply is a difficult task in network representation learning. In general, the influence of each node in the network is considered to be different. Generally speaking, the interaction relationship of nodes in the network is usually directly proportional to the influence of nodes and inversely proportional to the distance of nodes. Here the network as a whole is regarded as a data field with field effect. Different influence of nodes in the network is the corresponding potential energy in the data field. In this way, we can divide the structural role of nodes by topological potential, quantify the structural role of nodes, and obtain the complex coupling and interaction relationships and global structural information in the network. The random walk strategy based on role awareness under the guidance of meta-path proposed in this paper can distinguish different types of nodes and edges, and can obtain more potential information in the network.

Structural Role Proximity. Usually in real networks, some nodes have very important roles. These nodes usually have complex interactions and coupling relationships with other nodes in the network, and they contain a lot of potential information, which is of great significance to improve the effect of network representation learning. The structural role [17] proximity performance is a good representation of the special meaning of this class of nodes.

In this paper, the node topological potential is used to compute quantitative results on the structural role of nodes. Using this method, we can obtain far-distance node information, thus embedding the structural role proximity of nodes [17]. While quantifying the network structure, the network data field completely retains all the structural and semantic features of the real network. In this paper, the topological potential of nodes represented by a Gaussian potential function is used to calculate the structural role of nodes in the networks [17].

$$E_d\left(v_i\right) = \frac{1}{n} \sum_{j=1}^{n} d_j \times e^{-\left(\frac{wd_{ij}}{\gamma}\right)^2} \qquad (2)$$

where d_j is the node quality represented by the degree of node v_j. n is the number of all neighbor nodes of v_i. γ is an influence factor that can determine the influence range and interaction range of nodes in the network. wd_{ij} is the net-weighted shortest distance between nodes v_i and v_j.

Random Walk with Role-Aware Strategies. In order to retain more effective information and generate a meaningful node sequence, in this stage, a biased random walk is performed on the historical memory graph under the guidance of the meta-path through the role awareness strategy. There is a meta-path $\rho : K_1 \xrightarrow{R_1} K_2 \xrightarrow{R_2} \ldots \xrightarrow{R_c} K_{c+1} \xrightarrow{R_{c+1}} \ldots \xrightarrow{R_i} K_{i+1}$ in the historical memory graph. The walking path is generated according to the following allocation strategy.

$$P\left(v_{i+1} \mid v_i^c\right) =$$
$$\begin{cases} \alpha \dfrac{W(v_{i+1}|v_i^c)}{\sum_{v_j \in H_{c+1}(v_i^c)} W\left(v_j \mid v_i^c\right)} + \beta E_d\left(v_{i+1}\right) & \left(v_{i+1}, v_i^c\right) \in E, f\left(v_{i+1}\right) = c+1 \\ 0 & \left(v_{i+1}, v_i^c\right) \notin E \text{ or } f\left(v_{i+1}\right) \neq c+1 \end{cases}$$
$$(3)$$

where $v_i^c \in K_c$, the next node to be selected is v_{i+1}. $H_{c+1}(v_i^c)$ is a neighborhood of node v_i. The nodes in this neighborhood are all K_{c+1}. $H_{c+1}(v_i^c)$ can contain neighbor nodes belonging to v_i^c at any time in the time step. α and β are two equilibrium parameters used to adjust the degree of bias in the role-aware policy random walk.

3.3   Improved Skip-Gram Model Bases on Relational Awareness

The various heterogeneous relationships in dynamic heterogeneous networks have significantly different structural characteristics and need to be carefully handled using the modified model. In this paper, an improved skip-gram model based on relation-aware is used to learn the low-dimensional feature vectors of the nodes in the network.

Based on the original model, the improved model further considers that when two nodes have similar relationship structure with their neighbors, they can also be regarded as more similar nodes. In Fig. 3, there are atomic relations similar to A-P and P-C, and there are also composite interaction relations similar to A-P-A and A-P-C. The A-P structure is an equivalent relational structure. P-C structure is a kind of subordinate structure. In other words, unlike the equality structure, the dependency structure is a divergent relational structure. How to consider different interaction characteristics in embedding is another challenge of network embedding.

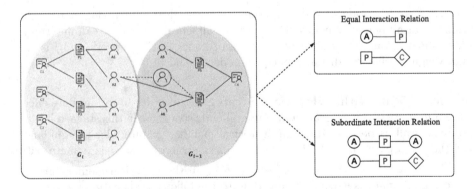

Fig. 3. Illustration of the interaction between nodes within the network.

Relation-Aware Strategy. Node degree can reflect some important characteristics of the network. Specifically, given nodes v_i and v_j and the connection interaction relationship r between them, a relationship metric score $D(r)$ can be used to sense the specific interaction relationship between nodes. The node relationship metric score $D(r)$ is specifically expressed as follows:

$$D(r) = \frac{max[\overline{d_{K_{v_i}}}, \overline{d_{K_{v_j}}}]}{min[\overline{d_{K_{v_i}}}, \overline{d_{K_{v_j}}}]} \tag{4}$$

K_{v_i} and K_{v_j} denote the respective node types of nodes v_i and v_j. $\overline{d_{K_{v_i}}}$ and $\overline{d_{K_{v_j}}}$ respectively corresponding to the type of node degrees on average. A larger $D(r)$ indicates a larger difference in the structural role between two nodes connected by relation r, and the interaction relationship is more inclined to the subordinate interaction relationship (SIR). On the contrary, it indicates that the average degree of the two nodes is compatible with each other, and the relationship is equal interaction (EIR).

Improved Skip-Gram Model. The $D(r)$'s distinction between interaction relationships is further extended to the improved skip-gram model based on relationship-aware: two nodes have similar relationship structure with their neighbor nodes, so these two nodes can be regarded as more similar nodes. The modified model can reduce the structural proximity and interaction proximity between node pairs, so as to integrate the structural and relational characteristics of nodes. We first use random walk to generate a large number of paths in the historical memory graph, and then obtain the neighbors of each node from these paths. For large-scale networks, in order to reduce the computational complexity, the negative sample sampling method is used to optimize the objective function.

$$log\sigma(X_{v_j} \cdot X_{v_i}) + \sum_{l=1}^{n} E_{n_c^l \sim Pn(n_c), h_c^l \sim Pn(h_c), r_c^l} \times log\sigma[-(X_{n_c^l} \cdot X_{v_i} + X_{h_c^l} \cdot X_{v_i})] \tag{5}$$

where $n_c \in N_c$, N_c is the set of current neighbors of type c of node v_i and h_c is the set of historical neighbors of type c of node v_i. r_c^l is the relationship between v_i and its neighbors. X_{v_i}, X_{v_j}, X_{n_c}, X_{h_c} are denoted as the embedding of the corresponding node, respectively. P_n is the set of negative samples of nodes. k is the number of negative nodes sampled. $\sigma = 1/(1 + exp(-x))$ is the sigmoid function. In research, the stochastic gradient descent method is generally used to optimize the above objective function.

3.4 The RRDNE Model

RRDNE constructs historical memory maps based on snapshots of historical maps and current maps within a given time step. According to the basis that the interaction behavior closer to the current time can have a greater impact on the target node, the historical memory map contains the weight of the interaction relationship between the historical node and the current node. For each node in the historical memory graph, a random walk based on the role-aware strategy is performed to generate a large number of node sequences, and they are input into the improved skip-gram model based on relational awareness for representation learning.

4   Experiments

4.1   Evaluation Datasets

Experiments are conducted on the public datasets AMiner and DBLP. The AMiner data of papers in various research fields from 1990 to 2005 are intercepted. DBLP is an author-centered academic information integration data set of computer science publications. The experiment uses a subset of bibliographic information containing different fields from 2000 to 2018. The details of the above two datasets are summarized in Table 1, Table 2 and Table 3.

Table 1. Description of the underlying dataset.

Dataset	Papers	Authors	Conferences	Labels
AMiner	107,623	134,472	34	7
DBLP	67,580	64,978	27	6

Table 2. Labels of AMiner dataset.

Label	Conferences/Journals
Machine Learning & Artificial Intelligence	PKDD, SDM, IJCAI, UAI, AISTATS, ICML, AAAI, COLT
Computer Science Theory	FOCS, SODA, STOC
Database	ICDE, SIGMOD, VLDB, PODS, EDBT
Visualization	CVPR, VAST, ICCV, BMVC, IEEE Visualization, Information Visualization, IEEE Trans.Vis.Comput.Graph.
Biomedical Technology	JAMIA, IEEE Trans.Med.Imaging , Artificial Intelligence in Medicine, Journal of Biomedical Informatics, IEEE Transactions on Information Technology in Biomedicine
Information Retrieval	SIGIR, WWW
Data Mining	ICDM, PAKDD, KDD, CIKM

Table 3. Labels of DBLP dataset.

Label	Conferences/Journals
Machine Learning & Artificial Intelligence	IJCAI, AAAI, ICML, UAI, AISTATS, PKDD
Computer Science Theory	FOCS, SODA, STOC, COLT
Database	CVPR, ICCV, ECCV, BMVC
Visualization	EDBT, ICDE, PODS, SIGMOD, VLDB
Biomedical Technology	KDD, PAKDD, SDM, ICDM, CIKM
Information Retrieval	SIGIR, WWW
Data Mining	SIGIR, ECIR, WWW

4.2 Experiment Settings

Baseline Methods. This work compares the performance of the RRDNE model with that of five state-of-art network embedding models. Among them, the first two are network embedding methods designed for homogeneous networks, and the rest include representation learning methods for static heterogeneous networks and dynamic homogeneous networks.

- DeepWalk [20] generates node sequences by random walk, which can retain network topology information.
- LINE [26] considers the first-order and second-order proximity in the network to construct the proximity matrix.
- HTNE [34] is a temporal network representation learning method based on Hawkes process, which can obtain historical and current information through event sequences.
- Metapath2vec [7] is a method to handle the graph representation of heterogeneous networks, generating node sequences by random walk based on meta-paths.
- Metapath2vec++ [7] is a modified model of Metapath2vec method. It optimizes the defect that Metapath2vec can only consider a single node type when negative sampling occurs.

Parameter Settings. In the experiments, the parameters of all the above basic methods are kept the same as the RRDNE model parameters setting as much as possible. Specifically, the vector embedding dimension is 128, the walk length is 100, the number of walks is 50, the neighborhood size is 7, the time step is 4, the number of negative samples is 5, and the gradient descent learning rate is 0.01.

4.3 Node Classification

Based on the node embeddings learned from the two datasets, we use the labels shown in Tables 1 and 2 to classify the AMiner dataset into seven classes and the DBLP dataset into six classes. 10%–80% of the nodes in the dataset are randomly selected as the training set in turn to train a linear SVM classifier to perform the classification task, and the Micro-F1 and Macro-F1 parameters are used as indicators to measure the classification results. Ten experiments are carried out, and the average score of Micro-F1 and Macro-F1 is taken as the final result of classification performance measurement.

The experimental results for the node classification task are shown in Table 4, where the best results are highlighted in bold. Experimental results show that the RRDNE model outperforms the existing state-of-art basic methods. In the AMiner dataset, the performance of the RRDNE model is 1.27%–22.11% higher than the Micro-F1 score of the baseline method when the training set is 60%, the performance is improved by 1.83%–22.24% when the training set is 70%, and the performance is improved by 1.58%–21.22% when the training set is 80%. The Macro-F1 score is increased by 1.34%–22.33%, 1.95%–22.51%, 1.91%–21.82% when the training set is 60%–80%. Similarly, in the DBLP dataset, the performance of RRDNE proposed in this work is improved over the indicators of the baseline methods, respectively. These results illustrate that RRDNE has better embedding performance than methods that only consider a single network characteristic without preserving network heterogeneity and dynamics.

Table 4. Multi-label node classification results in AMiner and DBLP datasets.

	Training sample ratio	DeepWalk	LINE	HTNE	Metapath2vec	Metapath2vec++	RRDNE		Training sample ratio	DeepWalk	LINE	HTNE	Metapath2vec	Metapath2vec++	RRDNE
AMiner Micro-F1	10%	0.7124	0.7118	0.8044	0.9001	0.9223	**0.9408**	**DBLP** Micro-F1	10%	0.6812	0.7009	0.7721	0.8911	0.9161	**0.9219**
	20%	0.7167	0.7154	0.8550	0.9139	0.9460	**0.9491**		20%	0.7122	0.7194	0.8364	0.9138	0.9359	**0.9403**
	30%	0.7232	0.7201	0.8743	0.9258	0.9499	**0.9503**		30%	0.7331	0.7367	0.8575	0.9426	0.9435	**0.9527**
	40%	0.7387	0.7327	0.8828	0.9346	0.9511	**0.9588**		40%	0.7382	0.7483	0.8740	0.9440	0.9533	**0.958**
	50%	0.7402	0.7369	0.8892	0.9389	0.9537	**0.9597**		50%	0.7398	0.7426	0.8713	0.9458	0.9557	**0.9599**
	60%	0.7451	0.7414	0.8936	0.9423	0.9535	**0.9662**		60%	0.7403	0.7375	0.8734	0.9452	0.9541	**0.9604**
	70%	0.7500	0.7462	0.8984	0.9456	0.9541	**0.9724**		70%	0.7558	0.7561	0.8954	0.9501	0.9567	**0.9689**
	80%	0.7589	0.7491	0.9061	0.9512	0.9553	**0.9711**		80%	0.7590	0.7600	0.8993	0.9552	0.9568	**0.9726**
Macro-F1	10%	0.7012	0.7109	0.7981	0.9013	0.9261	**0.9312**	Macro-F1	10%	0.6723	0.6807	0.7556	0.8856	0.9052	**0.9169**
	20%	0.7222	0.7195	0.8469	0.9203	0.9293	**0.9374**		20%	0.6868	0.6946	0.8298	0.9035	0.9089	**0.9237**
	30%	0.7254	0.7236	0.8673	0.9327	0.9425	**0.9459**		30%	0.7137	0.7285	0.8410	0.9261	0.9256	**0.9281**
	40%	0.7323	0.7392	0.8765	0.9389	0.9437	**0.9495**		40%	0.7254	0.7288	0.8529	0.9284	0.9289	**0.9377**
	50%	0.7367	0.7370	0.8836	0.9456	0.9458	**0.9574**		50%	0.7261	0.7297	0.8658	0.9287	0.9305	**0.9462**
	60%	0.7402	0.7467	0.8879	0.9458	0.9501	**0.9635**		60%	0.7276	0.7338	0.8622	0.9364	0.9397	**0.9538**
	70%	0.7451	0.7499	0.8920	0.9421	0.9507	**0.9702**		70%	0.7300	0.7497	0.8753	0.9442	0.9411	**0.9580**
	80%	0.7512	0.7568	0.9064	0.9458	0.9503	**0.9694**		80%	0.7342	0.7559	0.8802	0.9147	0.9480	**0.9635**

4.4   Link Prediction

In this part, the link prediction problem is modeled as a binary classification problem. In the training phase, the training set randomly retains 80 % of the existing relationships of the original historical memory network, and the test set

Table 5. Results of paper link prediction in the AMiner and DBLP datasets.

Baseline methods	AMiner		DBLP	
	AUC	F1	AUC	F1
DeepWalk	0.6415	0.6392	0.6386	0.6147
LINE	0.7853	0.7921	0.7894	0.7069
HTNE	0.8923	0.8724	0.8881	0.8709
Metapath2vec	0.9006	0.8328	0.9070	0.8225
Metapath2vec++	0.9148	0.8636	0.9111	0.8604
RRDNE	**0.9487**	**0.8918**	**0.9465**	**0.8944**

contains the remaining relationships. Then we use the evaluation index AUC to evaluate the prediction results on the test set. Each data set is repeated for 10 times, and finally the average AUC in the experiment is taken as the standard for performance evaluation.

The results for link prediction are shown in Table 5, where the best results for the dataset are shown in bold. It is clear that the RRDNE model outperforms all other baseline methods on both datasets. DeepWalk and LINE methods have similar prediction results and poor performance, which indicates that it is difficult to improve the embedding quality of heterogeneous networks without fully considering the node types. The performance of the HTNE method suitable for temporal networks in the link prediction task is better than that of the network embedding method suitable for static homogeneous networks, which indicates that considering the dynamic evolution characteristics of the network can effectively improve the quality of network embedding when embedding networks with time-varying characteristics. For Metapath2vec and Metapath2vec++ which are suitable for heterogeneous networks, although the network embedding quality is improved after considering the characteristics of node types, other potentially important information of the network is not retained, and the performance of the algorithm also needs to be improved. RRDNE fully considers the time-varying characteristics of dynamic heterogeneous networks, retains more potentially important information, and can better learn node embedding.

4.5   Parametric Analysis

In order to evaluate the effect of different hyperparameters in the model on the experimental results, this work investigates the effect of embedding dimension on the performance of link prediction task and the effect of time step on the performance of node classification task. Specifically, the dimensions of embedding dimensions are set to 25, 50, 128, 200 and 300, respectively, to analyze the AUC metric of link prediction performance. The time step was varied from 2 to 8 to analyze the Macro-F1 and Micro-F1 scores for the node classification task. The results are shown in Fig. 4.

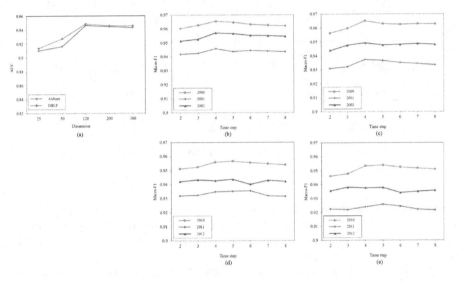

Fig. 4. (a) AUC for different embedding sizes. (b) (c) Micro-F1 and Macro-F1 scores at different time steps on AMiner. (d) (e) Micro-F1 and Macro-F1 scores at different time steps on DBLP.

As shown in Fig. 4(a), when the embedding dimension is less than 128, the performance of the connection prediction task improves as the number of dimensions increases. After the embedding dimension exceeds a certain value, the model performance slightly decreases. This shows that the model embedding dimension is not the bigger the better, but because too much unnecessary information is retained, the data redundancy is caused, and the time cost of the model operation is increased.

As shown in Fig. 4, the node classification task performance of the AMiner dataset reaches its maximum value when the time step $T = 4$, and slightly decreases as T increases or decreases. The reason for this result is that at $T < 4$, the embedding performance of the model is not ideal because the time step is too short, which causes a partial loss of information. However, the model performance is not significantly improved by increasing T, but rather by increasing the cost of randomly capturing key information in the history memory graph. On the other hand, the Micro-F1 and Macro-F1 scores for the classification task on the DBLP dataset are similar at 4 and 5. In this work, due to the different data selection, the frequency of node relationship changes on the AMiner dataset is more frequent than on the DBLP dataset. Due to the frequent and rapid relationship changes, the historical information with longer time is less valuable in the AMiner data set with frequent relationship changes, and the change information closer to the current time is needed for effective network embedding on the AMiner data set.

5   Conclusions

In this work, we propose RRDNE, a role and relation-aware representation learning framework for complex coupled dynamic heterogeneous networks, which aims to retain important historical information as well as global and local structural information during the dynamic change of networks. The influence of important nodes in the historical memory graph is increased, and the role awareness strategy based on structural role proximity is used to retain complex features. Then, the improved skip-gram model is used to learn the representation of the node sequence to improve the network embedding performance. Finally, various experiments are carried out on two real data sets, which fully demonstrate the effectiveness, superiority and feasibility of the proposed RRDNE method compared with the existing advanced baseline methods. This work does not consider the use of node attributes, which is a shortcoming of the model. Future work can also focus on how to further optimize the time and space costs of model learning.

References

1. Akujuobi, U., Yufei, H., Zhang, Q., Zhang, X.: Collaborative graph walk for semi-supervised multi-label node classification. In: 2019 IEEE International Conference on Data Mining (ICDM), pp. 1–10. IEEE (2019)
2. Cai, H., Zheng, V.W., Chang, K.C.C.: A comprehensive survey of graph embedding: problems, techniques, and applications. IEEE Trans. Knowl. Data Eng. **30**(9), 1616–1637 (2018)
3. Cao, S., Lu, W., Xu, Q.: Grarep: Learning graph representations with global structural information. In: Proceedings of the 24th ACM International on Conference on Information and Knowledge Management, pp. 891–900 (2015)
4. Chang, S., Han, W., Tang, J., Qi, G.J., Aggarwal, C.C., Huang, T.S.: Heterogeneous network embedding via deep architectures. In: Proceedings of the 21th ACM SIGKDD International Conference on Knowledge Discovery and Data Mining, pp. 119–128 (2015)
5. Chen, M.R., Huang, P., Lin, Y., Cai, S.M.: Ssne: effective node representation for link prediction in sparse networks. IEEE Access **9**, 57874–57885 (2021)
6. Ding, Y., Wei, H., Hu, G., Pan, Z., Wang, S.: Unifying community detection and network embedding in attributed networks. Knowl. Inf. Syst. **63**(5), 1221–1239 (2021)
7. Dong, Y., Chawla, N.V., Swami, A.: metapath2vec: scalable representation learning for heterogeneous networks. In: Proceedings of the 23rd ACM SIGKDD International Conference on Knowledge Discovery and Sata Mining, pp. 135–144 (2017)

8. Fu, T.y., Lee, W.C., Lei, Z.: Hin2vec: explore meta-paths in heterogeneous information networks for representation learning. In: Proceedings of the 2017 ACM on Conference on Information and Knowledge Management, pp. 1797–1806 (2017)

9. Gao, Y., Gong, M., Xie, Y., Zhong, H.: Community-oriented attributed network embedding. Knowl.-Based Syst. **193**, 105418 (2020)

10. Grover, A., Leskovec, J.: node2vec: scalable feature learning for networks. In: Proceedings of the 22nd ACM SIGKDD International Conference on Knowledge Discovery and Data Mining, pp. 855–864 (2016)

11. Hu, F., Zhu, Y., Wu, S., Wang, L., Tan, T.: Hierarchical graph convolutional networks for semi-supervised node classification. arXiv preprint arXiv:1902.06667 (2019)

12. Jacob, Y., Denoyer, L., Gallinari, P.: Learning latent representations of nodes for classifying in heterogeneous social networks. In: Proceedings of the 7th ACM International Conference on Web Search and Data Mining, pp. 373–382 (2014)

13. Kipf, T.N., Welling, M.: Semi-supervised classification with graph convolutional networks. arXiv preprint arXiv:1609.02907 (2016)

14. Kipf, T.N., Welling, M.: Variational graph auto-encoders. arXiv preprint arXiv:1611.07308 (2016)

15. Li, H., Wang, Y., Zhang, S., Song, Y., Qu, H.: Kg4vis: a knowledge graph-based approach for visualization recommendation. IEEE Trans. Visual Comput. Graphics **28**(1), 195–205 (2021)

16. Li, J., Dani, H., Hu, X., Tang, J., Chang, Y., Liu, H.: Attributed network embedding for learning in a dynamic environment. In: Proceedings of the 2017 ACM on Conference on Information and Knowledge Management, pp. 387–396 (2017)

17. Li, Z., Wang, X., Li, J., Zhang, Q.: Deep attributed network representation learning of complex coupling and interaction. Knowl.-Based Syst. **212**, 106618 (2021)

18. Ma, J., Cui, P., Zhu, W.: Depthlgp: learning embeddings of out-of-sample nodes in dynamic networks. In: Proceedings of the AAAI Conference on Artificial Intelligence, vol. 32 (2018)

19. Onn, R., Steinhardt, A.O., Bojanczyk, A.: The hyperbolic singular value decomposition and applications. In: Proceedings of the 32nd Midwest Symposium on Circuits and Systems, pp. 575–577. IEEE (1989)

20. Perozzi, B., Al-Rfou, R., Skiena, S.: Deepwalk: Online learning of social representations. In: Proceedings of the 20th ACM SIGKDD International Conference on Knowledge Discovery and Data Mining, pp. 701–710 (2014)

21. Qi, Y., Shi, G., Yu, X., Li, Y.: Visualization in media big data analysis. In: 2015 IEEE/ACIS 14th International Conference on Computer and Information Science (ICIS), pp. 571–574. IEEE (2015)

22. Ribeiro, L.F., Saverese, P.H., Figueiredo, D.R.: struc2vec: learning node representations from structural identity. In: Proceedings of the 23rd ACM SIGKDD International Conference on Knowledge Discovery and Data Mining, pp. 385–394 (2017)

23. Shi, C., Hu, B., Zhao, W.X., Philip, S.Y.: Heterogeneous information network embedding for recommendation. IEEE Trans. Knowl. Data Eng. **31**(2), 357–370 (2018)

24. Shi, M., Tang, Y., Zhu, X.: Mlne: multi-label network embedding. IEEE Trans. Neural Networks Learn. Syst. **31**(9), 3682–3695 (2019)

25. Tang, J., Qu, M., Mei, Q.: Pte: predictive text embedding through large-scale heterogeneous text networks. In: Proceedings of the 21th ACM SIGKDD International Conference on Knowledge Discovery and Data Mining, pp. 1165–1174 (2015)

26. Tang, J., Qu, M., Wang, M., Zhang, M., Yan, J., Mei, Q.: Line: large-scale information network embedding. In: Proceedings of the 24th International Conference on World Wide Web, pp. 1067–1077 (2015)

27. Tang, Y., Huang, Z., Cheng, J., Zhou, G., Feng, S., Zheng, H.: Graph neural network-based node classification with hard sample strategy. In: 2021 International Conference on Cyber-Physical Social Intelligence (ICCSI), pp. 1–4. IEEE (2021)

28. Tu, K., Cui, P., Wang, X., Wang, F., Zhu, W.: Structural deep embedding for hyper-networks. In: Proceedings of the AAAI Conference on Artificial Intelligence, vol. 32 (2018)

29. Wang, H., et al.: Graphgan: graph representation learning with generative adversarial nets. In: Proceedings of the AAAI Conference on Artificial Intelligence, vol. 32 (2018)

30. Wang, X., Cui, P., Wang, J., Pei, J., Zhu, W., Yang, S.: Community preserving network embedding. In: Proceedings of the AAAI Conference on Artificial Intelligence, vol. 31 (2017)

31. Wu, C., Zhou, Y., Tan, L., Teng, C.: Link prediction based on graph embedding method in unweighted networks. In: 2020 39th Chinese Control Conference (CCC), pp. 736–741. IEEE (2020)

32. Xia, T., Gu, Y., Yin, D.: Research on the link prediction model of dynamic multiplex social network based on improved graph representation learning. IEEE Access **9**, 412–420 (2020)

33. Yu, B., Li, Y., Zhang, C., Pan, K., Xie, Y.: Enhancing attributed network embedding via similarity measure. IEEE Access **7**, 166235–166245 (2019)

34. Zuo, Y., Liu, G., Lin, H., Guo, J., Hu, X., Wu, J.: Embedding temporal network via neighborhood formation. In: Proceedings of the 24th ACM SIGKDD International Conference on Knowledge Discovery & Data Mining, pp. 2857–2866 (2018)

Twin Graph Attention Network with Evolution Pattern Learner for Few-Shot Temporal Knowledge Graph Completion

Yi Liang[1], Shuai Zhao[1,2(✉)], Bo Cheng[1], and Hao Yang[3]

[1] State Key laboratory of Networking and Switching Technology,
Beijing University of Posts and Telecommunications,
No. 10. Xitucheng Road, Haidian District, Beijing, China
{liangyi,zhaoshuaiby,chengbo}@bupt.edu.cn
[2] Guangxi Key Laboratory of Cryptography and Information Security, Guilin, China
[3] 2012 Labs, Huawei Technologies Co., LTD, Beijing, China
yanghao30@huawei.com

Abstract. Recent years have witnessed a growing number of studies on few-shot knowledge graph completion (FSKGC), which aims to infer new facts for relations given its few-shot observed samples. Despite current research's great success in static knowledge graphs, few-shot temporal knowledge graph completion (FSTKGC) has not been well explored yet. Existing FSTKGC solutions mainly face two challenges. First, these models fail to **distinguish the contribution of neighbors** and model the difference between recurring and ever-changing facts. Second, they ignore **the latent evolution patterns** from observed temporal samples when learning relation representations. In this paper, we propose a novel framework named TwinGAT-VEDA with twin graph attention and an evolution pattern learner to address the above issues. First, our model devises two graph attention network (the twins) to aggregate most relative signals from recurring and dynamic neighbors separately and automatically fuses these futures based on the interaction between the subject and object. Secondly, we inject the time-differences to encode entity pairs and learn evolution patterns from few-shot reference sequence to represent few-shot relations. Comprehensive experiments on two benchmark datasets ICEWS-few-intp and GDELT-few-intp demonstrate that TwinGAT-VEDA achieves the state-of-the-art results.

Keywords: Knowledge Graph Completion · Link Prediction · Temporal Knowledge Graph · Few-Shot Learning · Graph Learning · Representation Learning

1 Introduction

Knowledge Graph (KG) is a powerful tool that stores facts as triple set $\{(s, r, o)\}$, in which s and o indicate the subject and object entity, and r represents the relation between subject and object. KG has been used in many downstream tasks

Z. Jin et al. (Eds.): KSEM 2023, LNAI 14117, pp. 234–246, 2023.
https://doi.org/10.1007/978-3-031-40283-8_20

such as question answering [5] and recommendation system [27]. A shortcoming of KGs is that they fail to account for the dynamic nature of facts that constantly changes over time [12]. In real-life scenarios, numerous facts are inherently associated with specific timestamp. Therefore, temporal knowledge graphs (TKGs) are introduced to inject time annotation to each fact, describing temporal facts in quadruple form (s, r, o, τ), where τ indicates the time when the fact is valid.

KGs and TKGs are generally incomplete [12,25]. Hence, Knowledge Graph Completion (KGC), which leverages existing facts to complete KG automatically, has garnered significant attention. Amount of methods are developed to complete KG [15,20] and TKG [12,24,25]. As research on KGC has deeply developed, the long-tail phenomenon [23] in real-world KG, *i.e.*, few-shot learning for knowledge graph completion, has attracted widespread research attention in recent years.

Though current researches have achieved significant improvement towards few-shot knowledge graph completion (FSKGC) [4,13,16,23,28] and few-shot temporal knowledge graph completion (FSTKGC) [1,7,14,29][1], they still face two major challenges on temporal scenario. First, the graph learning process of these models **failed to distinguish recurring and ever-changing facts**. We observe that some facts repeat hundreds of times in temporal knowledge graphs. For example, in ICEWS05-15 [2,8] knowledge graph, fact *("Mahmoud Ahmadinejad", "Make statement", "Iran")* repeats nearly 1400 times. Intuitively, this fact might tell less information about *"Iran"* than fact *("South Africa", "Impose embargo boycott or sanctions", "Iran")*, which only occurs two times in *2008-03-04* and *2012-02-03*, implying a sharp deterioration in the relationship between *"South Africa"* and *"Iran"*. Distinguishing the effects of these two kind of facts would help to learn more robust entity representations. In this paper, we call such constantly recurring neighbors as *"pseudo-static neighbors"*.

Second, these models **overlook the temporal order of instances** when learning relation representations, thereby ignoring the latent evolution patterns behind the observed temporal references, which have been proved valuable to temporal knowledge graph completion [22].

In this paper, we propose a novel framework TwinGAT-VEDA for few-shot temporal knowledge graph completion to tackle these challenges. Specifically, TwinGAT-VEDA contains three major components. First, TwinGAT applies two similar (**Twin**) Graph **AT**tention architecture to encode recurring neighbors and ever-changing neighbors separately for entities. A subject-object interaction-based gating function is leveraged to combine the output from the twins and filter noise. Then a time-**D**ifference p**A**ir encoder (DA) is proposed to represent entity pairs by injecting the divergence information between the support pair and query time. With time-difference injected pair representations, we devise e**V**olution-aware **E**ncoder (VE) that employs a Gate Recurrent Unit (GRU) [6] to capture hidden evolution within support pairs. Finally, a semantic-based decoder is applied to accomplish the prediction.

Our contributions could be summarized as: 1) This paper focuses on two major issues including heterogeneous temporal facts distinction and evolution

---

[1] More details about these models can be found on Sect. 2.

pattern learning in FSTKGC and proposes a novel model TwinGAT-VEDA to tackle these challenges 2) Experiments on two large-scale datasets reveal that TwinGAT-VEDA outperforms existing FSKGC and FSTKGC models. Ablation studies also prove the effectiveness of each module.

The rest of the paper is organized as follows. Section 2 is related work. Section 3 introduces basic definitions. Section 4 gives the details of TwinGAT-VEDA. Section 5 presents the experiments results. Finally, Sect. 6 concludes our work and points out potential future directions.

2   Related Work

Few-Shot Knowledge Graph Completion. Many studies have been proposed to tackle few-shot knowledge graph completion problem. GMatching [23] is the first study to tackle one-shot knowledge graph completion, using a sub-graph based convolution network to encode entities. To better leverage the heterogeneous feature of KG, researches [13,16,17,28] turn to graph attention network (GAT) to compute the different contribution of neighbors. Besides, studies [4,16,28] also highlight the importance of learning few-shot relation representations by exploiting the observed instances. However, these methods are tailored for static knowledge graph and ignore the dynamic characteristic of temporal KGs.

Few-Shot Temporal Knowledge Graph Completion. There have been some solutions for few-shot temporal knowledge graph completion (FSTKGC) [1,7,14, 29]. FTAG [14] and MOST [7] both focus on one-shot learning in FSTKGC and leverage sub-graph based convolution network similar to [23] to encode entities. More recently, FTMF [1] extends FTAG [14] to few-shot scenarios (more than one instances) and utilizes a fault-tolerant mechanism to handle errors. TFSC [29] is the most relevant study to our work, introducing a time-aware graph attention network to FSTKGC and employing self-attention to generate quadruple representations. However, the above methods neglect the difference between high-frequent repeat and ever-changing facts. Also, they fail to exploit the potential information behind the temporal instances in few-shot scenarios.

3   Background Knowledge

Temporal Knowledge Graph. We formulate the temporal knowledge graph $\mathcal{G}$ as $\mathcal{G} := \mathcal{E} \times \mathcal{R} \times \mathcal{E} \times \mathcal{T}$, where $\mathcal{E}$, $\mathcal{R}$ and $\mathcal{T}$ are the entity set, relation set and timestamp set respectively. Each fact in $\mathcal{G}$ is formulated as a quadruple $q = (s, r, o, \tau)$, s.t. $s, o \in \mathcal{E}$, $r \in \mathcal{R}$ and $\tau \in \mathcal{T}$. A group of seen quadruples as the background graph $\mathcal{BG} \subset \mathcal{G}$ is always available in training and validation.

Task Setting. Every new temporal few-shot relation $r \notin \mathcal{BG}$ is formulated as $\mathcal{D}_r = \{r, \mathbb{Q}_r\}$, in which $\mathbb{Q}_r := \{(s, o, \tau) | (s, r, o, \tau) \in \mathcal{G}\}$ represent relation specific quadruple set. The goal of FSTKGC is given a new few-shot relation r with

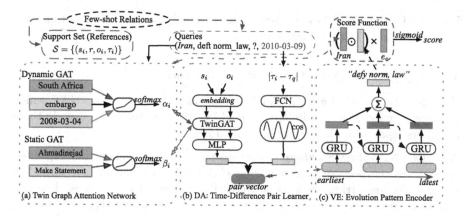

Fig. 1. The major architecture of each module in TwinGAT-VEDA.

K seen quadruples as support set $\mathcal{S}_r$, for a new query quadruple $(?, r, o, \tau_q)$ (or $(s, r, ?, \tau_q)$), predicting the golden subject entity (or golden object). In this work, we only consider predicting object and cast the subject prediction to inferring object for query $(o, r^{inv}, ?, \tau_q)$. To make our model closer to real-world challenge, we conduct the ranking process on the whole entity set $\mathcal{E}$ instead of a relation-specific candidate set. Furthermore, FSTKGC challenge can be categorized into interpolation (to predict events with known timestamps, *i.e.*, $\tau_q \in \mathcal{T}$) and extrapolation (*future* event prediction, *i.e.*, $\tau_q \notin \mathcal{T}$) manners [7]. We consider the *interpolation* scenario in our work and leave the extrapolation challenge to our future work.

Few-Shot Learning Process. Following [7,13,23], the learning process is divided into meta-training, meta-validation and meta-test stage. Every step in meta-training samples a few-shot relation $\mathcal{D}_{r_{tr}}$ from meta-training task set $\mathbb{T}_{tr}$, randomly choices K known instances from $\mathbb{Q}_{r_{tr}}$ to construct support set $\mathcal{S}_{r_{tr}}$ and selects query set $\mathcal{Q}_{r_{tr}}$ from $\mathbb{Q}_{r_{tr}} \setminus \mathcal{S}_{r_{tr}}$ for optimization. Meta-validation and meta-test conduct evaluation for each relation in meta-validation task set $\mathbb{T}_{val}$ and meta-testing task set $\mathbb{T}_{te}$, respectively. We select the very first K samples to formulate the $\mathcal{S}_{r_{eval}}$ for each relation r_{eval} in evaluation. Moreover, $\mathbb{T}_{tr}$, $\mathbb{T}_{val}$ and $\mathbb{T}_{te}$ are *disjoint*.

4   Model

The architecture of TwinGAT-VEDA is shown in Fig. 1. Given a query $(s_q, r, ?, \tau_q)$ of a few-shot relation r along with support set $\mathcal{S}_r$, TwinGAT-VEDA applies a twin graph attention network (TwinGAT) to capture both intrinsic and dynamic features from its one-hop neighbors separately. An entity interaction based gating mechanism is proposed to combine these two features to enhance entity embeddings. Then TwinGAT-VEDA sorts the references according to their timestamps and capture the evolution features with Gate Recurrent

Unit (GRU) to learn relation representation. Finally, a semantic function with Sigmoid is utilized to compute scores.

4.1   Twin Graph Attention Network for entities

To distinguish *pseudo-static facts* and *dynamic* facts, we design TwinGAT, which comprises two similar but independent GAT [15] (the twins) to encode these neighbors separately. Details are illustrated below.

Neighbor Sampling Strategy. We conduct a separate neighbor sampling strategy to construct pseudo-static neighbor set $\mathcal{N}_e^{st}$ and dynamic set $\mathcal{N}_e^{dy}$ for entity e. We collect recurring facts associated with e, and select the most frequent M_{st} facts, omit the timestamp to construct $\mathcal{N}_e^{st}$. Nearest neighbor sampling strategy [7] is applied to construct $\mathcal{N}_e^{dy}$, which selects the M_{dy} quadruples nearest to the latest time in $\mathcal{S}_r$. For $\mathcal{N}_e^{st}$ and $\mathcal{N}_e^{dy}$, we transform (s_j, r_j, e, τ_j) to $(e, r_j^{inv}, s_j, \tau_j)$ then only consider facts starting with e during sampling. Besides, M_{st} is much smaller than M_{dy} since most facts in temporal KG are dynamic.

Time Embedding. Considering the periodicity of time [10], we leverage a feed-forward network followed with cosine periodic activation function to embed τ:

$$\Phi(\tau) = \frac{1}{d_\tau}\cos(\mathbf{W}_1\tau + \mathbf{b}_1) \tag{1}$$

where $\mathbf{W}_1 \in \mathbb{R}^{d_\tau}$ and $\mathbf{b}_1 \in \mathbb{R}^{d_\tau}$. d_τ is the dimension of time representation.

Dynamic Graph Attention. Inspired by [3], we regard the time annotation of fact as an inherent attribute. For every dynamic neighbor $(e, r_i^{dy}, o_i^{dy}, \tau_i^{dy})$ in the temporal neighbor set $\mathcal{N}_e^{dy}$ of entity e, the hidden state $\mathbf{d}_i^{dy}$ and the attention weight are obtained as follows:

$$\mathbf{d}_i^{dy} = \text{LeakyReLU}(\mathbf{W}_2(\mathbf{r}_i^{dy}\|\mathbf{o}_i^{dy}\|\Phi(\tau_i^{dy})) + \mathbf{b}_2)$$
$$\alpha_i = \frac{\exp(\mathbf{u}_1\mathbf{d}_i^{dy})}{\sum_{j=1}^{|\mathcal{N}_e^{dy}|}(\exp(\mathbf{u}_1\mathbf{d}_j^{dy}))} \tag{2}$$

in which $\mathbf{W}_2 \in \mathbb{R}^{d_e \times (2d_e + d_\tau)}$, $\mathbf{b}_2 \in \mathbb{R}^{d_e}$ and $\mathbf{u}_1 \in \mathbb{R}^{1 \times d_e}$ are trainable parameters. d_e is the embedding dimension of entity and relation.

Pseudo-Static Graph Attention. Similar to previous studies [15,28], giving an entity e with its pseudo-static neighbors $\mathcal{N}_e^{st} = (e, r_i^{st}, o_i^{st})$, we compute the attention value of each pair as follows:

$$\mathbf{d}_i^{st} = \text{LeakyReLU}(\mathbf{W}_3(\mathbf{r}_i^{st}\|\mathbf{o}_i^{st}) + \mathbf{b}_3)$$
$$\beta_i = \frac{\exp(\mathbf{u}_2\mathbf{d}_i^{st})}{\sum_{j=1}^{|\mathcal{N}_e^{st}|}(\exp(\mathbf{u}_2\mathbf{d}_j^{st}))} \tag{3}$$

where $\mathbf{W}_3 \in \mathbb{R}^{d_e \times 2d_e}$, $\mathbf{b}_3 \in \mathbb{R}^{d_e}$ and $\mathbf{u}_2 \in \mathbb{R}^{1 \times d_e}$ are learnable parameters.

Interaction-Aware Fusion. Note that constructing such a pseudo-static neighbor set by simply omitting timestamps inevitably introduces noise. To relieve this issue, we leverage subject-object interactions [21] to obtain the final entity representation $\mathbf{e}$:

$$g_j = \text{Sigmoid}(\mathbf{u}_3(\mathbf{e}; \mathbf{e} - \mathbf{o}_j; \mathbf{e} \odot \mathbf{o}_j; \mathbf{o}_j) + \epsilon)$$

$$\mathbf{e} = \sum_{i=1}^{|\mathcal{N}_e^{dy}|} \alpha_i \mathbf{d}_i^{dy} + \sum_{j=1}^{|\mathcal{N}_e^{st}|} g_j \beta_j \mathbf{d}_j^{st} \tag{4}$$

where $\mathbf{u}_3 \in \mathbb{R}^{1 \times 4d_e}$ and $\epsilon \in \mathbb{R}$ are trainable. $\odot$ denotes Hadamard product.

4.2 DA: Query Time-Difference Pair Encoder

After obtaining enhanced representations of subject and object entities with TwinGAT, we are going to obtain representations for references. To fully exploit the dynamic characteristic of TKG, we devise a time differences aware network to encode the quadruple $\mathbf{q}_i = (s_i, r, o_i, \tau_i)$ in $\mathcal{S}$:

$$\hat{\mathbf{q}}_i = \text{MLP}(\mathbf{s}_i \| \mathbf{o}_i)$$

$$\mathbf{q}_i = \hat{\mathbf{q}}_i + \gamma \text{ReLU}(\mathbf{W}_4(\hat{\mathbf{q}}_i \| \Phi_d(|\tau_i - \tau_q|)) + \mathbf{b}_4) \tag{5}$$

wherein, $\mathbf{W}_4 \in \mathbb{R}^{d_e \times (d_e + d_\tau)}$, $\mathbf{b}_4 \in \mathbb{R}^{d_e}$ and γ are learnable parameters. τ_s and τ_q indicate the instance time and query time respectively. $\Phi_d(\cdot)$ is the time encoder sharing the same structure with $\Phi(\cdot)$ in Eq. 1.

4.3 VE: Evolution Pattern Encoder for Few-Shot Instances

Multiple references would provide valuable evolution signals of the few-shot relation. Inspired by the power of GRU [6] in modeling such features in TKGC [22], we propose an adaptive few-shot evolution encoder to learn relation representation from the references in $\mathcal{S}_r$. Specifically, we sort the references in chronological order from earliest to latest as $[\mathbf{q}_1^{\tau_1}, \mathbf{q}_2^{\tau_2}, \dots, \mathbf{q}_K^{\tau_K}]$, s.t. $\tau_1 \leq \tau_2 \leq \dots \leq \tau_K$. After gaining the quadruple representations $\mathbf{q}_1, \mathbf{q}_2, \dots, \mathbf{q}_K$ with Eq. 5, we update the hidden states and formulate the relation embedding $\mathbf{r}$ by considering the contribution of each final hidden state $\mathbf{h}_i$ as follows:

$$\mathbf{h}_k = \text{GRU}(\mathbf{h}_{k-1}, \mathbf{q}_k)$$

$$\alpha_i = \frac{\exp(\mathbf{u}_4 \mathbf{h}_i + \epsilon_2)}{\sum_K (\exp(\mathbf{u}_4 \mathbf{h}_j + \epsilon_2))}$$

$$\mathbf{r} = \sum_{i=1}^{K} \alpha_i \mathbf{h}_i \tag{6}$$

Finally, an infinity-norm regularization is used to filter noise [7] and the relation is represented as $\tilde{\mathbf{r}} = \frac{1}{\|\mathbf{r}\|_{\inf}} \mathbf{r}$. $\mathbf{u}_4 \in \mathbb{R}^{1 \times d_e}$ and $\epsilon_2 \in \mathbb{R}$ are tunable parameters.

4.4 Semantic Decode for Prediction

With well-encoded entity and relation embeddings, now we use a semantic decode to score query (s_q, r, e_c, τ_q). In particular, we extract latent semantic features and compute the score follow:

$$\Omega(s_q, r, e_c) = (\mathbf{s}_q \odot \tilde{\mathbf{r}}) \cdot \mathbf{e}_c^T$$

$$\text{sr}(s_q, r, e_c) = \text{Sigmoid}(\Omega(s_q, r, e_c)) = \frac{1}{1 + \exp(-\Omega(s_q, r, e_c))} \quad (7)$$

Optimization. During the learning stage, for each positive query (s_q, r, o_q, τ) from meta-training set, we use all entities *s.t.* $e_c^{'} \in \mathcal{E}, (s_q, r, o_q, e_c^{'}) \notin \mathcal{G}$ to construct negative samples $(y_{q'} = 0)$ and optimize model parameters with binary cross-entropy loss:

$$\ell(s_q, r, e_c) = y_q \log(\text{sr}(s_q, r, e_c)) + (1 - y_q)(1 - \text{sr}(s_q, r, e_c))$$

$$\mathcal{L} = -\frac{1}{|\mathcal{Q}_r|} \frac{1}{|\mathcal{E}|} \sum_{r \in \mathbb{T}_{tr}} \sum_{q \in \mathcal{Q}_r} \sum_{e_c \in \mathcal{E}} \ell(s_q, r, e_c) \quad (8)$$

5 Experiments

5.1 Datasets

We conduct experiments on two FSTKGC datasets ICEWS-few-intp and GDELT-few-intp[2]. ICEWS-few-intp is a subset of ICEWS (Integrated Crisis Early Warning System) temporal knowledge graph [2,8], containing political facts from 2005 to 2015 automatically extracting from news articles by the BBN ACCENT event coder[3]. We select relations with frequency between 50 and 500 as the few-shot relations. Relations with less than 50 quadruples are discarded and those with more than 500 facts are referred as background relations (relations in $\mathcal{BG}$). GDELT-few-intp derived from GDELT (global data on events, location, and tone) [9,19] is an event database collecting ethnic, religious, and other social and cultural relationships, including global social facts from Jan. 1, 2018 to Jan. 31, 2018. Similar to ICEWS-few-intp, relations with 100 and 1000 instances are selected as the few-shot relation set. Statistics of these two datasets are shown in Table 1.

5.2 Baselines

We compare our model with three categories of baselines:

- *Temporal Knowledge Graph Completion Models.* We employ TeRo [25], ATiSE [26] and TNTComplEx [12] for comparison. TeRo leverages rotation operation to model the temporal evolution of entity embeddings. ATiSE proposes an additive time series decomposition to inject time feature into entity and relation representations. TNTComplEx incorporates an order 4 tensor with ComplEx [20] to extract semantic meanings by tensor decomposition.

---

[2] We have uploaded our data to https://bit.ly/few-intp-data.
[3] https://github.com/BBN-E/data-online-cameo.

Table 1. Details of two datasets. $|Q_{bg}|$ is the number of quadruples in background graph. $|\mathcal{E}|$, $|\mathcal{T}|$, $|\mathcal{R}_{all}|$ and $|\mathcal{R}_{few}|$ represent the number of entities, timestamps, all relations (background graph relations and few-shot relations) and few-shot relations respectively. $|\mathbb{T}_{tr}|/|\mathbb{T}_{val}|/|\mathbb{T}_{te}|$ denote the size of train/validation/test task set.

Dataset	Time Interval	$|Q_{bg}|$	$|\mathcal{E}|$	$|\mathcal{T}|$	$|\mathcal{R}_{all}|$	$|\mathcal{R}_{few}|$	$|\mathbb{T}_{tr}|/|\mathbb{T}_{val}|/|\mathbb{T}_{te}|$
ICEWS-few-intp	day	441,553	10,356	4,017	155	93	74/9/10
GDELT-few-intp	hour	2,237,534	7,677	2,751	181	80	64/8/8

- *Static Few-shot Knowledge Graph Completion models.* To demonstrate the effectiveness of TwinGAT-VEDA, we compare it against five existing FSKGC models including GMatching [23], FSRL [28], FAAN [17], MetaR [4], GANA [16] and YANA [13]. GMatching enhances entity embeddings with a sub-graph based graph convolution network. FSRL takes the heterogeneity of KG into account and encodes relations using an LSTM auto-encoder. FAAN uses adaptive attentional networks to learn dynamic entity and relation representations. YANA addresses the solitary entities by introducing four abstract relations to describe entity correlations. MetaR utilizes gradient information to refine relation embeddings. GANA extends MetaR with a gating based GAT to handle the relation diversity of KG. We drop the timestamps of quadruples when training these models.
- *Temporal Few-shot Knowledge Graph Completion models.* We also compare TwinGAT-VEDA with four very recent researches in FSTKGC. FTAG [14] is the first research consider long-tail relations in TKGC. MOST [7] proposes a time-aware encoder to learn contextualized entity embeddings. FTMF [1] is the first model to concern few-shot problem in temporal knowledge graph completion, applying a snapshot based GCN to encode entities and incorporating fault-tolerant module to enhance model robustness. TFSC [29] uses GAT to embed entities and generates expressive pair representations via a Transformer encoder.

5.3   Implementation Details

We consider experiments under five-shot setting, *i.e.*, $K = 5$. We initialize the entity and relation embeddings in background graph with ComplEx [20], while the dimension is 100 for both datasets, then fine-tune with learning rate of $5e-5$. The dimension of time vector is set to 100. The hidden dimension of GRU is 200. The query set size is 64. The size of dynamic neighbor M_{dy} set is 256, and the static neighbor set size M_{st} is 15. We use the Adam [11] to optimize our model with learning rate of 0.001 for all modules except the embedding layer. Dropout [18] with rate tuned in $\{0.1, 0.3, 0.5\}$ is used to avoid over-fitting. We set the maximum training steps to 40,000 and perform evaluation on meta-validation set for every 1,000 steps.

Evaluation Protocol. We use MRR (Mean Reciprocal Rank) and Hist@N to measure model performance. The MRR is the average of the reciprocal ranks of

Table 2. Experiment Results. Best results are in **boldface**. <u>Underline</u> indicates the second-best results.

Model	ICEWS-few-intp				GDELT-few-intp			
	HITS@1	HITS@5	HITS@10	MRR	HITS@1	HITS@5	HITS@10	MRR
TNTComplEx [12]	.282	.397	.414	.345	.041	.114	.167	.083
TeRo [25]	.199	.420	.530	.307	.017	.088	.157	.066
ATiSE [26]	.246	.418	.502	.329	.038	.090	.132	.071
GMatching [23]	.226	.410	.512	.316	.073	.119	.159	.107
FSRL [28]	.319	.517	.584	.413	.070	.127	.167	.108
FAAN [17]	.276	.483	.583	.379	.052	.068	.082	.070
YANA [13]	.316	.541	.615	.418	.098	.135	.174	.128
MetaR [4]	.286	.492	.574	.381	.028	.068	.108	.060
GANA [16]	.251	.511	<u>.642</u>	.388	.050	.133	.185	.097
FTAG [14]	.206	.380	.455	.312	.097	.152	.239	.136
MOST [7]	.223	.516	.641	.364	.099	.184	.243	.148
FTMF [1]	<u>.334</u>	.480	.591	.403	<u>.101</u>	<u>.198</u>	<u>.258</u>	<u>.155</u>
TFSC [29]	.297	**.571**	.625	<u>.426</u>	.086	.170	.226	.133
TwinGAT-VEDA	**.349**	<u>.563</u>	**.644**	**.454**	**.114**	**.218**	**.283**	**.172**

all results for queries. Hits@N denotes the ratio of the test quadruple ranking among the top N quadruples. In this paper, $N = 1, 5, 10$.

5.4 Experimental Results

Overall results are listed in Table 2. From these results, we can conclude that:

1. Our model achieves the best MRR, Hits@10, Hits@1 results as well as the second best Hits@5 on two datasets, demonstrating that TwinGAT-VEDA is suitable for few-shot temporal knowledge graph completion challenge.
2. Compared with MOST and FTAG: these two models are based on graph convolution networks and utilize mean-pooling mechanism to obtain results. Our model achieves better performance on two datasets consistently, proving that modeling the contribution of entity neighbors is necessary.
3. Compared with FTMF and TFSC: these two models concern the few-shot scenarios in FSTKGC. FTMF used an LSTM auto-encoder to obtain few-shot relation embeddings but ignores the chronological order in the references. TFSC considered the different contribution of the one-hop temporal neighbors and utilizes time-aware GAT to encode entities but neglecting instance-level evolution patterns. Results show that TwinGAT-VEDA achieves superior performances, revealing that both temporal neighbor distinction and evolution patterns from references are essential in FSTKGC.
4. In general, the few-shot learning models could achieve better performance than the traditional temporal KGC models, implying that a well-designed model for FSTKGC requires to consider the few-shot nature of the task.

5. All three kind of models exhibit different performances on the two datasets. Although the FSKGC models could achieve comparable results on ICEWS-few-intp, their efficacy on GDELT-few-intp falls behind that of the FSTKGC models. This could be attributed to the finer time granularity in GDELT-few-intp, requiring the model to better consider temporal features to embed entities and relations. In addition, the results on GDELT-few-intp is less satisfactory compared to those on ICEWS-few-intp, indicating a significant potential for improvement in solving the FSTKGC challenge.

5.5   Ablation Study

To better understand the effectiveness of different module in TwinGAT-VEDA, we conduct ablation studies on both ICEWS-few-intp and GDELT-few-intp with 5-shot setting by removing or replacing key modules with alternative structures as follows. Overall results are listed in Table 3.

Effectiveness of TwinGAT. Our model devises a TwinGAT to capture pseudo-static and dynamic signals from the temporal graph. *AS1.1* remove the pseudo-static GAT module and encode entities with the time-aware attention network. *AS1.2* use just the pseudo-static GAT to obtain entity representations. Additionally, *AS1.3* replaces the cross-interaction with simply concatenated subject and object vector to calculate the gate values. The results of *AS1.1* and *AS1.2* reveal that both modules are essential. And the dynamic GAT has a more significant impact than the pseudo-static GAT since most facts change over time. Modeling such temporal features is necessary to tackle FSTKGC. *AS1.3* proves the effectiveness of the interaction gating function.

Effectiveness of VEDA. Another non-trivial contribution of our model is the VEDA, which comprises a Query time-difference aware pair encoder and the GRU-based evaluation encoder for few-shot instances. Model *AS2.1* and *AS2.2* apply the simple max pooling and mean pooling to pair representations to obtain relation representation, respectively. *AS2.3* skips the chronological sorting for references and replaces evolution pattern learner with LSTM auto-encoder used in FTMF [1] and FSRL [28]. Results suggest that our proposed VE module exhibits the strongest performance, showcasing the capacity of our module to capture the evolution patterns behind few-shot instances. *AS3* removes the time difference part in Eq. 5 and use the MLP to encode entity pairs like [7,23]. Results show the validness of our time-difference aware pair encoder.

5.6   Impacts of γ in DA

In DA (Query Time-Difference Pair Encoder), we introduce a learnable γ to dynamically combine time-injected data and the origin output from MLP. This part we conduct extensive studies on different shot setting and illustrate the learning curve of γ along with corresponding MRR on validation set (vMRR) on Fig. 2. We can observe that 1) Despite different settings, when the model

Table 3. Results of model variants on ICEWS-few-intp and GDELT-few-intp dataset with 5-shot. Best results are in **boldface**.

Models	ICEWS-few-intp				GDELT-few-intp			
	HITS@1	HITS@5	HITS@10	MRR	HITS@1	HITS@5	HITS@10	MRR
AS1.1	.320	.543	.635	.431	.110	.209	.262	.164
AS1.2	.257	.506	.563	.379	.078	.162	.216	.125
AS1.3	.312	.552	.624	.425	.104	.207	.274	.163
AS2.1	.260	.548	.615	.394	.077	.169	.232	.128
AS2.2	.296	.556	.618	.409	.094	.177	.239	.143
AS2.3	.304	.559	.629	.416	.095	.164	.228	.139
AS3	.317	.541	.600	.419	.091	.173	.221	.135
TwinGAT-VEDA	**.349**	**.563**	**.644**	**.454**	**.114**	**.218**	**.283**	**.172**

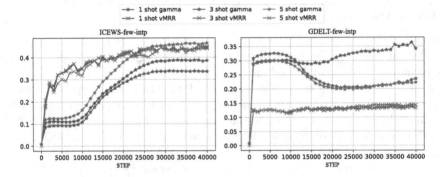

Fig. 2. The learning curve of γ and corresponding MRR in validation set (vMRR) for two datasets on 1, 3 and 5 shot scenarios.

coverages, the γ would stay in a non-negligible value, indicating that the time-difference aware representations are critical for encoding pairs. 2) The trend of γ is quite different in various experiment settings, proving that our design endows the model with strong flexibility and generalization ability to different datasets and various few-shot settings.

6   Conclusion

In this paper, we focus on the few-shot temporal knowledge graph completion in interpolation scenario and propose an innovative model TwinGAT-VEDA to solve this problem. TwinGAT-VEDA introduces TwinGAT to capture both instant and quasi-static signals in the temporal knowledge graph to represent entities and leverages GRU to extract evolution patterns in the few-shot references. Experiments on two datasets ICEWS-few-intp and GDELT-few-intp prove the superiority of our model. Ablation studies further verify the effectiveness of each module in TwinGAT-VEDA. The future work will extend TwinGAT-VEDA to extrapolation scenario and combine the TwinGAT with optimization-based methods to learn more robust relation representations.

Acknowledgements. This work is supported by National Natural Science Foundation of China (Grant No. U21A20468, 52071312), Guangxi Key Laboratory of Cryptography and Information Security (Grant No. GCIS202111), The Open Program of Zhejiang Lab (Grant No. 2021PD0AB02). Yi Liang is supported by BUPT Excellent Ph.D. Students Foundation under grant CX2019136. Shuai Zhao is the corresponding author.

References

1. Bai, L., Zhang, M., Zhang, H., Zhang, H.: FTMF: few-shot temporal knowledge graph completion based on meta-optimization and fault-tolerant mechanism. World Wide Web **26**(3), 1243–1270 (2023)
2. Boschee, E., Lautenschlager, J., O'Brien, S., Shellman, S., Starz, J., Ward, M.: ICEWS Coded Event Data (2015)
3. Chen, K., Li, C., Li, A., Gao, J., Ma, S.: Focus on inherent attributes for temporal knowledge graph completion. In: 2021 International Joint Conference on Neural Networks (IJCNN) (2021). https://doi.org/10.1109/IJCNN52387.2021.9533516
4. Chen, M., Zhang, W., Zhang, W., Chen, Q., Chen, H.: Meta relational learning for few-shot link prediction in knowledge graphs. In: EMNLP, pp. 4216–4225. Association for Computational Linguistics (2019)
5. Chen, Z., Zhao, X., Liao, J., Li, X., Kanoulas, E.: Temporal knowledge graph question answering via subgraph reasoning. Knowledge-Based Systems (2022)
6. Chung, J., Gülçehre, Ç., Cho, K., Bengio, Y.: Empirical evaluation of gated recurrent neural networks on sequence modeling. CoRR abs/1412.3555 (2014)
7. Ding, Z., He, B., Ma, Y., Han, Z., Tresp, V.: Learning meta representations of one-shot relations for temporal knowledge graph link prediction. arXiv preprint arXiv:2205.10621 (2022)
8. García-Durán, A., Dumancic, S., Niepert, M.: Learning sequence encoders for temporal knowledge graph completion. In: EMNLP (2018)
9. Jin, W., Qu, M., Jin, X., Ren, X.: Recurrent event network: autoregressive structure inference over temporal knowledge graphs. In: EMNLP (2020)
10. Kazemi, S.M., et al.: Time2vec: learning a vector representation of time. ArXiv abs/1907.05321 (2019)
11. Kingma, D.P., Ba, J.: Adam: a method for stochastic optimization. In: ICLR (2015)
12. Lacroix, T., Obozinski, G., Usunier, N.: Tensor decompositions for temporal knowledge base completion. In: International Conference on Learning Representations (2020)
13. Liang, Y., Zhao, S., Cheng, B., Yin, Y., Yang, H.: Tackling solitary entities for few-shot knowledge graph completion. In: Knowledge Science. Engineering and Management, pp. 227–239. Springer, Cham (2022). https://doi.org/10.1007/978-3-031-10983-6_18
14. Mirtaheri, M., Rostami, M., Ren, X., Morstatter, F., Galstyan, A.: One-shot learning for temporal knowledge graphs. AKBC (2021)
15. Nathani, D., Chauhan, J., Sharma, C., Kaul, M.: Learning attention-based embeddings for relation prediction in knowledge graphs. In: ACL (2019)

16. Niu, G., et al.: Relational learning with gated and attentive neighbor aggregator for few-shot knowledge graph completion. In: SIGIR (2021)
17. Sheng, J., Guo, S., Chen, Z., Yue, J., Wang, L., Liu, T., Xu, H.: Adaptive attentional network for few-shot knowledge graph completion. In: EMNLP (2020)
18. Srivastava, N., Hinton, G.E., Krizhevsky, A., Sutskever, I., Salakhutdinov, R.: Dropout: a simple way to prevent neural networks from overfitting. J. Mach. Learn. Res. **15**, 1929–1958 (2014)
19. Tone, A.: Global data on events, location and tone (gdelt) (2015)
20. Trouillon, T., Welbl, J., Riedel, S., Gaussier, É., Bouchard, G.: Complex embeddings for simple link prediction. In: ICML, vol. 48, pp. 2071–2080. JMLR.org (2016)
21. Wang, B., Shen, T., Long, G., Zhou, T., Chang, Y.: Structure-augmented text representation learning for efficient knowledge graph completion. In: The Web Conference 2021 (2020)
22. Wu, J., Cao, M., Cheung, J.C.K., Hamilton, W.L.: Temp: temporal message passing for temporal knowledge graph completion. In: Conference on EMNLP (2020)
23. Xiong, W., Yu, M., Chang, S., Guo, X., Wang, W.Y.: One-shot relational learning for knowledge graphs. In: EMNLP, pp. 1980–1990 (2018)
24. Xu, C., Nayyeri, M., Alkhoury, F., Lehmann, J., Yazdi, H.S.: Temporal knowledge graph embedding model based on additive time series decomposition. ArXiv abs/1911.07893 (2019)
25. Xu, C., Nayyeri, M., Alkhoury, F., Yazdi, H.S., Lehmann, J.: Tero: a time-aware knowledge graph embedding via temporal rotation. In: Proceedings of the 28th International Conference on Computational Linguistics, pp. 1583–1593 (2020)
26. Xu, C., Nayyeri, M., Alkhoury, F., Yazdi, H., Lehmann, J.: Temporal knowledge graph completion based on time series gaussian embedding. In: International Semantic Web Conference, pp. 654–671. Springer (2020)
27. Yang, Y., Huang, C., Xia, L., Li, C.: Knowledge graph contrastive learning for recommendation. In: Proceedings of the 45th International ACM SIGIR (2022)
28. Zhang, C., Yao, H., Huang, C., Jiang, M., Li, Z., Chawla, N.: Few-shot knowledge graph completion. In: AAAI, pp. 3041–3048 (2020)
29. Zhang, H., Bai, L.: Few-shot link prediction for temporal knowledge graphs based on time-aware translation and attention mechanism. Neural Networks (2023)

Subspace Clustering with Feature Grouping for Categorical Data

Hong Jia[✉] and Menghan Dong

Guangdong Key Laboratory of Intelligent Information Processing,
College of Electronics and Information Engineering, Shenzhen University,
Shenzhen, China
hongjia1102@szu.edu.cn, 2110436014@email.szu.edu.cn

Abstract. In clustering analysis, data clusters are usually associated with feature subsets rather than the whole space. Therefore, soft subspace clustering devote to find the corresponding subspace for each cluster by assigning weight to the features. However, since categorical data is qualitative rather than quantitative data, the study of subspace clustering for categorical data is relatively rare and challenging. Therefore, this paper presents a new two-step subspace clustering algorithm for categorical data. Firstly, an initial clustering method is proposed to obtain a reliable initial cluster structure, based on which, the feature-to-cluster groups are constructed by utilizing intrinsic relationships between features. Subsequently, the local and global clustering are defined to learn the local cluster relations between data objects and achieve the final clustering results, respectively. Experimental results on benchmark datasets demonstrate the effectiveness of proposed method.

Keywords: Soft subspace clustering · Categorical data · Feature group

1 Introduction

Subspace clustering is an important technique to find clusters in different feature subspaces, which is widely used in data mining and other scientific fields [6]. However, most traditional subspace clustering algorithms are proposed for numerical data, which are inapplicable to handle data with categorical attributes [8]. Therefore, in the literature, different subspace clustering methods that can be applied to categorical data have been presented [1,4]. For example, Oskouei et al. [5] proposed FKMAWCW algorithm based on a local attribute weighting mechanism and a cluster weighting mechanism. Jia and Cheung [3] proposed the WOCIL algorithm based on object-cluster similarity and attribute-cluster weight, which can be applied to pure numerical or categorical data, as well as mixed data. Nevertheless, the above algorithm analyzes the importance of each feature separately and some information about the feature groups may be ignored.

This work was supported by the National Natural Science Foundation of China under Grant 61806131 and the Natural Science Foundation of Guangdong Province under Grant 2018A030310510.

Z. Jin et al. (Eds.): KSEM 2023, LNAI 14117, pp. 247–254, 2023.
https://doi.org/10.1007/978-3-031-40283-8_21

In this paper, we present a new subspace clustering method for categorical data by exploring the group information of the features. By using the collaborative relationship between features, a feature-to-cluster group construction method is proposed to select the important features for different clusters. Since each feature group is targeted to specific cluster, local clustering is employed to collect category relations of data objects regarding to each feature group. Subsequently, a merging strategy is defined to obtain the global clustering labels. Moreover, an improved cluster center initialization approach is presented for the initial clustering, which enables the construction of reliable feature groups.

2   Related Work

Since the clustering framework of the proposed method is inspired by OCIL [2] and WOCIL [3] algorithms, in this section, we give a brief introduction to these two algorithms and make some symbolic definitions.

The OCIL algorithm was proposed based on the concept of object-cluster similarity. Specifically, suppose $X = \{x_1, x_2, \cdots, x_N\}$ is a categorical dataset with N objects, each of which is described by d features $\{A_1, A_2, \cdots, A_d\}$. Thus, x_i can be represented as $\{x_{i1}, x_{i2}, \cdots, x_{id}\}$. Moreover, to divide X into k different clusters, namely $\{C_1, C_2, \cdots, C_k\}$, the OCIL maximizes the following objective function:

$$\mathbf{Q}^* = \arg\max_{\mathbf{Q}} \left[\sum_{j=1}^{k} \sum_{i=1}^{N} \sum_{r=1}^{d} q_{ij} s\left(x_{ir}, C_j\right) \right] \tag{1}$$

where $\mathbf{Q} = (q_{ij})$ is an $N \times k$ partition matrix and $s\left(x_{ir}, C_j\right)$ is the object-cluster similarity for categorical data, which is defined as

$$s\left(x_{ir}, C_j\right) = \frac{\Psi_{A_r = x_{ir}}\left(C_j\right)}{\Psi_{A_r \neq \text{NULL}}\left(C_j\right)} \tag{2}$$

Here, C_j, A_r, x_{ir} symbolize the j-th cluster, the r-th attribute and the i-th object value of A_r, respectively. Moreover, Null denotes the empty, and $\Psi_{function}\left(x\right)$ is the number of objects in x that satisfies the condition of $function$.

On this basis, a soft subspace clustering algorithm namely WOCIL has been developed in [3], which aims to group data objects into several clusters based on both the model of attribute-cluster weights and the object-cluster similarity metric. The objective function of the WOCIL algorithm is:

$$\mathbf{Q}^* = \arg\max_{\mathbf{Q},\mathbf{W}} \left[\sum_{j=1}^{k} \sum_{i=1}^{N} \sum_{r=1}^{d} q_{ij} w_{rj} s\left(x_{ir}, C_j\right) \right] \tag{3}$$

where $\mathbf{W} = (w_{rj})$ is the attribute-cluster weight matrix. Specifically, it is measured based on two aspects: Hellinger distance is used to calculate the inter-cluster difference, denoted as F_{rj} and the average object-cluster similarity represents the intra-cluster similarity, denoted as M_{rj}. The specific definitions can be seen in [3]. Thus, the feature weight w_{ij} can be defined as

$$w_{rj} = \frac{F_{rj}M_{rj}}{\sum_{t=1}^{d}(F_{rj}M_{rj})}, r = 1, 2, \ldots, d, j = 1, 2, \ldots, k \tag{4}$$

3 Subspace Clustering with Feature Grouping Strategy

3.1 Initial Clustering

To build reliable feature-to-cluster groups, a reliable initial cluster structure should be obtained first. In general, randomly selecting the initial centers is a widely used initialization method, but the clustering results of different clustering centers are inconsistent [7]. Therefore, a new initialization method for cluster centers is proposed in this paper. Specifically, referring to the object-cluster similarity metric in [2], the similarity between object and dataset is given by

$$\text{sim}\,(\boldsymbol{x}_i, X) = \frac{1}{d}\sum_{r=1}^{d} s\,(x_{ir}, X) \tag{5}$$

where $s\,(x_{ir}, X)$ is calculated according to Eq. (2). The greater the similarity value of the object, the more possible it is to be a cluster center. Therefore, we utilize a threshold to select the candidate objects $\boldsymbol{x}_h \in X_h$ for cluster centers according to the following condition:

$$\text{sim}\,(\boldsymbol{x}_h, X) > 0.2 * \frac{1}{N}\sum_{i=1}^{N} \text{sim}\,(\boldsymbol{x}_i, X) \tag{6}$$

Then, the shortest distance between each points and the existing cluster center is calculated, and the one with the largest distance has been selected repeatedly until we find k cluster centers. Finally, we assign all data objects to each cluster according to Eq. (1) to attain the initial cluster labels. The procedure of initial clustering method can be summarized as Algorithm 1.

Algorithm 1. Initial Clustering

Input: dataset $X = \{\boldsymbol{x}_1, \boldsymbol{x}_2, \cdots, \boldsymbol{x}_N\}$ and the number of clusters k
Output: set of initial seed points S and initial cluster labels Y
1: For each $\boldsymbol{x}_i \in X$, calculate $\text{sim}\,(\boldsymbol{x}_i, X)$ according to Eq. (5).
2: Select $s_1 = \arg\max_{\boldsymbol{x}_i}\{\text{sim}\,(\boldsymbol{x}_i, X)\}$, let $S = s_1$ and get the candidate subset X_h according to Eq. (6).
3: **for all** $j = 2$ to k **do**
4:     For each $\boldsymbol{x}_i \in \{X_h \backslash S\}$, let $s_j = \max_{\boldsymbol{x}_i \in \{X_h \backslash S\}} \min_{s_l}\left\{\frac{1}{d}\sum_{r=1}^{d} 1(s_{lr} = x_{ir})\right\}$.
5: **end for**
6: Assign S to each cluster according to Eq. (1) to attain the initial cluster labels Y.

3.2   Construction of Feature-to-Cluster Groups

According to Eq. (4), the attribute-cluster weights can be calculated after obtaining the initial clustering results. Subsequently, we select features with higher weight to form the feature-to-cluster groups, denoted as $\{G_1, G_2, \cdots, G_k\}$. Specifically, for each cluster, the features whose weights are greater than the average weight are added to the group. That is, for the j-th cluster, if the following inequality is true, feature A_i will be added to group G_j.

$$w_{ij} > \frac{1}{d} \sum_{r=1}^{d} w_{rj}, \quad j = 1, 2, \cdots, k, \tag{7}$$

where w_{ij} represents the weight of the i-th feature on the j-th cluster. Features may repeat in different groups as long as they all play an important role in these clusters. Of course, it is possible that some features do not belong to any feature group, especially if they are noise features.

3.3   Local Clustering

In this part, local clustering is applied to k feature-to-cluster groups to obtain corresponding category information. Specifically, based on each feature-to-cluster group, we divide the dataset into two parts: in-cluster part and out-cluster part. For example, based on features in group G_t associated with cluster C_t, all data objects will be partitioned into two parts: in-cluster part C_t and out-cluster part $\overline{C_t}$. To this end, we first set the weight of out-group features to zero. That is, the feature weight can be refined as $\boldsymbol{\Gamma} = (\gamma_{rt})$ with

$$\gamma_{rt} = \begin{cases} w_{rt}, & \text{features in the group} \\ 0, & \text{features out of the group} \end{cases} \tag{8}$$

Then, the weighted similarities between the object $\boldsymbol{x}_i$ and the two parts C_t and $\overline{C_t}$ are calculated by

$$Lc\left(\boldsymbol{x}_i, C_t\right) = \sum_{r=1}^{d} \gamma_{rt} s\left(x_{ir}, C_t\right) \tag{9a}$$

$$Lc\left(\boldsymbol{x}_i, \overline{C_t}\right) = \sum_{r=1}^{d} \gamma_{rt} s\left(x_{ir}, \overline{C_t}\right) \tag{9b}$$

The values of Eqs. (9a) and (9b) are compared and $\boldsymbol{x}_i$ is assigned to C_t if the former is greater than the latter, and to $\overline{C_t}$ otherwise.

In particular, we utilize $\mathbf{U} = (\mu_{it})$ to record the local clustering information of each object, which is a $N \times k$ binary matrix that satisfies the following condition:

$$\mu_{it} = \begin{cases} 0, & \boldsymbol{x}_i \in \overline{C_t} \\ 1, & \boldsymbol{x}_i \in C_t \end{cases} \tag{10}$$

We repeat the operation for different feature groups to get k pieces of allocation information for each object, and they are all stored in $\mathbf{U}$.

Algorithm 2. The Proposed Subspace Clustering Algorithm

Input: dataset $X = \{x_1, x_2, \cdots, x_N\}$ and the number of clusters k
Output: cluster label $Y = \{y_1, y_2, \cdots, y_N\}$
1: Obtain initial clustering labels as $y^{(old)}$ according to Algorithm 1
2: **repeat**
3:    Initialize $noChange = true$.
4:    Update w_{rj} according to Eq. (4).
5:    Construct k feature-to-cluster groups for each cluster according to Eq. (7).
6:    **for all** $t = 1$ to k **do**
7:       Conduct local clustering for G_t according to Eqs. (9a) and (9b).
8:    **end for**
9:    Integrate the local information to obtain the global cluster labels $y^{(new)}$.
10:   **if** $y^{(new)} \neq y^{(old)}$ **then**
11:      $noChange$=$false$;
12:      $y^{(old)} = y^{(new)}$;
13:      Update the information of clusters $C_{y^{(new)}}$.
14:   **end if**
15: **until** $noChange$ is $true$

3.4   Global Clustering

To integrate the local clustering results, a cluster merging strategy is proposed to obtain the global cluster structure. According to the above analysis, each row of U represents the relationship between each object and different clusters. We further define a new variable $F_i = \sum_{t=1}^{k} \mu_{it}, i = 1, 2, \cdots, n$ to summarize the cluster relationship of x_i recorded in U. Obviously, the value range of F_i is $\{0, 1, ..., k\}$. For each object, there are three cases to discuss as follows:

1. $F_i = 1$. Actually, this is the ideal and most common situation. We directly assign the column label of the element 1 to the label of the object.
2. $1 < F_i \leq k$. In this case, the object is divided into different clusters with different feature groups. Assuming these clusters are $\{C_1, C_2, \cdots, C_{F_i}\}$. In order to figure out which cluster the object should be assigned to, we combined the correlative feature groups of $\{G_1, G_2, \cdots, G_{F_i}\}$ to form a new group G' and set the weights according to Eq. (8). Subsequently, the value of weighted similarities for these clusters are calculated respectively according to Eq. (9a), and the cluster label is determined by $c_i = \arg\max_C \{Lc(x_i, C)\}, C \in \{C_1, C_2, \cdots, C_{F_i}\}$.
3. $F_i = 0$. This means that the object has not been grouped into any cluster. Thus, we put all the features into the feature group and compare the weighted similarity values of all clusters according to Eq. (9a). Likewise, the cluster label of the object is $c_i = \arg\max_C \{Lc(x_i, C)\}, C \in \{C_1, C_2, \cdots, C_k\}$.

Subsequently, we get the global cluster labels of all the data objects. Based on the previous description, the pseudo-code of the proposed algorithm can be summarized as Algorithm 2.

4   Experiments

In this section, we evaluate the performance of proposed algorithm on categorical data in comparison with other state-of-the-art subspace clustering algorithms. The benchmark datasets are collected from the UCI machine learning repository (http://archive.ics.uci.edu/ml/), whose characteristics are summarized in Table 1. Three performance criteria, i.e., clustering accuracy(ACC), Rand index(RI) and normalized mutual information(NMI) [3], has been utilized to evaluate the clustering results. And the performance of WOCIL, WOCIL+OI, FKMAWCW [5], EWKM and OCIL [2] algorithms have also been recorded for comparative study. In the experiments, each algorithm was executed 50 times on each dataset, and the clustering results were statistically summarized.

Table 1. Characteristics of the benchmark data sets.

Datasets	Number of data points	Number of dimensions	Number of classes
Soybean	47	35	4
WBCD	699	9	2
Mushroom	5644	22	2
Tic-Tac-Toe	958	9	2
promoters	106	57	2
SPECT	267	22	2

The clustering results of different methods in the form of mean and standard deviation of ACC, RI and NMI are shown in Tables 2, 3 and 4 respectively. The best results are bold-faced and the second are underlined. From the results, it can be seen that the proposed algorithm achieves the best results on four of the six test datasets, outperforming the others. For the remaining two data sets, i.e. SPECT and WBCD, the best RI for the former belongs to the EWKM algorithm, while the proposed algorithm is is very close to it, and the ACC and NMI performance of our algorithm is better than that of EWKM. The OCIL algorithm surpasses the proposed algorithm on WBCD dataset, this may be due to the fact that the subspace structure of this dataset is not obvious. However, the proposed algorithm shows a large performance improvement over OCIL algorithm on other datasets, which can still shows that appropriate feature weights can improve the clustering accuracy in most of the datasets. In addition, our algorithm outperforms the WOCIL and WOCIL+OI algorithm on all datasets. This indicates that constructing feature-to-cluster groups can obviously improve the clustering performance in most cases.

Additionally, to reveal the effect of feature groups on clustering performance, mutual information (MI) and symmetric uncertainty (SU) metrics are further used to analyze the correlations between features [9]. The values of these two indices range from 0 to 1, where 1 indicating complete correlation and 0 indicating zero correlation. For each dataset, the values of these two criteria for each

Table 2. Clustering results in terms of ACC of different algorithms (Mean±Std.).

Datasets	Proposed	WOCIL+OI	WOCIL	FKMAWCW	EWKM	OCIL
Soybean	**1±0**	**1±0**	0.8609±0.1558	0.9438±0.1145	0.8089±0.1369	0.8498±0.1610
WBCD	0.8813±0	0.8798±0	0.8798±0.0000	0.3865±0.1754	0.8092±0.1411	**0.8937±0.0011**
Mushroom	**0.8505±0**	0.5237±0	0.5819±0.1187	0.7880±0.0844	0.7018±0.1215	0.5936±0.1137
Tic-Tac-Toe	**0.6326±0**	0.5216±0	0.5638±0.0307	0.5794±0.0075	0.5728±0.0401	0.5619±0.0315
promoters	**0.8113±0**	0.7547±0	0.7070±0.1106	0.5423±0.0329	0.6000±0.0662	0.6353±0.0650
SPECT	**0.6217±0**	0.5618±0	0.5630±0.0276	0.6196±0.0459	0.6066±0.0723	0.5585±0.0051

Table 3. Clustering results in terms of RI of different algorithms (Mean±Std.).

Datasets	Proposed	WOCIL+OI	WOCIL	FKMAWCW	EWKM	OCIL
Soybean	**1±0**	**1±0**	0.9641±0.0716	0.9641±0.0716	0.8765±0.0831	0.9255±0.0805
WBCD	0.7904±0	0.7882±0	0.7882±0.0001	0.4283±0.0798	0.7298±0.1482	**0.8097±0.0017**
Mushroom	**0.7456±0**	0.5010±0	0.5409±0.0902	0.6798±0.0637	0.6103±0.0945	0.5428±0.0901
Tic-Tac-Toe	**0.5347±0**	0.5008±0	0.5095±0.0086	0.5122±0.0032	0.5132±0.0124	0.5091±0.0082
promoters	**0.6909±0**	0.6262±0	0.6059±0.0807	0.5010±0.0083	0.5241±0.0335	0.5406±0.0366
SPECT	0.5279±0	0.5058±0	0.5076±0.0090	0.5310±0.0179	**0.5312±0.0385**	0.5050±0.0012

Table 4. Clustering results in terms of NMI of different algorithms (Mean±Std.).

Datasets	Proposed	WOCIL+OI	WOCIL	FKMAWCW	EWKM	OCIL
Soybean	**1±0**	**1±0**	0.8945±0.1078	0.9426±0.1135	0.8016±0.1413	0.8994±0.1083
WBCD	0.5061±0	0.5024±0	0.5024±0.0000	0.0492±0.0316	0.4012±0.2437	**0.5256±0.0033**
Mushroom	**0.4474±0**	0.0721±0	0.1287±0.1420	0.2824±0.0957	0.1838±0.1701	0.0811±0.1646
Tic-Tac-Toe	**0.0660±0**	0.0071±0	0.0097±0.0146	0.0083±0.0069	0.0085±0.0101	0.0109±0.0122
promoters	**0.3342±0**	0.2581±0	0.1981±0.1519	0.0087±0.0135	0.0504±0.0573	0.0749±0.0637
SPECT	**0.1232±0**	0.0999±0	0.0619±0.0430	0.1029±0.0435	0.0714±0.0346	0.0939±0.0023

pair of features are computed separately, and the maximum, minimum and mean values are recorded, as shown in Table 5. It can be observed that the difference between the maximum and minimum values is greater in Soybean and mushroom, which means that they have both highly correlated and less correlated feature pairs. On the contrary, the difference in the Tic-Tac-Toe is minimal, so its features are more independent and diverse. Specifically, from the results in Tables 2, 3 and 4, it can be concluded that the datasets with larger differences in the correlation between feature pairs are more suitable for the proposed algorithm, as this inherent difference allows the features to form meaningful groups that improve the ability to classify specific clusters.

Table 5. Correlation analysis of data features in terms of MI and SU.

Datasets	MI			SU		
	max	min	avg	max	min	avg
Soybean	1	0	0.0665	1	0	0.2166
WBCD	0.4435	0.1167	0.2097	0.4433	0.1058	0.2067
Mushroom	0.6980	0	0.1468	0.6972	0	0.1345
Tic-Tac-Toe	0.0348	0.0006	0.0123	0.0348	0.0006	0.0123
promoters	0.1332	0.0050	0.0371	0.1332	0.0050	0.0370
SPECT	0.4846	0	0.0519	0.4846	. 0	0.0517

5   Conclusion

In this paper, we presented a new subspace clustering algorithm for categorical data. This method constructed feature-to-cluster groups based on the collaborative relationship between features, and conducted clustering analysis with the most related feature group. The proposed algorithms not only takes advantage of the important interactions between features, but also provides new directions for efficiently clustering well-structured categorical data. Experimental results on benchmark datasets demonstrated the effectiveness of the proposed method.

References

1. Carbonera, J.L., Abel, M.: A subspace hierarchical clustering algorithm for categorical data. In: 2019 IEEE 31st International Conference on Tools with Artificial Intelligence (ICTAI), pp. 509–516. IEEE (2019)
2. Cheung, Y.M., Jia, H.: Categorical-and-numerical-attribute data clustering based on a unified similarity metric without knowing cluster number. Pattern Recogn. **46**(8), 2228–2238 (2013)
3. Jia, H., Cheung, Y.M.: Subspace clustering of categorical and numerical data with an unknown number of clusters. IEEE Trans. Neural Netw. Learn. Syst. **29**(8), 3308–3325 (2017)
4. Kuo, R.J., Zheng, Y., Nguyen, T.P.Q.: Metaheuristic-based possibilistic fuzzy k-modes algorithms for categorical data clustering. Inf. Sci. **557**, 1–15 (2021)
5. Oskouei, A.G., Balafar, M.A., Motamed, C.: FKMAWCW: categorical fuzzy k-modes clustering with automated attribute-weight and cluster-weight learning. Chaos Solitons Fract. **153**, 111–494 (2021)
6. Parsons, L., Haque, E., Liu, H.: Subspace clustering for high dimensional data: a review. ACM SIGKDD Explor. Newsl. **6**(1), 90–105 (2004)
7. Peng, L., Liu, Y.: Attribute weights-based clustering centres algorithm for initialising k-modes clustering. Clust. Comput. **22**, 6171–6179 (2019)
8. Qian, Y., Li, F., Liang, J., Liu, B., Dang, C.: Space structure and clustering of categorical data. IEEE Trans. Neural Netw. Learn. Syst. **27**(10), 2047–2059 (2015)
9. Yu, L., Liu, H.: Efficient feature selection via analysis of relevance and redundancy. J. Mach. Learn. Res. **5**, 1205–1224 (2004)

Learning Graph Neural Networks
on Feature-Missing Graphs

Jun Hu[1,2,3], Jinyan Wang[1,2,3(✉)], Quanmin Wei[3], Du Kai[3],
and Xianxian Li[1,2,3(✉)]

[1] Key Lab of Education Blockchain and Intelligent Technology,
Ministry of Education, Guangxi Normal University, Guilin 541004, China
{wangjy612,lixx}@gxnu.edu.cn
[2] Guangxi Key Lab of Multi-Source Information Mining and Security,
Guangxi Normal University, Guilin 541004, China
[3] School of Computer Science and Engineering, Guangxi Normal University,
Guilin 541004, China

Abstract. Graph neural networks have demonstrated state-of-the-art performance in many graph analysis tasks. However, relying on both node features and topology completeness can be challenging, especially as node features may be completely missing. Existing efforts that direct node feature completion suffer from several limitations on feature-missing graphs. In this paper, we propose a novel and general extension for running graph neural networks on feature-missing graphs via complete missing node feature information in the embedding space, called GNN-FIC. Specifically, it utilizes a Feature Information Generator to simulate missing feature information in the embedding space and then completes the node embedding using the predicted missing feature information. Additionally, GNN-FIC introduces two alignment mechanisms and a relation constraint mechanism, aiding in generating high-quality missing feature information. Extensive experiments on four benchmark datasets have shown that our proposed method provides consistent performance gains compared with several advanced methods.

Keywords: Graph neural network · Graph analysis · Node embedding · Graph representation learning · Feature-missing graph

1 Introduction

The graph is a general data format that models the relationships among entities in complex networks, typically composed of nodes and edges connecting the nodes. Graphs can represent data from a wide range of real-world domains, such as social networks, knowledge graphs, citation networks, etc. Numerous methods of graph representation learning have been proposed to extract implicit information and general patterns from graphs. More specifically, graph representation learning aims at mapping high-dimensional node features to low-dimensional and continuous vector representations while preserving the topological information whenever feasible. Graph neural network is a more sophisticated method that learns low-dimensional node embeddings by recursively aggregating information about the nodes and their local neighbors through non-linear transformations.

However, the existing graph neural networks assume that both node features and topology are available. In general, the completeness of topology is easily satisfied, but node features may be inaccessible. For example, the Weibo social network has technical limitations that prevent the crawl with users' specific sensitive information or all information of some users, which results in incomplete node features (called feature-incomplete graph) or missing features of some nodes (called feature-missing graph). Incomplete or missing node features pose difficulty for graph neural networks. This paper focuses on the more challenging problem of running graph neural networks on feature-missing graphs since feature-incomplete graphs have been well-studied.

Due to the different characteristics of graphs compared to traditional data [3,8], the data imputation methods are not applicable to graphs. The SAT [4] method, which relies on the shared-latent space assumption in graph representation learning, on the other hand, generates missing node features using the distribution alignment technique. The other advanced method, GCNmf [13], utilizes Gaussian mixture model in co-training with graph neural network to predict the missing node features in an end-to-end manner. However, these efforts to directly recover the missing node features in feature-missing graphs suffer from several limitations: 1) the high dimensionality of node features leads to a high computational cost of completing features directly; 2) node features are typically correlated with specific semantics, and direct completion of node features may result in out-of-domain features; and 3) existing methods cannot handle both discrete and continuous node features, which may introduce additional noise.

To address the above limitations, we propose a novel node feature information completion strategy, which completes nodes with missing feature information in the embedding space to avoid the disadvantageous effects of directly completing node features. Hinged on this strategy, as illustrated in Fig. 1, we realize a general extension for graph neural networks called the GNN-FIC framework. The framework is designed to complete missing feature information in the first layer of the embedding space. Furthermore, two alignment mechanisms and a relation constraint mechanism are introduced to guide the high-quality missing feature information for better matching the true value. The main contributions of this paper are summarised as follows:

- To our best knowledge, this is the first attempt to complete missing node feature information in the node embedding space for graph neural networks applied to feature-missing graphs.
- We propose a general and flexible graph neural network extension in an end-to-end manner, called GNN-FIC.
- We conduct extensive experiments on four real benchmark datasets. The proposed GNN-FIC obtains consistent performance gains in comparison to a comprehensive suite of baselines.

2 Methodology

2.1 Notation

Given a graph $G = (V, E)$ with node features X, where $V = \{v_1, v_2, ..., v_N\}$ is the set of nodes with N elements, E is the set of edges and is usually denoted by an adjacency matrix $A = \{0, 1\}^{N \times N}$, and $X \in \mathbb{R}^{N \times d_X}$ is the feature matrix with d_X dimensions. Let $V_o \subseteq V$ be the set of nodes with observed node features $X_o \subseteq X$, and $V_m \subseteq V$ be the set with missing features $X_m \subseteq X$. The mask matrix $\mathrm{M} = \{0, 1\}^{N \times N}$ is used to indicate whether a node feature is observed at each position in X.

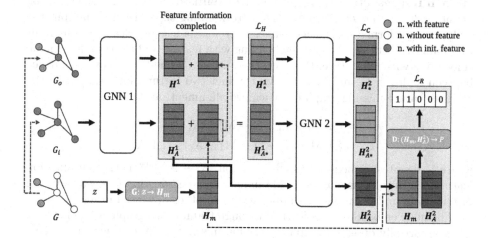

Fig. 1. Overall framework of GNN-FIC

2.2 Feature Information Completion

As discussed earlier, graph neural networks cannot work when node features are incomplete and missing. To address this issue on feature-missing graphs, previous methods that imputation missing node features before learning node embeddings may introduce unexpected noise, resulting in node embeddings in downstream tasks with poor performance. Hence, we attempt to complete feature information in the embedding space, as follows:

$$H + H_m = H_*, \tag{1}$$

where H is the learned node embedding, H_m is the output of the Feature Information Generator $G : z \to H_m$, and H_* is the completed node embedding. The Generator utilizes the latent variable $z \sim p_z(z)$, which follows the Gaussian distribution, as input. To enhance the expressive power, we integrate two layers of multi-layer perceptron into the Feature Information Generator G or another advanced model if needed.

2.3   Alignment Mechanisms

One way to complete the missing feature information in node embedding is to directly utilize the information H_m predicted by the Generator G. However, the unconstrained H_m may be an outlier or invalid values. Therefore, we introduce two alignment mechanisms in GNN-FIC to constrain the Generator G for simulating promising missing information in the embedding space. The first is the hidden representation alignment mechanism between the outputs of the first layer, H_*^1 and H_{A*}^1. The second is the consistency alignment among the outputs of the output layer, H_*^2, H_{A*}^2, and H_A^2.

Hidden Representation Alignment Mechanism. Simulating the promising missing information H_m requires the corresponding supervision signal, but the real missing information is inaccessible. Therefore, a feasible idea is to constraint the similarity between the node embedding with feature and the completed node embedding without feature. However, there exists no one-to-one correspondence between nodes in V_o and V_m, thus we conduct two feature initialization on the original feature-missing graph G to achieve alignment, as follows:

$$
\begin{aligned}
G_o &= (A, \mathrm{M} \odot X_o + (1 - \mathrm{M}) \odot X_i), \\
G_i &= (A, \mathrm{M} \odot X_i + (1 - \mathrm{M}) \odot X_i) = (A, X_i),
\end{aligned} \tag{2}
$$

where $\odot$ denotes element-wise multiplication, $X_i \in \mathbb{R}^{N \times d_X}$ is the initialization feature, which comprises a matrix of random noise vectors that follow a Gaussian distribution, and it can also be implemented in other advanced forms.

The node embeddings are learned through training the graph neural network using a partially observed graph G_o (global missing graph G_i), which will partially contain (without any) node feature information. Therefore, we impose the operation of completing the missing feature information in the embedding space. As an example, in the first layer of embedding space, the completed embeddings of the two initialization graphs are represented as follows, respectively:

$$
\begin{aligned}
H_*^1 &= \mathrm{M} \odot H^1 + (1 - \mathrm{M}) \odot \left(H^1 + H_m\right), \\
H_{A*}^1 &= \mathrm{M} \odot \left(H_A^1 + H_m\right) + (1 - \mathrm{M}) \odot \left(H_A^1 + H_m\right) = H_A^1 + H_m,
\end{aligned} \tag{3}
$$

where H^1 and H_A^1 are the uncompleted node embedding in the first layer of G_o and G_i, respectively.

There are two reasons that support completing the first layer's embedding rather than in other layers: 1) graph neural network model typically is a serial architecture. Completing potentially missing feature information in the first layer prevents performing similar operations in other layers to reduce computational complexity; 2) The hidden embedding in the first layer carries less information from neighbor nodes with missing features, resulting in an enhanced hidden representation alignment mechanism. Formally, this mechanism in the first embedding space is defined as the Frobenius norm between H_*^1 and H_{A*}^1:

$$
\mathcal{L}_H = \left\| H_*^1 - H_{A*}^1 \right\|_2^2. \tag{4}
$$

Consistency Alignment Mechanism. To enhance the generalization capability of the GNN-FIC model, we also introduce a consistency alignment mechanism [6] that ensures consistency among three different final node embeddings, including the partially completed node embedding $\boldsymbol{H}_*^2$, the fully completed node embedding $\boldsymbol{H}_{A*}^2$, and the node embedding $\boldsymbol{H}_A^2$ which only contains topological information. The significance of consistency alignment is that it enables GNN-FIC to produce the same output for similar inputs without over-emphasizing the node's feature information. Specifically, the label distribution center of the node embedding is first calculated by averaging three node embeddings, i.e. $\bar{\boldsymbol{H}} = \frac{1}{3}\sum_{i \in \{*, A*, A\}} \boldsymbol{H}_i^2$. Finally, the consistency alignment mechanism is formalized as the distance between the three node embeddings and the label distribution center:

$$\mathcal{L}_C = \frac{1}{3} \sum_{i \in \{*, A*, A\}} \left\| \bar{\boldsymbol{H}} - \boldsymbol{H}_i^2 \right\|_2^2. \tag{5}$$

2.4 Relation Constraint Mechanism

Graphs typically consist of nodes and connections between them, which are closely related. Therefore, the predicted missing feature information in node embedding should be supported using topological information. However, its design does not achieve this purpose. Inspired by BiGAN [5], which proposes that the concatenation of two vectors represents a mapping between them, we propose a relation constraint mechanism that constrains on GNN-FIC to ensure that the predicted $\boldsymbol{H}_m$ implicitly contains topological information. To implement this mechanism, we employ a multi-layer perceptron as a Relation Discriminator $\mathbf{D}$ to distinguish the concatenation of missing information and topological embeddings. Specifically, we utilize the following loss function for the Relation Discriminator $\mathbf{D}$:

$$\begin{aligned}
\mathcal{L}_R &= \min_{\mathbf{G}} \max_{\mathbf{D}} V(\mathbf{D}, \mathbf{G}) \\
&= E_{v \in V_o} \left[\log \mathbf{D} \left(\boldsymbol{H}_m[v], \boldsymbol{H}_A^2[v] \right) \right] \\
&\quad + E_{v \in V_m} \left[\log \left(1 - \mathbf{D} \left(\boldsymbol{H}_m[v], \boldsymbol{H}_A^2[v] \right) \right) \right].
\end{aligned} \tag{6}$$

2.5 Model Objective

GNN-FIC is trained through two objectives: task-related standard loss $\mathcal{L}_T$ and auxiliary losses for graph neural networks when dealing with feature-missing graphs. For instance, when considering the node classification task, the task-related loss is denoted as the cross-entropy between the node embedding $\boldsymbol{h}_v$ of the training node $v \in V_{tr}$ and the corresponding node class y_v, i.e. $\mathcal{L}_T = \sum_{v \in V_{tr}} \text{CrossEnt}(\boldsymbol{h}_v, y_v)$. And for the auxiliary losses, it is the combination of the hidden representation alignment loss $\mathcal{L}_H$, the consistency alignment loss $\mathcal{L}_C$, and the relation constraint loss $\mathcal{L}_R$. GNN-FIC's overall loss function is defined as:

$$\mathcal{L} = \mathcal{L}_T - a\mathcal{L}_R + b\mathcal{L}_H + c\mathcal{L}_C, \tag{7}$$

where a, b, and c are hyperparameters that balance the importance of different loss terms.

3   Experiments

3.1   Experimental Setup

Datasets. We conducted extensive experiments on four benchmark datasets for evaluation, including Cora, Citeseer, AmaPhoto, and AmaComp. Cora and Citeseer are citation networks, where each node represents a research paper, and the edges represent citation relationships between the papers. AmaPhoto and AmaComp are co-purchase graphs from Amazon, where each node is an entity, and each edge connects two entities in the same transaction. We follow the standard dataset splits of the literature [13] on all datasets.

Baselines. We proposed GNN-FIC is agnostic of the graph neural network and can be flexible in combination with various graph neural network models. By default, we employ the version implemented with GCN, named GCN-FIC, as an example in our experiments. To comprehensively evaluate GCN-FIC, we compare it to nine advanced methods, including MEAN [7], SoftImp [11], GAIN [14], K-NN [2], VAE [9], GINN [12], MFT [10], SAT [4], and GCNmf [13].

Environments and Settings. For the GCN and GCN variants, we adopt the two-layer architecture and utilize the Relu activation function for each hidden layer. We set the learning rate to 0.002, the weight decay to 0.01, the hidden layer dimension to 16, and the dropout rate to 0.5. Additionally, the maximum number of epochs is set as 10,000, and the epoch number for the early stopping is set as 100 to avoid over-fitting. For the importance coefficients in the final loss function $\mathcal{L}$ of GCN-FIC, we employ Optuna [1] for efficient hyperparameter search within the range of {0.01, 0.05, 0.1, 0.2, 0.3, 0.4, 0.5, 0.6, 0.7, 0.8, 0.9, 1.0}. To simulate feature-missing graphs, we randomly mask 10%, 30%, and 50% of node features that are completely available in the benchmark datasets. Finally, we train each model 5 times and report the average node classification accuracy to eliminate the effect of random factors.

3.2   Node Classification

Table 1 summarises the node classification accuracy on feature-missing graphs and the best performance of models is **bold**. Following the community conventions, the results of most baselines are reused from work [13] with the same experimental setup. For SAT(GCN) method with a different experimental setup, we fix the same setup and report the corresponding average accuracy. From

Table 1, the following observations are obtained. Firstly, our proposed GCN-FIC achieves consistently outperforms state-of-the-art methods over datasets. For example, the improvement in average accuracy compared to SAT (GCNmf) is 1.98% (1.45%), 9.2% (1.76%), 0.35% (0.62%), and 0.37% (0.49%) on different datasets. Secondly, GCN-FIC provides consistent performance gains for various mask rates across the four datasets, indicating its ability as a general method for insensitivity to missing features. Finally, the improvement in the performance of completing feature information in the output layer (GCN-FIC*) rather than the first hidden layer (GCN-FIC) is not significant. One possible explanation is that node embedding in the last layer is concealed by excessive information from nodes lacking features, which may weaken the alignment mechanisms' effectiveness.

Table 1. Evaluation on node classification

Mask rate	Cora			Citeseer			AmaPhoto			AmaComp		
	10	30	50	10	30	50	10	30	50	10	30	50
MEAN	80.92	79.05	75.22	69.55	67.30	53.64	92.06	91.59	90.59	82.53	81.35	79.59
SoftImp	79.71	69.31	44.71	44.06	25.83	25.59	91.75	90.55	88.00	82.64	81.32	79.68
GAIN	80.53	78.36	74.25	69.47	65.88	59.96	92.04	91.49	90.63	82.76	82.11	80.76
K-NN	80.76	78.63	74.51	69.67	66.09	56.86	92.04	91.43	90.37	82.59	81.57	80.25
VAE	80.63	78.57	74.69	69.63	66.34	60.46	92.11	91.50	90.46	82.76	81.72	79.23
GINN	80.85	78.88	74.76	69.64	66.24	55.76	92.09	91.53	90.43	82.55	81.46	79.59
MFT	80.91	78.93	74.47	69.84	66.67	51.08	92.08	91.59	90.56	82.48	81.43	79.40
SAT(GCN)	81.12	78.56	71.60	63.00	38.50	24.40	92.72	91.90	90.99	86.49	85.98	83.64
GCNmf	81.65	80.67	77.43	70.44	66.57	63.44	92.45	92.08	91.52	86.37	85.80	85.24
GCN-FIC*	82.85	80.70	77.30	69.10	67.95	64.00	92.89	92.50	92.00	86.72	85.92	85.20
GCN-FIC	**83.10**	**81.30**	**77.75**	**72.20**	**69.70**	**65.90**	**93.07**	**92.70**	**92.07**	**86.86**	**86.43**	**85.26**

4   Conclusion

In this paper, we propose a novel method called GNN-FIC that addresses the challenge of running graph neural networks on feature-missing graphs. GNN-FIC aims to bridge the gap between node embeddings with and without node features. Specifically, it addresses the issue of missing node features by completing potentially missing information within the node embedding space. Furthermore, the model constrains the generation of promising missing information through the inclusion of two alignment mechanisms and a relation constraint mechanism. Finally, experimental results on four public benchmark datasets demonstrate the superiority of our method over comparison methods on feature-missing graphs.

Acknowledgements. This paper was supported by the National Natural Science Foundation of China (No. 62162005 and U21A20474), Guangxi Science and Technology Project (GuikeAA22067070 and GuikeAD21220114), Center for Applied Mathematics of Guangxi (Guangxi Normal University), Guangxi "Bagui Scholar" Teams for Innovation and Research Project, and Guangxi Collaborative Innovation Center of Multi-source Information Integration and Intelligent Processing.

References

1. Akiba, T., Sano, S., Yanase, T., et al.: Optuna: a next-generation hyperparameter optimization framework. In: International Conference on Knowledge Discovery and Data Mining, pp. 2623–2631 (2019)
2. Batista, G.E.A.P.A., Monard, M.C.: A study of k-nearest neighbour as an imputation method. In: International Conference on Health Information Science, pp. 251–260 (2002)
3. Candès, E.J., Recht, B.: Exact matrix completion via convex optimization. Found. Comput. Math. **9**, 717–772 (2008)
4. Chen, X., Chen, S., Yao, J., et al.: Learning on attribute-missing graphs. IEEE Trans. Pattern Anal. Mach. Intell. **44**, 740–757 (2020)
5. Donahue, J., Krähenbühl, P., Darrell, T.: Adversarial feature learning. In: International Conference on Learning Representations (2016)
6. Feng, W., Zhang, J., Dong, Y., et al.: Graph random neural networks for semi-supervised learning on graphs. In: Neural Information Processing Systems, pp. 22092–22103 (2020)
7. García-Laencina, P.J., Sancho-Gómez, J.L., Figueiras-Vidal, A.R.: Pattern classification with missing data: a review. Neural Comput. Appl. **19**, 263–282 (2010)
8. Hu, X., Shen, Y., Pedrycz, W., Li, Y., Wu, G.: Granular fuzzy rule-based modeling with incomplete data representation. IEEE Trans. Cybern. **52**, 6420–6433 (2021)
9. Kingma, D.P., Welling, M.: Auto-encoding variational bayes. In: International Conference on Learning Representations (2014)
10. Koren, Y., Bell, R.M., Volinsky, C.: Matrix factorization techniques for recommender systems. Computer **42**, 30–37 (2009)
11. Mazumder, R., Hastie, T.J., Tibshirani, R.: Spectral regularization algorithms for learning large incomplete matrices. J. Mach. Learn. Res. **11**, 2287–2322 (2010)
12. Spinelli, I., Scardapane, S., Uncini, A.: Missing data imputation with adversarially-trained graph convolutional networks. Neural Netw. **129**, 249–260 (2020)
13. Taguchi, H., Liu, X., Murata, T.: Graph convolutional networks for graphs containing missing features. Futur. Gener. Comput. Syst. **117**, 155–168 (2020)
14. Yoon, J., Jordon, J., van der Schaar, M.: Gain: missing data imputation using generative adversarial nets. In: International Conference on Machine Learning, pp. 5689–5698 (2018)

Dealing with Over-Reliance
on Background Graph for Few-Shot
Knowledge Graph Completion

Ruiyin Yang and Xiao Wei$^{(\boxtimes)}$

School of Computer Engineering and Science, Shanghai University, Shanghai, China
{alisonyry,xwei}@shu.edu.cn

Abstract. Few-shot knowledge graph completion (FKGC) has drawn growing research attention recently, aiming at inferring new triples using only a small number of related references. Most existing FKGC methods encode few-shot relations by capturing signals from local neighbors of each entity. However, this process dramatically relies on a thorough background knowledge graph (background KG) that is space-consuming to storage and often inaccessible in real-life cases. Moreover, they tend to overlook the underlying correlational information coming with different relations. In this paper, we attempt to address FKGC task in a practical scenario where background KG is not provided and propose a novel framework called ICOM (**I C**an **C**ount **O**n **M**yself) which aims at making full use of few-shot instances within and across relations. Specifically, we go deep into the interaction between entity pairs within specific relation and devise a 3D convolutional meta-relation learner to extract relation-specific features straightly from triple. To accumulate knowledge across relations, an analogical enhancer is then built to leverage the semantic relational correlations attentively so that correlative relations can complement each other on representation learning for better link prediction. Finally, we introduce meta-learning technique for faster adaption. Empirical studies on three real-world FKGC datasets demonstrate that ICOM shows superiority over competitive baseline methods and achieves new state-of-the-art results with different few-shot sizes.

Keywords: Knowledge Graph Completion · Few-shot Learning · Representation Learning · Link Prediction

1 Introduction

Knowledge graphs (KGs) are known as suffering from incompleteness despite their large scale. Therefore, Knowledge Graph Completion (KGC) , which aims to automatically infer missing facts by learning from existing ones, has long been a question of great interest. To this end, many models [1,12,14,17] based on knowledge graph embedding (KGE) have been proposed. These methods embed KG components into a low-dimensional vector space and assess the plausibility of triples based on which. Although they have achieved considerable performance

© The Author(s), under exclusive license to Springer Nature Switzerland AG 2023
Z. Jin et al. (Eds.): KSEM 2023, LNAI 14117, pp. 263–275, 2023.
https://doi.org/10.1007/978-3-031-40283-8_23

on various datasets, their performance significantly drops when dealing with few-shot relations. Due to the long tail effect [20], low-resourced relations abundantly exist in most KGs. For instance, around 10% of relations in Wikidata have no more than 10 triples [5], and 96% of relations in Freebase have fewer than 5 triples. Furthermore, KGs in real life are primarily dynamic and evolving, new relations with limited instances will be added no matter when the new knowledge is acquired. Thus, it is crucial to equip the KGC models with the ability to complete relations with limited resources effectively. To accommodate the few-shot scenarios, Xiong et al. [16] made the first trial and proposed GMatching, in which a neighbor encoder is devised to enhance entity embeddings with their local one-hop neighbors. Following the fashion of GMatching, a series of models, including FSRL [19], FAAN [11], GANA [10] have been proposed successively. These models differ from each other in the way to aggregate different neighbors. For instance, GMatching simply assumes that all neighbors contribute equally, while the rest further leverage techniques like various attention mechanisms to selectively aggregate neighbor information.

Despite their variant designs, there remain two major limitations for these models as follows. **1) Over-reliance on background knowledge graphs**: Existing methods depend on the background KG to obtain entity embedding and background neighbors, while a thorough background KG is hard to obtain, especially in certain areas of expertise. Although it can be easier for common sense KG like NELL, Wiki to provide background graphs for few-shot entities, it is still space-consuming to store them. Thus, for more practical scenarios, we believe that the desired models should be able to handle the FKGC task without background KG provided. Moreover, our experimental results reveal that the performance of neighbor encoder is limited when the few-shot size is considerably small. Therefore, we posit that aggregating neighbors to encode few-shot relations is not necessarily the optimal solution to FKCG since this procedure is computationally expensive. **2) Underestimation of correlation among relations**: Previous approaches tend to view the relations in KG as independent and unrelated, ignoring their semantic correlations. According to the theory of human analogical reasoning, the presence of existing similarities between two systems indicates that there are likely to be further similarities. Therefore, we argue that the few-shot relations are not entirely independent but rather come with substantial similarities, and these similarities can benefit the embedding learning of relations. For instance, the relation *TopMemberOfOrganization* apparently shares a stronger similarity with the relation *CeoOf* compared with *HasOfficeInCountry*. Intuitively, these two similar relations could benefit from each other when learning their representation in latent space and there is no doubt that the neglect of such valuable information will lead to sub-optimal performance on FKGC.

In light of the above observations, we dive into a more realistic and challenging setting where background KG is not provided and propose a novel model ICOM (**I** **C**an **C**ount **O**n **M**yself). By fully exploiting the interactive features among entity pairs and analogically aggregating relations, ICOM can encode few-shot relations without neighbor aggregation, and therefore decreases the over-reliance on background KGs. Specifically, we devise a meta-relation learner module based on 3D convolution to capture detailed entity-relation interactions directly from entity pairs while maintaining the original transitional characteristics. In addition, inspired by the analogical reasoning process of humans, an analogical enhancer is implemented to alleviate the model's hypersensitivity towards long-tail distribution. It employs an attention mechanism to extract semantic correlations among relations and further fuse different relations accordingly. Finally, a hybrid score learner is introduced to access the plausibility of query triples by taking both translation theory and prototypical distance into consideration.

In summary, our contributions are as follows: 1) This paper aims to address the over reliance on background KG that is widespread in existing models, and propose an efficient FKGC framework that can make full use of provided instances and independent of the background KG in response to practical needs. 2) Extensive experiments are conducted on three public datasets. The results demonstrate that our method naturally addresses the task of FKGC and outperforms the competing state-of-the-art model with different few-shot sizes without accessing any background KG.

2   Related Work

To deal with the few-shot challenges for knowledge graph completion, various FKGC approaches have been proposed, which can be roughly categorized into three groups:

1) Sub-graph based methods: GMatching [16] is the first approach for one-shot KGC, which consists of a vanilla neighbor encoder to average information from direct neighbors and a matching processor to calculate the similarity between triples in the support set and query set. GMatching creates a paradigm of capturing neighborhood information and encoding few-shot relations. FSRL [19] extends GMatching to few-shot scenario and adopts an attention mechanism to aggregate neighbors selectively. FAAN [11] leverages a relation-specific dynamic attention mechanism that assigns dynamic weights to neighboring entities according to different relations. GANA [10] introduces a novel gated and attentive neighbor encoder that can filter the noise neighbors and incorporate it with meta-learning to better model complex relations. HARV [18] proposes a hierarchical attention neighbor encoder to aggregate fine-grained information at relation-level and entity-level in the neighborhood, respectively.

2) Full graph based methods: GNN-FSRP [15] is the first model that introduces graph neural network for few-shot scenario. It exploits the inter-layer and intra-layer neighborhood attention to alleviate over-smoothing tendencies of deep GNNs. YANA [8] constructs a local pattern graph network using four novel abstract relations representing correlations among entities in order to tackle the solitary entities in FKGC.

3) Meta-embedding methods: MetaP [6] proposes a meta-based pattern learning framework that uses a convolutional network to encode the few-shot relations. MetaR [2] solves the FKGC task utilizing a meta-learning based module to transfer relation-specific information to new, unseen relations.

3 Proposed Framework

The overall architecture of ICOM is illustrated in Fig. 1, it consists of three major modules: meta-relation learner, analogical enhancer and score learner. First, we randomly initialize the entity embeddings and generate initial relation embeddings using the translating mechanism. We then build negative samples for positive triples correspondingly by polluting the tail entity. Afterwards, 3D convolution based meta-relation learner is used to extract meta-relations from given triples, and the positive meta-relations extracted will be fed into analogical enhancer for further augmentation by leveraging the semantic correlations among relation prototypes stored in memory block. Finally, the plausibility of query triple will be calculated by score learner. Details of these modules will be demonstrated in the following subsections.

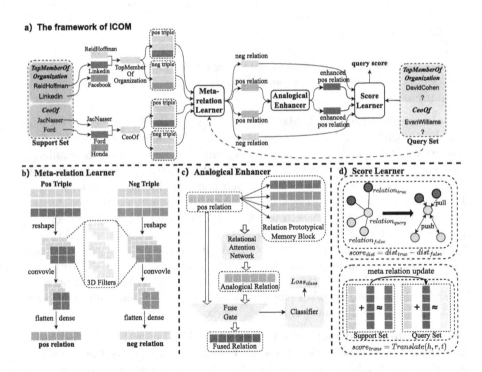

Fig. 1. An overview of our model ICOM.

3.1 Meta-relation Learner

To seek an alternative approach of neighbor encoder which is strongly dependent of background KG and computationally expensive, we utilize the power of convolutional neural network to directly extract the fundamental relation-specific pattern from the triple itself. Considering 2D convolution based ConvE [3] only focuses on the interaction between head entity and relation, therefore ignoring the translation property. We leverage 3D convolution to preserve the translation property, enabling deeper feature extraction.

Given a tripe (h, r, t), we first map the head entity and tail entity to vectors $e_h, e_t \in \mathbb{R}^k$ (k denotes the embedding dimension) using randomly initialized embedding layer to be more in line with practical needs in which pre-trained embeddings are not accessible. In light of the assumption that joint vector of head and tail entity is capable to represent the potential relation between them, we obtain a preliminary representation of relation $r \in \mathbb{R}^k$ based on given head entity e_h and tail entity e_t:

$$r = e_h - e_t \tag{1}$$

After the embedding representations are obtained, we reshape them into 2D matrix $S \in \mathbb{R}^{m \times n}(m \times n = k)$ respectively. Instead of simple concatenation, three matrices are stacked together to retain the original translation feature between entities and fed as input to a 3D convolutional layer. The stacked input is denoted as $C = [\overline{e_h}; \overline{r}; \overline{e_t}] \in \mathbb{R}^{3 \times m \times n}$, where $\overline{e_h}; \overline{r}; \overline{e_t}$ denote reshaped vectors.

After reshaping and stacking, our model convolves across the input C using a series of 3D filters. For each filter $\omega_i \in \mathbb{R}^{3 \times w_x \times w_y}$, a convolutional feature map will be generated accordingly. The feature map $v_i \in \mathbb{R}^{(m-w_x+1) \times (n-w_y+1)}$ can be calculated as:

$$v_i = g(\omega_i * C + b) = g(\omega_i * [\overline{e_h}; \overline{r}; \overline{e_t}] + b \tag{2}$$

where b is the bias and g is the activation function. We then apply for dropout on feature maps and flatten them into a vector x, the dimension of x is $(m - w_x + 1) \times (n - w_y + 1) \times 3$. Finally, we feed x into a fully connected neural network:

$$y = \sigma(W \times X + b) \tag{3}$$

where W and b are weights and bias in the neural network and y is the meta-relation extracted straightly from the interactions among specific triple (h, r, t). Note that unlike Conv3D [4], the features captured by convolutional network will not be projected, but feeded into analogical enhancer for further enhancement.

3.2 Analogical Enhancer

For few-shot relation r_i, we obtain the meta-relation representation for every triple in its support set:

$$r_i^j = MetaRelationLearner(h_j, r_i, t_j) \tag{4}$$

where r_i^j denotes the meta-relation representation of the j-th triples of the i-th relation in the support set, $j \in [1, k]$, k is the few-shot size and i, n is the total number of few-shot relations. Then we construct prototype P_{r_i} for each relation r_i by averaging all the meta-relations learned from triples in k-shot support set:

$$P_{r_n} = \frac{\sum_{j=1}^{k} r_i^j}{k} \tag{5}$$

We design a relation prototypical memory block P to store the prototype of each relation. The relation prototypical memory block will be updated synchronously with the meta-relation learner:

$$P = \{P_{r_1}, P_{r_2}, ..., P_{r_i}, ..., P_{r_n}\} \tag{6}$$

For a given relation r_i, we exploit its inherent correlation among other relations and utilize the correlation to enrich the embedding learned for r_i. An attention mechanism is adopted to adaptively adjust the correlational weight sim_i^j between different relation pair (P_{r_i}, P_{r_j}), since the degree of semantic correlation varies within relation:

$$\alpha_j = LeakyReLU(W_1^T P_{r_j}) \tag{7}$$

where α_j is the absolute attention value of the j-th relation prototype P_{r_j}, and W_1^T denotes a weight vector. The softmax function is applied afterwards:

$$\beta_j = \frac{exp(\alpha_j)}{\sum_{i=1}^{n} exp(\alpha_i)} \tag{8}$$

Not all relation prototypes can be helpful for analogical fusing. Thus, it is necessary to eliminate the noise relations due to the limited triples for each relation. To this end, we employ a gate value to let information through optionally:

$$gate = sigmoid(W_2^T \sum_{j=1}^{n} \beta_j P_{r_j}) \tag{9}$$

Based on the gating mechanism, we can obtain the final representation for relation r_i by adaptively determining the proportion between the original meta-relation prototype P_{r_i} and its correlational relation prototypes:

$$r_i' = \sum_{j=1}^{n} gate \cdot \beta_j + (1 - gate) \cdot W_3 \cdot P_{r_i} \tag{10}$$

To further minimize possible confusion during fusion, we introduce a cross entropy loss to make sure the representation learned is enhanced with the help of other relations while maintaining its own identity:

$$loss_{class} = \frac{1}{n} \sum_{i=1}^{n} -log(softmax(r_i'^T W_4)) \tag{11}$$

where W_4 is the classification weight matrix.

3.3   Score Learner

Score learner is designed to measure the validity of triples by taking two different scores into consideration: $score_{trans}$ and $score_{dist}$. The former measures the credibility of triple in the view of translation theory as well as the latter aims to pull the positive references closer to true query triples while pushing the negative references further.

We leverage the Model-Agnostic Meta-Learning algorithm to enable a rapid gradient update on the relation vector learned from the support set before optimize the whole model on query set. In light of the great success of translation model, we borrow the core idea of TransE and design the score function as follows:

$$score_{trans}(h, r, t) = \|h + r - t\| \tag{12}$$

where h,t represent the embedding of head entity and tail entity, r is the relation vector learned by analogical enhancer, $\|x\|$ denotes the L2 norm of vector x.

We first apply this score function on every triple in support set S_r and calculate the following loss as:

$$loss_{trans}(S_r) = \sum_{(h_i, r, t_i)} max[0, score_{trans}(h_i, r, t_i) - score_{trans}(h_i, r, t_i') + \gamma] \tag{13}$$

where γ is a margin which is a hyperparameter and (h_i, r, t_i') denote the negative triple generated by corrupting the tail entity in (h_i, r, t_i). Furthermore, the gradient of relation vector can be calculated based on $loss_{trans}(S_r)$ as follows:

$$Grad(r) = \nabla r Loss_{trans}(S_r) \tag{14}$$

Then, we can make a rapid update on relation vector before evaluate the query set by score learner since the gradients of parameters indicate how the parameters should be updated:

$$r' = r - \ell_r Grad(r) \tag{15}$$

where ℓ_r indicates the learning rate when updating relation vector on the support set. Afterward, we transfer the updated relation vector to query set and follow the same way to score the query set Q_r:

$$loss_{trans}(Q_r) = \sum_{(h_j, r', t_j)} max[0, score_{trans}(h_j, r', t_j) - score_{trans}(h_j, r', t_j') + \gamma]$$

$$\tag{16}$$

where (h_j, r', t_j) is a triple in query set with relation vector updated, and $loss_{trans}(Q_r)$ is one of our optimization objectives for training the whole model.Even though the score function built on translation theory has proven to be efficient, with a limited number of instances given, some negative query triples are misjudged as positive ones. To make full use of both positive samples and negative samples, we feed the triples from support set, negative set and query set to meta-relation learner to extract their relations respectively and introduce $score_{dist}$ as follows:

$$dist_{pos} = \|rel_{query} - rel_{pos}\|, dist_{neg} = \|rel_{query} - rel_{neg}\| \qquad (17)$$

$$score_{dist} = \|dist_{pos} - dist_{neg}\| \qquad (18)$$

where $\|x - y\|$ denotes the Euclidean distance between vector x and y and $score_{dist}$ should be large for true triples since our goal is to reduce the distance between rel_{query} and rel_{pos} but to increase which between rel_{query} and rel_{neg}.

3.4   Optimization

To take full advantage of two scores we designed for score learner and support the analogical enhancer, we follow the joint learning paradigm and design our overall optimization objective as:

$$\mathcal{L} = loss_{trans}(Q_r) + \lambda loss_{dist} + \mu loss_{class} \qquad (19)$$

wherein, λ and μ are trade-off hyperparameters for balancing the importance among different losses. We minimize the above function by gradient descent during training.

4   Experimental Results

4.1   Dataset and Baseline

Table 1. Details of experimental datasets. #BG denotes the number of relations in background KG. #Tasks denotes the number of few-shot relations

Dataset	#Entity	#Triples	#Relation	#BG	#Tasks	#Train	#Valid	#Test
NELL-One	68,545	181,109	358	291	67	51	5	11
Wiki-One	4,838,244	5,859,240	822	639	183	133	16	34
COVID19-One	4,800	6,872	18	0	18	9	5	4

Dataset: We conduct experiments on three real world public datasets: NELL-One, Wiki-One and COVID19-One. The first two datasets are constructed and released by GMatching [16], in order to meet the evaluating needs for FKGC tasks. In both datasets, relations with less than 500 but more than 50 triples are selected as few-shot tasks. As for COVID19-One, a medical dataset consisting entirely of few-shot relations and lacks the background KG, is built and released on the base of public COVID-19 dataset by MetaP [6]. More details are shown in Table 1.

Baseline: In order to verify the effectiveness of our method, we select the most representative and competitive KGC models as our baselines, and these models can fall into two categories:*1) Graph Neural Network Models*: These models mostly make link prediction by encoding all the entities in KG with multi-layer message passing neural network to capture features from their multi-hop neighbors, including **RA-GCN** [13], **GNN-FSRP** [15] and **YANA** [8]. *2) Few-shot Learning Models*: These models are proposed specifically to handle the FKGC tasks, following the fashion of few-shot learning paradigm, and therefore achieve state-of-the-art performance. We select **MetaR** [2], **MetaP** [6], **GMatching** [16], **FSRL** [19], **RSCL** [7], **FAAN** [11], **HARV** [18]**GANA** [10] as baselines.

4.2   Implementation Details and Evaluation Metrics

1) **Implementation Details:** To fully test the capabilities of our model, we use not only randomly initialized embeddings but also embeddings pretrained on available background KG using TransE [1]. The embedding dimension is set to 100, 50 and 100 for NELL-One, Wiki-One and COVID19-One respectively. We set the trade-off parameters λ, μ to 0.7 and 0.1 respectively, and the margin γ is fixed at 1.0. We tune all the hyperparameters for the proposed model by grid search on the validation set.

2) **Evaluation Metrics:** We utilize two traditional metrics MRR and Hits@N on both datasets to measure the performance of ICOM and baselines for FKGC task. With given head entity h_q and few-shot relation r_q, both metrics will evaluate the ranking of tail entity t_q among the candidates C_q. MRR is the mean reciprocal rank and Hits@N represent the proportion of correct tail entities ranked in the top N, with $N = 1, 5, 10$. For both of the metrics, the higher values are indicative of better performance of KG completion.

4.3   Main Results

Since our main goal is to reduce the dependence on the pre-trained embeddings and background KG, we first perform 1-shot, 3-shot and 5-shot FKGC task with randomly initialized entity embeddings on NELL-One, Wiki-One and COVID19-One. Table 2 shows that ICOM achieves consistently superiority over other baselines on three datasets in all metrics and achieves the state-of-the-art performance. Compared with the models taking advantage of the neighbor information, the performance lead of ICOM gradually decreases with the increase of few-shot size. We believe it is because as the few-shot size increases, such models have obtained enough information from neighbor aggregation to compensate for the lack of information in random embeddings. It also proves that the neighbor encoder is not cost-effective when the few-shot size is too small, such as 1-shot, 3-shot.

Table 2. Experiment results of FKGC with randomly initialized entity embeddings. **Bold** numbers are the best results. <u>Underline</u> numbers indicate the second-best results.

NELL-One	MRR			Hit@10			Hit@5			Hit@1		
	1-shot	3-shot	5-shot	1-shot	3-shot	5-shot	1-shot	3-shot	5-shot	1-shot	3-shot	5-shot
GMatching	0.151	0.178	0.189	0.252	0.287	0.291	0.186	0.192	0.204	0.103	0.129	0.136
MetaR	0.194	0.183	0.199	<u>0.312</u>	<u>0.305</u>	<u>0.338</u>	0.253	<u>0.248</u>	0.259	0.129	0.111	0.130
MetaP	<u>0.216</u>	0.171	0.172	0.303	0.235	0.242	<u>0.265</u>	0.199	0.195	<u>0.166</u>	0.138	0.136
FAAN	0.163	0.189	<u>0.215</u>	0.204	0.177	0.147	0.120	0.233	<u>0.288</u>	0.163	<u>0.159</u>	<u>0.153</u>
GANA	0.149	<u>0.198</u>	0.183	0.254	0.303	0.283	0.204	0.247	0.224	0.100	0.139	0.125
ICOM	**0.231**	**0.243**	**0.255**	**0.337**	**0.348**	**0.383**	**0.294**	**0.277**	**0.339**	**0.187**	**0.243**	**0.194**
Wiki-One	MRR			Hit@10			Hit@5			Hit@1		
	1-shot	3-shot	5-shot	1-shot	3-shot	5-shot	1-shot	3-shot	5-shot	1-shot	3-shot	5-shot
GMatching	0.198	0.213	0.222	0.286	0.305	0.315	0.260	0.288	0.291	0.133	0.142	0.151
MetaR	0.193	0.204	0.221	0.280	0.292	0.302	0.233	0.245	0.264	0.152	0.157	0.178
MetaP	<u>0.226</u>	0.232	0.229	0.291	0.320	0.311	0.265	0.304	0.288	<u>0.218</u>	0.197
FAAN	0.208	0.249	0.278	<u>0.278</u>	0.319	0.333	0.255	0.282	<u>0.327</u>	0.174	0.206	0.208
GANA	0.214	<u>0.256</u>	0.273	<u>0.299</u>	<u>0.324</u>	<u>0.342</u>	<u>0.274</u>	<u>0.315</u>	0.321	<u>0.187</u>	0.213	<u>0.231</u>
ICOM	**0.253**	**0.278**	**0.289**	**0.324**	**0.346**	**0.388**	**0.303**	**0.323**	**0.335**	**0.228**	**0.240**	**0.243**
COVID19-One	MRR			Hit@10			Hit@5			Hit@1		
	1-shot	3-shot	5-shot	1-shot	3-shot	5-shot	1-shot	3-shot	5-shot	1-shot	3-shot	5-shot
GMatching	0.184	0.193	0.202	0.213	0.234	0.237	0.201	0.222	0.227	0.139	0.151	0.157
MetaR	0.215	0.223	0.231	0.275	0.296	<u>0.314</u>	0.230	0.247	0.256	0.164	0.216	0.221
MetaP	<u>0.226</u>	<u>0.239</u>	0.250	<u>0.281</u>	<u>0.299</u>	0.289	<u>0.252</u>	<u>0.259</u>	0.265	<u>0.188</u>	<u>0.209</u>	0.215
FAAN	0.207	0.235	0.253	0.265	0.284	0.311	0.248	0.252	<u>0.269</u>	0.163	0.181	<u>0.227</u>
GANA	0.211	0.234	<u>0.256</u>	0.191	0.255	0.297	0.187	0.234	0.285	0.171	0.195	0.200
ICOM	**0.321**	**0.366**	**0.412**	**0.437**	**0.495**	**0.498**	**0.383**	**0.441**	**0.473**	**0.252**	**0.284**	**0.360**

To obtain a more comprehensive understanding of our proposed model, we also use pre-trained embedding based on TransE. Because COVID19-One lacks background KG, so we leave it out in this section. The results are shown in Table 3.

Compared together with the models which leverage, ICOM still outperforms all other models in all metrics except for GANA and GNN-FSRP on NELL-One. GNN-FSRP is a full graph model which encode the whole knowledge graph and GANA uses an adaptive gated neighbor encoder to enhance its entity representation. It is worth noting that NELL-One does not suffer from severe sparsity problem and can provide sufficient background neighborhood information for each entity. This therefore makes models capable to take advantage of rich graph contexts based on background KG can perform better on this dataset. Our model gains relatively stable improvements on Wiki-One expect for 5-shot scenario. Note that unlike NELL-One, Wiki-One is a large-scale and very sparse dataset, where nearly 99% of entities has less than 5 neighbors. This very sparsity prevents most models, including ours from fully performing on Wiki-One. YANA achieves the SOTA in 5-shot scenario, it is a graph neural network based model which focus specifically on the solitary entity issue and therefore very suitable for this dataset.

Table 3. Experiment results of FKGC using pre-trained embeddings and background KG. **Bold** numbers are the best results. Underline numbers indicate the second-best results.

NELL-One	MRR			Hit@10			Hit@5			Hit@1		
	1-shot	3-shot	5-shot	1-shot	3-shot	5-shot	1-shot	3-shot	5-shot	1-shot	3-shot	5-shot
RA-GCN	0.268	–	0.280	0.406	–	0.442	0.344	-	0.358	0.146	–	0.144
GNN-FSRP	0.322	–	0.336	0.479	–	0.518	**0.429**	–	**0.442**	0.221	–	0.218
YANA	–	–	0.294	–	–	0.421	–	–	0.364	–	–	0.230
GMatching	0.185	0.279	0.276	0.313	0.464	0.394	0.260	0.370	0.333	0.119	0.198	0.153
MetaR	0.164	0.183	0.209	0.331	0.346	0.355	0.238	0.265	0.280	0.093	0.129	0.141
MetaP	0.232	0.247	0.258	0.330	0.388	0.413	0.281	0.317	0.340	0.179	0.213	0.225
FSRL	0.192	0.197	0.184	0.326	0.331	0.272	0.262	0.267	0.234	0.119	0.121	0.136
HARV	–	0.293	–	–	0.433	–	–	0.365	–	–	0.221	–
FAAN	0.195	0.231	0.279	0.374	0.397	0.428	0.291	0.318	0.364	0.151	0.182	0.200
GANA	0.307	0.322	**0.344**	0.483	0.510	0.517	0.409	**0.432**	0.437	0.211	0.225	**0.246**
ICOM	**0.331**	**0.338**	0.342	**0.495**	**0.516**	**0.527**	0.418	0.419	0.424	**0.235**	**0.239**	0.243
Wiki-One	MRR			Hit@10			Hit@5			Hit@1		
	1-shot	3-shot	5-shot	1-shot	3-shot	5-shot	1-shot	3-shot	5-shot	1-shot	3-shot	5-shot
RA-GNN	0.211	–	0.241	0.337	–	0.364	0.283	–	0.321	0.125	–	0.146
GNN-FSRP	0.220	–	0.252	0.390	–	0.420	0.300	–	0.338	0.138	–	0.161
YANA	–	–	**0.380**	–	–	**0.523**	–	–	**0.442**	–	–	**0.327**
GMatching	0.200	0.171	0.263	0.336	0.324	0.387	0.272	0.235	0.337	0.120	0.095	0.197
MetaR	0.310	0.316	0.323	0.404	0.401	0.418	**0.375**	0.379	0.385	0.266	0.264	0.270
MetaP	0.245	0.298	0.201	0.337	0.366	0.282	0.279	0.329	0.249	0.207	0.263	0.157
FSRL	0.211	0.239	0.258	0.319	0.355	0.387	0.288	0.295	0.306	0.182	0.176	0.197
HARV	–	0.214	–	–	0.354	–	–	0.272	–	–	0.151	–
FAAN	0.226		0.341	0.374		0.463	0.302		0.395	0.153		0.281
GANA	0.301	0.331	0.351	0.416	0.425	0.446	0.350	**0.389**	0.407	0.231	0.283	0.299
ICOM	**0.328**	**0.336**	0.355	**0.424**	**0.441**	0.468	0.367	0.379	0.392	**0.284**	**0.295**	0.310

4.4   Ablation Study

To investigate the contribution of each module proposed and evaluate our method comprehensively, we conduct the following ablation studies on NELL-One in one-shot scenario. The experiment results are shown in Table 4.

1) **Impacts of Meta-Relation Learner:** We replace meta-relation learner with a 2-layers fully connected neural network to analyze the impact of which . we observe a significant performance drop when 3D convolutional based meta-relation learner is replaced by MLP, which emphasizes the need for capturing deep interactions between entity pairs while keeping translation property to learn

Table 4. Ablation Study on NELL-One in one-shot scenario

Models	MRR	Hits@10	Hits@5	Hits@1
whole model	0.231	0.337	0.294	0.187
w/o meta-relation learner	0.204	0.312	0.253	0.139
w/o analogical enhancer	0.219	0.320	0.266	0.161

relation-specific representation from limited instances. 2) **Impacts of Analogical Enhancer:** The performance drops when we remove the analogical enhancer from the whole model. It proves that learning from other correlational relations is beneficial to improve the quality of relation vector in few-shot scenario. In addition, we also provide the visualization of all relations on NELL-One using t-SNE [9]. As shown in Fig. 2, semantically similar relations get closer in embedding space when analogical enhancer is implemented.

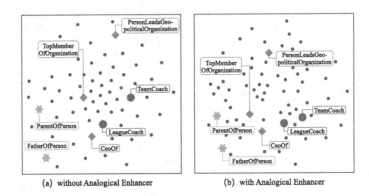

(a) without Analogical Enhancer   (b) with Analogical Enhancer

Fig. 2. t-SNE visualization of relation embeddings with and without analogical enhancer in NELL-One.

5   Conclusion

Previous studies rely heavily on background KG, ignoring the fact that a thorough background KG is often inaccessible in real life. Besides, they tend to neglect the correlations among relations which can benefit the relation embedding learning. Therefore, we propose a framework which is independent of background KG and can fully take advantage of relation's semantic correlations. The experimental results illustrate the superiority of our model over other competitive baselines on three few-shot datasets. Besides, we demonstrate the effectiveness of each component of the model through ablation studies. We notice that the very sparsity of Wiki-One has posed a challenge for our model, therefore, we will focus on reducing the impact of sparse data in our future work.

References

1. Bordes, A., Usunier, N., García-Durán, A., Weston, J., Yakhnenko, O.: Translating embeddings for modeling multi-relational data. In: NIPS (2013)
2. Chen, M., Zhang, W., Zhang, W., Chen, Q., Chen, H.: Meta relational learning for few-shot link prediction in knowledge graphs. arXiv abs/1909.01515 (2019)

3. Dettmers, T., Minervini, P., Stenetorp, P., Riedel, S.: Convolutional 2D knowledge graph embeddings. In: AAAI Conference on Artificial Intelligence (2017)
4. Feng, W.H., Zha, D., Wang, L., Guo, X.: Convolutional 3D embedding for knowledge graph completion. In: 2022 IEEE 25th International Conference on Computer Supported Cooperative Work in Design (CSCWD), pp. 1197–1202 (2022)
5. Gabrilovich, E., Markovitch, S.: Wikipedia-based semantic interpretation for natural language processing. J. Artif. Intell. Res. **34**, 443–498 (2014)
6. Jiang, Z., Gao, J., Lv, X.: Metap: meta pattern learning for one-shot knowledge graph completion. In: Proceedings of the 44th International ACM SIGIR Conference on Research and Development in Information Retrieval (2021)
7. Li, Y., Yu, K., Zhang, Y., Wu, X.: Learning relation-specific representations for few-shot knowledge graph completion. arXiv abs/2203.11639 (2022)
8. Liang, Y., Zhao, S., Cheng, B., Yin, Y., Yang, H.: Tackling solitary entities for few-shot knowledge graph completion. In: Knowledge Science, Engineering and Management (2022)
9. van der Maaten, L., Hinton, G.E.: Visualizing data using t-SNE. J. Mach. Learn. Res. **9**, 2579–2605 (2008)
10. Niu, G., et al.: Relational learning with gated and attentive neighbor aggregator for few-shot knowledge graph completion. In: Proceedings of the 44th International ACM SIGIR Conference on Research and Development in Information Retrieval (2021)
11. Sheng, J., et al.: Adaptive attentional network for few-shot knowledge graph completion. In: Conference on Empirical Methods in Natural Language Processing (2020)
12. Sun, Z., Deng, Z., Nie, J.Y., Tang, J.: Rotate: knowledge graph embedding by relational rotation in complex space. arXiv abs/1902.10197 (2018)
13. Tian, A., Zhang, C., Rang, M., Yang, X., Zhan, Z.: RA-GCN: relational aggregation graph convolutional network for knowledge graph completion. In: Proceedings of the 2020 12th International Conference on Machine Learning and Computing (2020)
14. Trouillon, T., Welbl, J., Riedel, S., Gaussier, É., Bouchard, G.: Complex embeddings for simple link prediction. In: International Conference on Machine Learning (2016)
15. Wang, Y., Zhang, H.: Introducing graph neural networks for few-shot relation prediction in knowledge graph completion task. In: Knowledge Science, Engineering and Management (2021)
16. Xiong, W., Yu, M., Chang, S., Guo, X., Wang, W.Y.: One-shot relational learning for knowledge graphs. In: Conference on Empirical Methods in Natural Language Processing (2018)
17. Yang, B., tau Yih, W., He, X., Gao, J., Deng, L.: Embedding entities and relations for learning and inference in knowledge bases. CoRR abs/1412.6575 (2014)
18. Yuan, X., Xu, C., Li, P., Chen, Z.: Relational learning with hierarchical attention encoder and recoding validator for few-shot knowledge graph completion. In: Proceedings of the 37th ACM/SIGAPP Symposium on Applied Computing (2022)
19. Zhang, C., Yao, H., Huang, C., Jiang, M., Li, Z.J., Chawla, N.: Few-shot knowledge graph completion. In: AAAI Conference on Artificial Intelligence (2019)
20. Zhang, N., et al.: Long-tail relation extraction via knowledge graph embeddings and graph convolution networks. In: North American Chapter of the Association for Computational Linguistics (2019)

Kernel-Based Feature Extraction for Time Series Clustering

Yuhang Liu[1], Yi Zhang[1], Yang Cao[2(✉)], Ye Zhu[2], Nayyar Zaidi[2],
Chathu Ranaweera[2], Gang Li[2], and Qingyi Zhu[1]

[1] School of Cyber Security and Information Law,
Chongqing University of Posts and Telecommunications,
Chongqing 400065, China
{S200231161,s220802019}@stu.cqupt.edu.cn, zhuqy@cqupt.edu.cn
[2] Centre for Cyber Resilience and Trust, Deakin University,
Burwood, VIC 3125, Australia
{charles.cao,ye.zhu}@ieee.org,
{nayyar.zaidi,schathu.ranaweera,gang.li}@deakin.edu.au

Abstract. Time series clustering is a key unsupervised data mining technique that has been widely applied in various domains for discovering patterns, insights and applications. Extracting meaningful features from time series is crucial for clustering. However, most existing feature extraction algorithms fail to capture the complex and dynamic patterns in time series data. In this paper, we propose a novel kernel-based feature extraction algorithm that utilizes a data-dependent kernel function with an efficient dimensionality reduction method. Our algorithm can adapt to the local data distribution and represent high-frequency subsequences of time series effectively. We demonstrate that, with a bag-of-words model, our feature extraction algorithm outperforms other existing methods for time series clustering on many real-world datasets from various domains.

Keywords: Time series clustering · Encoder · Feature descriptor · Isolation kernel · Dimensionality reduction

1 Introduction

A time series dataset is a sequence of data points arranged in chronological order, and it is a common data type that appears in many domains. Time series clustering, as a crucial unsupervised data mining technique, has become a popular research topic recently. The purpose of time series clustering is to identify hidden patterns and structures from time series and put similar time series data into related or homogeneous groups. This can be useful for applications such as healthcare [16], cyber security [10] and manufacturing [17].

Time series clustering can be roughly divided into three categories: similarity-based, model-based and feature-based. Similarity-based methods rely on the refinement of the predefined similarity measurement to improve the accuracy of clustering, such as dynamic time warping (DTW). However, most similarity-based

Z. Jin et al. (Eds.): KSEM 2023, LNAI 14117, pp. 276–283, 2023.
https://doi.org/10.1007/978-3-031-40283-8_24

methods cannot effectively consider the relationship between local matching between sequences and the time dependence of time series [21].

Model-based time series clustering methods accomplish the fitting of a training data set by using an algorithmic model and corresponding parameters, and use the fitted iterated parameter model to perform the category evaluation of the generalized data. However, these methods are based on a specific assumption of data distribution that may not be generalized. Moreover, feature-based methods extract features from the original time series data, and then carry out relevant coding for those features, before finally applying an appropriate clustering algorithm on the encoded sequences. Feature extraction methods can usually focus on either local features or global features. They usually require strong observation and feature processing experience, i.e., need to find out the features that can best describe time series data with good interpretation.

The Bag-of-Words (BoW) is an effective feature coding framework for machine learning and has achieved good results in the field of time series classification [9]. In order to identify more meaningful patterns from various kinds of time series, we propose a kernel-based time series feature descriptor in this paper. It can effectively extract feature representations from short subsequence representations of time series, and then encode and combine the representations with the BoW framework.

To the best of our knowledge, this work is the first to apply kernel functions to time series feature extraction for clustering. In this paper, we have the following two main contributions:

- Propose a kernel-based time series encoding framework to extract meaningful features of subsequences. It combines a data-dependent kernel function with efficient dimensionality reduction in a BoW framework. By leveraging the advantages of Isolation Kernel, it is adaptive to local data distribution and enables the clustering algorithm to discover more meaningful patterns.
- Verify the effectiveness of the proposed framework on 12 real-world datasets. Spectral clustering based on our encoded features usually achieved better clustering performance than other clustering/encoding methods.

This paper is organised as follows. Section 2 describes the relevant work about feature extraction for time series. We introduce the kernel functions and the encoding framework in detail in Sect. 3. Section 4 provides experimental evaluation. The conclusion and the future work are in Sect. 5.

2   Related Work

Most time series clustering algorithms can be divided into three important subtasks, including feature extraction, metric calculations on the extracted features, and clustering the extracted features according to their similarities.

Regarding feature extraction, Shapelet is a representative subsequence extraction method proposed by Ye et al. [18]. It measures the similarity between shapelets extracted from different time series. However, this feature ignores the information on the overall characteristics of the time series, although it provides good interpretability. Wang et al. [15] then introduce a piecewise aggregate approximation representation for shapelet classification.

Recently, Bag-of-Words (BoW) and Bag-of-Features (BoF) models have been applied in time-series analysis. These methods are originally used in natural language processing, typically for document classification characterized by the frequency of occurrence of each word. The key idea is to represent a time series by a histogram of words in a dictionary defined by quantized segments. Zhang and Alexander [19] use the statistical features based on BoF for modelling human activities. Hatami et al. [4] embedded recursive graphs on the basis of the BoF framework, converting traditional 1-dimensional time series data into 2-dimensional texture images, so that existing texture feature extraction algorithms can work well on time series.

Time series data essentially have high dimensionality which brings a range of challenges. Additionally, variable length and uncertain noise make it difficult to apply traditional point-to-point distance measures. The dimensionality reduction method can be used to preserve the original structural information of the sequence, for example, the most commonly used algorithms are PCA [2] and MDS [5]. Regarding the similarity search problem of variable-length sequences, Linardi et al. [7] propose the ULISSE method, an index capable of answering variable-length similarity search queries on both Z-normalized and non-Z-normalized sequences. To tackle the data noise problem, low-variance filtering or mean substitution is generally used to filter outliers before clustering.

3   Isolation Kernel-Based Time Series Encoding

In this paper, we adopt an existing BoW classification framework [20] for clustering time series. The main steps in the framework include detecting and describing local feature points, constructing feature codebooks and encoding subsequences. Here, we ultilise a data-dependent kernel (*Isolation Kernel* [11]) and a dimensionality reduction algorithm called Hierarchical 1-Nearest Neighbor graph based Embedding (*h-NNE*) [12] to effectively capture both local and global structure from time series, as shown in Fig. 1.

3.1   Detection Feature Points and Describing Representative Subsequences

This framework first selects local peak and valley points that distinguish local feature points and flat feature points, i.e., sampling more feature points in feature-rich regions, while uniformly sampling in flat regions. Afterwards, it extracts all representative subsequences of fixed length centred on these sampling points, i.e., obtaining sample subsequences as $S = \{s_1, s_2, ..., s_N\}$.

For extracting features from all representative subsequences, two local descriptors are used in the original framework. The first one is Histogram of Oriented Gradients of 1D time series (HOG-1D), introduced for object detection [6].

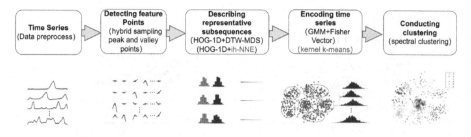

Fig. 1. Execution pipeline of our method, based on an existing encoding framework [20]. First, a hybrid sampling method is used to sample peak and valley points and identify representative subsequences. Then two descriptors are used to vectorise these subsequences. Our contributions are in both the second and third steps, i.e., using Isolation Kernel-based h-NNE and Isolation Kernel-based k-means in describing and encoding steps, respectively. Finally, it can directly apply an existing clustering algorithm on the encoded features to perform time series clustering. The red colour indicates the new proposed components to be used in the framework. (Color figure online)

It accumulates all the gradients by computing the slope between adjacent points in each subsequence. After that, it will accumulate gradient votes within orientation bins, and obtain HOG over bins. The other descriptor is Dynamic time warping-multidimensional scaling (DTW-MDS). However, DTW is sensitive to noise and magnitude shifts [3]. In order to improve the feature extraction performance, we propose to use a data-dependent kernel function (*Isolation Kernel* [11]) with an efficient dimensionality reduction method (*h-NNE* [12]) to replace the DTW-MDS in the original framework.

h-NNE [12] is a dimensionality reduction algorithm based on the hierarchy of 1-nearest neighbor graphs in the original space. h-NNE consists of three important steps: (1) constructing a tree hierarchy based on the 1-nearest neighbor graph; (2) calculating an initial projection using an approximate version of principal components analysis (PCA); (3) adjusting the projection point positions according to the constructed tree. The projection point position adjustment can be enhanced by an optional expansion step to the 1-nearest neighbor, which can be used to improve visualization using a hierarchy-based approach.

Isolation Kernel is the state-of-the-art data-dependent kernel [11,13]. The key idea of Isolation kernel is to use a space partitioning strategy to split the whole data space into ψ non-overlapping partitions based on a random sample of ψ objects from the given dataset D. The similarity between any two objects $x, y \in D$ represents how likely these two objects can be split into the same partition. Two points in a sparse region are more similar than two points of equal inter-point distance in a dense region.

Figure 2a shows an example of partitioning using the Voronoi diagram on a dataset generated from a normal distribution with the subsample size $\psi = 16$

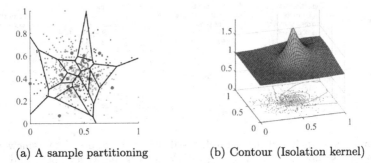

(a) A sample partitioning   (b) Contour (Isolation kernel)

Fig. 2. (a) is an example of partitioning H with $\psi = 16$, and red objects are a random subset. (b) is demonstrations of contours with reference to the point $(0.55, 0.55)$ using the Isolation kernel on a sample dataset from a normal distribution. (Color figure online)

using isolation kernel. It can be seen that there are more and smaller partitioning cells in the dense region than in the sparse region, i.e., points in a dense region are less likely to fall into the same cell and get a larger dissimilarity score to each other. For a point with equal inter-object distance from the reference object $x = (0.55, 0.55)$, points in the sparse region are more similar to x than objects in the dense region to x, as shown in Fig. 2b.

It is worth mentioning that Isolation Kernel has a finite-dimensional feature map with binary features. Here we use Isolation Kernel function as the pre-processing part of the feature descriptor encode, i.e., mapping each subsequence into the Hilbert space of Isolation Kernel before conducting h-NNE. We name the Isolation Kernel-based h-NNE as iTSE. This combination will significantly enhance h-NNE to extract the representations that consider both the local neighborhood properties and the global mass properties.

3.2 Encoding Time Series

The encoding process is to cluster time series features to construct a feature codebook. After each subsequence is described by a descriptor vector as $y_i \in \{y_1, y_2, ..., y_N\}$ from the last step, we can use a clustering method to fit the distribution of local descriptors and figure out a vector representation for each time series. The original framework uses the Fisher Vector (FV) encoding procedure with k component Gaussian mixture model (GMM) [1]. Here we propose to directly use Isolation kernel k-means to fit the distribution of local descriptors and figure out a vector representation for each time series.

Therefore, we call the new framework as *Isolation Kernel-based Time Series Encoding* (iTSE). The key procedures of iTSE are as follows.

1. Sampling the peaks and valley points using a hybrid sampling method and generating representative subsequences, i.e., sampling subsequences from landmarks in feature-rich regions, while sampling uniformly in other "flat" regions.

2. Describing representative subsequences by combining HOG-1D and *Isolation Kernel-based h-NNE* (ih-NNE).
3. Encoding each time series with a feature codebook using *Isolation kernel-based k-means*.
4. Applying an existing clustering algorithm such as spectral clustering on histogram vectors to perform time series.

4   Empirical Evaluation

In this section, we use iTSE with spectral clustering as the baseline, and compare it with two clustering algorithms k-means and k-Shape [8] that directly run on the original time series without any encoding process. To systematic evaluate the effectiveness of iTSE, we also compare other 4 variations used in the encoding process, including Zhao's original framework encoding [20], the bag-of-features (BoF) model, the h-NNE model, and ih-NNE model. For each algorithm, we search the best parameter settings in reasonable ranges, and report the best result in Adjusted Mutual Information (AMI) [14]. Note that because of randomisation for k-means like algorithms, we conduct 10 independent trials on the same dataset, and report the average AMI scores as their final results.

We collected 12 real-world datasets from a variety of fields. Before the experiments, standardization is used for each dataset to make all the feature values between -1 and 1. All experiments were conducted on a host with Intel(R) Core(TM) i5-9500 CPU @ 3.00 GHz and a 64-bit operating system, and Matlab2021a was used as the experimental development software.

Table 1 shows that iTSE achieves the highest average AMI score of 0.48 and performs better than other clustering/encoding methods on most datasets. Moreover, we have the following four key observations:

- Compared with the performance of classical k-means and k-shape algorithms, all clustering methods based on encoding have a great improvement. This confirms that better encoding will bring more meaningful features for time series clustering.
- All four variations of Zhao's framework, i..e, BoF, h-NNE, ih-NNE and TSE, achieves better performance than the original. This indicates that the extracted features can be enhanced with a better descriptor and encoder.
- It is interesting to see that there is only a tiny improvement when replacing the DTW-MDS with h-NNE for the original Zhao's framework. However, Isolation kernel can further improve the h-NNE, named as ih-NNE, to 0.46.
- iTSE shows a 2% improvement than the ih-NNE version. The only difference between iTSE and ih-NNE is that iTSE uses kernel k-means rather than GMM+Fisher Vector.

Table 1. Clustering performance of 7 algorithms on 12 datasets. The best performer on each dataset is boldfaced. n, d and c are the data size, dimensionality and number of clusters, respectively. BoF is the version replacing GMM with BoF in Zhao's model. h-NNE is the version that replaces DTW-MDS with h-NNE in Zhao's model. ih-NNE is the version that replaces DTW-MDS with Isolation Kernel-based h-NNE in Zhao's model.

Datasets	n	d	c	k-means	k-shape	Zhao's	BoF	h-NNE	ih-NNE	iTSE
Ascf1	200	1460	10	0.29	0.45	**0.54**	0.47	0.38	0.50	**0.54**
Beef	60	470	5	0.17	0.19	0.23	0.26	0.28	0.32	**0.35**
Chinatown	363	24	2	0.13	0.02	0.34	0.58	0.67	**0.82**	0.73
Fish	350	463	7	0.28	0.29	0.64	0.63	0.58	0.56	**0.72**
Ham	216	431	2	0.04	0.04	0.03	0.04	0.03	0.05	**0.08**
Lighting7	143	319	7	0.37	**0.48**	0.40	0.35	0.37	0.44	0.40
Osuleaf	441	427	6	0.20	0.36	0.42	0.51	0.45	0.51	**0.52**
Swedishleaf	1125	128	15	0.49	0.52	0.65	0.67	0.68	0.68	**0.69**
Trace	200	275	4	0.50	0.50	0.93	0.97	**1.00**	**1.00**	**1.00**
Wine	111	234	2	0.00	0.00	0.03	0.05	0.05	0.05	**0.16**
WordSynonyms	905	270	25	0.32	**0.38**	0.35	0.30	0.31	0.33	0.30
Worms	258	900	5	0.02	0.04	**0.33**	0.22	0.22	0.25	0.27
			Avg.	0.23	0.27	0.41	0.42	0.42	0.46	**0.48**

5 Conclusion

Time series clustering is challenging and has attracted a lot of attention recently. In this paper, we propose a new time series feature encoding framework iTSE for time series clustering. It utilises a data-dependent kernel function with an efficient dimensionality reduction method. This framework has the ability to encode time series focusing on high-frequent sub-sequence with the adoption of local density distribution. The experimental results on real-world datasets verify the effectiveness of our proposed framework iTSE.

Since iTSE has a few parameters involving different procedures, we will investigate how to automatically set those parameters in the future. Furthermore, we will explore the method to improve the efficiency of clustering on large time series datasets.

References

1. Baum, C.F., Schaffer, M.E., Stillman, S.: Instrumental variables and GMM: estimation and testing. Stand. Genom. Sci. **3**(1), 1–31 (2003)
2. Destefanis, G., Barge, M.T., Brugiapaglia, A., Tassone, S.: The use of principal component analysis (PCA) to characterize beef. Meat Sci. **56**(3), 255–259 (2000)
3. Dvornik, M., Hadji, I., Derpanis, K.G., Garg, A., Jepson, A.: Drop-DTW: aligning common signal between sequences while dropping outliers. Adv. Neural. Inf. Process. Syst. **34**, 13782–13793 (2021)

4. Hatami, N., Gavet, Y., Debayle, J.: Bag of recurrence patterns representation for time-series classification. Pattern Anal. Appl. **22**(3), 877–887 (2019)
5. Hout, M.C., Papesh, M.H., Goldinger, S.D.: Multidimensional scaling. Wiley Interdisc. Rev. Cogn. Sci. **4**(1), 93–103 (2013)
6. Klaser, A., Marszałek, M., Schmid, C.: A spatio-temporal descriptor based on 3D-gradients. In: BMVC 2008–19th British Machine Vision Conference, pp. 275–281. British Machine Vision Association (2008)
7. Linardi, M., Palpanas, T.: Scalable, variable-length similarity search in data series: the Ulisse approach. Proc. VLDB Endow. **11**(13), 2236–2248 (2018)
8. Paparrizos, J., Gravano, L.: k-shape: Efficient and accurate clustering of time series. In: Proceedings of the 2015 ACM SIGMOD International Conference on Management of Data, pp. 1855–1870 (2015)
9. Passalis, N., Tsantekidis, A., Tefas, A., Kanniainen, J., Gabbouj, M., Iosifidis, A.: Time-series classification using neural bag-of-features. In: 2017 25th European Signal Processing Conference (EUSIPCO), pp. 301–305. IEEE (2017)
10. Pérez, S.I., Moral-Rubio, S., Criado, R.: A new approach to combine multiplex networks and time series attributes: building intrusion detection systems (IDS) in cybersecurity. Chaos Solitons Fract. **150**, 111143 (2021)
11. Qin, X., Ting, K.M., Zhu, Y., Lee, V.C.: Nearest-neighbour-induced isolation similarity and its impact on density-based clustering. In: Proceedings of the AAAI Conference on Artificial Intelligence, vol. 33, pp. 4755–4762 (2019)
12. Sarfraz, S., Koulakis, M., Seibold, C., Stiefelhagen, R.: Hierarchical nearest neighbor graph embedding for efficient dimensionality reduction. In: Proceedings of the IEEE/CVF Conference on Computer Vision and Pattern Recognition, pp. 336–345 (2022)
13. Ting, K.M., Xu, B.C., Washio, T., Zhou, Z.H.: Isolation distributional kernel: a new tool for kernel based anomaly detection. In: Proceedings of the 26th ACM SIGKDD International Conference on Knowledge Discovery and Data Mining, pp. 198–206 (2020)
14. Vinh, N.X., Epps, J., Bailey, J.: Information theoretic measures for clusterings comparison: variants, properties, normalization and correction for chance. J. Mach. Learn. Res. **11**(Oct), 2837–2854 (2010)
15. Wang, H., Li, C., Sun, H., Guo, Z., Bai, Y.: Shapelet classification algorithm based on efficient subsequence matching. Data Sci. J. **17** (2018)
16. Wang, J., McDonald, N., Cochran, A.L., Oluyede, L., Wolfe, M., Prunkl, L.: Health care visits during the COVID-19 pandemic: a spatial and temporal analysis of mobile device data. Health and Place **72**, 102679 (2021)
17. Wang, Y., Perry, M., Whitlock, D., Sutherland, J.W.: Detecting anomalies in time series data from a manufacturing system using recurrent neural networks. J. Manuf. Syst. **62**, 823–834 (2022)
18. Ye, L., Keogh, E.: Time series shapelets: a new primitive for data mining. In: Proceedings of the 15th ACM SIGKDD International Conference on Knowledge Discovery and Data Mining, pp. 947–956 (2009)
19. Zhang, M., Sawchuk, A.A.: Motion primitive-based human activity recognition using a bag-of-features approach. In: Proceedings of the 2nd ACM SIGHIT International Health Informatics Symposium, pp. 631–640 (2012)
20. Zhao, J., Itti, L.: Classifying time series using local descriptors with hybrid sampling. IEEE Trans. Knowl. Data Eng. **28**(3), 623–637 (2015)
21. Zhao, J., Itti, L.: shapeDTW: shape dynamic time warping. Pattern Recogn. **74**, 171–184 (2018)

Cluster Robust Inference
for Embedding-Based Knowledge Graph
Completion

Simon Schramm[1,2]($\boxtimes$) (ID), Ulrich Niklas[2] (ID), and Ute Schmid[1] (ID)

[1] University of Bamberg, Kapuzinerstraße 16, 96047 Bamberg, Germany
{simon.schramm,ute.schmid}@uni-bamberg.de
[2] BMW Group, Knorrstraße 147, 80807 Munich, Germany
{simon.schramm,ulrich.niklas}@bmw.de
https://www.uni-bamberg.de/en/cogsys/, https://www.bmw.com

Abstract. Knowledge Graphs (KGs) are able to structure and represent knowledge in complex systems, whereby their completeness impacts the quality of any further application. Real world KGs are notoriously incomplete, which is why KG Completion (KGC) methods emerged. Most KGC methods rely on Knowledge Graph Embedding (KGE) based link prediction models, which provide completion candidates for a sparse KG. Metrics like the *Mean Rank*, the *Mean Reciprocal Rank* or *Hits@K* evaluate the quality of those models, like *TransR*, *DistMult* or *ComplEx*. Based on the principle of supervised learning, these metrics evaluate a KGC model trained on a training dataset, based on the partition of true completion candidates it achieves on a test dataset. Dealing with real world, complex KGs, we found that sparsity is not equally distributed across a KG, but rather grouped in clusters. We use modularity-based KG clustering, to approximate sparsity levels in a KG. Furthermore, we postulate that prediction errors of an embedding-based KGC model are correlated within clusters of a KG but uncorrelated between them and formalize a new, cluster-robust KGC evaluation metric. We test our metric using six benchmark dataset and one real-world industrial example dataset. Our experiments show its superiority to existing metrics with regards to the prediction of cluster-robust triplets[1] ([1]The code is available at https://github.com/simoncharmms/crmrr.).

Keywords: Knowledge graph completion · Knowledge graph embedding · Knowledge metrics · Knowledge in complex systems · Knowledge graph applications

1 Motivation, Objective and Related Work

1.1 Motivation and Objective

A Knowledge Graph (KG) is a network of entities (heads h and tails t), connected by directed and labelled relations (r). The composition of (h, r, t) is referred to as *triplet* and is set as a standard for KG construction [25]. Most KGs do not

Z. Jin et al. (Eds.): KSEM 2023, LNAI 14117, pp. 284–299, 2023.
https://doi.org/10.1007/978-3-031-40283-8_25

comprise the complete knowledge of their respective domain, but are notoriously incomplete. In order make correct inference from the relational information stored in a KG, models that try to impute the missing information via embeddings, referred to as embedding-based Knowledge Graph Completion (KGC), gained vast popularity [1,6,12]. Our motivation is to evaluate KGC results in a realistic setting, taking into account differing levels of sparsity in a KG. Current KGC evaluation metrics, such as Mean Rank (MR), Mean Reciprocal Rank (MRR) and *Hits@K*, neglect this circumstance. Our suggested approach is based on the assumption that modularity-based clustering results approximate sparsity levels in a KG and that embedding-based link prediction errors are correlated within clusters and uncorrelated between them. The latter property is a well-known concept from econometrics, referred to as cluster-robust errors [31].

Our objective is to create a KGC evaluation metric that identifies the KGC model which is least prone these errors. Therefore, a theoretical background on KGs, KGC and KG clustering is given in Sect. 3, which will also contain some reference and differentiation to unsupervised and semi-supervised Machine Learning (ML) models. In Sect. 3, we formalize a new method for embedding-based KGC evaluation using KG clustering. Furthermore, we will present six benchmark datasets as well as a real-world industrial KG in order to test our new metric in Sect. 4. Relevant notations can be found in Appendix A.

1.2   Related Work

In the field of econometrics, cluster-robust methods accumulated since [31] came up with their original paper, focusing on heteroscedasticity within clusters. The underlying principle divides a dataset into k disjoint clusters. Any pattern of heteroscedasticity and/or dependence is allowed within each cluster, but it is assumed that there is independence across clusters and that the assignment of observations to clusters is known. Under these assumptions, it is easy to compute cluster-robust standard errors that can be used to produce asymptotically valid inferences. Not only until [7] published their practitioner's guide in 2015, clustering regression model errors (being independent across cluster but correlated within) run rampant. Issues with cluster-robust methods are extensively studied (cf. [19]), after the application of clustered standard errors in widely-used econometric software packages [8]. In fact, cluster-robust methods are routinely used and updated, which can be seen in the regular update of guides for practical application of cluster-robust inference (cf. e.g. [20]).

When it comes to the application of cluster-robust methods to KG clustering, few approaches exist. One is [15], who focused on spectral partitioning and [17], who advised on how to construct KG clusters in a robust way. With regards to KGC evaluation metrics, a general overview is provided by [33] and a special view towards rank-based evaluation metric for KGC is provided by [12]. The latter ones outline why especially the most common rank-based evaluation metrics show grave deficiencies and thereby take the preliminary work of [11] a step further. Just as [21], they argue that current metrics solely rank a model's completion candidate suggestion within a likelihood space determined by all existing candidates. The authors focus on rank-based methods and provide an extension to the *TransE* model that allows for direct measuring of the quality of completion candidates by defining relation-specific regions in the translation vector space. None of the authors provide a metric that takes varying levels of sparsity into account.

2 Theoretical Background

2.1 Graphs, KGs, KG Clustering and KGC

In general, a graph is a set of connected *entities* $e \in \mathcal{E}$, e.g., *3-Series* or *BMW*, while connectors are referred to as *relations* $r \in \mathcal{R}$, e.g., *is model of*, in the context of a graph. Thus, a graph $\mathcal{G}$ consists of a set of nodes $\mathcal{E} = \{e_1, ..., e_i, ..., e_n\}$ and relations $\mathcal{R} = \{r_1, ..., r_j, ..., r_m\}$, which can be either directed or undirected. Given a directed relation r_1 from node e_1 to node e_2, e_1 is referred to as head h, while node e_2 is denoted tail t. A *triangle* $T(e)$ is a set of three entities connected by three different relations. A labeled graph is a graph in which holds $\forall e_i \in \mathcal{E}$ and $\forall r_j \in \mathcal{R}$ that *exactly* one element from a set of symbols $S = \{s_1, ..., s_k, ..., s_o\}$ is assigned to them. A symbol s_k is, in general, the name of an entity like *3-Series* or the name of a relationship like *is model of*. A head entity h connected via a relation r to a tail entity t, i.e., {3-Series ; is model of ; BMW} is called a triplet.

KGs are defined as a labeled, directed graphs. Graph entities can also carry properties, which are attributes of a pre-defined scheme, such as *Start of Sales* or *End of Sales*, whereby each property is provided with a respective value.[1] Assuming a simplified domain with a set of entities $\mathcal{E} = \{$ BMW; Tesla; 3-Series; Model 3; Germany; United States $\}$, a simple, domain-specific, one directional label property KG is depicted in Fig. 1. A sub-symbolic representation of KGs, referred to as *embedding*, is widely used. Embedding is defined as representing the entities of a KG as d-dimensional vectors $e_h, e_t \in \mathbb{R}^d$, while its relations $r \in \mathcal{R}$ can either be embedded as matrices $R_r \in \mathbb{R}^{d \times d}$ or vectors $r_r \in \mathbb{R}^d$ [2]. Hence, the basic idea is to embed the entities and relations of the KG into low dimensional numeric vector or matrix space, like a real-valued matrix or an adjacency matrix. Assuming such an adjacency matrix A, two types of *degree* of a node in a KG can be defined. The *outbound degree* describes the number of relations the node emits as $k_i^{out} = \sum_j a_{ji}$, while the *inbound degree* epitomizes the number of relations directed to that note as $k_i^{in} = \sum_j a_{ij}$ [5]. In contrary to the classical link prediction task, **KGC** is defined as the prediction of a missing tail t, given (h, r). Referring back to our example from exemplary Fig. 1, a typical task for KGC would be to predict all tails for $(h_{\text{Model Y}}, r_{\text{is sold in}})$. In this paper, we focus on embedding-based methods of KGC.

---

[1] In general, those graphs are referred to as *Label-Property-Graphs* and are opposed to graphs where also a pre-defined scheme for rules over entities, referred to as an ontology, is underlying [25]. In this paper, we focus on Label-Property-Graphs.

Clustering is the division of a dataset, based on some similarity metric [23]. In ML, clustering is usually an unsupervised learning task and usually aims at knowledge discovery and data mining [10,23].

With regards to KG clustering, the Leiden algorithm assigns nodes to arbitrary communities and then optimizes an objective function $\mathcal{H}_{Leiden} = \frac{1}{2m}\sum_{ij}(A_{ij} - \gamma n_i n_j)\delta(\sigma_i, \sigma_j)$, where σ is the cluster of a respective node i or j, which leads to $\delta(\sigma_i, \sigma_j) = 1$ if and only if $\sigma_i = \sigma_j$, 0 otherwise [28]. Notably A_{ij}, is the weight of relation from node i to node j and n_i is the weight of node i, which puts the Leiden algorithm in the position to take node and relation weights into account. The Leiden algorithm clusters triplets in a density-based manner, but ensures that detected clusters are not disconnected. This way, the algorithm can detect clusters as sketched in Fig. 1, where clusters may be inherently sparse but not disconnected to other clusters. A measure of how prone a KG is to form clusters is provided by the mean *clustering coefficient* $cco = \frac{T(e)}{2(deg(e)(deg(e)-1)-2deg'(e))}$, where $T(e)$ is the number of directed triangles through entity e, $deg(e)$ is the sum of inbound and outbound degree of e and $deg'(e)$ is the reciprocal degree of e [9].

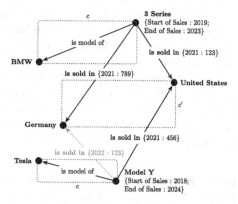

Fig. 1. A schematic Label-Property KG with clusters c and c' (blue frames). Triplets, such as $(h_{3\ Series}, r_{is\ model\ of}, t_{BMW})$, should ideally be clustered in a way that allows for the inference of different sparsity levels in a KG. Then, KGC systems can predict links (in gray) in order to create a close to complete representation of the real-world knowledge. (Color figure online)

Embedding-Based KGC models are characterized by a scoring function denoted $f_r(h,t) : \mathcal{E} \times \mathcal{R} \times \mathcal{E} \to \mathbb{R}$. Thereby, heads and tails are both *entities* in the KG, thus $h, t \in \mathcal{E}$. The straightforward idea of embedding-based KGC is that the embedding of a true prediction, referred to as *true completion candidate*, t should be close to the embedding of (h,r) in the embedding space, or, formally: $h + r \approx t$ for a true completion candidate [4]. A true completion candidate does not necessarily have to be the most *realistic* completion candidate, which could be an unknown triplet.

A popular example for an embedding-based, translational KGC model is *TransR*. The model embeds entities as vectors in $\mathbb{R}^d$ and each relation as vector in relation space $r_r \in \mathbb{R}^d$ but together with a relation-specific projection matrix $R_r \in \mathbb{R}^{d \times k}$. The scoring function of TransR is $f_r(h,t) = -||e_{h\perp} + r_r - e_{t\perp}||$, where $h_\perp = M_r h$ and $t_\perp = M_r t$. Put simply, TransR applies the projection matrix to heads and tails, which allows TransR to model $1-to-N$ relations, since $t_\perp = M_r t_1$ and $t_\perp = M_r t_2$ can simultaneously hold true [18].

Furthermore, *DistMult* is a tensor-factorization model with the scoring function $f_r(h,t) = <e_h, r_r, e_t> = \sum_i e_{h,i} \cdot r_{r,i} \cdot e_{t,i}$. Hence, it scores the multiplication and summation of the embeddings, which allows for a modeling of directed and $1-to-N$ relations [32]. Based on DistMult, *ComplEx* uses the concept of the complex conjugate from complex algebra to embed KG entities in a complex vector space. The scoring function of ComplEx is $f_r(h,t) = Re(\sum_i e_{h,i} \cdot r_{r,i} \cdot e_{\bar{t},i})$, where Re denotes the real part of the complex function and $\bar{t}$ is the conjugate of the vector of t. Thereby, ComplEx can model directed and multi-relational graphs as well [29]. All of the above-described embedding-based KGC models share a basic behaviour, namely the production of a similarity metric based on $e_h\_r_r$ and e_t, where _ epitomizes a placeholder for the respective operator in TransR, DistMult and ComplEx.

KGC Evaluation Metrics aim at detecting the prediction of non-cluster-robust completion candidates, such as $(h_{\text{Model Y}}, r_{\text{is sold in}}), (t_{\text{BMW}})$. Popular evaluation metrics for embedding-based KGC methods include the so-called Mean Rank, the Mean Reciprocal Rank, as well as *Hits@K* [1,6,12]. *Hits@k* (H_k) measures the partition of true completion candidates that occur in the first k hits, i.e. entries in a sorted rank-list. Formally, this parametric rank is defined as $H_k(r_1, ..., r_n) = \frac{1}{n} \sum_{i=1}^{n} \mathbb{I}[r_i \le k] \in [0,1]$, where $\mathbb{I}$ is the indicator function that equals 1 for $\mathbb{I}[x \le y]$ and 0 otherwise. Greater values of H_k would purportedly account for higher KGC precision. However, false completion candidates with a rank greater than k would not fall into this sorted rank list and thus would not affect this metric at all. *MR* is a non-parametric alternative to H_k, which reflects a measure of the rank of all true completion candidates. $MR(r_1, ..., r_n) = \frac{1}{n} \sum_{i=1}^{n} r_i \in [1, \infty]$. MR is nothing but the arithmetic mean over the ranks of true completion candidates, which allegedly renders smaller values better. *MRR* epitomizes a simple further evolution of MR, considering the inverse or reciprocal rank as summand of the arithmetic mean, with $MRR(r_1, ..., r_n) = \frac{1}{n} \sum_{i=1}^{n} r_i^{-1} \in (0,1]$. This adjustment results in a more cluster-robust metric, more sensitive to true completion candidates in lower ranks than H_k and less prone to outliers than MR.

2.2   KGC as a Semi-supervised ML Task

The applicability of a ML approach on KGs depends on the accessibility of *domain knowledge*. Domain knowledge in a KG is defined by the degree of availability of the independent variable y, which explains the set of observations x. **Supervised learning** techniques require *complete domain knowledge*. Complete domain knowledge is defined by a set of observations x and an independent variable y. Supervised learning attempts to learn a function f, based on x to predict the independent variable y [26]. One advantage in supervised learning is that due to the complete domain knowledge, the accuracy of the used model can be clearly determined [3].

Semi-supervised or **unsupervised learning** techniques can handle *incomplete* to *no domain knowledge* at all by inferring domain knowledge to data points with no domain knowledge by using concepts from supervised and unsupervised learning [30]. Its disadvantage is that the accuracy of the model and the identified patterns are difficult to measure [3]. Most real world KGs have incomplete domain knowledge, which renders KGC models a semi-supervised ML task. However, current evaluation metrics for KGC being trained on a training dataset, refer to the partition of true completion candidates in a test dataset. In the following section, we provide a metric that is able to handle KGC as the semi-supervised ML task it is.

3   Cluster-Robust Inference for KGC

3.1   Problem Statement

Definition 1. *Let $\mathcal{G}$ denote a network, in which the set $\mathcal{T} = \{(h, r, t)\}$ with labelled entities $(h_i, r_i) \in \mathcal{E}$ and labelled and directed relations $r_i \in \mathcal{R}$ exists. Then $\mathcal{G}$ is referred to as **Knowledge Graph** and $\mathcal{T}$ as the collection of triplets of G.*

We investigate the task of KGC, which can formally be defined as follows.

Definition 2. *The embedding-based prediction of $(h, r, t) \notin \mathcal{T}$ is referred to as **Knowledge Graph Completion**, whereby each prediction-triplet is called **completion candidate**. There is a scoring function $f_r(h, t)$ that assigns high scores to true completion candidates and low scores to false completion candidates, under the assumption that it holds that*

$$e_h \cdot r_r \approx e_t \tag{1}$$

During prediction, an arbitrary embedding-based KGC model ϕ assigns one element $\hat{y} = \hat{h} \oplus \hat{r} \oplus \hat{t}$ from preferably high-scored completion candidates to $(h, r, t) \notin \mathcal{T}$.

A pivotal problem in this setting is that the search space of ϕ for completion candidates is limited to $\mathcal{T}$, which limits all potential $\hat{y}$ to the existing knowledge in $\mathcal{G}$. Furthermore, $f_r(h, t)$ can only compute scores based on triplets already existent in $\mathcal{G}$. In supervised learning, the split of training, test and validation data allows to track the training performance of ϕ (on the test dataset) and compute accuracy metrics for its predictions on unseen data (the validation dataset). For embedding-based KGC models, the restriction to $\mathcal{T}$ distorts any rank-based metric for the link prediction task and renders it a mere representation of the likelihood of a true completion candidate *out of* $\mathcal{T}$. Table 1 presents the KGC models TransR, DistMult and ComplEx, which are applied to a real-world KG constructed from industrial data, comparable to Fig. 1. Therein, non-cluster-robust completion candidates are defined as follows.

Definition 3. *A true completion candidate is a predicted triple (h, r, t) which is also in $\mathcal{T}$. A completion candidate $(h, r, t) \notin \mathcal{T}$ is referred to as false completion candidate. For a given cluster c a true completion candidate is referred to as* **cluster-robust**, *if both $h, t \in \mathcal{T}_c$. If not the completion candidate shall be denoted a* **cross-cluster completion candidate** $(h, r, t)_{cc}$.

The Leiden algorithm follows a modularity-based approach and ensures that clusters may be inherently sparse but not disconnected [28]. Thus, we assume it as apt to infer different levels of sparsity within a KG (see Sect. 2). Hence, producing a high amount of cluster-robust true completion candidates would be a desirable property for an embedding-based KGC model, since the different sparsity levels of a KG, approximated by cluster affiliations of its triplets, would be considered. As Table 1 depicts, current KGC evaluation metrics fail in that regard, since MR, MRR as well as H_{10} would point at TransR, which produces the second highes amount of non-cluster robust true completion candidates. Our goal is to find a new metric that is able to determine the best KGC model with respect to cluster-robust true completion candidates and our suggested approach is presented in the following.

Table 1. Results of the embedding-based KGC task using three KGC models. Conventional rank-based evaluation metrics point at TransR as best embedding model for the KGC task (highest scores bold). However, DistMult would produce less non-cluster robust true completion candidates (lowest ratio bold).

	Model	non-cluster-robust true completion candidates	MR $\in (1, \infty]$	MRR $\in (0, 1]$	H_{10} $\in [0, 1]$
industry KG	TransR	13.41%	**8.312**	**0.120**	**0.727**
	DistMult	**11.91%**	54.854	0.018	0.578
	ComplEx	21.91%	470.813	0.002	0.184

3.2 Suggested Approach

Recall that the scoring function can be interpreted as a similarity metric between $e_h \cdot r_r$ and e_t, which is one for two vectors being exactly the same and zero for orthogonal vectors. In other words, the scoring function describes the error term ϵ in Eq. 1 as follows

$$e_h \cdot r_r \approx e_t \Longleftrightarrow e_h \cdot r_r = e_t + \epsilon \tag{2}$$

Transferred from known statements about cluster-robust inference for classical regression models (cf. [7,20]) our straightforward proposition is that ϵ is correlated within clusters but uncorrelated between clusters.

Lemma 1. *Let $e_{h,i}, r_{r,i}, e_{t,i}$ denote the embedding of any head, relation or tail of an arbitrary KG G and $e_{x,c}$ denote affiliation to a specific density-based cluster c then it holds that*

$$e_{h,i,c} \cdot r_{r,i,c} = e_{t,i,c} + \epsilon_{i,c}$$

It is assumed that $E[\epsilon_{i,c}|e_{t,i,c}] = 0$ *and thus*

$$E\left[\epsilon_{i,c}, \epsilon'_{j,c'}|e_{t,i,c}, e_{t,j,c'}\right] = 0, \text{ unless } c = c' \tag{3}$$

Proof. We follow the proof in [7], transferring it to embedding based KG clustering. Let c and c' be two distinct clusters, and let i and j be two individuals, possibly from different clusters. Let $e_{t,i,c}$ and $e_{t,j,c'}$ be the disturbances for individuals i and j, respectively, in time period t and clusters c and c'. Let $\epsilon_{i,c}$ and $\epsilon_{j,c'}$ be the corresponding errors in the regression equation for i and j, respectively. Then we want to show that

$$E\left[\epsilon_{i,c}, \epsilon'_{j,c'}|e_{t,i,c}, e_{t,j,c'}\right] = 0, \text{ unless } c = c'$$

By the Tower Rule, it holds that:

$$E\left[\epsilon_{i,c}, \epsilon'_{j,c'}|e_{t,i,c}, e_{t,j,c'}\right] = E\left[\epsilon_{i,c}|e_{t,i,c}, e_{t,j,c'}\right] + E\left[\epsilon'_{j,c'}|e_{t,i,c}, e_{t,j,c'}\right]$$

Now, since the disturbances $e_{t,i,c}$ and $e_{t,j,c'}$ are assumed to be uncorrelated across individuals and time periods, and not correlated with the covariates in the model, we have:

$$E[\epsilon_{i,c}|e_{t,i,c}, e_{t,j,c'}] = E[\epsilon_{i,c}] = 0,$$

and

$$E\left[\epsilon'_{j,c'}|e_{t,i,c}, e_{t,j,c'}\right] = E\left[\epsilon'_{j,c'}\right] = 0.$$

Therefore,

$$E\left[\epsilon_{i,c}, \epsilon'_{j,c'}|e_{t,i,c}, e_{t,j,c'}\right] = 0, \text{ unless } c = c'.$$

We thereby follow the argumentation of [7,20] but want to generalize their findings, which are limited to regression models, to the embedding-based KGC task. The basic idea of our approach is that any rank-based evaluation metric of embedding-based KGC models can be rendered more cluster-robust when evaluating completion candidates cluster-wise. The effect of the cluster-wise evaluation would be the scoring of completion candidates not based on $\mathcal{T}$, but based on all triplets within a certain cluster $\mathcal{T}_c$. As a result, scores of completion candidates that have a low error term ϵ (cf. Eq. 2) *and* are in $\mathcal{T}_c$ would be even higher than scores of completion candidates that have a high ϵ and are in $\mathcal{T}_c$. Completion candidates that are not in $\mathcal{T}_c$ however, would be assigned a score of zero, which would in turn impede the possibility of considering true completion candidates from another cluster. Thus, completion candidates from other clusters shall be *penalized in terms of their rank* in our approach, as follows.

Definition 4. *Let $MRR(r_1, ..., r_n)$ be the Mean Reciprocal Rank of all completion candidates scored by a scoring function $f_r(h, t)$ of an embedding-based KGC model ϕ on a clustered KG. Then, the* **Cluster-Robust Mean Reciprocal Rank** *is*

$$CRMRR(r_1, ..., r_n) = \underbrace{\frac{1}{n} \sum_{i=1}^{n} \sum_{j=1}^{m} r_i^{-1}}_{MRR(r_1, ..., r_n)} \underbrace{+|c|^{-\left(\frac{r_{j|cc}}{n}\right)} - 1}_{Penalty\ term} \quad (4)$$

where n is the total count of ranks r_i. $|c|$ is the count of clusters of a clustered KG. m is the count of cross-cluster ranks $r_{j|cc}$ from cross-cluster completion candidates $(h, r, t)_{cc}$.

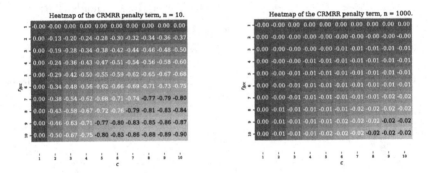

Fig. 2. Heatmap of the $CRMRR$ penalty term values at $n = 10$ and $n = 1000$. The penalty for KGs with a single clusters is zero, while for any cross-cluster completion candidate with rank 1, it is incrementally low (e.g. -0.002 for $n = 1000$).

This formulation provides the following, beneficial properties, which can easily be checked by inserting real numbers and is corroborated in Sect. 4.

- For predictions with $c = 1$, the latter, newly added part of the metric becomes zero.
- For predictions with $r_{j|cc} = 1$, the latter, newly added part of the metric becomes incremental as n grows.
- The higher $r_{nc,i}$, the greater the penalty for $n > 1$.
- The higher n, the lower the individual penalty.
- Though, the penalty-growth is stronger related to a high rank than to a large count of clusters.

Notably the last property is indeed beneficial, since a large count of clusters represents a rugged KG, which aggravates the stated problem of unknown true completion candidates. Figure 2 displays a heatmap of the $CRMRR$ penalty term values, which corroborates the above-described characteristics.

4   Experiments

4.1   Experimental Setup

Apart from the industry KG, six benchmark datasets are chosen for experiments on *CRMRR*. *sx-stackoverflow*, a large temporal network of interactions on the stack exchange Stack Overflow [24]. The popular *web-google* graph [16], a large, directed graph of web pages and hyperlinks between them. *soc-sign-bitcoin-otc* (*BTC_{otc}*) and *soc-sign-bitcoin-alpha* (*BTC_α*), two temporal, directed and weighted networks of mutual trust ratings of bitcoin traders [13,14]. *web-amazon*, a undirected, weighted network of Amazon reviews [22]. *musae-Facebook*, an undirected network of facebook pages with categorical node attributes [27]. Hence, the experimental setup covers different types of graph datasets. The key metrics of every dataset are presented in Fig. 3. Detailed metrics, such as $|c|$, can be found in Appendix B.

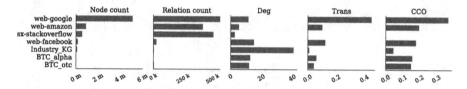

Fig. 3. Six benchmark datasets for testing *CRMRR* with varying density. Node counts reach from over 5 million to less than one million, whereby relation counts vary accordingly. The mean degree (Deg) is the mean number of edges an entity has, while the transitivity (Trans) is the probability of adjacent entities being related. The mean clustering coefficient (CCO) is the average of all local clustering coefficients, which describe how well connected entities in a neighbourhood are.

In order to test *CRMRR*, non-cluster-robust completion candidates in benchmark datasets need to be defined and labeled. We split the benchmark dataset into test (10%), validation (20%) and training data (70%) and conduct KGC using TransR, DistMult and ComplEx. The KGs are clustered using the Leiden algorithm, in order to consider both node and edge labels. Clustering is implemented using Leiden algorithm, starting from a singleton partition and optimising modularity as quality function [28]. Though, we are using $k_i^{out} k_j^{in}$ instead of K_c^2, since we are dealing with a directed graph. During training, the filtering approach from [5] is followed. Further information about the training settings and the exact results can be found in Appendix C.

4.2   Results

Figure 4 displays the result of the KGC task conducted by TransR, DistMult and ComplEx in terms of *MR*, *MRR* and H_{10} (the ten top scored completion candidates). The partitions of non-cluster-robust completion candidates r_{cc} are provided in the first row of the plot. The following rows contain the rank-based evaluation metrics *MR*, *MRR*, *Hits at 10* and the *CRMRR*. Each column of the figure depicts the respective metric result for the embedding-based KGC models TransR, DistMult and ComplEx for each of the analysed datasets. The respective lowest partition of non-cluster robust true completion candidates is framed green. At the same time, the respective metric value is framed gray if it indicated to not choose the model with the lowest partition of non-cluster robust true completion candidates and green if it did.

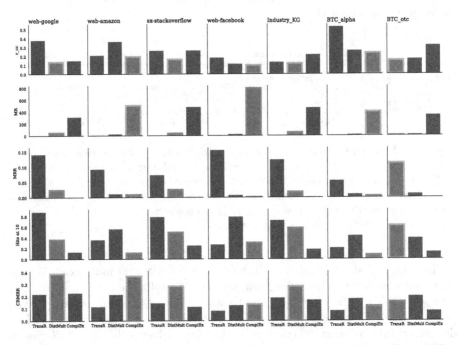

Fig. 4. The result of the KGC task conducted by TransR, DistMult and ComplEx in terms of *MP*, *MRR* and H_{10} for all datasets. The first row displays partitions of non-cluster-robust completion candidates, followed by rows contain the rank-based evaluation metrics *MR*, *MRR*, *Hits at 10* and the *CRMRR*. The respective lowest partition of non-cluster robust true completion candidates is framed green, its respective metric scores are framed green for correct indication and red for incorrect indication of the model that produces the lowest partition of non-cluster robust true completion candidates.

In five of seven cases (*web-google*, *web-amazon*, *sx-stackoverflow*, *web-facebook* and the *Industry KG*), $CRMRR$ was able to detect the KGC model that produced least r_{cc}. For KGs with relatively few nodes and relations, a relatively high transitivity and at the same time a relatively high clustering coefficient, such as both BTC KGs, $CRMRR$ failed to point at the correct KGC model, in contrast to MRR and H_{10}. In all other cases, $CRMRR$ outperformed MRR and H_{10} in indicating the KGC model with the least non-cluster robust completion candidates. Notably in some cases (*web − amazon* and BTC_{alpha}), the simple metric MR was able to indicate the KGC model with the lowest partition of non-cluster robust completion candidates as well.

5 Conclusion, Discussion and Outlook

5.1 Conclusion

Evaluating the results of any ML model using KG data under realistic settings is important for the practical application of those models. Especially in embedding-based KGC, conventional metrics fail to provide relevant information for this evaluation. We elaborated on the theoretical background of KGC, which is a semi-supervised task under the OWA and KG clustering, an unsupervised learning task. We proposed a new, rank-based evaluation metric for embedding-based KGC models which combines the two and presented its superiority to conventional metrics. We tested our metric using multiple real-world examples of KGs and multiple embedding-based KGC methods.

5.2 Discussion and Outlook

Further research has to be done in the field of KG clustering, so that clusters are not only well connected, which is what [28] contributed, but also add meaningful information about the edge weights to the KG [17]. Furthermore, it is imperative for the acceptance and wide usage of those methods, that also interpretability of especially unsupervised and semi-supervised ML methods has to be ensured. Eventually, our approach could be generalized in the future, since we only looked at embedding-based KGC methods so far. Future research could consider whether a graph may be too incomplete for embedding-based methods.

Appendix

Appendix A: Relevant Notations of this Paper

Notation	Meaning
G	A graph
$\{(h, r, t)\} \in \mathcal{T}$	A set of triples with heads, relations and tails
$e \in \mathcal{E}$	A set of entities e
$r \in \mathcal{R}$	A set of relations r
$R_r \in \mathbb{R}^{d \times d}$	A $d \times d$ dimensional matrix with coefficients a_{ji}
$r_r \in \mathbb{R}^d$	A d-dimensional vector
$k^{out} = \sum_j a_{ji}$	The *outbound degree*
$k_i^{in} = \sum_j a_{ij}$	The *inbound degree*
Deg	The total degree of a graph
$T(e)$	The number of triangles through entity e
$Trans$	The transitivity of a graph
CCO	The mean clustering coefficient of a graph
r_{cc}	The rank of a cross-cluster completion candidate
n	The total count of ranks r_i
m	The count of *cross-cluster* ranks $r_{j|cc}$ from $\{(h, r, t)_{cc}\}$
$|c|$	The count of clusters of a clustered KG
$(h, r, t)_{cc}$	A cross-cluster completion candidate

Appendix B: Metrics of Used Knowledge Graphs

	Industry KG	BTC_{alpha} [14]	BTC_{otc} [13]	$web-google$ [16]
Node count	116699	24185	35591	5105039
Relation count	5710	3782	5881	875713
Deg	40.875	12.789	12.103	11.659
$Trans$	0.012	0.063	0.045	0.449
CCO	0.044	0.158	0.151	0.369
$|c|$	61	79	87	29722
	$sx-stackoverflow$ [24]	$web-amazon$ [22]	$web-facebook$ [27]	
Node count	574795	925872	171002	
Relation count	406972	334863	22470	
Deg	2.824	5.529	15.220	
$Trans$	0.001	0.103	0.124	
CCO	0.001	0.198	0.179	
$|c|$	90266	31916	790	

Appendix C: Training Details and Results by KG and Model.

	Model	Epochs	Batch size	m/n	MR	MRR	H_{10}	CRMRR
$web - google$	TransR			0.381	6.070	0.142	0.887	0.221
	DistMult	510	32	0.137	49.370	0.024	0.362	0.389
	ComplEx			0.152	315.440	0.001	0.135	0.229
$web - amazon$	TransR			0.212	11.300	0.093	0.362	0.116
	DistMult	510	32	0.365	29.620	0.012	0.566	0.217
	ComplEx			0.195	508.480	0.009	0.112	0.368
$sx - stackoverflow$	TransR			0.262	7.150	0.074	0.791	0.145
	DistMult	510	32	0.165	38.400	0.025	0.498	0.285
	ComplEx			0.265	484.940	0.002	0.255	0.115
$web - facebook$	TransR			0.185	3.660	0.156	0.272	0.083
	DistMult	510	32	0.114	26.880	0.008	0.798	0.127
	ComplEx			0.098	795.670	0.001	0.302	0.136
Industry KG	TransR			0.134	8.312	0.124	0.727	0.189
	DistMult	510	32	0.119	54.854	0.018	0.578	0.283
	ComplEx			0.219	470.813	0.002	0.184	0.171
BTC_{alpha}	TransR			0.530	7.400	0.056	0.210	0.082
	DistMult	510	32	0.262	20.840	0.011	0.438	0.180
	ComplEx			0.235	404.900	0.004	0.076	0.119
BTC_{otc}	TransR			0.154	3.820	0.113	0.626	0.155
	DistMult	510	32	0.170	21.390	0.012	0.394	0.202
	ComplEx			0.32	348.40	0.001	0.134	0.081

References

1. Akrami, F., Saeef, M.S., Zhang, Q., Hu, W., Li, C.: Realistic re-evaluation of knowledge graph completion methods: an experimental study (2020). https://doi.org/10.1145/3318464.3380599
2. Ali, M., et al.: Bringing light into the dark: a large-scale evaluation of knowledge graph embedding models under a unified framework. CoRR (2020). https://doi.org/10.1109/TPAMI.2021.3124805
3. Bishop, C.M.: Pattern Recognition and Machine Learning. Springer, New York (2007). https://doi.org/10.1117/1.2819119
4. Biswas, R.: Embedding based link prediction for knowledge graph completion. In: Proceedings of the 29th ACM International Conference on Information and Knowledge Management, pp. 3221–3224. ACM, Virtual Event, Ireland (2020). https://doi.org/10.1145/3340531.3418512
5. Bordes, A., Usunier, N., Garcia-Durán, A., Weston, J., Yakhnenko, O.: Translating embeddings for modeling multi-relational data. In: Proceedings of the 26th International Conference on Neural Information Processing Systems, vol. 2, pp. 2787–2795. Curran Associates Inc., Red Hook, NY, USA (2013). https://doi.org/10.5555/2999792.2999923

6. Chen, Z., Wang, Y., Zhao, B., Cheng, J., Zhao, X., Duan, Z.: Knowledge graph completion: a review. IEEE Access **8**, 192435–192456 (2020). https://doi.org/10.1109/ACCESS.2020.3030076

7. Colin Cameron, A., Miller, D.L.: A practitioner's guide to cluster-robust inference. J. Hum. Resourc. **50**(2), 317–372 (2015). https://doi.org/10.3368/jhr.50.2.317

8. Esarey, J., Menger, A.: Practical and effective approaches to dealing with clustered data. Polit. Sci. Res. Methods **7**(3), 541–559 (2019). https://doi.org/10.1017/psrm.2017.42

9. Fagiolo, G.: Clustering in complex directed networks. Phys. Rev. E **76**, 026107 (2007). https://doi.org/10.1103/PhysRevE.76.026107

10. Fayyad, U., Smyth, P., Piatetsky-Shapiro, G.: From data mining to knowledge discovery in databases. AI Mag. **17**(3), 37–54 (1996). https://doi.org/10.1609/aimag.v17i3.1230

11. Fuhr, N.: Some common mistakes in IR evaluation, and how they can be avoided. ACM SIGIR Forum **51**(3), 32–41 (2018). https://doi.org/10.1145/3190580.3190586

12. Hoyt, C.T., Berrendorf, M., Galkin, M., Tresp, V., Gyori, B.M.: A unified framework for rank-based evaluation metrics for link prediction in knowledge graphs. Pre-print (2022). https://doi.org/10.48550/ARXIV.2203.07544

13. Kumar, S., Hooi, B., Makhija, D., Kumar, M., Faloutsos, C., Subrahmanian, V.: Rev2: fraudulent user prediction in rating platforms. In: Proceedings of the Eleventh ACM International Conference on Web Search and Data Mining, pp. 333–341. ACM (2018). https://doi.org/10.1145/3159652.3159729

14. Kumar, S., Spezzano, F., Subrahmanian, V., Faloutsos, C.: Edge weight prediction in weighted signed networks. In: 2016 IEEE 16th International Conference on Data Mining (ICDM), pp. 221–230. IEEE (2016). https://doi.org/10.1109/ICDM.2016.0033

15. Lee, J.R., Gharan, S.O., Trevisan, L.: Multiway spectral partitioning and higher-order Cheeger inequalities. J. ACM **61**(6), 1–30 (2014). https://doi.org/10.1145/2665063

16. Leskovec, J., Lang, K.J., Dasgupta, A., Mahoney, M.W.: Community structure in large networks: natural cluster sizes and the absence of large well-defined clusters (2008). https://doi.org/10.1080/15427951.2009.10129177

17. Leung, M.P.: Network cluster-robust inference. Pre-print (2021). https://doi.org/10.48550/ARXIV.2103.01470

18. Lin, Y., Liu, Z., Sun, M., Liu, Y., Zhu, X.: Learning entity and relation embeddings for knowledge graph completion. In: Proceedings of the AAAI Conference on Artificial Intelligence, vol. 29, no. 1 (2015). https://doi.org/10.1609/aaai.v29i1.9491

19. MacKinnon, J.G.: How cluster-robust inference is changing applied econometrics. Can. J. Econ./Revue canadienne d'économique **52**(3), 851–881 (2019). https://doi.org/10.1111/caje.12388

20. MacKinnon, J.G., Nielsen, M.Ø., Webb, M.D.: Cluster-robust inference: a guide to empirical practice. J. Econometrics, S0304407622000781 (2022). https://doi.org/10.1016/j.jeconom.2022.04.001

21. Marina Speranskaya, M.S.: Ranking vs. classifying: measuring knowledge base completion quality. Pre-print (2020). https://doi.org/10.24432/C57G65

22. McAuley, J., Leskovec, J.: Hidden factors and hidden topics: understanding rating dimensions with review text. In: Proceedings of the 7th ACM Conference on Recommender Systems. RecSys '13, pp. 165–172. Association for Computing Machinery, New York, NY, USA (2013). https://doi.org/10.1145/2507157.2507163

23. Mirkin, B.G.: Clustering for Data Mining: A Data Recovery Approach. No. 3 in Computer Science and Data Analysis Series, Chapman & Hall/CRC, Boca Raton, FL (2005). https://doi.org/10.1201/9781420034912

24. Paranjape, A., Benson, A.R., Leskovec, J.: Motifs in temporal networks. In: Proceedings of the Tenth ACM International Conference on Web Search and Data Mining. ACM (2017). https://doi.org/10.1145/3018661.3018731

25. Paulheim, H.: Knowledge graph refinement: a survey of approaches and evaluation methods. Semant. Web **8**(3), 489–508 (2016). https://doi.org/10.3233/SW-160218

26. Rosa, G.J.M.: The Elements of Statistical Learning: Data Mining, Inference, and Prediction by Hastie, T., Tibshirani, R., Friedman, J. Biometrics **66**(4), 1315–1315 (2010). https://doi.org/10.1111/j.1541-0420.2010.01516.x

27. Rozemberczki, B., Allen, C., Sarkar, R.: Multi-scale attributed node embedding (2019). https://doi.org/10.1093/comnet/cnab014

28. Traag, V.A., Waltman, L., van Eck, N.J.: From Louvain to Leiden: guaranteeing well-connected communities. Sci. Rep. **9**(1), 5233 (2019). https://doi.org/10.1038/s41598-019-41695-z

29. Trouillon, T., Welbl, J., Riedel, S., Gaussier, É., Bouchard, G.: Complex embeddings for simple link prediction. Pre-print (2016). https://doi.org/10.48550/ARXIV.1606.06357

30. van Engelen, J.E., Hoos, H.H.: A survey on semi-supervised learning. Mach. Learn. **109**(2), 373–440 (2019). https://doi.org/10.1007/s10994-019-05855-6

31. White, H.: A heteroskedasticity-consistent covariance matrix estimator and a direct test for heteroskedasticity. Econometrica **48**(4), 817 (1980). https://doi.org/10.2307/1912934

32. Yang, B., Yih, W.T., He, X., Gao, J., Deng, L.: Embedding entities and relations for learning and inference in knowledge bases. Pre-print (2014). https://doi.org/10.48550/ARXIV.1412.6575

33. Yang, H., Lin, Z., Zhang, M.: Rethinking knowledge graph evaluation under the open-world assumption (2022). https://doi.org/10.48550/ARXIV.2209.08858

Community-Enhanced Contrastive Siamese Networks for Graph Representation Learning

Yafang Li[1], Wenbo Wang[1], Guixiang Ma[2], and Baokai Zu[1(✉)]

[1] Beijing University of Technology, Beijing CHN 100123, China
{yafangli,wangwenbo,bzu}@bjut.edu.cn
[2] Intel Corporation, Hillsboro, OR 97124, USA
guixiang.ma@intel.com

Abstract. Graph representation learning is the encoding of graph nodes into a low-dimensional representation space, which can effectively improve graph information representation while reducing the information dimensionality. To overcome the heavy reliance on label information of previous graph representation learning, the graph contrastive learning method has received attention from researchers as a self-supervised learning method, but it introduces the problem of sample selection dependence. To address this issue, inspired by deep clustering methods and image contrastive learning methods, we propose a novel Siamese network method, namely Community-enhanced Contrastive Siamese networks for Graph Representation Learning (MEDC). Specifically, we employ a Siamese network architecture to contrast two augmented views of the original graph and guide the network training by minimizing the similarity of positive sample nodes and negative sample nodes. Meanwhile, to take full advantage of the potential community structure of graph, we add a deep clustering layer in the network architecture, and the perceived community structure information is used to guide the selection of positive and negative samples. To demonstrate the effectiveness of the proposed method, we conducted a series of comparative experiments on three real datasets to validate the performance of our method.

Keywords: graph embedding · Siamese networks · deep clustering · community structure

1 Introduction

Graph representation learning [1] refers to encoding graph nodes into LD representation space, which can effectively improve the ability of graph information representation while reducing the information dimension. Graph representation learning has attracted extensive research and exploration, and it has been widely applied and developed in the literature indexing network [4], biological information network [2], and social media network [3,5]. The existing graph representation learning methods can be categorized into (1) methods based on matrix factorization [6], (2) methods based on graph neural network [13], and (3) methods based on graph contrastive learning [7]. By comparing and enhancing the similarity of node representation, graph contrastive learning effectively reduces the dependence on label information.

Although the existing graph contrastive learning methods [7,10,11] have achieved promising results, they still have some defects. For example, the graph contrastive learning based mutual information (MI) [7] needs to maintain an additional MI estimator to evaluate the positive and negative sample pairs, which brings significant additional computational overhead. At the same time, the existing graph contrastive learning methods [11,20] lack the design for the selection of samples, leading to the introduction of quite several pseudo-negative samples into the model, which affects the contrastive learning ability. In addition, the existing graph contrastive learning methods rely on a large number of negative sample pairs to avoid model collapse during training, which also limits the performance of model.

To address the above problems, we designed a novel Siamese network graph contrastive learning framework and designed a negative sample debiasing mechanism with the guidance of deep clustering. Finally, we achieved an excellent representation learning effect without label information or a large number of negative samples. Our contribution is summarized as follows:

- We propose a novel framework to learn node representation by taking advantage of graph representation learning in the Siamese network and deep graph clustering. To the best of our knowledge, we are the first to use the Siamese network and deep graph clustering on node representation learning;
- We develop a debiased sampling strategy in the Siamese network to correct the bias of negative samples and use clustering results to reduce pseudo-negative samples. Both theoretical analysis and experimental results indicate that the proposed framework is conducive to improving the capabilities of representation learning.
- We conduct extensive experiments on various real-world datasets and demonstrate the effectiveness of the proposed method and its superior performance over state-of-the-art methods in self-supervised graph representation learning.

This paper is organized as follows: Sect. 2 discusses the related work, and Sect. 3 presents our proposed method. Then, we demonstrate the performance of our method compared to the baselines in Sect. 4. Section 5 concludes the paper and our further considerations.

2   Related Work

Graph Contrastive Learning design objective functions in latent space by contrasting positive and negative pairs. They usually aim to explore the relationship between nodes in complex graphs without using label information, unite graph structure and node feature information, and form more discriminative graph representation. Deep Graph Infomax (DGI [10]) obtains node representation by maximizing mutual information between patch representation and a high-level summary of the corresponding graph. Then, the multi-view graph representation learning method (MVGRL [11]) introduces different structural views into DGI for learning node and graph level representation. And Ming Jin et al. [12] use the Siamese networks for the first time in graph representation learning.

Siamese Network [14–16] consists of two identical sub-networks joined at their outputs. During training, the two sub-networks extract features from two signatures, while the joining neuron measures the distance between the two feature vectors. Verification involves comparing an extracted feature vector with a stored feature vector for the signer. Signatures closer to this stored representation than a chosen threshold are accepted and all other signatures are rejected as forgeries. BYOL [17] is the first to apply the Siamese network to computer vision. It constructively proposes to use two neural networks, referred to as online and target networks, that interact and learn from each other. From an augmented view of an image, BYOL trains the online network to predict the target network representation of the same image under a different augmented view. At the same time, BYOL updates the target network with a slow-moving average of the online network. MERIT [12] is the first to apply the Siamese network to graph representation learning, taking advantage of bootstrapping in the Siamese network and multi-scale graph contrastive learning. However, MERIT lacks an effective mechanism to remove the interference of pseudo-negative samples.

Graph Deep Clustering is committed to the integration of the embedding process and clustering process, using embedded subspace for clustering, achieving a better effect than that of the shallow clustering method. For example, deep embedding clustering (DEC) [9] learning mappings from graph data space to low-dimensional feature space to optimize clustering. Then, to make the autoencoder learn better data representation, Improved Deep Embedding Clustering (IDEC [8]) adds a reconstruction loss as a constraint in DEC and then learns better embedding representation. DGCL [18] took the lead in applying deep clustering to debiased sampling in graph contrastive learning, which improved the sampling bias phenomenon in graph self-supervised learning. Attention-driven Graph Clustering Network (AGCN [19]) develops a scale-wise fusion module to adaptively aggregate the multi-scale features embedded at different layers. Based on a unified optimization framework, AGCN can jointly perform feature learning and cluster assignment in an unsupervised fashion. However, the existing methods rely on a large number of sample pairs to avoid model collapse during training, which also limits the performance of model.

3   Method

Overall Framework. MEDC consists of four parts, which are shown in Fig. 1. Graph augmentations use the combination of four graph augmentation strategies to obtain two augmentation graphs (views), which strengthens the global or local characteristics and other information of the graph. Siamese Graph Network embeds these two augmentation graphs (views) in an online network and target network with the same parameters to learn four graph representations. Deep clustering optimization clusters the representations learned from the online network, and uses clustering information as a pseudo-label to guide graph contrastive learning. By repeating the above steps through the momentum update mechanism, we get an optimized Siamese network framework for learning the best representation of the graph.

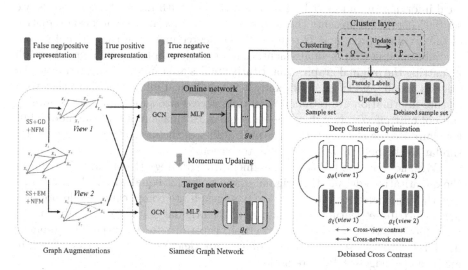

Fig. 1. The framework of MEDC is shown in Fig. 1, which contains four main parts. MEDC first generates two augmented views (View 1 and View2) from the original graph, then learns the original embeddings of each view in each network. The online network embeddings are used to cluster, and guide cross-network contrastive learning and cross-view contrastive learning.

3.1   Graph Augmentations

Graph augmentations are the first step of graph contrastive learning. Through graph diffusion, edge modification, sub-sampling, and node feature mask, the global information and local information of the original graph can be retained or highlighted, and the topological information and feature information of the original graph can be fully utilized, thereby significantly improving the effort of contrastive learning. We use the combination of four graph augmentation strategies to obtain two graphs, namely, *view 1* is obtained by the combination of sub-sampling + graph diffusion + node feature mask, and *view 2* is obtained by the combination of sub-sampling + edge modification + node feature mask. The four basic augmentation strategies we used are as follows:

Graph Diffusion (GD) is an augmentation strategy that introduces the global information of the graph into the original graph. Through a series of operations on the adjacency matrix and degree matrix of the original graph, the graph contains topological information at all levels. Specifically, the graph diffusion strategy adopted in this scheme can be described as :

$$S = \alpha(I - (1 - \alpha)D^{-\frac{1}{2}}AD^{-\frac{1}{2}})^{-1} \qquad (1)$$

where S represents the adjacency matrix of the graph obtained by graph diffusion, α is the predefined hyper-parameter used to balance the proportion of local information and global information (In line with many classical works, we set 0.05 here), I represents the unit matrix, A represents the adjacency matrix of the original graph, and D represents the degree matrix of the original graph.

Subsampling (SS) is an augmentation strategy to obtain a smaller sub-graph by cutting the original graph. Quantitative nodes are randomly selected from the original graph, and these nodes and their topological information together with feature information are retained to obtain a fixed-size sub-graph. Sub-sampling can not only effectively reduce the subsequent calculation cost of the model, but also improve the representation learning ability of the model to a certain extent, similar to the pooling layer in computer vision.

Edge modification (EM) is an augmentation strategy that randomly removes the quantitative edges in the original graph and adds equal edges. By this strategy, the topological results of the original graph are complicated while preserving the attribute (feature) information of the original graph. Specifically, for the adjacency matrix A of the original graph, according to the given edge replacement ratio P (e.g. 0.2), the edges of $P/2$ are deleted from the original graph, and the new edges of $P/2$ are added.

Node Feature Masking (NFM) is an augmentation strategy to randomly select some nodes in the original graph and set their feature information to Null. Specifically, a node is sampled from the attribute matrix X of the original graph at a fixed ratio P (e.g. 0.2), and all features (attributes) of the sampled node are set to zero vector.

3.2   Siamese Graph Network

Inspired by the Siamese network in computer vision, we design a novel graph contrastive learning framework with an online network and target network. We input the two augmented graphs (*view* 1, *view* 2) into the online network and the target network, and gain four graph node representations (*online h*1, *online h*2, *target h*1, *target h*2). The online network and the target network are composed of a graph convolution network and a 512-layer multi-layer perception. The parameters of the two networks are initialized to the same random value. The parameters of the online network are updated with the gradient descent when training. The parameters of the target network are not updated with the gradient but are updated gradually by the momentum update mechanism.

The momentum update mechanism adopted by the target network is a mechanism that updates according to a fixed ratio (momentum m) based on the historical parameters of the model. By using this update mechanism, the target network can be maintained relatively stable, thus ensuring that the online network is iterative in a relatively stable direction. Specifically, the momentum update mechanism adopted in this scheme can be described as the following formula:

$$\xi^t = m \cdot \xi^{t-1} + (1 - m) \cdot \theta^t \tag{2}$$

where ξ^{t-1} represents the parameters of the target network after $t - 1$ update, θ^t represents the parameters of the online network after t gradient update, ξ^t represents the new parameters of the target network, and momentum m is a predefined super parameter for adjusting the momentum update ratio. When m is set to 0, it is equivalent to directly copying the parameters of the online network in each iteration of the target network; when m is set to 1, it is equivalent to the target network keeping the initial random parameters to stop updating. We discuss the effects of hyper-parameter m in Sect. 4.3.

3.3   Deep Clustering Optimization

The clustering layer in the framework is used to cluster the representation (*online h1*) obtained by the online network of an augmented graph *view 1*, and the clustering loss L_{kl} can be used to describe the similarity of the representation learned by the online network and the target network of an augmented graph *view 1* obtained in Sect. 3.1.

Firstly, we calculated the soft label distribution Q_1 and Q_2 of the graph node representation (*online h1* and *target h1*), which are learned by the online network and target network. Taking *online h1* as an example, the soft label distribution Q_1 measured by $student - t$ distribution, which indicates that the node x_k in online $h1$ belongs to the similarity of the j cluster. The definition of $q_{kj}^{(1)} \in Q_1$ is as follows:

$$q_{kj}^{(1)} = \frac{\left(1 + \| g_\theta(x_k) - \mu_j \|^2\right)^{-1}}{\sum_j \left(1 + \| g_\theta(x_k) - \mu_j \|^2\right)^{-1}} \tag{3}$$

where $g_\theta(x_k)$ represents the embedding of node x_k in *online h1* and μ_j represents the j cluster center.

Similarly, the soft label distribution Q_2 of the *target h1* is also measured by $student - t$ distribution, which indicates that the node x_k in target $h1$ belongs to the similarity of the j cluster. The definition of $q_{kj}^{(2)} \in Q_2$ is as follows:

$$q_{kj}^{(2)} = \frac{\left(1 + \| g_\xi(x_k) - \mu_j \|^2\right)^{-1}}{\sum_j \left(1 + \| g_\xi(x_k) - \mu_j \|^2\right)^{-1}} \tag{4}$$

We define $f_j = \sum_{k=1}^{n} q_{kj}^{(1)}$ and introduce auxiliary target distribution P, which is derived from Q_1:

$$p_{kj} = \frac{q_{kj}^{(1)} \cdot q_{kj}^{(1)} / f_j}{\sum_{j'} q_{kj'}^{(1)} \cdot q_{kj'}^{(1)} / f_{j'}} \tag{5}$$

Then, we can calculate the average distribution Q_m and the KL divergence of target P distribution with Q_m. These variables can be used for measuring the similarity of the graph node representation *online h*1 and *target h*1) obtained by the online network and target network of *view* 1. The KL divergence of target P and the average distribution Q_m is defined as:

$$L_{kl} = KL(P\|Q_m) = \sum_k \sum_j p_{ij} log \frac{p_{kj}}{q_{kj}^{(m)}} \tag{6}$$

where Q_m is the mean of Q_1 and Q_2, and $q_{kj}^{(m)}$ represents the average similarity of node x_k belonging to the j cluster.

$$Q_m = (Q_1 + Q_2)/2 \tag{7}$$

3.4   Debiased Cross Contrast

The clustering information can not only be used in the clustering layer but also can be used for conducting graph contrastive learning. We call this clustering information as "pseudo label", which can be regarded as the categories of nodes and used for debiased sampling.

Taking *online h*1 and *target h*1 for example, we take node x in *online h*1 as a target, and the negative samples are usually selected as all nodes except x in *target h*1. The negative samples may have "false negative" nodes that are highly similar to x. Referring to these "pseudo labels", we believe that a node y in a negative sample set is "false negative" if it belongs to the same cluster as x.

We design a cross-contrast mechanism with debiasing, which is divided into two parts: cross-view contrast and cross-network contrast.

Cross-view contrast. We choose *online h*1 as the target and select positive and negative samples from *onlie h*2. Taking node x in *online h*1 as an example, those neighbor nodes to x in *online h*2 and belonging to the same cluster are positive samples, while those not adjacent and not belonging to the same cluster are negative samples. The contrast loss is denoted as $L_{clv}(x_i)$.

Cross-network contrast. Similar to cross-view contrast, we choose *online h*1 as the target and select positive and negative samples from *target h*1. The cross-network contrast loss is denoted as $L_{cln}(x_i)$.

The calculation formula of contrast loss in cross-network contrast and cross-view contrast is:

$$L_{cln}(x_i) = -\log \frac{e^{g_\theta(x_i)^T g_\xi(x_i^+)}}{e^{g_\theta(x_i)^T g_\xi(x_i^+)} + \sum_{t=1}^{M} e^{g_\theta(x_i)^T g_\xi(x_{it}^-)}} \tag{8}$$

$$L_{clv}(x_i) = -\log \frac{e^{g_\theta(x_i)^T g_\theta(x_i^+)}}{e^{g_\theta(x_i)^T g_\theta(x_i^+)} + \sum_{t=1}^{M} e^{g_\theta(x_i)^T g_\theta(x_{it}^-)}} \tag{9}$$

Among them, $g_\theta(x_i)$ represents the representation of node x_i learned by the online network in *view* 1, $g_\xi(x_i^+)$ represents the representation of node x_i learned by target network in *view* 1, $g_\theta(x_i^+)$ represents the representation of node x_i^+ learned by the online network in *view* 2.

The calculation methods of $L_{cln}(x_i)$ and $L_{clv}(x_i)$ are consistent, and the difference is the input network representation. Taking cross-network contrast as an example, where $g_\theta(x_i)$ represents the embedding representation of node x_i in *online* $h1$, $g_\xi(x_i^+)$ represents the embedding representation of positive samples selected from *target* $h1$ with the same clustering pseudo labels as x_i, $g_\theta(x_{it}^-)$ represents the embedding representation of negative samples selected from *target* $h1$ with different clustering pseudo labels as x_i, M is the predefined number of negative samples.

The overall loss function of the model is obtained by synthesizing the cross-view contrast loss and cross-network contrast loss, as well as the clustering loss obtained in Sect. 3.3. The overall objective function L of the model is defined as follows :

$$L = \beta * L_{kl} + L_{cln} + L_{clv} \tag{10}$$

where, L_{kl}, L_{cln} and L_{clv} represent the clustering loss, the cross-network contrast loss, and the cross-view contrast loss, and β represents the hyper-parameter(discussed in Chap. 4.3) regulating the clustering loss and the debiased contrast loss.

The original graph is input into the trained online network and the target network, and the sum of the two representations is used as the final representation, which is applied to the downstream node classification, node clustering, and other tasks, namely:

$$g = g_\theta + g_\xi \tag{11}$$

where g represents the representation of the graph learned in MEDC, and g_θ and g_ξ represent the representation of the original graph obtained by the trained online network and the target network.

3.5 MEDC Algorithm

As shown in Algorithm 1, MEDC consists of four parts: Graph Augmentations, Siamese network for graph, Deep Clustering Optimization, and Debiased Cross Contrast. The input of MEDC is an attributed graph G, and the output is the representation g corresponding to graph G. The representation g can be used for downstream tasks such as node classification, node clustering, and link prediction.

4   Experiments and Analysis

To evaluate the effect of our proposed MEDC for self-supervised graph representation learning, we compare the node classification and clustering performance with four existing state-of-the-art graph contrastive learning methods on classical benchmark networks.

Algorithm 1: The MEDC algorithm

Input: The attributed graph $G = (V, E)$ with adjacency matrix A and degree
   matrix D, the hyper-parameter m and β
Output: Graph embedding representation g
MEDC()
   Obtain *view* 1 and *view* 2 with graph enhancement;
   Initialize online network and target network with random parameters;
   while *epoch* < *epochs* **do**
      Embedding *view* 1 and *view* 2 in online network and target network;
      Calculate the soft label distribution $Q1$ and $Q2$ according to (3) and (4);
      Get the target distribution P use (5);
      Calculate cluster loss L_{kl} of P and $Q1$, $Q2$ according to (6) and (7);
      Sampling and de-biasing with clustering P;
      Calculate contrastive loss L_{cln} and L_{clv} according to (8) to (9);
      Assemble L_{kl}, L_{cln} and L_{clv} with β according to (10);
      Back-propagation and momentum update with m use (1);
   end
   Output graph embedding g according to (11);

4.1   Experimental Settings

Benchmark Datasets. In our experiments, we use three commonly used benchmark real-world networks to evaluate the performance: Cora, Citseer, and Pubmed [22]. Table 1 summarizes their data characteristics. The Cora dataset is composed of machine-learning papers. Each paper in the dataset cites or is cited by at least one other paper, and the label indicates the category to which the paper belongs. The Citeseer paper network database contains 3,327 papers with 4,732 citations, and each paper corresponds to one of the 6 types of labels. Pubmed is a biomedical paper database, which contains 19,717 papers, 44,338 citations, and 3 types of labels.

Table 1. Statistics of datasets used in our experiments.

Dataset	Nodes	Edges	Features	Classes
Cora	2708	5429	1433	7
Citeseer	3327	4732	3703	6
Pubmed	19717	44338	500	3

Parameter Settings. In the method proposed in this paper, the graph diffusion hyperparameter α (set to 0.05), the momentum m (set to 0.5), and the number of neurons in the embedding layer used by an encoder (set to 512) are identical in Cora, Citeseer, and Pubmed. But the hyper-parameters β represent the regulating the clustering loss and the debiased Contrastive loss is set to 0.5 in Cora and Citeseer, set to 0.7 in Pubmed. We will analyze the effect of this parameter on the results in the next subsection.

Benchmark Methods. We compare MEDC with the following representative graph contrastive learning methods: GMI [20], MVGRL [11], GRACE [21], and MERIT [12]. GMI is trained by maximizing the graph mutual information between the input graph and the high-level hidden representation. MVGRL introduces the concept of graph multi-view contrastive learning by discriminating the patch-global representations over two augmented views derived from the input graph. GRACE proposes a hybrid scheme to generate graph views at the structure and attribute levels, providing diverse node contexts for comparison targets. MERIT is the first to apply the Siamese network to graph representation learning, taking advantage of the boot-strapping in the Siamese network and multi-scale graph contrastive learning.

Experimental Environment. We run all the experiments on a Linux machine with a 12th Gen Intel(R) Core(TM) i7-12700KF CPU (12 cores @ 4.90GHz), 128 GB of RAM, and two RTX 3090 GPU. For all methods, we used the same hyper-parameter settings as in the original paper to achieve the highest possible accuracy on original datasets.

4.2   Results and Analysis

Node Classification. To ensure the reliability of our experiments, we adopt a linear evaluation protocol to train a logistic regression classifier. Specifically, we take the learned graph embedding as the input of the classifier, train it with the same hyper-parameters, and compare the node classification accuracy [23] of our proposed method with the four excellent graph contrastive learning methods. The larger the value of this accuracy rate, the better the classification performance of the method.

We repeat the experiments for 10 times and report the average accuracy rate and standard deviation in the node classification result. As shown in Table 2, we can observe that MEDC achieves the highest performance on all three datasets. This result can be attributed to the three key components in our framework: (1) The Siamese network architecture introduced is more beneficial to contrastive learning without node label information. (2) An additional clustering layer to eliminate the pseudo labels in nodes. (3) A more consummate objective function that introduces node clustering loss and multiple contrasts within and across different views and networks.

Benefiting from the combination of graph contrastive learning on the Siamese network and the extract clustering layer used for debiasing, MEDC achieves the best classification accuracy on three datasets. However, three still exist performance gaps between graph contrastive learning methods in CiteSeer and Pubmed, even though the five contrastive learning methods have achieved similar even better classification accuracy in the Cora dataset.

Table 2. Classification accuracies on three benchmark datasets.

Method	Cora	CiteSeer	PubMed
GMI	0.816±0.00	0.683±0.01	0.785±0.00
MVGRL	0.820±0.00	0.702±0.00	0.714±0.00
GRACE	0.827±0.01	0.697±0.00	0.764±0.01
MERIT	0.831±0.60	0.733±0.40	0.801±0.70
MEDC(ours)	**0.833±0.01**	**0.737±0.00**	**0.815±0.01**

Node Clustering. In addition, we compare the performance of these methods on graph node clustering tasks based on three benchmark datasets. We choose three widely recognized evaluation metrics for the clustering task, namely, Clustering Accuracy (ACC), Normalized Mutual Information (NMI [24]), and Adjusted Rand Index (ARI [25]), where NMI is used to describe the similarity of clustering results and ARI is used to describe the consistency of clustering results. As with the Clustering Accuracy(ACC), the larger the value of NMI and ARI, the better the clustering effect.

Table 3. Clustering performance on three benchmark datasets.

Method	Cora			CiteSeer			PubMed		
	ACC	NMI	ARI	ACC	NMI	ARI	ACC	NMI	ARI
GMI	0.7087	0.6804	0.5575	0.5003	0.3689	0.2458	0.4533	0.4195	0.265
MVGRL	0.7286	0.6383	0.5137	0.4525	0.3063	0.1629	0.435	0.3193	0.2308
GRACE	0.6967	0.5461	0.4956	0.6346	0.3838	0.3677	0.4851	0.1703	0.0784
MERIT	0.6928	0.6972	0.5346	0.65	0.4778	**0.4112**	0.7833	0.4919	0.5488
MEDC(ours)	**0.7714**	**0.7228**	**0.5895**	**0.6667**	0.4825	0.3902	**0.7967**	**0.4953**	**0.5701**

As shown in Table 3, our proposed method achieves optimal results in most of the metrics for all three data sets. Compared with MERIT, which also uses a twin network architecture, we significantly improve ACC and NMI on Cora, while maintaining the excellent performance of the CiteSeer and Pubmed datasets. We attribute this to the fact that our proposed clustering guidance mechanism improves MERIT's inadequate comparison on smaller datasets.

Efficiency (Training Time and Memory Cost). In Table 4, we compare the performance of MEDC with the state-of-the-art methods including GRACE and MERIT in terms of their training time and the memory overhead. We tested node classification in three datasets, and recorded the training time and memory required to achieve optimal results for each method. Here, the training time refers to the time for model training and the memory overhead refers to the total memory costs of model parameters and all hidden representations of a batch.

As can be observed, MEDC achieved the best results on the Cora in a shorter time, leading GRACE by 2.163 s and MERIT by 3.616 s. The significant lead on PubMed demonstrates that MEDC has better generalization capabilities on large-scale graphs. It must be acknowledged that MEDC utilizes more network parameters, resulting in higher memory consumption, but this trade-off is worthwhile considering the improvement in its performance.

Table 4. Comparisons of efficiency on three graph datasets.

Dataset	Algorithm	Training Time	Memory
Cora	GRACE	11.680 s	296 MB
	MERIT	13.133 s	838 MB
	MEDC(ours)	9.517 s	1254 MB
CiteSeer	GRACE	2.805 s	596 MB
	MERIT	3.627 s	868 MB
	MEDC(ours)	3.461 s	1238 MB
PubMed	GRACE	311.806 s	11298 MB
	MERIT	20.934 s	770 MB
	MEDC(ours)	11.304 s	1122 MB

4.3 Parameter Sensitivity Analysis

In graph diffusion, we use the hyper-parameters α to balance the proportion of local information and global information. On the other hand, we use the important hyper-parameters β to balance the relationship with cross-graph contrast loss, cross-network contrast loss, and clustering loss. In addition, we use the hyper-parameters m to control the target network and keep relatively stable in the momentum update mechanism.

As can be observed in Fig. 2, the effectiveness of graph diffusion is different for Cora, Citeseer, and Pubmed. But in general, the best performance was achieved for all datasets when α is set to 0.05.

In Fig. 2, for a fixed momentum update rate m (set to 0.8), we observe that β value around 0.5 achieved the best classification performance in Cora and CiteSeer, which achieved the best performance in 0.7 in PubMed. We believe this is due to the fact that PubMed has far more nodes and edges than Cora and CiteSeer, and fewer feature dimensions. In other words, PubMed easier to have pseudo-labels. When the value of β is set to 0.7, the clustering loss is more important in the objective function, and then the model has a stronger debiasing ability to adapt to the Pumed dataset.

On the other hand, for a certain β value (such as 0.6), MEDC achieves the best classification accuracy when the momentum update rate m is set between 0.4 to 0.6. We hypothesize that a moderate m can control the direction of graph contrast learning well and avoid over-fitting (m set to 1) or freezing (m set to 0).

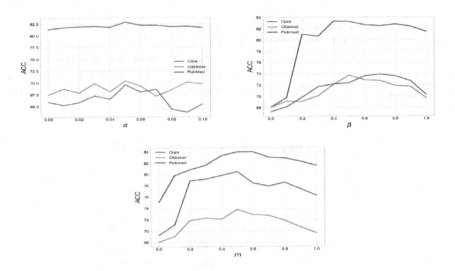

Fig. 2. Effect of α, β and m in Cora, Citeseer and Pubmed

5   Conclusion

In this paper, we proposed a novel Siamese graph representation learning method based on community structure enhancement. To demonstrate the effect of the proposed method, we conducted experiments on four real datasets, showing that our method does not depend on the quality of the dataset and always achieves optimal results. As a novel graph contrastive learning method, our proposed approach can be applied in areas such as drug discovery and social network analysis. There are two promising avenues for future work: (1) exploring how to reduce the dependence on graph enhancement. (2) applying the Contrastive Siamese networks to more real-world tasks including biochemistry and recommender system.

References

1. Zhang, D., Yin, J., Zhu, X., Zhang, C.: Network representation learning: a survey. IEEE Transactions on Big Data, pp. 3–28 (2018). https://doi.org/10.1109/tbdata.2018.2850013
2. Ktena, S.I., et al.: Distance metric learning using graph convolutional networks: application to functional brain networks. In: Descoteaux, M., Maier-Hein, L., Franz, A., Jannin, P., Collins, D.L., Duchesne, S. (eds.) MICCAI 2017. LNCS, vol. 10433, pp. 469–477. Springer, Cham (2017). https://doi.org/10.1007/978-3-319-66182-7_54
3. Lin, H., Ma, J., Cheng, M., Yang, Z., Chen, L., Chen, G.: Rumor detection on twitter with claim-guided hierarchical graph attention networks. In: Proceedings of the 2021 Conference on Empirical Methods in Natural Language Processing, pp. 10035–10047 (2021)

4. Bastings, J., Titov, I., Aziz, W., Marcheggiani, D., Sima'an, K.: Graph convolutional encoders for syntax-aware neural machine translation. The Association for Computational Linguistics (2017)

5. Ma, J., Zhou, C., Cui, P., Yang, H., Zhu, W.: Learning disentangled representations for a recommendation. In: Advances in Neural Information Processing Systems 32 (2019)

6. Yang, C., Liu, Z., Zhao, D., Sun, M., Chang, E.Y.: Network representation learning with rich text information. In: Proceedings of the 24th International Joint Conference on Artifcial Intelligence, pp. 2111–2117 (2015)

7. Oord, A.V.D., Li, Y., Vinyals, O.: Representation learning with contrastive predictive coding. arXiv preprint arXiv:1807.03748 (2018)

8. Guo, X., Gao, L., Liu, X., Yin, J.: Improved deep embedded clustering with local structure preservation. In: IJCAI, pp. 1753–1759 (2017)

9. Xie, J., Girshick, R., Farhadi, A.: Unsupervised deep embedding for clustering analysis. In: International Conference on Machine Learning, pp. 478–487. PMLR (2016)

10. You, Y., Chen, T., Sui, Y., Chen, T., Wang, Z., Shen, Y.: Graph contrastive learning with augmentations. Adv. Neural. Inf. Process. Syst. **33**, 5812–5823 (2020)

11. Hassani, K., Khasahmadi, A.H.: Contrastive multi-view representation learning on graphs. In: International Conference on Machine Learning, pp. 4116–4126. PMLR (2020)

12. Jin, M., Zheng, Y., Li, Y.F., Gong, C., Zhou, C., Pan, S. Multi-scale contrastive Siamese networks for self-supervised graph representation learning. arXiv preprint arXiv:2105.05682 (2021)

13. Kipf, T.N., Welling, M.: Semi-supervised classification with graph convolutional networks. In: Proceedings of the International Conference on Learning Representations (ICLR) (2016)

14. Hadsell, R., Chopra, S., LeCun, Y.: Dimensionality reduction by learning an invariant mapping. In: Proceedings of the 2006 IEEE Computer Society Conference on Computer Vision and Pattern Recognition, vol. 2, pp. 1735–1742 (2006)

15. Mueller, J., Thyagarajan, A., Doshi-Velez, F.: Siamese recurrent architectures for learning sentence similarity. In: Thirty-First AAAI Conference on Artificial Intelligence (2016)

16. Schroff, F., Kalenichenko, D., Philbin, J.: FaceNet: a unified embedding for face recognition and clustering. In: Proceedings of the 2015 IEEE Conference on Computer Vision and Pattern Recognition, pp. 815–823 (2015)

17. Grill, J.B., et al.: Bootstrap your own latent-a new approach to self-supervised learning. In: Advances in Neural Information Processing Systems 33, pp. 21271–21284 (2020)

18. Zhao, H., Yang, X., Wang, Z., Yang, E., Deng, C.: Graph debiased contrastive learning with joint representation clustering. In: IJCAI, pp. 3434–3440 (2021)

19. Peng, Z., Liu, H., Jia, Y., Hou, J.: Attention-driven graph clustering network. In: Proceedings of the 29th ACM International Conference on Multimedia, pp. 935–943 (2021)

20. Peng, Z., et al.: Graph representation learning via graphical mutual information maximization. In: Proceedings of The Web Conference 2020, pp. 259–270 (2020)

21. Zhu, Y., Xu, Y., Yu, F., Liu, Q., Wu, S., Wang, L.: Deep graph contrastive representation learning. In: ICML Workshop on Graph Representation Learning and Beyond (2020)

22. Shchur, O., Mumme, M., Bojchevski, A., Günnemann, S.: Pitfalls of graph neural network evaluation. Computing Research Repository, abs/1811.05868 (2018)

23. Ghamrawi, N., McCallum, A.: Collective multi-label classification. In: Proceedings of the 14th ACM International Conference on Information and Knowledge Management, pp. 195–200 (2005)
24. Younis, O., Krunz, M., Ramasubramanian, S.: Node clustering in wireless sensor networks: recent developments and deployment challenges. IEEE Network **20**(3), 20–25 (2006)
25. Rendón, E., Abundez, I., Arizmendi, A., Quiroz, E.M.: Internal versus external cluster validation indexes. Int. J. Comput. Commun. **5**(1), 27-34 (2011)

Distant Supervision Relation Extraction with Improved PCNN and Multi-level Attention

Yang Zou[✉], Qifei Wang, Zhen Wang, Jian Zhou, and Xiaoqin Zeng

Institute of Intelligence Science and Technology, School of Computer and Information,
Hohai University, Nanjing 210098, China
{yzou,qfwang,zwang,211607010098,xzeng}@hhu.edu.cn

Abstract. In the research field of relation extraction, a large amount of labeled training data can be quickly obtained through distant supervision. However, distant supervision will be inevitably accompanied by the problem of wrong labelling, and the noisy data can substantially hurt the performance of relation extraction model. Previous studies mainly focus on de-noising by designing neural networks with intra-bag or inter-bag attention, but do not sufficiently take noise interference at different levels into account. Moreover, the conventional approach Piecewise Convolutional Neural Network (PCNN) encodes sentences based on an assumption that each segmented feature contributes equally to the relation, which is unreasonable. To alleviate these issues, we propose a distant supervision relation extraction model with Improved PCNN (I-PCNN) and multi-level attention. By incorporating word-level, sentence-level and bag-level attention into the model, it can effectively reduce the noisy data in a data set. Besides, it also enhances PCNN by augmenting self-attention, which can promote the encoding quality of sentences. Experiments conducted on New York Times (NYT) data set show that the proposed model evidently outperforms several baseline models in terms of the metrics *Precision*, *Recall*, *AUC*, and *P@N*.

Keywords: relation extraction · distant supervision · I-PCNN · multi-level attention

1 Introduction

Relation extraction is one of the fundamental tasks in constructing Knowledge Graph, which aims to extract semantic relations between entity pairs in unstructured text. According to the degree of dependence on manually annotated data, mainstream methods of relation extraction are mainly divided into four categories: supervised relation extraction, semi-supervised relation extraction, distant supervision relation extraction, and unsupervised relation extraction.

Generally, supervision relation extraction can achieve good training results, but it relies heavily on high-quality manual annotation data, which requires a large amount of human and financial costs. Moreover, most of those annotated data are domain-specific and not highly scalable, and thus the models trained on them cannot be effortlessly generalized.

Z. Jin et al. (Eds.): KSEM 2023, LNAI 14117, pp. 315–327, 2023.
https://doi.org/10.1007/978-3-031-40283-8_27

To address the above issue, Mintz et al. [1] proposed the usage of distant supervision instead of manually tagging data. The core idea of distant supervision is: If there is a certain entity relation triple (entity 1, entity 2, relation R) in the Knowledge Base (KB), it can be determined that all text sentences containing entity 1 and entity 2 in the corresponding corpus can express the meaning of relation R. For example, if there is a triple entity relation (*Biden, United States, President*) in the KB such as Freebase proposed by Bollacker et al. [2], all sentences in the corpus that appear simultaneously with "*Biden*" and "*United States*" will be marked as the "*President*" relation. Obviously, the extremely strong hypothesis of distant supervision inevitably leads to incorrect tagging of labeled sentence data.

In order to reduce the adverse impact of noisy data generated by distant supervision on the performance of relation extraction model, quite a few works have been proposed, including converting the strong constraints into weaker ones, or introducing attention to dynamically adjust the weights made by each sentence on the relation, and identify and correct noisy data. Although these methods have achieved some good denoising results on distant supervision data set, there is still room for improvement. Zeng et al. [3] proposed PCNN, which directly splices each segmented feature after max-pooling. Lin et al. [4] utilized PCNN and sentence-level attention to represent sentences and assign weights to them in the bag, respectively. Jat et al. [5] adopted word and entity-based attention to reduce noisy interference in sentences. Ye et al. [6] obtained a new representation of sentences by increasing the attention across the bag within the bag.

Nevertheless, the above methods of expressing sentences ignore the real distribution of data in a data set. As a matter of fact, the contribution of each segmented feature to the relation is quite different. In addition, there is much noisy data in the data set generated by distant supervision, and there are even situations where all the sentences in a bag cannot represent the relation. Therefore, these methods do not sufficiently take noise interference at different levels into account.

In order to tackle the above problems, this paper proposes a novel distant supervision relation extraction model with I-PCNN and multi-level attention. Firstly, it improves the processing method after sentence max-pooling by using the self-attention to dynamically obtain the specific contribution of each segmented feature to the relation. Then, considering the existence of the case where no positive example sample exists in the whole bag, it simultaneously fuses word-level, sentence-level and bag-level attention to acquire a feature representation of the relation. Finally, it inputs the feature into a *softmax* layer to train the relation extraction model.

In summary, the main contributions of this paper are as follows:

- In the proposed model, the self-attention is integrated into PCNN to dynamically acquire the specific contribution of each segmented feature to the relation so as to determine which segmented features have greater contributions, and thus can achieve more accurate feature representation of the relation.
- By incorporating word-level, sentence-level and bag-level attention into the framework, the proposed model can process noisy data from all dimensions, which effectively improves the performance of relation extraction.

- Experimental results on the distant supervision data set NYT show that compared with several baseline models, the proposed model achieves preferable performance with respect to the metrics such as *PR* plots, *AUC* values, and *P@N*.

2 Related Work

In order to alleviate the problem of mislabeling generated by distant supervision, Riedel et al. [7] proposed a method that combines the Multi-Instance Learning (MIL) with distant supervision. It appropriately relaxes the distant supervision assumption and proposes the following hypothesis: the data set generated by distant supervision is divided into multiple bags, where each bag consists of sentences of the same entity pair, and there is at least one sentence in each bag that can express the relation, which can effectively alleviate the problem of wrong labels in distant supervision data set. Zeng et al. [3] adopted piecewise convolutional neural networks to solve the error propagation problem caused by relying on natural language processing tools. Lin et al. [4] provided a sentence-level attention, so that the relation extraction model can fully utilize all the sentence information in each bag.

To address the problem of data false negatives caused by incomplete KB, Xie et al. [8] employed the RERE model to detect sentence-level relations for effective training of samples. Li et al. [9] utilized the multi-head attention layer to calculate and assign weights, avoiding the usage of noisy relation labels as the basis for attention assignment, so as to reduce the impact of noise. Ji et al. [10] exploited TransH pre-trained entity vectors to select attention together with sentence features to further improve the encoding quality of sentences. Ye et al. [6] introduced the Inter-Bag attention to alleviate noisy data existing in the data set marked by the distant supervision, obtaining high-quality feature representation for training relation extraction model.

The above-mentioned methods process the sentence feature after PCNN, neglecting the fact that each segmented feature contributes differently to the sentence representation. Based on this observation, this paper introduces the self-attention to the PCNN stage to dynamically select the important segmented features for the sentence feature representation. In addition, it integrates the attention into the model at word-level, sentence-level, and bag-level simultaneously.

3 Relation Extraction with I-PCNN and Multi-level Attention

In this section, we propose a model with I-PCNN and multi-level attention for distant supervision relation extraction. The framework of the model is shown in Fig. 1, which consists of three main modules.

- Sentence Encoder. Given a sentence and two target entities, the I-PCNN can be used to construct a distributed representation of the sentence.
- Selective Attention over Sentences. When the distributed feature representation of all sentences is learnt, sentence-level attention can be utilized to select the sentences which exactly express the corresponding relation and obtain the distributed representation of the bag.

- Selective Attention over Bags. When the distributed feature representation of all bags is learnt, bag-level attention can be adopted to attain the representation of the bag group.

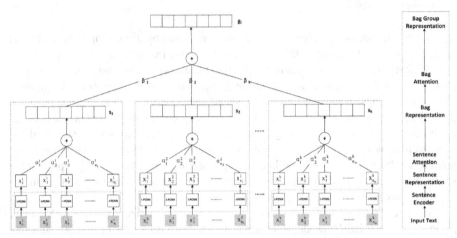

Fig. 1. The framework of the proposed model with I-PCNN and multi-level attention for relation extraction. I-PCNN is showed in the dashed blue box, whereas the process within each bag is shown in the dashed red box.

3.1 Sentence Encoder

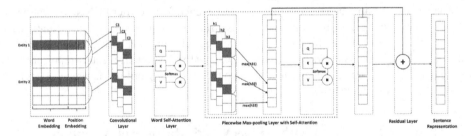

Fig. 2. The architecture of I-PCNN.

In this subsection, a module called Piecewise Max-pooling Layer with Self-Attention is introduced, as shown in the red dashed box in Fig. 2, which incorporates the self-attention layer to the conventional PCNN to more precisely assign weights to the segmented features after piecewise max-pooling.

Word Representation. Word vectors refer to the distributed representation of words, which map each word in a text to a low-dimensional dense vector [11]. Let $x = \{w_1, w_2, \ldots, w_n\}$ be a sentence, and n the number of words in the sentence. Each word w_i within x is mapped into a d_w-dimensional word embedding by the word embedding matrix named $WE \in R^{d_w \times |V|}$, where $|V|$ denotes the number of all words in the corpus, and the final feature representation is denoted as $w_i = \{d_1^i, d_2^i, \ldots, d_w^i\}$.

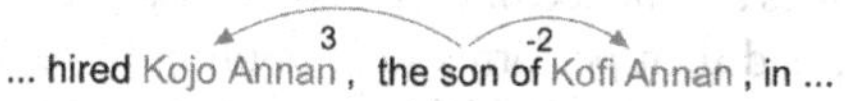

$$\overset{3}{\overbrace{\ldots \text{ hired Kojo Annan}}} , \quad \text{the son } \overset{-2}{\overbrace{\text{of Kofi Annan}}} , \text{ in } \ldots$$

Fig. 3. An example of relative positions.

Let $P1_i$ and $P2_i$, $(i = 1, 2, 3, \ldots, n)$, be the relative distances of the i-th word from the two entities respectively. In line with the previous word embedding matrix, the position vector matrix is defined by $PE \in R^{d_p \times |X|}$, where d_p denotes the vector dimension of each position and $|X|$ denotes the number of relative positions in the range of values. The relative positions are shown in Fig. 3, where "son" is at a distance of 3 from the first entity "Kojo Annan" and -2 from the second entity "Kofi Annan".

As shown in Fig. 2, each word w_i in sentence x consists of a word vector and two position vectors, where $w_i \in R^d$, and $d = d_w + 2 \times d_p$.

Convolutional Layer. It can effectively capture the n-gram features, as well as key local information in a text, and fuse all the local features together to achieve global prediction [12]. The set of m convolutional kernels is denoted as $F_c = \{f_c^1, f_c^2, \ldots, f_c^m\}$, where $f_c^j \in R^{l \times d}$ of size l, and the j-th convolutional operation is formulated as Eq. 1, where $w_{i:i+l-1}$ denotes the splicing matrix from w_i to w_{i+l-1}.

$$c_i^j = f_c^j w_{i:i+l-1}, 1 \le i \le n - l + 1, 1 \le j \le m \tag{1}$$

Finally, sentence $x = \{w_1, w_2, \ldots, w_n\}$ is represented by the results of convolutional operation as $C = \{c^1, c^2, c^3, \ldots, c^m\}$, where each c^j is the concatenation of c_i^j ($1 \le i \le n - l + 1$) and $C \in R^{(m \times (n-l+1))}$.

Word Self-Attention Layer. Word self-attention is to dynamically assign a weight to each word in the sentence by calculating the correlation between words and filtering the negative impact of irrelevant words [13]. The specific process includes two steps: First, the features C captured by the convolutional layer are processed by three different linear transformations to obtain three matrices Q_c, K_c and V_c, respectively; and then the sentence representation $H = \{h^1, h^2, h^3, \ldots, h^m\}$ after self-attention is obtained by the scaled dot-product attention, where $H \in R^{(m \times (n-l+1))}$. The corresponding two calculations are expressed as Eqs. 2, 3, respectively, where d_k represents the dimension of matrix K_c.

$$Q_C = W_{Q_C}C, K_C = W_{K_C}C, V_C = W_{V_C}C \tag{2}$$

$$H = softmax\left(\frac{Q_C K_C^T}{\sqrt{d_k}}\right)V_C \tag{3}$$

Piecewise Max-pooling Layer with Self-Attention. In the field of Natural Language Processing (NLP), the extraction of features using convolutional layers is regularly followed by a pooling layer for reducing the number of parameters [14]. However, if the common method of maximum pooling is used, a problem will be encountered that the granularity of the feature data after processing by max-pooling is too large, and then it is difficult to obtain the important feature about the entity pairs. The piecewise max-pooling method [3], divides a sentence into three parts based on the positions of the two entities in the sentence, and then performs max-pooling to each of the three parts, as shown in Fig. 2. The sentence feature, which is extracted by the word self-attention, can be represented as $H = \{h^1, h^2, h^3, \ldots, h^m\}$, where each h^j is divided into $\left\{h_1^j, h_2^j, h_3^j\right\}$. The calculation is shown in Eq. 4:

$$p_r^j = \max\left(h_r^j\right), 1 \leq r \leq 3, 1 \leq j \leq m \tag{4}$$

The final result is expressed as $P = \{p^1, p^2, p^3, \ldots, p^m\}$.

The above is the basic process of the conventional PCNN. However, from the viewpoint of data distribution, it can be observed that the contribution of each segmented feature to the relation is quite different. To address this, we introduce the self-attention to dynamically assign weights to the m segmented features after piecewise max-pooling processing so as to discover the important feature among them. The specific process is described as follows: The features P captured by piecewise max-pooling operation is processed by three different linear transformations to obtain three matrices Q, K, and V, respectively, and then the feature representation $Z = \{z^1, z^2, z^3, \ldots, z^m\}$ is achieved from the self-attention layer by the scaled dot-product attention. The calculations in the process can be formulated as Eqs. 5, 6:

$$Q_P = W_{Q_P}P, \ K_P = W_{K_P}P, \ V_P = W_{V_P}P \tag{5}$$

$$Z = softmax\left(\frac{Q_P K_P{}^T}{\sqrt{d_k}}\right)V_P \tag{6}$$

Finally, through a residual layer, all vectors are stitched together and fed into the activation function *tanh* to obtain a feature representation as Eqs. 7, 8, where $x \in R^{3m}$.

$$Z = P + Z \tag{7}$$

$$x = tanh\left(z^{1:m}\right) \tag{8}$$

3.2 Selective Attention over Sentences

From a sentence feature representation extracted by Sentence Encoder it can be known which words in the sentence have greater contributions to the relation. Lin et al. [4] exploit the attention at the sentence-level to dynamically assign different weights to the sentences in each bag, and thus filter out the undesirable effects of noisy sentences. The architecture of the sentence-level attention is given in Fig. 4, where $s = \{x_1, x_2, \ldots, x_n\}$ is a set comprised of n sentences that contain the same entity pair $(head, tail)$ and r is the corresponding relation.

The specific process is presented as follows: After obtaining the corresponding feature representation from I-PCNN processing, each sentence gains its weight through the sentence-level attention; and then the scaled dot-product attention is done to the sentences and their weights to achieve the final bag representation s. The calculations involved are expressed as Eqs. 9, 10, 11:

$$s = \sum_{i=1}^{n} \alpha_i x_i \tag{9}$$

$$\alpha_i = \frac{\exp(e_i)}{\sum_{j=1}^{n} \exp(e_j)} \tag{10}$$

$$e_i = x_i A r \tag{11}$$

where x_i denotes the i-th sentence in a bag, r denotes the one-hot representation of the relation, A denotes the diagonal weight matrix, α_i denotes the weight of the i-th sentence in the bag, and s denotes the feature representation of the whole bag.

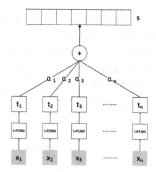

Fig. 4. The architecture of the sentence-level attention.

3.3 Selective Attention over Bags

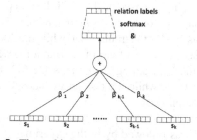

Fig. 5. The architecture of the bag-level attention.

The training data provided by distant supervision is divided into multiple bag groups, where each bag in a bag group represents the same relationship and the sentences in each bag contain the same entity pairs. The core idea of the bag attention is that after obtaining the feature representation of each bag, the attention for the bags will be computed within each bag group, so as to assign different weights to each bag. Figure 5 represents the architecture of the bag-level attention.

The processing of the bag-level attention is basically the same as that of the sentence-level attention, and the difference only lies in the input and output. Consequently, the calculation of the bag-level attention can be similarly achieved by using Eqs. 9, 10, 11, where x_i and α_i are replaced by s_i and β_i.

The feature representation of a bag group is expressed as $g_i \in T$, which corresponds to the i-th relation as preset in the data set, where T is the set of achieved feature representations corresponding to all the bag groups in the data set. A *softmax* layer is employed as in Eqs. 12, 13:

$$p(i|g_i) = \frac{o_i}{\sum_{j=1}^{n_r} \exp(o_j)} \tag{12}$$

$$o_i = Mg_i + d \tag{13}$$

where g_i denotes the feature representation of a bag group with the i-th relation, n_r denotes the total number of all relations, M denotes the weight parameter matrix of all the relations, $d \in R^{n_r}$ denotes the bias term, o_i denotes the score of the i-th relation, and $p(i|g_i)$ denotes the probability that bag group g_i is classified into the i-th relation.

The loss of the model is calculated by using a cross-entropy loss function, where θ denotes all the parameters in the model. The loss function is minimized by *Adadelt*, as in Eq. 14:

$$J(\theta) = -\sum_{g_i \in T} log p(i|g_i; \theta) \tag{14}$$

4   Experiments and Analysis

4.1   Data Set and Evaluation Metrics

The proposed model was evaluated based on the NYT data set proposed in [7] which was established using distant supervision by aligning the Freebase KB with the NYT corpus. The 2005–2006 corpus was used as the training set, while the 2007 corpus was employed as the test set. The data set includes a total of 53 relations, where "NA" indicates no relation between entity pairs. The training set contains 522,611 sentences, 281,270 entity pairs, and 18,252 relation facts, while the test set includes 172,448 sentences, 96,678 entity pairs, and 1,950 relation facts.

Zeng et al. [3] proposed a complete evaluation paradigm for distant supervision relation extraction, which was followed by in the experiments. The paradigm comprehensively evaluates the model performance from four aspects: *Precision, Recall, AUC* values, and *P@N*. *Precision* indicates the proportion of correctly predicted positive sentences among all predicted positive sentences. *Recall* calculates the proportion of predicted positive sentences among all predicted sentences. *AUC* values are used to measure the classifier's ability to distinguish between positive and negative samples, providing a more comprehensive assessment of the model's performance. $P@N$ metric denotes the accuracy of the N-th record after sorting by confidence level, where N takes the values of 100, 200, and 300 respectively.

4.2 Configurations

A pre-trained Word2Vec word embedding model on the NYT corpus is utilized to map words to 50-dimensional vectors, and position vectors are initialized randomly to 5-dimensional vectors. As a word has a relative position with respect to both the head and tail entities, each word vector and its two position vectors are concatenated to form a 60-dimensional input embedding. The maximum length of input sentences is set to 100, and any input exceeding this limit will be truncated.

In the experiments, a gird search is employed using training set to determine the optimal parameters. The learning rate lr is 0.01, the number of filters k is 100, the sliding window size w is 3, the batch size B is 10, and the neuron random dropout probability p is 0.5.

4.3 Comparison with Baseline Models

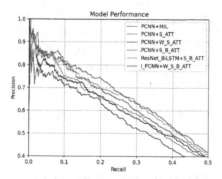

Fig. 6. Performance comparison of proposed model and baseline models.

To evaluate the proposed method, we select the following five related baseline models for comparison through held-out evaluation (Fig. 6):

1. **PCNN + MIL** Zeng et al. [3] proposed a combination of piecewise convolutional max-pooling and Multi-Instance Learning (MIL) to select the best quality sentence in the entity bag to represent the whole entity bag.
2. **PCNN + S_ATT** Lin et al. [4] introduced a sentence-level attention (S_ATT) instead of MIL to assign different weights to sentences in the entity bag and then summed them for relational classification training.
3. **PCNN + W_S_ATT** Jat et al. [5] proposed an approach to fusing word-level and sentence-level attention (W_S_ATT) to filter the undesirable effects of noisy data in entity bag.

4. **PCNN + S_B_ATT** Ye et al. [6] presented an entity bag-level attention (S_B_ATT) to handle noisy data at sentence and bag levels respectively, and then constructed bag-level feature representations for relational classification.

5. **ResNet_BiLSTM + S_B_ATT** Jiang et al. [15] used ResNet_BiLSTM to encode sentences, followed by the sentence-level and bag-level attention (S_B_ATT) to filter noisy data in the NYT data set.

6. **I_PCNN + W_S_B_ATT** The proposed model employs both I-PCNN and word-level attention, sentence-level and bag-level attention (W_S_B_ATT) to represent sentences and reduce noisy data in the NYT data set.

Table 1 shows the $P@N$ for these models in three test settings.

- **One**: For each testing entity pair, randomly select one sentence to predict relation.
- **Two**: For each testing entity pair, randomly select two sentences to conduct relation extraction.
- **All**: Use all the sentences of each entity pair for relation extraction.

Table 1. $P@N$ for relation extraction in the entity pairs with different number of sentences

Test Setting	One				Two				All			
$P@N$	100	200	300	Mean	100	200	300	Mean	100	200	300	Mean
PCNN + MIL	72.3	64.8	56.8	65.0	70.3	67.2	63.1	66.9	72.3	69.7	64.1	68.7
PCNN + S_ATT	78.3	72.2	63.8	71.4	81.2	71.6	66.1	73.0	79.2	73.1	70.4	74.2
PCNN + W_S_ATT	80.1	74.1	65.9	73.4	86.6	73.1	71.1	76.9	87.1	80.1	77.1	81.4
PCNN + S_B_ATT	86.8	**77.6**	73.9	79.4	91.2	79.2	75.4	81.9	91.8	84.0	78.7	84.8
ResNet_BiLSTM + S_B_ATT	87.2	75.1	74.2	78.8	89.9	**80.6**	**76.9**	82.4	92.9	84.1	**79.5**	85.5
I_PCNN + W_S_B_ATT	**88.2**	76.2	**75.1**	**79.5**	**92.3**	78.4	**76.9**	**82.5**	**93.4**	**85.1**	79.1	**85.9**

Table 2. AUC values of different models

No	Model	AUC
1	PCNN + MIL	0.355
2	PCNN + S_ATT	0.388
3	PCNN + W_S_ATT	0.391
4	PCNN + S_B_ATT	0.422
5	ResNet_BiLSTM + S_B_ATT	0.430
6	I_PCNN + W_S_B_ATT	**0.436**

From the above experimental results, it can be shown that the proposed model outperforms all the baseline models in terms of PR curve and various metrics. This is due to that the proposed model reduces the noisy interference in the feature data at each level and promotes the traditional PCNN processing, allowing the model to focus on the feature data that contributes more to the relation and thus effectively alleviate the mislabeling problem of distant supervision.

In order to demonstrate the validity of the experimental results, we also quantify the results using the *AUC* values, and Table 2. AUC values of different models shows the *AUC* values of all baseline models and the proposed model. Compared with the current deep learning models, the proposed model gains an improvement of approximately 0.081 over the model proposed by Zeng et al. [3], and also outperforms other four attention-based models, achieving a maximum value of 0.436. Furthermore, it can be concluded from No.1 to No.2, No.2 to No.3, and No.2 to No.4 in Table 2. AUC values of different models that sentence-level, word-level, and bag-level attention are actually effective, respectively.

P@N is the accuracy of the N-th sentence of confidence ranking. The experimental results exhibits that the proposed model can effectively filter the negative effects of noisy data in the distant supervision NYT data set and improve the performance of the relation extraction model.

4.4 Effect of I-PCNN

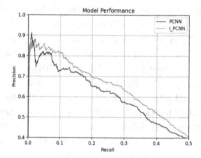

Fig. 7. Performance comparison of PCNN and I-PCNN

In order to verify the effect of I-PCNN, we conduct an ablation experiment. The setting of the experiment is as follows: (1) use PCNN to represent sentences; (2) use I-PCNN to represent sentences; and the rest of the settings remains the same. The experimental results are illustrated in Fig. 7.

The results illustrate that I-PCNN achieves a clear performance improvement over PCNN, which suggests that the contributions of segmented features to the relation after max-pooling processing are indeed different, and the usage of self-attention allows the relation extraction model to focus on more important segmented features. This verifies the positive effect of the I-PCNN.

5 Conclusion

This paper proposes a distant supervision relation extraction model based on I-PCNN and multi-level attention. The main differences between the proposed model and the baseline models lie in two aspects. First, traditional PCNN is improved in a way that the feature data obtained from piecewise max-pooling processing is subject to self-attention. Second, it fuses word-level, sentence-level and bag-level attention to better eliminate the interference of noisy data in the distant supervision data set. The experimental results show that the proposed model outperforms all the baseline models. In addition, the positive effect of I-PCNN is verified by an ablation study. In the future work, we attempt to exploit pre-trained language models to integrate external information to improve the generalization and robustness of the relation extraction model.

References

1. Mintz, M., Bills, S., Snow, R., et al.: Distant supervision for relation extraction without labeled data. In: Proceedings of the Joint Conference of the 47th Annual Meeting of the ACL, pp. 1003–1011 (2009)
2. Bollacker, K., Evans, C., Paritosh, P., et al.: Freebase: a collaboratively created graph database for structuring human knowledge. In: Proceedings of the 2008 ACM SIGMOD International Conference on Management of Data, pp. 1247–1250 (2008)
3. Zeng, D., Liu, K., Chen, Y., et al.: Distant supervision for relation extraction via piecewise convolutional neural networks. In: Proceedings of the 2015 Conference on Empirical Methods in Natural Language Processing, pp. 1753–1762 (2015)
4. Lin, Y., Shen, S., Liu, Z., et al.: Neural relation extraction with selective attention over instances. In: Proceedings of the 54th Annual Meeting of the Association for Computational Linguistics (Volume 1: Long Papers), pp. 2124–2133 (2016)
5. Jat, S., Khandelwal, S., Talukdar, P.: Improving distantly supervised relation extraction using word and entity based attention. In: Proceedings of the 6th Workshop on Automated Knowledge Base Construction (AKBC) at NIPS 2017, Long Beach, CA, USA (2017)
6. Ye, Z.X., Ling, Z.H.: Distant supervision relation extraction with intra-bag and inter-bag attentions. In: Proceedings of the North American Chapter of the Association for Computational Linguistics. Minneapolis, USA, pp. 2810–2819 (2019)
7. Riedel, S., Yao, L., McCallum, A.: Modeling relations and their mentions without labeled text. In: Balcázar, J.L., Bonchi, F., Gionis, A., Sebag, M. (eds.) ECML PKDD 2010. LNCS (LNAI), vol. 6323, pp. 148–163. Springer, Heidelberg (2010). https://doi.org/10.1007/978-3-642-15939-8_10
8. Xie, C., Liang, J., Liu, J., et al.: Revisiting the negative data of distantly supervised relation extraction. In: Proceedings of the 59th Annual Meeting of the Association for Computational Linguistics and the 11th International Joint Conference on Natural Language Processing (Volume 1: Long Papers). Association for Computational Linguistics, pp. 3572–3581 (2021)
9. Li, S.Q., Zhu, Q., Chen, Y.F., et al.: A distant supervision relation extraction method incorporating multi-headed self-attention. Inf. Eng. 7(6), 045–057 (2022)
10. Ji, Y.M., Tang, S.N., Liu, Z.D., et al.: Distant supervision relation extraction algorithm based on TransH with double attention mechanism. J. Nanjing Univ. Posts Telecommun. Nat. Sci. Ed. 42(6), 9 (2022)
11. Mikolov, T., Sutskever, I., Chen, K., et al.: Distributed representations of words and phrases and their compositionality. In: Advances in Neural Information Processing Systems, vol. 26 (2013)

12. Gu, J., Wang, Z., Kuen, J., et al.: Recent advances in convolutional neural networks. Pattern Recogn. **77**, 354–377 (2018)
13. Vaswani, A., Shazeer, N., Parmar, N., et al.: Attention is all you need. In: Advances in Neural Information Processing Systems, vol. 30 (2017)
14. Li, Y., Hao, Z., Lei, H.: Survey of convolutional neural network. J. Comput. Appl. **36**(9), 2508 (2016)
15. Jiang, X., Qian, X.Z., Song, W.: Combining residual BiLSTM with sentence and bag attention for distant supervision relation extraction. Comput. Eng. **10**, 110–122 (2022)

Enhancing Adversarial Robustness via Anomaly-aware Adversarial Training

Keke Tang[1], Tianrui Lou[1(✉)], Xu He[1], Yawen Shi[1], Peican Zhu[2(✉)],
and Zhaoquan Gu[3]

[1] Cyberspace Institute of Advanced Technology,
Guangzhou University, Guangzhou 510006, China
`loutianrui@gmail.com`
[2] School of Artificial Intelligence, Optics, and Electronics (iOPEN),
Northwestern Polytechnical University, Xi'an 710072, China
`ericcan@nwpu.edu.cn`
[3] Department of Computer Science and Technology, Harbin Institute
of Technology (Shenzhen), Shenzhen 518055, China
`guzhaoquan@hit.edu.cn`

Abstract. Adversarial training (AT) is one of the most promising solutions for defending adversarial attacks. By exploiting the adversarial examples generated in the maximization step of AT, a large improvement on the robustness can be brought. However, by analyzing the original natural examples and the corresponding adversarial examples, we observe that a certain part of them are abnormal. In this paper, we propose a novel AT framework called anomaly-aware adversarial training (A^3T), which utilizes different learning strategies for handling the one normal case and two abnormal cases of generating adversarial examples. Extensive experiments on three publicly available datasets with classifiers in three major network architectures demonstrate that A^3T is effective in robustifying networks to adversarial attacks in both white/black-box settings and outperforms the state-of-the-art AT methods.

Keywords: Adversarial attack · Adversarial training · Adversarial defense · Adversarial example · Anomaly

1 Introduction

With the development of deep neural networks(DNNs) [16,26,27], they are playing an increasingly important role in many computer vision applications. However, even the state-of-the-art DNN classifiers have been validated to be vulnerable to adversarial attacks, i.e., an imperceptible adversarial perturbation applied on the input image will lead to an error prediction of category [20,24]. Since the vulnerability of DNNs brings hidden risks for their application to real-world tasks, e.g., robotic grasping [18] and autonomous driving [6], the research

---

K. Tang and T. Lou—Contributed equally to this work.

Z. Jin et al. (Eds.): KSEM 2023, LNAI 14117, pp. 328–342, 2023.
https://doi.org/10.1007/978-3-031-40283-8_28

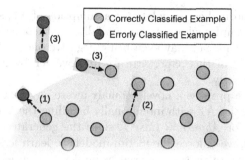

Fig. 1. The demonstration of three cases in the process of adversarial attack: (1) The normal case where the original natural examples can be correctly classified but the generated examples can not; (2) *Abnormal Case I* where both the original natural examples and generated examples can be correctly classified; (3) *Abnormal Case II* where the original natural examples can not be correctly classified.

on promoting the robustness of DNNs to adversarial attacks has attracted much attention. Among them, adversarial training (AT) [5] is considered to be one of the most promising methods to robustify DNNs for its simplicity and effectiveness.

AT is essentially a data argumentation method, which can be formulated as a min-max problem [19], with a maximization step to find adversarial examples of the victim models first, followed by a minimization step to train the models augmented with the generated adversarial examples. Therefore, there are two mainstream directions of research on improving AT. For improving the maximization step of AT, the main focus is to find better adversarial examples, e.g., worst cases that make classification loss larger [2] and special cases that are closer to the decision boundaries [4], but with fewer iterations, e.g., by recycling the gradient when updating model parameters [22] and by restricting most of the forward and back propagation within the first layer when updating adversary [34]. For improving the minimization step of AT, the main focus instead becomes to better utilize the adversarial examples. Indeed, many recent studies show that by adopting suitable strategies, even common adversarial examples, that are neither worst cases nor special cases, can bring large improvement on robustifying the victim models [25,35].

However, by analyzing the original natural examples and the corresponding adversarial examples generated in the maximization step of AT, we observe that a certain part of them are not as expected, and fall into two different abnormal cases:

- *Abnormal Case I*: Both the original natural examples and the generated adversarial examples can be correctly classified by the victim models.
- *Abnormal Case II*: The original natural examples themselves can not be correctly classified by the victim models.

Since these two abnormal cases violate the assumption of AT, see Fig. 1, training with adversarial examples whose generation falls into them can hardly bring any positive effects, and instead may even bring negative ones. Therefore, it brings us to the main topic of this paper: can we improve AT by handling these two abnormal cases properly?

In this paper, we propose a novel anomaly-aware adversarial training (A^3T) framework that applies AT with intentionally handling the above two abnormal cases. Specifically, for *Abnormal Case I*, since the generated examples are not adversarial enough, we enforce the victim models to learn less from them, such that more knowledge of real adversarial examples can be learned. For *Abnormal Case II*, since the original natural examples can not be correctly classified already, we enforce the victim models to learn from them first instead of their corresponding adversarial ones, such that these natural examples can be correctly classified and utilized to produce real adversarial examples in the subsequent iterations. Extensive experiments on the three publicly available datasets, e.g., CIFAR-10, CIFAR-100 [13], and Tiny ImageNet [15], with DNN classifiers in three representative network architectures, e.g., PreAct ResNet-18 [9], MobileNet-V2 [21] and VGG-16 [23], validate the effectiveness of A^3T framework in robustifying DNN models to adversarial attacks under both white-box and black-box settings, and its superiority to the state-of-the-art AT methods.

Overall, our contribution is at least three-fold.

- We are the first to summarize the two abnormal cases of generating adversarial examples in the maximization step of AT.
- We propose a novel anomaly-aware adversarial training (A^3T) framework that handles both two abnormal cases.
- We validate the superiority of the A^3T framework to the state-of-the-art AT methods via extensive experiments.

2   Related Work

2.1   Adversarial Attack and Defense

Since Szegedy et al. [24] reported the vulnerability of deep neural networks (DNNs), that adversarial examples generated by applying imperceptible perturbation on the input can fool them to make error predictions, a large body of researches have been conducted on adversarial attack [10,28,29,36].

To alleviate the influence brought by adversarial attacks and thus facilitate the deployment of DNN systems to real-world scenarios, various adversarial defense strategies have been devised. Mainstream adversarial defense directions include detecting and then rejecting adversarial examples [8], defending certain types of adversarial attacks by modifying network architectures [17], denoising adversarial examples in the image level [7] or in the feature level [32], and adversarial training [5]. While these defense methods are claimed to raise the robustness of DNNs, Athalye et al. [1] criticized that the improved robustness brought by most of these methods relies on gradient masking, leading to a false sense of security. By contrast, adversarial training is considered as one of the most promising defense solutions for its simplicity and effectiveness.

2.2 Adversarial Training

The concept of adversarial training (AT) was first introduced by Goodfellow et al. [5], where DNN classifiers are trained with a mixture of natural examples and adversarial examples generated by the fast gradient sign method (FGSM). Although the above solution brings improved robustness to the FGSM attack, the strengthened DNN classifiers are reported to be still susceptible to stronger multi-step attacks [14]. Madry et al. [19] mathematically defined AT as a min-max problem and proposed the projected gradient descent adversarial training (PGD-AT) framework, showing robustness to multi-step attacks.

Later, researches on AT are mainly focused on improving the maximization step and the minimization step of AT [2,4,11,12,25,30,31,35]. To improve the maximization step of AT, Cai et al. [2] proposed to generate stronger adversarial examples by using more iteration steps and increasing convergence quality. Besides pursuing the worst cases, Ding et al. [4] proposed to find adversarial examples that are close to the class boundaries by using adaptive perturbation sizes. The improvement on the minimization step of AT is instead to make better use of the generated adversarial examples. By owing the existence of adversarial images to the small distance between natural examples and decision boundaries, Zhang et al. [35] intentionally enforced the classifiers not only to classify the adversarial examples correctly but also to push them far away from the boundaries by using a regulation term of boundary loss. By observing that misclassified natural examples have a larger impact on the final robustness, Wang et al. [31] proposed to emphasize these misclassified examples. To prevent the overfitting of PGD-AT, Tack et al. [25] proposed to force the adversarial predictive distributions from different augmentations to be similar.

We also aim to improve AT from the perspective of the minimization step. Differently, we intentionally divide the generation of adversarial examples in the maximization step into three cases, e.g., one normal case and two abnormal cases, and apply different learning strategies to them.

3 Problem Formulation

3.1 Notations

We consider a C-category image classification problem. Let $\mathcal{D}$ denote a training dataset, containing a set of natural examples and corresponding labels $\mathcal{D} = \{(x_i, y_i)\}_{i=1}^{n}$. Let $f_\theta(\cdot)$ denote a classifier which predicts the category of input data with model parameter θ and $p_f(\cdot)$ indicate the prediction probabilities of $f_\theta(\cdot)$ on all the C categories. Besides, we denote $\mathcal{L}$ as the classification loss of classifier $f_\theta(\cdot)$.

3.2   Formulation of Adversarial Training

AT aims to strengthen the DNN classifier f_θ by solving the below min-max problem [19],

$$\min_\theta \max_{x' \in \mathcal{B}_\epsilon(x_i)} \mathbb{E}_{(x_i, y_i) \sim \mathcal{D}} \mathcal{L}(x_i', y_i; \theta), \tag{1}$$

where x_i' is the corresponding adversarial example generated from x_i, which is limited within a l_∞-ball, i.e., $\mathcal{B}_\epsilon$.

3.3   Formulation of Normal/Abnormal Cases

Formally, we denote the generation of an adversarial example with a 3-tuple vector,

$$s_i = <x_i, x_i', y_i>.$$

By analyzing the original natural examples and the corresponding adversarial examples generated in the maximization step of AT, we find that the whole set $\mathcal{S} = \{s_1, ..., s_n\}$ can be divided into one subset of normal case, i.e., $\mathcal{S}_n$, and two subsets of abnormal cases, i.e., $\mathcal{S}_a^1$ and $\mathcal{S}_a^2$,

(1) $\mathcal{S}_n = \{s_i \mid f(x_i) = y_i, f(x_i') \neq y_i\}$;
(2) $\mathcal{S}_a^1 = \{s_i \mid f(x_i) = y_i, f(x_i') = y_i\}$;
(3) $\mathcal{S}_a^2 = \{s_i \mid f(x_i) \neq y_i\}$.

3.4   Our Solution

Since the above three cases have different effects on AT, we thus propose to utilize them for the minimization step of AT by solving the below equation instead,

$$\min_\theta \sum_{s_i \in \mathcal{S}_n} \mathcal{L}_n(s_i) + \lambda_1 \sum_{s_i \in \mathcal{S}_a^1} \mathcal{L}_a^1(s_i) + \lambda_2 \sum_{s_i \in \mathcal{S}_a^2} \mathcal{L}_a^2(s_i), \tag{2}$$

where $\mathcal{L}_n(\cdot)$, $\mathcal{L}_a^1(\cdot)$ and $\mathcal{L}_a^2(\cdot)$ are the three loss functions with applying different learning strategies, and λ_1 and λ_2 are the weighting parameters.

For the set of normal case $\mathcal{S}_n$, we propose to learn from them normally as common AT solutions. For the set of *Abnormal Case I*, i.e., $\mathcal{S}_a^1$, since the generated examples are not adversarial enough, we propose to learn less from them. For the set of *Abnormal Case II*, i.e., $\mathcal{S}_a^2$, where natural examples can not be correctly classified originally, we propose to learn from natural examples instead.

4   Method

In this section, we will first describe the learning strategies for handling the normal case and two abnormal cases, and then the indicator functions for determining which cases the generation of adversarial example falls, and finally introduce our anomaly-aware adversarial training (A³T) framework. Please refer to Fig. 2 for a demonstration of our framework.

4.1 Anomaly-aware Learning Strategy

In this subsection, we describe the learning strategies for handling normal/abnormal cases, and the corresponding mathematical loss functions.

Learning Strategy for $\mathcal{S}_n$. For a normal case $s_i =< x_i, x_i', y_i >\in \mathcal{S}_n$, we utilize the adversarial example x_i' as a sample for training classification. Instead of adopting the traditional cross-entropy loss, we enforce the difference between the prediction of natural example $p_f(x_i)$ and that of adversarial example $p_f(x_i')$ to be close following [35], such that the decision boundary of the classifier can be pushed away from the sample instances. It can be implemented by minimizing the KL divergence,

$$\mathrm{KL}(p_f(x)\|p_f(x')) = \sum_{c=1}^{C} p_f(x)[c]log\frac{p_f(x)[c]}{p_f(x')[c]}, \tag{3}$$

where $p_f(x)[c]$ indicates the predicted probability of classifier $f_\theta(\cdot)$ on category c. Therefore, $\mathcal{L}_n(s_i)$ can be defined as,

$$\mathcal{L}_n(s_i) = \mathrm{KL}(p_f(x)\|p_f(x')) \tag{4}$$

Learning Strategy for $\mathcal{S}_a^1$. For a case that belongs to the *Abnormal Case I*, i.e., $s_i =< x_i, x_i', y_i >\in \mathcal{S}_a^1$, since x_i' can not fool the classifier, it is actually not an adversarial example. Even though, x_i' is more likely to be close to the decision boundary than x_i. Therefore, by applying a similar KL divergence minimization scheme, the decision boundary can be also pushed away to make the classifier more robust. Namely, we define $\mathcal{L}_n(s_i)$ as,

$$\mathcal{L}_a^1(s_i) = \mathrm{KL}(p_f(x)\|p_f(x')). \tag{5}$$

As we will show in the experimental section, the samples in the set $\mathcal{S}_a^1$ are in a much larger amount than those in the set $\mathcal{S}_n$. Therefore, we set the value of λ_1 in the Eq. 2 to be smaller than 1, such that the adversarial training will not be dominated by those abnormal samples in the set $\mathcal{S}_n$.

Learning Strategy for $\mathcal{S}_a^2$. For a case that belongs to the *Abnormal Case II*, i.e., $s_i =< x_i, x_i', y_i >\in \mathcal{S}_a^2$, we propose to enforce the classifier $f_\theta(\cdot)$ to correctly classify x_i first. Specifically, we implement it by applying the boosted cross-entropy (BCE) loss, which is reported to be able to make the classifier stronger than the traditional cross-entropy loss, following [31],

$$\mathrm{BCE}(p_f(x), y) = -log(p_f(x)[y]) - log(1 - \max_{c\neq y} p_f(x)[c]). \tag{6}$$

Therefore, $\mathcal{L}_a^2(s_i)$ can be defined as,

$$\mathcal{L}_a^2(s_i) = \mathrm{BCE}(p_f(x), y). \tag{7}$$

Similarly, we set λ_2 in the Eq. 2 to be smaller than 1. Note that, the *Abnormal Case II* can be transformed to the normal case or *Abnormal Case I* if the learning strategy works.

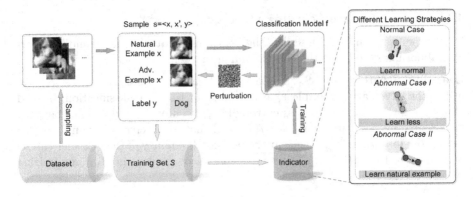

Fig. 2. Overview of the anomaly-aware adversarial training (A³T) framework.

4.2 Anomaly-aware Case Indicator

In this subsection, we first describe the indicator functions for determining which case the generation of adversarial example falls in a 0-1 form and then convert them into differential forms.

Indicator for $\mathcal{S}_n$. For a normal case $s_i =< x_i, x_i', y_i >\in \mathcal{S}_n$, its indicator function is

$$\mathbb{1}(f_\theta(x_i) = y_i) \cdot \mathbb{1}(f_\theta(x_i') \neq y_i),$$

To make it differential, we use the prediction probability $p_f(x_i)[y_i]$ to represent $\mathbb{1}(f_\theta(x_i) = y_i)$, which is approximately 1 if x_i is classified correctly. Similarly, we use $(1 - p_f(x_i')[y_i])$ to represent $\mathbb{1}(f_\theta(x_i') \neq y_i)$ which is approximately 1 if x_i' correctly is misclassified. Overall, the differential indication function of the normal case is,

$$\text{Ind}_n(s_i) = p_f(x_i)[y_i] \cdot (1 - p_f(x_i')[y_i]). \tag{8}$$

Indicator for $\mathcal{S}_a^1$. For a case that belongs to *Abnormal Case I*, i.e., $s_i =< x_i, x_i', y_i >\in \mathcal{S}_a^2$, its indicator function is

$$\mathbb{1}(f_\theta(x_i) = y_i) \cdot \mathbb{1}(f_\theta(x_i') = y_i),$$

To make it differential, we replace the above function with,

$$\text{Ind}_a^1(s_i) = p_f(x_i)[y_i] \cdot p_f(x_i')[y_i], \tag{9}$$

which is approximately 1 if both x_i and x_i' are classified as y_i.

Indicator for $\mathcal{S}_a^2$. For a case that belongs to *Abnormal Case II*, i.e., $s_i =< x_i, x_i', y_i >\in \mathcal{S}_a^2$, its indicator function is

$$\mathbb{1}(f_\theta(x_i) \neq y_i),$$

Algorithm 1. Anomaly-aware Adversarial Training (A^3T)

Input: Batch size m, training epochs T; number of iterations K, step size α and maximum perturbation size ϵ for generating adversarial examples in the inner optimization; step size η for network updating in the outer optimization.

Output: Robust network f_θ.

1: **Initialization:** Standard random initialization of f_θ.
2: **for** $t = 1, ..., T$ **do**
3:   Read mini-batch $B^{(t)} = \{(x_1, y_1), ..., (x_m, y_m)\}$ from training dataset.
4:   **for** $i = 1, ..., m$ **do**
5:     $x_i' = x_i + \epsilon \cdot \xi, with\ \xi \sim U(-1, 1)$ # U is a uniform distribution.
6:     **for** $k = 1, ..., K$ **do**
7:       $x_i' \leftarrow \prod_{\mathcal{B}_\epsilon}(x_i' + \alpha \cdot sign(\nabla_{x_i'} CE(p(x_i', \theta), y_i)))$ # $\prod$ is a projection operator.
8:     **end for**
9:     Construct the 3-tuple vector $s_i = <x_i, x_i', y_i>$ for training.
10:     Calculate indicators for three different cases $\text{Ind}_n(s_i), \text{Ind}_a^1(s_i), \text{Ind}_a^2(s_i)$ using Eqs. 8, 9, 10.
11:     Calculate the losses $\mathcal{L}_n(s_i), \mathcal{L}_a^1(s_i), \mathcal{L}_a^2(s_i)$ corresponding to different cases using Eqs. 4, 5, 7.
12:   **end for**
13:   $\theta \leftarrow \theta - \eta \nabla_\theta [\sum_{i=1}^m \text{Ind}_n(s_i) \cdot \mathcal{L}_n(s_i) + \lambda_1 \sum_{i=1}^m \text{Ind}_a^1(s_i) \cdot \mathcal{L}_a^1(s_i) + \lambda_2 \sum_{i=1}^m \text{Ind}_a^2(s_i) \cdot \mathcal{L}_a^2(s_i)]$
14: **end for**

To make it differential, we replace the above function with,

$$\text{Ind}_a^2(s_i) = 1 - p_f(x_i)[y_i], \tag{10}$$

which is approximately 1 if x_i is misclassified.

4.3   Anomaly-aware Adversarial Training Framework

Given a dataset $\mathcal{D}$, we first generate adversarial example x_i' for each x_i by conducting the maximization step,

$$x_i' = \arg\max_{x_i' \in \mathcal{B}_\epsilon(x_i)} CE(p_f(x_i'), y_i), \tag{11}$$

where CE is the cross entropy loss. Then we get the 3-tuple vector $s_i = <x_i, x_i', y_i>$ for conducting the minimization step,

$$\min_\theta \quad \sum_{i=1}^n \text{Ind}_n(s_i) \cdot \mathcal{L}_n(s_i) + \lambda_1 \sum_{i=1}^n \text{Ind}_a^1(s_i) \cdot \mathcal{L}_a^1(s_i)$$
$$+ \lambda_2 \sum_{i=1}^n \text{Ind}_a^2(s_i) \cdot \mathcal{L}_a^2(s_i). \tag{12}$$

Table 1. Adversarial accuracy (%) ↑ of models strengthened by different adversarial training methods on CIFAR-10 and CIFAR-100.

Dataset	Model	AT Method	White-Box				Black-Box	AutoAttack
			-	FGSM	MI-FGSM-7	PGD-50	Transfer	
CIFAR-10	PreAct ResNet-18	-	**95.05**	33.43	2.69	0.00	34.45	0.00
		PGD-AT	84.46	51.84	49.46	47.52	83.80	45.05
		TRADES	81.96	57.86	54.39	50.36	84.42	46.59
		MART	81.65	**60.77**	57.61	52.67	81.35	47.11
		Consistency	84.25	60.48	57.94	56.31	82.84	48.51
		A³T	82.17	60.11	**58.43**	**56.96**	**84.87**	**49.25**
	MobileNet-V2	-	**91.88**	23.37	0.52	0.00	32.97	0.00
		PGD-AT	75.90	49.89	47.87	42.93	75.13	38.31
		TRADES	72.93	**50.81**	49.20	45.07	76.35	39.73
		MART	70.85	50.15	48.33	46.68	67.41	39.15
		Consistency	78.55	48.98	47.89	46.57	75.20	40.57
		A³T	73.72	50.33	**49.76**	**47.97**	**77.31**	**41.72**
	VGG-16	-	**93.60**	31.86	2.35	0.00	31.08	0.00
		PGD-AT	80.03	51.55	47.73	44.80	79.37	41.80
		TRADES	75.64	53.21	51.26	47.31	80.04	43.52
		MART	75.34	52.03	50.37	48.31	78.60	42.07
		Consistency	79.90	51.57	50.69	48.32	79.75	43.39
		A³T	75.17	**53.86**	**51.79**	**49.43**	**80.84**	**44.27**
CIFAR-100	PreAct ResNet-18	-	**76.70**	7.40	0.05	0.00	12.25	0.00
		PGD-AT	54.67	25.45	23.11	20.01	53.35	18.73
		TRADES	52.70	31.86	30.04	27.94	**53.99**	24.06
		MART	52.18	32.63	30.30	27.77	50.02	23.53
		Consistency	59.70	32.18	30.81	30.18	52.84	24.54
		A³T	52.12	**32.77**	**31.31**	**30.10**	53.54	**25.12**
	MobileNet-V2	-	**70.14**	7.76	0.04	0.00	17.09	0.00
		PGD-AT	46.35	24.67	22.58	19.78	50.96	17.30
		TRADES	42.05	26.21	25.15	24.65	52.43	19.25
		MART	43.07	27.43	26.22	25.41	51.63	19.76
		Consistency	46.30	27.18	26.71	26.07	52.07	19.01
		A³T	43.84	**28.48**	**27.20**	**26.43**	**52.90**	**20.68**
	VGG-16	-	**72.85**	15.36	2.05	0.08	19.22	0.00
		PGD-AT	51.08	20.92	19.41	17.38	47.25	15.01
		TRADES	46.18	24.14	21.93	19.69	48.34	16.93
		MART	44.27	21.54	20.76	20.04	47.16	15.50
		Consistency	49.75	23.11	21.30	20.82	47.78	16.70
		A³T	46.44	**24.23**	**22.73**	**21.67**	**49.37**	**17.85**

Note that the learning strategies, e.g., loss functions, and the indicator functions are defined in Subsec. 4.1 and Subsec. 4.2, respectively. The pseudocode of the whole A³T framework is displayed in Algorithm 1.

5 Experimental Results

5.1 Experimental Setup

Implementation. We implement the A^3T framework using PyTorch, and run it on a workstation with four NVIDIA RTX 2080Ti GPUs. We set the hyperparameter λ_1 as 0.01 and λ_2 as 0.1 in Eq. 12, and use 10-step PGD with $\epsilon = 8/255$, step size $\alpha = 2/255$ for generating adversarial examples in the maximum step. For experiments on CIFAR-10 and CIFAR-100, we train all networks using the SGD optimizer with an initial learning rate of 0.1, which decays with a factor of 0.1 at 60, 80, and 100 epochs, for a total of 105 epochs. The momentum and weight decay of the SGD optimizer are set as 0.9 and $5e-4$, respectively. For experiments on Tiny ImageNet [15], we set the learning rate to be 0.1 initially and drop it at 100 and 150 epochs with a decay factor 0.1 following [25].

DNN Classifiers. We choose three different DNN classifiers, i.e., PreAct ResNet-18 [9], MobileNet-V2 [21] and VGG-16 [23].

Baseline at Methods. We compare A^3T with four state-of-the-art baseline solutions, i.e., projected gradient decent adversarial training (PGD-AT) [19], TRADES [35], misclassification aware adversarial training (MART) [31] and consistency regularization adversarial training (Consistency) [25]. Besides, we also report the results of normal training denoted with "-" for reference.

Evaluation Metric. We evaluate the performance of different AT solutions by measuring the *adversarial accuracy* (larger is better, ↑) of DNN classifiers that are strengthened by them, which is defined as the percentage of adversarial examples that are correctly classified.

Adversarial Attack Methods. We adopt five adversarial attack methods to attack the DNN classifiers strengthened by different AT solutions, including three while-box attack methods, i.e., FGSM, MI-FGSM-7 (7 iterations), PGD-50 (50 iterations, step size $2/255$), one black-box attack method, i.e., adversarial images generated by PGD-50 to attack Wide-ResNet-40-10 [33] trained on clean images (Transfer), in addition to the strongest AutoAttack [3], which combines adaptive white-box attacks and powerful black-box attacks. For all white-box attack methods and AutoAttack, we set the perturbation size ϵ as $8/255$.

5.2 Performance Analysis

White-box Performance. The results reported in Table 1 show that all three DNN classifiers trained on the two datasets are vulnerable to adversarial attacks, and the adversarial accuracy can be decreased to nearly 0% under the PGD-50

Table 2. Adversarial accuracy (%) ↑ of PreAct ResNet-18 strengthened by different adversarial training methods on Tiny ImageNet.

AT Method	-	FGSM	MI-FGSM-7	PGD-50	AutoAttack
PGD-AT	43.71	22.33	15.85	12.71	10.48
TRADES	40.81	25.31	20.23	16.87	13.92
MART	42.53	28.90	23.48	18.24	15.28
Consistency	**46.15**	33.82	24.57	20.83	15.47
A3T	42.29	**35.13**	**25.91**	**22.56**	**17.05**

attack. By applying AT, their robustness to the three adversarial attacks is significantly improved. In particular, our A^3T framework brings the largest improvement in robustness, especially to the two iterative-based attacks, validating its effectiveness and superiority.

Black-box Performance. To further validate the effectiveness of A^3T, we also report the comparison results with the state-of-the-art AT methods in the black-box setting. The results reported in Table 1 show that A^3T brings the largest improvements in the robustness to the Transfer attack in almost all cases, validating the effectiveness of our framework.

AutoAttack Performance. We also demonstrate the effectiveness of our A^3T framework by evaluating its strengthened DNN classifiers to the AutoAttack [3] framework which is an integrated system with two strong white-box attack methods and two strong black-box attack methods. Since AutoAttack sets hyperparameters adaptively and can detect whether the evaluated method gets pseudo robustness due to gradient masking [1], it is considered as the most authoritative attack method for evaluating adversarial robustness. The results reported in Table 1 show that A^3T outperforms all the other state-of-the-art AT methods, validating the effectiveness and superiority of our A^3T framework.

5.3 Performance on Tiny ImageNet

To further validate the effectiveness of A^3T on larger datasets, we compare it with TRADES, MART and Consistency in strengthening PreAct ResNet-18 on Tiny ImageNet. The results in Table 2 show that A^3T brings the largest robustness to three white-box attacks and AutoAttack, validating its effectiveness.

5.4 Ablation Studies and Additional Discussion

Effect of Both Abnormal Cases. To demonstrate the importance of handling the two abnormal cases in A^3T, we evaluate the performance of the A^3T framework with only one of the abnormal cases to be handled. Specifically, we strengthen the DNN classifiers using the A^3T framework by ablating the regularization on *Abnormal Case I* and *Abnormal Case II*, respectively. The results

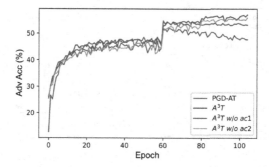

Fig. 3. Adversarial accuracy (%) ↑ of networks strengthened by PGD-AT and A^3T under different ablation settings on CIFAR-10. These methods are applied to PreAct ResNet-18.

Table 3. Ablation studies on the effects of handling abnormal case I (ac1) and abnormal case II (ac2) of A^3T for strengthening PreAct ResNet-18.

Dataset	AT Method	-	FGSM	MI-FGSM-7	PGD-50
CIFAR-10	A^3T w/o ac1	76.95	58.56	56.71	54.57
	A^3T w/o ac2	76.53	58.65	57.12	55.92
	A^3T	**77.17**	**60.11**	**58.43**	**56.96**
CIFAR-100	A^3T w/o ac1	51.15	31.34	29.95	28.21
	A^3T w/o ac2	50.21	31.59	30.27	29.15
	A^3T	**52.12**	**32.77**	**31.31**	**30.10**

reported in Table 3 show that the adversarial accuracies of the above two settings are lower than that of the setting with the full A^3T framework, validating the importance of handling both abnormal cases.

We also visualize the adversarial accuracies of PGD-AT, A^3T, and its two ablated versions for the whole training epochs. The curves drawn in Fig. 3 validate the effectiveness of our framework, and also the importance on handling the two abnormal cases.

The Amount of Three Cases. We count the number of adversarial examples generated by PGD-AT for strengthening PreAct ResNet-18 on CIFAR-10 that fall into the set of three different cases, i.e., one normal case and two abnormal cases, at different epochs. In particular, we also report the two subcases of *Abnormal Case II*. The curves drawn in Fig. 4 show that the two abnormal cases occupy at the beginning. As the training progresses, the number of *Abnormal Case I* keeps increasing, while that of *Abnormal Case II* decreases. Throughout the training process, abnormal cases account for the majority, validating the importance of handling abnormal cases in AT.

Can Delete Adversarial Examples in *Abnormal Case I* Directly? We investigate whether we can delete adversarial examples in *Abnormal Case I*

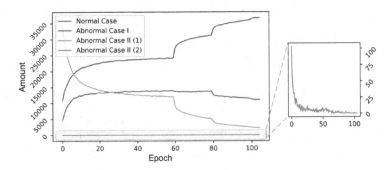

Fig. 4. The number of adversarial examples generated by PGD-AT for strengthening PreAct ResNet-18 on CIFAR-10 that fall into the normal case and the two abnormal cases. Note that *Abnormal Case II (1)* represents the case where both the original natural examples and generated examples are errorly classified, and *Abnormal Case II (2)* represents the case where the original natural examples are errorly classified but generated examples are correctly classified.

Table 4. Adversarial accuracy (%) ↑ of PreAct ResNet-18 strengthened by PGD-AT (del n/%), i.e., PGD-AT with deleting n/% of the adversarial examples in the abnormal case I, and A^{3}T on CIFAR-10.

AT Method	-	FGSM	MI-FGSM-7	PGD-50	AutoAttack
PGD-AT (del 0/%)	84.46	51.84	49.46	47.52	45.05
PGD-AT (del 25/%)	81.16	57.20	54.97	52.40	43.79
PGD-AT (del 50/%)	81.63	58.00	55.42	53.02	43.89
PGD-AT (del 75/%)	**84.03**	58.40	56.45	55.77	42.40
PGD-AT (del 100/%)	79.76	59.49	**59.94**	56.91	30.20
A^{3}T	82.17	**60.11**	58.43	**56.96**	**49.25**

directly without learning from them. The results reported in Table 4 show that although this solution improves the robustness against white-box attacks slightly, the performance against AutoAttack drops significantly. Indeed, although those samples are not adversarial, they are much close to the decision boundary, and thus can be utilized for robustifying the classifiers. However, if we delete those samples that are in a large amount as reported in Fig. 4, the classifiers can only learn from a specific type of adversarial examples, leading to overfitting.

6   Conclusion

This paper has proposed a novel adversarial training framework, i.e., anomaly-aware adversarial training (A^{3}T). The rationale is to handle the two abnormal cases of generating adversarial examples using different minimization strategies. Extensive experiments validate the effectiveness of the A^{3}T framework and its superiority to the state-of-the-art methods. We hope our framework can inspire more research on delving into the two steps of adversarial training. In the future, we plan to develop more powerful strategies to handle these abnormal cases.

Acknowledgment. This work was supported in part by the National Key R&D Program of China (2020AAA0107704), the National Natural Science Foundation of China (62102105 and 62073263), the Guangdong Basic and Applied Basic Research Foundation (2020A1515110997 and 2022A1515011501).

References

1. Athalye, A., Carlini, N., Wagner, D.: Obfuscated gradients give a false sense of security: Circumventing defenses to adversarial examples. In: ICML, pp. 274–283 (2018)
2. Cai, Q.Z., Liu, C., Song, D.: Curriculum adversarial training. In: IJCAI, pp. 3740–3747 (2018)
3. Croce, F., Hein, M.: Reliable evaluation of adversarial robustness with an ensemble of diverse parameter-free attacks. In: ICML, pp. 2206–2216 (2020)
4. Ding, G.W., Sharma, Y., Lui, K.Y.C., Huang, R.: MMA training: direct input space margin maximization through adversarial training. In: ICLR (2019)
5. Goodfellow, I.J., Shlens, J., Szegedy, C.: Explaining and harnessing adversarial examples. In: ICLR (2015)
6. Grigorescu, S., Trasnea, B., Cocias, T., Macesanu, G.: A survey of deep learning techniques for autonomous driving. J. Field Robot. **37**(3), 362–386 (2020)
7. Guo, C., Rana, M., Cisse, M., Van Der Maaten, L.: Countering adversarial images using input transformations. In: ICLR (2018)
8. Guo, S., Li, X., Zhu, P., Mu, Z.: ADS-Detector: an attention-based dual stream adversarial example detection method. Knowl.-Based Syst. **265**, 110388 (2023)
9. He, K., Zhang, X., Ren, S., Sun, J.: Deep residual learning for image recognition. In: CVPR, pp. 770–778 (2016)
10. Hong, J., Tang, K., Gao, C., Wang, S., Guo, S., Zhu, P.: GM-Attack: improving the transferability of adversarial attacks. In: KSEM, pp. 489–500 (2022)
11. Jia, X., et al.: Prior-guided adversarial initialization for fast adversarial training. In: Avidan, S., Brostow, G., Cisse, M., Farinella, G.M., Hassner, T. (eds.) Computer Vision – ECCV 2022. ECCV 2022. Lecture Notes in Computer Science, vol. 13664, pp. 567–584. Springer, Cham (2022). https://doi.org/10.1007/978-3-031-19772-7_33
12. Jia, X., Zhang, Y., Wu, B., Wang, J., Cao, X.: Boosting fast adversarial training with learnable adversarial initialization. IEEE Trans. Image Process. **31**, 4417–4430 (2022). https://doi.org/10.1109/TIP.2022.3184255
13. Krizhevsky, A., Hinton, G., et al.: Learning multiple layers of features from tiny images (2009)
14. Kurakin, A., Goodfellow, I., Bengio, S.: Adversarial machine learning at scale. arXiv preprint arXiv:1611.01236 (2016)
15. Le, Y., Yang, X.S.: Tiny imagenet visual recognition challenge (2015)
16. LeCun, Y., Bengio, Y., Hinton, G.: Deep learning. Nature **521**(7553), 436–444 (2015)
17. Li, Y., Cheng, S., Su, H., Zhu, J.: Defense against adversarial attacks via controlling gradient leaking on embedded manifolds. In: Vedaldi, A., Bischof, H., Brox, T., Frahm, J.-M. (eds.) ECCV 2020. LNCS, vol. 12373, pp. 753–769. Springer, Cham (2020). https://doi.org/10.1007/978-3-030-58604-1_45

18. Lin, N., et al.: Manipulation planning from demonstration via goal-conditioned prior action primitive decomposition and alignment. IEEE Robot. Autom. Lett. **7**(2), 1387–1394 (2022)

19. Madry, A., Makelov, A., Schmidt, L., Tsipras, D., Vladu, A.: Towards deep learning models resistant to adversarial attacks. In: ICLR (2018)

20. Papernot, N., McDaniel, P., Jha, S., Fredrikson, M., Celik, Z.B., Swami, A.: The limitations of deep learning in adversarial settings, pp. 372–387 (2016)

21. Sandler, M., Howard, A., Zhu, M., Zhmoginov, A., Chen, L.C.: Mobilenetv 2: Inverted residuals and linear bottlenecks. In: CVPR, pp. 4510–4520 (2018)

22. Shafahi, A., et al.: Adversarial training for free! In: NeurIPS, pp. 3358–3369 (2019)

23. Simonyan, K., Zisserman, A.: Very deep convolutional networks for large-scale image recognition. arXiv preprint arXiv:1409.1556 (2014)

24. Szegedy, C., et al.: Intriguing properties of neural networks. In: ICLR (2014)

25. Tack, J., Yu, S., Jeong, J., Kim, M., Hwang, S.J., Shin, J.: Consistency regularization for adversarial robustness. In: AAAI, vol. 36, pp. 8414–8422 (2022)

26. Tang, K., et al.: RepPVConv: attentively fusing reparameterized voxel features for efficient 3d point cloud perception. The Visual Computer, pp. 1–12 (2022). https://doi.org/10.1007/s00371-022-02682-0

27. Tang, K., Ma, Y., Miao, D., Song, P., Gu, Z., Wang, W.: Decision fusion networks for image classification. IEEE Transactions on Neural Networks and Learning Systems, pp. 1–14 (2022). https://doi.org/10.1109/TNNLS.2022.3196129

28. Tang, K., et al.: Rethinking perturbation directions for imperceptible adversarial attacks on point clouds. IEEE Internet Things J. **10**(6), 5158–5169 (2023). https://doi.org/10.1109/JIOT.2022.3222159

29. Tang, K., et al.: NormalAttack: curvature-aware shape deformation along normals for imperceptible point cloud attack. Security and Communication Networks 2022 (2022)

30. Wang, Y., Ma, X., Bailey, J., Yi, J., Zhou, B., Gu, Q.: On the convergence and robustness of adversarial training. In: ICML, pp. 6586–6595. PMLR (2019)

31. Wang, Y., Zou, D., Yi, J., Bailey, J., Ma, X., Gu, Q.: Improving adversarial robustness requires revisiting misclassified examples. In: ICLR (2019)

32. Xie, C., Wu, Y., van der Maaten, L., Yuille, A.L., He, K.: Feature denoising for improving adversarial robustness. In: CVPR, pp. 501–509 (2019)

33. Zagoruyko, S., Komodakis, N.: Wide residual networks. In: BMVC (2016)

34. Zhang, D., Zhang, T., Lu, Y., Zhu, Z., Dong, B.: You only propagate once: accelerating adversarial training via maximal principle. In: NeurIPS, vol. 32, pp. 227–238 (2019)

35. Zhang, H., Yu, Y., Jiao, J., Xing, E., El Ghaoui, L., Jordan, M.: Theoretically principled trade-off between robustness and accuracy. In: ICML, pp. 7472–7482 (2019)

36. Zhu, P., Hong, J., Li, X., Tang, K., Wang, Z.: SGMA: a novel adversarial attack approach with improved transferability. Complex & Intelligent Systems, pp. 1–13 (2023). https://doi.org/10.1007/s40747-023-01060-0

An Improved Cross-Validated Adversarial Validation Method

Wen Zhang[1], Zhengjiang Liu[1], Yan Xue[2], Ruibo Wang[3(✉)]⬤, Xuefei Cao[1], and Jihong Li[3]

[1] School of Automation and Software Engineering, Shanxi University, Taiyuan 030006, China
[2] School of Computer and Information Technology, Shanxi University, Taiyuan 030006, China
[3] School of Modern Education Technology, Shanxi University, Taiyuan 030006, China
wangruibo@sxu.edu.cn

Abstract. As a widely-used strategy among Kaggle competitors, adversarial validation provides a novel selection framework of a reasonable training and validation sets. An adversarial validation heavily depends on an accurate identification of the difference between the distributions of the training and test sets released in a Kaggle competition. However, the typical adversarial validation merely uses a K-fold cross-validated point estimator to measure the difference regardless of the variation of the estimator. Therefore, the typical adversarial validation tends to produce unpromising false positive conclusions. In this study, we reconsider the adversarial validation from a perspective of algorithm comparison. Specifically, we formulate the adversarial validation into a comparison task of a well-trained classifier with a random-guessing classifier on an adversarial data set. Then, we investigate the state-of-the-art algorithm comparison methods to improve the adversarial validation method for reducing false positive conclusions. We conducted sufficient simulated and real-world experiments, and we showed the recently-proposed 5×2 BCV McNemar's test can significantly improve the performance of the adversarial validation method.

Keywords: Adversarial Validation · Cross Validation · Algorithm Comparison · Significance Testing · Distribution Shift

1 Introduction

In a Kaggle competition, an adversarial validation is recommended for ensuring that the model trained on a training set has a good generalization ability on a test set especially when the training and test sets possess a distribution shift [1,3]. To date, an adversarial validation has shown the state-of-the-art performance in the applications of user targeting automation [14], credit scoring [15], text complexity estimation [12], e-commerce purchase intent prediction [10], causal analysis [9], and etc.

© The Author(s), under exclusive license to Springer Nature Switzerland AG 2023
Z. Jin et al. (Eds.): KSEM 2023, LNAI 14117, pp. 343–353, 2023.
https://doi.org/10.1007/978-3-031-40283-8_29

An adversarial validation provides several novel methods of automated feature selection, validation data set selection, and inverse propensity weighting strategy of a training set based on an identification mechanism of the difference between the distributions of a training set and a test set [14]. The effectiveness of an adversarial validation depends on the quality of the identification mechanism. If an adversarial validation incorrectly recognizes that training set and a test set are IID distributed, then the model trained on the training set would achieve a poor generalization ability on the test set.

To implement the identification mechanism, an adversarial validation first combines a training set and a test set into a binary classification data set of which the class labels indicate whether a data record comes from the training set. The combined data set is named an adversarial data set. Then, an adversarial validation trains an adversarial classifier to separate the training and test sets. If the classification results degrade to a random guessing, then we consider the training and test sets are IID; otherwise, they are not IID and possess a distribution shift.

In practical, researchers frequently perform a K-fold cross-validation (CV) to estimate the accuracy (or AUC) of the adversarial classifier and then compare the K-fold cross-validated point estimator of the accuracy (or AUC) with the accuracy (or AUC) of a random guessing, i.e., 0.5, to infer the conclusion. However, direct comparison on the point estimation regardless of the variance is unreasonable and results in less replicable conclusions [16]. For example, Pan et al. performed 5-fold CV on an adversarial data set, and they considered a point estimator of 0.49 as a close-to-random score and inferred that the distributions of the training and test sets are consistent without providing sufficient statistical evidences [14]. It is also unreasonable to infer that the distributions of the training set and test sets are significant different when the point estimated score tends to one. Similar weaknesses can also be found in the work of [10,15].

To address the above-mentioned weaknesses, we regard the identification mechanism in an adversarial validation as a comparison task of two classification algorithms. As far as we know, no previous research has investigated an adversarial validation from the perspective of algorithm comparison. Furthermore, we borrow various algorithm comparison methods to improve the adversarial validation method. The existing state-of-the-art algorithm comparison methods comprehensively consider the expectation and variance of a CV estimator and construct test statistics for obtaining a reliable conclusion. Over the past few decades, dozens of significance tests based algorithm comparison methods were proposed, including widely-used K-fold CV t-tests, 5×2 CV t-tests and F-tests [2,8]. Blocked 3×2 CV t-test [19], and 5×2 BCV McNemer's test [17], and etc. Therefore, we use an algorithm comparison method as a play-and-plug technique to improve the adversarial validation. To investigate the improvement of different algorithm comparison methods on an adversarial validation, we constructed several adversarial data sets based on some synthetic and real-world data sets. Then, we perform sufficient experiments with multiple adversarial data sets and classifiers. The results illustrate that the typical 5-fold CV point estimator performs worse in an adversarial validation, and we recommend the 5×2 BCV McNemar's test because it can significantly improve an adversarial validation among all candidate algorithm comparison methods.

2 Our Proposed Improved Adversarial Validation

2.1 Formalization of an Adversarial Validation

In a data science competition, we gets a training and test sets note as $\mathcal{D}$ and $\mathcal{T}$, respectively, where the sizes of the training and test sets are $|\mathcal{D}| = n_1$ and $|\mathcal{T}| = n_2$. Data records contained in $\mathcal{D}$ and $\mathcal{T}$ are denoted as $z_{\mathcal{D}}$ and $z_{\mathcal{T}}$, respectively, and we further assume that $z_{\mathcal{D}} \sim \mathbf{P}_{\mathcal{D}}$ and $z_{\mathcal{T}} \sim \mathbf{P}_{\mathcal{T}}$. Then, a competitor aims to use the training set $\mathcal{D}$ and a machine learning algorithm $\mathbb{A}$ to train a model that can achieve the state-of-the-art generalization ability on the test set $\mathcal{T}$. Nevertheless, the generalization ability of $\mathbb{A}$ has a close relationship with the difference $\mathbf{P}_{\mathcal{D}}$ and $\mathbf{P}_{\mathcal{T}}$. Therefore, an adversarial validation aims to identify whether $\mathbf{P}_{\mathcal{D}}$ and $\mathbf{P}_{\mathcal{T}}$ are identical. Then an adversarial validation is performed based on the identification problem for subsequent operations.

Formally, the identification problem in an adversarial validation can be regarded as a hypothesis testing problem as follows.

$$H_0 : \mathbf{P}_{\mathcal{D}} = \mathbf{P}_{\mathcal{T}} \quad v.s. \quad H_1 : \mathbf{P}_{\mathcal{D}} \neq \mathbf{P}_{\mathcal{T}} \tag{1}$$

Unfortunately, distributions $\mathbf{P}_{\mathcal{D}}$ and $\mathbf{P}_{\mathcal{T}}$ are difficult to compare and estimate. Nevertheless, we can use the data records from the two distributions, $\mathcal{D}$ and $\mathcal{T}$, to construct some useful statistics to address Problem (1).

Specifically, an adversarial validation constructs an adversarial data set $\tilde{D} = \{(z_i, \tilde{y}_i)\}_{i=1}^{n}$ where $z_i \in \mathcal{D} \cup \mathcal{T}$, $n = n_1 + n_2$ is the data set size, and $\tilde{y}_i \in \{'train', 'test'\}$ is a binary class label to indicate whether a record z_i comes from $\mathcal{D}$ or $\mathcal{T}$. Then, a binary classification algorithm $\tilde{\mathbb{A}}$ is trained and validated on the adversarial data set $\tilde{D}$, and then we can obtain the estimation of the performance of $\tilde{\mathbb{A}}$, denoted as $\widehat{\mathbb{M}}(\tilde{\mathbb{A}}(\tilde{D}))$, where $\mathbb{M}$ indicates an evaluation metric. As a rule of thumb, a 5-fold CV is frequently used in the estimation of $\widehat{\mathbb{M}}$ [14,15]. Moreover, without loss of generality, we merely consider that $\mathbb{M}$ is accuracy.

Furthermore, to solve Problem (1), an adversarial validation considers that if the null hypothesis H_0 in Problem (1) holds, then the data records in $\tilde{D}$ can not be separated in the sense of probability, thus the accuracy of $\tilde{\mathbb{A}}$, $\widetilde{\mathbb{M}}(\tilde{\mathbb{A}}(\tilde{D}))$, should degrade to that of a random guessing, i.e., 0.5. In contrast, if $\mathbb{M}(\tilde{\mathbb{A}}(\tilde{D})) \neq 0.5$, then we consider the null hypothesis H_0 is rejected, and the distributions of $\mathcal{D}$ and $\mathcal{T}$ are different. In a short word, an adversarial validation converts Problem (1) to the following hypothesis testing problem.

$$H_0' : \mathbb{M}(\tilde{\mathbb{A}}(\tilde{D})) = 0.5 \quad v.s. \quad H_1' : \mathbb{M}(\tilde{\mathbb{A}}(\tilde{D})) \neq 0.5 \tag{2}$$

On the basis of the estimator of $\mathbb{M}(\tilde{\mathbb{A}}(\tilde{D}))$, i.e., $\widehat{\mathbb{M}}(\tilde{\mathbb{A}}(\tilde{D}))$, an adversarial validation outputs a decision as follows: *if* $|\widehat{\mathbb{M}}(\tilde{\mathbb{A}}(\tilde{D})) - 0.5| > \epsilon$, *then* H_0' *is*

Algorithm 1: An adversarial validation.

Input: A training set, $\mathcal{D}$; a test set, $\mathcal{T}$; an adversarial classifier, $\tilde{\mathbb{A}}$; a decision threshold, ϵ.

Output: Whether $\mathbf{P}_{\mathcal{D}}$ and $\mathbf{P}_{\mathcal{T}}$ are identical?

1 Construct an adversarial data set $\tilde{D} = \{(z_i, \tilde{y}_i)\}_{i=1}^n$ based on $\mathcal{D}$ and $\mathcal{T}$;

2 Perform a 5-fold CV on the adversarial data set $\tilde{D}$;

3 Train and validate classifier $\tilde{\mathbb{A}}$ on the 5 folds of $\tilde{D}$;

4 Obtain the 5-fold CV estimator of the accuracy of $\tilde{\mathbb{A}}$, denoted as $\widehat{\mathbb{M}}(\tilde{\mathbb{A}}(\tilde{D}))$;

5 **if** $|\widehat{\mathbb{M}}(\tilde{\mathbb{A}}(\tilde{D})) - 0.5| < \epsilon$ **then**

6 $\quad$ Output $\mathbf{P}_{\mathcal{D}} = \mathbf{P}_{\mathcal{T}}$;

7 **else**

8 $\quad$ Output $\mathbf{P}_{\mathcal{D}} \neq \mathbf{P}_{\mathcal{T}}$.

---

rejected, and $\mathbf{P}_{\mathcal{D}} \neq \mathbf{P}_{\mathcal{T}}$*; otherwise, distributions* $\mathbf{P}_{\mathcal{D}}$ *and* $\mathbf{P}_{\mathcal{T}}$ *are identical.* The sketch of a typical adversarial validation is given in Algorithm 1.

Several weaknesses of an adversarial validation can be observed from Algorithm 1. We list them as follows.

- The decision rule in Step 5 of Algorithm 1 merely uses a point estimator of $\mathbb{M}(\tilde{\mathbb{A}}(\tilde{D}))$ regardless of the variance of the estimator, which can not provide sufficient statistical evidences of the final decision.
- A 5-fold CV frequently performs unpromisingly in an adversarial validation, it frequently tends to output false positive conclusion in an algorithm comparison task [8].
- It is difficult to provide an universal optimal value of the decision threshold, ϵ. A reasonable value of ϵ heavily depends on the distribution of the estimator $\widehat{\mathbb{M}}$. Thus, a reasonable setting of ϵ is very challenging.

2.2 Our Proposed Improved Adversarial Validation

The core aim of the adversarial validation, i.e., Problem (2), is essentially an algorithm comparison problem. It is a comparison of the accuracy of an adversarial classifier on $\tilde{D}$ and that of a random guessing. In addition, a promising solution to Problem (2) is applying the state-of-the-art algorithm comparison methods. To date, various algorithm comparison methods have been proposed, and the mainstream is the CV based algorithm comparison methods [8,17]. In this study,therefore, we concentrate on the CV based algorithm comparison methods to improve an adversarial validation.

Formally, given an adversarial data set $\tilde{D}$, a CV is performed on it and a partition set of $\tilde{D}$ is obtained. The partition set is denoted as $\mathcal{P} = \{(\tilde{D}_k^{(t)}, \tilde{D}_k^{(v)})\}_{k=1}^K$ where $\tilde{D}_k^{(t)}$ is the k-th training adversarial set, $\tilde{D}_k^{(v)}$ is the validation adversarial set, and $|\mathcal{P}| = K$ is the partition set size. Then, an adversarial classifier $\tilde{\mathbb{A}}$ is trained and validated on the partition set $\mathcal{P}$ and K estimators of the accuracy of

---

Algorithm 2: An improved cross-validated adversarial validation.

Input: A training set, $\mathcal{D}$; a test set, $\mathcal{T}$; an adversarial classifier, $\tilde{\mathbb{A}}$; a CV-based
    algorithm comparison method; a significance level, α.
Output: Whether $\mathbf{P}_{\mathcal{D}}$ and $\mathbf{P}_{\mathcal{T}}$ are identical?

1   Construct an adversarial data set $\tilde{D} = \{(z_i, \tilde{y}_i)\}_{i=1}^{n}$ based on $\mathcal{D}$ and $\mathcal{T}$;
2   Perform a CV on the adversarial data set $\tilde{D}$ according to the input algorithm
   comparison method, and obtain the corresponding partition set $\mathcal{P}$;
3   Train and validate classifier $\tilde{\mathbb{A}}$ on the partition set $\mathcal{P}$, and obtain the
   corresponding estimators $\widehat{\mathcal{M}}$;
4   Construct a test statistic $Q(\widehat{\mathcal{M}})$ according to the input algorithm comparison
   method;
5   Obtain the quantile q_α based on the distribution of $Q(\widehat{\mathcal{M}})$ and α;
6   **if** $Q(\widehat{\mathcal{M}}) > q_\alpha$ **then**
7 | Output $\mathbf{P}_{\mathcal{D}} \neq \mathbf{P}_{\mathcal{T}}$
8   **else**
9 | Output $\mathbf{P}_{\mathcal{D}} = \mathbf{P}_{\mathcal{T}}$

$\tilde{\mathbb{A}}$ are obtained, denoted as $\widehat{\mathcal{M}} = \{\widehat{\mathbb{M}}_k\}_{k=1}^{K}$. Furthermore, the estimators in $\widehat{\mathcal{M}}$ are used to estimate the expectation and variance of the distribution of $\widehat{\mathbb{M}}$ and construct a test statistic $Q(\widehat{\mathcal{M}})$ for solving Problem (2). Finally, we obtain the decision according to the commonly-used significance testing rule: *Reject H_0' iff* $|Q(\mathcal{M})| > q_\alpha$; *otherwise, H_0' is not rejected.* In the rule, α is a significance level, and q_α is the corresponding quantile, and we assume that a smaller absolute value of $Q(\widehat{\mathcal{M}})$ indicates a smaller difference between $\mathbf{P}_{\mathcal{D}}$ and $\mathbf{P}_{\mathcal{T}}$.

In sum, the sketch of an improved cross-validated adversarial validation is presented in Algorithm 2. Different from Algorithm 1, Algorithm 2 uses a suitable algorithm comparison method to produce a decision. Therefore, the proposed method improves the identification mechanism of an adversarial validation. Moreover the improvement of Algorithm 2 depends on the quality of the play-and-plug algorithm comparison method. Therefore, in order to maximize the improvement, it is indispensable to select an appropriate algorithm comparison method for the improved adversarial validation method.

3   Investigation of the Existing Play-and-Plug Algorithm Comparison Methods

It is important to select a promising algorithm comparison method to ensure the superiority of the proposed improved adversarial validation method.

To date, there exists about 17 different CV based algorithm comparison methods which can be categorized into four families.

(i) **t-test family** (containing 9 tests). (1) Repeated hold-out (RHO) paired t-test [8]. (2) K-fold CV paired t-test [8]. (3) 5×2 CV paired t-test [8]. (4)

Corrected RHO t-test [13]. (5) Pseudo bootstrap test [13]. (6) Corrected pseudo bootstrap test [13]. (7) Corrected 10×10 CV t-test [5]. (8) Combined 5 × 2 CV t-test [20]. (9) Blocked 3 × 2 CV t-test [19].

(ii) **F-test family** (containing 2 tests). (1) Combined 5 × 2 CV F-test [2]. (2) Calibrated 5 × 2 BCV F-test [18].

(iii) **Z-test family** (containing 3 tests). (1) Proportional test [8]. (2) Conservative Z-test [13]. (3) K-fold CV-CI Z-test [4].

(iv) **McNemar's (MCN) test family** (containing 3 tests). (1) Conventional HO MCN test [8]. (2) K-fold CV MCN test [17]. (3) 5 × 2 BCV MCN test [17].

The conservative Z-test, pseudo bootstrap test, and corrected pseudo bootstrap test are excluded in all experiments because it has been found that the three tests are less powerful and more expensive than the corrected RHO t-test [13]. In the next section, we select the best algorithm out of 14 through simulation experiments.

4   Experiments

4.1   Experimental Data Sets and Settings

We use a synthetic data set and several real-world data sets to simulate adversarial data sets in our experiments. According to Problem, we need to produce data records from two populations, namely $\mathbf{P}_\mathcal{D}$ and $\mathbf{P}_\mathcal{T}$, respectively. Therefore, motivated by the simple binary classification data set in [17], we use the following synthetic setting of an adversarial data set.

In a simple adversarial data set (marked as S in Table 2), we use two univariant normal distributions to formalize $\mathbf{P}_\mathcal{D}$ and $\mathbf{P}_\mathcal{T}$ where $\mathbf{P}_\mathcal{D}$ is $N(0,1)$ and $\mathbf{P}_\mathcal{T}$ is $N(\Delta, 1)$. Obviously, when $\Delta = 0$, we obtain $\mathbf{P}_\mathcal{D} = \mathbf{P}_\mathcal{T}$; otherwise, $\mathbf{P}_\mathcal{D} \neq \mathbf{P}_\mathcal{T}$. Furthermore, we define an adversarial data set as $\tilde{D} = \{(z_i, \tilde{y}_i)\}_{i=1}^{1000}$ where $\tilde{y} \in \{'train', 'test'\}$, and $z_i|\tilde{y}_i =' train' \sim N(0,1)$ and $z_i|\tilde{y}_i =' test' \sim N(\Delta, 1)$. The synthetic data set, simple, determines the degree of distribution difference between $\mathbf{P}_\mathcal{D}$ and $\mathbf{P}_\mathcal{T}$ based on changes in Δ.

Besides the synthetic adversarial data set, we also choose eight real-world binary classification data sets from the KEEL data repository [7] to construct the corresponding adversarial data sets, the inspiration for choosing this binary data set comes from [11].

The information about eight KEEL data sets is given in Table 1, covering different levels of numbers of attributes and data records. For each binary data set, we randomly select a fraction of positive records with a proportion parameter of $\Delta \in [0.5, 1]$ and a fraction of negative records with a proportion of $1 - \Delta$ in a without-replacement manner. For example, when Delta=0.6, we select data with a ratio of 0.6 from the original positive class label and a ratio of 0.4 from the original negative class label to merge them as the dataset for the new label $'train'$, and the rest as the dataset for $'test'$. An adversarial data set consists of

Table 1. Information about eight data sets in the KEEL repository.

Data set	Abbreviation	No. of attributes	No. of examples
Pima	P_i	8	768
Appendicitis	A_p	7	106
Australian	A_u	14	690
Banana	B_a	2	5,300
Bupa	B_u	6	345
Haberman	H	3	306
Phoneme	P_h	5	5,400
Mammographic	M	5	830

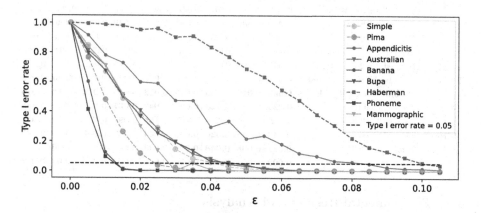

Fig. 1. Type I errors of Algorithm 1 with an increasing ϵ.

the above two fractions of records with an adversarial class label of *'train'* and the remainder records of which the adversarial class label is *'test'*.

In this study, a logistic regression is used as an adversarial classification algorithm. Because an adversarial validation corresponds to a hypothesis testing, we adopt two commonly-used evaluation measures, namely, type I error and power curve [6], to compare the performance of Algorithm 2 with that of Algorithm 1. The type I error is the probability of rejecting the null hypothesis H_0' when H_0' holds. Type II error is the probability of not rejecting H_0' when H_0' doesn't hold. Correspondingly, when H_0' holds, the power value equals to the type I error; otherwise, the power value is one minus the type II error.

Moreover, because type I and II errors are probability, we have to approximate their values with empirical frequencies. Therefore, in our experiments, we randomly and independently produce 1,000 adversarial data sets. It mains we perform Algorithms 1 and 2 to obtain 1,000 decisions of Problem (2). Finally, we use the results to compute the numerical values of type I and II errors.

Given a significance level α, a promising adversarial validation algorithm should own two properties simultaneously: (1) a type I error lower than α, and

(2) the most skew power curve. Therefore, the two properties are used as the criteria for comparing Algorithms 1 and 2. Moreover, the value of $\alpha = 0.05$ is used in this study.

Table 2. Type I errors of different algorithms on nine data sets.

Family	Test	S	P_i	A_p	A_u	B_a	B_u	H	P_h	M
Algorithm 1										
Baseline	$\epsilon = 0.01$	0.669	**0.480**	0.779	0.710	0.123	0.675	0.988	0.095	0.711
	$\epsilon = 0.05$	**0.015**	**0.000**	0.215	**0.031**	**0.000**	**0.040**	0.688	**0.000**	**0.000**
	$\epsilon = 0.1$	**0.000**	**0.000**	**0.015**	**0.000**	**0.000**	**0.000**	0.054	**0.000**	**0.000**
Algorithm 2										
t-test	RHO paired t-test	0.421	0.292	0.350	0.299	0.380	0.288	0.328	0.332	0.330
	K-fold CV paired t-test	0.100	0.139	0.127	0.116	0.174	0.116	0.184	0.138	0.132
	5×2 CV paired t-test	0.079	0.073	0.076	0.071	0.068	0.063	0.064	0.065	0.061
	Corrected RHO t-test	**0.050**	**0.039**	0.073	**0.041**	0.090	**0.049**	0.077	**0.046**	**0.045**
	Corrected 10×10 CV t-test	0.082	0.051	0.127	0.073	0.117	0.070	0.103	0.083	0.056
	Combined 5×2 CV t-test	0.094	0.095	0.083	0.101	0.107	0.082	0.099	0.094	0.086
	Blocked 3×2 CV t-test	**0.045**	0.051	0.057	0.051	0.057	**0.049**	0.057	0.060	0.060
F-test	Combined 5×2 CV F-test	**0.012**	**0.020**	**0.012**	**0.030**	**0.012**	**0.020**	**0.017**	**0.014**	**0.018**
	Calibrated 5×2 BCV F-test	**0.009**	**0.019**	**0.010**	**0.029**	**0.012**	**0.018**	**0.014**	**0.013**	**0.015**
Z-test	Proportional test	**0.029**	0.056	**0.028**	**0.036**	**0.042**	**0.037**	**0.035**	0.055	**0.035**
	K-fold CV-CI Z-test	0.122	0.274	0.313	0.247	0.326	0.266	0.350	0.251	0.309
MCN-test	HO MCN test	**0.044**	**0.048**	**0.020**	**0.038**	**0.044**	**0.037**	**0.041**	**0.046**	**0.035**
	K-fold CV MCN test	**0.021**	**0.008**	**0.008**	**0.009**	**0.033**	**0.006**	**0.007**	**0.040**	**0.012**
	5×2 BCV MCN test	**0.002**	**0.005**	**0.002**	**0.006**	**0.004**	**0.002**	**0.004**	**0.004**	**0.007**

4.2 Experimental Results and Analysis

To illustrate the weaknesses of Algorithm 1, we plot the type I errors of the algorithm with an increasing value of ϵ in Fig. 1. The black horizontal line indicates an acceptable type I error, i.e., 0.05. From Figure 1, we obtain several observations as follows. (1) For The type I error of Algorithm 1 heavily depends on a specific data set. (3) There exists no an universal optimal setting of ϵ, and the optimal setting of ϵ depends on a specific data set.

The type I errors of Algorithms 1 and 2 are further compared in Table 2. In the table, a value in bold indicates that the corresponding type I error is acceptable. For Algorithm 1, we obtain that when $\epsilon = 0.1$, the values of type I error on all the data sets are acceptable. Thus, we merely use $\epsilon = 0.1$ to further obtain the power curve of Algorithm 1.

We also obtain that the value of type I error varies along with the type of a play-and-plug algorithm comparison method in Table 2. Specifically, we obtain several observations. (1) The methods in the t-test family perform worse because most values of type I error exceed 0.05. (2) The RHO paired t-test and K-fold CV paired t-test achieve the worst performance. (3) The methods in the F-test and MCN test families achieve acceptable type I errors over all the nine data sets. In particular, the 5×2 BCV MCN test achieves the smallest type I error that indicates that this method can effectively reduce the false positive decisions in Problem (2).

On each data set, Fig. 2 illustrates that the power curves of the adversarial validation methods with different play-and-plug algorithm comparison methods owning an acceptable type I error. From Fig. 2, we obtain that (1) Algorithm 1 frequently performs worse. (2) The 5 × 2 BCV MCN test based algorithm comparison method constantly possesses the most skew power curves over all the data sets.

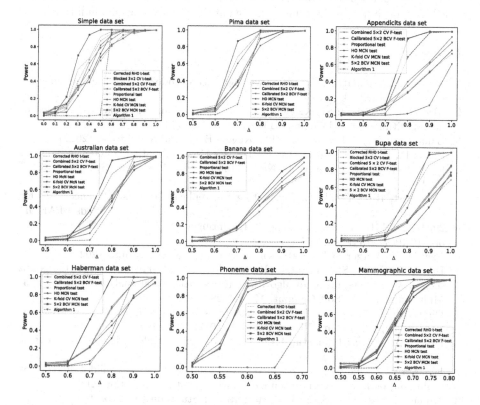

Fig. 2. Powers curves of adversarial validation algorithms on different data sets.

Comprehensively integrating the results in Table 2 and Fig. 2, we consider that Algorithm 2 coupled with a 5 × 2 BCV MCN test performs the best in an adversarial validation. Therefore, we recommend a 5 BCV MCN test based adversarial validation method to identify the difference of the distributions of a training set and a test set in a data competition.

5 Conclusions

In this study, we first investigate the weaknesses of a typical adversarial validation and then propose a novel cross-validated adversarial validation coupled with a play-and-plug algorithm comparison method to improve the identification accuracy of the difference between the distributions of a training set and a test set. Through an investigation of the existing 17 algorithm comparison methods, we show that the proposed adversarial validation based on a 5×2 BCV MCN test owns a promising improvement. Therefore, as a guideline, we recommend the practitioners to use the 5×2 BCV MCN test based adversarial validation in a data competition to properly assess a machine learning data set. In future, we will further improve the other components in an adversarial validation.

References

1. Adversarial validation. https://www.kaggle.com/code/kevinbonnes/adversarial-validation/notebook (2018)
2. Alpaydin, E.: Combined 5×2 cv f test for comparing supervised classification learning algorithms. Neural Comput. **11**(8), 1885–1892 (1999)
3. Banachewicz, K., Massaron, L.: The Kaggle Book. Packt Publisher (2022)
4. Bayle, P., Bayle, A., Janson, L., Mackey, L.: Cross-validation confidence intervals for test error. In: Advances in Neural Information Processing Systems, vol. 33 (2020)
5. Bouckaert, R.R., Frank, E.: Evaluating the replicability of significance tests for comparing learning algorithms. In: Dai, H., Srikant, R., Zhang, C. (eds.) PAKDD 2004. LNCS (LNAI), vol. 3056, pp. 3–12. Springer, Heidelberg (2004). https://doi.org/10.1007/978-3-540-24775-3_3
6. Casella, G., Berger, R.L.: Statistical inference. Cengage Learning (2021)
7. Derrac, J., Garcia, S., Sanchez, L., Herrera, F.: Keel data-mining software tool: data set repository, integration of algorithms and experimental analysis framework. J. Mult. Valued Logic Soft Comput. **17**, 255-287 (2015)
8. Dietterich, T.G.: Approximate statistical tests for comparing supervised classification learning algorithms. Neural Comput. **10**(7), 1895–1923 (1998)
9. Dragomiretskiy, S.: Influential ML: towards detection of algorithmic influence drift through causal analysis. Master's thesis (2022)
10. Ishihara, S., Goda, S., Arai, H.: Adversarial validation to select validation data for evaluating performance in e-commerce purchase intent prediction (2021)
11. Moreno-Torres, J.G., Sáez, J.A., Herrera, F.: Study on the impact of partition-induced dataset shift on k-fold cross-validation. IEEE Trans. Neural Netw. Learn. Syst. **23**(8), 1304–1312 (2012)
12. Mosquera, A.: Tackling data drift with adversarial validation: an application for German text complexity estimation. In: Proceedings of the GermEval 2022 Workshop on Text Complexity Assessment of German Text, pp. 39–44 (2022)
13. Nadeau, C., Bengio, Y.: Inference for the generalization error. Mach. Learn. **52**(3), 239–281 (2003)
14. Pan, J., Pham, V., Dorairaj, M., Chen, H., Lee, J.Y.: Adversarial validation approach to concept drift problem in user targeting automation systems at uber. arXiv preprint arXiv:2004.03045 (2020)
15. Qian, H., Wang, B., Ma, P., Peng, L., Gao, S., Song, Y.: Managing dataset shift by adversarial validation for credit scoring. In: Khanna, S., Cao, J., Bai, Q., Xu, G. (eds.) PRICAI 2022: Trends in Artificial Intelligence. PRICAI 2022. Lecture Notes in Computer Science, vol. 13629, pp. 477–488. Springer, Cham (2022). https://doi.org/10.1007/978-3-031-20862-1_35

16. Wang, R., Li, J.: Bayes test of precision, recall, and f1 measure for comparison of two natural language processing models. In: Proceedings of the 57th Annual Meeting of the Association for Computational Linguistics, pp. 4135–4145 (2019)
17. Wang, R., Li, J.: Block-regularized 5×2 cross-validated mcnemar's test for comparing two classification algorithms. arXiv preprint arXiv:2304.03990 (2023)
18. Wang, Yu., Li, J., Li, Y.: Choosing between two classification learning algorithms based on calibrated balanced 5×2 cross-validated F-test. Neural Process. Lett. $46(1)$, 1–13 (2016). https://doi.org/10.1007/s11063-016-9569-z
19. Wang, Y., Wang, R., Jia, H., Li, J.: Blocked 3×2 cross-validated t-test for comparing supervised classification learning algorithms. Neural Comput. $26(1)$, 208–235 (2014)
20. Yildiz, O.T.: Omnivariate rule induction using a novel pairwise statistical test. IEEE Trans. Knowl. Data Eng. $25(9)$, 2105–2118 (2013)

EACCNet: Enhanced Auto-Cross Correlation Network for Few-Shot Classification

Jiuqiang Li[✉][iD]

Southwest Jiaotong University, Chengdu 611756, Sichuan, China
jiuqiangli@my.swjtu.edu.cn

Abstract. Few-shot classification, which belongs to a popular direction in few-shot learning, can be said to bridge the gap between human intelligence and machine models at present, aiming at rapid classification of new classes encountered in downstream tasks with only a small number of samples after the model has learned a certain class of data. However, the current approach suffers from two fatal problems, which are a very complicated training process and the presence of irrelevant information in the captured semantic features, resulting in low accuracy. We propose two core modules that can be learned: the enhanced auto-correlation representation (EACR) module and the enhanced cross-correlation attention (ECCA) module. The EACR module takes the representations computed by enhanced auto-correlation and learns the auto-correlation representation by convolutional operations to reveal the structural patterns of the images. The ECCA module works together from both meta-learning and representation cosine similarity to construct the query image and support enhanced cross-correlation attention maps between images. In the experiments, the EACCNet consisting of these two modules performs quit well on three standard benchmarks, achieving end-to-end few-shot classification with guaranteed high accuracy.

Keywords: Few-Shot classification · Auto-Correlation · Cross-Correlation · Deep learning · Convolutional neural networks

1 Introduction

Few-shot image classification aims to learn new visual concepts with just a few samples, and evaluate the ability to classify new classes with only a small number of support images. This task has significant implications for reducing labeling costs and bridging the gap between human and machine intelligence. Vision transformer [3,7,16,20] has emerged as a powerful alternative to convolutional neural networks [11,28] in various computer vision tasks. However, transformers lack some of the inductive biases inherent in Convolutional neural networks (CNNs) and rely heavily on large datasets. Recent methods [9,11,28] have mitigated this issue through meta-learning a deep embedding function, but there are still challenges in effectively converting images into representations and filtering out irrelevant features.

Z. Jin et al. (Eds.): KSEM 2023, LNAI 14117, pp. 354–365, 2023.
https://doi.org/10.1007/978-3-031-40283-8_30

Our Work: Our approach focuses on enhancing auto-cross correlation to better mine relational patterns in a base feature map for joint attention of query and support images. We propose two core modules: the enhanced auto-correlation representation (EACR) module, which obtains reliable auto-correlation representations using enhanced computation and convolution operations, and the enhanced cross-correlation attention (ECCA) module, which learns cross-attention maps between query and support images using meta-learning and cosine similarity comparison, and filters with four-dimensional convolution for improved classification. These modules are combined in EACCNet for end-to-end training and evaluation of few-shot classification with improved accuracy and reduced computational and time costs.

The contributions of this paper are as follows:

- We propose the enhanced auto-correlation representation (EACR) module for few-shot classification. It converts deep neural features into enhanced and effective feature representations that assist in learning transferable structural patterns in an image.
- We introduce the enhanced cross-correlation Attention (ECCA) module for few-shot classification. It learns to filter out irrelevant features and generate common attention between images through enhanced convolutional filtering and cross-correlation.
- Experiments demonstrate that our EACCNet mainly composed of EACR and ECCA modules achieves end-to-end training and performs remarkably well on multiple standard few-shot classification benchmarks with a short training duration, and ablation studies validate the effectiveness of the components.

2   Related Work

2.1   Few-Shot Classification

Few-shot classification requires learning how to learn. Three broad approaches to few-shot classification include transfer-learning, transformer-based, and metric-based approaches. The transfer-learning approach [21] involves pre-training and fine-tuning, which is powerful but time-consuming. The transformer-based approach [7,8] incorporates semantic hierarchies of images into transformers but requires high computational effort. The metric-based approach learns an embedding function to map images to the metric space and calculate their distance, but may learn useless features. Our method also belongs to the metric-based approach, but we improve the transferability of embeddings and filter out irrelevant features by strengthening auto-correlation and cross-correlation embeddings through learning to learn. This allows for better discrimination between unseen categories in the test stage.

2.2   Auto-Correlation

Auto-correlation measures the correlation of data with itself, commonly used in time series forecasting. The combination of Transformers and Auto-Correlation in Autoformer [26] has shown good performance in long time series forecasting. Auto-Correlation can also reveal the structural pattern of an image and is useful for feature extraction in deep learning networks. The EACR module for few-shot classification uses image auto-correlation to mine potential structural patterns in images, which is learned by convolution for representation learning.

2.3 Cross-Correlation

Cross-Correlation is used in time series forecasting to compare two time series for correlation. In computer vision, it is used for tasks like semantic segmentation [17] and video object segmentation [18]. Some few-shot classification methods use cross-correlation, but they can learn unreliable correlations and miss the geometric relationship of features. The ECCA module improves cross-correlation attention by filtering out unreliable correlations using two parallel routes. The first route uses a meta-learning model to learn the cross-correlation attention graph, while the second route uses four-dimensional convolution to compare cosine similarity and filter out useless information. The final cross-correlation attention graph is obtained by combining the two routes.

3   Proposed Approach

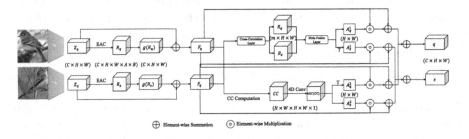

Fig. 1. The Overall Architecture of the Proposed EACCNet Model.

In this section, we introduce the *Enhanced Auto-Cross Correlation Network* (**EACCNet**) for few-shot classification via enhanced auto-correlation and enhanced cross-correlation. Figure 1 illustrates the overall architecture of EAC-CNet, which is composed of enhanced auto-correlation representation (EACR) module and enhanced cross-correlation attention (ECCA) module.

3.1   Preliminary on Few-Shot Classification

For few-shot classification tasks, the proposed method in the model training phase performs training and tuning optimization in a training data $\mathcal{D}_{\text{train}}$ with classes $\mathcal{C}_{\text{train}}$. In the model evaluation phase, the trained model is evaluated on a test data $\mathcal{D}_{\text{test}}$ containing classes $\mathcal{C}_{\text{test}}$ not seen in the model training phase, where it is worth noting that $\mathcal{C}_{\text{train}} \cap \mathcal{C}_{\text{test}} = \varnothing$. The overall model training and model evaluation process we use the episode training mode, and in the episode mode both $\mathcal{D}_{\text{train}}$ and $\mathcal{D}_{\text{test}}$ contain multiple episodes, and they both provide a support set $\mathcal{S} = \left\{ \left(\mathbf{I}_s^{(l)}, y_s^{(l)} \right) \right\}_{l=1}^{NK}$ and a query set $\mathcal{Q} = (\mathbf{I}_q, y_q)$ containing N classes and K pairs of images with labels.

3.2 Architecture Overview of EACCNet

EACCNet effectively combines Auto-Correlation and Cross-Correlation enhancements for new-shot classification, aiming at learning reliable structural patterns of a given image to form more reliable auto-correlation representations for classification tasks, filtering out irrelevant representations by enhanced convolution operations and weighted aggregation to draw attention to the target object to form a common attention between the support image and the query image.

3.3 Enhanced Auto-Correlation Representation (EACR)

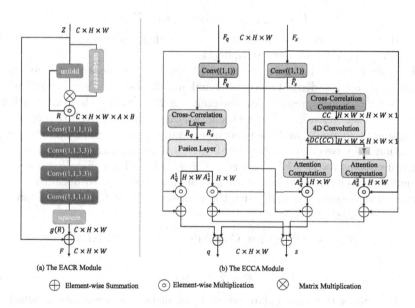

(a) The EACR Module   (b) The ECCA Module

⊕ Element-wise Summation   ⊙ Element-wise Multiplication   ⊗ Matrix Multiplication

Fig. 2. The Architecture of EACR and ECCA Modules.

In the evaluation phase of small-sample classification methods, it is very challenging to identify images in categories that have not been seen in the training process, so how to make the model learn to learn how to mine the structure in the image so that it can accurately determine the category of a given image in the test is the problem we need to solve. From this reflection, we propose the EACR module to learn to mine the structural patterns of a given image and to provide a reliable feature representation for the subsequent ECCA module and classification tasks. In the following we will detail the technical details of the EACR module, and similarly, Fig. 2 (a) illustrates the architecture of the EACR module.

First, it needs to be stated that the input to the EACR module is the underlying representation Z provided by the backbone network ResNet [6], with dimensions $C \times H \times W$. Then, the autocorrelation calculation part of our cleverly designed EACR module has to be described in detail. It can be generally easy to think of performing the unfold operation on the representation Z to obtain the offset representation of Z for each direction of a given scale, and then go to the original Z to do the Hadamard product with each offset representation to obtain the autocorrelation representation of the given representation. The specific implementation can be achieved by Eqs. 1 and 2.

$$\mathbf{Z_p} = \frac{\mathbf{Z(x+o)}}{\|\mathbf{Z(x+o)}\|} \tag{1}$$

$$\mathbf{R_1(x,o)} = \frac{\mathbf{Z(x)}}{\|\mathbf{Z(x)}\|} \odot \mathbf{Z_p} \tag{2}$$

$$\mathbf{R} = \mathbf{Z_p} \odot (\text{Unsequeeze}\,(\mathbf{Z}) \otimes \mathbf{Z_p}) \tag{3}$$

where $\mathbf{R}$ denotes the auto-correlation tensor, $\odot$ denotes element-wise multiplication, and $\otimes$ denotes matrix multiplication.

To analyze the structural patterns of the resulting auto-correlation representations R, we use a series of two-dimensional and three-dimensional convolutions for auto-correlation representation learning. First, to reduce the computational effort of representation learning, we use a two-dimensional convolution to reduce the number of channels, and then convolve along the $A \times B$ direction of the representation R by two three-dimensional convolutions, thus changing the scale of the feature from $C \times H \times W \times A \times B$ to $C \times H \times W \times 1 \times 1$. Finally, we recover the number of channels by a two-dimensional convolution to obtain an auto-correlation representation $g(R)$ with the final size of $C \times H \times W$. This process can be represented as Eq. 4.

$$g(R) = \text{Conv2d}(\text{View}(\text{Conv3d}(\text{Conv3d}(\text{Conv2d}(R))))) \tag{4}$$

$$\mathbf{F} = \mathbf{Z} + g(\mathbf{R}) \tag{5}$$

where F denotes the final enhanced auto-correlation representation, which is similar to a residual connection.

3.4   Enhanced Cross-Correlation Attention (ECCA)

For the first direction, the generated representations $\hat{\mathbf{F}}_q$, $\hat{\mathbf{F}}_s$ are introduced into the cross-correlation layer to compute cross-correlation to capture the cross-correlation patterns between the images in the support set and the images in the query set, generating cross-correlation representations $\mathbf{R_q}$, $\mathbf{R_s}$ with each other, respectively, which is described in Eq. 6.

$$R_c = \left(\frac{\hat{\mathbf{F}}_s}{\|\hat{\mathbf{F}}_s\|_2}\right)^T \left(\frac{\hat{\mathbf{F}}_q}{\|\hat{\mathbf{F}}_q\|_2}\right) \tag{6}$$

where $R_q = R_c$, $R_s = R_c^T$ and R_q, R_s are the cross-correlation representations of the support set image and the query set image, respectively.

We then employ a meta-fusion layer to generate the attention of the support image and the query image based on the corresponding cross-correlation representations, respectively. For the design of the meta-learner w in the meta-fusion layer can be described by the following Eq. 7.

$$w = W_1 \left(RELU \left(W_2 \left(GAP \left(R_s\right)\right)\right) \tag{7}$$

where $W_1 \in \mathbb{R}^{m \times \frac{m}{r}}$ and $W_2 \in \mathbb{R}^{\frac{m}{r} \times m}$ are the parameters of the meta-learner, and r is the reduction ratio. RELU denotes the RELU activation function and GAP means global average pooling. After designing the meta-learner, we will describe how the meta-fusion layer works with the example of generating cross-correlation attention to support ensemble images, as detailed in Eq. 8.

$$A_s^1 = \frac{\exp \left(\left(w^T R_s\right)/\varrho\right)}{\sum_{j=1}^{h \times w} \exp \left(\left(w^T R_s^j\right)/\varrho\right)} \tag{8}$$

where ϱ is the temperature hyperparameter and Lower temperature leading to lower entropy make the distribution concentrate on a few high confidence positions. By the same method as above we can obtain the cross-correlation attention A_q^1 of the query image.

For the second direction, we also used the cross-correlation calculation, but unlike the first direction, we used to calculate the cosine similarity of the two auto-correlated representations $\hat{\mathbf{F}}_q$ and $\hat{\mathbf{F}}_s$ to obtain the cross-correlation representation $\mathbf{CC}$.

$$\mathbf{CC} = \sim \left(\hat{\mathbf{F}}_q, \hat{\mathbf{F}}_s\right) \tag{9}$$

where $\sim(\cdot,\cdot)$ means the cosine similarity between two tensors, and the size of $\mathbf{CC}$ is $H \times W \times H \times W \times 1$. Calculations in this way not only yield reliable cross-correlation representations, but also reduce the computational effort. The cross-correlation representation obtained so far is still irrelevant to the classification task, so it needs to be filtered to obtain a more reliable cross-correlation representation, and we solve this problem by using 4D convolution, i.e., *4D Convolution* (4DC) block. *4D Convolution* block consists of two 4-dimensional convolution layer operations, which not only performs the filtering operation for the previously obtained cross-correlation representation, but also provides a more reliable input for the subsequent generation of cross-attention.

After obtaining more reliable cross-correlation representations, we need to establish the common cross-attention between the support set images and the query set images.

$$\mathbf{A}_s^2(\mathbf{x}_s) = \frac{1}{HW} \sum_{\mathbf{x}_q} \frac{\exp\left(\hat{\mathbf{C}}(\mathbf{x}_s, \mathbf{x}_q)/\varrho\right)}{\sum_{\mathbf{x}_s'} \exp\left(\hat{\mathbf{C}}(\mathbf{x}_s', \mathbf{x}_q)/\varrho\right)} \tag{10}$$

where ϱ is the temperature hyperparameter, $\mathbf{x}$ is a position at the feature map, $\hat{\mathbf{C}}(\mathbf{x}_q, \mathbf{x}_s)$ is a matching score between the positions $\mathbf{x}_q$ and $\mathbf{x}_s$. $\mathbf{A}_s^2$ can be interpreted as the average probability of matching the support image with a position on the query image to obtain the common cross-attention of both. The common cross-attention $\mathbf{A}_q^2$ of the query image with respect to the support image can also be calculated in a similar way for the query image.

The above two directions yield a common cross-attention between the two query images and the support image, i.e., $\mathbf{A}_s^1$ and $\mathbf{A}_q^1$, and $\mathbf{A}_s^2$ and $\mathbf{A}_q^2$. To obtain a more reliable and comprehensive joint cross-attention, we further fuse the above two directions to enhance the joint cross-attention of the query and support images. Specifically, the attention maps generated in both directions are made Hadamard products with the original representations respectively, and then combined with the original representations, and finally the attentions of the query images or support images in both directions are combined to obtain the final common cross-attention map.

$$\mathbf{A}_q = \left(\mathbf{A}_q^1 \odot \mathbf{F}_q\right) + \left(\mathbf{A}_q^2 \odot \mathbf{F}_q\right) + \mathbf{F}_q \tag{11}$$

$$\mathbf{A}_s = \left(\mathbf{A}_s^1 \odot \mathbf{F}_s\right) + \left(\mathbf{A}_s^2 \odot \mathbf{F}_s\right) + \mathbf{F}_s \tag{12}$$

where $\mathbf{A}_q$, $\mathbf{A}_s$ are the common cross-attention maps of the query image or the support image, respectively. $\odot$ is the Hadamard product.

3.5   Training Strategy of EACCNet

The proposed EACCNet is an end-to-end training approach that jointly trains the proposed model by combining two types of losses: anchor-based classification loss $\mathcal{L}_1$ and metric-based classification loss $\mathcal{L}_2$.

$$\mathcal{L}_1 = -\log \frac{\exp\left(\mathbf{w}_c^\top \mathbf{z}_q + \mathbf{b}_c\right)}{\sum_{c'=1}^{|\mathcal{C}_{\text{trin}}|} \exp\left(\mathbf{w}_{c'}^\top \mathbf{z}_q + \mathbf{b}_{c'}\right)} \tag{13}$$

where $[\mathbf{b}_1, \cdots, \mathbf{b}_{|\mathcal{C}_{\text{train}}|}]$ and $[\mathbf{w}_1^\top, \cdots, \mathbf{w}_{|\mathcal{C}_{\text{trin}}|}^\top]$ are biases and weights in the fully-connected layer, respectively.

$$\mathcal{L}_2 = -\log \frac{\exp\left(\text{sim}\left(\overline{\mathbf{s}}^{(n)}, \overline{\mathbf{q}}^{(n)}\right)/\varrho\right)}{\sum_{n'=1}^{N} \exp\left(\text{sim}\left(\overline{\mathbf{s}}^{(n')}, \overline{\mathbf{q}}^{(n')}\right)/\varrho\right)} \tag{14}$$

where ϱ is a temperature hyperparameter and sim is cosine similarity. The final loss function is expressed as:

$$\mathcal{L} = \mathcal{L}_1 + \lambda \mathcal{L}_2 \tag{15}$$

where λ is a hyper-parameter which balances the loss terms.

4   Experiments

In this section, we evaluate EACCNet on standard benchmarks and compare the results with the recent state of the arts. We also conduct ablation studies to validate the effect of the major components.

4.1   Datasets

We perform experiments to train and evaluate our methods on three popular and standard benchmarks for few-shot classification, including miniImageNet, CIFAR-FS and CUB-200-2011. In order to validate the effect of the major components, we also use some of the three datasets in our ablation studies. *mini*ImageNet [24] contains 100 classes from the ImageNet[54] [4], randomly split into 64 bases, 16 validation, and 20 novel classes, and each class contains 600 images. **CIFAR-FS** [1] contains 100 classes from the CIFAR100 [12], randomly split into 64 bases, 16 validation, adn 20 novel calsses, and each class contains 600 images. **CUB-200-2011** (CUB) [25] is a dataset for fine-grained classification of bird species, consisting of 100/50/50 object classes for train/validation/test splits, respectively.

4.2   Implementation Details

All experiments are run on ResNet12 [6], which provides a base representation **Z**. We set $A = B = 5$ in our experiments. The hyperparameter λ is set to 0.3, 0.45, 1.25 for *mini*ImageNet, CIFAR-FS, CUB, respectively. ϱ is set to 2 for CUB and 5 otherwise. We implement our PyTorch-based approach by training on an NVIDIA RTX 3090 GPU with 24 GB of video memory. The base learning rate value is $1e^{-4}$, the batch size is 64, the training epoch is 100, and the cosine annealing learning rate strategy is adopted.

4.3   Experimental Results

In Tables 1, 2, and 3, we compare our method EACCNet with the now existing methods experimentally on three standard benchmarks, where N-way K-shot means that in the support set, there are n species and k samples for each species. It can be found that the proposed EACCNet outperforms the best method in the experimental comparison on three datasets, which verifies from the experimental point of view that the EACCNet performs very well for the few-shot image classification task.

Table 1. Experiment Results on *mini*ImageNet Dataset

Method	Backbone	5-way 1-shot	5-way 5-shot
ProtoNet [19]	*ResNet12*	62.39±0.21	80.53±0.14
MetaOptNet [13]	*ResNet12*	62.64±0.82	78.63±0.46
MatchNet [24]	*ResNet12*	63.08±0.80	75.99±0.60
CAN [10]	*ResNet12*	63.85±0.48	79.44±0.34
NegMargin [15]	*ResNet12*	63.85±0.81	81.57±0.56
CTM [14]	*ResNet18*	64.12±0.82	80.51±0.13
DeepEMD [28]	*ResNet12*	65.91±0.82	82.41±0.56
FEAT [27]	*ResNet12*	66.78±0.20	82.05±0.14
RENet [11]	*ResNet12*	67.60±0.44	82.58±0.30
ECCANet (ours)	*ResNet12*	**68.57±0.52**	**83.26±0.46**

Table 2. Experiment Results on CIFAR-FS Dataset

Method	Backbone	5-way 1-shot	5-way 5-shot
RFS-simple [23]	*ResNet12*	71.5±0.8	86.0±0.5
ProtoNet [19]	*ResNet12*	72.2±0.7	83.5±0.5
MetaOptNet [13]	*ResNet12*	72.6±0.7	84.3±0.5
Boosting [5]	*WRN-28-10*	73.6±0.3	86.0±0.2
RENet [11]	*ResNet12*	74.51±0.46	86.60±0.32
ECCANet (ours)	*ResNet12*	**75.42±0.29**	**87.02±0.26**

Table 3. Experiment Results on CUB-200-2011 Dataset

Method	Backbone	5-way 1-shot	5-way 5-shot
ProtoNet [19]	*ResNet12*	66.09±0.92	82.50±0.58
RelationNet [22]	*ResNet34*	66.20±0.99	82.30±0.58
MAML [4]	*ResNet34*	67.28±1.08	83.47±0.59
cosine classifier [2]	*ResNet12*	67.30±0.86	84.75±0.60
MatchNet [24]	*ResNet12*	71.87±0.85	85.08±0.57
NegMargin [15]	*ResNet18*	72.66±0.85	89.40±0.43
FEAT [27]	*ResNet12*	73.27±0.22	85.77±0.14
DeepEMD [28]	*ResNet12*	75.65±0.83	88.69±0.50
RENet [11]	*ResNet12*	79.49±0.44	91.11±0.24
ECCANet (ours)	*ResNet12*	**81.36±0.34**	**92.04±0.41**

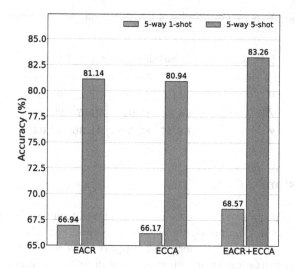

Fig. 3. Visualization of the Ablation Experimental Results of the Proposed EACCNet Model on the *mini*ImageNet dataset.

It is worth noting that the training process of our proposed method is single-stage end-to-end and does not require any pre-training process or post-processing operations. At the same time, the model training is fast, and the proposed method takes rough two minutes to evaluate 2,000 5-way 5-shot episodes with an Intel i7-8550U CPU and an NVIDIA RTX 3090 GPU during the model training.

4.4   Ablation Studies

To verify the validity of the proposed method, we also performed ablation experiments, mainly to verify the effectiveness of the EACR module and the ECCA module. Table 4 shows the results of the ablation experiments, where we use the base representation as input when only the ECCA module is available, and we use its output directly for classification when only the EACR module is available.

The ablation experimental results show that the reliable representations provided by the EACR module are crucial for subsequent classification, while the ECCA module can further filter the representations provided by EACR to strengthen the cross-correlation, resulting in better results. Figure 3 shows the visualization of the ablation experimental results of the proposed method EAC-CNet on miniImageNet. For this intuitive experimental result we can find that if the EACR module is missing to mine the structural patterns and provide reliable autocorrelation characterization, then the ECCA module alone does not reach good results, or even better than using the EACR module alone.

Table 4. Ablation Experiment Results of EACCNet on miniImageNet and CUB-200-2011 dataset.

EACR	ECCA	*mini*ImageNet		CUB-200-2011	
		1-shot	5-shot	1-shot	5-shot
✔	✗	66.94	81.14	79.83	90.92
✗	✔	66.17	80.94	79.67	90.58
✔	✔	**68.57**	**83.26**	**81.36**	**92.04**

5   Conclusion

In this work, we propose enhanced auto-cross correlation to mine the enhanced relational patterns in the underlying feature maps and are able to learn the joint reliable enhanced attention of query and support images to overcome the problem of poor generalization in unseen categories in few-shot image classification. The EACR module focuses on providing more reliable feature criteria and revealing structural patterns of images. The ECCA module mines the cross-correlation attention of query images and support images to provide reliable semantic representations for classification tasks. In the experiments, the proposed model EAC-CNet performs well on three standard benchmarks and validates the effectiveness of the model components by ablation experiments, providing an end-to-end and efficient method for few-shot classification.

References

1. Bertinetto, L., Henriques, J.F., Torr, P.H., Vedaldi, A.: Meta-learning with differentiable closed-form solvers. arXiv preprint arXiv:1805.08136 (2018)
2. Chen, W.Y., Liu, Y.C., Kira, Z., Wang, Y.C.F., Huang, J.B.: A closer look at few-shot classification. arXiv preprint arXiv:1904.04232 (2019)
3. Dosovitskiy, A., et al.: An image is worth 16x16 words: transformers for image recognition at scale. In: ICLR (2021)
4. Finn, C., Abbeel, P., Levine, S.: Model-agnostic meta-learning for fast adaptation of deep networks. In: ICML, pp. 1126–1135. PMLR (2017)
5. Gidaris, S., Bursuc, A., Komodakis, N., Pérez, P., Cord, M.: Boosting few-shot visual learning with self-supervision. In: ICCV, pp. 8059–8068 (2019)
6. He, K., Zhang, X., Ren, S., Sun, J.: Deep residual learning for image recognition. In: CVPR, pp. 770–778 (2016)
7. He, Y., et al.: Attribute surrogates learning and spectral tokens pooling in transformers for few-shot learning. In: CVPR, pp. 9109–9119 (2022). https://doi.org/10.1109/CVPR52688.2022.00891
8. Hiller, M., Ma, R., Harandi, M., Drummond, T.: Rethinking generalization in few-shot classification. In: Oh, A.H., Agarwal, A., Belgrave, D., Cho, K. (eds.) NeurIPS (2022). https://openreview.net/forum?id=p_g2nHlMus
9. Hou, R., Chang, H., Ma, B., Shan, S., Chen, X.: Cross Attention Network for Few-Shot Classification. Curran Associates Inc., Red Hook (2019)

10. Hou, R., Chang, H., Ma, B., Shan, S., Chen, X.: Cross attention network for few-shot classification. In: Advances in Neural Information Processing Systems, vol. 32 (2019)

11. Kang, D., Kwon, H., Min, J., Cho, M.: Relational embedding for few-shot classification. In: Proceedings of the IEEE/CVF International Conference on Computer Vision, pp. 8822–8833 (2021)

12. Krizhevsky, A., Hinton, G., et al.: Learning multiple layers of features from tiny images (2009)

13. Lee, K., Maji, S., Ravichandran, A., Soatto, S.: Meta-learning with differentiable convex optimization. IEEE (2019)

14. Li, H., Eigen, D., Dodge, S., Zeiler, M., Wang, X.: Finding task-relevant features for few-shot learning by category traversal. In: Proceedings of the IEEE/CVF Conference on Computer Vision and Pattern Recognition, pp. 1–10 (2019)

15. Liu, B., et al.: Negative margin matters: understanding margin in few-shot classification. In: Vedaldi, A., Bischof, H., Brox, T., Frahm, J.-M. (eds.) ECCV 2020. LNCS, vol. 12349, pp. 438–455. Springer, Cham (2020). https://doi.org/10.1007/978-3-030-58548-8_26

16. Liu, Z., et al.: Swin transformer: hierarchical vision transformer using shifted windows. In: ICCV, pp. 10012–10022 (2021)

17. Min, J., Kang, D., Cho, M.: Hypercorrelation squeeze for few-shot segmentation. In: ICCV, pp. 6941–6952 (2021)

18. Oh, S.W., Lee, J.Y., Xu, N., Kim, S.J.: Video object segmentation using space-time memory networks. In: ICCV, pp. 9226–9235 (2019)

19. Snell, J., Swersky, K., Zemel, R.: Prototypical networks for few-shot learning. In: Advances in Neural Information Processing Systems, vol. 30 (2017)

20. Srinivas, A., Lin, T.Y., Parmar, N., Shlens, J., Abbeel, P., Vaswani, A.: Bottleneck transformers for visual recognition. In: CVPR, pp. 16519–16529 (2021)

21. Sun, Q., Liu, Y., Chua, T.S., Schiele, B.: Meta-transfer learning for few-shot learning. In: 2019 IEEE/CVF Conference on Computer Vision and Pattern Recognition (CVPR), pp. 403–412 (2019). https://doi.org/10.1109/CVPR.2019.00049

22. Sung, F., Yang, Y., Zhang, L., Xiang, T., Torr, P.H., Hospedales, T.M.: Learning to compare: relation network for few-shot learning. In: Proceedings of the IEEE Conference on Computer Vision and Pattern Recognition, pp. 1199–1208 (2018)

23. Tian, Y., Wang, Y., Krishnan, D., Tenenbaum, J.B., Isola, P.: Rethinking few-shot image classification: a good embedding is all you need? In: Vedaldi, A., Bischof, H., Brox, T., Frahm, J.-M. (eds.) ECCV 2020. LNCS, vol. 12359, pp. 266–282. Springer, Cham (2020). https://doi.org/10.1007/978-3-030-58568-6_16

24. Vinyals, O., Blundell, C., Lillicrap, T., Wierstra, D., et al.: Matching networks for one shot learning. In: Advances in Neural Information Processing Systems, vol. 29 (2016)

25. Wah, C., Branson, S., Welinder, P., Perona, P., Belongie, S.: The caltech-ucsd birds-200-2011 dataset (2011)

26. Wu, H., Xu, J., Wang, J., Long, M.: Autoformer: decomposition transformers with auto-correlation for long-term series forecasting. Adv. Neural. Inf. Process. Syst. **34**, 22419–22430 (2021)

27. Ye, H.J., Hu, H., Zhan, D.C., Sha, F.: Few-shot learning via embedding adaptation with set-to-set functions. In: CVPR, pp. 8808–8817 (2020)

28. Zhao, H., Jia, J., Koltun, V.: Exploring self-attention for image recognition. In: CVPR, pp. 10076–10085 (2020)

A Flexible Generative Model for Joint Label-Structure Estimation from Multifaceted Graph Data

Qianqian Peng[1], Ziming Tang[2], Xinzhi Yao[1], Sizhuo Ouyang[1], Zhihan He[1,2], and Jingbo Xia[1(✉)]

[1] Hubei Key Lab of Agricultural Bioinformatics, College of Informatics, Huazhong Agricultural University, Wuhan, Hubei, People's Republic of China
hezhihan@webmail.hzau.edu.cn, xiajingbo.math@gmail.com
[2] College of Science, Huazhong Agricultural University, Wuhan, Hubei, People's Republic of China

Abstract. Learning an optimal graph structure for graph neural networks (GNNs) is crucial for solving graph-based node classification, while current methods mainly apply in the scenario that there is only one or no observed graph structure, ignoring a real and important multifaceted scenario. In the multifaceted scenario, a set of graphs are derived from different measurements and trade-off considerations applied to the same complex system. In this paper, we proposed a Flexible Generative model for joint label-structure Estimation from Multifaceted graph data (FGEM), which formulated a joint probabilistic distribution of the observations including node features, labels, and multifaceted graph structures. To explore the general relationship among these observations, our model took a flexible setting by considering various prior distributions over graphs, rather than assuming implicit label independence in GNNs. We derived a learning objective with a scalable variational inference algorithm, which considered the posterior inference of missing labels and underlying optimal graph, along with the parameter optimization of GNNs. We conducted thorough experiments on one real and three pseudo multifaceted graph datasets, and the results demonstrated the state-of-the-art performance of our model in both settings.

Keywords: Graph structure learning · Graph convolution networks · Semi-supervised learning · Bayesian learning

1 Introduction

Graphs have drawn a great attention in various domains, such as biological, technological and social systems. Applying graph neural networks (GNNs) to model graph-structured data has achieved state-of-the-art performance in a variety of graph analysis tasks such as node classification and link prediction. Although many previous GNN

The work is supported by Hubei Province Funds for Natural Science (No.2662021JC008, No.2662022XXQD001), and the Major Project of Hubei Hongshan Laboratory (No. 2022HSZD031).

researches treated the observed graph as complete ground-truth information, it is noted that the graph observations suffer from noise and measurement error [16]. Such graph structures containing uncertain, wrong and missing interactions have been reported to significantly limit the capability of GNNs [5,30].

To handle the noise problem, there has been a significant amount of work on graph structure learning (GSL). These methods restrict the GSL under prior knowledge of Stochastic Block Model (SBM) and smoothness, and then the resulting graph and GNNs are employed to solve node classification [23,30]. To improve the adaptability between GNNs and reconstructed graphs, many methods jointly optimize the parameters of the adjacency matrix and GNNs by solving a downstream task [5,11,16,27]. Without any external supervision information (i.e., labels), [19] jointly optimize the adjacency matrix and GNNs in a self-supervised way.

However, most existing GSL methods mainly consider the scenario, where there is only one or no observation graph and ignore a real and important challenge that graph data can be multifaceted, i.e. a set of graphs derived from different measurements and trade-off considerations applied to the same complex system. Actually, many complex systems can be measured repeatedly, such as friendship network, ecological network and World Wide Web [22]. From the view of Bayesian GSL, multifaceted data provide more observations on the underlying optimal graph, which is useful for estimating the optimal graph. Estimating an optimal graph from the multifaceted graph data for downstream analysis not only facilitates the use of complementary interaction information, but also corrects for bias or errors in single measurement [15,22].

Although various methods have been proposed to estimate a single-graph from multifaceted graphs [1,15,21,22], they have two following limitations: (1) Inadaptability with semi-supervised scenarios. They are either in a fully-supervised (i.e. all nodes are uniquely labeled) [1,21] or unsupervised setting (i.e. no label information is used) [15,22]. When the node labels are limited in general cases, these methods fail to joint graph structure and semi-supervised learning. (2) Deviation from graph representation learning. A more promising approach boosting the performance for downstream task is to jointly optimize parameters of adjacency matrix and GNNs [11,27].

We frame above issues as graph-based joint label-structure estimation from multifaceted graph data. To deal with this new scenario, we propose a Flexible Generative model for joint label-structure Estimation from Multifaceted graph data (FGEM), which bridges semi-supervised node classification and optimal graph estimation from multifaceted graph data, along with parameters optimization of GNNs.

Multifaceted setting vs. Multi-view setting. We remark that multifaceted setting we study in this work is a distinct concept from multi-view setting. The most significant difference is that multi-view setting emphasize the heterogeneity of data. In our multifaceted setting, there is only one type of data features and relationship in the graph set. From a Bayesian point of view, each observed graph is treated as a sample of the optimal graph.

In summary, the paper highlights are following three-fold:

- **Problem**. The focus is to joint graph-based semi-supervised learning and GSL estimation from multifaceted graph data. To the best of our knowledge, this is the first attempt to handle such scenario.

- **Algorithm**. We propose a novel generative model, which derives an Evidence Lower Bound to bridge semi-supervised node classification and optimal graph estimation from multifaceted graph data, along with parameters optimization of GNNs.
- **Evaluation**. We evaluate our model via comparisons with baseline methods on one real and three pseudo multifaceted graph data.

2 Background

2.1 Graph Neural Networks for Semi-supervised Node Classification

A typical GNN recursively updates node representation by aggregating neighboring information according to graph topology structure [7]. Recent years have witnessed boosted development of GNN on semi-supervised learning [14,16] and the goal is to learn a function that maps the unlabelled nodes to a class label based on the node features, graph structure and partial label information.

2.2 Graph Structure Learning

There has been great amount of conventional machine learning work on GSL, e.g., network science [21] and signal processing [12], and they are known to be weak in handling graph data with high-dimensional features.

More recently, a large number of significant efforts are dedicated to joint GSL and GNNs for boosting downstream task, leading to the named deep graph structure learning (DGSL) [5,11,16,17,19,27]. One of the active area is designing generative models for graph-based semi-supervised learning and DGSL. Observation graph is considered as generated object [20], while [3,16] treat the graph as an object to be inferred, taking into account the case where the observation graph does not exist or where there are particularly few edges are observed, respectively. However, all of the above DGSL methods are not capable of handling the multifaceted GSL. Although some methods have been proposed to estimate a single-graph from multifaceted graphs [1,15,21,22], they have two following limitations: inadaptability with semi-supervised scenarios and deviation from graph representation learning.

3 Problem Statement

We start by introducing the problem of multifaceted graph-based semi-supervised node classification, as shown in Fig. 1a. Let $\mathcal{D} = \{(x_i, y_i)\}_{i=1}^n$ be a set of data samples, where $x_i \in \mathbb{R}^d$ and $y_i \in \mathbb{R}^l$ represent the feature and label vectors of nodes, respectively. All of the features and label vectors thus form a feature matrix $X \in \mathbb{R}^{n \times d}$ and a label matrix $Y \in \mathbb{R}^{n \times l}$. In the common semi-supervised learning setting, only partial labels of nodes are observed and the others are missing, which are defined as Y_{obs} and Y_{mis}, respectively. In particular, there is a multifaceted data pattern depicting the relationships between these nodes, as defined below.

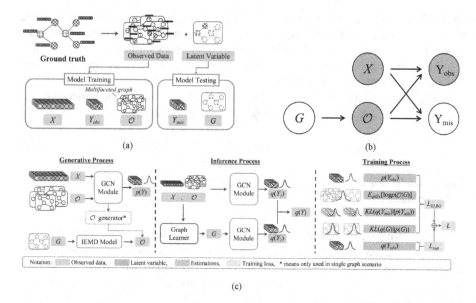

(a)   (b)

(c)

Fig. 1. (a) Problem setup illustration. Given observed node feature X, label Y_{obs} and multifacted graph set $\mathcal{O}$, the goal is to jointly estimate the latent Y_{mis} and the underlying optimal graph G. (b) Probabilistic graphical model of the generative process. (c) Flowchart of the FGEM model on generative process, inference process and training process.

Definition 1 (Multifaceted graph dataset). Let $\mathcal{O} = \{O^{(m)}|O^{(m)} = (V, E^{(m)}), V = 1, \cdots, n, E^{(m)} = (e_{ij}^{(m)})^{n \times n}, m = 1, \cdots, M\}$ be a multifaceted graph dataset, where each $O^{(m)}$ reflects a graph structure retrieved by the m-th measurement of the same complex system, which is treated as a sample of the underlying optimal graph G.

Given the graph feature and label data $\mathcal{D}$ and multiple graphs with noise $\mathcal{O}$, our goal is to jointly estimate the missing label Y_{mis} and an underlying optimal graph $G = (V, E)$, where $V = 1, \cdots, n, E = (e_{ij})^{n \times n}$.

4 Our Proposed Model

4.1 Probabilistic Bayesian Model

FGEM model include three main processes including generative process, inference process and training process.

Generative Process. As presented in the probabilistic graphical model (PGM, Fig. 1b) as shown in Fig. 1c, the joint probability is decomposed as

$$
\begin{aligned}
p(X, Y_{obs}, \mathcal{O}) &= \int p(Y_{obs}, Y_{mis}, X, \mathcal{O}, G) dY_{mis} dG \\
&= \int p(Y_{obs}, Y_{mis}|X, \mathcal{O}) p(\mathcal{O}|G) p(G) p(X) dY_{mis} dG,
\end{aligned}
\tag{1}
$$

where the conditional probabilities $p(Y_{obs}, Y_{mis}|X, \mathcal{O})$ and $p(\mathcal{O}|G)$ can be modeled by flexible families distribution $p_\theta(Y_{obs}, Y_{mis}|X, \mathcal{O})$ and $p_\theta(\mathcal{O}|G)$, parameterized by generation parameters θ. It is flexible to specify $p(G)$ with various priors over graph. For simplicity, it is not necessary to specify the distribution $p(X)$ as almost all of the variables are conditioned on X in this paper.

To infer the missing labels Y_{mis} and optimal graph structure G, the posterior distribution $p_\theta(Y_{mis}, G|X, Y_{obs}, \mathcal{O})$ is obtained by the Bayes' theorem:

$$p_\theta(Y_{mis}, G|X, Y_{obs}, \mathcal{O}) = \frac{p_\theta(Y_{mis}, G, Y_{obs}, \mathcal{O}|X)}{p_\theta(Y_{obs}, \mathcal{O}|X)}. \tag{2}$$

Unfortunately, this computation is intractable due to the high-dimensional integration in denominator of (2).

Inference Process. Since the true posterior distribution $p_\theta(Y_{mis}, G|X, Y_{obs}, \mathcal{O})$ in (2) is intractable, we utilize the scalable variational inference algorithm [13] to approximate the true posterior by introducing a variational posterior distribution $q_\phi(Y_{mis}, G|X, Y_{obs}, \mathcal{O})$, parameterized by approximate posterior parameters ϕ. $q_\phi(Y_{mis}, G|X, Y_{obs}, \mathcal{O})$ is decomposed as $q_\phi(G|X, \mathcal{O})q_\phi(Y_{mis}|X, Y_{obs}, G, \mathcal{O})$. Specifically, we can achieve this purpose by deriving an Evidence Lower Bound (ELBO) loss, $\mathcal{L}_{ELBO}$, for the log-likelihood of observed data as:

$$\begin{aligned}
&\log p_\theta(Y_{obs}, \mathcal{O}|X) \\
&\geq E_{q_\phi(Y_{mis}, G)}[\log p_\theta(Y_{obs}, \mathcal{O}, Y_{mis}, G|X)] - E_{q_\phi(Y_{mis}, G)}[\log q_\phi(Y_{mis}, G)] \\
&= \log p_\theta(Y_{obs}|X, \mathcal{O}) + E_{q_\phi(G)}[\log p_\theta(\mathcal{O}|G)] \\
&\quad - \mathcal{D}_{KL}(q_\phi(Y_{mis})||p_\theta(Y_{mis})) - \mathcal{D}_{KL}(q_\phi(G)||p_\theta(G)) \\
&:= \mathcal{L}_{ELBO}(\theta, \phi; X, Y_{obs}, \mathcal{O}).
\end{aligned} \tag{3}$$

For simplicity, we leave out the conditions in probability. We obtain the optimal generation parameters $\hat{\theta}$ and approximate posterior parameters $\hat{\phi}$ by minimizing the above loss:

$$\hat{\theta}, \hat{\phi} = \arg\min_{\theta, \phi}(-\mathcal{L}_{ELBO}(\theta, \phi; X, Y_{obs}, \mathcal{O})).$$

4.2   Model Instantiations

In this section, we show the key step how the parameter form of each probability distribution in the model is instantiated. And we describe how our model can flexibly handle single noisy observed graph scenario and flexibly consider different graph priors.

Instantiantion of $p_\theta(Y|X, \mathcal{O})$. We instantiate it by a GCN with strong learning capacity, which takes $(X, \mathcal{O})$ as input and outputs the probability of Y. Since GCN by default takes a single graph as input, rather than a set of multifaceted graphs, we replace $\mathcal{O}$ with a variant graph $\hat{O}$ which contains all edges in $\mathcal{O}$.

Instantiantion of $p_\theta(\mathcal{O}|G)$. In order to instantiate $p_\theta(\mathcal{O}|G)$, inspired by [22], we introduce the simple yet effective independent edge measurements model:

$$p_\theta(\mathcal{O}|G) = \prod_{i,j} [\alpha^{B_{ij}}(1-\alpha)^{M-B_{ij}}]^{e_{ij}} [\beta^{B_{ij}}(1-\beta)^{M-B_{ij}}]^{1-e_{ij}}, \qquad (4)$$

where e_{ij} is 1 or 0 indicating that whether there is an edge between i and j in optimal graph G that needs to be estimated. $\theta = \{\alpha, \beta\}$ and α is the true-positive rate, which is the probability of observing an edge that truly exists in the optimal graph G. β is the false-positive rate, which is the probability of observing an edge that none exists in optimal graph G. And thus, the true-negative rate and false-negative rate are $1 - \beta$ and $1 - \alpha$, respectively. Moreover, M is the number of observed graphs (i.e., $|\mathcal{O}|$), and B_{ij} represents the number of times that edge e_{ij} is observed in $\mathcal{O}$. Therefore, if an edge e_{ij} truly exists in the optimal graph G, the probability of observing edge e_{ij} with B_{ij} times is formulated as $\alpha^{B_{ij}}(1-\alpha)^{M-B_{ij}}$. Otherwise, the probability is $\beta^{B_{ij}}(1-\beta)^{M-B_{ij}}$.

Instantiantion of $q_\phi(G|X, \mathcal{O})$. In generative models for graphs, it is assumed that the edges are conditionally independent. Based on common assumption, the probability of the optimal graph G is decomposed by

$$q_\phi(G|X, \mathcal{O}) = \prod_{i,j} q_\phi(e_{ij}|X, \mathcal{O}), \qquad (5)$$

where $q_\phi(e_{ij} = 1|X, \mathcal{O}) = \rho_{ij}$ and $q_\phi(e_{ij} = 0|X, \mathcal{O}) = 1 - \rho_{ij}$, ρ_{ij} is a weight value between 0 and 1. The inference of $q_\phi(G|X, \mathcal{O})$ is performed and instantiated by a graph learner to derive edge weights [31]. Specifically, it first generates a new graph through the multi-head weighted cosine similarity learning method previously utilized by [16]. Subsequently, the original graph $\mathcal{O}$ is incorporated into the new graph to generate the optimal graph G. We refer readers of interest to [31] for a comprehensive survey about graph structure modeling approaches.

We define $\{w_s\}_{s=1}^{S}$ as S learnable weight vectors. The multi-head weighted cosine similarity computation is performed as $c_{ij} = \frac{1}{S} \sum_{s=1}^{S} \cos(w_s \odot x_i, w_s \odot x_j)$, where x_i and x_j are the node features of node pair i and j. All c_{ij} form the new graph.

To inherit the information in original graph $\mathcal{O}$, we employ a smoothing parameter λ to combine the learned new graph and original graph set $\mathcal{O}$ and get the optimal graph G:

$$\rho_{ij} = \lambda \times \hat{O}_{ij} + (1 - \lambda) \times c_{ij} \qquad (6)$$

where $\hat{O}$ is an integrated graph containing all edges in $\mathcal{O}$. Here, $\hat{O}_{ij}$ equals to 1 or 0 indicating that whether the edge between nodes i and j is observed in graph set $\mathcal{O}$.

Instantiation of $q_\phi(Y_{mis}|X, Y_{obs}, \mathcal{O})$. We also instantiate it by a GCN module with strong learning capacity. We implement the approximation by $q_\phi(Y_{mis}|X, \mathcal{O}, G)$ as GCN by-default takes node features and graph structure as input. This approximation assumes an independence between labels, known as the mean-field assumption.

To infer the missing Y_{mis} and optimal graph G jointly, we design an joint-learning architecture that takes $(X, \mathcal{O}, G)$ as input and outputs the probability of Y_{mis}. Figure 1c shows the details during the inference process. In brief, the final inference of Y_{mis} is the weighted sum of two terms: (1) the output Y_1 of GCN that takes $(X, \hat{O})$ as input; (2) the output Y_2 of GCN that takes (X, G) as input.

Flexible Model Setting over Graph Priors. FGEM is flexible to adapt various graph priors for $p(G)$. In our experiment setting, we used two popular priors over graph, i.e., SBM [10] and LSM [9], thus formulating two algorithmic variants of FGEM, namely, FGEM-SBM and FGEM-LSM. We refer readers of interest to [20] for more details about these two priors.

Flexible Model Setting upon Single-graph Scenario by Generating Pseudo Multi-faceted Data. FGEM is flexible to be applied to the single-graph scenario by generating pseudo multifaceted graph set. To achieve this purpose, inspired by [27], we employ an multifaceted graphs generator. Figure 2 shows the process.

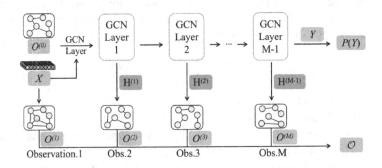

Fig. 2. $\mathcal{O}$ generator for generating pseudo multifaceted graph data.

Specifically, we first extract the output of each GCN layer in the GCN module used to compute $P(Y)$. And then the original node features and outputs of GCNs are used to calculate kNN graphs based cosine similarity, thus resulting a set of graphs, i.e., $\mathcal{O}$. The node features in different GCN layers reflect multi-order neighborhood information. Therefore, these graphs derived from different GCN layers capture proximity information from different facets. The intuition of above idea stems from the observation that node pair with similar neighborhoods is apt to be connected, although they may be far away in the graph. For example, implicit connections may still exist between papers with similar citations, even though they are not explicitly stated by citation [18].

4.3 Model Training

Supervise Loss. As our main task is to perform node classification with the variational posterior model, we introduce an additional supervise loss to better train the variational model similar with [20]:

$$\mathcal{L}_{sup}(\phi) = -\log q_\phi(Y_{obs}|X, \mathcal{O}, G). \tag{7}$$

The total loss is the combination of ELBO loss and supervise loss with a weight hyper-parameter η:

$$\mathcal{L}_{total}(\theta, \phi) = -\mathcal{L}_{ELBO}(\theta, \phi; X, Y_{obs}, \mathcal{O}) + \eta \mathcal{L}_{sup}(\phi). \tag{8}$$

The loss is reformulated as

$$\begin{aligned}
\mathcal{L}_{total}(\theta, \phi) = &- \log p_\theta(Y_{obs}) - E_{q_\phi(Y_{mis}, G)} \log p_\theta(\mathcal{O}|G) \\
&+ \mathcal{D}_{KL}(q_\phi(Y_{mis})\|p_\theta(Y_{mis})) + \mathcal{D}_{KL}(q_\phi(G)\|p(G)) - \eta \cdot \log q_\phi(Y_{obs}),
\end{aligned} \tag{9}$$

where the first, the second and the last terms provide supervise information for estimating Y_{mis} and optimal graph G, and the other two terms provide additional KL-divergence regularizations: the inferred Y_{mis} and optimal graph G are restricted to be close to their priors.

4.4 Computational Complexity

Computing $p(Y)$ and $q(Y)$ requires $O(n^2 dDl)$, where D is the hidden dimension of two-layer GCN. Computing $p(\mathcal{O}|G)$, $q(G)$ and the KL-divergences in Eq. (9) requires $O(n^2)$, $O(nSl + n^2l)$ and $O(n^2 + nl)$, respectively, all of which can be trivially parallelized. An additional $O(n^2l)$ computation is required when the proposed model is applied to single-graph scenario, which also can be parallelized. The computational complexity of $p(\mathcal{O}|G)$ and $\mathcal{D}_{KL}(q_\phi(G)\|p(G))$ can be reduced to $O(T)$, where T is the number of sampled edges.

5 Experiments

5.1 Experimental Settings

Datasets. GSL w.r.t., multifaceted scenario is in its cradle and the benchmark dataset is limited. Recently, EMOGI [24] provided a multifaceted protein-protein interaction (MPPI) dataset, which consists of five PPI graphs. Hence, we set the MPPI dataset as the benchmark dataset for multifaceted GSL. We also evaluate the flexibility and capability of our model on three pseudo multifaceted graph datasets drived from three benchmark single graph datasets.

- **MPPI dataset for multifaceted GSL.** The PPI dataset was collected from [24], including five PPI graphs: CPDB, IREF, IREF 2015, MULTINET and STRINGdb. These PPI graphs record the interaction information of 22,193 proteins (or genes). Only 3,759 genes have labels recording whether these genes are cancer driver genes (labeled with 1) or not (labeled with 0). For training and evaluating our model and baselines, we took a common approach to dataset partitioning: 0.6, 0.2, 0.2 for training, validating and testing.
- **Three benchmark datasets for pseudo multifaceted data.** The three standard benchmark datasets are Cora, Citeseer and Pubmed [25,29], which are used for generating Pseudo Multifaceted Cora (PMCora), Citeseer (PMCiteseer) and Pubmed (PMPubmed) data. We collected these datasets from the PyTorch-Geometric library [4] in our experiments and adopt their datasets partitioning approach for our model and all baselines.

Comparative Methods. We designed comparative experiments in three dimensions:

- **Multifaceted GSL algorithms.** We implemented two multifaceted graphs estimation algorithms: Random graph estimate [22] and Poisson graph estimate [15], which are either in an unsupervised setting. Additionally, we adapt a simple merging strategy that generates a graph containing all edges in multifaceted graphs dataset $\mathcal{O}$. The resulting three graphs are fed to single-graph structure learning algorithm and several representative GNNs for node classification.
- **Single GSL algorithms.** We compare our model with four single-graph structure learning models, G^{3}NN [20], LDS [5], GEN [27] and SUBLIME [19] on three benchmark datasets and three graphs estimated by multifaceted GSL algorithms.
- **Representative GNNs.** We also compare our model with three spectral-based methods, i.e., SGC [28], GCN [14] and ChebNet [2], and three spatial-based methods, i.e., GAT [26], APPNP [6] and GraphSAGE [8].

Data Scarce Settings. Generative models usually are expected to have advantage when observed data are scarce. In this paper, we also evaluate our model under two types of data scarce settings on the three benchmark datasets: reduced-label setting and missing-edge setting. Under reduced-label setting, half of the node labels in the training set are masked. Under missing-edge setting, half of observed edges are masked.

Implementation. We utilize two-layer GCNs to estimate the probability of missing labels Y_{mis} both in generation and inference process. We adapt the grid search strategy for the heads number S of graph learner, hidden dimension D used for GCN, K used for the $\mathcal{O}$ generator and η used for supervise loss, the search space of which are $\{2, 4, 6, 8\}$, $\{32, 64, 128\}$, $\{3, .., 13\}$, $\{0.5, 1, 10\}$, respectively. For the constants (p_0, p_1) used for SBM, we use two settings:(0.9, 0.1) and (0.5, 0.6). For the output dimension for LSM, we set it the same as D. We utilize Adam optimizer to train our model and adapt early stopping strategy. The learning rate is 0.01. For the comparative methods, we use one of three implementation PyTorch-Geometric [4] library, the source codes provided by their authors and the iterative formula provided in their papers.

5.2   Experimental Results

Ablation Study of Multifaceted Data over Single Graph. From the view of Bayesian GSL, multifaceted data provide more observations on G, making it possible for better node classification. The results in Table 1 confirm the above idea. Here, almost all GNNs perform better on the merged graph containing multifaceted information except GraphSAGE, compared with the results on five single PPI graphs. Furthermore, we apply our multifaceted GSL framework to pseudo multifaceted data by introducing an $\mathcal{O}$ generator, and therefore perform three experiments as shown in Table 2. Results show that in most settings, FGEM-SBM outperforms other single GSL baselines.

Advantages of Adapting Data Scarce. We design our model under a generative framework. Hence, it is expected to have advantages when observed data are scarce. Table 2 shows the results over various data scarce settings and normal setting, of which the

Table 1. Test accuracy result of label prediction over single and multifaceted PPI graphs. Bold texts refer to the highest accuracy.

	Single-graph learning					Multifaceted GSL
	CPDB (%)	IREF (%)	IREF 2015 (%)	MULTINET (%)	STRINGdb (%)	Direct graph merge (%)
SGC	72.4 ± 0.5	73.0 ± 0.2	70.2 ± 1.0	68.8 ± 0.8	70.7 ± 0.9	**76.5 ± 0.2**
GCN	75.8 ± 0.7	73.6 ± 0.3	71.2 ± 0.6	72.1 ± 0.5	70.7 ± 0.5	**77.2 ± 0.3**
ChebNet	72.4 ± 0.5	73.2 ± 0.4	74.8 ± 0.1	75.1 ± 0.2	73.2 ± 0.5	**76.7 ± 0.6**
GAT	75.0 ± 0.1	72.9 ± 0.6	74.2 ± 0.2	74.9 ± 0.1	75.8 ± 0.4	**76.4 ± 0.4**
APPNP	66.7 ± 0.2	69.1 ± 1.5	67.2 ± 0.4	66.5 ± 0.7	71.1 ± 1.5	**72.5 ± 0.5**
GraphSAGE	73.7 ± 0.1	68.6 ± 0.7	72.3 ± 0.1	**75.5 ± 0.3**	72.1 ± 0.1	73.3 ± 0.8

Table 2. Test accuracy results of FGEM on Pseudo Multifaceted data and results of baseline methods on standard data. LC and ER mean the number of labels per class for training and the ratio of reserved edges, respectively.

Datasets	LC-ER	SGC	GCN	ChebNet	GAT	APPNP	GraphSAGE	G³NN	LDS	GEN	SUBLIME	FGEM-SBM	FGEM-LSM
Cora	20-1.0	81.8 ± 0.3	81.3 ± 0.2	79.9 ± 0.2	81.9 ± 0.3	81.8 ± 0.3	80.2 ± 0.3	82.9 ± 0.3	82.7 ± 0.9	82.2 ± 0.5	83.1 ± 0.6	**83.4 ± 0.4**	82.7 ± 0.3
(PMCora-FGEM)	10-1.0	74.7 ± 0.3	74.6 ± 0.5	70.1 ± 0.2	74.2 ± 0.9	76.1 ± 0.1	73.1 ± 0.2	**79.4 ± 0.5**	77.5 ± 1.5	76.2 ± 0.7	79.2 ± 0.5	79.4 ± 0.3	78.2 ± 0.2
	20-0.5	76.3 ± 0.3	76.5 ± 0.2	48.5 ± 1.7	76.4 ± 0.6	77.4 ± 0.3	71.6 ± 0.5	79.6 ± 0.6	77.9 ± 1.2	76.5 ± 0.6	68.9 ± 0.3	**80.5 ± 0.5**	78.8 ± 0.6
	10-0.5	65.9 ± 0.3	66.1 ± 0.3	33.7 ± 0.5	69.5 ± 0.5	69.0 ± 0.3	60.2 ± 0.6	73.3 ± 0.6	72.6 ± 0.8	71.3 ± 0.9	66.3 ± 0.6	**74.1 ± 0.9**	71.1 ± 0.7
Citeseer	20-1.0	71.5 ± 0.1	71.6 ± 0.2	70.7 ± 0.4	72.2 ± 0.3	72.0 ± 0.2	71.3 ± 0.7	74.5 ± 0.4	72.5 ± 0.8	73.4 ± 1.2	72.6 ± 0.8	**74.9 ± 0.4**	73.1 ± 0.3
(PMCiteseer-FGEM)	10-1.0	69.1 ± 0.5	68.4 ± 0.4	68.8 ± 1.2	69.6 ± 0.6	68.7 ± 0.5	67.5 ± 0.9	70.9 ± 0.8	70.4 ± 1.1	70.3 ± 0.4	70.0 ± 0.5	**73.1 ± 0.5**	71.5 ± 0.2
	20-0.5	66.9 ± 0.2	66.7 ± 0.5	65.5 ± 0.2	70.0 ± 0.3	68.0 ± 0.3	64.5 ± 0.7	71.7 ± 0.7	71.5 ± 0.9	70.2 ± 0.6	72.1 ± 0.4	**72.6 ± 0.6**	71.1 ± 1.1
	10-0.5	62.6 ± 0.6	62.5 ± 0.5	57.9 ± 1.1	65.5 ± 0.6	63.4 ± 0.8	56.3 ± 0.5	67.5 ± 0.8	68.6 ± 0.7	68.4 ± 0.8	**69.2 ± 1.3**	68.1 ± 0.5	66.5 ± 0.9
Pubmed	20-1.0	79.5 ± 0.3	79.4 ± 0.4	78.6 ± 0.1	77.9 ± 0.2	79.0 ± 0.2	77.2 ± 0.3	78.4 ± 0.6	78.2 ± 0.4	80.9 ± 0.8	80.8 ± 0.6	**81.3 ± 0.5**	80.7 ± 0.4
(PMPubmed-FGEM)	10-1.0	72.7 ± 0.5	73.2 ± 0.4	72.2 ± 0.7	72.8 ± 0.7	73.1 ± 0.1	72.8 ± 0.5	76.0 ± 0.8	74.4 ± 0.9	75.6 ± 1.1	**77.3 ± 0.6**	76.4 ± 0.4	74.9 ± 0.8
	20-0.5	76.5 ± 0.3	75.9 ± 0.3	76.2 ± 0.3	76.0 ± 0.7	76.0 ± 0.7	75.2 ± 0.4	74.3 ± 1.2	77.5 ± 1.1	76.0 ± 0.7	80.2 ± 0.6	**80.9 ± 1.2**	78.3 ± 1.1
	10-0.5	69.9 ± 0.2	70.4 ± 0.2	68.4 ± 0.3	71.3 ± 0.8	71.4 ± 0.7	67.3 ± 0.8	69.3 ± 0.9	70.3 ± 0.7	71.8 ± 0.8	**76.1 ± 1.0**	73.3 ± 1.1	72.4 ± 1.2

Table 3. Test accuracy result of FGEM and baseline methods on one real multifaceted graph data. OOM means out of memory.

Dataset	Approach for multifaceted GSL	SGC	GCN	ChebNet	GAT	APPNP	GraphSAGE	G3NN	LDS	GEN	SUBLIME	FGEM-SBM	FGEM-LSM
MPPI	Direct graph merge	76.5±0.2	77.2±0.3	76.7±0.6	76.4±0.4	72.5±0.5	73.3±0.8	77.6±0.3	OOM	OOM	72.5 ± 0.4	-	-
	Random Graph Estimate	73.3±0.1	73.5±0.1	74.3±0.4	73.7±0.6	69.3±0.8	70.6±0.8	74.5±0.4	OOM	OOM	72.3 ± 0.9	-	-
	Poisson Graph Estimate	73.9±0.2	73.1±0.1	74.1±0.1	74.6±0.8	68.7±0.8	70.1±0.8	73.3±0.5	OOM	OOM	73.2 ± 1.0	-	-
	Label-structure joint learning for multifaceted graphs	-	-	-	-	-	-	-	-	-	-	**78.6 ± 0.4**	77.5±0.5

number of labels per class (LC) equals 20 and edge ratio equals (ER) 1.0 is the normal setting, the remaining are the data scarce settings. Our model outperforms almost all baselines except SUBLIME over settings of (dataset: Citeseer, LC: 10, ER: 0.5), (dataset: Pubmed, LC: 10, ER: 1.0) and (dataset: Pubmed, LC: 10, ER: 0.5).

Advantages of Joint Label-Structure Estimation in Multifaceted GSL. Table 3 shows the comparison between our model with three multifaceted GSL algorithms. Although the graphs estimated by the three algorithms can be applied to various GNNs and GSL methods, results shows that estimating node label and optimal graph structure from multifaceted graph data jointly, along with the parameter optimization of GCN, is a more promising approach for node classification task.

Hyper-parameter Sensitivity. An important parameter that needs to be carefully fine-tuned is K used for computing kNN graph in single GSL scenario. Figure 3 shows the trend of accuracy w.r.t K. Roughly, accuracy first increases as K increases and then decreases. This may be because a small K would result in not providing enough useful observed edges, while a large K tends to introduce excessive false-positive edges.

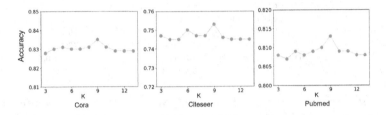

Fig. 3. Sensitivity of K on three benchmark datasets.

5.3 Conclusion

In this research, we presented a flexible generative model for joint label-structure estimation from multifaceted graph data. Its flexibility is reflected in two aspects: (1) applicability to different scenarios: multifaceted graph scenario and single-graph scenario; (2) explorability to various priors over optimal graph structure. We have experimentally verified that the use of multifaceted graph data is able to improve node classification both with real multifaceted graph data and pseudo multifaceted graph data. We perform label-structure estimation jointly along with the parameter optimization of GCNs, which enhanced the adaptability of estimated optimal graph and GCNs for node classification. We also showed that the proposed generative model had promising potential in data scarce settings. For future work, we expect to explore more priors over graphs and investigate underlying principles under which the observed data are generated for graph-based semi-supervised learning under generative framework.

References

1. Butts, C.T.: Network inference, error, and informant (in) accuracy: a Bayesian approach. Social Netw. **25**(2), 103–140 (2003)
2. Defferrard, M., Bresson, X., Vandergheynst, P.: Convolutional neural networks on graphs with fast localized spectral filtering. In: Advances in Neural Information Processing Systems 29 (2016)
3. Elinas, P., Bonilla, E.V., Tiao, L.: Variational inference for graph convolutional networks in the absence of graph data and adversarial settings. Adv. Neural. Inf. Process. Syst. **33**, 18648–18660 (2020)
4. Fey, M., Lenssen, J.E.: Fast graph representation learning with pyTorch geometric. arXiv preprint arXiv:1903.02428 (2019)
5. Franceschi, L., Niepert, M., Pontil, M., He, X.: Learning discrete structures for graph neural networks. In: International Conference on Machine Learning, pp. 1972–1982. PMLR (2019)
6. Gasteiger, J., Bojchevski, A., Günnemann, S.: Predict then propagate: graph neural networks meet personalized pagerank. arXiv preprint arXiv:1810.05997 (2018)

7. Gilmer, J., Schoenholz, S.S., Riley, P.F., Vinyals, O., Dahl, G.E.: Neural message passing for quantum chemistry. In: International Conference on Machine Learning, pp. 1263–1272. PMLR (2017)
8. Hamilton, W., Ying, Z., Leskovec, J.: Inductive representation learning on large graphs. In: Advances in Neural Information Processing Systems 30 (2017)
9. Hoff, P.D., Raftery, A.E., Handcock, M.S.: Latent space approaches to social network analysis. J. Am. Stat. Assoc. **97**(460), 1090–1098 (2002)
10. Holland, P.W., Laskey, K.B., Leinhardt, S.: Stochastic blockmodels: first steps. Social networks **5**(2), 109–137 (1983)
11. Hu, M., Chang, H., Ma, B., Shan, S.: Learning continuous graph structure with bilevel programming for graph neural networks (2022)
12. Kalofolias, V.: How to learn a graph from smooth signals. In: Artificial Intelligence and Statistics, pp. 920–929. PMLR (2016)
13. Kingma, D.P., Mohamed, S., Jimenez Rezende, D., Welling, M.: Semi-supervised learning with deep generative models. In: Advances in Neural Information Processing Systems 27 (2014)
14. Kipf, T.N., Welling, M.: Semi-supervised classification with graph convolutional networks. arXiv preprint arXiv:1609.02907 (2016)
15. Kuang, J., Scoglio, C.: A principled approach for weighted multilayer network aggregation. arXiv preprint arXiv:2103.05774 (2021)
16. Lao, D., Yang, X., Wu, Q., Yan, J.: Variational inference for training graph neural networks in low-data regime through joint structure-label estimation. In: Proceedings of the 28th ACM SIGKDD Conference on Knowledge Discovery and Data Mining, pp. 824–834 (2022)
17. Lin, S., Dong, C., Shen, Y.: Cross-perspective graph contrastive learning. In: Memmi, G., Yang, B., Kong, L., Zhang, T., Qiu, M. (eds.) Knowledge Science, Engineering and Management. KSEM 2022. Lecture Notes in Computer Science, vol. 13368, pp. 58–70. Springer, Cham (2022). https://doi.org/10.1007/978-3-031-10983-6_5
18. Liu, H., Kou, H., Yan, C., Qi, L.: Link prediction in paper citation network to construct paper correlation graph. EURASIP J. Wirel. Commun. Netw. **2019**(1), 1–12 (2019). https://doi.org/10.1186/s13638-019-1561-7
19. Liu, Y., Zheng, Y., Zhang, D., Chen, H., Peng, H., Pan, S.: Towards unsupervised deep graph structure learning. In: Proceedings of the ACM Web Conference 2022, pp. 1392–1403 (2022)
20. Ma, J., Tang, W., Zhu, J., Mei, Q.: A flexible generative framework for graph-based semi-supervised learning. In: Advances in Neural Information Processing Systems 32 (2019)
21. Martin, T., Ball, B., Newman, M.E.: Structural inference for uncertain networks. Phys. Rev. E **93**(1), 012306 (2016)
22. Newman, M.E.: Estimating network structure from unreliable measurements. Phys. Rev. E **98**(6), 062321 (2018)
23. Pal, S., Valkanas, A., Regol, F., Coates, M.: Bag graph: multiple instance learning using Bayesian graph neural networks. In: Proceedings AAAI Conference on Artificial Intelligence (2022)
24. Schulte-Sasse, R., Budach, S., Hnisz, D., Marsico, A.: Integration of multiomics data with graph convolutional networks to identify new cancer genes and their associated molecular mechanisms. Nat. Mach. Intell. **3**(6), 513–526 (2021)
25. Sen, P., Namata, G., Bilgic, M., Getoor, L., Galligher, B., Eliassi-Rad, T.: Collective classification in network data. AI Mag. **29**(3), 93 (2008)
26. Veličković, P., Cucurull, G., Casanova, A., Romero, A., Lio, P., Bengio, Y.: Graph attention networks. arXiv preprint arXiv:1710.10903 (2017)
27. Wang, R., et al.: Graph structure estimation neural networks. In: Proceedings of the Web Conference 2021, pp. 342–353 (2021)

28. Wu, F., Souza, A., Zhang, T., Fifty, C., Yu, T., Weinberger, K.: Simplifying graph convolutional networks. In: International Conference on Machine Learning, pp. 6861–6871. PMLR (2019)
29. Yang, Z., Cohen, W., Salakhudinov, R.: Revisiting semi-supervised learning with graph embeddings. In: International Conference on Machine Learning, pp. 40–48. PMLR (2016)
30. Zhang, Y., Pal, S., Coates, M., Ustebay, D.: Bayesian graph convolutional neural networks for semi-supervised classification. In: Proceedings of the AAAI Conference on Artificial Intelligence, vol. 33, pp. 5829–5836 (2019)
31. Zhu, Y., et al.: A survey on graph structure learning: Progress and opportunities. arXiv e-prints pp. arXiv-2103 (2021)

Dual Channel Knowledge Graph Embedding with Ontology Guided Data Augmentation

Tengwei Song[ID], Long Yin, Xudong Ma, and Jie Luo[✉][ID]

State Key Laboratory of Software Development Environment,
School of Computer Science and Engineering, Beihang University, Beijing, China
{songtengwei,long_yin,Macaronlin,luojie}@buaa.edu.cn

Abstract. Current knowledge graph completion suffers from two major issues: data sparsity and false negatives. To address these challenges, we propose an ontology-guided joint embedding framework that utilizes dual data augmentation channels and a joint loss function to learn embeddings of knowledge graphs. Our approach spontaneously generates positive and negative instances from two distinct ontology axiom sets, leading to improved completion rates for originally sparse knowledge graphs while also producing true-negative samples. Additionally, we propose two novel metrics for evaluating a model's reasoning capabilities in predicting relations or links using KG and ontology data, thus avoiding incorrect predictions. Empirical results demonstrate that our framework outperforms existing models in most tasks and datasets, with significantly better performance in many cases for reasoning capability evaluation metrics.

Keywords: Knowledge graph · Representation learning · Data augmentation · Relation property · Ontology

1 Introduction

Knowledge graph embedding (KGE) aims to map the entities and relations in Knowledge Graphs (KGs) to low-dimensional vectors and capture their semantics. This reduces the dependence of machine learning algorithms on feature engineering [14] in natural language processing [23,32], question answering [10,21], recommendation systems [6,31], and other fields that could be guided by domain knowledge.

KGE-based KG completion faces significant challenges due to data sparsity and false negatives [28]. The former can hinder the model's ability to capture the underlying relation patterns between entities, while the latter occurs when two entities are related but not explicitly connected in the KG. To address the first challenge, existing works typically model the relation patterns in the KG through geometric transformations to enhance the generalization and reasoning abilities of KGE models. For example, RotatE [26] models relations as rotations between source and target entities to capture various relation patterns such as symmetry and inverse. However, there is currently no universal way to model all relation patterns in a KG, and hence need to design different geometric methods for different relation patterns. To address the second challenge, PUDA [28] uses adversarial training to generate synthetic entities, while NS-KGE [11] proposes a method to avoid negative sampling. However, the complexity of these methods is relatively high.

To alleviate these challenges, we propose a genetic **D**ual channel **KGE** framework based on **O**ntology-**G**uided data augmentation (DKOG). Our framework leverages the two types of axiom sets defined in the Web Ontology Language (OWL) [15] to augment the KG, which are *conformance* axioms, and *violence* axioms. The former defines a specific semantic type of relations that can generate additional positive inferences from the original KG. The latter identifies relations that generate negative examples, which are contrary to the existing triples of these relations in the knowledge base. Furthermore, we use semantic reasoning rules to spontaneously find corresponding relations and generate true-positive and true-negative triples to alleviate the challenges of data sparsity and false negatives. Moreover, a joint loss function is used to aggregate the dual channel to optimize the embeddings. Additionally, our framework proposes two novel evaluation metrics to measure the reasoning capability of a model in predicting whether the inference results of the model obey or violate the axioms in the ontology. Importantly, DKOG is scalable and can be used with a range of KGE methods.

To summarize, the main contributions of this paper are as follows:

- We introduce an ontology-guided data augmentation approach for using conformance and violence axioms to spontaneously derive true positive and true negative instances of the KG.
- We propose a generic joint embedding framework for KGE learning through a loss function to make the framework adaptable to the vast majority of KGE models.
- We define two evaluation metrics for measuring the capability of KGE models for predicting triples that are derived from KG and avoiding miss-predictions for triples that contradict the KG.
- Experiments on typical KGE models demonstrated that models with our framework obtained better performance on both general evaluation metrics and the proposed metrics on different datasets.

2   Related Work

Geometry Based Models. Geometry methods build the relations as different geometric transformation to model relation patterns. TransE [2] first proposed to regard the relations as the translation between subject and object entities. Following TransE, many variants and extensions such as TransH [33], TransR [12], and TransD [7] were proposed to enhance the expressive power of the model. In addition, Rotational models such as RotatE [26] and Rotate3D[5] regard the relations as the rotation between subject and object entities. To further model the transitive pattern, Rot-Pro [25] imposes a projection on both subject and object entities to express transitivity, and uses a rotation operation as RotatE to support other relation patterns.

Tensor Decomposition Based Models. Tensor decomposition (TD) method aims to decompose the tensor into a set of low-rank factor matrices that can be used to represent entities and relations in the vector space. RESCAL [18] first imposes a score function of a bilinear product on the entity vectors and predicate matrix. DistMult [35] simplifies RESCAL by diagonalizing the predicate matrix. To expand Euclidean space, ComplEx [30] first introduces a complex vector space that can capture both symmetric and asymmetric relations, while QuatE [36] uses a quaternion inner product to capture the latent dependency within a four-dimensional space of relations and entities. Recently, SimplE [8] and TuckER [1] proposed state-of-the-art methods based on Canonical Polyadic decomposition and Tucker decomposition respectively.

Deep Learning Based Models. Deep Learning (DL) methods represent another branch of encoding and have yielded remarkable performance in recent studies. ConvE [4] and ConvKB [17] apply convolutional neural networks (CNNs) to learning deep expressive features. Moreover, with the popularity of graph neural networks (GNNs), R-GCN [22] and SCAN [24] apply graph convolutional networks (GCNs) [9] to act as a graph encoder on relational knowledge bases. KBGAT [16] used an attention-based embedding model that considers both entity embedding and relation embedding.

3   Ontology-Guided Data Augmentation

We define KG $\mathcal{G}$ as $\mathcal{G}(\mathcal{E}, \mathcal{R}, \mathcal{I})$, where $\mathcal{E}, \mathcal{R}, \mathcal{I}$ denotes the set of entities, relations and instances in the KG. Each instance in $\mathcal{I}$ is a triple of the form (s, r, o), where s is the subject entity, r is a relation (or predicate), and o is the object entity. We list the main notations and descriptions of this paper in Table 1.

Table 1. Main notations and descriptions.

Notation	Description
$\mathcal{I}$	Instances in KG
$\mathcal{R}_C$	Relation set with C-axiom
$\mathcal{R}_V$	Relation set with V-axiom
$\mathcal{I}_C$	Instances in KG related to the $\mathcal{R}_C$
$\mathcal{I}_V$	Instances in KG related to the $\mathcal{R}_V$
$\mathcal{D}^+(\mathcal{I}_C)$	True-positive instances derived from $\mathcal{I}_C$
$\mathcal{D}^-(\mathcal{I}_V)$	True-negative instances derived from $\mathcal{I}_V$

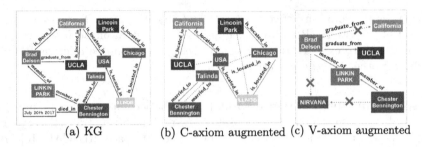

(a) KG   (b) C-axiom augmented   (c) V-axiom augmented

Fig. 1. An illustration of a KG (a) and its augmented KGs by C-axiom (b) and V-axiom (c).

Table 2. Semantic reasoning rules for relation property axioms.

	Relation Property	Semantic Reasoning Rule
C-Axiom	symmetry	$(s, r, o) \in \mathcal{I}_C \Rightarrow (o, r, s) \in \mathcal{D}^+(\mathcal{I}_C)$
	transitivity	$(a, r, b), (b, r, c) \in \mathcal{I}_C \Rightarrow (a, r, c) \in \mathcal{D}^+(\mathcal{I}_C)$
	inverse to	$r = p^{-1} \wedge (s, r, o) \in \mathcal{I}_C \Rightarrow (o, p, s) \in \mathcal{D}^+(\mathcal{I}_C)$
	subproperty of	$r_1 \subseteq r_2 \wedge (s, r_1, o) \in \mathcal{I}_C \Rightarrow (s, r_2, o) \in \mathcal{D}^+(\mathcal{I}_C)$
V-Axiom	asymmetry	$(s, r, o) \in \mathcal{I}_V \Rightarrow (o, r, s) \in \mathcal{D}^-(\mathcal{I}_V)$
	functionality	$b \neq c \Rightarrow (a, r, b) \in \mathcal{I}_V \Rightarrow (a, r, c) \in \mathcal{D}^-(\mathcal{I}_V)$
	inverse functionality	$a \neq c \wedge (a, r, b) \in \mathcal{I}_V \Rightarrow (c, r, b) \in \mathcal{D}^-(\mathcal{I}_V)$

As mentioned before, conformance axioms (C-axiom for short) refer to a set of semantic type relations that generate additional positive inferences from the original KG, as illustrated in Fig. 1(b). These relations are denoted as $\mathcal{R}_C$. For a relation $r_C \in \mathcal{R}_C$, the set of instances in $\mathcal{I}$ with r_C are denoted by $\mathcal{I}_C$. The positive instances derived from $\mathcal{I}_C$ based on axioms in $\mathcal{R}_C$ are denoted by $\mathcal{D}^+(\mathcal{I}_C)$. Violence axioms (V-axiom for short), on the other hand, identify relations that generate negative examples, which are contrary to the existing triples in the knowledge base. The V-axiom related KG is illustrated in Fig. 1(c). These relations are denoted as $\mathcal{R}_V$. For a relation $r_V \in \mathcal{R}_V$, the set of instances in $\mathcal{I}$ with r_V are denoted by $\mathcal{I}_V$ and the negative instances derived from $\mathcal{I}_V$ based on axioms in $\mathcal{R}_V$ are denoted by $\mathcal{D}^-(\mathcal{I}_V)$. We construct two sets of relation properties according to the C-axiom and V-axiom, and define the corresponding semantic reasoning rule, which is illustrated in Table 2. Noticeably, in practice, to avoid the problem of label leaking, $\mathcal{D}^+(\mathcal{I}_C)$ is a set that filtered out the testing triples.

4 Joint Embedding Framework

The general structure of the DKOG framework is illustrated in Fig. 2, which contains the following core modules.

4.1 Dual Channel Data Augmentation

In the preprocessing of data augmentation, we first use semantic reasoning rules to find corresponding relations that satisfy the relation properties in C-axiom

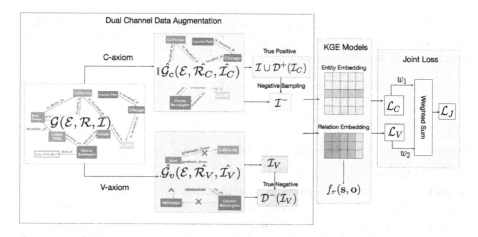

Fig. 2. The structure of the DKOG framework. Given a KG $\mathcal{G}$, dual channel data augmentation will simultaneously generate its augmented KGs by C-axiom ($\hat{\mathcal{G}}_c(\mathcal{E}, \hat{\mathcal{R}}_C, \hat{\mathcal{I}}_C)$) and by V-axiom ($\hat{\mathcal{G}}_v(\mathcal{E}, \hat{\mathcal{R}}_V, \hat{\mathcal{I}}_V)$). Then the pair-wised positive and negative instances from both channels are fed to the KGE models and calculate the conformance loss $\mathcal{L}_C$ and violence loss $\mathcal{L}_V$ according to the specific score function $f_r(s, o)$. Finally the joint loss $\mathcal{L}_J$ is obtained by a weighted sum.

and V-axiom. Specifically, we compare the proportion of instances that match relation property among all instances of the relation with a threshold value η. For relations that fulfill the axioms, we use the semantic reasoning rules to augment the subgraph related to $\mathcal{R}_C$ and get the augmented KG $\hat{\mathcal{G}}_c(\mathcal{E}, \hat{\mathcal{R}}_C, \hat{\mathcal{I}}_C)$, where $\hat{\mathcal{I}}_C = \{\mathcal{I} \cup \mathcal{D}^+(\mathcal{I}_C)\}$. Similarly, we augment the subgraph related to $\mathcal{R}_V$ and get the augmented KG $\hat{\mathcal{G}}_v(\mathcal{E}, \hat{\mathcal{R}}_V, \hat{\mathcal{I}}_V)$, where $\hat{\mathcal{I}}_V = \{\mathcal{I}_V \cup \mathcal{D}^-(\mathcal{I}_V)\}$.

4.2 Joint Loss

We introduce two loss functions, which are *conformance loss* $\mathcal{L}_C$ and *violation loss* $\mathcal{L}_V$ on the basis of two types of loss functions that are commonly used by KGE models. They measure the fitness of the model with true positives and true negatives respectively.

Conformance Loss $\mathcal{L}_C$. After obtaining the augmented instances $\mathcal{D}^+(\mathcal{I}_C)$, we consider them as true positives along with the instances in the original KG, i.e., $\hat{\mathcal{I}}_C$. Conformance loss $\mathcal{L}_C$ is defined similarly to the original pairwise ranking loss $\mathcal{L}_{marg}$ and logistic loss $\mathcal{L}_{logi}$. Given a positive instance $\tau^+ = (s, r, o) \in \hat{\mathcal{I}}_C$ and negative instance $\tau^- = (s', r, o') \in \hat{\mathcal{I}}_C^{\,c}$, the construction of $\mathcal{L}_C$ is as follows:

$$\mathcal{L}_C = \sum_{\substack{\tau^+ \in \hat{\mathcal{I}}_C \\ \tau^- \in \hat{\mathcal{I}}_C^{\,c}}} \max\left(0, \gamma - f_r(s, o) + f_r(s', o')\right), \tag{1}$$

where $\hat{\mathcal{I}_C}^C$ is the set of negative instances obtained by random negative sampling or self-adversarial negative sampling [26]. In the case of the logistic loss, The formulation of logistic loss is as:

$$\mathcal{L}_{logi} = \sum_{\substack{\tau^+ \in \hat{\mathcal{I}_C} \\ \tau^- \in \hat{\mathcal{I}_C}^C}} \log\left(1 + \exp\left(-l_{(s,r,o)} \cdot f_r(s,o)\right)\right), \tag{2}$$

where $\tau = (s,r,o)$ is a training instance in $\hat{\mathcal{I}_C}$ or $\hat{\mathcal{I}_C}^C$, and $l_{(s,r,o)}$ is the label of τ. If $\tau \in \hat{\mathcal{I}_C}$, $l_{(s,r,o)}$ is 1; otherwise it is -1.

Violation Loss $\mathcal{L}_V$. Following the basic idea that the instances in $\mathcal{D}^-(\mathcal{I}_V)$ are "more negative" than the instances that are generated by negative sampling, the form of the loss functions for the pairwise ranking loss and logistic loss also need to be corrected slightly. In the case of the pairwise ranking loss, the violation loss $\mathcal{L}_V$ is defined as follows:

$$\mathcal{L}_V = \sum_{\substack{\tau^+ \in \mathcal{I}_V \\ \tau^- \in \mathcal{D}^-(\mathcal{I}_V)}} \max\left(0, \gamma' - f_r(s,o) + f_r(s',o')\right) \tag{3}$$

Specifically, an additional hyperparameter γ' is introduced to replace the discriminative margin γ in $\mathcal{L}_V$. γ' is set to be larger than γ to ensure that $\mathcal{D}^-(\mathcal{I}_V)$ is "more negative" by making the margin between $\hat{\mathcal{I}_C}$ and $\hat{\mathcal{I}_C^C}$ smaller than that between $\mathcal{I}_V$ and $\mathcal{D}^-(\mathcal{I}_V)$.

In the case of the logistic loss, another hyperparameter θ ($\theta > 1$) is introduced as the label of instances in $\mathcal{D}^-(\mathcal{I}_V)$ to make it "more negative" and the label function is corrected accordingly:

$$l_{(s,r,o)} = \begin{cases} 1, & \text{if } (s,r,o) \in \mathcal{I} \cup \mathcal{D}^+(\mathcal{I}_C) \\ -1, & \text{if } (s,r,o) \in \mathcal{I}^- \\ -\theta, & \text{if } (s,r,o) \in \mathcal{D}^-(\mathcal{I}_V) \end{cases} \tag{4}$$

Joint Loss. The original loss is combined with the conformance loss and violation loss in the *ontology-guided joint loss function*, which is defined as follows:

$$\mathcal{L}_J = w_1 \cdot \mathcal{L}_C + w_2 \cdot \mathcal{L}_V, \tag{5}$$

where w_1 and w_2 are hyperparameters for tuning the weights between the two losses.

The above correction to the loss function makes the framework conform more to the Open World Assumption (OWA) [20] by differentiating positive instances, true negative instances, and potentially negative instances.

4.3   Empirical Evaluation Metrics on C-axiom and V-axiom

To evaluate the capability of KGE models to predict implicit positive instances of the KG and avoid the derivation of true negative instances, we propose two new empirical evaluation metrics. We denote the instances in the test set that are related to the C-axiom and V-axiom as T_C and T_V respectively. The true positive instances and true negative instances derived from them are denoted by $\mathcal{D}^+(T_C)$ and $\mathcal{D}^-(T_V)$ respectively.

Metrics on C-axiom. We measure the capability of KGE methods learning C-axiom by defining the top-k Hit Ratio on $\mathcal{D}^+(T_C)$ as:

$$\text{Hit}_{\mathcal{D}^+(T_C)}@k = \frac{|\mathcal{D}^+(T_C)@k|}{|\mathcal{D}^+(T_C)|}, \tag{6}$$

where $|\mathcal{D}^+(T_C)|$ is the number of instances in $\mathcal{D}^+(T_C)$ and $|\mathcal{D}^+(T_C)@k|$ is the number of instances in $\mathcal{D}^+(T_C)$ that appear in the top-k rank list during prediction. Higher $\text{Hit}_{\mathcal{D}^+(T_C)}@k$ means better capability of model on learning C-axiom.

Metrics on V-axiom. We further define the top-k Hit Ratio on $\mathcal{D}^-(T_V)$ as

$$\text{Hit}_{\mathcal{D}^-(T_V)}@k = \frac{|\mathcal{D}^-(T_V)@k|}{|\mathcal{D}^-(T_V)|}, \tag{7}$$

where $|\mathcal{D}^-(T_V)|$ is the number of instances in $\mathcal{D}^-(T_V)$ and $|\mathcal{D}^-(T_V)@k|$ is the number of instances in $\mathcal{D}^-(T_V)$ that appear in the top-k rank list during prediction. Lower $\text{Hit}_{\mathcal{D}^-(T_V)}@k$ means better capability of model on learning V-axiom.

To further evaluate the extent that KGE models correctly distinguish between positive and negative samples, we use another V-axiom evaluation metric NDCG. For relations in $\mathcal{R}_V$, we expect that the correct entity should not only be hit but also separated from the false entities as far as possible, i.e., we care about the specific ranking of the missing entities. We intuitively consider that the correlation of the correct entity is 1 and that of the wrong entities is 0, and hence, the NDCG indicator can be written as

$$\text{NDCG} = \frac{1}{\log_2(i+1)},$$

where i denotes the rank of the missing entity.

5   Experiments

5.1   Experimental Setup

Datasets Description. We evaluated the effectiveness of our DKOG framework on the following three widely adopted benchmark datasets, which are FB15k-237 [29], NELL-995 [34], and YAGO3-10 [13]. FB15k-237 is a modified version of FB15k that excludes inverse relations to resolve a flaw with FB15k [4]. YAGO3-10 is a subset of the YAGO3 dataset which is a relatively large-scale graph compared to FB15k-237 and NELL-995. NELL-995 is a sparser graph with lower relation and entity density. The statistics of datasets are listed in Table 3.

Evaluation Protocol. We evaluated the effectiveness of the DKOG on the link prediction task. The purpose of link prediction is to infer s given (r, o) or infer

Table 3. Statistics of datasets. The density of entity and relation are calculated as [19].

	entities	relations	Number of Triples							Density	
			train	valid	test	$\mathcal{I}_C$	$\mathcal{I}_V$	$\mathcal{T}_C$	$\mathcal{T}_V$	$\mathcal{D}$(rel)	$\mathcal{D}$(ent)
FB15k-237	14,541	237	272,115	17,535	20,466	7,810	10,698	396	933	1148.16	37.43
NELL-995	75,492	200	149,678	543	3,992	3,263	10,771	0	3,992	748.39	3.97
YAGO3-10	123,182	37	1,079,040	5,000	5,000	124,484	122,955	578	569	29163.24	17.52

o given (s, r). We evaluated all the models using both the evaluation metrics proposed in Sect. 4.3, and three common evaluation metrics: mean rank (MR), mean reciprocal rank (MRR), and Hit@k. The lower the MR, the higher the MRR, or the higher the Hit@k, the better the performance.

Following previous works [2,4,16,36], we evaluated all the models in a *filtered* setting, that is, we removed corrupt triples that appeared in the training, validation, or test sets during ranking. We ranked the valid triple and filtered corrupted triples in ascending order of their prediction scores.

Additionally, it was recently proposed [27] that the position at which the correct triplet is inserted can substantially affect the prediction results since certain KG embedding models derive the same score for different triples. Therefore, we use the robust evaluation protocol proposed in [27] to minimize the evaluation bias.

Hyperparameters Selection. For the newly introduced hyperparameters, we trained the DKOG enhanced models using a grid search of the hyperparameters: weight tuning hyperparameters for $\mathcal{L}_C, \mathcal{L}_V$, $w_1, w_2 \in \{0.3, 0.5, 0.6, 1.0\}$, discriminative margin for true negative instances in pairwise ranking loss $\gamma' \in \{1, 1.5, 2.0\}$, label of true negative instances in logistic loss $\theta \in \{1.1, 1.2, 1.3, 1.5, 2.0\}$, ratio of used derived true positive instances $\{0.1, 0.2, 0.5, 0.8\}$, and ratio of generating true negative instances $\{8, 10, 20, 40\}$.

Baseline Models. We selected several representative baselines and applied our DKOG method to them. For geometry-based models, we chose TransE [2] and PairRE [3]. For tensor decomposition models, we chose ComplEx [30], QuatE [36] and SimplE [8]. For deep neural networks based models, we choose CNN-based model ConvKB [17] and GNN-based model KBGAT [16].

To ensure that the implemented environment consisted of the DKOG enhanced models, we reproduced the baseline models using publicly available source code. The overall deviation of the reproduction results was within ±4%of the reported results in [4,16].

5.2 Result and Discussion

We list the link prediction results on three datasets. The results on common evaluation metrics are presented in Table 4 and the results on our proposed metrics are listed in Table 5. We represent the baseline models as [name](base) and the models enhanced by our framework as [name]-DKOG.

Table 4. Link prediction results on FB15k-237, NELL-995, and YAGO3-10 on three common evaluation metrics. The results of ConvKB (base) and KBGAT (base) are taken from the revised version from [27]. Better results are in **bold**.

		FB15k-237			NELL-995			YAGO3-10		
		MR	MRR	Hit@10	MR	MRR	Hit@10	MR	MRR	Hit@10
Geometry	TransE (base)	329.9	0.282	42.56	**6773.6**	0.224	38.06	**1335.3**	0.150	40.62
	TransE-DKOG	**266.0**	**0.297**	**47.14**	6774.8	**0.226**	**38.77**	1366.8	**0.179**	**45.64**
	PairRE (base)	**156.1**	0.345	53.91	10413.4	0.328	44.22	866.7	0.527	68.83
	PairRE-DKOG	176.7	**0.348**	**53.95**	**9516.4**	**0.378**	**47.23**	**760.2**	**0.539**	**69.04**
TD	ComplEx (base)	378.8	0.258	**45.14**	**12128.2**	0.309	39.03	7093.6	0.417	57.28
	ComplEx-DKOG	**276.8**	**0.264**	44.32	12635.6	**0.384**	**47.07**	**3509.8**	**0.441**	**60.18**
	QuatE (base)	95.6	0.350	53.92	166.8	0.468	58.72	381.7	0.450	65.78
	QuatE-DKOG	**75.3**	**0.408**	**59.80**	**163.1**	**0.493**	**62.65**	**264.3**	**0.542**	**74.70**
	SimplE (base)	**215.1**	0.255	**42.30**	8830.8	0.354	43.50	7201.5	0.427	58.80
	SimplE-DKOG	237.9	**0.257**	42.15	9266.7	**0.378**	**45.28**	**5443.4**	**0.447**	**60.41**
DL	ConvKB (base)	372.1	0.213	39.60	4788.7	0.347	48.18	6635.4	0.451	57.80
	ConvKB-DKOG	**243.6**	**0.422**	**54.76**	**4052.7**	**0.370**	**48.68**	**6238.1**	**0.459**	**63.30**
	KBGAT (base)	360.1	0.167	31.89	3032.4	0.310	46.96	3815.9	0.075	13.88
	KBGAT-DKOG	**266.2**	**0.189**	**36.90**	**1194.2**	**0.421**	**60.61**	**1018.1**	**0.253**	**46.83**

Table 5. Link prediction results on two reasoning capability evaluation metrics.

		FB15k-237		NELL-995	YAGO3-10	
		$\text{Hit}_{\mathcal{D}^{+}(T_C)}@10$	$\text{Hit}_{\mathcal{D}^{-}(T_V)}@10$	$\text{Hit}_{\mathcal{D}^{-}(T_V)}@10$	$\text{Hit}_{\mathcal{D}^{+}(T_C)}@10$	$\text{Hit}_{\mathcal{D}^{-}(T_V)}@10$
Geometry	TransE (base)	30.09	**0.00**	4.94	16.38	**0.00**
	TransE-DKOG	**57.10**	0.05	**4.17**	**65.15**	**0.00**
	PairRE (base)	**61.44**	**6.54**	18.78	69.51	28.12
	PairRE-DKOG	52.45	**0.00**	**1.91**	**70.26**	26.88
TD	ComplEx (base)	54.30	1.01	**2.17**	44.15	19.77
	ComplEx-DKOG	**56.68**	**0.00**	3.37	**52.41**	1.23
	QuatE (base)	23.71	1.39	35.88	19.15	**0.53**
	QuatE-DKOG	**49.45**	**0.64**	15.98	**78.13**	0.70
	SimplE (base)	33.47	0.65	9.17	47.21	17.22
	SimplE-DKOG	**35.78**	**0.00**	**0.48**	**49.54**	6.85
DL	ConvKB (base)	24.85	0.16	1.04	18.47	60.28
	ConvKB-DKOG	**57.44**	0.16	**0.36**	**62.28**	55.36
	KBGAT (base)	22.61	0.05	16.87	10.09	**0.00**
	KBGAT-DKOG	**36.73**	0.05	**13.98**	**16.42**	**0.00**

Improvement on The Common Evaluation Metrics. The common evaluation metrics (MR, MRR, Hit@k) measure the general prediction capability of models. From Table 4, we found that models with our framework performed better in most cases for the common evaluation metrics, which indicates that the DKOG did not damage the original advantages of the baseline models, and in most cases could enhance the performance of different KGE models. In particular, for deep learning methods such as ConvKB and KBGAT, the original model tends to have difficulty distinguishing the prediction scores to different candidate triples in a test case, and thus cause bad performance on the revised results in [27]. It could be seen that DKOG could significantly fix such problems and improve the general performance on the robust evaluation protocol.

Improvement on The Proposed Evaluation Metrics. The proposed evaluation metrics measure the effectiveness of the DKOG for inferring hidden relation instances in the KG and avoiding deriving relation instances that contradict the KG. The experimental results on link prediction tasks demonstrated significant improvements to the reasoning capability evaluation metrics for the models with the DKOG framework. From Table 5, the best $\text{Hit}_{\mathcal{D}+(T_C)}@k$ and $\text{Hit}_{\mathcal{D}-(T_V)}@k$ achieved significant improvement. This indicates that our framework improved the capability of the KGE models for learning C-axiom and V-axiom.

Table 6. Case study on link prediction task for DKOG enhanced models. For each query, we list the top-5 results ranked by prediction scores. Ground truths are marked in **bold**.

Query	Top 5 triples with highest score
(Henry_VII_of_England, isMarriedTo, ?)	**Elizabeth_of_York**(1.71)
	Mary_Tudor,_Queen_of_France(1.56)
	Catherine_of_Valois(0.99)
	Margaret_Tudor(0.83)
	Beatrice_of_England(0.72)
(?, isMarriedTo, Elizabeth_of_York)	**Henry_VII_of_England**(1.71)
	Elizabeth_Woodville (0.97)
	Edward_IV_of_England (0.94)
	Henry_VIII_of_England(0.80)
	Margaret_Tudor(0.63)
(Aleksei_Yuryevich_German, diedIn, ?)	**Saint_Petersburg**(0.61)
	Moscow (-1.30)
	Minsk (-1.78)
	Riga (-2.06)
	Samara,_Russia (-2.24)
(?, hasCapital, Kandy)	**Central_Province_Sri_Lanka**(1.52)
	Northern_Province,_Sri_Lanka (0.47)
	Central_Province,_Sri_Lanka(0.45)
	North_Central_Province,_Sri_Lanka (0.24)
	Kandy_District (-0.24)

5.3 Case Study

Table 6 shows the top-5 prediction results for the DKOG enhanced models. Among the queries, relation *isMarriedTo* is in $\mathcal{R}_C$. The first two queries were the source and target predictions for the same triple with symmetric relation *isMarriedTo*. The results demonstrated that the top-1 predictions were exactly entities of the married couples.

Meanwhile, relation *diedIn* and *hasCapital* were functional and inverse functional relations specified by axioms in $\mathcal{R}_V$. The results demonstrated that the top-1 prediction not only accurately hit the unique ground truth but also had a significantly higher prediction score than the left, which means that the DKOG enhanced model was capable of capturing the semantic property of functionality and inverse functionality.

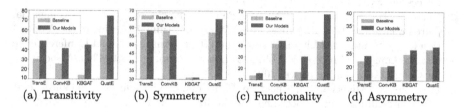

(a) Transitivity   (b) Symmetry   (c) Functionality   (d) Asymmetry

Fig. 3. Histograms of relational study results. We report the Hit@10 (%) value on transitivity and symmetry and NDCG@1 (%) on functionality and asymmetry.

We further evaluate the performance on specific relation of C-axiom and V-axiom. The results are shown in Fig. 3. The histograms directly show that the improvement for a specific relation pattern was rather significant for some models, such as TransE and ConvKB for the transitive property and QuatE for the transitive, symmetric, and functional properties. The results indicate that models with the DKOG framework learned the relation semantic property better.

6   Conclusion

In this paper, we proposed an ontology-guided data augmentation joint embedding framework that can be easily embedded in existing KGE models. The basic idea of this framework is to incorporate the constraints specified in the ontology through a joint loss function with two losses defined on the derived positive and negative instance sets. We also proposed two evaluation metrics to evaluate the capability of the model to predict positive triples whose derivation requires complex reasoning and avoid mistaken predictions of true negative triples. The experimental results demonstrated that models with our framework generally performed better than their corresponding baseline models on most evaluation metrics for different datasets.

Acknowledgement. This work was supported by the National Key R&D Program of China (Grant No. 2021ZD0112901) and National Natural Science Foundation of China (Grant No. 62276014)

References

1. Balažević, I., Allen, C., Hospedales, T.: Tucker: tensor factorization for knowledge graph completion. In: Proceedings of the 2019 Conference on Empirical Methods in Natural Language Processing and the 9th International Joint Conference on Natural Language Processing (EMNLP-IJCNLP), pp. 5185–5194 (2019)
2. Bordes, A., Usunier, N., Garcia-Duran, A., Weston, J., Yakhnenko, O.: Translating embeddings for modeling multi-relational data. In: Advances in Neural Information Processing Systems 26, pp. 2787–2795 (2013)
3. Chao, L., He, J., Wang, T., Chu, W.: PairRE: knowledge graph embeddings via paired relation vectors. In: Proceedings of the 59th Annual Meeting of the Association for Computational Linguistics and the 11th International Joint Conference on Natural Language Processing (Volume 1: Long Papers), pp. 4360–4369. Association for Computational Linguistics (2021)
4. Dettmers, T., Minervini, P., Stenetorp, P., Riedel, S.: Convolutional 2D knowledge graph embeddings. In: Proceedings of the 32nd AAAI Conference on Artificial Intelligence (2018)
5. Gao, C., Sun, C., Shan, L., Lin, L., Wang, M.: Rotate3D: representing relations as rotations in three-dimensional space for knowledge graph embedding. In: Proceedings of the 29th ACM International Conference on Information & Knowledge Management, pp. 385–394 (2020)
6. Guo, Q., et al.: A survey on knowledge graph-based recommender systems (2020)
7. Ji, G., He, S., Xu, L., Liu, K., Zhao, J.: Knowledge graph embedding via dynamic mapping matrix. In: Proceedings of the 53rd Annual Meeting of the Association for Computational Linguistics and the 7th International Joint Conference on Natural Language Processing, pp. 687–696. Association for Computational Linguistics (2015)
8. Kazemi, S.M., Poole, D.: Simple embedding for link prediction in knowledge graphs. In: Advances in Neural Information Processing Systems 31 (2018)
9. Kipf, T., Welling, M.: Semi-supervised classification with graph convolutional networks. In: Proceedings of ICLR, pp. 1–14 (2017)
10. Lan, Y., He, G., Jiang, J., Jiang, J., Zhao, W.X., Wen, J.R.: A survey on complex knowledge base question answering: methods, challenges and solutions (2021)
11. Li, Z., et al.: Efficient non-sampling knowledge graph embedding. In: Proceedings of the Web Conference 2021, pp. 1727–1736. WWW 2021, Association for Computing Machinery (2021)
12. Lin, Y., Liu, Z., Sun, M., Liu, Y., Zhu, X.: Learning entity and relation embeddings for knowledge graph completion. In: Proceedings of the 29th AAAI Conference on Artificial Intelligence, pp. 2181–2187 (2015)
13. Mahdisoltani, F., Biega, J., Suchanek, F.M.: YAGO3: a knowledge base from multilingual wikipedias. In: Proceedings of CIDR 2015 (2015)
14. Mintz, M., Bills, S., Snow, R., Jurafsky, D.: Distant supervision for relation extraction without labeled data, pp. 1003–1011 (2009)
15. Motik, B., Grau, B.C., Horrocks, I., Wu, Z., Fokoue, A., Lutz, C.: OWL 2 web ontology language profiles (second edition). W3C Recommendation 11 December 2012 (2012)
16. Nathani, D., Chauhan, J., Sharma, C., Kaul, M.: Learning attention-based embeddings for relation prediction in knowledge graphs. In: Proceedings of the 57th Annual Meeting of the Association for Computational Linguistics, pp. 4710–4723. Association for Computational Linguistics (2019)

17. Nguyen, D.Q., Nguyen, T.D., Nguyen, D.Q., Phung, D.: A novel embedding model for knowledge base completion based on convolutional neural network, vol. 2, pp. 327–333 (2018)

18. Nickel, M., Tresp, V., Kriegel, H.P.: A three-way model for collective learning on multi-relational data. In: Proceedings of the 28th International Conference on International Conference on Machine Learning, pp. 809–816. ICML2011, Omnipress (2011)

19. Pujara, J., Augustine, E., Getoor, L.: Sparsity and noise: where knowledge graph embeddings fall short. In: Proceedings of the 2017 Conference on Empirical Methods in Natural Language Processing, pp. 1751–1756. Association for Computational Linguistics, Copenhagen, Denmark (2017)

20. Reiter, R.: Deductive question-answering on relational data bases. In: Gallaire, H., Minker, J. (eds.) Logic and Data Bases, pp. 149–177. Springer, US, Boston, MA (1978). https://doi.org/10.1007/978-1-4684-3384-5_6

21. Saxena, A., Tripathi, A., Talukdar, P.: Improving multi-hop question answering over knowledge graphs using knowledge base embeddings. In: Proceedings of the 58th Annual Meeting of the Association for Computational Linguistics, pp. 4498–4507. Association for Computational Linguistics (2020)

22. Schlichtkrull, M., Kipf, T.N., Bloem, P., Berg, R.V.D., Titov, I., Welling, M.: Modeling relational data with graph convolutional networks. In: ESWC, pp. 593–607 (2018)

23. Schneider, P., Schopf, T., Vladika, J., Galkin, M., Simperl, E., Matthes, F.: A decade of knowledge graphs in natural language processing: a survey (2022)

24. Shang, C., Tang, Y., Huang, J., Bi, J., He, X., Zhou, B.: End-to-end structure-aware convolutional networks for knowledge base completion. In: Proceedings of the AAAI Conference on Artificial Intelligence, vol. 33, pp. 3060–3067 (2019)

25. Song, T., Luo, J., Huang, L.: Rot-Pro: modeling transitivity by projection in knowledge graph embedding. In: Proceedings of the Thirty-Fifth Annual Conference on Advances in Neural Information Processing Systems (NeurIPS) (2021)

26. Sun, Z., Deng, Z.H., Nie, J.Y., Tang, J.: Rotate: Knowledge graph embedding by relational rotation in complex space. In: International Conference on Learning Representations, pp. 1–18 (2019)

27. Sun, Z., Vashishth, S., Sanyal, S., Talukdar, P., Yang, Y.: A re-evaluation of knowledge graph completion methods. In: Proceedings of the 58th Annual Meeting of the Association for Computational Linguistics, pp. 5516–5522. Association for Computational Linguistics (2020)

28. Tang, Z., et al.: Positive-unlabeled learning with adversarial data augmentation for knowledge graph completion. In: Raedt, L.D. (ed.) Proceedings of the Thirty-First International Joint Conference on Artificial Intelligence, IJCAI-22, pp. 2248–2254. International Joint Conferences on Artificial Intelligence Organization (2022)

29. Toutanova, K., Chen, D.: Observed versus latent features for knowledge base and text inference. In: Proceedings of the 3rd Workshop on Continuous Vector Space Models and their Compositionality, pp. 57–66 (2015)

30. Trouillon, T., Welbl, J., S. Riedel, E.G., Bouchard, G.: Complex embeddings for simple link prediction. In: Proceedings of 33rd International Conference Machine Learning, pp. 2071–2080 (2016)

31. Wang, H., et al.: Knowledge-aware graph neural networks with label smoothness regularization for recommender systems, pp. 968–977. KDD 2019, Association for Computing Machinery, New York, NY, USA (2019)

32. Wang, X., et al.: KEPLER: a Unified Model for Knowledge Embedding and Pre-trained Language Representation. Trans. Assoc. Comput. Linguist. **9**, 176–194 (2021)
33. Wang, Z., Zhang, J., Feng, J., Chen, Z.: Knowledge graph embedding by translating on hyperplanes. In: AAAI Conference on Artificial Intelligence, pp. 1112–1119 (2014)
34. Xiong, T.H.W., Wang, W.Y.: DeepPath: a reinforcement learning method for knowledge graph reasoning. In: Proceedings of the 2017 Conference on Empirical Methods in Natural Language Processing (EMNLP) (2017)
35. Yang, B., Yih, W., He, X., Gao, J., Deng, L.: Embedding entities and relations for learning and inference in knowledge bases. In: ICLR, pp. 1–13 (2015)
36. Zhang, S., Tay, Y., Yao, L., Liu, Q.: Quaternion knowledge graph embedding. Adv. Neural. Inf. Process. Syst. **32**, 2731–2741 (2019)

Multi-Dimensional Graph Rule Learner

Jiayang Wu[1] , Zhenlian Qi[2], and Wensheng Gan[1,3(✉)]

[1] Jinan University, Guangzhou 510632, China
[2] Guangdong Eco-Engineering Polytechnic, Guangzhou 510520, China
[3] Pazhou Lab, Guangzhou 510330, China
`wsgan001@gmail.com`

Abstract. Knowledge graph completion plays a pivotal role in the era of artificial intelligence. To harness the interpretability benefits of logical rules, we propose a cross-level position constraint template based on graph path feature learning (GPFL). For improving prediction performance, we place significant emphasis on the rule evaluation stage, specifically how to effectively learn the rules. To this end, we propose a Multi-Dimensional Graph Rule Learner (MDGRL) that calculates features from different dimensions for every rule. We assign weights to features of different dimensions based on their rule learning abilities and integrate them into rule learning. Our experiments demonstrate effectiveness across various dataset sizes, showcasing improved prediction performance in rule evaluation. The fusion of features substantially aids in enhancing prediction performance.

Keywords: Logical rules · Rule learning · Similarity · Path reasoning · Knowledge graph · Knowledge learning

1 Introduction

In today's data-driven era, big data mining [7] has emerged as a crucial method for acquiring and understanding information about the world. Traditional data processing techniques have become less competitive due to the overwhelming volume of data. In response to this challenge, Google introduced the concept of the Knowledge Graph (KG) in 2012 [1]. The knowledge graph, built upon semantic web technology, connects distinct knowledge points via entities, attributes, and relationships, forming a large-scale knowledge base [5,17]. As an efficient graphical structure for representing and storing knowledge, the knowledge graph can be employed to accomplish various tasks, including semantic search [22], intelligent question answering [13] and personalized recommendations [18]. In GPFL (Graph Path Feature Learning) [8], a rule template is proposed. Based on the template, completely abstract rules (CAR and OAR) and instantiated rules (HAR and BAR) can be generated. Instantiated rules replace variables in the abstract rule with constants according to the constraints of the template. The utilization of the instantiated rules improves the generalization capabilities and has achieved positive results in predicting unknown triples. Moreover,

Z. Jin et al. (Eds.): KSEM 2023, LNAI 14117, pp. 393–404, 2023.
https://doi.org/10.1007/978-3-031-40283-8_33

mining the rules with the template can yield good interpretative performance for the mining results. A two-stage mining pattern is also adopted. In rule generation, a termination policy is utilized to stop generating rules according to the value of rule space coverage [15]. This value is proposed to measure the expressive ability of the rule space and determine the termination conditions. Moreover, in every iteration of the rule generation, the rules are put into a batch of fixed size; rule space coverage is calculated as the overlap ratio between the current batch and the total rule set; and then the process terminates when the coverage reaches the threshold. In rule evaluation, smooth confidence (SC) is used for pruning and scoring rules. With the cross-level template, when executing the grounding step, GPFL only needs to traverse the completely abstract rules instead of traversing every instantiated rule, which can greatly reduce the time consumed in rule evaluation. Then, it uses these rules to generate potential triples for knowledge graph completion, which could achieve better results than many other algorithms. However, we found that it can still be improved.

In rule evaluation, only SC was used for evaluation. This feature can represent the rules' head and rules' body similarity. However, single-dimensional features can only provide limited information, which could lead to data overfitting or weak generalization ability, potentially causing misunderstanding and bias in graph reasoning. Therefore, we have adopted multiple feature learning to alleviate this problem. To improve the rules learning ability, we also take the feature from another two dimensions, i.e., path transfer probability from path reasoning [12] and embedding distance [3] from knowledge representation learning, as two more features. We conducted a comprehensive experiment comparing the experimental results to the baseline GPFL and a detailed analysis of each feature to analyze how to obtain the best predictive performance for the individual features. Finally, we integrate these features and extract the best weight expression through individual experiments. The results show that our improvement can achieve the best prediction performance, surpassing the baseline and every individual feature. Our contributions can be summarized as follows:

- Based on the rule template of GPFL, we propose a more readable cross-level position constraint template.
- Based on the cross-level position constraint template, we propose three dimensions of features to learn the rules. The first dimension involves rules' set similarity from association learning; the second considers the path transfer probability from path reasoning; and the third incorporates the embedding distance from representation learning.
- We analyze the prediction performance for every individual feature and obtain the weighted combination according to their single performance. Finally, we integrate these features into the rule learning process. The results show that prediction with multi-feature learning can outperform the baseline and every individual feature.

The rest of the paper is organized as follows. Section 2 reviews the related work. Section 3 describes the related definitions. Section 4 explains the details of the proposed MDGRL algorithm. We evaluate the experimental results in Sect. 5 and conclude this paper in Sect. 6.

2   Related Work

The related work of this study includes knowledge representation learning, path-based reasoning, and rule-based learning. Details are reviewed below.

Knowledge Representation Learning. Knowledge representation learning utilizes machine learning algorithms to represent entities and relationships as vectors, predicting relationships between entities by calculating embedding distances [3]. Notable algorithms in this category include TransE, TransH, DistMult, PTransE, and CSPM [14, 21]. These methods represent entities and relationships in vector form, which facilitates computation and inference. Furthermore, they can capture semantic similarities between entities and relationships, enhancing their prediction ability [20]. Nonetheless, they may encounter issues such as over-fitting or under-fitting in cases where there is insufficient or sparse data. To mitigate these drawbacks, researchers should consider refining the algorithm or incorporating additional sources of information to improve the model's performance and robustness.

Path-Based Reasoning. Path reasoning involves knowledge inference and completion by identifying meaningful paths between entities and relationships in a knowledge graph. The Path Ranking Algorithm (PRA) is a path-based knowledge graph link prediction algorithm [10]. This algorithm discovers paths between nodes in the knowledge graph and assigns a weight to each path to predict whether a link relationship exists between two nodes. Advantages of path reasoning algorithms include the ability to capture complex relationships between nodes and represent these relationships through paths. These algorithms improve the accuracy of link prediction by identifying intricate connections between nodes. Additionally, path reasoning algorithms are computationally efficient, enabling link prediction on large-scale knowledge graphs. However, the performance of path reasoning algorithms may be impacted when the knowledge graph is exceptionally sparse. To overcome these limitations, researchers should combine path reasoning algorithms with other methods to enhance performance and reliability.

Rule-Based Learning. Algorithms for rule-based learning describe the logical relationships between entities and relationships in a knowledge graph. Methods like AMIE, RuleN, AnyBURL, and GPFL fall under this category [16]. Logic rules are primarily utilized in rule-based methods for knowledge inference and completion. The AMIE (Association Rule Mining under Incomplete Evidence) [6] is a top-down learning approach rooted in association rule mining. It generates rules by continuously specializing rules derived from top-level rules, adding new atoms or instantiated rules that replace constants for abstract rules. During the traversal of the graph database, it can generate a great number of useful rules for reasoning. A key disadvantage of logic rule algorithms is their limited generalization ability and the production of overfitting rules, which may lead to issues such as inaccurate rules for reasoning. Moreover, these limitations can negatively impact the reasoning process.

3   Definitions

The knowledge graph is a directed multigraph that can be represented as $G = (E, R, T)$, consisting of many triples.

Definition 1. (Triple and path). Each triplet contains two entities and relationships and can be represented as $r_i(e_j, e_k) \in T$, where $r_i \in R$ is the relation type (predicate), and $e_j, e_k \in E$ are entities (constants). Paths formed by these triplets can be represented as $r_0(e_0, e_1), r_1(e_1, e_2), ..., r_n(e_n, e_{n+1})$, where these paths or rules consisting of triplets, and paths that satisfy the rule conditions are called "grounding" paths.

Definition 2. (Language bias). In the knowledge graph, the paths can take various forms and can be on a large scale. Therefore, many algorithms have proposed some semantic biases to limit the extension of paths based on predefined constraints, such as path length, path form, etc. This paper continues to use these constraints to extend the paths. In the proposed algorithm, atoms are limited to binary $r_i(e_j, e_k)$ instead of $r_i(e_j, e_k, e')$, and adjacent atoms are connected by the same entity, such as e_1 in the previous example. Furthermore, a constant cannot appear more than twice in the same path to avoid infinite loops, and self-loop paths, such as $r_0(e_0, e_1), r_1(e_1, e_2), ..., r_n(e_n, e_0)$, are filtered out.

Definition 3. (The form of the rule). These paths and triplets can be converted into the form of rule deduction, such as $r_0(e_0, e_{n+1}) \leftarrow r_0(e_0, e_1), r_1(e_1, e_2), ..., r_n(e_n, e_{n+1})$, where the left arrow represents the rule head, which is the conclusion of the deduction, and the right arrow represents the rule body, which is the premise of the deduction. The number of triplets in the rule body is equal to the length of the path (rule).

Definition 4. (Cross-level position constraint template). In the cross-level position constraint template, there are three types of rules: completely abstract rules (CAR), instantiated rules with one constant (HAR), and rules with two constants (BAR). These rules are designed to help convert paths into corresponding rules and are summarized in Table 1. CAR is the abstract rule, which only contains variables in the rule's head and body. To convert a path into a CAR, the following steps are taken: First, both the first entity and the last entity of the rule's head and rule's body are represented by X and Y: $r_0(X_1, Y_1) \leftarrow r_0(X_2, e_1), r_2(e_1, Y_2)$. Next, the remaining entities in the positions are sequentially replaced with variables V: $r_0(X_1, Y_1) \leftarrow r_1(X_2, V_0), r_2(V_0, Y_2)$. OAR can be instantiated into HAR and BAR by replacing one or two variables with the entities in the specified positions of the rules. OAR can be instantiated by replacing one variable with the entity e_1 in the rule's head to obtain HAR: $r_0(X_1, e_1) \leftarrow r_1(X_2, V_0), r_2(V_0, Y_2)$ or $r_0(e_1, Y_1) \leftarrow r_1(X_2, V_0), r_2(V_0, Y_2)$. Replacing the variable with entity e_2 at the last index of the rule's body yields BAR: $r_0(X_1, e_1) \leftarrow r_1(X_2, V_0), r_2(V_0, e_2)$ or $r_0(e_1, Y_1) \leftarrow r_1(X_2, V_0), r_2(V_0, e_2)$.

Table 1. Cross-level position constraint template

Rule	Potential Constraint triple
CAR	$X_1=X_2,Y_1=Y_2$
OAR	$1.X_1=X_2,Y_1\neq Y_2$ $2.X_1\neq X_2,Y_1=Y_2$
HAR	1.if $X_1=X_2$, $Y_1\neq Y_2$, then instantiate Y_1 as e_1 2.if $X_1\neq X_2$, $Y_1=Y_2$, then instantiate X_1 as e_1
BAR	1.if $X_1=X_2,Y_1\neq Y_2$, then instantiate Y_1 as e_1 and instantiate Y_2 as e_1 2.if $X_1\neq X_2,Y_1=Y_2$, then instantiate X_1 as e_1 and instantiate X_2 as e_2

4 Proposed Algorithm

Path Transfer Probability. The Path Ranking Algorithm (PRA) [10] proposes a formula for path transfer probability that assigns weights to different paths through iterative optimization to calculate scores for predicting entity relationships. However, this approach has the limitation that the training of the weight optimization process requires a significant amount of time. To address this, we try to combine the position template to enhance path inference. The formula for path transfer probability consists of two parts: the probability of the next node selection and the probability of the path selection. The selection probability depends on the number of next nodes. If there are no next nodes, then the transfer probability is 0. If there are multiple nodes to choose from, then the transfer probability is $1/|nodes|$. The selection probability of the path is $1/|path|$, which represents how many paths can reach one of the next nodes. To balance the relationship between the nearest and farthest nodes, we can multiply a decreasing *rate* at each step, which gradually reduces the influence of future nodes. This can help focus more on the nearest nodes and achieve a better balance between multiple-hop paths and one-hop paths [23].

In our framework, the paths are the rule's grounding and can be represented as $P = \{p_1, p_2, ..., p_m\}$. However, the grounding's head and tail entities may be different. Therefore, we need to classify the grounding according to keys incorporating head and tail entities. A path can be represented as $p_i = (e_{i,1}, r_{i,1}, e_{i,2}, r_{i,2}, ..., r_{i,k-1}, e_{i,k})$, representing the ith path passing through these entities and relations. The next node transfer can be represented by a triple, such as $(e_{i,j}, r_{i,j}, e_{i,j+1})$. The probability of the next node selection is $p_{i,j} = r_{i,j}, \mathrm{p}(e_{i,j}, r_{i,j})$, representing the one-hop probability of the jth node $e_{i,j}$ passing through the relation $r_{i,j}$. The path selection probability is $q_{i,j} = \mathrm{q}(r_{i,j}, e_{i,j+1})$, representing the one-hop probability of the jth node reaching the next node $e_{i,j+1}$ through $r_{i,j}$. The transfer probability of each step or triple is represented by $p_{i,j} * q_{i,j}$. To increase the influence of the nearest nodes, we introduce a decreasing coefficient d. Moreover, d multiplies itself for each step, assuming the coefficient is d, and the coefficient for the jth step is d^{j-1}. For calculation on the entire path, the probability needs to be recursively multiplied from left to right. The equation $p_i = \prod_{j=1}^{k-1} p_{i,j} * q_{i,j} * d^{j-1}$ calculates the transfer probability recursively in a path, where d is a decreasing factor. To calculate the rule, the probabilities of all paths that satisfy the rules need to be added up: $\sum_{i=1}^{m} p_i$. The final score of a rule is represented as:

$$P = \sum_{i=1}^{m} \prod_{j=1}^{k-1} p_{i,j} \cdot q_{i,j} \cdot d^{j-1}. \tag{1}$$

Algorithm 1 introduces the specific steps for calculating the path transfer probability. First, it initializes M, which is used to store different paths sorted by their head and tail (line 1). It then initializes the list S to keep track of the scores of different head-tail paths (line 2). P is used to obtain the probabilities of nodes and different direction relations, which can be directly obtained by calling the Neo4j API interface (line 3). Next, it searches for the paths that can satisfy the $r.body$ assigned to $r.Ground$, sorts them into different categories based on their head and tail, and finally stores them in M (lines 4-5). Using Formula 1, we calculate the scores for different keys in M and store these scores in S (line 6). It takes the average of these scores in S and finally returns it as an attribute (lines 7-8).

Algorithm 1: Path transfer probability

Input: r: the rule, D: the dataset
Output: S: the path transition probability of the rule.
1 initialize map M;
2 initialize empty list S;
3 $P \leftarrow$ Get all the probability between the nodes and relations;
4 $r.Ground \leftarrow$ Search for all the paths that can satisfy the $r.body$;
5 map $r.Ground$ into M according to their head and tail;
6 calculate with Formula 1 for different keys in M and put the scores into S;
7 $S = \text{mean}(S)$;
8 **return** S

Embedding Distance. Rule-based learning and knowledge representation learning algorithms are two different approaches that each have their own strengths and weaknesses. Therefore, we try to combine rule-based learning and knowledge representation learning to leverage their strengths and improve the robustness of the algorithms, thus obtaining better inference performance. First, we continue to use the rule's framework to generate rules, as mentioned before, but in the evaluation of rules, we add the calculation of embedding distance. Although there are many embedding formulas, to better integrate them into our logic rule calculations, we use the most basic distance formula $||h + r(pr) - t||$. The algorithms that use this formula include TransE [3] and PTransE [11], which are trained to obtain the optimal expression vectors for entities on a single plane. TransE is designed to learn embedding representations of entities and relations. Each entity and relationship is mapped to a low-dimensional vector space and

---

Algorithm 2: Embedding distance

Input: r: the rule, D: the dataset, *tar*: the target relations.
Output: S: the score of the rule.

1 initialize empty array E, h, r, t;
2 initialize empty list S;
3 $E \leftarrow$ Train the embedding from TransE or PTransE;
4 $r = E.get(tar)$;
5 $len = |r.B|$ - 1;
6 **if** $r.type == 0$ **then**
7   **for** $g \in r.B$ **do**
8          $h = E.get(g[0])$;
9          $t = E.get(g[len])$;
10         $pr = E.get(r.B.tar[0]) + E.get(r.B.tar[1])... + E.get(r.B.tar[len])$;
11         $S.add(Dis(h, r(pr), t))$;
12   **end**
13 **else**
14   **if** $r.type == 1 \,||\, r.type == 2$ **then**
15   **if** $((r.x_1 == r.x_2) \,\&\&\, (r.y_1 \neq r.y_2))||((r.x_1 \neq r.x_2) \,\&\&\, (r.y_1 == r.y_2))$
           then
16   **for** $g \in r.B$ **do**
17                 $h = E.get(g[0(len)])$;
18   **for** $s \in r.A$ **do**
19                       $t = E.get(s.tail(head))$;
20                       $pr = E.get(r.B.tar[0]) + E.get(r.B.tar[1])... +$
                         $E.get(r.B.tar[len])$;
21                       $S.add(Dis(h, r(pr), t))$;
22   **end**
23   **end**
24   **end**
25   **end**
26 **end**
27 $S = sigmoid(-mean(S))$;
28 **return** S

---

optimized by gradient descent. Specifically, TransE learns embedding representations of entities and relations through negative sampling and gradient descent, where negative sampling refers to randomly selecting some incorrect triples during training to update vector representations to better distinguish between correct and incorrect triples. PTransE is an improved version of the TransE algorithm that adds the concept of paths for gradient descent, thus allowing for better modeling of relations between entities.

Algorithm 2 first initializes an array E to store vectors for all entities and relations. Additionally, arrays h, r, and t are initialized to store vectors during calculations (line 1). A list S is initialized to store the value of scores (line 2). The vectors for all entities and relations are obtained through training with TransE or PTransE and stored in the array E (line 3). The vector for the relation r

is obtained from E, and the path length is assigned to *len* (lines 4-5). If the type of the rule is CAR, we directly extract the head entity and tail entity from $r.B$, and the vector is obtained from E. The head entity vector is stored in h, while the tail entity vector is stored in t. The pr vector used in PTransE is obtained by accumulating the vectors among relations in $r.B$. In TransE, the score is calculated using the TransE vector with $||h + r - t||$, and the score is calculated using the PTransE vector with $||h + pr - t||$. Moreover, the scores are stored in the S list (lines 6-12). If the type of the rule is HAR or BAR, and if the condition $((r.x_1 == r.x_2)\ \&\&\ (r.y_1 \neq r.y_2))$ is satisfied, we traverse the rule's body. h is obtained as the vector from the first element of grounding in E, t is obtained as the vector from the tail element of the rule's head, and pr is obtained by adding the relation vectors from left to right. When the condition is $((r.x_1 \neq r.x_2)\ \&\&\ (r.y_1 == r.y_2))$, h is obtained as the vector from the last element of grounding in E, and t is obtained as the vector from the head element of the rule's head. Then, the distance score is calculated using the existing h, $r(pr)$, and t vectors (lines 14-26). The mean value of the S is normalized using the sigmoid function after being negated. In this way, higher scores represent better performance. With the calculation, the value is assigned to S once more. Finally, the score is returned (lines 27-28).

5   Experimental Evaluation

For a detailed evaluation, we conduct comprehensive experiments on a computer with an 11th Gen Intel(R) Core(TM) i7-11700 @ 2.50 GHz (16 CPUs) to 2.5 GHz and 32 GB of RAM. The upper bound of the rule's body length is set to 3. We perform more in-depth experiments to investigate the performance of different feature dimensions, such as feature I based on SC in GPFL, feature II path transfer probability, and feature III embedding distance. Finally, based on these findings, we make the optimal weighted combinations among the features. To evaluate the experimental results, we use the common evaluation metrics in information retrieval and machine learning tasks, including Hits@1, Hits@3, Hits@10, and mean reciprocal ranking (MRR) [3]. Moreover, we use the filtered ranking method, which only considers the data in the prediction set and unknown data for the calculation of knowledge ranking [9].

5.1   Datasets

Five datasets are used to evaluate the performance of various improvements to our algorithm. Each dataset comes from a different field and has a unique set of entities, relationships, and quantities, making them diverse and challenging benchmarks for evaluating the effectiveness of the models. These datasets are publicly accessible. Moreover, all the datasets are split into 6:2:2. FB15K-237 is a subset of the larger Freebase dataset [19]. WN18RR[1] is a subset of the WordNet

---

[1] https://github.com/irokin/GPFL.

dataset [4]. Kinship[2] is a synthetic dataset that was created to evaluate the ability of models to make inferences in small-scale knowledge graphs [24]. UMLS is a biomedical knowledge graph that integrates various biomedical vocabularies, classifications, and ontologies [2]. Security[3] is a knowledge graph of software vulnerabilities [25].

5.2   Path Transfer Probability (F II)

According to Formula 1, we incorporate a decreasing rate in our path transfer calculation to balance the effect of closer nodes and long-distance nodes. We first conduct an experiment on the Kinship dataset to observe the curve change when the rate d ranges from 0.1 to 1. As shown in Fig. 1 (a), Hits@10 increases before 0.7, and we find that when d is between 0.8 and 0.9, the results stabilize and yield better performance. However, without the rate, i.e., when d is 1, the results are worse than those at the peak. To test the effectiveness of d and search for the best setting, we perform experiments on all datasets with d values of 0.8, 0.9, and 1. As shown in Fig. 1 (b), when d is 0.8 or 0.9, the Hits@10 values surpass those without a decreasing rate. Therefore, we can conclude that the decreasing rate helps in learning the nodes at different distances and improves prediction performance compared to not using a decreasing rate in the path transfer probability. Furthermore, for the four datasets, a d value of 0.9 yields higher Hits@10 values than 0.8. Thus, $d = 0.9$ is the most appropriate rate for the d setting.

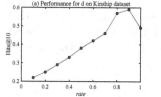 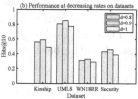

Fig. 1. Comparison of Hits@10 performance on various datasets with different decrease rates.

5.3   Embedding Distance (F III)

As shown in Algorithm 2, we can use TransE or PTransE to train and obtain the embedding values for every entity and relation. We have limited the length of both entity and relation vectors to 100. We discuss the experimental results for Feature III, the embedding distance, as shown in Table 2. The results show that PTransE+Rule achieves the best performance, surpassing TransE+Rule,

---

[2] https://github.com/ZhenfengLei/KGDatasets.

[3] https://github.com/kgembedding2019/Embedding-and-Predicting-Software-Security.

TransE, and PTransE in terms of Hits@3, Hits@5, Hits@10, and MRR metrics on both UMLS and Security datasets. Moreover, the results demonstrate that combining the rule framework with embedding methods, such as TransE and PTransE, leads to better performance compared to using only the embedding methods. For example, when comparing PTransE+Rule with PTransE, we observe an improvement in performance across all evaluation metrics. A similar pattern is observed when comparing TransE+Rule with TransE. Furthermore, the results reveal the impact of embedding quality on overall performance when combined with the rule framework. PTransE, which generally provides better embeddings than TransE, leads to higher performance when combined with the rule framework.

Table 2. Performance of datasets on Feature III

Algorithm	UMLS				Security			
	Hits@3	Hits@5	Hits@10	MRR	Hits@3	Hits@5	Hits@10	MRR
TransE	0.76	0.80	0.84	0.55	0.30	0.32	0.37	0.25
PTransE	0.80	0.83	0.87	0.39	0.33	0.35	0.39	0.27
TransE+Rule	0.81	0.84	0.88	0.55	0.38	0.40	0.42	0.33
PTransE+Rule	0.83	0.86	0.90	0.75	0.40	0.44	0.48	0.35

5.4 The Prediction Performance of MDGRL (Multi-F)

We further evaluate the experimental results for the integration of all features, with assigned weights of 0.5 to F I, 0.2 to F II, and 0.3 to F III, based on their individual performances. Table 3 shows the results of the integrated features (Multi-F) compared to the baseline GPFL (F I) and the individual features F II and F III.

Table 3. Performance of datasets on various dimensions feature

Algorithm	FB15K				WN18RR				Kinship				UMLS				Security			
	Hits@3	Hits@5	Hits@10	MRR	Hits@3	Hits@5	Hits@10	MRR	Hits@3	Hits@5	Hits@10	MRR	Hits@3	Hits@5	Hits@10	MRR	Hits@3	Hits@5	Hits@10	MRR
GPFL (F I)	0.25	0.32	0.36	0.18	0.30	0.32	0.35	0.29	0.67	0.77	0.80	0.58	0.85	0.87	0.89	0.80	0.39	0.46	0.51	0.37
F II	0.19	0.23	0.27	0.12	0.29	0.31	0.33	0.28	0.54	0.57	0.59	0.43	0.75	0.80	0.85	0.71	0.38	0.41	0.46	0.33
F III	0.20	0.25	0.28	0.14	0.33	0.40	0.43	0.25	0.60	0.65	0.72	0.40	0.83	0.86	0.90	0.75	0.40	0.44	0.48	0.35
Multi-F	0.33	0.39	0.46	0.27	0.38	0.42	0.46	0.37	0.70	0.73	0.83	0.60	0.88	0.90	0.92	0.88	0.42	0.48	0.53	0.42

From Table 3, we can observe that the Multi-F approach outperforms the baseline GPFL and all individual features in terms of Hits@3, Hits@5, Hits@10, and MRR metrics across all datasets. This demonstrates the effectiveness of integrating multiple features and assigning appropriate weights to improve the prediction performance of the model. These results strongly indicate that the integration of the proposed features, along with the optimized weight assignments, significantly enhances the prediction performance of the model. In conclusion, the experimental results clearly demonstrate the effectiveness of our proposed improvements. By integrating different dimension features and optimizing the weights assigned to them, our MDGRL approach can achieve the best prediction performance, outperforming the baseline GPFL and all individual features.

6   Conclusion

In this paper, we propose a novel Multi-Dimensional Graph Rule Learner (MDGRL) framework to enhance knowledge graph completion by leveraging the interpretability benefits of logical rules. By considering features from three different dimensions, including rules' set similarity, path transfer probability, and embedding distance, we significantly improve rule learning ability and prediction performance. The integration of features from multiple dimensions leads to a more robust and contextually relevant decision-making process in knowledge graph completion tasks. The detailed results show that our multi-feature learning approach surpasses the baseline and every individual feature, paving the way for future advancements in knowledge graph completion and AI applications.

Acknowledgment. This research was supported in part by the National Natural Science Foundation of China (Nos. 62002136 and 62272196), Natural Science Foundation of Guangdong Province (No. 2022A1515011861), Fundamental Research Funds for the Central Universities of Jinan University (No. 21622416), and the Young Scholar Program of Pazhou Lab (No. PZL2021KF0023).

References

1. Abu-Salih, B.: Domain-specific knowledge graphs: a survey. J. Netw. Comput. Appl. **185**, 103076 (2021)
2. Bodenreider, O.: The unified medical language system: integrating biomedical terminology. Nucleic Acids Res. **32**, 267–270 (2004)
3. Bordes, A., Usunier, N., Garcia-Duran, A., Weston, J., Yakhnenko, O.: Translating embeddings for modeling multi-relational data. In: Advances in Neural Information Processing Systems 26 (2013)
4. Dettmers, T., Pasumarthi, R.K., Bansal, K.: Convolutional 2D knowledge graph embeddings. In: Conference on Empirical Methods in Natural Language Processing, pp. 2071–2081 (2018)
5. Duan, Y., Shao, L., Hu, G., Zhou, Z., Zou, Q., Lin, Z.: Specifying architecture of knowledge graph with data graph, information graph, knowledge graph and wisdom graph. In: IEEE 15th International Conference on Software Engineering Research, Management and Applications, pp. 327–332. IEEE (2017)
6. Galárraga, L.A., Teflioudi, C., Hose, K., Suchanek, F.: AMIE: association rule mining under incomplete evidence in ontological knowledge bases. In: The 22nd International Conference on World Wide Web, pp. 413–422 (2013)
7. Gan, W., Lin, J.C.W., Chao, H.C., Zhan, J.: Data mining in distributed environment: a survey. Wiley Interdiscip. Rev. Data Min. Knowl. Discov. **7**(6), e1216 (2017)
8. Gu, Y., Guan, Y., Missier, P.: Towards learning instantiated logical rules from knowledge graphs. arXiv preprint arXiv:2003.06071 (2020)

9. Ji, G., He, S., Xu, L., Liu, K., Zhao, J.: Knowledge graph embedding via dynamic mapping matrix. In: The 7th International Joint Conference on Natural Language Processing, pp. 687–696 (2015)
10. Lao, N., Cohen, W.W.: Relational retrieval using a combination of path-constrained random walks. Mach. Learn. **81**, 53–67 (2010)
11. Lin, Y., Liu, Z., Luan, H., Sun, M., Rao, S., Liu, S.: Modeling relation paths for representation learning of knowledge bases. In: Conference on Empirical Methods in Natural Language Processing, pp. 705–714 (2015)
12. Lin, Y., Liu, Z., Sun, M., Liu, Y., Zhu, X.: Gated path ranking: learning to rank for knowledge graph completion. In: Conference on Empirical Methods in Natural Language Processing, pp. 1052–1058 (2015)
13. Lin, Z.Q., et al.: Intelligent development environment and software knowledge graph. J. Comput. Sci. Technol. **32**, 242–249 (2017)
14. Liu, J., Zhou, M., Fournier-Viger, P., Yang, M., Pan, L., Nouioua, M.: Discovering representative attribute-stars via minimum description length. In: IEEE 38th International Conference on Data Engineering, pp. 68–80. IEEE (2022)
15. Meilicke, C., Chekol, M.W., Ruffinelli, D., Stuckenschmidt, H.: Anytime bottom-up rule learning for knowledge graph completion. In: International Joint Conference on Artificial Intelligence, pp. 3137–3143 (2019)
16. Meilicke, C., Fink, M., Wang, Y., Ruffinelli, D., Gemulla, R., Stuckenschmidt, H.: Fine-grained evaluation of rule- and embedding-based systems for knowledge graph completion. In: Vrandečić, D., et al. (eds.) ISWC 2018. LNCS, vol. 11136, pp. 3–20. Springer, Cham (2018). https://doi.org/10.1007/978-3-030-00671-6_1
17. Oldman, D., Tanase, D.: Reshaping the knowledge graph by connecting researchers, data and practices in researchspace. In: Vrandečić, D., et al. (eds.) ISWC 2018. LNCS, vol. 11137, pp. 325–340. Springer, Cham (2018). https://doi.org/10.1007/978-3-030-00668-6_20
18. Sha, X., Sun, Z., Zhang, J.: Hierarchical attentive knowledge graph embedding for personalized recommendation. Electron. Commer. Res. Appl. **48**, 101071 (2021)
19. Toutanova, K., Chen, D., Pantel, P.: Representing text for joint embedding of text and knowledge bases. In: Conference on Empirical Methods in Natural Language Processing, pp. 1499–1509 (2015)
20. Trouillon, T., Welbl, J., Riedel, S., Gaussier, É., Bouchard, G.: Complex embeddings for simple link prediction. In: International Conference on Machine Learning, pp. 2071–2080. PMLR (2016)
21. Wang, Q., Mao, Z., Wang, B., Guo, L.: Knowledge graph embedding: a survey of approaches and applications. IEEE Trans. Knowl. Data Eng. **29**(12), 2724–2743 (2017)
22. Xiong, C., Power, R., Callan, J.: Explicit semantic ranking for academic search via knowledge graph embedding. In: The 26th International Conference on World Wide Web, pp. 1271–1279 (2017)
23. Xiong, W., Hoang, T., Wang, W.Y.: DeepPath: a reinforcement learning method for knowledge graph reasoning. In: Conference on Empirical Methods in Natural Language Processing, pp. 564–573 (2017)
24. Yang, Y., Hospedales, T.M.: Modeling relations and their mentions without labeled text. In: Conference on Empirical Methods in Natural Language Processing, pp. 1746–1751 (2015)
25. Zhang, W., Liu, P., Wang, T., Xue, M., Wang, G., Yang, X.: Embedding and predicting software security entity relationships: a knowledge graph based approach. In: The 35th Annual ACM Symposium on Applied Computing, pp. 1016–1023 (2020)

MixUNet: A Hybrid Retinal Vessels Segmentation Model Combining The Latest CNN and MLPs

Ziyan Ke[1], Lingxi Peng[2], Yiduan Chen[1(✉)], Jie Liu[2(✉)], Xuebing Luo[1], Jinhui Lin[1], and Zhiwen Yu[3]

[1] School of Mechanical and Electrical Engineering, Guangzhou University, Guangzhou 510006, China
ydchen@gzhu.edu.cn
[2] Experimental Center, Guangzhou University, Guangzhou 510006, China
manplx@163.com
[3] School of Computer Science and Engineering, SouthChina University of Technology, Guangzhou 510650, Guangdong, China

Abstract. The success of Vision Transformer has led to an increased emphasis on combining global and local context, and its high training cost spawned numerous alternative works. The latest MLP architecture has achieved excellent results as the alternative to Transformer, but the large number of parameters make it difficult to perform on segmentation independently. A U-shaped network MixUNet combining CNN and MLP is proposed to reduce the limitation among data samples by External AttentionMLP in the encoder and decoder, while adding a global context path based on Mix-Scale MLP to capture global information directly, and designing a Multi-scale Vision Attention Module containing multi-scale features and dynamic weights. The experimental validation on DRIVE and STARE shows that MixUNet can achieve better comprehensive performance compared with other medical image segmentation networks.

Keywords: Retinal vessels segmentation · Hybrid model · CNN · MLP

1 Introduction

The status of retinal vessels not only reflects various ophthalmic diseases, but also provides assistance in the diagnosis of cardiovascular and cerebrovascular disease [1]. With the rise in the number of related patients, manual observation alone is inefficient and subjective. Therefore, automatic detection of blood vessels in segmented fundus images by computer has important clinical significance. Some complete CNNs(convolutional neural networks) based on U-Net [2] achieved remarkable results in the field of image

The paper is supported by the Tertiary Education Scientific research project of Guangzhou Municipal Education Bureau under grant No. 202235165.
Z. Ke and L. Peng—Denotes the Co-first author,

processing [3]. However, due to the small receptive field, Transformer [4] is superior to traditional convolutions in capturing global context and long-range relations [5]. Therefore, there have been many works that combine CNN and Transformer [6, 7], enabling network structures to better integrate global and local features. These models have made progress in medical imaging tasks, but also have obvious drawbacks, such as the extensive training costs required for the training process. Therefore, some subsequent works focused on finding alternatives to Transformer [8], and MLP(Multi-Layer Perceptron) becoming the center of attention.

MLP consists of two or more FC(Fully-Connected) layers and is far superior to convolutions in capturing global information [5, 9]. However, the huge number of parameters and the easy overfitting make it difficult for MLP to be widely used in early work [5], until the emergence of MLP-Mixer [8]to make a breakthrough. MLP-Mixer divides the image into blocks and sends them into multiple Mixer Layers, which consists of token-mixing and channel-mixing. The former uses MLP to linearly map the flattened spatial dimensions, achieving spatial domain information fusion, while the latter uses MLP to linearly map the channel dimensions, promoting inter-channel information exchange. These two methods are alternately stacked to obtain global information. On the ImageNet, MLP-Mixer demonstrating the potential of the MLP-based architecture. Since then, various new MLPs have emerged.

Despite the impressive success of MLP-Mixer and other MLPs in image classification tasks, they are difficult to migrate to image segmentation tasks because the multilevel semantic feature generated by sufficient downsampling are crucial, but the coupling of the number of parameters to the image size leads to the huge size of pure MLP-based hierarchical architectures that are difficult to use [9].

To address the above situation, MixUNet, a hybrid U-shaped network of CNN and MLP, is proposed and experimentally validated it on two well-known fundus datasets. The results show that MixUNet has good performance in retinal blood vessels segmentation, outperforming U-Net and other mainstream hybrid medical image segmentation algorithms. The main contributions are as follows:

(1) EAMLP (External Attention MLP) [10] is added to the codec of the first three layers to enhance the correlation between data samples and improve the effect.
(2) We use MVAM (Multiscale Visual Attention Module) at the bottom of the encoder to capture multiscale information and introduce dynamic weights to address the segmentation difficulties caused by retinal vascular changes.
(3) A global token-mixing MiS MLP incorporating a pyramid strategy is proposed to improve network representation by combining GCP(Global Context Path) to capture global information of feature maps at different scales.

2   Method

Figure 1 shows the overall architecture of MixUNet, and we describe the architecture of the proposed MixUNet in detail in this section.

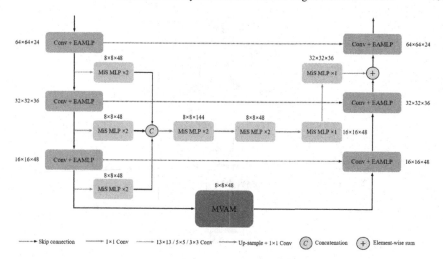

Fig. 1. Overall architecture of MixUNet

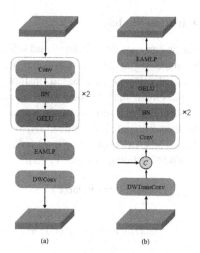

Fig. 2. Conv + EAMLP of (a)Encoder (b)Decoder

2.1 Encoder-Decoder

The encoder and decoder consist of convolution and EAMLP, as shown in Fig. 2. Convolution captures the gradient and underlying information of the image, facilitating accurate edge detection, and each convolution is followed by BN and GELU; An EAMLP is also added at the end of each layer to enhance the correlation between samples, which has a huge boost for learning features of the same scale across the dataset. In addition, dw-conv(depthwise convolution) and dw-transconv with step size 2 and kernel size 2×2 are used as downsampling and upsampling, respectively.

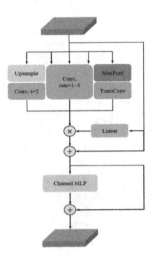

Fig. 3. Structure of MVAM

2.2 Mutil-scale Vision Attention Module

Multi-scale context information can capture rich detail and semantic information, which is a common strategy for image segmentation, while the attention mechanisms can be considered as an adaptive selection process based on input features, i.e., dynamic weights. Several studies have shown that the new type of attention for feature map element multiplication is as beneficial as traditional attention for improving the modeling ability of CNN models, and even more advantageous in terms of outputting key features [11]. For this reason we design MVAM shown in Fig. 3 to replace the fourth encoder. The spatial interaction of MVAM is shown in Eqs. (1)–(3):

$$\text{Attention=Linear}(F) \tag{1}$$

$$F_{new} = \sum_i^3 Conv_{3\times3,\, r=i}(F) + TransConv(MP(F)) + Conv_{3\times3,\, s=2}(UP(F)) \tag{2}$$

$$F_{out} = Conv_{3\times3}\left(\frac{Attention \otimes F_{new}}{d}\right) + F \tag{3}$$

MP and UP represent maxpooling and bilinear upsampling, $\otimes$ denotes element-wise multiplication. We manually add a factor d to prevent the features from being too large.

2.3 Mix-Scale MLP

MiS MLP adopts the permutation in ViP [12], but combines the three branches to perform feature projection in the C, H, and W dimensions of the feature maps, fully considering the interaction between dimensions. Specifically, it first performs a linear mapping on the channel dimension after the first LN (Layer Normalization), then divides the channel dimension into multiple segments and performs Height-Channel and Width-Channel

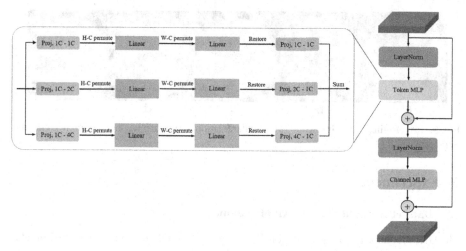

Fig. 4. Detailed architecture of MiS MLP

permutation accordingly i.e., combining the number of channel segments with the corresponding space dimensions. A FC layer is added after each permutation, so that the spatial information can be encoded from different spatial dimensions to obtain the global information of feature map. Considering that most MLP works have insufficient multiscale feature extraction [13], we introduce a pyramid strategy in the token mixing stage. The channel projecting is expanded by three different multiples, and due to the difference in channel numbers, the H-C and W-C permutations on each branch are different. This allows for feature extraction at different scales on the two dimensions, enhancing the multi-scale feature perception of MiS MLP. Finally, the feature maps of different scales are restored and added together, completing the spatial information fusion. Figure 4 shows the detail of MiS MLP.

2.4 Global Context Path

Considering the traditional U-Net architecture can only extract global information by stacking encoders, we add a GCP based on MiS MLP. It consists of three hierarchical encoders, an aggregation encoder and decoder. Hierarchical encoders use convolution of steps 4, 2, and 1 to resize the feature maps of each layer of the main encoder to the same size, respectively, and obtain the global semantic of each features maps by MiS MLPs, and then send them to the aggregation encoder after concatenate, which reduces the number of channels to 1/3 after 2 MiS MLPs, as the input feature decoding stage. The bilinear upsampling and MiS MLP blocks are used alternately in the decoder to obtain multi-level global features while recovering the size, and they are sent to the last layer of the main decoder to achieve the fusion of global and local information.

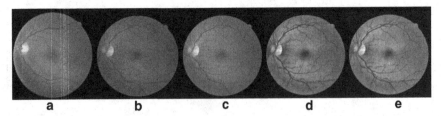

Fig. 5. (a) Original (b) Grayscale (c) Standardization (d) Adaptive histogram (e) Gamma transform

3 Experiment

3.1 Dataset Introduction and Amplification

The DRIVE dataset consists of 40 color training and test images of size 584 × 565 pixels, where both training and test images are equipped with manual vascular segmentation maps; The STARE dataset is a collection of 20 color retinal fundus images with an image size of 700 × 605, 10 of which contain lesions, and two different manual segmentation maps are available for each image. STARE use the first expert segmentation as the gold standard. Each original image is cropped into multiple 64 × 64 pixel image patches using a random interception and rotation. For DRIVE/START, 8000/13000 image patches are arbitrarily clipped from each training image.

To improve the segmentation effect, We use the method shown in Fig. 5 as the pre-processing, which are grayscale, standardization, adaptive histogram, gamma transform.

3.2 Experimental Environment

Adam optimizer is used to optimize the network, with learning rate of 0.001, the loss function is the cross-entropy, the number of iterations set to 50 and batch size is 32. We use AUC(Area Under Curve), F1(F1-Score), ACC(Accuracy), SE(Sensitivity), and SP(Specificity) as the evaluation metrics for network performance.

3.3 Experimental Results and Analysis

Ablation Experiments. To verify the validity of the three modules, five ablation experiments were performed on DRIVE. The improvements in each of the five evaluation metrics in Table 1 validate the effectiveness of each module.

Comparison Experiment of Different MLPs. From Table 2, it can be seen that MiS MLPs outperform some global dependencies MLPs in a certain extent. Meanwhile, it is found that global token-mixing MLPs can also perform the segmentation task through reasonable model construction.

Comparative Analysis of Different Algorithms. The results shown in Table 3 and the segmentation images are shown in Fig. 6, from left to right, for the original images, segmentation results of MixUNet, AFNet, UTNet and the gold standard, with the DRIVE in the first row and the STARE in the second row. These data and images show that

Table 1. Performance Analysis of Three Modules on the DRIVE dataset

Methods	AUC	F1	ACC	SE	SP
U-Net	0.9794	0.8209	0.9560	0.7927	0.9787
U-Net + EAMLP	0.9812	0.8252	0.9574	0.7877	**0.9823**
U-Net + MiS MLP	0.9812	0.8292	0.9571	**0.8177**	0.9775
U-Net + MVAM	0.9810	0.8262	0.9572	0.7984	0.9804
MixUNet	**0.9822**	**0.8309**	**0.9579**	0.8137	0.9789

Table 2. MixUNet performance of different MLPs on the DRIVE dataset

Mixing	Methods	AUC	F1	ACC	SE	SP
Global	MLP-Mixer [8]	0.9816	0.8245	0.9575	0.7839	**0.9829**
	Permute MLP [12]	0.9816	0.8248	0.9575	0.7865	0.9824
	MixUNet	**0.9822**	**0.8309**	**0.9579**	**0.8137**	0.9789
Local	AS-MLP [14]	0.9819	0.8289	0.9578	0.8032	0.9803
	S^2 MLP [15]	0.9815	0.8258	0.9575	0.7906	0.9819
	Hire MLP [16]	0.9813	0.8276	0.9572	0.8074	0.9790

MixUNet can successfully segment the missed fine vessels and details, demonstrating excellent retinal vessels segmentation performance.

Table 3. The results of different networks on DRIVE and STARE

Dataset	Methods	AUC	F1	ACC	SE	SP
DRIVE	U-Net [2]	0.9794	0.8209	0.9560	0.7927	0.9787
	AFNet [3]	0.9814	0.8287	0.9572	0.8134	0.9782
	UNet-2022 [6]	0.9811	0.8258	0.9568	0.8047	0.9790
	UTNet [7]	0.9814	0.8245	0.9575	0.7836	**0.9829**
	MixUNet	**0.9822**	**0.8309**	**0.9579**	**0.8137**	0.9789
STARE	U-Net	0.9858	0.8276	0.9668	0.8275	0.9816
	AFNet	0.9887	0.8362	0.9676	**0.8592**	0.9791
	UNet-2022	0.9893	0.8366	0.9689	0.8277	0.9839
	UTNet	0.9888	0.8396	0.9694	0.8324	0.9840
	MixUNet	**0.9895**	**0.8411**	**0.9697**	0.8331	**0.9843**

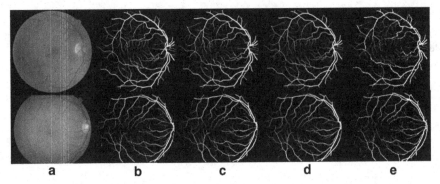

Fig. 6. (a) Original (b) MixUNet (c) AFNet (d) UTNet (e) Gold standard

4   Conclusion

In this paper, we propose MixUNet, a U-shaped hybrid network combining convolution, EAMLP and MiS MLP for retinal vessel segmentation. The MiS MLP is able to extract image global information in a multi-scale manner; we upgrade the convolutional attention based on the latest work, enabling MixUNet to obtain better representation capability. In the experimental analysis of two publicly datasets, MixUNet retains more subtle vascular features and outperforms the state-of-the-art CNN and hybrid structured medical image segmentation networks in evaluation metrics. In the future, we will apply the MixUNet on more medical image datasets to validate its scalability.

References

1. Cheung, C.Y., Ikram, M.K., Sabanayagam, C.: Retinal microvasculature as a model to study the manifestations of hypertension. Hypertension **60**(5), 1094–1103 (2012)
2. Ronneberger, O., Fischer, P., Brox, T.: U-Net: Convolutional Networks for Biomedical Image Segmentation. In: Navab, N., Hornegger, J., Wells, W.M., Frangi, A.F. (eds.) MICCAI 2015. LNCS, vol. 9351, pp. 234–241. Springer, Cham (2015). https://doi.org/10.1007/978-3-319-24574-4_28
3. Li, D., Peng, L., Peng, S., et al.: Retinal vessel segmentation by using AFNet. Vis Comput **39**, 1929–1941 (2022). https://doi.org/10.1007/s00371-022-02456-8
4. Vaswani, Ashish, et al.: Attention is all you need. Adv. Neural Inf. Process. Syst. **30,** (2017)
5. Zhao, Y., et al.: A battle of network structures: an empirical study of CNN, transformer, and MLP. arXiv preprint arXiv:2108.13002 (2021)
6. Guo, J., et al.: UNet-2022: Exploring dynamics in non-isomorphic architecture. arXiv preprint arXiv:2210.15566 (2022)
7. Gao, Y., Zhou, M., Metaxas, D.N.: UTNet: A Hybrid Transformer Architecture for Medical Image Segmentation. In: de Bruijne, M., et al. (eds.) MICCAI 2021. LNCS, vol. 12903, pp. 61–71. Springer, Cham (2021). https://doi.org/10.1007/978-3-030-87199-4_6
8. Tolstikhin, I., et al.: MLP-Mixer: an all-MLP architecture for vision. Adv. Neural Inf. Process. Syst. **34**, 24261–24272 (2021)
9. Ding, Xiaohan, et al. "Repmlpnet: hierarchical vision MLP with re-parameterized locality. In: Proceedings of the IEEE/CVF Conference on Computer Vision and Pattern Recognition (2022)

10. Guo, M.-H., Liu, Z.-N., Tai-Jiang, M., Shi-Min, H.: Beyond self-attention: external attention using two linear layers for visual tasks. IEEE Trans. Pattern Anal. Mach. Intell. **45**, 1–13 (2022)
11. Guo, Meng-Hao, et al.: Visual attention network. arXiv preprint arXiv:2202.09741 (2022)
12. Hou, Q., Jiang, Z., Yuan, L., Cheng, M.-M., Yan, S., Feng, J.: Vision permutator: a permutable MLP-like architecture for visual recognition. IEEE Trans. Pattern Anal. Mach. Intell. **45**(1), 1328–1334 (2023)
13. Zheng, H., et al.: Mixing and shifting: exploiting global and local dependencies in vision MLPs. arXiv preprint arXiv:2202.06510 (2022)
14. Lian, Dongze, et al.: As-mlp: an axial shifted MLP architecture for vision. arXiv preprint arXiv:2107.08391 (2021)
15. Yu, Tan, et al.: S ^{2}-MLPv2: improved spatial-shift MLP architecture for vision. arXiv preprint arXiv:2108.01072 (2021)
16. Guo, Jianyuan, et al.: Hire-mlp: vision MLP via hierarchical rearrangement. In: Proceedings of the IEEE/CVF Conference on Computer Vision and Pattern Recognition (2022)

Robust Few-Shot Graph Anomaly Detection via Graph Coarsening

Liting Li[1,2], Yueheng Sun[1,2], Tianpeng Li[1,2], and Minglai Shao[2,3(✉)]

[1] College of Intelligence and Computing, Tianjin University, Tianjin, China
{liliting,yhs,ltpnimeia}@tju.edu.cn
[2] Georgia Tech Shenzhen Institute, Tianjin University, Tianjin, China
shaoml@tju.edu.cn
[3] School of New Media and Communication, Tianjin University, Tianjin, China

Abstract. Graph anomaly detection is an important aspect of anomaly detection, especially the graph-level anomaly detection, which can be used into biomolecular research or drug molecular detection and so on. It is necessary to identify anomalies within a limited sample size as the real-world scenarios always lack of anomalous graph labels. Graph-level anomaly detection with few samples mainly faces the following problems: 1) There are not enough samples for the model to effectively learn anomalies; 2) There is noise or irrelevant information in the graph, which makes it difficult to quickly learn the key structural information of the graph. To address these issues, we propose a Robust Meta-learning-based Graph Anomaly Detection Framework via Graph Coarsening (RCM-GAD). Specifically, we employ meta-learning to effectively extract and integrate abnormal information from similar networks. Then, we use the Graph Coarsening module to obtain the key structural information of the graph for anomaly detection. We apply this framework to detect anomalies at both the graph-level and subgraph-level. We conduct experiments on four datasets, demonstrating the superiority of our proposed framework, RCM-GAD, over state-of-the-art baselines in graph-level and subgraph-level anomaly detection tasks.

Keywords: Few-shot learning · Graph-level anomaly detection · Subgraph-level anomaly detection · Graph Coarsening

1 Introduction

With rapid growth of the social network [26] and biomolecular research [12], graphs have become an increasingly popular means of representing data relationships in fields such as real networks, daily life, and social interactions. The occurrence of network intrusions, harmful molecular substances, social spam, and other issues have led to some graphs polluted, resulting in anomalous graphs or anomalous subgraphs. Consequently, research on graph-level anomaly detection has gained increasing attention.

Existing graph anomaly detection models [14–16] that employ deep learning often require a large number of labeled samples for training. In the real world,

Z. Jin et al. (Eds.): KSEM 2023, LNAI 14117, pp. 414–429, 2023.
https://doi.org/10.1007/978-3-031-40283-8_35

due to the high cost of manual labeling, limited intrusion account labeling information in social network databases, or constrained data samples in the early stages of drug and molecular research, few-shot anomaly detection research has received more and more attention. However, there is currently no work dedicated specifically to few-shot graph-level anomaly detection.

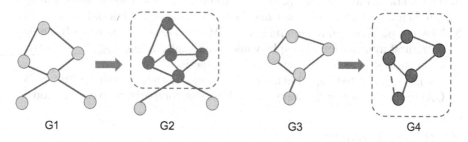

G1   G2   G3   G4

Fig. 1. An example of graph anomalies: G1 and G3 represent normal graphs. G2 is a partially polluted version of G1 with an abnormal subgraph present. Compared to G3, G4 exhibits both abnormal structure and node attributes, rendering the entire graph anomalous.

Moreover, noise is inevitable in graph data, as is the presence of structural information that is irrelevant to the anomaly detection task. While the graph aggregation operation leverages the information from all nodes in the graph, it can be affected by random noise or invalid structural information, leading to poor model robustness. Consequently, it is essential to continue exploring the field of few-shot graph anomaly detection and consider addressing the interference of noise and irrelevant structures in model design.

Conducting this work presents the following challenges: (1) How to use only a limited number of samples to train an effective detection model? (2) How to eliminate data noise in the graph or the information that is not relevant for a specific task, to accurately obtain the effective information of the graph?

To address the aforementioned challenges, we propose a new framework Robust Meta-learning-based Graph Anomaly Detection Framework via Graph Coarsening, called RCM-GAD. Specifically, meta-learning - a "learn to learn" method - has demonstrated impressive performance on few-shot tasks by training a general learning algorithm that can be applied across different tasks through the correlation of information in similar networks. This approach results in a well-generalized initialized network, which can achieve good performance with only a small amount of data when applied to new learning tasks. To address the noise issue, we employ the coarsening method based on spectral graph theory to reduce the graph's dimensionality and merge nodes that are highly related in structure. With theoretical guarantees, this approach can extract key structural information from the graph and provide effective information for the meta-network.

We conduct experiments on two specific tasks: graph-level anomaly detection and subgraph-level anomaly detection (Two kinds of anomaly are shown in Fig. 1). Our experimental results demonstrate that our model outperforms previous state-of-the-art models in few-shot graph-level anomaly detection, and achieves a high accuracy.

Our main contributions in this paper can be summarized as follows:

1. We implements a few-shot graph-level anomaly detection framework (RCM-GAD), which is the first work in this area.
2. The Meta module in the RCM-GAD framework has cross-network learning capabilities, which can extract and fuse cross-network abnormal information.
3. The Graph Coarsening module in RCM-GAD framework can obtain key structural information of graphs while significantly improving the robustness of our model, which has been proved in practice.
4. We have conducted experiments on four datasets to demonstrate that RCM-GAD achieves better accuracy and robustness compared to baseline models.

2   Related Work

2.1   Graph Anomaly Detection

Graph anomaly detection has gained increasing attention in recent years, as the development of deep learning and GNN has greatly improved the ability of graph learning. However, research on graph anomaly detection mainly focuses on node anomaly detection [4,21]. There is relatively less research on graph-level anomaly detection. Graph-level anomaly detection can be mainly divided into two categories: subgraph-level anomaly detection and graph-level anomaly detection. Subgraph-level anomaly detection focuses on local anomalous structures within graphs. FRAUDAR [11] searches for tightly coupled sub-networks, providing provable limits for undetectable fraud. DeepFD [20], designed for fraud detection, discovers suspiciously dense blocks in attribute bipartite graphs. AS-GAE [28] is an unsupervised and weakly supervised deep sub-network graph anomaly detection network, which develops a position-aware autoencoder and uncovers abnormal subgraphs in the graph through graph reconstruction. Du et al. [5] represents the e-commerce network as a heterogeneous information graph, performing multi-view clustering to detect anomalous users within the network.

Graph-level anomaly detection concentrates on the abnormal behavior of the entire graph. GLocalKD [15] takes into account both global and local abnormal information through knowledge distillation. GLAD [14] uses contrastive learning to reconstruct the graph through graph convolutional autoencoders, obtaining abnormal information from different levels and capturing graph anomalies. The iGAD [27] perceives both substructures and attributes in the graph at the same time and uses point mutual information (PMI) to solve the problem of distribution imbalance.

Although the above studies have made significant progress in graph anomaly detection, they do not address the problems we raised very well when dealing with small samples. Currently, there is no graph-level anomaly detection method specifically designed for small-sample scenarios.

2.2   Meta-Learning on Graphs

Meta-learning [6] is a method that distills knowledge from multiple learning processes, which can be used to develop general learning algorithms for different tasks. The goal of meta-learning is to train a model on various learning tasks so that it can solve new learning tasks using only a small number of training samples while ensuring good performance on each new learned task. This "learning to learn" approach has advantages such as data and computational efficiency and is akin to lifelong learning in human society.

In the graph field, meta-learning has become an important research direction. The current research in the direction of deep learning can be divided into two categories. One is to use meta-learning to simultaneously optimize graph structures and CNN parameters. Franceschi et al. [7] simultaneously learns graphs and GNN parameters for semi-supervised classification; Zügner et al. [30] improve the overall classification performance of the model through adversarial attacks, and take into account the bilevel optimization problem. Another way to learn a good initialization model through meta-learning. MetaR [1] and Xiong et al. [24] study knowledge map prediction; X-FNC [22], Cheng et al. [2], GFL [25] and Meta-GNN [29] research node classification tasks. Meta-learning has significant advantages in addressing graph-related problems.

Although meta-learning has achieved some success in the field of graph representation learning, its application to graph anomaly detection tasks remains understudied, particularly in few-shot scenarios. For few-shot node anomaly detection, Meta-GDN [4], GLITTER [21] and Guo et al. [8] utilize cross-network knowledge to improve anomaly detection performance. However, there is currently no research that combines meta-learning with few-shot graph-level anomaly detection. Thus, exploring how to apply meta-learning to few-shot graph-level anomaly detection has important theoretical and practical value.

3   Framework

In this section, we introduce our RCM-GAD framework. The RCM-GAD framework is illustrated in Fig. 2. The key structure and information in the graph are captured through Graph Coarsening. Then, prior knowledge about anomalies is obtained from the relevant domain of the target network, and this valuable prior knowledge is used to learn an initialization model with high generalization capabilities.

By implementing a fine-tuning process on the target network, we can get a effective anomaly detection model. This compensates for shortcomings stemming from limited sample sizes, enhancing the anomaly detection performance, and demonstrating robustness against perturbations.

3.1   Problem Definition

We investigate a framework for few-shot graph-level anomaly detection. A graph dataset comprising m graphs can be denoted as $\mathcal{G} = \{G_1, G_2, \cdots, G_m\}$, where

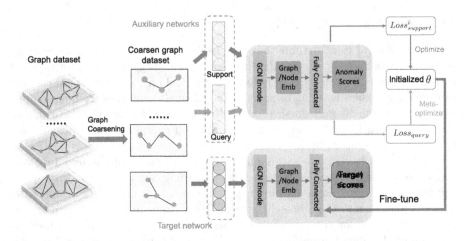

Fig. 2. The overall framework of RCM-GAD. First, we employ the Graph Coarsening module to coarsen the graphs in the graph collection. Then, we divide the dataset to create auxiliary networks and a target network, and further partition the support and query sets within the auxiliary networks. These sets are used as input for the model, and we obtain embeddings through GCN. Next, a fully connected layer is utilized to learn the anomaly scores and compute the loss, followed by meta-optimization on the loss. After training the initial value of θ and performing fine-tuning, we finally obtain the anomaly scores for the target network.

$G_i = (V_i, \varepsilon_i, X_i)$ represents an attributed network, $V_i = \{v_1, v_2, \cdots, v_N\}$ signifies the node set, $\varepsilon_i = \{e_1, e_2, \cdots, e_N\}$ indicates the edge set and $X_i = \{x_1, x_2, \cdots, x_N\}$ denotes node attributes. G_i can also be expressed as $G_i = (A_i, X_i)$, where A_i is an adjacency matrix. In graph G_i, if $A_i(u, j) = 1$, there's an edge between node v_u and node v_j; if $A_i(u, j) = 0$, there's no edge. A_i does not consider self-loop; that is, $A_i(u, u) = 0$.

Our objective is to learn an anomaly detection framework that is able to leverage the ground truth anomaly knowledge from multiple auxiliary networks, specifically $\{\mathcal{G}_1^A, \mathcal{G}_2^A, \cdots, \mathcal{G}_k^A\}$. For each $\mathcal{G}_i^A = (G_1, G_2, \cdots, G_p)$, where p < n, and $\mathcal{G}_i^A$ is a subset of $\mathcal{G}$, the framework aims to detect anomalous graphs or subgraphs in the target network $\mathcal{G}^T$ $(\mathcal{G}^T \subset \mathcal{G})$. We detect abnormal graphs or subgraphs by assigning scores to them.

3.2 Graph Embedding with Graph Coarsening

In few-shot learning, it is crucial to efficiently extract key information from graphs. Our objective is to simplify the graph structure while preserving its essential properties. To achieve this, we employ Graph Coarsening techniques to reduce graph size without significantly altering their fundamental attributes. Graph Coarsening is an interpretable scaling operation that allows the construction of coarse graphs that capture the global problem structure.

Firstly, we utilize the local variational method to construct the contraction set. Various local variational algorithms consider different criteria when constructing the contraction set. We adopt multi-level coarsening, adopt edge-based variant [13] in each level, and construct the edge set as a contraction set based on the edge-based local variation algorithm. For the coarsening of layer l, we first construct a contraction set $\mathcal{V}_{l-1}$ as follows:

$$\mathcal{V}_{l-1} = \left\{ \mathcal{V}_{l-1}^{(1)}, \mathcal{V}_{l-1}^{(2)}, \cdots, \mathcal{V}_{l-1}^{(p)} \right\}, \text{ where } \mathcal{V}_{l-1}^{(i)} = \{ v \in \mathcal{V}_{l-1} : \phi_l(v) \} \tag{1}$$

where $\phi_l(v)$ represents the constraint on the contraction set, signifying that the subgraph coarsened by the contraction set $\mathcal{V}_{l-1}^{(i)}$ must be a connected graph. This is a subjective map.

In general, the contraction set must satisfy two requirements: (1) Full mapping, meaning that all nodes at the upper level have and only have one $\mathcal{V}_{l-1}^{(i)}$ corresponds to it. The contraction set divides the upper-level nodes into N subgraphs, with each subgraph corresponding to a single node at this level of nodes; (2) The nodes within the same $\mathcal{V}_{l-1}^{(i)}$ are connected to each other. Then, the coarsening matrix $C_l(i, k)$ at level l can be computed using the contraction set $\mathcal{V}_{l-1}$:

$$C_l(i, k) = \begin{cases} \frac{1}{|\mathcal{V}_{l-1}^{(i)}|} & \text{if } v_k \in \mathcal{V}_{l-1}^{(i)} \\ 0 & \text{otherwise} \end{cases} \text{ and } \left[C_l^+ \right](k, i) = \begin{cases} 1 & \text{if } v_k \in \mathcal{V}_{l-1}^{(i)} \\ 0 & \text{otherwise} \end{cases} \tag{2}$$

where $C_l(i, k) \in \mathbb{R}^{N_l \times N_{l-1}}$, and $\left[C_l^+ \right](k, i)$ represents the pseudo-inverse matrix of $C_l(i, k)$.

We can represent a graph G by the Laplacian operator as follows:

$$Laplac_0(i, j) = \begin{cases} d_i & \text{if } i = j \\ -w_{ij} & \text{if } e_{ij} \in \varepsilon \\ 0 & \text{otherwise} \end{cases} \tag{3}$$

where w_{ij} is the weight of edge e_{ij} and d_i is the weighted degree of v_i.

Then, for a graph G represented by $Laplac_0$, we can perform coarsening as follows:

$$Laplac_l = C_l^{\mp} Laplac_{l-1} C_l^+ \tag{4}$$

where $C_l^{\mp}$ is the transposed pseudoinverse matrix of C_l.

According to our definition of the graph, we can obtain the adjacency matrix A_l of the coarsened graph G_l by removing the diagonal values of $Laplac_l$ and taking their absolute values. For the coarsened label y_l and coarsened feature X_l of the graph, this method can also be applied to compute them.

For each $G_i = (A_i, X_i)$, we implement multi-level coarsening, initially converting it to $Laplac_0$, followed by utilizing Eq. (4). We can get

$$G_0 = (A_0, X_0), G_1 = (A_1, X_1), \cdots G_l = (A_l, X_l) \tag{5}$$

where the size of these graphs $N = N_0 > N_1 > \cdots > N_l = n$, and the coarsening ratio is $r = 1 - \frac{n}{N}$.

After obtaining each coarsened graph G_l. We utilize graph convolutional networks (GCNs), which exploit graph structure information and node features to learn vector representations of nodes. In this study, a two-layer GCN algorithm is implemented, as described below:

$$h^1 = f^1_{GCN}(A_l, X_l),$$
$$z_v = f^2_{GCN}(A_l, h^1) \tag{6}$$

where z_v represents the node representation, and f^i_{GCN} represents the i-th GCN layer. Considering that the complexity inherited from neural networks in GCN may not be necessary, we employ two layers of SGC [23] (Simple Graph Convolution) to construct a node encoder on the coarsening set.

We utilize the readout layer to aggregate node representations, thereby obtaining the feature representation of the entire graph, as follows:

$$z_G = F_{readout}\{z_v, v \in V_l\} \tag{7}$$

where, $F_{readout}$ represents the node aggregation function, which can encompass different operations such as averaging, maximum, and others.

3.3 Loss Function

Input the embedding into the abnormal evaluation module to obtain the abnormal score:

$$s_i = W_2(\sigma(W_1 z_i + b_1)) + b_2 \tag{8}$$

where W_1 and W_2 represent the weights of the hidden layer and the output layer, respectively, while b_1 and b_2 denote bias terms. The activation function is represented by σ. In this study, we employ the ReLU (Rectified Linear Unit) activation function.

We use Deviation Loss [18] to construct loss. It can increase the difference between normal and abnormal nodes by enforcing a greater distance between them. We assume that the distribution of q anomaly scores follows a Gaussian distribution, denoted by $s_1, s_2, \ldots, s_q \sim N(\mu, \sigma^2)$.

To compute the mean of this Gaussian distribution, we calculate the average of all the scores as follows:

$$\mu = \frac{1}{q}\sum_{i=1}^{q} s_i \tag{9}$$

We define the loss function as:

$$Loss = (1 - y_i) \cdot |dev(v_i)| + y_i \cdot max(0, m - dev(v_i)) \tag{10}$$

where $dev(v_i) = \frac{s_i - \mu}{\sigma}$ represents the deviation between the reference score and the normal score. For graph-level anomaly detection, y_i denotes the ground truth label for each graph. In the case of subgraph-level anomaly detection, y_i represents the ground truth label of each node within the coarsened graph, and m stands for the confidence range.

3.4   Meta-Learning for Networks

The meta-learning component of our approach employs the MAML [6] (Model-Agnostic Meta-Learning) algorithm. Our objective is to train a set of initialization parameters that allow for rapid convergence with only a small amount of data.

For the auxiliary graph set, we perform optimization through a two-stage gradient descent process, dividing each auxiliary graph set into a support set and a query set. Initially, a batch is constructed from the support set, comprising data from each auxiliary graph set. During each training process, a batch is sampled, the data goes through forward propagation, and the θ parameter is updated. This process corresponds to the inner loop:

$$\theta_i' = \theta_i - \alpha \nabla_{\theta_i} Loss_{support}^i \tag{11}$$

where α is step size, and $Loss_{support}^i$ represents the loss on the support set calculated by Eq. (10).

Then we perform forward propagation on the query set. Sum the calculated losses, and apply gradient descent to update the weight of θ. This process corresponds to the outer loop:

$$\theta \leftarrow \theta - \beta \nabla_{\theta_i} \sum_{i=1}^{k} Loss_{query} \tag{12}$$

where β is meta step size, and $Loss_{query}$ represents the loss on the query set calculated by Eq. (10).

Given that the MAML model necessitates second-order derivatives during training, substantial computational overhead can arise. Therefore, we also employ Reptile [17], which simplifies the parameter update approach. It uses $\theta^0 - \theta'$ as the gradient for updating the parameters, and avoids calculating the loss gradient in the outer loop process.

After training the initialization model, we only need to perform a simple fine-tuning to obtain the anomaly detection model for the target network set and the anomaly scores of the graphs in the target network set.

3.5   Anomaly Detection Using RCM-GAD

In this section, we apply the proposed framework to specific anomaly detection tasks. Taking graph-level anomaly detection and subgraph-level anomaly detection as examples, we provide concrete algorithms for these two tasks.

Graph-Level Anomaly Detection. Given a graph set $\mathcal{G} = \{G_1, G_2, \cdots, G_n\}$, our goal is to identify graphs that deviate from normal graphs due to attributes, graph structures, or partial graph contamination. For each graph G_i, if the corresponding ground truth is 1, it indicates an anomalous graph, whereas a ground truth of 0 signifies a normal graph.

Subgraph-Level Anomaly Detection. Given a graph set $\mathcal{G} = \{G_1, G_2, \cdots, G_n\}$, the objective is to identify all abnormal blocks or nodes within the target graph set. These abnormal blocks appear as nodes in the coarsened, low-dimensional graph space. For each coarsened node v_i in V_l, if the corresponding ground truth is 1, it indicates an abnormal block, whereas a ground truth of 0 signifies a normal block.

4   Experiments and Results

We evaluate the efficacy of our framework through experiments, addressing the following research questions:

- Q1: How effective is RCM-GAD on graph-level anomaly detection?
- Q2: How effective is RCM-GAD on subgraph-level anomaly detection?
- Q3: Is each component of RCM-GAD effective?
- Q4: Can the Graph Coarsening module extract the key information in the graph, and is the coarsened graph consistent with the original graph?

4.1   Experimental Setup

Dataset. In this experiment, we select four public datasets to test the effectiveness of the proposed RCM-GAD framework (shown in Table 1). For graphs without attribute information, we construct identity matrices as features of nodes. The information on the four graph-level anomaly datasets is as follows:

- **MUTAG** [3]. A widely-used molecular graph dataset consisting of 188 compound samples, which include basic graphs and mutant base graphs.
- **AIDS** [19]. A dataset of compounds targeting HIV, constructed based on their antiviral activity against AIDS.
- **PTC-FM** [10] and **PTC-MM** [10]. These datasets consist of carcinogenically labeled compound collections for female mice and male mice, respectively. The datasets include two types of compounds: carcinogenic and non-carcinogenic.

Baselines. We compare RCM-GAD with two types of anomaly detection baselines. The details of these baselines are as follows:

(1) Graph-level anomaly detection algorithms.
- **GLocalKD** [15]. This approach introduces knowledge distillation to combine global and local information for the detection of anomalous graphs.
- **GLAD** [14]. This method employs contrastive learning to increase the distance between normal and abnormal graphs, and utilizes graph convolutional autoencoders to obtain abnormal information at different levels.
- **iGAD** [27]. This technique simultaneously perceives substructure and attribute information in graphs, and addresses distribution imbalance using PMI.

(2) Subgraph-level anomaly detection algorithms.
- **GraphSAGE** [9]. A graph representation learning method based on graph neural networks that randomly samples neighbors and aggregates embeddings of neighbor nodes through multi-layer aggregation functions to obtain node representations. This method is applied for subgraph-level anomaly detection tasks.
- **AS-GAE** [28]. An unsupervised subgraph-level anomaly detection model that combines local subgraph features with global network information to identify anomalous subgraphs. It measures the similarity between subgraphs through a graph autoencoder.

Table 1. Statistics for Graph Anomaly Dataset.

Dataset	#Graph	#Node	#Edge	#Anomaly Ratio
AIDS	2000	31385	64780	0.2
MUTAG	188	3371	7442	0.335
PTC-FM	349	4925	10110	0.41
PTC-MM	336	4695	9624	0.384

Evaluation Metric. In this study, we employ AUC-ROC (Area Under the Receiver Operating Characteristic Curve) to evaluate the performance of our anomaly detection model. AUC-ROC is defined as the area under the ROC curve, with a value closer to 1.0 indicating better performance. This metric has also been utilized in previous anomaly detection research.

In addition, we borrow from Loukas [13] restricted spectral approximation method, and use a coarse similarity metric ϵ to define the closeness of $Laplac_l$ and $Laplac$. We construct the isometry guarantee (i.e., induced semi-norms):

$$\|x\|_{Laplac} = \sqrt{x^\top Laplac x} \quad \text{and} \quad \|x_c\|_{Laplac_l} = \sqrt{x_c^\top Laplac_l x_c} \quad (13)$$

for all $x \in \mathbb{R}^N$.

For R is a k-dimensional subspace of $\mathbb{R}^N$, if $Laplac_l$ and $Laplac$ are similar, then there is a $\epsilon >= 0$ such that:

$$\|x - \tilde{x}\|_{Laplac} \le \epsilon \|x\|_{Laplac} \quad for \ all \quad x \in \mathbf{R}, \quad (14)$$

where $\tilde{x} = C^+ C x$. In particular, when $\epsilon < 1$, we consider the graphs before and after coarsening to be highly similar.

Implementation Details. We configure the auxiliary networks to include four networks, with the query set and support set each comprising 50% of the data. For the target networks, we allocate one network with the following distribution: 40% for the training set, 20% for the validation set, and 40% for the test set. In Eq. (7), we use the average operation to denote $F_{readout}$, which is

$z_G = \frac{1}{|V|} \sum_{v \in V_l} z_v$. In Eq. (8), the hidden layer consists of 512 units, and the output layer contains 1 unit. We set the confidence bound (i.e., m) in Eq. (10) to 5.

In the node encoding section, we utilize the SGC [23] method to learn node representations. For the meta-learning component, we employ two models MAML [6] and Reptile [17], denoted as RCM-GAD and ReRCM-GAD respectively, and record their experimental outcomes.

During model training, RCM-GAD undergoes 100 epochs with a batch size of 8 per epoch. In meta-training, we set the inner loop learning rate (i.e., α) to 0.01, the outer loop learning rate (i.e., β) to 0.008, and compute θ' using a 5-step gradient update for meta-optimization. In the fine-tuning process, we update the model on the training data for 15 steps. For the baseline, we run it on the dataset, select the best-performing hyperparameters, and document the experimental results. To account for potential performance degradation due to random data selection, we repeated 30 times on RCM-GAD and baseline, and averaged the results as the final experimental results.

4.2   Graph-Level Anomaly Detection

The experimental results for graph anomaly detection are shown in Table 2. We observe that our method RCM-GAD achieves state-of-the-art performance on most datasets, indicating that it can effectively detect anomalistic graphs in graph sets. Regarding the baseline experimental results, we provide the following analysis: 1) GLocalKD performs poorly on the some datasets. A possible reason is that this method relies on knowledge distillation to learn abnormal graph features, and limited data may hinder its ability to fully learn abnormal knowledge. 2) GLAD, which uses contrastive learning to capture abnormal graphs, may suffer from reduced performance under small sample conditions, as contrastive learning requires a large number of samples for training. 3) The structures of the three models are relatively complex, and underfitting might occur in the case of limited data, which could be one reason for their poor experimental performance.

Table 2. Result for Graph-level Anomaly Detection.

Model	AIDS	MUTAG	PTC-FM	PTC-MM
iGAD	0.625	0.8000	0.4750	0.6375
GlocalKD	0.1333	0.2000	0.4833	0.5916
GLADC	**1.0000**	0.8333	0.5666	0.4000
RCM-GAD w/o Meta	0.9667	0.6833	0.5667	0.5250
RCM-GAD w/o Coarsening	0.9333	0.9200	0.6167	0.5000
RCM-GAD	0.9833	0.9333	0.5667	**0.6417**
ReRCM-GAD	0.9500	**1.0000**	**0.7000**	0.5250

4.3 Subgraph-Level Anomaly Detection

Comparing our model, RCM-GAD, with the baseline methods for subgraph-level anomaly detection, the results are shown in Table 3. Our method achieves state-of-the-art accuracy on most datasets. We attempt to analyze the experimental results: 1) Our method outperforms the baseline models in detecting abnormal blocks within graph collections. 2) The AS-GAE method is an unsupervised approach that primarily relies on a large amount of data to learn the internal structure and distribution of the data. When the data is scarce, it is challenging to fully capture the underlying anomalistic patterns. 3) GraphSAGE, as a supervised method, performs better. However, since it randomly samples neighbor nodes when learning node representations, it may struggle to identify abnormal information. 4) Similarly, the structures of both models might underfit when the amount of data is small, affecting their performance in subgraph-level anomaly detection.

Table 3. Result for Subgraph-level Anomaly Detection.

Model	AIDS	MUTAG	PTC-FM	PTC-MM
AS-GAE	0.4812	0.5350	0.5060	0.5140
GraphSAGE	0.7736	0.9541	0.9571	**0.9570**
RCM-GAD w/o Meta	0.8440	0.7516	0.6891	0.7742
RCM-GAD w/o Coarsening	0.8553	0.8213	0.9217	0.8282
RCM-GAD	**0.9005**	0.9073	**0.9701**	0.8317
ReRCM-GAD	0.8652	**0.9585**	0.9057	0.8427

4.4 Ablation Experiments

We conduct ablation experiments to investigate the effectiveness of each component in RCM-GAD. By removing or replacing individual components and comparing the performance of the modified models to the original RCM-GAD, we can assess the contribution of each component to the framework's overall performance. Specifically, we propose two variants: RCM-GAD w/o Meta and RCM-GAD w/o Coarsening. RCM-GAD w/o Meta does not learn cross-network knowledge. RCM-GAD w/o Coarsening does not use the Graph Coarsening module, instead it employs GCN to learn the node representation, and then directly obtains the graph representation through the readout module.

The ablation experiment results for graph-level anomaly detection are shown in Table 2, and the ablation experiment results for subgraph-level anomaly detection are shown in Table 3. The following results are observed: (1) The RCM-GAD model outperforms the two variants, indicating that each component of our RCM-GAD plays a key role. (2) Both RCM-GAD w/o Meta and RCM-GAD w/o Coarsening can effectively complete the task of graph-level anomaly detection, but the performance of RCM-GAD w/o Meta drops more noticeably, revealing that the Meta module plays a more important role in graph-level anomaly detection.

4.5 Effectiveness of Graph Coarsening Module

Taking the application of graph-level anomaly detection as an example, we use a case study to illustrate the effectiveness of Graph Coarsening module.

Robustness Analysis. We selected a graph randomly from the MUTAG dataset, and applied coarsening to it with the coarsening ratio $r = 0.6$. We recorded the results of each layer of coarsening, as illustrated in Fig. 3(1). The graph underwent two rounds of coarsening, which reduced the number of nodes from 17 to 7. Next, we apply a perturbation to the graph to alter its structure and perform two coarsening operations, as demonstrated in Fig. 3(2). We can observe that, although the model graphs before coarsening are different, the coarsened graphs obtained after coarsening are consistent. This demonstrates that coarsening can effectively handle high-frequency disturbances (in spectral graph theory, high-frequency disturbances refer to noise in the network or components that have little impact on the key structure), resulting in the robust extraction of the graph's key structural features.

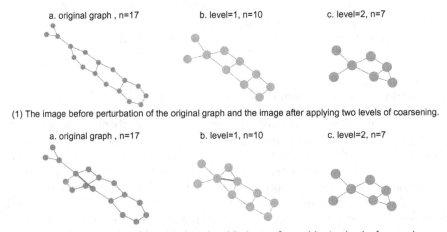

(1) The image before perturbation of the original graph and the image after applying two levels of coarsening.

(2) The image after perturbation of the original graph and the image after applying two levels of coarsening.

Fig. 3. The Graph Coarsening effect image of the graph before and after the disturbance, where a represents the original graph, b illustrates the effect after the first layer of coarsening, and c depicts the effect after the second layer of coarsening.

Simultaneously, we input the pre-perturbation and post-perturbation images into the baseline GLADC and our RCM-GAD model, with the results displayed in the Table 4. The ground truth label for this graph is 0. GLADC's prediction for this graph changes before and after the perturbation, while RCM-GAD's prediction remains consistent. This demonstrates the robustness of the RCM-GAD model in handling graph perturbations.

Similarity Analysis. We analyze the structural similarity between the coarsened graph and the original graph. Taking the previously sampled graph and the perturbed graph as examples (denoted as sample1 and sample2), after two layers of coarsening, we calculate the smallest ϵ that satisfies Eq. (14). The results obtained are shown in Table 5.

Table 4. We perturb the sample graph and input both pre-disturbance and post-disturbance graphs into the GLADC and RCM-GAD models. The results are recorded in the table below, noting that the ground truth value for this graph is 0.

Input	GLADC	RCM-GAD
pre-disturbance graph	0	0
post-disturbance graph	1	0

Table 5. We select two samples (sample1 and sample2, along with their corresponding coarsened graphs) to evaluate the coarsening similarity. This involves calculating the minimum ϵ that satisfies Eq. (14). When $\epsilon < 1$, it indicates that the two graphs exhibit strong similarity before and after coarsening.

Metric	sample1	sample2
ϵ	0.8998	0.6756

It can be observed that, regardless of whether it is before or after perturbation, the similarity between the graphs before and after coarsening remains very high.

To sum up, the Graph Coarsening module can effectively extract the key structure of the graph, and can overcome some small perturbations, and has good robustness.

5   Conclusion

In this paper, we investigate the issue of noisy few-shot graph-level anomaly detection. We proposed the RCM-GAD framework, in which the Meta module can extract and fuse cross-network information well, and the Graph Coarsening module efficiently and stably extracts key abnormal information in the graph. We conduct experiments on two specific tasks of graph-level anomaly detection and subgraph-level anomaly detection, and demonstrate that our RCM-GAD framework outperforms state-of-the-art methods.

In the future, we will continue to explore this field. On the one hand, we will use spectral theory to provide theoretical proof for the coarsening part. On the other hand, we will investigate improvements to the Meta module. Existing meta-learning methods are mostly designed for images or audio data, which are relatively easy to collect cross-domain knowledge. We aim to further develop meta-learning methods that are more suitable for graph structures.

Acknowledgement. This work is supported by the Project of Shenzhen Higher Education Stability Support Program (No.20220618160306001) and NSFC program (No. 62272338).

References

1. Chen, M., Zhang, W., Zhang, W., Chen, Q., Chen, H.: Meta relational learning for few-shot link prediction in knowledge graphs. arXiv preprint arXiv:1909.01515 (2019)
2. Cheng, H., Zhou, J.T., Tay, W.P., Wen, B.: Graph neural networks with triple attention for few-shot learning. IEEE Transactions on Multimedia (2023)
3. Debnath, A.K., de Compadre, R.L.L., Debnath, G., Shusterman, A.J., Hansch, C.: Structure-activity relationship of mutagenic aromatic and heteroaromatic nitro compounds. correlation with molecular orbital energies and hydrophobicity. J. Med. Chemis. **34**(2), 786–797 (1991)
4. Ding, K., Zhou, Q., Tong, H., Liu, H.: Few-shot network anomaly detection via cross-network meta-learning. In: Proceedings of the Web Conference 2021, pp. 2448–2456 (2021)
5. Du, H., Li, D., Wang, W.: Abnormal user detection via multiview graph clustering in the mobile e-commerce network. Wireless Communications and Mobile Computing 2022 (2022)
6. Finn, C., Abbeel, P., Levine, S.: Model-agnostic meta-learning for fast adaptation of deep networks. In: International Conference on Machine Learning, pp. 1126–1135. PMLR (2017)
7. Franceschi, L., Niepert, M., Pontil, M., He, X.: Learning discrete structures for graph neural networks. In: International Conference on Machine Learning, pp. 1972–1982. PMLR (2019)
8. Guo, Q., Zhao, X., Fang, Y., Yang, S., Lin, X., Ouyang, D.: Learning hypersphere for few-shot anomaly detection on attributed networks. In: Proceedings of the 31st ACM International Conference on Information & Knowledge Management, pp. 635–645 (2022)
9. Hamilton, W., Ying, Z., Leskovec, J.: Inductive representation learning on large graphs. In: Advances in Neural Information Processing Systems 30 (2017)
10. Helma, C., King, R.D., Kramer, S., Srinivasan, A.: The Predictive Toxicology Challenge 2000-2001. Bioinformatics **17**(1), 107–108 (2001). https://doi.org/10.1093/bioinformatics/17.1.107. http://bioinformatics.oxfordjournals.org/cgi/doi/10.1093/bioinformatics/17.1.107
11. Hooi, B., Song, H.A., Beutel, A., Shah, N., Shin, K., Faloutsos, C.: FRAUDAR: bounding graph fraud in the face of camouflage. In: Proceedings of the 22nd ACM SIGKDD International Conference on Knowledge Discovery and Data Mining, pp. 895–904 (2016)

12. Lee, C.Y., Chen, Y.P.P.: Descriptive prediction of drug side-effects using a hybrid deep learning model. Int. J. Intell. Syst. **36**(6), 2491–2510 (2021)
13. Loukas, A.: Graph reduction with spectral and cut guarantees. J. Mach. Learn. Res. **20**(116), 1–42 (2019)
14. Luo, X., et al.: Deep graph level anomaly detection with contrastive learning. Sci. Rep. **12**(1), 19867 (2022)
15. Ma, R., Pang, G., Chen, L., van den Hengel, A.: Deep graph-level anomaly detection by glocal knowledge distillation. In: Proceedings of the Fifteenth ACM International Conference on Web Search and Data Mining, pp. 704–714 (2022)
16. Ma, X., et al.: A comprehensive survey on graph anomaly detection with deep learning. IEEE Transactions on Knowledge and Data Engineering (2021)
17. Nichol, A., Achiam, J., Schulman, J.: On first-order meta-learning algorithms. arXiv preprint arXiv:1803.02999 (2018)
18. Pang, G., Shen, C., van den Hengel, A.: Deep anomaly detection with deviation networks. In: Proceedings of the 25th ACM SIGKDD International Conference on Knowledge Discovery & Data Mining, pp. 353–362 (2019)
19. Rossi, R.A., Ahmed, N.K.: The network data repository with interactive graph analytics and visualization. In: AAAI (2015). https://networkrepository.com/
20. Wang, H., Zhou, C., Wu, J., Dang, W., Zhu, X., Wang, J.: Deep structure learning for fraud detection. In: 2018 IEEE International Conference on Data Mining (ICDM), pp. 567–576. IEEE (2018)
21. Wang, S., Chen, C., Li, J.: Graph few-shot learning with task-specific structures. arXiv preprint arXiv:2210.12130 (2022)
22. Wang, S., Dong, Y., Ding, K., Chen, C., Li, J.: Few-shot node classification with extremely weak supervision. arXiv preprint arXiv:2301.02708 (2023)
23. Wu, F., Souza, A., Zhang, T., Fifty, C., Yu, T., Weinberger, K.: Simplifying graph convolutional networks. In: International Conference on Machine Learning, pp. 6861–6871. PMLR (2019)
24. Xiong, W., Yu, M., Chang, S., Guo, X., Wang, W.Y.: One-shot relational learning for knowledge graphs. arXiv preprint arXiv:1808.09040 (2018)
25. Yao, H., et al.: Graph few-shot learning via knowledge transfer. In: Proceedings of the AAAI Conference on Artificial Intelligence, vol. 34, pp. 6656–6663 (2020)
26. Zafarani, R., Abbasi, M.A., Liu, H.: Social media mining: an introduction. Cambridge University Press (2014)
27. Zhang, G., et al.: Dual-discriminative graph neural network for imbalanced graph-level anomaly detection. Adv. Neural. Inf. Process. Syst. **35**, 24144–24157 (2022)
28. Zhang, Z., Zhao, L.: Unsupervised deep subgraph anomaly detection. In: 2022 IEEE International Conference on Data Mining (ICDM), pp. 753–762. IEEE (2022)
29. Zhou, F., Cao, C., Zhang, K., Trajcevski, G., Zhong, T., Geng, J.: Meta-GNN: on few-shot node classification in graph meta-learning. In: Proceedings of the 28th ACM International Conference on Information and Knowledge Management, pp. 2357–2360 (2019)
30. Zügner, D., Günnemann, S.: Adversarial attacks on graph neural networks via meta learning (2019)

An Evaluation Metric for Prediction Stability with Imprecise Data

Ye Li[1], Mei Wang[1(✉)], and Jianwen Su[2]

[1] Donghua University, Shanghai 201620, China
2212498@mail.dhu.edu.cn, wangmei@dhu.edu.cn
[2] University of California, Santa Barbara, CA, USA
su@cs.ucsb.edu

Abstract. Application of machine learning techniques for analysis and prediction in healthcare heavily relies on patient data. Lab tests, medical instruments, and other sources generate a significant portion of patient healthcare data, which may contain imprecision ranges of up to 20%. However, previous studies have shown that prediction models built from such imprecise data tend to be "brittle" or *unstable*. Even a minor deviation within the normal imprecision range can lead to varying prediction results. Measuring the stability of such models is a crucial challenge for public health agencies in large cities in China. In this paper, we report our preliminary results on measuring stability, specifically, develop a "voting" based metric to assess the predictive stability of a model. We also formulate an effective method to calculate this metric that allows us to observe, understand, and compare the predictive stability of a model at a finer granularity. We conducted experiments on the MIMIC dataset and a predefined dataset to test the baseline method and two commonly used improved methods for handling noisy and imprecise data. The results showed that the improved methods demonstrated lower instability than the original method, highlighting the soundness of our evaluation metrics. Notably, when two models had similar accuracy for the same task, our evaluation metric identifies varying levels of stability among the models, suggesting that our proposed method provides a valuable perspective for model selection that deserves further explanation.

Keywords: data imprecision · prediction stability · evaluation metric

1 Introduction

Over the recent years, there is a rapid increase of public and academic interest in applying machine learning (ML) techniques in healthcare [1,2]. Intelligent diagnostic and decision-making systems have been developed for specific diseases, which train deep learning models based on historical electronic health record (EHR) data. These systems can overcome the limitations of individual doctor's experience, and their accuracy can rival that of experienced doctors [3,4]. In 2018, the US Food and Drug Administration (FDA) approved the world's first

© The Author(s), under exclusive license to Springer Nature Switzerland AG 2023
Z. Jin et al. (Eds.): KSEM 2023, LNAI 14117, pp. 430–441, 2023.
https://doi.org/10.1007/978-3-031-40283-8_36

automatic artificial intelligence (AI) diagnostic equipment [5]. While ML techniques can achieve high accuracy, a main barrier preventing wide scope adoption of ML techniques in healthcare is the inadequacy of ML techniques in dealing with data imprecision.

Imprecision of clinical lab test results is often due to systematic and random factors. Systematic factors are mostly reproducible and tend to skew results consistently in the same direction. For examples, the attenuation of the light source of the instrument will cause the test result to shift to one side. Random factors are unpredictable during operations. Also, the expired reagents, expired controls or calibrators, or failure in sampling system. Since random factors can not be easily attributed to certain reasons, it is difficult to eliminate error. Usually large imprecision margins are unallowable for lab tests. Therefore, each lab follows some specified quality control and process control protocols to ensure that the test results are within respective tolerable ranges (or imprecision ranges, values in this range are acceptable, though imprecise).

Existing research suggests that small perturbations can alter model outputs, leading to unstable and unreliable predictions [6]. While data imprecision can lead to unclear prediction results, it is not always the case every learned model is always weak on imprecise data. For example, Sheng Kang Corp. (SKC) (that manages all patient data from about 40 top hospitals in Shanghai) is eager to select models are strong and can be adopted in practice. Clearly, in real-world applications such as SKC's, prediction stability and reliability are highly demanded and critically important. Therefore, it is crucial to develop practical methods for the user to evaluate such stability when choosing and effectively utilizing prediction models.

It is a challenging task to develop an evaluation metric to access the stability of a model. A straightforward idea is to measure the variability of model outputs under noisy input or directly count the number of samples in which the prediction result changes due to imprecision. The occurrence of events where the prediction result changes are rare, making it difficult to distinguish different models directly by the number of occurrences [7]. Furthermore, observations obtained from this method can vary significantly for each sample, posing difficulties in acquiring consistent measurement values to evaluate the model comprehensively. Consequently, it is challenging to assess the stability of the model using this approach, and no clear measurement method exists for this purpose.

In this paper, we propose an effective evaluation metric to assess the predictive stability of a model. We first interpret the prediction as a voting process for each predicted value in the acceptable range, with consistency indicating stability. Based on the above understanding, we then define and propose an evaluate metric for prediction stability at the sample level. The value range of all sample evaluation scores is partitioned into fixed intervals. The number of samples falling in each interval is counted. The interval as well as the corresponding number construct a new distribution, which allows us to observe, understand, and compare the predictive stability of a model at a finer granularity and also provides greater distinguishability. We conducted experiments on the MIMIC dataset and a predefined dataset for the classification tasks, testing the baseline method and two commonly used improved methods for handling noisy and imprecise data. Our results showed that the improved methods demonstrated higher stability than the original method, witnessing the effectiveness of the proposed evaluation metrics. Moreover, when two models had similar accuracy for the same task, our evaluation metrics identified varying levels of stability among the models, suggesting that our proposed method provides a valuable perspective for model selection.

In summary, our main contributions are highlighted as:

- We define and propose evaluation metrics for prediction stability at the sample level and model level. The proposed measure is highly sensitive to differences in model stability, making it an effective tool for assessing and comparing the performance of different models.
- We propose a new way to calculate the metric, which allows us to observe, understand, and compare the predictive stability of a model at a finer granularity.
- We extend the metric to multiple classification situations, achieving the equivalent evaluation ability for different tasks.

2   Related Work

Model stability has long been a topic of interest. Most current research focuses on enhancing model robustness, Evaluation methods commonly rely solely on experimental verifications, which often adopt traditional evaluation metrics to assess overall sample performance of the model on validation or test datasets [8,9]. Evaluating the model using these methods requires generating perturbed samples, which may cause biased verification results due to the variations among perturbed samples. Meanwhile, in practical applications, we are more concerned with the variation of samples. Traditional evaluation metrics are inadequate in evaluating the predictive performance of the model on a sample level.

Certified robustness is typically based on mathematical methods that provide rigorous proofs of a model's robustness. Random Smoothing [10] improves model robustness by randomizing input data and can also provide certified robustness radii for each sample, proving that inputs within the radius range will result in stable model outputs. SortNet [11] was designed to achieve higher certified robustness than Lipschitz neural networks on benchmark datasets. These methods can provide rigorous mathematical guarantees, but in practice, they may be limited by computational complexity, running time, and scalability, and do not provide a robustness metric for a model.

A statistical method has been proposed to assess the robustness of prediction models when applied to given samples [7]. The method involves uniformly perturbing the input within an l_p ball with a radius of ϵ, and the evaluation is based on whether the prediction result changes due to the perturbation. However, we believe that this method has three limitations. Firstly, the occurrence of events where the prediction result changes is rare, resulting in small values that make it difficult to distinguish between different models. Secondly, although the measurement range is increased to negative infinity to 0 through function mapping, it is still challenging to calculate statistical values for all samples, which only allows for sample-level measurement, not model-level measurement. Lastly, existing methods do not consider that the same evaluation metric value should reflect the same stability prediction ability for multi-class classification with different numbers of categories. Therefore, we propose that the evaluation metric for model stability should possess three properties: 1) the evaluation value should be within a specific range, such as between 0 and 1; 2) the same evaluation metric value should reflect the same stability prediction ability for different models; 3) the measurement metric should guide model improvement.

3   Stability

In this section, we first present the stability evaluation metric for each sample. Next, we formally define our stability evaluation metrics for prediction models. Then, we introduce an extended metric that can measure equivalently under multiple classification situations. Finally, we provide the algorithm for calculating the metric.

3.1   Stability of a Sample

Let f be the learning model that maps the input space χ to the output space Y. In real-world applications, the model f can serve as a prediction model to diagnose or monitor the progress of a disease for a given patient based on the patient's Electronic Health Record (EHR) data. Here the variable in input space could be the basic patient information such as age, gender, and so on as well as lab test results, or other information. The output variable could be the label, which represents the corresponding disease type.

As we all know, inaccuracies in data are a common occurrence in real-world applications. This means that the variable x in input space has an imprecision range space, denoted as $Ipr(x)$. Values in $Ipr(x)$ are also acceptable, in this way the prediction result for a given patient could be obtained by a voting strategy. Each sample in imprecision range space generates the label. All of the labels are aggregated into a single one. If the model is stable, there will be no inconsistent predictions, that is, all labels are the same. Let P_{major} to represent the proportion of samples with the majority label in the space. It can be seen that the larger P_{major} is, the more stable the model is. Let c_{max} denote the majority class label, that is $c_{max} = argmax_c f(x)$, $x \in Ipr(x)$. The prediction stability for sample x is:

$$s(x) = \int_{Ipr(x)} sign(f(x) = c_{max})q(x). \tag{1}$$

where $q(x)$ is the probability distribution of the imprecise sample in imprecision range space. $sign()$ is the function, when the input is true, it output 1; else 0.

To calculate $s(x)$ in Eq. 1, we randomly sample N points in the imprecision range space $Ipr(x)$ of sample x. These sampled points are then input to a K-classification neural network model f_K for prediction, and the proportion of major class samples in the predicted categories is obtained as the stability measure of x.

The definition presented in Eq. 1 is similar to the robustness measurement introduced in [7]. However, there is a fundamental difference between the two. In [7], the samples in the neighborhood of a given input are considered to be the noisy samples, and the number of samples where $f(x') \neq f(x)$ is used to measure the robustness. As we discussed earlier, the prediction result for a given patient can be obtained using a voting strategy. Our definition of stability is more reasonable and can be easily extended to measure the stability of the model. In addition, in a K-classification problem, if the model has no prediction ability, resulting in totally unstable predictions in $Ipr(x)$. In this worst-case scenario, for each point sampled from $Ipr(x)$, the model randomly outputs the label, with $P_{major} = 1/K$, which means that $min(s_x) = 1/K$. The stability values measured for the 2-classification and 100-classification problems are different in the worst case scenario. However, we aim to use the same value to measure stability in both cases. Furthermore, smaller values of s_x have a greater impact on measuring the model's stability.

Based on above observations, we modify the stability measure for sample x as follows:

$$s_x = -log_K\left(P_{major}\right) \tag{2}$$

In the worst-case scenario where the model has no prediction ability, for a 100-classification problem, the model randomly outputs the label with a probability of $P_{major} = 1/100$ for each point sampled from Ipr(x), and $S_k = 1$; Similarly, for a binary classification problem with two classes, $S_k = 1$ even when $P_{major} = 1/2$. When the class labels are different, s_k outputs the same value for the same predictive power of the model.

On the other hand, the closer P_{major} to $1/k$, the worse the predictive power of the model. The contribution of different p to the prediction stability is different. For example, in a binary classification task, the least stable scenario is when $P_{major} = 0.5$, while the most stable is when $P_{major} = 1$. When $P_{major} = 0.95$, we consider the sample to be relatively stable. The impact on model instability of transitioning from a relatively stable to the most stable scenario is insignificant. However, if $P_{major} = 0.5$ changes to $P_{major} = 0.55$, the sample is considered to transition from an unstable, randomly classified scenario to a relatively unstable one. Therefore, we are more interested in the impact of such samples on model instability. Consequently, our designed stability metric is more sensitive to the decrease in sample instability when P_{major} is smaller, and the same growth occurs. The $-log$ function possesses this ability, and our stability metric, denoted by s_x, measures instability in this way.

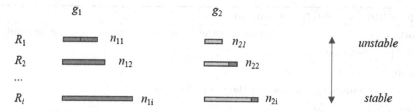

Fig. 1. Two models with the interval and the number of samples falling in each interval.

3.2   Stability of a Model

Based on the stability measure for each input sample, the stability for model f could be defined as:

$$S_f = \int s_x \, p(x) dx \tag{3}$$

where $p(x)$ is the probability distribution of input variables.

Since integrating over the entire sample space is challenging. Assume for model users, they have a sequence of input variables $X = \{x_1, x_2, ..., x_T\}$, Eq. 3 could be written as:

$$S_f = \sum_{i=0}^{T} s_{x_i} P(x_i) \tag{4}$$

Although Eq. 4 gives a measure of model stability, this measure is still not intuitive enough for model selection and comparison. we further divide the range space formed by all the values of s_x into fixed-length intervals. Let min, max denote the minimum and maximum of s_x the range space could be denoted as $[min, max]$. Divide the space with fixed space, we can obtain fixed-length interval R_m, where $m \in \{1, ..., M\}, R_1 < R_2, ..., < R_m$. Taking binary classification as an example, as defined in Sect. 3.1, s_x is the proportion of majority labels, min is 0.5 and max is 1. Then the whole range space is $[0.5, 1]$, Divide an interval with fixed step 0.05, then we can obtain 10 intervals.

Then we count the number of s_x falling in each interval. The interval R_j with the number n_j of samples which falls on the interval constitutes a distribution D. For different Model $g1$ and $g2$, assume they are trained for the same task. Then we can obtain $D_1 = \{\{R_1, n_{11}\}, \{R_2, n_{12}\}, ..., \{R_m, n_{1m}\}$, $D_2 = \{\{R_1, n_{21}\}, \{R_2, n_{22}\}, ..., \{R_m, n_{2m}\}$. Figure 1 illustrates an example. As we know, the smaller R_j, the more instability. If the sample originally located at R_j in D_1 enters R_k of D_2, where $k > j$, it means that the stability of model 2 at this sample is higher than that of model 1. The larger the number of such samples, the higher the stability of Model 2 than Model 1. And the smaller the original R_j value, the larger the stability of Model 2.

Algorithm 1. stability calculation

Input: k-classification neural network model f_k, uncertain range space $Ipr(x)$, dataset
$\{x_i\}_{i=1}^{N'}$, Intervals R_m;

Output: Measure of stability S_f;

1: Initialize number of samples in the interval *counts*

2: **for** $i = 1 \rightarrow \mathbf{N}'$ **do**

3:     sample $\{\mathbf{x}_i^{(j)}\}_{j=1}^N$ i.i.d. from $Ipr(\mathbf{x}_i)$;

4:     counts0 $\leftarrow COUNTPREDICTS(f_k, \{\mathbf{x}_i^{(j)}\}_{j=1}^N)$;

5:     $c_A \leftarrow$ major class in counts0;

6:     $n_A \leftarrow counts0[c_A]$;

7:     $P_{major} \leftarrow n_A/N$;

8:     calculate $s_x(\mathbf{x}_i)$ with P_{major};

9:     Update *counts* based on $s_x(\mathbf{x}_i)$;

10: **end for**

11: P(m) $\leftarrow \{counts(m)/N'\}$;

12: calculate S_f with $P(m)$;

13: **return** S_f

After generating distribution D, the model stability is calculated based on the expectation as:

$$S_f = \frac{1}{T} \sum_{i=0}^{M} s_{ix} n_r \tag{5}$$

where s_{ix} is the median of interval R_i.

The detailed stability calculation is shown in Algorithm 1. The function $COUNTPREDICTS(f_k, \{\mathbf{x}_i^{(j)}\}_{j=1}^N)$ in the pseudocode takes input $\{\mathbf{x}_i^{(j)}\}_{j=1}^N$, feeds them into the neural network model f_k, and returns count0, which is a queue containing k numbers where each number represents the count of samples for the corresponding index class.

4   Experiments

In this section, we begin by introducing the experimental settings, including the dataset and implementation details. Then, we proceed to discuss the experimental results and provide a detailed analysis to demonstrate the effectiveness of the proposed metric.

4.1   Datasets

We conducted experiments using the MIMIC-III (Medical Information Mart for Intensive Care) dataset, as described in Johnson et al. (2016) [12]. This dataset is a comprehensive single-center database that contains information on

Table 1. dataset statistics.

Dataset	# of samples	# of positive	# of negative
MIMIC-III	21139	18342	2797

patients admitted to the intensive care units of a large tertiary care hospital. The dataset includes vital signs, medications, laboratory measurements, orders, procedure codes, diagnosis codes, imaging reports, length of stay, survival data, and other variables, which may contain imprecise data. MIMIC-III includes data from 53,423 unique adult patients (16 years or older) admitted to the ICU between 2001 and 2012, as well as data from 7,870 neonates admitted between 2001 and 2008. To construct our in-hospital mortality prediction dataset, we followed the MIMIC-based benchmark proposed by Harutyunyan et al. [13]. Our objective is to predict in-hospital mortality using patients' ICU data from the 48 h preceding admission.

Table 1 describes some statistics about the dataset. The table shows that the real-world MIMIC dataset suffers from severe imbalances. To remove the influence of data imbalanced, we conducted experiments on a simple and balanced predifined dataset. This dataset was generated using the `sklearn.datasets.make_moons` method and was used for binary classification tasks.

4.2 Implementation Details

Our software environment contains ubuntu 20.04, PyTorch v1.13.0, and python 3.9.15. All experiments were conducted on a machine equipped with two GPUs (NVIDIA GeForce GTX 4090) and 64 GB of memory. With a batch size of 64 for the in-hospital mortality prediction dataset, and a batch size of 200 for the predefined dataset. For the learning rate, we set it at $1e-3$ for the in-hospital mortality prediction dataset and $5e-3$ for another dataset. To evaluate the proposed metric, for each task, we calculated the measurement based on the proposed metric using three prediction models. One model is the baseline model, while the other two models are the PGD adversarial training method [14] and the IR loss method [15], which have been proven to improve robustness and stability. Since data in MIMIC is organized as time series, we use the Long Short-Term Memory (LSTM) as the base model f. In order to compare different models, we also unfold the temporal data and use MLP model for comparison. As for the predefined dataset, we utilized residual neural networks as the base model. Finally, we applied dropout to the classification layer of all classification task models, with a dropout rate of 0.3 and $N = 100,000$. These hyper-parameters were selected based on the performance on the validation set.

4.3 Result and Analysis

The Effectiveness of the Metric: Figure 2 illustrates the results of running base model and two improved models, evaluating against the proposed metric.

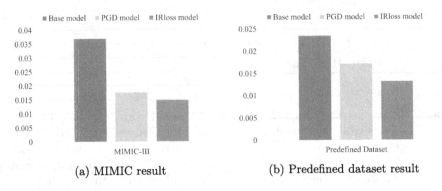

(a) MIMIC result   (b) Predefined dataset result

Fig. 2. The performance of the baseline models and improved models on the two tasks. On both tasks, the stability metrics of the improved methods are significantly lower than those of the baseline model.

According to Eq. 2, the lower our measure of stability, the more stable the system is. Based on the results, we observe the following: Firstly, the experimental results confirm the effectiveness of the proposed metric. Specifically, the stability metric of the PGD method and IR loss are lower than that of the baseline model. Secondly, our proposed stability metric is sensitive in measuring differences in model stability. As seen in the comparison of the measurement results of the baseline and improved models on the MIMIC and predefined dataset, the stability metric of the baseline models reaches the level of 10^{-2}, but the evaluation differences with the improved models are still more than 50%. This indicates that our proposed metric is highly sensitive to the stability factors of the models. Finally, our stability metric can be applied to various task scenarios, ranging from complex public real-world dataset to simple predefined dataset, making it an effective evaluation tool. Furthermore, our metric is applicable to both LSTM and residual neural network models. It is simple yet effective, and can be used to evaluate the stability of neural network models in a wide range of neural network architectures and use cases.

The Advantages of Interval Partition: To validate the model's stability and analyze the characteristics of the samples that affect their stability, we conducted a statistical analysis of the number of samples in each interval of the stability measure, which is one of the advantages of interval. The statistical results of stability on the MIMIC dataset and predefined dataset are presented in Fig. 3 and Fig. 4, respectively. The x-axis represents the intervals based on P_{major} used to calculate sample stability, and the y-axis represents the number of samples falling in the corresponding interval. Since the most unstable state for binary classification is when $P_{major} = 0.5$ and the most stable state is achieved when $P_{major} = 1$ with an stability measure of 0, which has no impact on model stability, we ignore the statistics for samples with $P_{major} = 1$. Next, we analyze the statistical results on the two datasets:

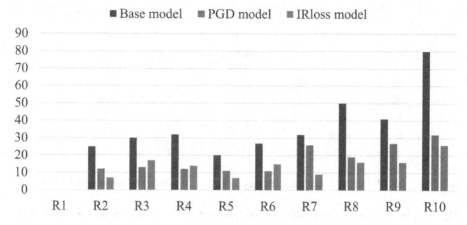

Fig. 3. The statistical results of the number of samples in each interval on the MIMIC dataset.

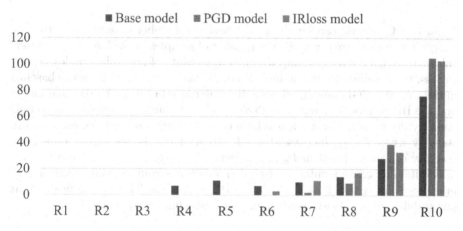

Fig. 4. The statistical results of the number of samples in each interval on the predefined dataset.

In Fig. 3, it can be observed that the number of samples in each unstable interval of the MIMIC dataset is significantly lower in the improved model results compared to the baseline model. Many samples with higher P_{major} values, indicating higher stability, in the improved model are reduced in comparison to the baseline model. This suggests that the stability measure is effective in identifying unstable samples, and the improved model has lower stability compared to the baseline model. The use of interval allows for a clear validation of the effectiveness of stability metric and identification of unstable samples in the MIMIC dataset. This information can be used to propose new model improvement methods specifically targeting the unstable samples, thereby further enhancing the model's performance.

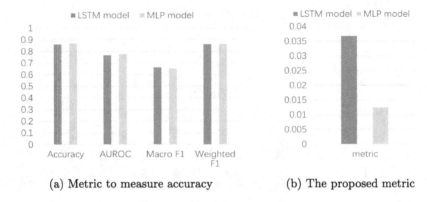

(a) Metric to measure accuracy   (b) The proposed metric

Fig. 5. The performance of different models on the same task using the MIMIC-III dataset, evaluated on both metrics to measure prediction accuracy and the proposed metric to measure stability.

In Fig. 4, a trend can be observed where the number of samples in the low P_{major} intervals decreases while the number of samples in the high P_{major} intervals increases, indicating an improvement in stability of unstable samples. Nevertheless, the stability metrics indicates a difference of 26.9% between the baseline model and the PGD model, whereas the difference between the baseline model and the IRloss model amounts to 43.8%. This is because we believe that sample stability does not follow a linear relationship. We suppose that the reduction in stability when P_{major} increases from R_1 to R_2 has a larger impact on sample stability compared to when P_{major} increases from R_9 to R_{10}. This discrepancy in results may cause similar statistical trends but significant differences in stability measure results for the PGD and IRloss models. This also indicates that our stability metric takes into account such non-linearity accurately.

The Proposed Metric Can Be Use for Model Selection: Our proposed stability metric can assist in selecting more effective models. As depicted in Fig. 5 (a), when utilizing LSTM and MLP models for MIMIC-III datasets, the difference in traditional metrics such as accuracy, AUROC, and weighted F1 is minimal, making it challenging to choose between the two models. However it is evident on our metrics that the stability of the LSTM model is significantly lower than that of the MLP model as illustrated in Fig. 5 (b). This can help us choose more stable MLP model.

5   Conclusion

This paper reports a new metric to assess the predictive stability at the sample level and model level, and a method to calculate the metric. The definition and the calculate process provide a new way to observe, understand, and compare the predictive stability of a model. The experiments conducted on the real world healthcare dataset and a predefined dataset testify the effectiveness of the proposed method. In the experiments, we can see that when two models had similar accuracy for the same task, the stability of the models obtained using our metrics may be different, suggesting that our proposed method provides a new perspective for model selection. Future work will focus on exploring the relationships between different levels of stability and different models and identifying the key factors that can improve the stability of a sample from one interval to another.

References

1. Mckinney, S.M., et al.: International evaluation of an AI system for breast cancer screening. Nature **577**, 89–94 (2020)
2. Mckinney, S.M., et al.: Artificial intelligence will soon change the landscape of medical physics research and practice. Med. Phys. **45**(5), 1791–1793 (2018)
3. Gulshan, V., et al.: Development and validation of a deep learning algorithm for detection of diabetic retinopathy in retinal fundus photographs. JAMA **316**(22), 2402–2410 (2016)
4. Esteva, A., et al.: Dermatologist-level classification of skin cancer with deep neural networks. Nature **542**(7639), 115–118 (2017)
5. Lipkovich, I., Dmitrienko, A., d'agostino, R.B.: Tutorial in biostatistics: data-driven subgroup identification and analysis in clinical trials. Stat. Med. **36**, 08 (2016)
6. Wang, M., Su, J., Lu, H.Q.: Impact of medical data imprecision on learning results. In: Proceedings of SIGKDD Workshop (2020)
7. Webb, S., Rainforth, T., Teh, Y.W., Pawan Kumar, M.: A statistical approach to assessing neural network robustness. In: 7th International Conference on Learning Representations, ICLR 2019, New Orleans, LA, USA, 6–9 May 2019. OpenReview.net (2019)
8. Qin, M., Vucinic, D.: Training recurrent neural networks against noisy computations during inference (2018)
9. Yeo, K.: Short note on the behavior of recurrent neural network for noisy dynamical system. ArXiv, abs/1904.05158 (2019)
10. Cohen, J., Rosenfeld, E., Kolter, Z.: Certified adversarial robustness via randomized smoothing. In: International Conference on Machine Learning, pp. 1310–1320. PMLR (2019)
11. Zhang, B., Jiang, D., He, D., Wang, L.: Rethinking Lipschitz neural networks and certified robustness. A boolean function perspective. In: Advances in Neural Information Processing Systems (2022)
12. Johnson, A.E.W.: Mimic-III, a freely accessible critical care database. Sci. Data **3**(1), 1–9 (2016)
13. Harutyunyan, H., Khachatrian, H., Kale, D.C., Steeg, G.V., Galstyan, A.: Multitask learning and benchmarking with clinical time series data. Sci. Data **6**(1), 96 (2019)
14. Madry, A., Makelov, A., Schmidt, L., Tsipras, D., Vladu, A.: Towards deep learning models resistant to adversarial attacks. arXiv preprint arXiv:1706.06083 (2017)
15. Wang, M., Lin, Z., Li, R., Li, Y., Jianwen, S.: Predicting disease progress with imprecise lab test results. Artif. Intell. Med. **132**, 102373 (2022)

Reducing the Teacher-Student Gap via Elastic Student

Haorong Li, Zihao Chen, Jingtao Zhou, and Shuangyin Li[✉]

School of Computer, South China Normal University, Guangzhou, China
{haorongli,zihaochen,jingtaozhou}@m.scnu.edu.cn, shuangyinli@scnu.edu.cn

Abstract. The application of knowledge distillation (KD) has shown promise in transferring knowledge from a larger teacher model to a smaller student model. Nevertheless, a prevalent phenomenon in knowledge distillation is that student performance decreases when the teacher-student gap becomes large. Our contention is that the degradation from teacher to student is predominantly attributable to two gaps, namely the capacity gap and the knowledge gap. In this paper, we introduce Elastic Student Knowledge Distillation (ESKD), an innovative method that comprises Elastic Architecture and Elastic Learning to bridge the two gaps. The Elastic Architecture temporarily increases the number of student's parameters during training and subsequently reverts to its original size while inference. It improves the learning ability of the model without increasing the cost at inference time. The Elastic Learning strategy introduces mask matrix and progressive learning strategies that facilitates the student in comprehending the intricate knowledge of the teacher and accomplishing the effect of regularization. We conducted extensive experiments on CIFAR-100 and ImageNet datasets, demonstrating that ESKD outperforms existing methods while preserving computational efficiency.

Keywords: Knowledge distillation · Image classification · Knowledge transfer

1 Introduction

Deep neural networks (DNN) have shown remarkable performance in computer vision tasks, but their high computational and storage demands hinder their deployment on mobile devices. One promising solution to address the challenges is knowledge distillation. Popularized by Hinton et al. [1], this approach enhances the student network's learning by mimicking the teacher network's behavior. However, a prevalent phenomenon in knowledge distillation is that student performance decreases when the teacher-student gap becomes large [20].

We believe that the performance degradation is mainly credited to two gaps, namely the capacity gap and the knowledge gap. Specifically, the capacity gap refers to the discrepancy in the number of trainable parameters between the teacher and student networks. Obviously, the teacher network possesses more

Z. Jin et al. (Eds.): KSEM 2023, LNAI 14117, pp. 442–453, 2023.
https://doi.org/10.1007/978-3-031-40283-8_37

parameters than the student, leading to a higher learning ability. On the other hand, the knowledge gap refers to the discrepancy between the deep features encoded by the teacher and those of the student. In general, the deep features extracted by the teacher are more easily linearly distinguishable.

Nevertheless, previous methods predominantly focused on reducing the trainable parameters of teacher models to accommodate the student [14], rather than exploring the potential for enhancing the capacity of student models. Therefore, we introduce a novel Elastic Architecture strategy, which leverages structural reparameterization to bridge the capacity gap between teacher and student models. Specifically, during the training phase, the elastic architecture allows for an increase in the capacity of the student model, thus enhancing its learning potential. Notably, during inference, the elastic architecture reverts the student model's capacity to its original level without requiring additional parameters.

Meanwhile, we have observed that complete teacher-student feature alignment can be challenging. Therefore, it is crucial for the teacher model to not only impart feature knowledge directly but also dynamically control the amount of knowledge imparted. Our proposed method, termed Elastic Learning, allows the teacher model to control knowledge transfer. Ideally, this approach can minimize the knowledge gap and induce a regularization effect, thereby preventing the student from acquiring redundant knowledge from the teacher. To accommodate varying model architectures, we apply a 3×3 convolution as a transformation layer following the student feature encoder, effectively addressing potential dimension mismatches between the teacher and student. Using these methods improves the student model's learning from the teacher, reducing the performance gap. Our technique surpasses current methods and maintains computational efficiency, as demonstrated on multiple benchmark datasets.

Overall, our contributions are summarized as follows:

- We raise the issue of the capacity and knowledge gap between teacher and student models and then propose a framework termed Elastic Student Knowledge Distillation to tackle the aforementioned challenges.
- We present two strategies, called Elastic Architecture and Elastic Learning. The former is used to increase the capacity of students, while the latter works to transfer knowledge to students more efficiently.
- We conducted experiments on CIFAR100 and ImageNet using multiple teacher-student architectures. Experimental results show that the proposed method is effective and outperforms state-of-the-arts on both datasets.

2   Related Work

2.1   Knowledge Distillation

Knowledge distillation (KD) has emerged as a prevalent technique for model compression. A highly proficient teacher model is leveraged to transfer its knowledge to a smaller and more compact student model. This approach involves imparting the knowledge encoded in logits based on input samples [1]. To further enhance student performance, researchers have explored diverse knowledge besides logits.

A viable strategy involves leveraging insights from the pre-existing teacher's intermediate layers, which has led to the emergence of feature distillation. In feature distillation, researchers propose various representations to capture transferred knowledge effectively. These include coarse intermediate feature maps as suggested by Fitnets [2], angle-wise relations encoded by similarity matrices as demonstrated by RKD [3], or those modeled through contrastive learning techniques [4]. Chen et al. [6] introduced semantic calibration, a method that assigns target teacher layers to corresponding student layers across multiple levels.

However, little attention has been paid for enhancing the capacity of the student, potentially limiting the effectiveness of knowledge distillation. Our proposed methodology diverges from prior works by concurrently focusing on the capacity gap and knowledge gap.

2.2   Re-parameterization

Throughout the years, numerous techniques have been proposed to re-parameterize convolutional neural networks with the objective of enhancing their efficiency and performance. These methods typically concentrate on altering the network structure during training without increasing the complexity during inference.

RepVGG [11] proposes a VGG-like architecture, where the network's body uses only 3×3 convolutions for inference. RepMLP [12] constructs convolutional layers and merges them into the FC for inference. The Diverse Branch Block (DBB) [13], is a versatile building block for ConvNets that integrates diverse branches to enhance the feature space.

In light of the aforementioned techniques, our proposed method, known as Elastic Architecture, endeavors to mitigate the limitations of the original architecture without incurring additional inference-time costs. As such, this technique offers a promising avenue for optimizing convolutional network performance.

3   Method

3.1   Elastic Architecture

In the realm of convolutional networks, homogeneity and additivity are two fundamental properties that provide significant guidance for the design and training of these networks.

Transform via Homogeneity. Homogeneity is characterized by the property that scaling the convolutional kernel leads to a proportional scaling of the output feature maps. Specifically, let us assume that s is a constant factor. Let $I \in R^{C \times H \times W}$ be the input and $O \in R^{D \times H_0 \times W_0}$ be the output. The following relation can describe the property:

$$s \cdot O_{d,x,y} = s\left(\sum_{c=1}^{C}\sum_{i=1}^{K}\sum_{j=1}^{K} w_{d,c,i,j} I_{c,(x-1+i),(y-1+j)}\right)$$

$$= \sum_{c=1}^{C}\sum_{i=1}^{K}\sum_{j=1}^{K}(s \cdot w_{d,c,i,j}) I_{c,(x-1+i),(y-1+j)} \tag{1}$$

where the number of the output channels is denoted by d, while x and y refer to the row and column of the output, respectively. C denotes the number of channels in the input and K denotes the size of the convolutional kernel. Thus, when considering two sequential convolutions, $w_1 \in R^{C_1 \times C \times 1 \times 1}$ and $w_2 \in R^{D \times C_1 \times K \times K}$, the merging formula can be expressed as

$$w' \leftarrow w_2 \circledast p(w_1) \tag{2}$$

where $p(w_1) \in R^{C \times C_1 \times 1 \times 1}$ is the result of permuting w_1 such that its input channels and output channels are swapped.

Transform via Additivity. Suppose we have n convolutional kernels. When we independently perform the convolution operation with these n kernels on the input I, we generate n outputs. The sum of these output feature maps is equal to the output O' obtained by performing a convolution operation using the sum of the kernels $\sum_{i=1}^{n} w_i$ on the input I. The property can be expressed as follows:

$$\sum_{i=1}^{n} O_{d,x,y} = \sum_{i=1}^{n}\sum_{c=1}^{C}\sum_{j=1}^{K}\sum_{k=1}^{K} w_{i,d,c,j,k} I_{c,(x-1+j),(y-1+k)}$$

$$= \sum_{c=1}^{C}\sum_{j=1}^{K}\sum_{k=1}^{K}\left(\sum_{i=1}^{n} w_{i,d,c,j,k}\right) I_{c,(x-1+j),(y-1+k)} \tag{3}$$

where n denotes the number of convolutional kernels employed for the convolution operation.Hence, when considering two parallel convolutions, $w_1, w_2 \in R^{D \times C \times k \times k}$, the merging formula can be expressed as:

$$w' \leftarrow w_1 + w_2 \tag{4}$$

The homogeneity and additivity illustrate that it is mathematically feasible to merge two convolution kernels. Considering the linear nature of convolutional operations, it is possible to increase the capacity of the student model during training. And the student reverts to its initial capacity at inference time to avoid incurring additional computational costs. We utilize this property to address the capacity gap issue between the teacher and the student. For different types of network structures, we propose two convolutional kernel conversion strategies.

During training, for student models without branches, such as VGG, we design a triple parallel KxK convolutional kernel to replace the original one, as illustrated in Fig. 1(a). Conversely, for wider or already-branched student models,

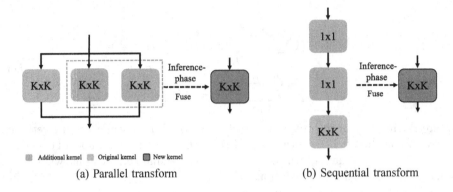

(a) Parallel transform   (b) Sequential transform

Fig. 1. Elastic Architecture transformations. Here we only show how a layer of convolution is transformed. Note that for networks without branches, the left scheme is employed, whereas for others, the right scheme is utilized.

such as ResNet, we propose a different transformation. Two 1×1 convolutional kernels are serially connected in front of the original KxK convolutional kernel, as depicted in Fig. 1(b). During the inference phase, those kernels are then fused with the original kernel to form a more efficient and powerful single kernel. Note that there is no nonlinear activation after the extra convolution layer, otherwise the linear nature required for convolutional kernel merging is not satisfied.

These Elastic Architecture schemes can alleviate the limitations of the original architecture without incurring additional inference time costs, ultimately producing a more robust and efficient architecture.

3.2   Elastic Learning

The last layer of the teacher's network usually generates highly abstract feature maps. The students' feature maps, on the other hand, tend to be less expressive than the teacher's, reflecting the gap in knowledge. However, the teacher's image features are often redundant. In practice, it has been observed that maintaining alignment between students' and teachers' feature map throughout all training epochs resulted in learning redundant knowledge. This is due to the fact that the L2 loss function aims to minimize the mean squared error, which may inadvertently cause the student to become overly reliant on the teacher and potentially fit to redundant knowledge, as shown in Fig. 2(a)(b).

A potential solution to mitigate overfitting involves introducing masks that selectively conceal specific pixels in both the teacher and student feature maps. Previous studies have shown that masking an image does not necessarily impair model performance [21]. On the contrary, this approach enables the student to learn from a subset of the teacher's knowledge, thus reducing the impact of redundant knowledge and the difficulty of learning. By leveraging masking, the student can effectively learn a simplified version of the teacher's knowledge, paving the way for more effective knowledge transfer. Specifically, The last fea-

| | | |
| (a) teacher | (b) w/o EL | (c) w/ EL |

Fig. 2. Visualisation of feature maps. EL refers to Elastic Learning. a) illustrates the feature maps of the teacher's final layer output, b) depicts the feature maps obtained when the student model learns the full knowledge of the teacher's feature maps, and c) demonstrates the feature maps acquired by the student model when using the Elastic Learning masking strategy, which allows the student model to learn partial knowledge.

ture maps of the teacher and student models are denoted by $T \in \mathbb{R}^{C \times H \times W}$ and $S \in \mathbb{R}^{C \times H \times W}$, respectively. In order to randomly mask both feature maps, we define a binary mask matrix $M \in {0, 1}^{H \times W}$ as follows:

$$M_{i,j} \doteq \begin{cases} 0 & \text{if } U_{i,j} < \gamma \\ 1 & \text{otherwise} \end{cases} \tag{5}$$

where $U_{i,j}$ is a random number uniformly distributed in the interval $(0, 1)$, while i and j represent the horizontal and vertical coordinates of the feature map, respectively. The parameter γ signifies the masking ratio, controlling the proportion of masked elements within the feature maps.

We propose that the teacher model's function should not be limited to knowledge transfer but also include modulating the complexity and quantity of knowledge imparted to the student. Specifically, the teacher model should provide comprehensive knowledge at the beginning of training and then gradually reduce the amount of information provided. By adjusting the ratio, the student model can further bridge the knowledge gap based on the mask matrix strategy while achieving a regularization effect. Moreover, by incrementally lessening guidance, the student model can develop its own problem-solving strategies instead of excessively fitting the teacher's redundant knowledge.

That is, the proposed approach involves the parameter γ, which is dependent on the current training epoch. This parameter update scheme ensures that γ increases linearly as the number of training epochs increases. Specifically, γ is defined as follows:

$$\gamma = \frac{e_i}{e_m} \tag{6}$$

where e_i denotes the current training epoch, and e_m denotes the stopping epoch of the teacher's assistance. Next, we align the masked student feature map with the masked teacher feature map, as described in Eq. 7.

$$\mathcal{L}_{\text{dis}} = \|T \cdot M - f_{align}(S) \cdot M\|_2^2 \tag{7}$$

where $\mathcal{L}_{\mathrm{dis}}$ is distillation loss and f_{align} is an alignment layer that utilizes a 3×3 convolutional operation to align the student feature map S with the teacher feature map T. M denotes the mask matrix, and $\| \cdot \|_2^2$ is ℓ_2 loss function.

Finally, the objective of our method can be expressed as follows:

$$\mathcal{L}_{ESKD} = \alpha \mathcal{L}_{ce} + \beta \mathcal{L}_{dis} \tag{8}$$

where $\mathcal{L}_{ce}$ is the cross-entropy loss. α and β denote the weight factors. An illustrative diagram of the proposed method is shown in Fig. 3.

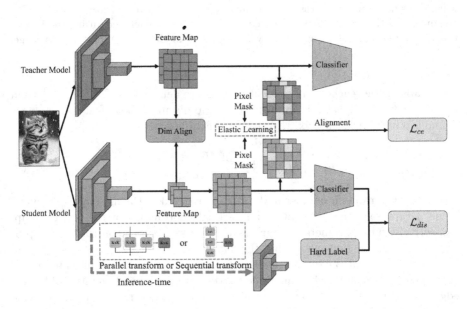

Fig. 3. An illustrative diagram of the proposed method.

4 Experiments

Within this section, we perform a comprehensive series of experiments to showcase the efficacy of our newly proposed ESKD method.

Datasets. We employ two image classification datasets, namely CIFAR-100 [19] and ImageNet [18], for our series of experiments. CIFAR-100 comprises 32×32 images classified into 100 categories, with 50k and 10k images in the training and validation sets. ImageNet is a large-scale dataset with 1.28 million images in the training set and 50k images in the validation set, categorized into 1000 classes.

Baselines and Model Architectures. To evaluate the proposed method's efficacy, we reproduce KD [1], FitNet [2], CC [10], RKD [3], VID [7], NST [5], AT [8], SP [9], which are 8 advanced knowledge distillation methods. The selected teacher networks comprise ResNet110 [15], WRN-40-2 [16], VGG13 [17], and ResNet32 × 4 [15], while the student networks include ResNet18 [15], ResNet32 [15], WRN-16-2 [16], WRN-40-1 [16], VGG8 [17], and ResNet8 × 4 [15].

Implementation Details. We employ the SGD optimizer with 0.9 Nesterov momentum for all datasets. In the case of CIFAR-100, the training process spans 240 epochs. The learning rate is adjusted by a factor of 10 at the 150th, 180th, and 210th epochs. The mini-batch size is 64. The weight decay is 5×10^{-4}. The initial learning rate is 0.05. For ImageNet, the training lasts for 120 epochs, and the initial learning rate is 0.1. The learning rate is reduced by a factor of 10 at the 30th, 60th, and 90th epochs. The mini-batch size is 128, and the weight decay is 1×10^{-4}. For consistency in the knowledge distillation process, we keep the temperature T at 4 and e_m at 100.

Table 1. Top-1 accuracy (%) of different knowledge distillation approaches on Cifar-100 testing set. Results averaged over 5 trials.

Teacher	ResNet110	ResNet110	VGG13	WRN-40-2	ResNet32 × 4	ResNet32 × 4	ResNet32 × 4
	74.31	74.31	74.64	75.61	79.42	79.42	79.42
Student	ResNet32	ResNet8 × 4	VGG8	ResNet32	ResNet32	ResNet8 × 4	WRN-16-2
	71.14	72.5	70.36	71.14	71.14	72.5	73.26
KD	73.08	73.43	72.98	72.12	72.19	73.33	73.94
FitNet	71.01	70.98	71.03	71.43	70.62	73.51	73.62
AT	72.31	73.15	71.43	72.42	72.53	73.44	74.09
SP	72.65	72.33	72.65	72.89	72.81	72.91	73.28
CC	71.48	72.81	70.71	71.49	71.52	72.97	73.56
RKD	71.83	72.23	71.46	71.75	71.05	71.52	72.31
VID	72.16	73.38	72.93	71.66	71.07	72.59	73.28
NST	72.48	73.05	71.53	72.52	72.16	73.25	73.21
Ours	**73.11**	**73.51**	**73.16**	**73.18**	**73.55**	**74.12**	**74.18**

4.1   Main Results

Results on Cifar-100. Table 1 provides a comprehensive comparison of different knowledge distillation techniques. Our proposed method, ESKD, consistently outperforms the baseline and vanilla KD techniques on all teacher-student pairs. Specifically, we achieve an improvement of $1 - 3\%$ in the teacher-student pairs, indicating the effectiveness of our approach. Besides, multiple methods offer tiny improvements to vanilla KD. Vanilla KD exceeds half of the other distillation methods in all teacher-student architecture. An intriguing observation emerged when the teacher model remained constant while the student model varied. The performance differences between the student models are significantly reduced through our proposed elastic distillation framework. For instance, when the teacher is ResNet32 × 4, and the students are ResNet8 × 4 and WRN-16-2, respectively, the difference between the students obtained through KD is 0.61%, whereas with ESKD, the difference is reduced to 0.06%. This shows that our method can significantly narrow the gap between the teacher and the lower-performing students, as the learning ability of the lower-performing students is improved and can be on par with the stronger students. These results strongly support the efficacy of ESKD.

Table 2. Top-1 accuracy (%) of different knowledge distillation approaches on ImageNet testing set. Results averaged over 5 trials.

	Student	KD	FitNet	AT	SP	CC	RKD	VID	NST	**ESKD**(Ours)
Top-1	71.12	72.52	71.23	72.65	72.46	72.34	71.89	71.28	72.61	**72.72**
Top-5	90.13	91.35	90.41	91.47	91.26	91.02	90.54	90.38	91.44	**91.51**

Results on ImageNet. Table 2 presents the top-1 and top-5 accuracies for image classification on ImageNet, with ResNet32 × 4 as the teacher and ResNet32 as the student. It is noteworthy that our method achieved a significant improvement over the baseline results, with a Top-1 accuracy of 72.72% and a Top-5 accuracy of 91.51% for ResNet32. Compared with the other prevalent knowledge distillation methods, our ESKD exhibits distinct advantages. Our approach results in an increase of 1.6% from the base student. These results highlight the effectiveness of our proposed method in improving the performance of ResNet32 on the ImageNet validation set.

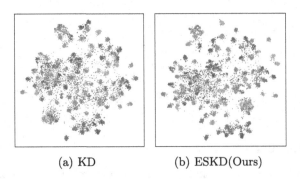

(a) KD   (b) ESKD(Ours)

Fig. 4. T-SNE Visualizations.

Visualizations. We utilize a teacher-student framework with VGG13 as the teacher and VGG8 as the student on CIFAR-100. Visualizations via t-SNE showed that ESKD (Fig. 4(b))generated more separable representations than KD (Fig. 4(a)), indicating that ESKD enhances the discriminability of deep features.

4.2   Ablation Study

Effect of Elastic Architecture and Elastic Learning. In Table 3, we present the experimental results comparing the effects of elastic architecture and elastic learning strategies on two different teacher-student architecture pairs: Vgg13-Vgg8 and ResNet32 × 4-ResNet8 × 4. The results are summarized in six categories: Vanilla, feature alignment w/o Elastic Learning(i.e., full alignment in all training epochs), feature alignment w/ Elastic Learning, Elastic Architecture w/o feature alignment, Elastic Architecture w/o Elastic Learning, and the combination of Elastic Learning and Elastic Architecture. It is evident that the Elastic Learning approach achieves improvements for both teacher-student pairs. Specifically, the VGG13-VGG8 pair achieves 72.42% accuracy with Elastic Learning, compared to 70.36% for the Vanilla setting and 72.38% without Elastic Learning. Similarly, the ResNet32 × 4-ResNet8 × 4 pair obtains 73.85% accuracy using Elastic Learning, while the Vanilla and without Elastic Learning settings yield 72.5% and 73.57% accuracy, respectively. The table also indicates that the Elastic Architecture strategy enhances the learning potential of the student model. The most significant improvement can be seen when both elastic learning and elastic architecture strategies are combined, yielding the highest performance for both student models.

Table 3. Ablation study of ESKD. It shows Top-1 accuracy (%) of two teacher-student pairs on CIFAR100. Without Elastic Learning means that no mask strategy is used in Eq. 1.

Teacher	VGG13	ResNet32 × 4
Student	VGG8	ResNet8 × 4
Vanilla	70.36	72.5
Feature alignment w/o Elastic Learning	72.38	73.57
Feature alignment w/ Elastic Learning	72.42	73.85
Elastic Architecture w/o feature alignment	71.37	72.46
Elastic Architecture w/o Elastic Learning	72.82	73.65
Elastic Architecture+Elastic Learning	**73.16**	**74.12**

Analysis of the Elastic Architecture. Table 4 demonstrates the effectiveness of our elastic architecture. For VGG architectures, adding parallel structures can lead to greater performance gains. VGG8 achieves the highest accuracy of 71.37% in this transformation. However, for ResNet32, WRN-16-2, and ResNet8 × 4, introducing additional serial 1 × 1 convolutions leads to a noticeable improvement. ResNet32 exhibits a higher accuracy of 71.45% via sequential transform. Note that only cross-entropy is used as the loss function.

Table 4. Analysis of the Elastic Architecture

	VGG8	ResNet32	WRN-16-2	ResNet8 × 4
None	70.36	71.14	73.26	72.5
Sequential	71.21	**71.45**	**73.47**	**72.66**
Parallel	**71.37**	71.35	73.31	72.62

Effect of e_m. Table 5 illustrates the influence of e_m. For the ResNet8 × 4, the highest accuracy of 74.74% is achieved when e_m is 130. As the e_m increases beyond this value, the performance starts to degrade, suggesting that student models necessitate a period for autonomous learning and should avoid excessive dependence on the teacher model's knowledge. It is worth noting that the performance remains stable in an interval of e_m values, 70-190 for ResNet8 × 4 and 70-130 for VGG8, with only minor fluctuations in accuracy. This phenomenon is intuitive because smaller models do not need large training rounds to achieve the best performance. This experiment indicates that the Elastic Learning strategy achieves a regularization effect by introducing randomness.

Table 5. Effect of e_m

e_m	70	100	130	160	190	220	240
ResNet8 × 4	74.61	74.72	**74.74**	74.66	74.62	74.21	74.18
VGG8	73.01	**73.16**	73.09	72.56	72.54	72.46	72.35

5   Conclusion

In this study, we introduced two novel strategies, Elastic Learning and Elastic Architecture, to bridge the gap between teacher and student models in knowledge distillation. Elastic Architecture enlarges the student model's capacity during training and overcomes the limitations of the original architecture, while the Elastic Learning strategy provides the student with a knowledge acquisition direction from the teacher model. The proposed ESKD method achieved significant improvements on both the CIFAR-100 and ImageNet datasets.

Acknowledgements. This work was supported by Natural Science Foundation of Guangdong (2023A1515012073), National Natural Science Foundation of China(No. 62006083) and South China Normal University Student Innovation and Entrepreneurship Training Program(No. 202321004).

References

1. Hinton, G., Vinyals, O., Dean, J.: Distilling the knowledge in a neural network. arXiv preprint arXiv:1503.02531 (2015)
2. Romero, A., Ballas, N., Kahou, S.E., Chassang, A., Gatta, C., Bengio, Y.: FitNets: hints for thin deep nets. arXiv preprint arXiv:1412.6550(2014)
3. Park, W., Kim, D., Lu, Y., Cho, M.: Relational knowledge distillation. In: CVPR, pp. 3967–3976 (2019)
4. Tian, Y., Krishnan, D., Isola, P.: Contrastive representation distillation. arXiv preprint arXiv:1910.10699 (2019)
5. Huang, Z., Wang, N.: Like what you like: knowledge distill via neuron selectivity transfer. arXiv preprint arXiv:1707.01219 (2017)
6. Chen, D., et al.: Cross-layer distillation with semantic calibration. In: AAAI, pp. 7028–7036 (2021)
7. Ahn, S., Hu, S.X., Damianou, A., Lawrence, N.D., Dai, Z.: Variational information distillation for knowledge transfer. In: CVPR, pp. 9163–9171 (2019)
8. Komodakis, N., Zagoruyko, S.: Paying more attention to attention: improving the performance of convolutional neural networks via attention transfer. In ICLR (2017)
9. Tung, F., Mori, G.: Similarity-preserving knowledge distillation. In: ICCV, pp. 1365–1374 (2019)
10. Peng, B., Jin, X., Liu, J., Li, D., Wu, Y., Liu, Y., Zhang, Z.: Correlation congruence for knowledge distillation. In: ICCV, pp. 5007–5016 (2019)
11. Ding, X., Zhang, X., Ma, N., Han, J., Ding, G., Sun, J.: RepVGG: making VGG-style convnets great again. In: CVPR, pp. 13733–13742 (2021)
12. Ding, X., Xia, C., Zhang, X., Chu, X., Han, J., Ding, G.: RepMLP: re-parameterizing convolutions into fully-connected layers for image recognition. arXiv preprint arXiv:2105.01883 (2021)
13. Ding, X., Zhang, X., Han, J., Ding, G.: Diverse branch block: Building a convolution as an inception-like unit. In: CVPR, pp. 10886–10895 (2021)
14. Zhang, K., Zhang, C., Li, S., Zeng, D., Ge, S.: Student network learning via evolutionary knowledge distillation.In: IEEE Trans. Circuits Syst. Video Technol. **32**(4), 2251–2263 (2021)
15. He, K., Zhang, X., Ren, S., Sun, J.: Deep residual learning for image recognition. In: CVPR, pp. 770–778 (2016)
16. Zagoruyko, S., Komodakis, N.: Wide residual networks. arXiv preprint arXiv:1605.07146 (2016)
17. Simonyan, K., Zisserman, A.: Very deep convolutional networks for large-scale image recognition. arXiv preprint arXiv:1409.1556 (2014)
18. Russakovsky, O., et al.: ImageNet large scale visual recognition challenge. Int. J. Comput. Vis. **115**, 211–252 (2015). https://doi.org/10.1007/s11263-015-0816-y
19. Krizhevsky, A., Hinton, G.: Learning multiple layers of features from tiny images (2009)
20. Mirzadeh, S.I., Farajtabar, M., Li, A., Levine, N., Matsukawa, A., Ghasemzadeh, H.: Improved knowledge distillation via teacher assistant. In: AAAI, vol. 34, no. 04, pp. 5191–5198 (2020)
21. He, K., Chen, X., Xie, S., Li, Y., Dollár, P., Girshick, R.: Masked autoencoders are scalable vision learners. In: CVPR, pp. 16000–16009 (2022)

Author Index

Z. Jin et al. (Eds.): KSEM 2023, LNAI 14117, pp. 455–457, 2023.
https://doi.org/10.1007/978-3-031-40283-8

Printed in the United States
by Baker & Taylor Publisher Services